MARRIAGE BONDS
OF
TRYON AND LINCOLN COUNTIES
NORTH CAROLINA

Abstracted and Indexed by
Curtis Bynum

CLEARFIELD

Originally published under the auspices of
the Catawba County Historical Association, Inc.
Newton, North Carolina and
the Lincoln County Historical Association, Inc.
Lincolnton, North Carolina
1929

Reprinted for Clearfield Company by
Genealogical Publishing Company
Baltimore, Maryland
1996, 2012

ISBN 978-0-8063-4654-0

Made in the United States of America

Introduction

*L*INCOLN COUNTY was formed from Tryon; Tryon, from Mecklenburg; Mecklenburg, from Anson; Anson, from Bladen; Bladen, from New Hanover precinct of Bath. As each of these counties was successively formed it was allotted all the territory settled and unsettled to the westward, the western boundary of the new county being the western boundary of the Colony or State. The Charter of Charles II fixed the westward boundary "as far as the South-Seas." This boundary was affirmed in the Bill of Rights in 1776. Hence Bladen and its western successors until 1777 extended to the "South-Seas."

In 1749 Bladen was divided by a line equidistant from Saxapahaw and Great Pee Dee rivers—the western part to be Anson County. Anson then included the whole of the western part of North Carolina from the Virginia line to the South Carolina line and evidently west to the Pacific. But in 1753 Rowan County was cut off from Anson, taking with it all the territory north of Earl Granville's line, which had been fixed as latitude 35° 34′.

In 1762 Mecklenburg was cut off from Anson, its eastern boundary being a line "beginning at Lord Carteret's (Earl Granville's) line six miles northeast from Capt Charles Hart's plantation on Buffalo Creek, and to run from thence to the mouth of Clear Creek which empties itself into Rocky River, below Capt Adam Alexander's, and from thence due south, to the bounds of the province of South Carolina." Mecklenburg's northern boundary was evidently Earl Granville's line; its southern boundary, the South Carolina line; and its western boundary, the Pacific Ocean.

In 1768, effective 10th April 1769, Tryon County was cut off from Mecklenburg. Tryon's eastern boundary was a line "beginning at Earl Granville's line where it crosses the Catawba River, and the said river to be the line to the South Carolina line." The northern boundary was Earl Granville's line. The southern boundary was the South Carolina line. The western boundary was indefinitely westward, the Pacific Ocean. In 1777 this western boundary was however definitely fixed by the formation of Washington County, comprising all the territory west of the mountains, and the western boundary of Tryon became approximately what is now the boundary line between North Carolina and Tennessee.

In 1779 Lincoln County was formed. Tryon was cut by a line "beginning at the south line near Broad River on the dividing ridge between Buffaloe Creek and Little Broad River, thence along the said ridge to the line of Burke County." All of Tryon to the west of this line became Rutherford County; all to the east became Lincoln. The western boundary of Lincoln then ran thru the middle of what is now Cleveland County. The northern boundary was Earl Granville's line. The southern boundary was the South Carolina line. The eastern boundary was the Catawba River.

In 1782 the size of Lincoln was increased by addition of a part of Burke County. The northern line of Lincoln was to run as follows: "Beginning at Sharrol's ford, running with the road leading towards Henry Whitner's as far

3

as Mathew Wilson's; thence a direct course to Simon Horse's, on the waters of Clark's creek, thence a direct course to the fish-dam ford of the south fork of the Catawba river, between James Wilson and David Robinson, and from thence a southwest course to Earl Granville's old line." This line was amended in 1784 so that "the boundary line between the counties of Burke and Lincoln shall hereafter be as follows, to wit, beginning at the Horse-Ford on Catawba river, running thence to John Hawn's on Hendry river, thence to William Orr's on Jacob's river, and thence to the intersection of the counties of Burke, Lincoln, and Rutherford." These two enactments were somehow interpreted as extending the county northward to the Catawba River, and the county is so shown on maps dated about 1820. Thus from 1784 until the formation of Cleveland in 1841 the county included all of what is now Lincoln, Catawba, and Gaston, and a large part of what is now Cleveland. This is an area about 56 miles long and about 33 miles wide.

In 1841 Cleveland County was cut off from Lincoln and Rutherford. The part of the line that affected Lincoln was to run with the dividing line of Burke and Rutherford to the Lincoln line, thence to the 13 mile post on the Lucas Ford Road, thence to the 12 mile post on the New Post Road from Rutherfordton to Lincolnton, thence to the 12 mile post on the road from Lincolnton to Quinn's Ferry, thence to the 12 mile post on the road from Morganton to Yorkville, S. C., thence with the road passing Abernathy's store by the Gold Mine at King's Mountain to the South Carolina line.

In 1842 Catawba County was cut off from Lincoln. All that portion of Lincoln north of an east and west line running 1½ miles north of Lincolnton was taken away. A part of this territory was returned to Lincoln when Gaston was formed four years later.

In 1846 Gaston County was cut off. All that portion of Lincoln which lay south of an east and west line running 6 miles south of the dividing line between Lincoln and Catawba (that is 4½ miles south of Lincolnton) was taken away. At the same time the dividing line between Lincoln and Catawba was moved 4 miles north, to a line 5½ miles north of Lincolnton. This should have left the county 10 miles long from north to south.

When these changes were made in the boundaries, commissioners were appointed to mark the new lines. This fact may account for certain divergences from the statutory boundaries.

POPULATION

The population of the county from 1769 to 1870 was as follows:

1769..... 8500 (estimate based on number of Taxables which was 1221)
1770.....11000 (estimate based on number of Taxables which was 1614)
1785..... 9000 (estimate based on number of Polls which was 1460)
1790..... 9319 (of which 935 slaves)
1800.....12660
1810.....16359
1820.....18147 (of which 3356 negroes)
1830.....22455 (second largest in the State)
1840.....26160 (largest in the State)
1850..... 7746
1860..... 8195
1870..... 9573

4

LIST OF COUNTY COURT CLERKS

Ezekiel Polk	1769, Apl	to 1772, Jul
Andrew Neel	1772, Oct 28	to 1776, Apl (about)
William Graham	1776, Apl (about)	to 1777, Jul
Andrew Neel	1777, Jul	to 1780, Apl
David Dickey	1780, Oct 23	to 1781, Apl
Joseph Dickson	1781, Apl 16	to 1788, Oct 8
John Dickson	1788, Oct 8	to 1804, Oct 3
Lawson Henderson	1804, Oct 3	to 1807, Apl 13
Daniel M Forney	1807, Jul 7	to 1812, May 22
Vardry McBee	1812, Jul 21	to 1833, Jul
Miles W Abernathy	1833, Oct 28	to 1837, Sep 4
Henry Cansler	1837, Sep 4	to 1844, Jun
Cyrus L Hunter	1844, Jun	to 1845, Sep
Robert Williamson	1845, Sep	to 1853, Oct
John A Huss	1853, Oct	to 1857, Oct
William R Clark	1857, Oct	to 1865, Jun
A Sidney Haynes	1865, Jun	to 1866, Jan 31
William R Clark	1866, Jan 31	to 1868 (end of County Court)

MARRIAGE BONDS

Marriage Bonds were first required in North Carolina by the Act of April 4th, 1741. This act provided that "every clergyman of the Church of England, or for want of such, any lawful Magistrate, within this Government, shall . . . join together in the holy estate of martimony, such persons who may lawfully enter into such a relation, and have complied with the directions herein after contained. . . . No Minister or Justice of the Peace . . . . shall celebrate the rites of matrimony . . . without license . . . or thrice publication of the banns as prescribed by the rubrick in the book of common prayer." License must be issued by the Clerk of the County Court of the county where the feme shall have her usual residence. The prospective groom, in order to obtain this license, must make a bond with sufficient security in the sum of fifty pounds proclamation money, with condition that there is no lawful cause to obstruct the marriage; if either of the persons should be under the age of twenty one years, consent of the parent or guardian must be had.

It should be particularly noted that there is an alternative provision herein: the marriage might be by license or by banns. If the banns were properly published according to the rubrick and the customs of the Church of England, the marriage might take place without a license and consequently without a bond. This may account for the absence of bonds for many marriages which are known to have taken place. The same was true in Virginia, as is made clear in the introduction to Mr Landon C Bell's valuable book "Cumberland Parish."

The Act of April 4th, 1741, was confirmed in 1749. In 1766 the Presbyterian or dissenting clergy were permitted to perform the ceremony, as they had been doing, apparently illegally, for some time. And in 1778 it was enacted that all regular ministers of the gospel of every denomination, having the cure of souls, and all justices of the peace are "authorized to solemnize the rites of matrimony according to the rites of their respective churches and agreeable to the rules in this act prescribed." Provision was again made for marriage by license or by banns published three times by any minister of the gospel. The amount of the bond required for license was raised to five hundred pounds lawful money of the State. In the Revised Statutes of 1836-7 the amount of the bond was changed to $1000. In the Revised Code of 1854 the regulations remain the same. Finally, by Chapter LXIX, Laws of 1866-7, Section 1, "so much of section 2 of . . . Revised Code chapter 68 as requires the Clerk to take bond . . . is hereby repealed"; this act was ratified 26 Feb 1867. Thus the marriage bonds of North Carolina should cover the period from 1741 to 1867. Those of Tryon and Lincoln Counties cover the period from 1769, when Tryon was organized, to 1867.

The law of 1867 requires that the Clerk shall keep a register of marriages. It may be noted in passing that as early as 1715 it was enacted that "the Register of every precinct, when there is no clerk of the church in that precinct, shall register all births, marriages, and burials." And in 1850 a further provision for a register was enacted. Apparently all such injunctions were obstinately disobeyed in North Carolina as they were in Virginia. (Compare Mr L C Bell's Old Free State, Vol. II, page 388). An incomplete register was kept in Lincoln County for a few years between 1850 and 1865. After the act of 1867 the register was resumed 26 July 1868 and continues thereafter, tho in a highly unsatisfactory state.

The bonds herein abstracted are all that are on file in the Court House in Lincolnton. There are more than 6000. It is thought that few have been lost. For the period after 1867 resort must be had to the file of licenses, which is doubtless fairly complete, and to the register. The compilation herein covers only the period from 1769 to 1867.

ACKNOWLEDGMENTS

Acknowledgments are gratefully made to Mr Lawrence S Holt Jr for invaluable assistance in preparing the abstracts; to Miss Adelaide L Fries for her kindly interest and help in deciphering some of the difficult German script; and to Mr Landon C Bell for most useful information given me in his books and in his letters.

No worker among the records of Lincoln County can fail to do honor to the memory of the late Alfred Nixon, for many years faithful Clerk of the Court. His unremitting labor has done more to preserve the history of his county than any one else can ever do.

EXPLANATIONS

(1)   The bonds abstracted below have been carefully studied and all the material contained in the instrument except the formal legal phraseology has been incorporated in the abstract.   The names of the groom, of the bride, of the surety, and of the witnesses are shown, as is also the date.   Examination of the original bond will reveal nothing more unless the handwriting is important.   As the bonds are many of them crumbling with age, it is earnestly urged that they be not taken from the files.

(2)   Names are spelled precisely as they are spelled in the bond, if the writing is legible.   No corrections have been made even where errors are obvious.   The spelling given first is that of the signature if any and if legible. If the signature is omitted or is illegible the Clerk's spelling is given.   Variant spellings in the bond are shown in parentheses.

(3)   If initials appear in the signature and the full name is given in the body of the bond, the full name is shown in the abstract as if so signed.

(4)   An x after a name indicates that the signature was by mark.   This does not mean that the signer was necessarily illiterate.

(5)   Some signatures are in German script.   In such cases the first spelling shown is that of the Clerk, and the German signature is shown in parentheses preceded by the abbreviation Ger.

(6)   The bride did not sign the bond; hence the spelling shown is not her own but in every case that of the Clerk.

(7)   In searching for a name, look for possible variant spellings.   The following table shows some of the letters that are frequently indistinguishable in manuscripts:

> e, i, c
> s, r
> u, n, ie, or
> t, l
> m, nn, en, in
> Capital S, L, T, F, J, I

(8)   The date shown is not the date of marriage but the date of the bond; the marriage followed within a few days thereafter.   Where the date is omitted from the bond every effort has been made to fix it.   Resort is had to the endorsement that usually appears on the outside of the folded bond, to the reference to the Governor for the time being which appears regularly in the bonds, to the watermark in the paper, or even to the handwriting of the Clerk. Any such clues are given parenthetically in the abstract.

(9)   Comparison of the abstracts with the incomplete Register mentioned above has been made and any additional information on the Register has been incorporated.   Comparison has also been made with a partial list prepared some years ago by the late Alfred Nixon and additions and corrections have been made from this list; abstracts marked (N) are taken from his list, the original having disappeared.   In some cases after 1850 licenses and certificates are on file with the bonds: any additional information contained in them has also been incorporated in the abstracts.

(10)   Abbreviations used:

Ambiguous. . uncertain which is groom and which is surety
B . . . . Bond
C . . . . Certificate of Minister or Justice of the Peace
CC . . . . Clerk of County Court
CCC . . . . Clerk of County Court
DC . . . . Deputy Clerk
DCC . . . . Deputy Clerk of Court
Doubtful . . . . incomplete, partial, illegible, or self contradictory
End . . . . endorsed
Ger . . . . German script
JP . . . . Justice of the Peace
L . . . . License
M . . . . married
MG . . . . Minister of the Gospel
Mst . . . . Minister
N . . . . A list of bonds prepared by Mr Alfred Nixon
R . . . . The Register of Marriages from 1850 to 1865
Uncertain . . . same as doubtful
x . . . . signed with mark
. . . . omission or illegible

(11)   The abstracts are arranged in alphabetical order of grooms; the index at the end is in alphabetical order of brides.   Grooms' names and brides' names are reversed, the surname being put first; all other names are in natural order, the surname last.

(12)   The abstracts are arranged and punctuated as follows:

Groom;   Bride;   Surety or Sureties;   Date;   Witness or Witnesses;   Other Information.

Abstracts

Abee, James; Stillwell, Margaret; Daniel D Hudson; 2 Oct 1841; L E Thompson

Abernathy, Aaron; Vaughen, Suckey; James Abernathy; 27 Feb 1802; Jos Dickson

Abernathy, Alfred; Friday, Magdalene; Grief Abernathy; 11 Mar 1824; V McBee

Abernathy, Andrew x; Wilfong, Eve; David Killian; 1 Jul 1820; Jas T Alexander

Abernathy, Battee; Beale, Mary; Joseph Beale, Charles x Abernathy; 13 Nov 1778; Andrew Neel; Written consent of John Beale father of Mary

Abernathy, Battee (Jr); Nance, Polly; Randolph Barnett; 10 Jul 1810; Danl M Forney

Abernathy, Berryman; Tarr, Rebeckah; Jacob Forney; 1 May 1824; V McBee

Abernathy, Buckner; Harwell, Patsey; Gardner Harwell; 25 Mar 1805; Lwn Henderson; Signed by G Harwell for B Abernathy

Abernathy, C M; Goodson, Hetty (Hilton); Martin Loftin; 2 Nov 1851; Elisha Saunders; M same date by Elisha Saunders JP

Abernathy, Caleb x; Goodson, Jane; D O Wilkinson; 23 Feb 1866; W R Clark; M 4 Mar 1866 by Elisha Saunders JP

Abernathy, Charles; Cobb, Barbary; Ambrose x Cobb Jr; 4 Sep 1782; Jno Moore

Abernathy, D M; Reel, Mary; M L Abernathy; 5 Mar 1849; Robt Williamson

Abernathy, Daniel A; Abernathy, Franky; Henderson Abernathy; 6 Aug 1837; M W Abernathy

Abernathy, David; Forney, Christina; Peter Forney; 27 May 1782

Abernathy, David x; Whisenhant, Catherine; Moses Seitz (Sides); 24 Jul 1820; V McBee

Abernathy, David x; Summit, Polly; John x Moose; 27 Jan 1834; Miles W Abernathy

Abernathy, David M; Nixon, Eliza; Milton S Abernathy; 5 Jul 1855; J A Huss; M 11 Jul 1855 by R H Morrison

Abernathy, Eli; Havner, Mary; Elisha Sanders; 28 Oct 1823; V McBee

Abernathy, Elijah x; Sullivan, Nancy; Isaiah x Abernathy; 30 Aug 1830; J T Alexander

Abernathy, Enock x; Fisher, Mary; Mathew Kirksy; 10 Oct 1857; W R Clark; M 15 Oct 1857 by Robt Blackburn JP

Abernathy, Fredrick; Long, Eleanor; Smith Abernathy; 16 Jan 1835

Abernathy, George W; Goodson, Holly; Franklin Abernathy; 29 May 1848; Robt Williamson

Abernathy, George W; Barnett, Susan A; Daniel Barnett; 5 Aug 1861; W R Clark; M 6 Aug 1861 by D A Lowe JP

Abernathy, H W; Rush, Eliza A; William Ramsour; 22 May 1850

Abernathy, Isaac (Isaah) x; Fortner, Mary; James x Abernathy; 15 Jun 1833; L McBee

Abernathy, Isaiah x; Low, Salley; William Low; 2 Feb 1813

Abernathy, James x; Clore, Elisabeth; Andw x Cline; 4 Jan 1803

Abernathy, James; Rockett, Polly; Nathan Abernathy; 15 Apl 1808; Phil Whitener JP

Abernathy, James; Clodfelter, Fanny; William x Abernathy; 7 Dec 1821; James T Alexander

Abernathy, James; Abernathy, Ritty; Michael Abernathy; 25 Sep 1838; L E Thompson

Abernathy, Jeremiah x; Ward, Rue; Henry Gross; 11 Aug 1824; V McBee

Abernathy, John; Forney, Susan; Turner Abernathy, James Rutledge; 21 Apl 1784

Abernathy, John; Nance, Catey; Robt Abernathy; 9 Jul 1791

Abernathy, John; Linebarger, Mary; James Sherrill (Sherrel); 28 Dec 1812; Vardry McBee

Abernathy, John x; Farewell, Polly; Isaiah x Abernathy; 4 Nov 1840; H Cansler

Abernathy, John R; Morris, Stacy; Drury G Abernathy; ------ 182-- (endorsed 1829); V McBee

Abernathy, Joseph x; Abernathy, Glaffira; Sterling Abernathy; 16 Apl 1804

Abernathy, Joseph x; Keller, Nancy; Isaiah x Abernathy; 28 Jan 1819; V McBee

Abernathy, Joseph T x; Nance, Olly; Sherod S Little; 2 ---- 1832; Jno D Graham

Abernathy, Larkin; Little, Jane; Bary Abernathy; 30 Sep 1816; V McBee

Abernathy, Lawson H; Rankin, Margaret E; J (or I) W Gabriel (Wilson Gabriel); 22 Sep 1838; H Cansler CC

Abernathy, Michal; West, Izabellar; Larkin Bradshaw; 18 Nov 1826; J T Alexander

Abernathy, Miles; Bracher, Usley; Vincent Cox, John Abernathy; 6 Oct 1781

Abernathy, Miles x; Cobb, Nancey; Philip Cline; 7 Sep 1808

Abernathy, Miles; Rocket, Nancy; Harley Abernathy; 12 Dec 1809; Ligt Williams

Abernathy, Miles; Bomgarner, Nancy; John D Hoke; 6 Sep 1826; J T Alexander

Abernathy, Miles; Abernathy, Frances; William L Nantz (Nance); 3 Dec 1835; J D King

Abernathy, Miles J; Lutz, Malinda; Henry Sumerowe (Summerow); 13 Feb 1841

Abernathy, Miles S; Lorance, Catharine M; W H Gibbs; 17 Nov 1840; H Cansler

9

Abernathy, Miles W; Lorantz, Catharine C; Alexander Lorance (Lourance); __ Aug 1832; Fr Hoke JP; Torn
Abernathy, Miles W; Hoke, Ann; John W Vogler; 17 Jun 1835; Carlos Leonard
Abernathy, Milton S; Nixon, Susan; David M Abernathy; 20 Feb 1856; J A Huss; M 28 Feb 1856 by R H Morrison
Abernathy, Moses; Bynum, Susana; Jas Abernathy; 29 Jan 1803; Jo Dickson
Abernathy, Moses; Short, Polley; David Troutman; 3 Aug 1824; V McBee
Abernathy, Nathan x; Burk, Emeline; Jesse Sanders (Saunders); 28 Aug 1835; Elisha Saunders JP
Abernathy, Nathen x; Cline, Eve; Andrew x Cline; 28 Jan 1808; Jacob Reinhardt
Abernathy, Philip x; Orents, Polly; Miles C Abernathy; 26 May 1836; Elisha Saunders JP
Abernathy, Robert; Nicols, Sarah; John Farrar (Pharow); 23 Jun 1783; James Dickson
Abernathy, Robert; Byianm, Dice; Harley Abernathy; 24 Jan 1809; Thos Wheeler
Abernathy, Robert x; Huskins, Rosy; Philip Cline; 17 Nov 1817; Andrew Loretz
Abernathy, Samuel; Sherrel, Sally; Temple Shelton; 2 (or 26) Jan 1810; Danl M Forney
Abernathy, Samuel; Harill (or Havill), Nancy; Wilson x Turbyfield; 9 Dec 1838; H Cansler CC
Abernathy, Seth x; Cline, Polly; Henry Finger (Ger Heinrich Finger); 12 Feb 1803
Abernathy, Seth x; Bradshaw, Elizabeth; Miles A Sanders; 2 Aug 1834; John D Hoke
Abernathy, Shadrach; Hager, Anne; H H (or St) Abernathy; 8 Nov 1805; Lwn Henderson
Abernathy, Sidney T; Davenport, Elizabeth C; A W Davenport; 18 Jan 1843; R M Alexander JP
Abernathy, Turner; Abernathy, Disey; William Haker (Heger); 15 Dec 1788; Eliza Dickson
Abernathy, Turner; Gooding, Susanna; William Daniel (?); 27 Dec 1813; Jesse Perkins
Abernathy, Turner; Whitener, Fanney; Jacob Link; 25 Oct 1821; James T Alexander
Abernathy, Turner; Lourance, Elizabeth J; Milton Abernathy; 10 Feb 1842; H Cansler
Abernathy, Valentine x; Coldwell, Elizabeth; Andrew Colwell (Coldwell); 20 Jul 1824; Jas T Alexander
Abernathy, Wiliferd (Williford); Turbifield, Polly; Benjamin Fisher; 6 Nov 1838; Alexander Ward JP
Abernathy, William; Kimbrel, Winifred; John Dickson; 1 Jan 1799; Abraham Martin
Abernathy, William x; Law (or Low), Nancy; Isaiah x Abernathy; 11 Jan 1820; V McBee
Abernathy, William; Roberson, Leah; B T Kirby; 20 Jan 1837; M W Abernathy
Abernathy, William I; Reinhardt, Barbara; Wilson Gabriel; 26 Mar 1833; J T Alexander
Abey see Eaby
Abrams, Joseph x; Lee, Elizabeth; Isam (?) Douglass; 7 Jan 1830; Alexander Ward
Abrams, Lewis D H; Faulkner, Nancy A; Michael Quickel; 26 Aug 1843; Carlos Leonard
Aby, Henry; Stamey, Sally; Benjamin Howard; 17 Jan 1814; V McBee
Acer, Peter (Ger Peter Ecker); Kiser, Jean; David Short; 6 Sep 1792
Acock, John H; M'Cord, Martha R; Wm Hanks; 8 Jun 1843
Adams (Addams), Andrew; Taylor, Ann; Thomas Little; 17 Sep 1836; M W Abernathy CC by J A Ramsour DC
Adams, David x; Oxford, Katrine; James B Meredith (James Myridith), James x James; 29 Sep 1784; Joseph Steel
Adams, James; Baird, Betsy; Robert Baird; 5 Jan 1804; Polly D Greaves
Adams, James; Patterson, Catharine; Zenas Baird; 14 Jan 1829; Wm Wilson
Adams, James; Burton, Eliza; Henry Fulenwider; 29 Dec 1834
Adams, James; McCarty, Mary; Henry Fulenwider; 13 May 1836; John B Harry
Adams, James P; Proctor, Julia; Robert Sumerville (Somerville); 18 Oct 1859; W R Clark Clk; M same date by M J H Morrison (MG)
Adams, John x; Cox, Hexxey; John Campbell; 6 Jan 1819; V McBee
Adams, John B; McAlly (?), Eliza; John B Patterson; 19 Dec 1825; And Hoyl JP
Adams, Joseph W; Winters, Margaret; Samuel E Winter (Winters); 20 Oct 1836; John Dickson
Adams, R J; Lindsay, Mary D; T B Maclean (McLean); 1 Jan 1844; Isaac Holland
Adams, Robert; Barber, Jane; John Barber, James Martin; 31 Mar 1795; Samuel Wilson, T (or J) Wilson
Adams, Robert E; Perkins, Eliza T; Miles W Abernathy; 25 Nov 1835
Adams, Wm C; Rudisill, F L; A Alexander; 17 Jul 1862; W R Clark; M same date by R N Davis Minister
Adams, William E; Hayes, Margaret J; Rufus J Adams; 5 Sep 1836; L E Thompson
Adderholt, David; Rudisill, Sally; T William Aderhold (Adderholt); 13 Sep 1827; J T Alexander

10

Aderhold (Aderholdt), Abraham; Rudisel, Margaret; Andrew x Prevet; 5 Aug 1829; V McBee

Aderholdt, Emanuel M; Brown, Rebecca E; Philip Plonk; 30 Aug 1862; W R Clark; M 31 Aug 1862 by A J Fox MG

Aderholdt, John A F; Hoover, Martha Ann; Jonas S Cloninger; 18 Nov 1860; W R Clark; M 22 Nov 1860 by A J Fox MG

Aderholdt (Adderholdt), John A F; Crouse, Barbara A; J S Cloninger; 16 Sep 1865; A S Haynes; M 20 Sep 1865 by A J Fox MG

Aderholdt, Marcus; Heedick, E C; --------; 7 Jul 1866; W R Clark Clerk; M 8 Jul 1866 by Alfred J Fox MG; L and C, no B

Aderholt, William; Carrol, Esther; Lewis Vandyke (Joshua Vendike); 4 Jul 1822; V McBee

Adkins, Gervis G x; Dillen, Polly; Mark Massey; 27 Apl 1815; I Holland --

Aker see Eake and Eaker

Albright, James; Lantz, Linny; John P Anthony; 13 Dec 1848; Robt Williamson

Alexander, Abraham; McCorkle, Jenny; William Beatty; 3 Mar 1808; Henry Conner

Alexander, David M x; Spratt, Jane; Richard x Wright; 22 Jan 1859; W R Clark; M 23 Jan 1859 by Philip Carpenter JP

Alexander, Elias J; Summey, Barbara L; David Welsh; 2 Jun 1851; Robt Williamson; M 3 Jun 1851 by George Coon JP

Alexander, Frank R; `Magness, Levina; Joseph Morris; 24 Jul 1799

Alexander, Isaac; Sadler, Lucey; William R Sadler; 17 Apl 1802; Jos Dickson

Alexander, James; Armstrong, Ann; Wm Henry, David Alexander; 29 Aug 1769; Ezekiel Polk

Alexander, James L; Wells, Frances A; J H Boyd; 21 May 1862; M same date by G W Ivy MG

Alexander, John x; Morison, Mary; William x Morison; 20 Jul 1779; John Baldridg; This bond is written on back of a license issued by Clerk of Mecklenburg County in favor of John Alexander and Mary Morrison "of this County", dated 19 Jul 1779

Alexander, John; Marison, Magaret; Charles Williams; 2 Sep 1807; D M Forney

Alexander, John (Jr); Ferguson, Polly; John Alexander (Sr), Moses Ferguson; 3 Sep 1812; Dvd Warlick JP

Alexander, John F; Beam, Mary Ann M; John A Roberts; 18 Jan 1848; Robt Williamson

Alexander, Josiah; Paterson, Agnes; Thos Paterson; 15 Aug 1800

Alexander, Moses; Wilson, Polley; Maxwell Wilson; 9 Sep 1806; John Willfong

Alexander, Moses; Fronabarger, Nancy; William Hager; 4 Mar 1845

Alexander, Moses W; Graham, Vilet W; Robert D Alexander; 20 Dec 1821; V McBee

Alexander, Newman; Carpenter, Catherine; Wm Barr (Bar); 1 Feb 1820; V McBee

Alexander, Newman; Harris, Eve; Wm Baxter; 23 Mar 1850; Robt Williamson

Alexander, Robert; ----------; John Smith; 27 Dec 1825; D Reinhardt

Alexander, Robert J (Alexander, Robert Jr); Moore, Louisa; James Martin; 16 Jul 1800; Jno Dickson

Alexander, Robt J; McCorkle, Charity A; Joseph M Gabriel; 11 Sep 1841; H Cansler

Alexander, Sample; Philips, Abigal; David Phillipes (Philips); 10 Nov 1829; V McBee

Alexander, William; Fish, Elisabeth; James Lee; 4 Apl 1797

Allen, A G (Green); Mires, B; John Ballard; 19 Apl 1839; J T Alexander

Allen, Benjamin; Palmer, Anne; John Allen; 1 Nov 1804

Allen (or Allan), Burrell C; Hoke, Rhoda L; Frederick Hoke (yu); 31 Oct 1832 (end 1833)

Allen, Henry H (H K); Edwards, Viry (Viney); Joel H Howard; 1 Oct 1859; J (or I) Lowe JP; M 2 Oct 1859 by J W Naylor (MG)

Allen (Allan), Hinchea E; Little, Catherina; Burrel C Allen (Allan); 11 Aug 1835; Fr Hoke JP

Allen, James; Litten, Tabitha; Isaac Litton (Litten); 26 Apl 1794; Joseph Steel

Allen, John; Beaty, Susannah; John McCorkle; 25 Jan 1830; Luther M McBee

Allen (Allean), John Y; Davies, Dealph (?); Isaiah M (or U) Davis (Davies); 24 Jun 1841; J Yount JP

Allen, Levi x; Howard, Polly; Franklin M Abernathy; 28 Oct 1835; Miles W Abernathy

Allen, Stanley see Black, Autison

Allen, William; Linebarger, Elizabeth; Rufus Fisher; 15 Apl 1834; Miles W Abernathy

Allison, Greenberry; Smith, Nancy; Robert Smith; 21 Nov 1835; Isaac Holland

Allison, Henry; Erwin, Margaret; James N Todd (Dodd); 2 Mar 1821; V McBee

Allison, James M; Ewing, ------; Hugh Ewing; 29 Jul 1833; I Holland

Allison, Robert; Neel, Rosanna F; Nobel Niell (or Nall); 1-th Nov 1819; G Milligan

Allison, Samuel; Dickson, Margaret; William Dickson; 13 July 1795; Jo Dickson

Allison, Thomas J; Neill, Jane; William Neill; 11 Jul 1825; Fr Hoke
Allison, William M; Erwine, Maryan; Samuel B Hill; 2 Aug 1821; V McBee
Allran, John; Nance, Mary; Jacob Allran; 20 Aug 1854; Daniel A Haines
Alston see Austin
Anders, Elias M; Stroup, Carline; William R Holland; 14 Dec 1846; Isaac Holland
Anderson, Isaac; Curtis, Sarah; John Curtis, John Murphey; 2 Oct 1797
Anderson, Isaac; Bridges, Dycy; John M Sherill (Sherril); 15 Sep 1826; V McBee
Anderson, John; Neagle, Elizabeth; Andrew Neagle; 6 May 1820; V McBee
Anderson, Lewis x (Freedman); Hunter, Lusinda (Freedwoman); Abraham x McDowel
    (Freedman); 25 Aug 1866; D A Lowe; M same date by D A Lowe JP
Anderson, Matison x; Brevard, Nancy; Stephain x Brevard; 29 Jun 1867; M same
    date by J Helderman JP; "Freed man and freedwoman"
Andras, Henry; Litton, Rebecka; Isaac Litten (Litton); 6 May 1809; Danl M Forney
Andres (Anders), James; Hovis, Malinda; J Cline; 12 Sep 1839; Jesse Gantt
Angel, John; Wilson, Ruth; Andrew Wilson; 25 Jul 1811
Angel, Joseph A; Johnson, Susanah; David Warlick; 25 Dec 1826; V McBee
Angle (Angel), David; Wells, Sarah; Daniel Leonard; 3 Sep 1838; W M Reinhardt
Anthony, Daniel; Rinehardt, Eve; Paul Anthony; 5 Apl 1807; Peter Hoyle JP
Anthony (or Anthoney), Daniel; Bangle, Sarah; Paul Anthony (or Anthoney); 3 Jan
    1831; J T Alexander
Anthony, Darling x; Nance, Betsy; James x Brown; 6 Apl 1824; J Blackwood Esq
Anthony, Gideon; Henry, Sarah; John Michal (Michael); 4 Feb 1834; M W Abernathy
Anthony, Gideon x; Shull, Mary Ann; G J Connor; 24 Aug 1859; W R Clark;
    M 25 Aug 1859 by A J Fox MG
Anthony, Jacob; Beam, Elizabeth; David Warlick; 13 Jan 1818; Drury Dobbins,
    Wm White
Anthony, John; Carson, Martha; James M Carson; 18 Mar 1829; Isaac Holland
Anthony, John A; Hull, Hannah; David x Anthony; 21 Mar 1859; W R Clark;
    M 24 Mar 1859 by G L Hunt MG
Anthony, John J (?); Wilkinson, Margaret L; W Lander; 13 Sep 1846; Robt
    Williamson
Anthony, John P; Wilson, Mary; Robt Williamson; 28 Nov 1853; M same date by
    Saml Lander (Rev)
Anthony, Jonathan x; Hawkins, Anna; John Harris; 28 Oct 1830; J T Alexander
Anthony, Joseph D; Hobbs, Susannah; P V Cauble; 19 Dec 1853; J A Huss;
    M 28 Dec 1853 by F J Jetton JP
Anthony, Paul; Rhodes, Magalina; Daniel Anthony; 3 Jan 1831; J T Alexander
Anthony, Philip x; Dellinger, Elvira; John Harris; 17 May 1834; G Hoke
Apley see Epply
Apley, Daniel x; Keebler, Catherine; David Keebler (Ger David Kübler); 10 Mar 1800;
    Danl McKisick
Aprey, Joseph x; Berry, Nancy; Isaiah Dane (?); 30 May 1807; Ligt Williams JP
Arawood, Lawed x; Arrawood, Dacey; Henry Costner (Ger Henrich Castner), Litleton
    Bill (Littleton Petillo); 6 Apl 1810
Arends, David x; Finger, Catharine; J G Milster; 4 Apl 1835
Arent (Arnt), Jacob; Rutledge, Jane; Elisha Sanders (Saunders); 15 Jul 1823; V McBee
Arents, Wesley x; Derr, Dinah; Benjamin x Friday; 18 Jan 1867; P A Summey DC;
    M 23 Jan 1867 by Elisha Saunders JP; "Colored man and Colored Woman"
Arewood, William x; Shuck, Susanna; Philip Speegle (Ger Philib Spiegel); 12 Oct
    1807; Phil Whitener JP
Armour, Arthur; Shelton, Susan; John F Brevard; 3 Aug 1824
Armour (Armer, Armers), Robert; Wyatt, Elisabeth; Ezekiel Hazlet (Heslet); 7 Nov
    1786; Jo Dickson
Armstrong, A S; Wise, Catherine E; Absalom Wise; 2 Jan 1866; A S Haynes CCC;
    M same date by P Carpenter JP
Armstrong, Andrew; Oliver, Harriot; James Henry; 27 Apl 1821; V McBee
Armstrong, Andrew; Beard, Sarah; Jno M x M'Carver (Milton McCarver); 1 Jan
    1835; E Hanks
Armstrong, Francis; Brimer, Mary; Samuel Brymer; 7 Feb 1811; Joseph Neel
Armstrong, James; Robison, Margaret; Robert Robison; 21 Jun 1779; Andr Neel
Armstrong, John; Huggins, Ann; John Huggins; 23 Jul 1788; Eliza Dickson
Armstrong, John; Bond, Mary; Abner Womack; 15 Aug 1791; Jo Dickson
Armstrong, John; Dobbins, Mary; --------; 27 Mar 1793; Note from Alexander
    Dobbins to Clerk asking that license be issued; "my daughter Mary." Not a bond
Armstrong, John x (Jr); Fite, Peggy; Willis Rives (Reeves); 27 Mar 1828
Armstrong, John; Goodson, Margaret; John x Goodson; 16 Jan 1838; H Cansler CC

12

Armstrong, John; Martin, Margaret; James Smith; 29 May 1838; And Hoyl JP
Armstrong, John; West, Visey; James Leeper; 27 Feb 1845; C L Hunter
Armstrong, John M; Martin, Martha S; William S Martin; 7 Aug 1844
Armstrong, John R x; Hinkle, Winnie M; Simon S Hager; 1 Jul 1845; Rob Williamson
Armstrong, Mathew; Titmon, Cathrine; Samuel Armstrong; 21 Nov 1831; Isaac Holland
Armstrong, Mathew R; Moore, Rosey; Robert Edwards; 3 Feb 1838; H Cansler CC
Armstrong, Matthew; Marriner, Mary; John Mariner (Marriner); 23 Apl 1816; James T Alexander
Armstrong, Samuel; Oliver, Elizabeth; Abner Berry; 27 Mar 1815; James T Alexander
Armstrong, Thomas; Hansel, Martha; Robert Edwards; 23 Apl 1842
Armstrong, W J; Wise, Mary M; Jacob Wise; 8 Dec 1865; A S Haynes CCC; M 17 Dec 1865 by P Carpenter JP
Armstrong, William x; Beal, Mary; Jeremiah Goodson; 8 Jan 1816; James T Alexander
Arndt, Henry x; Finger, Ann; John x Finger; 24 Mar 1837; M W Abernathy
Arney see Earney
Arney (Earney), Christian; Vendike, Salley; Jacob Rush; 8 Nov 1819; V McBee
Arney, Jacob; Derr, Sally; John Ramsaur (Ramsour); 12 Aug 1813; Vardry McBee
Arney, John; Tevebough, Betsey; David Ramsour; 28 Jan 1808; Danl Forney
Arowood, Zachariah; Arrowood, Anna; William Whitt; 17 Nov 1818; James T Alexander
Arrowwood, Zacharias x; Commins, Elisabeth; James x Arrowwood; 29 Jan 1786
Asberry (Arsberry), Daniel; Morris, Nancey; William Mayes, Samuel Harwell; 4 Jan 1790
Asbury, Daniel M; Clipperd, Sarah; James M Smith; 7 Nov 1866; H Asbury; M 11 Nov 1866 by L A Fox MG
Asbury, Francis; Linebarger, Elizabeth; John Leinberger (Linebarger); 17 Oct 1812; Vardry McBee
Asbury, Henry; Robinson, Elizabeth; Thomas S (or L) Mays; 10 Aug 1821; V McBee
Asbury, Henry; Bradshaw, Emily; Isaac Lowe (Low); 17 Jul 1838; N M Reinhardt
Asbury, John F; Drew, Mary T; Lewis P Rothrock (Rotherick); 27 Jun 1838; H Cansler CC
Asbury, Josiah; Finger, Sarah A C; R A Bready; 1 Mar 1859; H Asbury; M same date by Saml Lander
Asbury, Wesley (Westly); Abernathy, Susannah; Elisha Sherrill; 25 Jun 1830; J T Alexander
Ash, William x; Spencer, Sally; Philip Fry (Ger Philib Frey); __th Jul 1823; Mic Cline
Ashabrand, Henry x; Kyser, Sarah; Henry x Kistler; 27 Jan 1807; Peter Hoyle JP
Ashabraner, John x; Troughbock, Barbara; Jacob x Troughbock; 4 Jun 1814; V McBee
Ashe (Ash), Joseph; Phillips, Barbary; Isaac Ashe (Ash); 20 Aug 1818; Joseph Fisher
Ashebrener, Abraham x; Grose, Mary; Henry x Ashebrener; 22 May 1814; Phil Whitener JP
Ashebrener, Daniel x; Froy, Cathrein; Jhon Seegle; 21 Aug 1806; Paul Whitener JP
Atkinson, William; Massangale, Mary; Joseph Morris; 1 Apl 1792; Jno Moore
Atris see Eatris
Aurends (Arends), John x; Bysinger, Susanna; Henry Rudisall Jr (Rudisile); 6 Sep 1808
Austin (Alston), Samuel; Bolick, Sally; Frederick Miller (Ger Friedrich Miller); 5 Mar 1818; Mic Cline
Auten, Powell (Auten, Paul; Fulmauten, Powell) x; Jenkins, Anne; John Henry, Ebenezer Keener (?); 15 Oct 1811; Joseph Neel
Auter (Otter), Fulcard; Bonim, Eliza; John x Titman; 17 Jun 1788
Avery, A C; Morrison, Susan W; B S Johnson; 26 Feb 1861; M 27 Feb 1861 by J L Kirkpatrick (MG)
Avery, Absalom x; Shuford, Elizabeth; Emmanuel Houser; 29 Oct 1850; Robt Williamson
Avery, Daniel x; Speak, Sally; John Cook; 22 Mar 1824; Jas T Alexander
Avery, George; Plonk, Susan; J L Carpenter; 9 Sep 1858; W R Clark; M same date by G L Hunt MG
Avery, John; Carpenter, Mary A; Franklin Taylor; 25 Jun 1853; R Williamson; M 7 Jul 1853 by George Coon JP
Avery, Philip x; Plonk, Catharine; Lawson - Shuford; 16 Nov 1858; Wm J Hoke DC; M 17 Nov 1858 by G L Hunt MG
Ayle see Oel

Baggs, William (Billy); Dickson, Sarah; Thomas Dickson; 5 Aug 1817; Saml Wilson
Bailes (Bayles), John (Jr); Willis, Susannah; Daniel Willis; 7 Sep 1833; M Hull JP
Bailey (Baily), David; Leinhardt, Sally; William x Baily; 13 Aug 1810; H Y Webb

Bailey, David; Keistler, Catharine; Abraham Keistler; 7 Aug 1828; B J Thompson
Bailey, William; Rhom, Lucinda; Daniel Carpenter; 25 Dec 1834; G Hoke
Bails (Bayles), David; Lackey, Effy; David Williams; 15 Dec 1835; M Hull JP
Baily (Bailey), Cox; Walker, Mary; Robert Abernathy; 25 Jul 1789; Jo Dickson
Baily, Samuel C; Bess, Mary Ann; N H Mauney; 11 Jun 1859; M 16 Jun 1859 by
P. Carpenter JP
Baird, Adam; Spenser, Sarah; Robert Floyd; 7 Dec 1819; I Holland for Vardry McBee
Baird (Beard), William; Martin, Abigal; George Witherspoon; 12 Sep 1803; Jonathan
Greaves
Baker, Allen; Rudisill, Betsey; Edward Baker; 12 Dec 1825; J T Alexander
Baker, Allen; Plunk, Elizabeth; John Rudasill (Rudisill); 16 Jun 1847; V A McBee
Baker, Edward; Butz, Mary; Daniel Eaker; 8 Mar 1817; V McBee
Baker, Edward; Beam, Mrs Elizabeth; John Michal; 2 Jun 1841; H Cansler
Baker, Eli x; Reinhardt, Mary; Robert Smith; 13 Feb 1844
Baker, Henry; Linebarger, Harriet; Charles D Conner; 1 Jun 1852; Robt Williamson;
M 6 Jun 1852 by F J Jetton JP; Uncertain; groom may be Jacob Henry
Baker, Jacob; Sellers, Susannah; Henry Sellers; 10 Jun 1819; James T Alexander
Baker, John (Ger Hannes Baker); Yoder, Cathn; John Miller; 8 May 1798; Jno Dickson
Baker, John; Jenkins, Sarah; Robert x Smith; 29 Mar 1814; James Taylor Alexander
Baker, John (Ger ____); Sellers, Margaret; Jacob Sellers; 3 Jan 1816; V McBee
Baker, John x; West, Sarah; Levi Clanton; 27 Nov 1850; Robt Williamson
Baker, Jose (Jr) x; Reynolds, Betcy; Peter Eaker; 1 Sep 1821; V McBee
Baker, Joseph x; Jinkins, Betsey; Benjamin x Jinkins; 23 Jul 1787; Jo Dickson
Baker, Joseph x; Stine, Catharine; Daniel Hoke; 3 Mar 1830; Fr Hoke
Baker, Jos Anderson x; Lamasters, Elizabeth; Wiley W Reynolds; 30 Dec 1857; W R
Clark; M 31 Dec 1857 by F J Jetton JP
Baker, Levi; Ingle, Christena; G L Brown; 8 Sep 1849; V A McBee
Baker, Philip (Ger Phillip Becker); Sigman, Polly; Joshua White; 24 Apl 1821;
James T Alexander
Baker, Silas; Vestal, Rachel; John Smith; 28 Jun 1806; Lwn Henderson
Baker, V E; Harris, Elisabeth; A G Harrill (Harral); 6 Oct 1863; S P Sherrill;
M same date by F J Jetton JP
Baker, William; Bynum, Sarah; William Hager; 25 Nov 1837; H Cansler
Baldasor, Andrew x; Hawn, Eve; Benedick x Hawn; 11 Oct 1785; Joseph Steel
Baldon, Squire; ____, ____; David Rhyne (Ryne); 18 Nov 1816; John Blackwood JP
Baldridge, Dornton; Boggs, Mary; James Boggs; 9 Oct 1810; Saml Wilson ____
Baldrige, Michael; Lytle, Isabella; Henry Little; 24 Jul 1798
Baldwin, Armsted; Pinner, Patience; John Gibson; 27 Apl 1819; I Holland for
Vardry McBee CC
Baldwin, Johnathen x; Kenedy, Janey; William Spencer; 13 Apl 1842; D Hoffman JP
Ballard, Isaah W x; Farewell, Ebbe; John Ballard, Osburn Munday; 4 Aug 1831;
Wm Little
Ballard, Jacob x; Kidd, Catharine; John Myers; 23 Jul 1839; H Cansler CC
Ballard, James; West, Martha; _____; 8 Oct 1857; M this date by F J Jetton JP;
C only, no B
Ballard, Jno x; Childress, Salley; William Kids (Kidds); 1 Nov 1815; V McBee
Ballard, John; Meiers, Caty; James x Ballard, William Childress (Childers); 8 Mar
1821; Henry x Meiers
Ballard, John H; Patterson, Lovina; Rufus J Myers (Miars); 9 Feb 1843; J Helderman
Ballard, Philip; Huggins, Margarett E; J M Kids; 17 Mar 1864; John H Ballard;
M same date by H A T Harris
Ballard, Reuben; Linebarger, Molly; James Ballard; 30 Jan 1810; Thos Wheeler
Ballard, Thomas J x; Holdbrooks, Catharine A; A S Haynes; 29 Oct 1859; W R Clark
Ballard, William; Daily, Sarah K; Henry Brotherton; 2 Sep 1866; Philip Ballard;
M same date by J A Huggins Minister M P Church
Ballard, William L; Whitney, Mina (?); Benjamin Ballard; 6 Mar 1833; L McBee
Ballard (Ballad), Wm L; McCorkle, Elizabeth; James Sherrill; 10 Oct 1837
Ballew, W A; Cline, Harriet; John L Jones; 3 Sep 1850; W M Reinhardt
Baly, John x; Mathus, Elezabeth; William x Baly; 10 Jun 1824; Fr Hoke JP
Bamber, Jurdan x; Hoagens, Salley; Wm Beatty, John x Hoagens; 22 Jul 1806;
Hy Conner JP
Banday, John; Hollar, Christina; Jacob Reinhardt; 4 Nov 1817; V McBee
Banday (Bandy), Thomas; Gooding, Rebecca; Jno x Caldwell; 18 Oct 1809; Danl M
Forney
Bandy, Alexander M; Young (Yount), Susan; Eli Johnson; 27 Feb 1855; J A Huss;
M 1 Mar 1855 by A J Fox MG

14

Bandy, George; Gibbs, Martha; John D Abernethy (Abernathy); 19 Jan 1819; James T Alexander

Bandy, Hugh Q; Monday (Munday), Elizabeth; John A Barkly; 10 Mar 1855; M 11 Mar 1855 by H Asbury Mst

Bandy, James M; Leonard, Mattie (Marthe) J; Samuel S Gregory Jr; 4 Nov 1866; Henry Rhodes; M same date by D A Haines JP

Bandy, Rufus; Abernathy, Letty; Daniel A Abernathy; 29 Feb 1840

Bandy, William; Wilfong, Elizabeth; John Johnson (Johnston); 24 Dec 1811; Jacob Reinhardt

Bangle, Henry; Helms, Catharine; Andrew Hauss; 14 Apl 1849; Robt Williamson

Bangle (Pangle), John; Spake, Catharine; John Cook; 10 Mar 1823; Jas T Alexander

Barber, George; Neel, Anna; Adam Niell (Neel); 28 Aug 1824; V McBee

Barber, John; Davis, Polley; Ephraim Davis; 30 Dec 1818; V McBee

Barber, John; Ferguson, S A; William Ferguson; 4 Mar 1844

Barber, Richard x; Rook, Susey; Wm Temple Coles; 12 Mar 1794; John Carruth

Barcley (Barkley), John; Hunter, Judith; John Hunter; 27 Feb 1786

Barger, David; Hawn, Charity; Simeon Barger; 15 Dec 1829; Jonas Bost

Barger (Berger), Isaac; Collance, Polly; George Seitz; 5 Feb 1809; Mic Cline

Barger, Isaac x; Bolch, Elizabeth; Andrew Herman; 21 Aug 1834; Henry Cline

Barger, Jesse; Herman, Leah; John Barger; 30 Jul 1831; Henry Cline

Barger, John; Hawn, Elizabeth; Jacob Yoder; 15 Aug 1828; V McBee

Barger, John; Bolick, Rachel; Henry Cloninger; 31 Mar 1836

Barger, Moses; Dietz, Sarah; Jacob Burnes; 28 May 1841; A J Cansler

Barger, Simeon Jr; Pitts, Fanny; John Barger; 18 Apl 1830; Henry Cline

Barger, Thomas; Sigman, Harriet; Simeon Barger; 13 Jul 1837; Danl Miller

Barkley, Archd C; Hill, Elizabeth; Henry Barkley, Thos Beatty; 10 Jan 1811 (end 1810); Henry Conner

Barkley, James; James, Delina; Henry Barkley, Henry Little; 22 Apl 1813; Henry Conner

Barkley (Bartley), Thomas J; Harvill, Catherine E; Robert L Barkley (Bartley); 28 Aug 1834; Wm Little

Barkly, Henry; Brotherton, Eliz; J W (or I W) Lowe; 3 Mar 1840

Barnes, Jasper N x; Denham, Margaret D; William C D Mclure; 27 Oct 1845; W Reeves JP

Barnes, John x; Sherril, Elizabeth; William Gilliland; 6 Oct 1806

Barnet, Daniel; Barnet, Winiford Balsora; Absolom Barnet; 12 Sep 1864; J A Huggins; M same date by J A Huggins Minister M P Church

Barnet, James; Smith, Jane E; Arthur F Barnet; 22 Nov 1858; D A Lowe; M 25 Nov 1858 by D A Lowe JP

Barnet, Joseph; Hager, Ann; --------; 31 Dec 1851; M this date by J W Moore JP; C only, no B

Barnet, Philip; Flanegen, Susanah; Daniel x Campbell; 15 Jul 1824; V McBee

Barnet, Randolph; Bynum, Barbara; Abraham Dayley (Dailey); 2 Aug 1814; V McBee

Barnett, Arthur F; Hager (Hoyle), Isabella; Jonas Sifford; 27 Dec 1851; V A McBee; M 7 Jan 1852 by J W Moore JP

Barnett, William; Mosteller, Elizabeth; Peter x Mosteller; 27 Mar 1813; V McBee

Barnhill, Samuel S; Nealey, Rebeca; Joseph Gladen; 24 Aug 1791

Barns, Eli; Fisher, Catherine; George Brown; 24 Nov 1833 (end 1832); Alexander Ward JP

Barnwell, James A; Armstrong, Mary C; Joseph O Daniel; 12 May 1845

Barret, Isaac; Baker, Margaret; James Baker; 22 Mar 1793; Joseph Steel

Barrier, Richard; Messey, Katrine; William Thomas; 20 Aug 1789; Joseph Steel

Barringer, David; Fry, Catharina; Solomon Shell; 3 Oct 1820; Mic Cline

Barringer, Joseph; Rudisel, Mary E; William Rudisell (Rudisel); 17 Oct 1832; V McBee

Barringer, Mathies; Pritched, Catharine; Michael Rudisill (Rudisale); 10 Oct 1810; J Summy

Barringer, Matthias; Bullinger, Susanna; Joseph Bollinger (Bullinger); 21 Mar 1804; John Dickson

Barringer, Rufus; Morrison, Eugenia E; C C Henderson; 1 May 1854; M 23 May 1854 by P T Penick (MG); "Rufus Barringer of Cabarrus Co"

Barron (Barren), Thomas; Martin, Elisabeth; James Martin; 12 Feb 1796; Jo Dickson

Baty (Beaty), Gabriel; Tucker, Eliza; Andrew Neel; 22 Mar 1823; V McBee

Baulding, Alfred x; York, Eliza; Joseph Saine; 17 Oct 1861; David Boiles Esq; M same date by David Boiles JP

Bauman, Daniel x; Moser, Barbara; George Herman; 28 Sep 1834; J D Herman

Bauman, Henry x; Bolick, Elissabeth; (Ger) Johannes Bauman; 29 Apl 1809; John Willfong

Baxter, Burr x; Odum, Delian; George x Baxter; 15 Dec 1866; W R Clark; "Freedman"; M same date by Wm J Hoke JP
Baxter, David; Martin, Mary; James Martin; 29 Jun 1791; Jo Dickson
Baxter, Henry x; Leonhardt, Ealzabeth; Joseph Carpenter; 10 Feb 1848
Baxter, Peter; Goodin, Elizabeth; William Baxter; 9 Sep 1824; M Hull JP
Baxter, Peter; Baxter, Sarah; William McClurg (McClurd); 22 Apl 1843; H Cansler
Baxter, Thos H; Bess, Euphemia; H H Alexander; 19 Sep 1866; W R Clark; M same date by H A T Harris
Baxter, William; Carpenter, Salley; John Carpenter; 14 Jan 1819; V McBee
Beach, Benjamin; Cox, Sarah; James x Cob; 17 Feb 1792; Robert Dickson
Beal, Benjamin x; William, Betsey; David x Abernathy; 2 Apl 1803; Jos Dickson
Beal, Christopher x; Sronce, Salley; Giles Beel (Beal); 7 Apl 1832; V McBee
Beal, John F; Forney, M C; Peter S Beel (Beal); 26 Oct 1859; M 27 Oct 1859 by H Asbury (MG)
Beal, Turner x; Bealk, Nancy; Stephen x West; 23 Nov 1798; Jno Dickson
Beal, William; Nixon, Isabella; James Nixon; 29 Sep 1789
Bealk, Payton x; Sutton, Betsy; James x Gutry; 27 Jul 1804; John Dickson
Bealt (Belt), William; West, Mary; Stephen x West; 10 May 1792; Robert Dickson
Beam, Andrew; Adams, Margaret; John Beam; 18 Aug 1832; Vardry McBee
Beam, Aron; Shull, Mary; Saml B Tucker; 4 Dec 1840; H Cansler
Beam, David; Shidle, Barbara; Charles Reinhardt; 1 Aug 1820; V McBee
Beam, David; Wilkiser, Marey; William Aderholt; 27 Dec 1821; Peter Hoyle for Verdry McBee
Beam, David C; Huss, Catharine; Andrew Roseman; 4 Jan 1858; W R Clark; M 7 Jan 1858 by Logan H Lowrance JP
Beam, David F; Bess, Susannah; Wesley Williams; 19 Dec 1855; D Williams; M 20 Dec 1855 by David Williams JP
Beam, Jacob M; Hoke, Euphemia; Frederick L Hoke; 7 Sep 1847; Robt Williamson
Beam, John; Carpenter, Mary; Jonas Rudisill (Rudisel); 17 Feb 1822; V McBee
Beam, John; Carpenter, Leanah; Newman Alexander; 1 Nov 1831; J T Alexander
Beam, John T; Doggett, Eveline; Aaron Beam; 4 Jan 1834; Carlos Leonard
Beam, John T; Hermon, Nercisis; John Harmon (Hermon); 28 Jan 1836; John Dickson
Beam, Joshua; Mooney, Mitilda; Wallace A Mooney; 27 Sep 1830; Jacob Reinhardt
Beam, Joshua; Havner, Susan; Levi Hafner; 18 Apl 1848; Robt Williamson
Beam, M R; Warlick, Sarah; W L Baker; 17 Dec 1866; W R Clark CC; M 18 Dec 1866 by Rev J W Naylor
Beam, Micheal; Warlick, Susannah; John Hearn (Heron); 6 Jul 1836; M W Abernathy
Beam, Moses; Mooney, Elizabeth; Michael Rudasil (Rudisill); 23 Mar 1831; Jno D Hoke
Beam, Peter; Houser, Elizabeth; John Chandler; 10 May 1851; Robt Williamson
Beam, Teter; Dickson, Letty; Nicholas J Tucker; 20 Sep 1821; V McBee
Beanack, Henry; Hedick, Polley; Thomas Williams; 17 Feb 1831; M Hull JP
Bear, Christian x; Dohertie, Molly; Nicholas x Hafner; 20 Oct 1788; Eliza Dickson
Beate, Robert x; Mays, Rebeca; Henry x Weathers; 12 Sep 1815; James T Alexander
Beatey, Francis; Gabriel, Mary; Joseph Henry; 17 Dec 1788; Eliza Dickson
Beatey, John, of Mecklenburg County; Gabrial, Susana; --------; 13 Feb 1788
Beatey, John; Smith, Jane; Dari (or Dav) Smith; 30 Dec 1797; Jo Dickson
Beatey (Beaty), Samuel; Devenport, Sally; Jonathan Beaty; 1 Aug 1816; V McBee
Beatty (Beatie), Charles; Sherrill, Judith; Theophilus Sherill (Sherrill); 10 Jan 1821; James T Alexander
Beatty (Beattie), Edmund; Lockman, Ibby; Franklin Caldwell; 5 Feb 1842
Beatty (Beaty), Franklin; Farwell, Elenor; Uriah Long; 30 May 1839; Wm Long JP
Beatty, John; Reed, Mary; William Childress; 4 Nov 1820; V McBee
Beaty, James U; Boyd, ____; Benjamin Smith; 5 Nov 1832; Eli Hoyl
Beaty, John; Black, Elizabeth; Henry Conner; 3 Sep 1806; Lwn Henderson CC; Note from Henry Conner to Clerk
Beaty, Jonathan; Chetham, Peggy; Samuel Ewing; 13 Mar 1818; V McBee
Beaty (Beatty), Joseph; Huson, Rebecca; John Chittam (Chittim); 19 Mar 1800; Jno Dickson
Beaty, Robert A; Leeper, Nancy E; John D Leeper; 19 Apl 1819; V McBee
Beaty, Thomas; Cornelias, Nancy; Thomas Brotherton; 20 Aug 1825; V McBee
Beaver, Hezekiah; Saunders, Patsey; Jacob x Painter; 17 Mar 1807; Lwn Henderson
Beaver, William x; Newton, Mary; Robert Will Davis; 13 Mar 1864; M same date by David Boiles JP
Beavin, Joseph x; Brendle, Margret; John Brendle (Ger Johannes Brendel); 16 Aug 1800; Ligt Williams JP

Bechtler, J A; Warlick, Maggie; F M Bechtler; 28 Nov 1865; A S Haynes; M same date by R N Davis Minister

Bedford, George P; Killian, Harriat; Richard Tallant; 29 Apl 1830; V McBee

Beel, Benjamin; Keener, Mary; Christopher Beel; 15 Jan 1850; Robt Williamson

Beel (Beal), Charles; Keaner, Molly; Christ Beel (Beal); 13 Nov 1835; M W Abernathy

Beel (Beal), Giles; Cleppard, Lovina; Henry Keever; 16 Jan 1828; V McBee

Beel, John x; Statia, Nancy; William Heaker (Heger); 15 Dec 1788; Eliza Dickson

Beel (Beal), Marcus; Keener Elizabeth; Charles Beel (Beal); 24 Dec 1839; Elisha Saunders

Beel (Beal), Richard; Arawood, Caroline; P Cannon (?); 21 May 1841; H Cansler

Beenick, Henry; Williams, Sarah; Peter x Cook; 8 Dec 1807; R Williamson

Beever, Henry (Ger Bieber); Sellars, Betcy; Michael Sellers (Sellars); 31 July 1815; V McBee

Belew, James x; Anderson, Jean; Christopher x Boston; 18 Jan 1803; Jonn Greaves

Belew, John; Warlick, Mary;. Westley Conley; ____ Nov 1835; Abel H Shuford JP

Belk, Chamberlain x; Beal, Nancey; Stephen x West; 24 Aug 1798; Jo Dickson

Belk, John; Earwood, Lucy; Fredk x Earwood; 2 Sep 1808; Danl M Forney

Belk, Thomas S; Norton, Elizabeth; Benjamin B x Conner; 27 Jul 1824; V McBee

Belk, West x; Gadberry, Nancy; John Rumfelt; 28 Oct 1822; Laws W Caldwell

Bell, Alexander; Oats, Mary; Wm D Hannah; 26 Jan 1836; Isaac Holland

Bell, Hugh; Black, Elizabeth; Abner Berry; 26 Aug 1830; J T Alexander

Bell, James; Grissum, Sopphia; Jesse Hallom (Holland); 1 Jan 1808; Jacob Forney

Bell, John; Clonger, Susanah; Elisha Jones; 10 Sep 1840 ((end 1843); Dl Hoffman JP

Bell, Lewis x; Coffey, Milley; Thomas Kennedy (Kenady); 11 Aug 1821; I Holland

Bell, R M; Ramsour, Lydia J; W G Ramsour; 8 Oct 1858; W R Clark Clk; M 10 Oct 1858 by J Ingold

Bell, Robert H; Rudisill, Ann; Samuel F D Baird; 13 Mar 1840; I H (or J H) Holland

Bell, Thomas M; Barkly, Nancy C; Thomas Bell; 15 Dec 1835; M W Abernathy

Belt, Isaac x; West, Phreby; Charles Witt (Whit); 26 Oct 1819; V McBee

Belt, Stephen x; West, Salley; Jonathan West; 26 Oct 1819; V McBee

Benfield, Daniel (Ger Daniel Benfiel); Pitts, Elisabeth; John Benfield (Ger Johannes Benfiel); 23 Mar 1823; Mic Cline

Benfield, Henry x; Bolick, Fanny; John Benfield; 10 Jul 1809

Benfield, John (Jr) (Ger Johannes Benfiel); Bolick, Margarate; Adam Bolick (Sr) (Ger Adam Bolch); 19 Aug 1820

Benfield, Joseph; Mingis, Betsy; Edwin B Torrence; 17 Sep 1836; J A Ramsour DC

Bengle (Pangle), Henry; Gross, Sary; Daniel Lore (Loore); 23 Sep 1813; Ligt Williams JP

Benick, Philip; Hinkle, Susana; Aaron S Robinson; 2 Sep 1833; V McBee

Bennett, Abraham; Hevener, Haty; John Huggins; 6 Jul 1808; Danl Forney

Bennett, Jacob; Coxe, Margt; Wm Ramsey; 27 May 1800; Jas McEwin

Bennett, William T; Alexander, Nancy C; Maxwell Wilson; 18 Aug 1836; Elkanah P Coulter

Bennick (Beanack), David R; Reinhardt, Maryann; Henry Beenick (Beanack); 14 Feb 1828; Major Hull JP

Benton, Buckley K; Harry, Mary Nell; Jacob Rush; 27 Mar 1823; V McBee

Benton, Calvin; Armstrong, Sarah; Pleasant x Fite; 9 Nov 1834; H N Gaston

Berrey (Berry), Alexander; Falls, Amanda; James A Falls; 21 Apl 1842; James Ferguson

Berrey (Berry), John; Blanton, Bazila; A L Hoke; 21 Dec 1841

Berrey (Barry), Richard; Burns, Polly; Wm A Compton; 12 Jun 1830; Isaac Holland

Berrier, Henry J; Hartzog, Mary E; A S Haynes; 22 Apl 1861

Berriman (Berryman), James C; Lowrance, Elizabeth B; Elkanah Shuford; 1 May 1828; M W Abernathy JP

Berry, Adam x; Abernathy, Milla; Matthias x Berry (Sr); 17 Jul 1825; Wm Little

Berry, Ebizur (Elizur) M; Acock, Harriot; Jacob Linebarger (Leinbarger); 24 May 1838; S C Robinson

Berry, George x; Lincoln, Patsey; Peter Costner; 12 May 1812; Lwn Henderson

Berry, Henry x; Bumgarner, Rutha; Francis M'Corkle (McOrkle); 12 Nov 1812; James•T Alexander

Berry, Hiram x; Linkhorn, Milley; David Stroup; 20 Aug 1813; V McBee

Berry, James; Gullick, Jane; _____; 1812; (N)

Berry, John x; Froy, Barbara; Peter x Froy; 10 Jan 1813; Phil Whitener JP

Berry, John; Rader, Charity; _____; 1817; (N)

Berry, Milton; Mellon, Cynthey; Robert Glenn; 27 Dec 1825; Isaac Holland

Berry, Thomas;· Summey, Catharine; Jacob Carpenter; 1807; (N)

Berry, Wm; Dorsey, Polly; Bassett Dorsey; 1801; (N)

17

Berry, Wm; Cox, Peggy M; --------; 1818; (N)

Bess, Boston; Lacky, Elizabet; --------; 5 Feb 1852; M this date by D Williams JP; R only, no B

Bess, Hiram; Wilson, Elizabeth; Joseph Wise; 11 Mar 1835; M W Abernathy

Bess, J F; Houser, S A F; Philip A Shull; 19 Sep 1866; W R Clark; M 27 Sep 1866 by H A T Harris

Bess (Best), Lawson; Beam, Catherine; Henry Carpenter; 22 Dec 1842; F A Hoke

Bess, Noah; Baggs, Sally ----; William Baggs; 17 Jan 1833; M Hull JP

Bess, Noah; Grigg, Jane; Wm T Williams; 1 Feb 1855; D Williams; M same date by J Finger (MG)

Bess (Biss), Peter x; Weathers, Leanna; Samuel x Hawkins; 8 Dec 1810; Jacob Ramsour

Bess, Thomas; Leonhardt, Louisa; R E Johnston; 19 Nov 1845; R Williamson

Best, Bosten (Bastian); Carpenter, Polly; Thomas x Carpenter; 10 Feb 1810; J Ramsour; Ambiguous

Best, Christin (Christian); Hoyl, Betsey; Fredk Best; 17 Feb 1796; Jo Dickson

Best, Daniel (Ger same); Rhoads, Mary; George Cathy (Cathey); 16 Dec 1794; Jo Dickson

Best (Bast), Jonas; Meheffey, Rosannah; James Mehaffey; 26 Feb 1818; Mic Cline

Best, Michael; Costner, Fanny; William Froneberger; 2 Mar 1818; V McBee

Best, Michael; Rhyne, Fany; Samuel Sarvies (Sarvis); 18 Dec 1843 (end 1842); ---- Reeves; Ambiguous

Best, Peter; Beam, Sarah; John H Roberts; 28 Nov 1840; H Cansler

Best, Petter (Jr?); Whitenbarger, Cristina; Boston Best; 13 Oct 1779; Adam Baird

Best, Samuel; Rhyne, Mary; John Rhyne; 14 May 1821; V McBee

Bevins, Jacob; Hubbard, Eliza; David Rhodes; 4 Mar 1859; D A Hanes; M same date by D A Hanes JP

Bevins, John x; Brillhardt, Catharine; John Brindle; 18 Jan 1831; J T Alexander

Bevins, John H; Hill, Sarah M C; William Robinson; 23 Mar 1830; J T Alexander

Bevins (or Bivins), Joseph x; Helms, Elisabeth; Jeremiah Seitz; 19 Jul 1832; P Stamey JP

Bigam, Samuel x; Carpenter, Barbary; William Davis; 17 Dec 1807; Maxl Chambers

Bigger (Bigars), James; Wilson, Eidey; John Wilson; 12 Jun 1786; Danl McKisick

Bigger, Samuel; Wilson, Sarah; John Wilson; 16 Feb 1790; John Moore .

Bigham, R H; Oats, Margaret M; John Oats; 13 Jan 1846; John Falls JP; Ambiguous

Bigham, Robert; Clark, Margret; James Clark; 28 Mar 1810; Saml Wilson JP

Bigham (Bighem), William; McClure, Jane; Isaac Henry; 22 Jan 1819; ---- Henry

Bigham, William; Wilson, Isabella; Wm J Wilson; 28 (or 20) Jul 1835; G Hoke

Biles (Boyls), Charles; Williams, Ann; William Biles (Boyls); 2 Oct 1821; V McBee

Biles (Boyles), Enoch; Eaton, Nancy; David Brendel (Brindle); 8 Nov 1815; V McBee

Biles, Noah; Mauney, Catharine; Miles x Williams; 6 Oct 1844; R Williamson Jr

Biles, William; Johnston, Dosey; Elisha Dyer; 20 Nov 1824

Bird, Benjamin; Willbanks, Elizabeth; Dexter Carpenter; 1 Nov 1830; V McBee

Bird, Francis; Abernathy, Franky; Temple Shelton; 29 Jul 1808; Danl M Forney

Bird, Frank x (Frdm); Rheindhart, Anna F (Frdwm); Alexander x Johnson (Frdm); 24 Dec 1866; H Asbury for W R Clark Clerk; M 25 Dec 1866 by D M Asbury JP

Bird, Henry x; Queen, Margaret; Richard B Smith; 6 Feb 1845; R Williamson Jr

Bird, John x; Drake, Margaret; Thomas x Adams; 12 Aug 1805; Lwn Henderson

Bird, John; McCarty, Barbara; Jonas Paysur (Paysour); 9 Nov 1844

Birk, James x; Vials, Betcy; Jesse Sanders; 21 Oct 1828; J T Alexander

Bisanar (Beisanar), Moses; Pelt, Margaret A; John V Pelt; 13 May 1838; Elisha Saunders JP

Bisaner (Bysinger), Jacob; Jetton, Sarah; Allen Alexander; 24 Mar 1836; M W Abernathy

Bisaner, Wm H (M); Asbury, Rebecca; A B Laney; 28 Sep 1865; A S Haynes; M 1 Oct 1865 by Elisha Saunders JP

Bishop, Beal; Childers, Mary; Wm x Bishop, Matthew x Goodson; 28 Jun 1790; Jo Dickson

Bishop, Edmond N (Nash); Huffstotler, Polley; John Huggin (Huggins); 22 Jun 1822; V McBee

Bishop, Jeremiah x; Parker, Jenny; Wm Guinn, Wm Bishop Senr, Beal Bishop; 24 Nov 1796

Black, Autison; Allen, Stanly; John Allen, Jere Sadler; 13 Oct 1808; Hy Conner; Doubtful

Black, C N; Harris, C A J; Saml Lander; 13 Jul 1866; W R Clark

Black, Daniel; Neil, Lucinda; Wiley Black; 24 Mar 1837; M W Abernathy

18

Black, David, of Iredell Co; Johnston, Elisabeth; Joseph Steel; 5 May 1791; Isaac Lorance
Black, Ephraim; Hamsley, Doshey; Joshua Roberts; 21 Dec 1790
Black, Ephraim; Homesly, Hester; Amos B Homesley (Homesly); 9 Jan 1844
Black, Ephraim; Smith, Sarah Ann; Lawrence Black; 23 Jun 1860; David Bailey JP; M same date by David Bailey JP
Black, James; Allen, Susanna; John x Allen; 1806; (N)
Black, James G (or S); Hansel, Sarah S; Joseph H Stroup; 16 May 1867; J A Huggins; M same date by J A Huggins Minister
Black, John; Ingle, Susannah; Rob Luckey; 1816; (N)
Black, John; Cody, Nancy; _____; 30 Nov 1851; M this date at Mosteller's Paper Mill by Rev B Jones; R only, no B
Black, Joseph; Wrenweeks, Sally; Danl Eaker; 1804; (N)
Black, Joseph; Havener, Polley; John Hafner (Havener); 22 Aug 1815; V McBee
Black, Joseph; Allen, Margaret; Aught Black; 1816; (N)
Black, Joseph x; Shull, Frances; Lawson Mauny; 9 Dec 1859; W R Clark; M 14 Dec 1859 by Alfred Black JP
Black, Lorenzo D; Weaver, Malinda; Lawrence Black; 12 Feb 1844
Black, Milas D; Helderman, Mary Ann C; J A G Potts; 17 Dec 1855; Elisha Saunders; M 20 Dec 1855 by Elisha Saunders JP
Black, Robert; Clark, Sally; Archibald (Archibald C) Barkley; 11 Jul 1826; Wm Little
Black, Samuel; Baldwin, Patsey; Jon Beaty (?); 3 Mar 1807; Hy Conner JP
Black, Samuel; Carpenter, Ann; Ephraim Mauney; 16 Nov 1835
Black, Samuel x; Cherry, Jane; Milton McGahey; 25 Nov 1862; R Nixon JP; M same date by Alex Ranson
Black, Stephen; Brown, Elizabeth; Michl Mauney; 1821; (N)
Black, Thomas; Lenhart, Barbara; Peter Mauny; 8 Jul 1815; James T Alexander
Black, Thomas; Stroup, Rebeckah; Peter Summey; 23 Sep 1825; V McBee
Black, Thomas P; Wilkinson, Martha S; Henry Nixon; 26 Mar 1842
Black, Vincent x; King, Sarah; L A Burch; 4 Nov 1866; R Nixon JP; M same date by R Nixon JP
Black, William; Forsyth, Elisabeth; William Nixon; 8 Dec 1795; John M Dickson
Black, William; Nixon, Elisabeth; Robert Nixon; 1 Jul 1797; Jno Dickson
Black, William Sr; Winters, Mime (?); James Back; 12 Oct 1809; Henry Conner
Blackburn, Daniel; Hause, Elizabeth; John x Waycaster; 14 Apl 1828; B J Thompson
Blackburn, Eli; Finger, Barbara; William Blackburn; 4 Jun 1793; W Alexander
Blackburn, Ephraim; Carpenter, Lavina; Martin Zimmerman; 1 Oct 1834; M W Abernathy
Blackburn, George; Warlick, Rachel E; Wm McCaslin; 14 Mar 1853; R Williamson; M 17 Mar 1853 by J R Peterson (Rev)
Blackburn, James; Heltebrand, Susanna; Wm Blackburn; 21 Mar 1803; John Dickson
Blackburn, John; Holman, _____; Joseph Morris; 23 Feb 1805; Js McEwin
Blackburn, John; Wells, Polly; Peter Hoyl; 7 Jan 1834; Major Hull JP
Blackburn, John H; Dellinger, Lavinia C; John P Anthony; 1 Aug 1846; Robt Williamson
Blackburn, Robert; Sherril, Polley A; Benjamin S Johnson; 12 May 1824; V McBee
Blackburn, Robert; Shell, Salley; David x Shell; 2 Nov 1825; V McBee
Blackburn, Robert x; Flanigan, Susan; David x Hoover; 20 Jan 1860; W R Clark
Blackburn, Saml; Shuford, Elizabeth; A H Ramsaur (Ramsour); 16 Nov 1841; L E Thompson
Blackburn, William; Davis, Esther M; James T Alexander; 23 Sep 1832; V McBee
Blackburn, Wm M S; Jacobs, Harriet L; John F Hinson; 25 Sep 1866; W R Clark CC; M 26 Sep 1866 by J Finger MG
Blackwood, Gideon; Mauney, Affy; Lawson Mooney (?); 1 Mar 1837; M W Abernathy
Blackwood, John; Stroup, Sarah Ann; H W Burton; 25 Apl 1846; R Williamson
Blackwood, Samuel; Falls, Rebeccah; John F Oats; 1 Feb 1837; M W Abernathy
Blake, Aaron x; Esterbrook, Ann; B F Foster; 19 Jul 1865; A S Haynes CCC, Jno P Anthony
Blake, Aaron x; Holdbrooks, Ann; John E McIvor; 25 Jul 1865; A S Haynes CCC, S P Sherrill; M same date by S P Sherrill JP
Blaloc (Blalock), John; Spain, Betcy; Richard Proctor; 17 Jul 1822; V McBee
Blalock, Andrew A x; Hicks, Epsey; Singleton x Hicks; 11 Apl 1842
Blalock (Blaylock), James; Sadler, Assenath; _____; 4 Jan 1837 Robert Abernathy
Blalock, Thomas R; Beattie, Charlotte R; Winslow F Blalock; 29 Jun 1844
Blalock, Winslow F; Beatty, Dovey B; A A Norwood; 21 Jul 1846; Robert Williamson
Blaylock (Blalock), David Jr; Sides, Louisa; Green Abernathy; 12 Oct 1822; V McBee

19

Blaylock, Hubbard x; Dellinger, Nancy; Andrew Dellinner (Dellinger); 5 Jun 1819; James T Alexander

Blaylock, William x; Armstrong, Mary; Robert Lucky, James Black; 28 Sep 1821; Wm Little JP

Bleckley, Charles; Cook, Anne; Barryman (Berriman) Cook; 4 Jul 1821; D Reinhardt, James McGinnas

Bleckley (Blakely), James; Lutz, Catherine; Hiriam x Ward; 3 Apl 1824; V McBee

Bleckley, Thomas C; Hooper, Eletha B; Maxwell Wilson; 15 Jun 1837

Blithe (Blythe), Stephen; Millican, Jane; Abraham Devenport; 7 Dec 1802; Lwn Henderson

Bluford, Daniel; Simson, Ann; Charles Witt; 19 Dec 1826

Bobo, Charles D; Simpson, Sarah A; J C Jenkins (Jinkins); 27 May 1847

Bodine (Bordine), Peter; Lollar, Jean; Augustus Perkins; 16 Aug 1792; Joseph Steel

Boger, John E; Ramsour, Mary Ann; James C Jenkins (Jinkins); 5 Dec 1848; Robt Williamson

Boggs, Andrew N; Hafner (Havner), Margaret A; David Williams; 22 Sep 1858; R Williamson; M 23 Sep 1858 by Danl Siegel JP

Boggs, David; Best, Sally; Thomas Williams; 1 Jan 1830; L M McBee

Boggs, Joseph; Wyont, Mary; Daniel Wyont; 5 Oct 1839; J A Ramsour

Boggs, Noah; Leonhardt, Temperance; Peter Baxter; 25 Nov 1850; Robt Williamson

Boggs, Thomas D; Williams, Anna; Joseph B Boggs; 16 Dec 1841; M Hull JP

Boggs, William; Cherry, ------; Jonathan Gullick; 15 May 1800; Jonn Greaves

Boiles, Joseph; Brindle, Viney; Elias Hull; 5 Jun 1858; W R Clark

Boiles (Boyles), Joseph; Greenhill, Luiza; Lawson Greenhill; 1 Sep 1858; Joshua Pendleton JP

Boils (Boiles), Alexander; McCaslin, Angeline; A C McCaslin; 8 Aug 1860

Boils, David; Young, Faney ; Joseph Stamey; 9 Jan 1832; P Stamey

Boils, John W; Stamey, Adaline; Andrew Roseman; 20 Jul 1861; W R Clark Clk; M 23 (25) Jul 1861 by Daniel Siegel JP

Bolch, Andrew; Bollinger, ------; Joseph Bovey; 20 Mar 1832; Henry Cline

Bolch (Bolick), Andrew; Deal, Rosanna; Joseph Bolch (Bolick); 17 Apl 1835; G Hoke

Bolch, Casper; Huffman, Julianna; John Seaboch; 28 Oct 1823; Mic Cline

Bolch, Elias; Mowser, Catherine; Solomon Bolch; 8 Jun 1837; Henry Cline

Bolch (Bolick), Godfrey; Probst, Sabina; Caspar Bolick (Ger Caspar Bolch); 8 Jan 1824; Mic Cline

Bolch, Hiram; Miller, Susannah; Henry Miller; 8 Jan 1843; Epm Yount JP

Bolch (Bolick), Jacob; Moroson, Sofiah; G I (or J) Willkie; ---- Jun 1841; J Yount JP

Bolch (Bolick), Jonas; Bolick, Sarah; John Tutherow (Totherow); 12 Jan 1842; R Williamson Jr

Bolch (Bolick), Joseph; Bollinger, Jolly; Andrew Bolch (Bolick); 17 Apl 1835; G Hoke

Bolch, Sebastian (Boston); Bolch, Catherine; Solomon Bolch; 2 May 1839; Henry Cline

Bolch (Bolick), Solomon; Bolick, Elizabeth; Casper Bolch (Bolick); 20 Oct 1825; Mic Cline

Boldwin, Armsted x; Groves, Anny; John Gibson; 14 Jun 1815; I Holland JP

Bolick, Adam x; Huffmon, Catherine; William x Deal; 22 Dec 1822; Zachary Stacy

Bolick, Ambrose; Shell, Rebecca; John Coulter; 2 Apl 1838

Bolick, Daniel (Ger Bolch); Simon, Susanah; John x Simon; 20 Jan 1811; John Willfong

Bolick, David (Ger Bolch); Simon, Rachael; Jacob Bolick (Ger Bolch); 8 Apl 1815; John Willfong JP

Bolick, David x; Null, Elizabeth; Adam Bolick, (Ger) Michael Hermon; 30 Nov 1820; Zachariah Stacy

Bolick, Gotfree (Ger Gottfred Bolch); Hertle, Cathrine, widow; John Benfield (Ger Benfiel); 16 Apl 1814; Mic Cline

Bolick, Henry; Hunsecker, Sally; Henry Cline; 24 Oct 1826; J T Alexander

Bolick, Jacob; Reder, Margered; Daniel Bolick (Ger Bolch); 23 Dec 1819; Mic Cline

Bolick, Jacob x; Dietz, Barbara; Jacob Bolick Sr (Ger Bolch); 11 Mar 1821; Mic Cline

Bolick, Joseph x; Sigman, Sally; Jacob x Longcrier (?); 27 Apl 1830; Mic Cline

Bolick, Robert; Hallman, Mary J; Monroe P Finger; 9 Sep 1861; W R Clark

Bolick, William x; Eikerd, Caty; Simon x Eikerd; 26 Mar 1814; Mic Cline JP

Bolinger, Abraham A; Grise, Martha E; Philip Plonk; 11 Oct 1859; M same date by Philip Plonk (JP)

Bolinger (Bullinger), Daniel J; Plonk, Mary; Robt E Johnston; 17 Jan 1848; Robt Williamson

Bollinger (Bullinger), Abraham; Oliver, Mary; Abner Berry; 5 Jul 1819; James T Alexander
Bollinger (Bullenger), Daniel; Trevelstedt, Betsy; James T Alexander; 14 Nov 1818; V McBee
Bollinger, David; Herbeson, Rebecca; Nancy Harbeson, Conrad Ward; 2 Oct 1808; Mic Cline
Bollinger (Bullinger), George F; Ramsour, Sally; Jno Hoke; 26 Jul 1802; Jno Dickson
Bollinger (Bullinger), Jacob A; Whitener, Rhoda; Michael Bollinger (Bullinger); 4 Nov 1841; R Williamson Jr
Bolton, Wm M; Delane, Mary A; J The Adams; 14 Sep 1865; A S Haynes CCC; M same date by E G Gage
Boman, Isaac F; McCullow, Harriet E; Allen Alexander; 22 Aug 1837; J A Ramsour DCC
Bomgarner, Luis x; Parker, Catherine; Jacobs Helms; 17 Feb 1814; Saml Wilson
Bomgarner, Philip G x; Styles, Rebecca; David x Keener; 11 Apl 1827; V McBee
Boncard, Oscar T de; Wesson, Rose; William J Hoke; 19 Apl 1849; Robt Williamson
Bond, Isaac; Reid, Rebecky; Robert Reed; 26 Oct 1791; Robert Dickson
Bonham, Absalom; Cock, Rebacka; Frs Cunningham; 8 Apl 1785; Danl McKisick
Bonham, Arnold; McMurry, Poley; Elijah Campbell; 10 Dec 1807; Danl Forney
Bonham, John; Spencer, Isabella; Joseph Spencer; 4 Sep 1799; Jno Dickson
Bookout (Beekout), Levi; Swaringame, Nancy; Joseph Bookout (Beekout); 7 Aug 1817
Bookout, Silas; Seury (?), Mary; David Bookout; 18 Jan (or Jul) 1833; L McBee
Boovey, David x; Smyer, Salley; David Smyer; 18 Dec 1820; V McBee
Borland (Borlin), John; Ormond, Mary; William Sims; 27 Jul 1769; Ezekiel Polk CC
Bost, Daniel; Cline, Anna Barbara; Jonathan Miller; 21 Feb 1832; L McB
Bost, David; Killian, Barbara; Daniel Smyer; 22 Oct 1814; Mic Cline
Bost, Eli; Smyre, Adaline; O C Green; 9 May 1835; M W Abernathy
Bost, Jacob; Mosteller, Frances; John R Smyer; 22 Sep 1838; H Cansler
Bost, Jesse; Wilson, Belina; Franklin Witherspoon (Weatherspoon); 3 May 1833; V McBee
Bost, Jonathan; Lutz, Sally; Conrad Fry; 11 Nov 1823; Mic Cline
Bost, Joseph; Bost, Polly; John Smyer (Smyre); 29 Apl 1830; Jonas Bost
Bost, Lawson; Killian, Susannah; Abel J Probst; 1 (?) Jan 1835; Mic Cline
Bost, Marcus L; Loretz, Mary J E; John P Anthony; 7 Sep 1849; Robt Williamson
Bostick, Littleberry; Graham, Sophynealy; William Graham; 28 Feb 1818; James T Alexander
Bovey, Conrad x; Moose, Sally; Matthias x Bovey; 15 Mar 1818; Mic Cline
Bovey, Joseph; Bolick, Mary; David Smyer; 9 Apl 1832; Mic Cline
Bovey, Matthias; Herman, Polly; Matthias x Bovey Sr; 24 Jan 1811
Bovey, Matthias; Ikerd, Margaret; Jacob Sepaugh Seapach); 13 Jan 1835; Henry Cline
Bovey, William; Mauney, Harriet; David x Bovey; 5 Apl 1824; Mic Cline
Bovy, John; Herman, Cathrine; Mathias x Bovey; 28 Mar 1811
Bower (Bowers), Thomas x; Senter, Judea; James Senter Jr; 2 Dec 1779; Andw Neel
Bowers, Gillan G (Powers, Gillum); Rhine, Barbara; James Moore; 13 Nov 1822; V McBee
Bowman, Boston; Mowser, Polly; John Bowman; 29 Nov 1836; Henry Cline
Bowman, Daniel (Ger Bauman); Isenhower, Catharina; Peter x Bowman; 24 Feb 1822; Fr Hoke
Bowman (Boman), Drewrey; Froy, Elisebeth; Peter Froy (Ger Peter Frey); 24 Nov 1803; Phil Whitener
Bowman, Jesse x; Hefner, Sarah; J White; 16 Apl 1837; John Moretz
Bowman, John; Raden, Lidia; Jonas Raden; 9 Jan 1834; J D Herman; Ambiguous
Bowman, John; Bollinger, Ann; Boston (Sebastian) Bowman; 6 Dec 1839; H Cansler
Bowman, Jonas; Little, Elizabeth; Daniel x Bowman; 2 Jan 1831; Fr Hoke
Bowman, Joseph; Little, Sary; Jacob Little; 21 Nov 1824; Fr Hoke
Bowman, Solomon x; Hawn, Sally; Absalom Miller; 18 Feb 1837; Ambiguous
Boyck, John Henry; Rine, Hannah; John M Call; 11 Dec 1805; Lwn Henderson
Boyd, Edward; Olliver, Sarah; John Oliver (Olliver); 26 Feb 1817; V McBee
Boyd, James; McGill, Rachel; John Oats, Ephraim McLean; 18 Dec 1794; Thomas x Miller, J Wilson
Boyd, John; Bomgarner, Michel; Thos Ward; 27 Oct 1820; V McBee
Boyd, John; Linch, Sarah; Willburn Boyd; 26 Dec 1861; M 15 Jan 1862 by J M Smith JP
Boyd, Moses; Barkly, Letty L; J H Bartley (Barkly); 31 Jan 1837; M W Abernathy
Boyd, Perry L F; Kelly, Margaret; P S Rush; 28 Aug 1856; J A Huss; M same date by Elisha Saunders JP

21

Boyd, Robert M; Rhyne, Elizebeth; Jacob Rhyne; 23 Sep 1833; Isaac Holland
Boyles (Boiles), Marcus W; Wood Susan A; Allen Alexander; 13 Mar 1866; M 14 Mar
    1866 by David Boiles JP
Bracket, George x; Williams, Mary Ann; John x Helms, Peter x Helms; 30 Sep 1858;
    P Carpenter JP; M same date by P Carpenter JP
Bradburn, Thomas; Reed, Elizabeth; Martin Sigman; 26 Apl 1831; L M McBee
Bradley, Alexander x; Smith, Eliza; David x Smith; 6 Aug 1834; Isaac Holland
Bradley, James A; Stinson, Martina; John Wm Bradley; 22 Sep 1824; Isaac Holland
Bradley, Joseph W; Jenkins, Mary; John Thomas; 25 Jul 1827; Isaac Holland
Bradley, Richard; Williams, Winifred; Richard Ledbetter, John Potts; 24 Dec 1778;
    Jonathn Hampton
Bradley, William D; Gibson, Elizebeth; William Gibson; 24 Oct 1823; I Holland
Bradly, Willis x; Self, Ruthey; James Lacky, John Oneel; 17 Nov 1812; Saml
    Wilson Dp C
Bradshaw, Field; Cloer, Nancey; Robert Haskins; 6 Feb 1811; Danl M Forney
Bradshaw, Fields x; Keener, Hanah; (Ger) Johannes Schlunker (?); 31 Aug 1798;
    Jno Dickson
Bradshaw, John; Bradshaw, Frances; Leml Sanders; 3 Jan 1804; Jno Dickson
Bradshaw, John; Shutly, Polly; Pride x Bradshaw; 2 Oct 1804; Jno Dickson
Bradshaw, John; Lowe, Francess; Thomas Lowe; 7 Aug 1817; John Allen
Bradshaw, John; Englifinger, Anna; Jonas Bradshaw; 18 Jan 1820; James T Alexander
Bradshaw, John F; Miller, Mary R; Wellington Miller; 4 Nov 1844; R Williamson
Bradshaw, Jonas; White, Elizabeth; Pride Bradshaw; 28 Mar 1818; James T Alexander
Bradshaw, Jonas; Barnett, Nancey; John H White; 27 Feb 1832; L McBee
Bradshaw (Bradsha), Josiah; Hogan, Betsey; Benjemin Bradshaw; 7 Aug 1789;
    Jo Dickson
Bradshaw, Josiah; Gaultney, Cenith; Larkin Bradshaw; 12 Mar 1831; L McBee
Bradshaw, Larkin; Parker, Nancy; William Williams; 17 Oct 1820; Joshua Roberts
Bradshaw, Larkin; Drum, Sarah; Michael C Abernathy; 16 Feb 1838; J T Alexander
Bradshaw, Pride; White, Sally; John Bradshaw; 13 Apl 1807
Bradshaw, Pride x; Newton, Sarah S; David F Clanton; 27 Sep 1855; J A Huss;
    M same date by P S Kistler (JP)
Bradshaw, William; McGinnas, Patsey; William Penny; 22 Jun 1829; J T Alexander
Brady, Albert x; Hoke, Polly; Marcus Smith; 16 Jul 1840; J Yount JP
Brady, James; Huffstetler, Elizabeth; John B Roneche; 2 Jun 1843; A J Cansler
Bragg, Benjamin; Myers, Catharine; Richard x Perkins; 13 Apl 1825; Thomas Low
Brandon, Larken P; Millon, Sarah; William E Millon (or Mellon); 13 Mar 1839;
    Isaac Holland; Married 14 March 1839
Brandon, Thomas L; Lewis, Louisa R; James J Lewis; 18 Dec 1845; J G Lewis JP
Braneman, Christen; Crismore, Mary; --------; no date; no B, notation on back of
    James Bigger's bond of 1786
Braneman, Christian; ------ ------; Henry Summerour; 13 Sep 1785; Danl McKisick
Brannum (Brenhem), William x; Glenn, Milley; Abner McAfee; 14 Oct 1793
Branon, William; Gregory, Susan; Joseph Gregory; 29 Oct 1828; Isaac Holland
Brawner, Lewis; Benton, Dulsinea; William McClure; 17 Mar 1821; Saml M'Kee
Brem, George; Wallace, Kitty G; George Shuford (Shufford); 29 Apl 1828
Brem, Jacob; Hoover, Eve; John x Smith; 9 May 1812; Lwn Henderson
Brendel (Brindle), David; Williams, Dicy; William Biles (Byles); 22 Jul 1823;
    Jas T Alexander
Brendel (Brendle), David; Leonhardt, Susan; V A McBee; 18 Feb 1852; M 19 Feb
    1852 by J H Robinson JP
Brendel (Brendle), Joseph H; Baily, Sarah L; John R Brendel (Brendle); 20 Oct 1853;
    Danl Siegel JP; M same date by Danl Siegel JP
Brendle (Brindel), Henry; Bivens, Mary; John Brindel (Ger Johannes Brendel); 5 Jun
    1810; Ligt Williams JP
Brian (Briant), James; Collins, Susan; --------; 29 Aug 1820; V McBee; Note from
    Abraham Collins: . . Jas Brian Jun a Citizen of York District . . So Carolina . .
    to marry my grand Daughter . . Witness: Jehu Evans . . Aug 28, 1820
Bridenbo, John x; Moore, Levira; Willard Boyden; 1 Jun 1832; J T Alexander
Bridgers, Nicholas; ------ ------; Thos C Bleckley; 21 Sep 1836
Bridges, Alfred; Neill, Salley; James Bridges; 27 Jul 1822; V McBee
Bridges, Elisha; Drum, Anne; John Bridges; 12 Dec 1817; V McBee
Bridges, Elisha L; ------ ------; Lawson Ward; 15 Oct 1835
Bridges, Gilbert; Havener, Mahala; Carlos Leonard; 27 Apl 1836; John B Harry
Bridges (Briges), John; Kinton, Mary; Edward Cason; 23 Jul 1802; John Dickson
Bridges, John L; Hollman, Mary Catharine; Abner McCoy; 12 May 1849; Robt
    Williamson

Bridges, Moses; Yarborough, Elizabeth; Lewis Yarbrough (Yarborough); 13 Nov 1826; Luther M McBee

Bridges, Thomas; Harry, Ann Elizabeth; John B Harry; 26 Jul 1831; John H Harry

Briles, Adam; Michel, Sussana; Daniel Michael (Michel); 3 Sep 1820; D Lutz JP; "Adam Brilse of the Staite of the Intiana"

Brilhart, Jacob (Ger Jacob Brilhardt ?); Lingerfelt, Catharine; Henry Hoke; 31 Jan 1806; Js McEwin

Brilhart, Peter x; Kizer, Ann M; John Goings; 3 May 1834; M W Abernathy

Brimer, Moses x; Mitchel, Elizebeth; Jonathan G Hand; 11 Jan 1828

Brimer, Samuel; Porter, Sally Ann; Jonathan G Hand; 19 Dec 1828; Isaac Holland

Brindel (Brindle), Joseph H; Nance, Francis S; Jacob J Brown; 8 Dec 1855; J A Huss; M 9 Dec 1855 by J Helderman JP

Brindle, David; Boiles, Abygail; Joseph Brindal (Brindle); 14 Feb 1813 (end 1815); Ligt Williams JP

Brindle, John; Williams, Polly; Christian Hambright (Hamright); 10 Nov 1823; Jas T Alexander

Brindle, Wesley; Greenhill, Eliza A; Jos H Brendel; 21 Apl 1861; M same date by David Boiles (JP)

Bringle, Lorenz (Lorance); Reep, Anna Catharine; William F Whetstine (Whetstone); 12 Aug 1828; M Hull JP

Brison, George R; Clark, Harriet E; Alexander Robinson; 21 Sep 1837

Broadway (Bradaway), Alen; Clifton, Edey; Philip Pollard; 2 Apl 1822; Jas T Alexander

Brodaway (Broadaway), Samuel; Rogers, Adiline; Robt Williamson; 6 Mar 1855; J A Huss; M same date by P S Kistler JP

Brooks, Abram x; Williams, Susan; Milton A Smith (?); 11 Dec 1832; L McBee

Brooks, Samuel (J); Fitchjerrold, Nancy; James Leonard; 15 Mar 1830; V McBee

Brooks, Walter; Smith, Rachel; John Alexander; 11 Nov 1788

Broomhead, John J x; Gardner, Antoinette; Charles D Conner (Connor); 10 Jul 1852; Robt Williamson; M 13 Jul 1852 by F J Jetton JP

Brotherton, George; Linebarger, Nancy; John Linebarger; 11 Oct 1810; Jeremiah Munday

Brotherton, George; Edwards, Rachel; George C Brotherton; 23 (?) May 1821; Samuel __ Turner

Brotherton, Hiram; Serat, Dorcas; George Brotherton; 22 Aug 1816; John Allen

Brotherton, Hiram; Hunicut (Honeycut), Rhoda; 22 Dec 1857; W R Clark Clk; M same date by Wm W Munday JP; L and C, no B

Brotherton, Hua; Little, Fanny; _____; 24 Mar 1852; M this date by W W Munday JP; R only, no B

Brotherton, Hugh x; Nantz, Martha K; Clement N Blythe; 10 May 1856; W B Withers JP; M 13 May 1856 by R H Morrison

Brotherton, James x; Crongleton, Margaret; John W x Brotherton; 20 May 1814; V McBee

Brotherton, John x; Howard, Minerva; Franklin Howard; 21 Mar 1851; Robt Williamson; M 23 Mar 1851 by W W Munday JP

Brotherton, Joseph; Dinkin, Polley; John Dinkin; 20 Feb 1806

Brotherton, Thomas; Brotherton, Martha; James Sherrill (Sherril); 29 Dec 1836

Brotherton (Brutherton), Thomas; Howard, Nancy; George x Brutherton; 7 Sep 1837; H Cansler Clk

Brotherton, William H; Brotherton, Nancy; James Brotherton; 16 Dec 1866; R Nixon JP; M same date by R Nixon JP

Browan (?) (Broun), Samuel; Dellinger, Mary; John Rudasill (Rudisel); 10 Aug 1826; V McBee

Brower, John x; Hefnar, Catherina; Philip x Hefnar; 3 May 1819; Fr Hoke; Ambiguous

Brown, A A (Anderson); Davis, R C; C J Frazier (Fraser); 24 Aug 1859; M 26 (25) Aug 1859 by A J Fox MG

Brown, Absalom; Killian, Elizabeth; Christopher _____; 25 (?) Oct 1814; _____ Cline

Brown, Absalom; Shull, Barbara; R Williamson Jr; 10 May 1845

Brown, Amos; Brown, Elisabeth; James Johnston; 17 Mar 1788

Brown, Andrew; Miller, Sarah; Joseph Stevenson; 19 Jul 1815; V McBee

Brown, Arthur; Dellinger, Mary M; Lewis Dellinger; 22 Jan 1822; James T Alexander

Brown, Daniel x; Cooper, Margaret; William Johnson; 21 May 1818; V McBee

Brown, Elijah P; Glenn, Rachel; Milton W Grissom; 29 Mar 1827; I Holland, Polly Holland

Brown, George; Helderman, Fany (?); Jacob Helderman; 18 Apl 1809; Thos Wheeler

Brown, George; Litten, Viney; John Litten; 7 Mar 1838; Wm Long

23

Brown, George; Havner, Sarah; Jonas Brown, Stephen Hafner (Havener); 22 Dec 1850; Robt Williamson; Uncertain; groom may be Jonas Brown

Brown, H H; Abernathy, Sarah A; John x Morrison; 8 Sep 1860; W R Clark; M same date by Philip Plonk JP

Brown, Jacob J; Plonk, Christena; E M Sullivan; 20 Feb 1854; M 23 Feb 1854 by David Crouse JP

Brown, James x; Antoney, Salley; Simon x Hager; 3 Apl 1800; John Crouse JP

Brown, James; McCarver, Nancy; James McCarver; 1 Jun 1803; Eliza Greaves

Brown, John; Dellinger, Betcy; James Bevings (Bivings); 25 Jan 1819; V McBee

Brown, John; Mauney, Catharine; Jacob McCarty; 23 Oct 1821; James T Alexander

Brown, John; Robinson, Eliza; E F M (E F N) Lewis; 14 Dec 1849; Robt Williamson

Brown, John x; Hedspeth (Hedgpeth), Caroline; Jonas x Brown; 26 Nov 1857; Robt Williamson; M 27 Nov 1857 by David Crouse JP

Brown, John A; Reel, Susan A; Lauson A Dellinger; 1 Feb 1850; Robt Williamson

Brown, John P (or T); McCombs, Rosannah; Alexander McNight; 14 Nov 1814; James T Alexander

Brown, Jonas see Brown, George

Brown, Levi; Roseman, Lile; Daniel Roseman; 12 Nov 1835

Brown, Levi; Roseman, Nancy; Daniel Deal; 27 Apl 1841; Fr Hoke JP

Brown, Logan x; Cosner, Catharine; Joshua x Cosner; 29 Oct 1833; Miles W Abernathy CC

Brown, Luke; Hanks, Ann; Richard x Hanks; 12 Sep 1821; Saml MKee

Brown, Martin L (Dr); Bost, Catharine E; Henry Pharr; 31 Dec 1855; M 1 Jan 1856 by A J Fox MG

Brown, Moses; Hedgecock, Elisabeth; Thomas Hedgcock; 26 Dec 1808; Saml Wilson

Brown, Parker; Ellison, Margaret; Josiah Brown; 4 Nov 1818

Brown, Philip x; Morrison, Nancy; John x Reynolds; 8 May 1834; M W Abernathy CC

Brown, Robt F x; Hullet, Martha E; J M Carpenter; 28 Nov 1865; A S Haynes; M 30 Nov 1865 by J W Naylor MG

Brown, Robert H; Self, Nancy; Wilson Norman; 9 Dec 1828; V McBee

Brown, Robert H; Reynolds, Rachael; W W McGinnas; 11 May 1840; H Cansler

Brown, William x; McCallister, Patsey; Wm McCallister; No date; Williams Governor 1799-1802

Brown, William; Davis, Mary; William Moore, Isaac Davis; 23 Sep 1806; Betsey Henderson

Brown, William x; Mauney, Sarah; Christian Eaker; 23 Nov 1833; M W Abernathy

Brumby, Richard T; Brevard, Mary M; Charles C Henderson; 18 Apl 1828; J T Alexander

Brunt (or Breent), William R; Downs, Mary Ann; _____; 6 Mar 1859; W R Clark Clk; M same date by R Nixon JP; L and C, no B

Bryan, John; Hager, Mary; Simon Hager; 22 Dec 1789

Bryant (Briant), James; Hager, Ebby; Henry Edleman; 20 Oct 1812

Buchanan, James; Johnston, Sally; Robert McCall; 16 Dec 1816; James T Alexander

Buchanan, Thomas; Nowlan, Nancy; John Nolan (Nowlan); 12 Oct 1813; James T Alexander

Buchanan (Buchannan), Thomas; Shiphard, Polly; Willis Reeves; 12 Aug 1830; Isaac Holland

Buckhannon (Buchannan), John N; Beatie, Mary; Abner Berry; 8 Jan 1819; Jas T Alexander

Buff, Henry; Howser, Anna; Abraham Hafner (Havener); 25 May 1836; John B Harry

Buff, Martin x; Kline, Rosannah; George x Buff; 22 Dec 1789; James Dickson

Buise, Elisha; Ireland, Elizabeth; M Reuben Perkins; 6 Jan 1836; M W Abernathy

Bulingar, George F x; Springs, Margaret; William x Wells; 5 Apl 1843; And Hoyl

Bullenger (Bolinger), Christen; Reynolds, Sally; Martin Smith; 9 Jan 1837; M W Abernathy

Bullinger, Matthias (Ger Mattheus Bollinger); Peterson, Pricilla; Thomas Fisher; 13 Nov 1789; Joseph Steel

Bullinger (Bollinger), Michael; Whitener, Catherine; Andrew Bolch (Bolick), Joseph Bolch (Bolick); 12 May 1835; Abs Miller

Bumgardner (Bomgarner), Moses x; Mathews, Rachael; Thomas x Bumgardner (Bomgarner); 22 Sep 1837; Wm Herman JP

Bumgarner, Andrew x; Bandy, Nancy; Absalom Bumgarner; 20 Aug 1814; James Taylor Alexander

Bumgarner, Andrew; Triplet, Lavina; John Bumgarner; 17 Dec 1834; M W Abernathy

Bumgarner (Bomgarner), Charles; Odom, Rebeckah; Robert Murell (Murrel); 29 Aug 1821; V McBee

Bumgarner, John x; Ward, Katrine; Fredrick x Ward; 24 Jun 1793; Joseph Steel
Bumgarner, John A; Abernathy, Mary; George Moose; 26 Feb 1828; Electious Conner JP
Bumgarner, Melcher x; Troutman, Mary Ann; Isaac Taylor; 13 Aug 1811; D M Forney
Bumgarner, Moses; Ichard, Charity; Elias Plott; 8 May 1798; Jno Dickson
Bumgarner, Peter x; Wates, Elender; James x Collis, Leijah x Self; 1 Oct 1835; John Bumgarner, Andrew Dickson
Bumgarner, Thomas x; Bolick, Regina; Joseph x Flowers; 23 Oct 1831; Henry Cline
Bumgarner, Thomas G x; Deal, Sally; John Bumgarner; 30 Dec 1823; Jas T Alexander
Bumgarner, Wallace x; Lefever, Jemimah; Noe Sullivan; 30 Dec 1835; M W Abernathy
Bumgerner, John x; Odam, Elisabeth; Jacob Wike (Ger Weik), Daniel Setzer; 29 Dec 181__ (end 1815)
Burch, R E; Kincaid, Mary C; L A Kayler; 25 Feb 1866; R Nixon JP; M same date by J Finger MG
Burch, Richard; King, Elisabeth; Peter Kimball; 25 Jul 1800; Jno Dickson
Burch, Thos F; Ward, Mira; Richd E Burch; 30 Oct 1842; John D King
Burk, Monroe x; Cronester, Rachael; Thomas L Painter; 22 Sep 1838; H Cansler CC
Burk, Yancy x; Beal, Salley; James x Burk; 18 Oct 1827; V McBee
Burke, Green x; Henkle, Eliza; James x Burke; 2 Apl 1827; V McBee
Burnett, A Jenkins; Crouse, Margaret; William Armstrong; 26 Oct 1826; Luther M McBee
Burns, Daniel; O'Neel, Faney (?); Christopher Oneel, Saml Waller; 1 Jan 1801
Burns, Jacob; Barger, Jemima; Abram (Abraham) Cook; 18 May 1834; Jonas Bost
Burns, James x; Parker, Elizabeth; Christopher Carpenter; 2 Nov 1822; V McBee
Burns, James x; Clippard, Nancy; Morgan x Robinson; 17 Jan 1831; James T Alexander
Burns, John; Hause, Christina; Philip Rudisell (Rudisill); 20 Dec 1830; J T Alexander
Burns, Philip; Bost, Elizabeth E; Silas Bost; 2 Feb 1835; G Hoke
Burton, Alfred M; Fulenwider, Elizabeth; Jacob Ramsour; 1 Jun 1811
Burton, James M; Johnston, Martha; Jacob Summey; 8 Feb 1812; H Y Webb
Burton, Robert H; Fulenwider, Mary; Robert Williamson; 11 May 1813; V McBee
Buthof (or Butloof), Gasper x; Shull, Elizabeth; Joseph Henry; 27 Mar 1785; Jo Henry
Butler, Thornton; Middlekauff, Mary A E; Andrew Ramsaur (Ramsour); 3 Sep 1850; Robt Williamson
Butt, Zephaniah; McIlvaine, Anna; R Williamson Jr; 25 Feb 1845
Butts, David; Shuford, Elizabeth M; Alfred Hoke; 8 Jan 1834; Carlos Leonard
Butts, Henry; Cline, Charity; John Petry (Ger Johannes Pettri); 21 Jan 1820; V McBee
Butts, John; Mauney, Elizabeth; David Reinhardt; 26 Jul 1835
Butz, Michael (Ger Botz); Dellinger, Betcy; Solomon x Stroup; 12 Sep 1812; V McBee
Byars, Edward (per W J W); Henry, Jane; Wm J Wilson; 27 Feb 1812; Lwn Henderson
Byars, Robert x; Houston, Jane; William x Tucker; 24 Mar 1804; John Dickson
Byers, Wm x; _____ _____; Wm x Earwood (Carwood); 8 Jan 1796
Bynum, Albert A; Abernathy, Mary M; M D x Dellinger; 28 Aug 1866; W R Clark CC; M 8 Sep 1866 by L M Nolen Minister
Bynum, Arthur; Williams, Mary; Robert Abernathy (Jr); 19 Sep 1777; Andr Neel
Bynum, Gray; Cox, Elisabeth; Benjamin Beech; 23 Apl 1791; Jo Dickson
Bynum, James x; Beale, Betsy; John Bynum; 6 Mar 1809
Bynum, John; Heaker, Elizabeth; John (?) Heaker; 18 Jan 1814; Blair M'Gee
Bynum, John x; Hovis, Fanny; Monroe x Burke; 28 Mar 1849; Robt Williamson
Bynum, John G; Litton, Candis; Elias M Kelley; 7 Feb 1822; V McBee
Bynum, John S x; Williams, Elizabeth; Philip G Regan (Regans); 29 Jul 1857; W B Withers JP; M 9 Aug 1857 by Robert Nixon Esq
Bynum, Rufus L x; McMinn, Martha; Larkin Bradshaw; 3 Nov 1839; H Cansler CC
Bynum, Vincent x; Robeson, Elizabeth; John x Bynum; 14 Mar 1834; Elisha Saunders
Bynum, W P; Shipp, A E; W H Miller; 2 Dec 1846
Bynum (Binam), William; Richards, Margaret; Valentine Richards; 21 Feb 1818; James T Alexander
Bynum, Wm L; Bradshaw, Catharine; Rufus Lour; 27 Dec 1852; M 30 Dec 1852 by Elisha Saunders JP
Byres (Byers), Franklin x; Wilson, Mary; R F Harriss (Robt T Harris); 7 Dec 1859; M 8 Dec 1859 by R G Ramsey (JP)
Byrum, Upton; Cloninger, Mary; Moses Cloninger; 18 Jan 1831; J T Alexander
Bysinger, John x; Richardson, Nancy; Jacob Link; 6 Oct 1835; G Hoke

Cahill, John P; McGinnas (Maginnas), Alice E; --------; 9 Sep 1857; J A Huss
    Clerk by R Williamson DC; M 15 Sep 1857 by Revrd A T McNeal; L and C, no B
Caldwell, Andrew; Wagener, Polley; William Little; 6 Nov 1807; Thos Wheeler
Caldwell, Elam; Motz, Elizabeth; Franklin A Hoke; 19 Aug 1840; H Cansler
Caldwell, Franklin; Lockman, Mary; --------; 10 Apl 1852; M this date by W W
    Munday JP; R only, no B
Caldwell, J F; Williams, Martha; R W Munday; 5 Sep 1865; A S Haynes CCC;
    M 6 Sep 1865 by H Munday
Caldwell, James; Boggs, Jien; James Boggs; 31 Aug 1795; Jo Dickson
Caldwell, Samuel; Cauble, Rachael; Jonathan Gullick; 13 Apl 1785; Jo Dickson
Caldwell, Thomas; Lockman, Sarah; Hail M Munday (Monday); 8 Dec 1841
Caldwell, William; Campbel, Elizabeth; Robert Campbell; 30 Nov 1785
Caldwell, William; Waggoner, Rebecah; Edmond Waggener; 13 Dec 1804; Thos Wheeler
Calloway, Joseph W; Johnston, Ann; W H Miller; 5 Nov 1845; R Williamson
Camel, Abel x; Finger, Ann; Israel A Spencer; 29 Mar 1837; Miles W Abernathy
Camel, William x; Johnson, Elizabeth Ann; A S (Amen S) Johnson; 10 May 1840;
    M Hull JP
Campbel (Campbell), James; McCord, Sarah; William McCord; 16 Mar 1789
Campbell, Andrew x; Hartzog, Julia Ann; Leander x Campbell; 24 Apl 1852; Robt
    Williamson; M 30 Apl 1852 by Rev David Crooks
Campbell, Daniel x; Willis, Rosena; Jacob Eply (Ger Eble ?); 9 Jun 1809; H Y Webb
Campbell, Henry; Lutz, Leah; James Wilson; 10 Aug 1823; V McBee
Campbell, James; Abernathy, Elizabeth; Nathaniel Cline; 23 Dec 1833; Carlos Leonard
Campbell, James A; Dailey, Jane M; A P James; 1 Apl 1857; W R Clark; M 2 Apl
    1857 by J W Moore JP
Campbell, John; Sleagle, Sarar; (Ger) Friederich Schlegel, David Bailey; 16 Oct 1812;
    Saml Wilson ____
Campbell, John; Halman, Elizabeth; Daniel x Halman; 2 Nov 1819; Jas T Alexander
Campbell, John; Bumgar, Elizabeth; Robert Boyd; 11 Feb 1834; M W Abernathy
Campbell, Joseph B; Jenkins, Leanna; Robison Moore; 17 Jul 1810; H Y Webb
Campbell, William; Maclean, Eliza J; Richard D S McLean (Maclean); 15 Jul 1823;
    Mary McKee
Campble, Matthew (of Iredell); Steel, Ruth; Saml Steel; 23 Feb 1790; Joseph Steel
Canada, Alexander (Ger Cannada); Lutz, Mary; John Willfong Sr; 21 Apl 1830;
    J T Alexander
Canipe, Daniel x; Hubard, Luisa; Daniel x Hubard (Hubbard); 15 Nov 1855; D A
    Haines; M 15 (or 18) Nov 1855 by D A Haines JP
Canipe, Joseph J; Wilson, Sarah Emet; Alexander W Pool; 5 Feb 1861; G W Hull;
    M same date by G W Hull
Cannon, William F; Linebarger, Eliner; Eli Linebarger; 12 Apl 1830; And Hoyl
Canseler (Cansler), Henry; Ornt, Mary; Henry Schenck; 23 Mar 1824; Jas T Alexander
Canseler (Cansler), Henry; Hinson, Mary; F M Reinhardt; 28 Oct 1840; H Cansler
Canseler (Cansler), Peter; Rozzel, Nancy; Henry Schenck Jr; 19 Feb 1825; Jos E Bell
Canseler (Cansler), Philip Jr; Smith, Evilene; John Zimmerman; 15 Aug 1826; V McBee
Cansler, Daniel; Smith, Sarah; Drury G Abernathy; 4 Oct 1831; J T Alexander
Cansler, Henry; Shuford, Fanny; James M Erwin; 13 Jun 1822
Cansler, John; Brown, Synthia; Willington Miller; 17 Apl 1838; H Cansler
Cansler, Philip (Ger Philip Gansler); Quigle, Mary; Michael Quigle (Ger Michael
    Quickel); 12 Jun 1790
Capps, Franklin x; Fite, Esther; John x Brimer; 10 Jun 1833; Isaac Holland
Capps, Thomas B; Smith, Martha; Andrew C Fulenwider; 11 May 1842; And Hoyl JP
Carl, Joseph; Henry, Isabella; Robt Patterson; 1 Apl 1810 (end 19 Jul 1810)
Carns, David B (of Mecklenburg Co); Scott, Nancy; Charles Carnes (of Mecklenburg
    Co); 27 Feb 1812; Wm Scott
Carouthers, Edmond; Lewis, Haney; James Clifton, John x Martin; 30 Aug 1807;
    Hy Conner JP
Carpanter, Peter x; Carpanter, Mary; James Kiesr (Kizer); 4 Aug 1827; J T Alexander
Carpenter, Adolphus; Lingfelt, Mary; W F Carpenter; 5 May 1866; D A Haines JP;
    M same date by D A Haines JP
Carpenter, Alford (Alfred); Warlick, Abigail; Benjamin Carpenter; 1 Oct 1842
Carpenter, Andrew; Ellmore, Anne; George Carpenter; 26 Apl 1825
Carpenter, Andrew; Smith, Sophia; John R Dunn; 19 Apl 1831; L M McBee
Carpenter, Christopher; Dellinger, Mary E; Christopher Carpenter; 26 Sep 1818;
    V McBee; One of above is Christopher Carpenter Jr, the other is Jacob's Son
Carpenter, Christopher (Christian); Eaker, Sally; Christopher han Bright (Christian
    Hamright); 16 Dec 1818; V McBee; ("Christian Carpenter, Jacob's son")

Carpenter, Christopher x; Carpenter, Anna; Martin x Carpenter; 14 Nov 1831; L McBee
Carpenter, Christopher; Williams, Martha; Andrew Gilbert; 13 Aug 1833; V McBee
Carpenter, Daniel (Ger Daniel Zimmerman); Pasehaur, Betsey; Jonas Mosteler (Mosteller); 12 Nov 1809; Danl M Forney
Carpenter, Daniel; Hager, Margaret; Michael Carpenter; 27 Aug 1834; M W Abernathy
Carpenter, David (Ger David Zimmerman); Rhinehart, Elizabeth; Daniel Stricknan (Ger Daniel Stricker); 1 Aug 1789
Carpenter, David; Childress, Rosanah; William Conner; 13 Jun 1818; V McBee
Carpenter, Elias x; Johnson, Sally S; Christopher x Carpenter; 26 Sep 1832; J T Alexander
Carpenter, Emmanuel; Cloninger, Nancy; Joshua Carpenter; 18 Mar 1837
Carpenter, Fredk (Ger Friderich Zimmermann); Kyser, Catharine; Henry Carpenter; 8 Apl 1800
Carpenter, Frederick; Fronebarger, Barbara; Daniel Caustner (Costner); 8 Mar 1821; James T Alexander
Carpenter, George; Carpenter, Barbara; Peter x Carpenter; 9 May 1827; V McBee
Carpenter, George x; Kizer, Narcissa; David x Carpenter; 28 Feb 1863; W R Clark; M 5 Mar 1863 by David Crouse JP
Carpenter, George; Lourance, Elizabeth; Daniel Carpenter; 13 Feb 1865; W R Clark; M 14 Feb 1865 by R H Abernethy JP
Carpenter, H F (Franklin); Carpenter, Mary Ann; Daniel Carpenter; 29 Mar 1852; Robt Williamson; M 7 Apl 1852 by Rev David Crooks
Carpenter, Henry; Laymen, Fanny; Martin Friday (Ger Freitag); 5 Feb 1790
Carpenter, Henry (Ger Henrich Zimmermann); Mostiller, Catharine; John Carpenter; 8 Dec 1801; Jno Dickson
Carpenter, Henry; Hoyle, Anne; Samuel Bigham; 12 May 1816; Daniel Lutz
Carpenter, Henry; Blackburn, Elizabeth M; J C Jenkins (Jinkins); 19 Dec 1848
Carpenter, Isaac W; Matthews, Eliza; James A Hardy (Hardie); 14 Nov 1839; H Cansler
Carpenter, J M; Bess, Jane Catharine; J A Huss; 23 Sep 1861; W R Clark
Carpenter, Jacob; Quickiel, Catherine; Jacob Carpenter (?); 27 Feb 1800; Peter Hoyl
Carpenter, Jacob; Jinkens, Anne; Lwn Henderson; 7 Feb 1805
Carpenter, Jacob (Jr); Barringer, Betsy; John Campbell; 27 Oct 1818; V McBee
Carpenter, Jacob; Weaver, Elizabeth; Valentine x Harris; 6 Jan 1834; G Hoke
Carpenter, Jacob; Loretz, Mary; Samuel Blackburn; 20 Sep 1837; H Cansler
Carpenter, Jacob x; Keener, Margaret; Joshua Carpenter; 30 Aug 1859; M 1 Sep 1859 by Robt Blackburn JP
Carpenter, Jacob x; Hoyl, Violet; Thos W Lindsay (Lindsey); 2 Mar 1866; A Costner
Carpenter, James; Simon, Rachel; John x Ashe; 6 Dec 1796; John Dickson
Carpenter, Joel; Hovis, Sally; Marcus L Hoke; 2 Jun 1835; M W Abernathy; Ambiguous
Carpenter, John; Carpenter, Mary; John Carpenter; 6 Jan 1803; Jno Dickson; One is John Carpenter Senr; one signs with mark
Carpenter, John; Ramsey, Margret; Henry Summerour; 11 Jul 1812; Ligt Williams JP
Carpenter, John; Whisenhunt, Anne; John Whisnant (Whisenhunt); 31 May 1813; V McBee
Carpenter, John; Carpenter, Rebeckah; Samuel Bigham; 20 Dec 1813; V McBee
Carpenter, John; Ramsour, Mary; John Heedick; 9 Oct 1815; James T Alexander
Carpenter, John; Baker, Olly; Joshua Clark; 12 Aug 1830; J T Alexander
Carpenter, John x; Baker, Hetty; Absalom x Carpenter; 27 Dec 1849; Robt Williamson
Carpenter, John J; Shuford, Catharine; Jacob F Dailey; 16 Mar 1842; R Williamson Jr
Carpenter, Jonas; Kizer, Mary; Jacob Carpenter; 22 Dec 1806
Carpenter, Jonas; Roberts, Sally; Michael Quickel (Quickle); 28 Aug 1824; V McBee
Carpenter, Jonathan; Kistler, Barbara; Henry x Kistler; 27 Jul 1819; V McBee
Carpenter, Jonathan; Clay, Anna; H Cansler; 20 Aug 1856; M 21 Aug 1856 by Maxll Warlick JP
Carpenter, Joseph; Carpenter, Elizabeth; Jonas Mosteller; 15 Oct 1814; V McBee
Carpenter, Joseph; Bess, Mary; Thomas Bess; 31 Mar 1847; George Coon JP
Carpenter, Joshua; Summey, Elizabeth; Joel Carpenter; 10 Jul 1837; M W Abernathy
Carpenter, Joshua; Keener, Mary; D W Carpenter; 2 Jan 1866; A S Haynes CCC; M 4 Jan 1866 by Elisha Saunders JP
Carpenter, Joshua P; Beam, Barbara C; Philip Plonk; 8 Oct 1856; W R Clark; M 9 Oct 1856 by David Crouse JP
Carpenter, Lawson; Kizer, Ruthy; Martin Zimmerman; 18 Dec 1834; M W Abernathy
Carpenter, Levi; Perkins, Salley; Jacob M Allen; 6 Jan 1827; V McBee
Carpenter, Levi; Keener, Elizabeth; Joel Carpenter; 4 Sep 1838; H Cansler CC

Carpenter, Martin; Carpenter, Anna; James Kizer; 8 Dec 1827; V McBee
Carpenter, Michael; Conner, Mary; William Conner; 13 Jan 1823; V McBee
Carpenter, Michael; Carpenter, Rebeccah; Miles W Abernathy; 16 Mar 1835
Carpenter, Michael; Carpenter, Elithabeth; Lawson D (or A) Reinhardt; 24 Sep 1835;
    M W Abernathy; Ambiguous
Carpenter, Moses; Costner, Abatine; Peter Carpenter; 18 Jun 1827; V McBee
Carpenter, Nicholas; Plunk, Cathrine; Jonas Mosteller; 5 Dec 1812
Carpenter, Nicholas (Ger Nicklus Zimmerman); Wheard, Catherine; John Lourance
    (Lorance); 5 Nov 1832; Z Stacy JP
Carpenter, Noah; Kiser, Barbara; Henry Kiser (Ger Heinrich Kaiser); 7 Jun 1823;
    Jas T Alexander
Carpenter, Noah C; Hoyle, Mary A; W M Hull; 8 Jan 1867; W R Clark; M 10 Jan
    1867 by H A T Harris
Carpenter, P H; Harriss, Sarah; J M Carpenter; 5 Jan 1861; M 8 Jan 1861 by
    P Carpenter JP
Carpenter, Paul x; Lavender, Vina; John Helton (Hilton); 28 Dec 1840; H Cansler
Carpenter, Peter; Lutz, Susannah; Thomas Williams; 8 Jan 1829; M Hull JP
Carpenter, Peter; Setzer, Sally; James Leonard; 12 Apl 1830; J T Alexander
Carpenter (Carpanter), Philip; Carpanter, Sally; David Rudisill; 22 Sep 1827; J T
    Alexander
Carpenter, Robert C; Shitle, Martha; Wm Towery; 20 Dec 1865; A S Haynes CCC;
    M 21 Dec 1865 by Rev C A Pickens Supt Cleavland Ct
Carpenter, Samuel; Rudesell, Elisabeth; (Ger) Pete Zimerman; 4 Oct 1804; John
    Dickson
Carpenter, Samuel; McCormick, Jane; John S McCormick; 8 Jan 1824; Jas T Alexander
Carpenter, Samuel; Mauney, Catharine; Philip Carpenter; 9 Mar 1824; Jas T Alexander
Carpenter, Samuel; Brown, Polly; M W Abernathy; 30 Sep 1835
Carpenter, Samuel; Carpenter, Elizabeth; John F Leonhardt; 30 Mar 1841
Carpenter, Solomon; Carpenter, Sally Salina; John F Hill; 7 Mar 1843
Carpenter, Thomas; Kiser, Polly; Bosten (Bastian) Best; 5 Oct 1810; Jacob Ramsour
Carpenter, William; Rudicell, Milly; Abraham Carpenter; 18 Dec 1807; Maxl Chambers
Carpenter, William x; Kizer, Barbara; Edward McClurg (E Nathaniel McClerd);
    5 Feb 1844; W Williamson
Carpenter, William; Baker, Elizabeth; Allen Baker; 1 Nov 1845; R Williamson
Carpenter, William A I (or J); Dellinger, Rosannah; Adam Dellinger; 24 Mar 1848;
    Robt Williamson
Carpenter, William J; Fullbright, Catharine; Nicholas Carpenter (Ger Nicklus Zimmer-
    man); 9 Feb 1832; Miles W Abernathy JP
Carrigan, John; Clark, Martha; George Davis; 20 Jan 1790; Jo Dickson
Carroll (Carrel), Henry W; Wethers, Nancy Lavina; Thos K Pursley; 15 Aug 1839;
    Eli Hoyl
Carroll, James x; Lusk (?), Ann; Henry Hauss (Huss); 14 Mar 1837; M W Abernathy
Carroll, John; Baker, Sary Delany; John Eaker; 4 Oct 1840; C Stroup JP
Carroll(Carrel), Joseph M; Endsley, Elizabeth; Silas Williams; 31 May 1831;
    M Hull JP
Carrothers, Ezekiel; Ratchford, Jane C; Joseph Rathford (Ratchford); 5 Dec 1826;
    Isaac Holland
Carruth, Adam; Graham, Nancy; --------; 16 Mar 1814; V McBee
Carson, Andrew; Whitesides, Isebella; Jas Carson; ---- ---- 183--; This printed
    form used in 1837
Carson, Peter; Cox, Rachael; Robert Weer (Wier); 5 Jul 1786; Wm Maclean
Carson, Tench C; McBee, Martha A; Alen Smith; 6 Oct 1835
Carter, Daniel Randolph x; Luvsey, Rosanah Hovis Nore; John x Proctor; 1 Mar
    1837; Daniel Hoffman JP
Carter, Erwin x; Gregorey, Margret; Martin Grisom (Grissom); 10 Jan 1822; I Holland
Carter, John; Brown, Polly; Jos (?) Stevenson; 10 Apl 1806
Carter, Joshua C; Sherrel, Margaret R; James Sherrill (Sherrel); 10 May 1865; Elisha
    Saunders; M same date by Elisha Saunders JP
Carvolt, Richard; Earney, Mrs Sarah; John B Roneche; 21 Oct 1844
Cashion (Cashon), James; Clark, Ann; James x Bartley; 12 Jan 1826; Wm Little
Cashion, James H; Little, Frances C; W P Sherrill; 21 Jan 1861; M same date by
    Wm W Munday JP
Cashion, William J; Hager, Jane; Starling Wamac (or Warnac); 25 Apl 1858; Robert
    Nixon JP
Caslin (McCasland), Matthew; Wilson, Margaret; Ezekiel Wilson; 6 Apl 1833; V McBee
Cathcart (Cathcard), Allen; Bayley, Margret; David Fowlar; 4 Oct 1814; Phil
    Whitener JP

28

Cathcart, John; Baily, Elizabeth; Thomas Hill; 2 Oct 1810; H Y Webb
Cathey, Alexander; Ford, Patsy; George M (?) King; 5 Feb 1821; V McBee
Cathey, Andrew; Owens, Mary Ann; James Owens; 18 Nov 1789
Cathey, Archibald; Wiley, Ellen; Abner McAfee; 20 Dec 1808
Cathey, Cyrus; Smith, Nancy L; Thos H Jones; 13 Jan 1828; Eli Hoyl
Cathey, George; Leeper, Margarat; Robert Leeper; 24 Jan 1846; Isaac Holland
Cathey, James; Beaty, _____a; Thomas Hoover; 11 Sep 1832; Eli Hoyl
Cathey (Cathy), William; Beaty, Nancy; Smith Beaty; 4 Feb 1828; V McBee
Cathy (Cathey), George; Morason (Morrison), Mary; Samuel Kuykendal; 11 Jun 1779; Adam Baird
Cathy, George; Shufford, Elizabeth; Andrew H L Shufford; 3 Mar 1830; V McBee
Cathy, John; Mcarver, Sarah; George Cathy; 7 Jan 1830; Eli Hoyl
Cathy (Cathey), Robert F; Cox, Lucinda; Peter Fite; 11 Oct 1836; R M Alexander
Cauble, E H; Carpenter, Frances; W R Edwards; 16 Apl 1862; M 17 Apl 1862 by L M Berry (MG)
Cauble, Harrison; White, Nancey; C P Johnson; 6 Mar 1867; W R Clark CC; M 7 Mar 1867 by B S Johnson JP
Cauble, Henry; Miller, Catharine; Jas T Alexander; 8 Apl 1824; V McBee
Cauble, P V; Hobbs, Nancy; Jonas Elmore; 3 Aug 1854; J A Huss
Cauble, Peter V; Mosteller, Mary A; A G Harrill (Harrell); 23 Jan 1857; W R Clark; M 25 Jan 1857 by F J Jetton JP
Cauble, Robt W; Garrison, Nancy; Ephraim Garrison; 5 Apl 1859; W R Clark; M same date by J R Peterson
Caustner (Costner), Daniel; Kizer, Sarah; Michael Best (Bess); 13 Feb 1823; V McBee
Cellers see Sellers
Center, James x; Niell, Poley; Joseph x Beakr, Jacob Mc Erty (?); 28 Aug 1806; William Cline, James Wright
Center, Steven; Holland, Anne; James Sentter (Center), Jinkin Jinkins; 26 Jan 1779; And Neel
Chambers, John J; Danizeln, Elizabeth; John Thomas; 8 Jan 1828; Isaac Holland
Chandler, John J; Long, Fanny; John Dickson; 17 Jul 1838; W M Reinhardt'
Chandler, Milchisedeck; Oats, Mary; Henry A Dilling (Dillen); 3 Dec 1840
Chapman, George; Vanderver, Nancy; Nicholas x Chapman; 1 Jul 1809; Ligt Williams JP
Chapman, Jones; Williams, ____ney (or ____ncy); James Ramsey; 26 Mar 1833; P Stamey JP
Chapman, Thomas; Williams, Susannah; Marthew x Hubbord; Ruben x Tallant; 25 Oct 1827; M Hull JP
Cherry, John; _____er, Martha; David Cherry (Sr); __ Dec 1832; John D King
Cherry, Robert; Thomson, Sally; John Burch; 15 Sep 1840; John __ King
Cheser, Wilson; Keller, Nancy; David x Clubb; 26 Apl 1825; Jas T Alexander
Cheser, Wilson; Hunt, Rebecca; Larkin Bradshaw; 19 Sep 1834; G Hoke
Childers, Isom x; Parker, Patience; Thomas x Parker; 8 Sep 1791
Childers (Childres), John; Howard, Nancy; Gilbert x Milligan; 17 Oct 1820; James T Alexander
Childers, Nelson; Favell, Elizabeth; Isaiah W Ballard; 22 Jul 1834; Wm Little
Childers, W C; Wehunt, M A; P P (J J) Davis; 28 Jun 1866; W R Clark; M 1 Jul 1866 by H A T Harris
Childers, William x; Brown, Marthew; Robert Weer (Weear); 2 Nov 1788
Childers, William x; Howard, Patsy; Robert Murrel; 23 Sep 1820; V McBee
Childris (Childers), Alfred; Wamick, Elizabeth; Adam Engle (Ingle); 13 Dec 1837; Alexander Ward
Childs, Lysander D; Hoke, Nancy; Andrew Motz; 10 Jun 1843; R Williamson Jr
Chism, Daniel x; Jinkins, Susannah; William Wilson; 7 Jan 1819; Jacob Carpenter JP
Chittim (Chittam), Thomas; Alexander, Elisa; Jonathan Beatey; 26 Jul 1821; Saml M'Kee
Chrisman (Crisman), Henry; West, Nancy; Henry Foster; 5 Nov 1805; Wm Scott
Chrisman (Creasman), Henry; Skidmore, Cynthia; Turner x Skidmore; 12 Jul 1830; Eli Hoyl
Christenbury, Daniel F; Wells, Susanah; James Bivings; 30 Oct 1822; V McBee
Christofar, Peter x; Sigman, Fanny; Peter x Deel; 10 July 1821; Fr Hoke
Clanton, David F; Hope, Eliza Phoebe; Levi Clanton; 15 Jun 1850; Robt Williamson
Clanton, Isaac; Englefinger, Salley; Benjamin S Johnson (Johnston); 27 Oct 1824; V McBee
Clanton, Levi; Sanders, Frances; A H Robison (Roberson); 1 Apl 1852; V A McBee
Clanton, William; Murrel, Martha; Isaac Clanton; 1 Mar 1825; V McBee

29

Clapp, Jacob; Reinhardt, Katharine; David Hoke; 10 Mar 1830; J T Alexander
Clark, Anthony; Dunlop, Sarah; James Clark; 23 Sep 1813; Da'd Warlick JP
Clark, Archibald M; Leeper, Mary M; John Beaty; 13 Mar 1837; Isaac Holland
Clark, Burgess; Gilliland (Gilleland), Lydia; _____; 8 Mar 1856; John A Huss
    Clerk by Robt Williamson DC; M 9 Mar 1856 by Jephthae Clark (MG); L and C,
    no B
Clark, Christopher; Moore, R; Franklin B Moore; 20 Nov 1841; A J Cansler
Clark, Cornelius; Litle (?), Elizabeth; James Clark; 5 Nov 1791; Robert Dickson
Clark, Jacob F 'x; Wheard, Eliza; W Williamson; 1 Jan 1855; J A Huss; M same
    date by Saml Lander (MG)
Clark, James; Bigham, Jane; _____; 16 Sep 1812
Clark, James x; Heltenbrand, Mary; Jacob Kistler; 2 Oct 1817; Peter Hoyle
Clark, James; Hart, Elizabeth; Robert Nixon; 19 Nov 1854; R E Burch JP; M same
    date by R E Burch JP
Clark, James; Robinson, Sarah; _____; 30 Dec 1857; W R Clark Clk; M same
    date by D A Lowe JP; L and C, no B
Clark, James W; Blackwood, Polly; Zenas S Ormand (Orman); 2 Aug 1828; J T
    Alexander
Clark, James W; Dickey, Mary M; John Mauney; 6 Jun 1839; H Cansler
Clark, Jephtha; Holman, Catherine; Daniel Killian; 5 Apl 1825; V McBee
Clark, Jephthae; Maize, Susannah; M L Hoke; 12 Apl 1836; John B Harry
Clark, Johnston; Wright, Sarah; Benjamin Walker; No date (Alexander Martin Govr)
Clark, Jonathan; Hager, Salley; John Huggin (Huggins); 14 Jun 1818; V McBee
Clark, Joshua; Kizer, Jemimah; Robert Clark; 14 Feb 1822; V McBee
Clark, Owen; Duncan, Effey; Randolph Barnet; 29 May 1813; V McBee
Clark, Robert; Jenkins, Jincy O; Benjamin Ormand; 2 Dec 1823; Jas T Alexander
Clark, Robt H; Hill, Sarah; B Hager; 23 Sep 1849; R E Burch JP
Clark, Washington B x; Kizer, Ruthy; Jonathan Clark; 22 Apl 1818; V McBee
Clark (Clerk), William; Johnston, Rebeckah; John x Hanson (Hansell); 3 Mar 1784;
    James Dickson
Clark, William; Lytle, Mary; John Thompson; 9 Oct 1787
Clark, William A C x; Wear, Charlotte D; John Mauney; 27 Jan 1843
Clark, William R; McCulloh, Charlotte A; A H Loretz; 9 Oct 1837; H Cansler
Clay, Abraham; Jones, Mary; Josaph Jones; 11 Dec 1789; Joseph Steel
Clay, Andrew; Buff, Elizabeth; David Huss; 19 May 1842; H Cansler
Clay (Cley), Daniel; Reep, Barbara; Daniel Huver; 9 Jan 1816; Jacob Reinhardt
Clay, David; Shufford, Rebecca; Philip Huver (Hoover); 24 May 1830
Clay, G P; Michal, S J; P M Mull (Mulle); 31 Oct 1864
Clay (Cley), Isaac; Seagle, Barbara; John Sigel (Seagle), Christian Seaback; 18 Nov
    1793; Jo Dickson
Clay, Jacob; Bangle, Salley; Henry Bangle; 15 Jan 1822; V McBee
Clay, John; Shufford, Polly; Ephraim Whisenhunt; 19 Jul 1831; J T Alexander
Clay, Joseph; Loretz, Judith; John Hafner (Havner); 3 May 1837; M W Abernathy;
    Ambiguous
Clay, M C; Houser, Harriet S; Andrew Hauss; 26 Sep 1860; W R Clark; M 27 Sep
    1860 by J Finger (MG)
Clemer, John; Hufman, Hannah; Michael Rhyne (Rhine); 6 Apl 1803; Jas McKisick
Clemmer, Andrew; Rhyne, Marry; Jesse Elmore; 16 Jun 1832; B T Kirby; 'Ambiguous
Clemmer, Eli; Rhoads, Cathrine; George W M'Callister; 10 Nov 1825; Isaac Holland
Clemmer, Fety (Valentine); Linebarger, Barbara; Jacob Propst; 26 Feb 1827; J T
    Alexander
Clemmer, George; Weathers, Mary; Moses Cloninger; 22 Jul 1834
Clemmer, John; Linebarger, Susannah; Jacob Hovis; 21 Jul 1829; J T Alexander
Clemmer, John M L; Delinger, Elisabeth; L L Suggs; 23 Feb 1864; M 25 Feb 1864
    by J R Peterson
Clemmer(Clemer), Levi (E); Featherston, Sarah; George Clemmer (Clemer); 20 Nov
    1846; And Hoyl
Clemor (Clemmer), Adam; Rhyne, Louisa; Eli Hoyl; 8 Jan 1841; And Hoyl
Clemor (Clemmer), David; Canon, Nancy; Jacob Roades (?); 15 Aug 1835
Clifton, Jacob; Lovesey, Elizabeth; William Rutlege (Rutledge); 17 Feb 1819; Jas T
    Alexander
Clifton, Jacob; Bradshaw, Susan; Pleasant Green; 21 Mar 1838; H Cansler
Clifton, Robert; Cashon, Martha; Philip Pollard; 13 Dec 1822; Saml M'Kee
Clifton, Samuel; Walker, Winna; Philip Pollard; 3 Dec 1821; Jas T Alexander
Clifton, Warren; Baringer, Mary; Jas M Leonard; 25 Jul 1830; J T Alexander
Clifton, William x; Hicks, Phebba; Thomas x Ownby; 9 Mar 1813; V McBee

Cline, Amen (?) x; Bolick, Liney; Ambrose Bolick; 3 Oct 1838; L E Thompson
Cline, Amon (Amen); Harris, Nancy; Daniel D Hudson; 17 Apl 1841; L E Thompson
Cline, Andrew x; Taylor, Mary; Henry Finger (Ger Henrich Finger); 13 Jun 1801; John Dickson
Cline, Daniel; Wike, Susanna; H Bollinger; 25 May 1813
Cline, David (Jr); Holman, Barbara; Daniel Holman per V McBee; 12 Oct 1819; V McBee
Cline, Elkana x; Green, Joanna; John Cline; 14 May 1836; John B Harry
Cline, Ephraim; Eckerd, Mary; Absalom Miller; 22 Apl 1835; Mic Cline
Cline, George; Peterson, Polly; Michael Herman (Ger same); 7 Mar 1813; Mic Cline
Cline, Henry (Ger Henrich Klein); Carpenter, Elisabeth; John McGaughey; 11 Jan 1787
Cline, Henry; Eckerd, Elizabeth; Daniel Bolick (Ger Daniel Bolch); 28 Mar 1819; Mic Cline
Cline, Henry; Boovey, Sally; Anthonay Hallman (Holman); 25 Apl 1820; Jas T Alexander
Cline, Jacob; Wilfong, Elisabeth; John Wilfong; 28 Nov 1786; Joseph Steel
Cline, Jacob; Eckard, Molly; Conrad x Pitts; 4 Sep 1810; Mic Cline
Cline, Jacob; Shufford, Salley; John Roberts (Robards); 4 Mar 1821; V McBee
Cline, Jacob Sr x; Halman, Barbara; Abel J x Probst; 23 Oct 1841; Wm Herman JP
Cline, Jessa (Jesse); Hauss, Margaret; Henry Bolick; 2 Oct 1834; Miles W Abernathy
Cline, John x; _____ _____; Jacob x Lutze; 24 Jan 1810; Wm Nesbitt; Ambiguous
Cline, John; Sullivan, Margaret; William Cline; 27 Apl 1821; V McBee
Cline, John (Ger Johannes Klein); Holman, Rachel; Caleb Miller; 20 Oct 1822; V McBee
Cline, John x; Cockran, Elizabeth; Jacob x Burns; 16 Jul 1826; V McBee
Cline, Martin x; Fresham, Elizabeth; Jacob x Tommey; 15 Feb 1814; V McBee
Cline, Mathias; Sigman, Polly; Paul Setzer; 6 Jan 1831; Mic Cline
Cline, Michael; Amburn, Susanah; Jacob x Rumple; 18 (or 10) Aug 1819; John Willfong
Cline, Miles x; Abernathy, Susannah; Moses Abernathy; 26 Mar 1829; V McBee
Cline, Nathaniel; Frye, Barbara; John x Summitt; 23 Sep 1830; J T Alexander
Cline, Paul; Bost, Selina; Silas Bost; 3 (or 5) May 1835; H W Robinson
Cline, Philip; Abernathy, Betsy; Seth x Abernathy; 12 Aug 1808; Danl Forney
Cline, Sebastian; Eakerd, Margaret; John Probst (Propst); 9 Jun 1820; V McBee
Cline, Solomon x; Amburn, Sally; Christopher x Cline, Samuel Amburn; 1 Mar 1821; Mic Cline
Cline (Kline), Thomas; Mitchum, Sally; Thomas Williams; 18 Oct 1825; M Hull JP
Cline, William; Raden, Sally; William Bost; 6 May 1809; Mic Cline
Cline, William; Huffman, Polly; Gasper Bolick (Ger Caspar Bolch); 11 Apl 1816; Mic Cline
Cline, William; Starr, Susannah; Jacob Seapaugh; 27 Jul 1825
Cline, Wm A; Martin, S J; A S Haynes; 5 Nov 1860; W R Clark; M 6 Nov 1860 by J Finger (MG)
Clipard (Clippard), Andrew; Bumgarner, Rebecca; Green Burk; 31 May 1832; J T Alexander
Clipard (Clippard), David; Swanson, Dyza; Blair McGee; 9 Dec 1823; Saml M'Kee
Clipard, John x; Lailors (?), Nancy; Martin x Cline; 15 Oct 1814; V McBee
Clippard, D E; Helderman, S R D; R M Helderman; 15 Oct 1859; W R Clark; M 19 Oct 1859 by J R Peterson (MG)
Clippard, Henry; Ingle, Viney; James M x Armstrong; 20 Nov 1858; W R Clark; M 21 Nov 1858 by J Helderman JP
Clipperd, Rufus; Richards, Christina; Jesse Walden; 5 (?) Apl 1841; J A Ramsour D C
Clodfelter, Daniel; Lutz, Mary; George x Lutz; 29 Aug 1815; V McBee
Clodfelter, Felix; Scrum, Christina; John Shrum (Srum); 1 Jan 1829; D Reinhardt
Clodfelter, Peter x; Wilfong, Salley; Jacob x Stilwell; 19 Dec 1814; V McBee
Cloer, Elisha x; Houston, Easter; Archibald Ray; 10 Dec 1829; Miles W Abernathy
Cloneger, David x; Paysaur Rebeca; Eli Huffstettler; 13 Apl 1845; W Reeves JP
Cloninger, Adam; Clemer, Susanah; Philip Cloninger; 1 Nov 1803; Jos Dickson
Cloninger, Adam; Plonk, Elizabeth; Upton Byrum; 29 Jun 1830; J T Alexander
Cloninger, Daniel x; Barey, Catey; Henry x Barey; 18 Jul 1819; John Allen; Ambiguous
Cloninger, Daniel; Nichademus, Lucinda; Henry Cloninger; 7 Sep 1842; A J Cansler
Cloninger, David; Centre, Susanna; Thomas Cloninger; 6 Feb 1808; Jacob Forney
Cloninger, Henry x; Berry, Mary; Matthias x Berry (Barey); 11 Mar 1819; Gilbert Milligan
Cloninger, Henry; Bolch, Suannah; John Barger; 24 Jul 1836; Jesse Gantt

31

Cloninger, Henry; Clipperd, Susanah; John Rabb; 29 Jan 1842; A J Cansler

Cloninger, Jacob; Clemmon (or Clemmor), Elizabeth; Thomas Cloninger; 24 June 1810; H Y Webb

Cloninger (Cloniger), Jacob; Linebarger, Margaret E; Laben J Linebarger; 16 Jan 1847; Isaac H Holland

Cloninger, John (Jonathan); Connor, Epsey C; Peter Little; 24 Sep 1838; H Cansler

Cloninger, Michael see Hovis, John P

Cloninger, Michael; Hovis, Catharine; Moses Cloninger; 16 Mar 1839

Cloninger, Michal Jr x; Cresemore, Salley; Michal x Cloninger Sr; 27 Nov 1817; John Allen

Cloninger, Moses; McGinas, Ebby; Lawson McGinnas (McGinas); 11 Jul 1825; V McBee

Cloninger, Moses; Little, Christina; Willard Boyden (Barden); 11 Oct 1830; V McBee

Cloninger, Moses; Bolinger, Catharine; Edwin B Torrence; 11 Dec 1834; Miles W Abernathy

Cloninger, Moses x; Hovis, Elizabeth; Daniel Carpenter; 31 Oct 1863; W R Clark; M 5 Nov 1863 by R H Abernethy JP

Cloninger, Noah; Weatherspoon, Pelina ((or Telina); Alexander Frazer; 10 Dec 1840; Henry Cline

Cloninger, Philip; Hovis, Sally; Johe Seits (?); 22 Feb 1803; Jos Dickson

Cloninger, Thomas; Rhine, Mary; David Linebarger; 31 Oct 1812; Vardry McBee

Cloninger, Valentine; Long, Mary; Upton Byrum; 27 Nov 1830; Peregrine Roberts

Cloninger, William x; Thompson, Martha; Elihu Lockman; 3 Jul 1867; J Finger; M same date by J Finger MG

Clore, Elisha; Williams, Elisabeth; Leml Sanders; 3 Jan 1804; Jno Dickson

Clotfelter, Alius x (Clodfelter, Elias); Nebb (?), Mary; (Ger) David Killian, George Clodfelter; 8 Jan 1822; Zachary Stacy

Clotfelter, David A; Clotfelter, Hannah L; George Penick; 4 Dec 1842; Epm Yount JP

Clotfelter, John x; Abernathy, Katherine; George Clodfelter, James Abernathy; 14 Feb 1822; Zachary Stacy

Clouney (Clowney), Samuel; Armstrong, Esther; John Leeper; 3 Jan 1782

Club, John; Williams, Polly; Daniel McGee; 9 Mar 1805; Betsey Henderson

Clubb, David x; Long, Caroline; William x Huskins; 10 Dec 1840; H Cansler

Clubb, George; Masters, Eave; George N Clubb; 4 Feb 180__ (Alexander Gov 1805-7); Betsey Henderson

Clubb, George; Cobb, Kessy; William Clubb (William Thradekule); 8 Mar 1843

Clubb, Jacob; Stiles, Elender; Henry Pitts; 7 Mar 1821; James T Alexander

Clubb, Moses x; Sherrell, Easter; William J Abernathy; 8 Feb 1821; James T Alexander

Clyne (Kline), Henry; Sullivan, Polley; Charles Biles (Byles); 12 Jan 1813; V McBee

Clyne (Cline), John; Cathy, Betcy; John Cathy; 9 Feb 1820; V McBee

Cobb, Ambrose x; Black, Rachael; Moses Scott; 18 Mar 1783

Cobb, Bartlett Y; Henderson, Barbara M; J A Caldwell; 11 Oct 1853; Robt Williamson; M same date by R N Davis (MG)

Cobb, David; Bird, Kitty; Barney West; 5 Oct 1785; Will Boldrige

Cobb, Enoch; Shelley, Susannah; Andrew x Abernathy; 20 Oct 1821; D Reinhardt.

Cobb, Henry x; Shitly, Betsy; Miles x Abernathy Jr; 27 Aug 1817; V McBee

Cobb, Henry x; Hilton, Nancy; James Wilson; 16 Dec 1840; H Cansler

Cobb, James x; Beach, Sarah; Benjamin Beech (Beach); 23 Oct 1790; Jo Dickson

Cobb, James; Hilton, Frances; Wilson x Turbyfield; 3 Feb 1838; H Cansler CC

Cobb, John; Bomgarner, Sarah; Henry Sides; 18 Apl 1821; James Hanes (or Keener)

Cobb, John x; Huchison, Elizabeth; Randolph x Helton; 21 Sep 1839; J A Ramsour D C

Cobb, John; Long, Ann; Randall x Helton; 27 Feb 1841; A J Cansler

Cobb, Joseph C; Butts, Margaret E; J W (William) Kerr; 25 Oct 1847; V A McBee

Cobb, Philip x; Penny, Louisa; James x Cox; 20 Jan 1820; Jno Coulter

Cobb, Robert; Phillips, Elenor; Isaiah x Abernathy; 15 Feb 1813; Jas T Alexander

Cobb, Robert; Miller, Elisabeth; Daniel x Whitener (Sr); 13 Mar 1818; John Willfong

Cobb, Robert x; Hope, Leana; William x Tuttle; 14 Dec 1841; R Williamson Jr

Cobb, Starling; Penney, Nancy; Miles x Abernathy; 11 Oct 1817; V McBee

Cobb, Stephen x; Steeley, Luveey (?); John Sadler; 8 Nov 1822; Saml M'Kee

Cobb, Thomas; Hager, Hannah; Wilie (Willie) Harris); 8 Oct 1811; Lwn Henderson

Cobb, Waulter; Cox, Esabella; James Cox; 22 Jan 1816; V McBee

Cobb, William x; _____; Charles Abernathy; 7 Aug 1787; Jo Dickson

Cobb, William; Harmon, Martha; John Harmon; 15 Feb 1827; George Willkie; Ambiguous

Cobb, William W; Cline, Margaret A; V A McBee; 8 Sep 1845; R Williamson

Cobbs, Ralph; Lamkin, Jane; Robert Abernathy, George Lamkin Jr; 10 Mar 1779; Andw Neel; Ambiguous

Cochran, Asa F; Motz, Caroline R; E S Caldwell; 27 Jul 1847

Cochrane, William x; Keizer, Sarah; John Sadler (Saddler); 5 Mar 1827; Charles L Torrence

Cochren (Cochran), Robert; Reed, Leteetia; John Reed; 8 Nov 1791; Robert Dickson

Cody, Curtis (Cody, Charles) x; Hull, Polly; James x Cody; 11 Nov 1834

Cody, D L; Leonard, Emeline; Absalom Wood; 24 Nov 1865; A S Haynes Cty Ct Clk; M 2 Dec 1865 by P Carpenter JP

Cody, James; Moore, Sarah F; J Mason Spainhour; 7 Dec 1865; A S Haynes; M same date by P Carpenter JP

Cody, Murphia x; Cook, Ann; Curtis x Cody; 6 Dec 1841; George Coon JP

Cody, Perry; Darte, Biddy (Dougherty, Bridget); J W Paysour; 10 Feb 1851; V A McBee; M same date by F J Jetton JP

Cody, Turner x; Mauney, Anna; John A Jetton; 5 Oct 1844; C L Hunter

Cogswell (Gookswill), William; Howerd, Pecky; Nimrod Winsor (Ger _____); 26 Mar 1820; D Lutz JP

Coiner, John K; Rudisill, Paulina; P S Kistler; 8 Apl 1853; R Williamson; M 10 Apl 1853 by David Crooks

Cole, Ephraim; Hambleton, Ran (?); Ephraim West; 14 Nov 1815; V McBee

Colding, J D; Shuford, Susen E; W T Shuford; 4 Dec 1860; M same date by L M Berry MG

Collier, Henry; Tucker, Louisa; Thomas Sadler; 12 Dec 1817; V McBee

Collier, Wm T; Hedick, Barbara E; J W Wilfong; 5 Apl 1849

Collins, Isaac x; Login, Frankey; Ab McAfee; 3 Oct 1815

Collins, John; Leeper, Peggy; Philip Youn__; 4 Jun 1810

Collins, John x; Earles, Rebekah; Ab McAfee; 27 Jul 1815

Collins (Collance), Josiah; Dickson, Jean; Thomas Dickson; 12 Sep 1816; Saml Wilson __

Collins, Richard x; Dillon (or Dillow), Susannah; Henry Smethers (Ger Schmetter); 21 Jan 1815; Mic Cline

Collins, William; Endsley, Marey; Archibald Endsley, Alexander Collins; 6 Dec 1814; Da'd Warlick

Collins, William; Benfiele (or Benfield), Catherine; Isaac Barger (Berger); 28 Oct 1815; Mic Cline

Colter, John x; Hortan, Sarah; Martin Coulter (Martin Colter Jr); 22 Oct 1789; Joseph Steel

Colwell (Coldwell), Andrew; Mins, Fanney; John x Moody; 1 Mar 1822; Jas T Alexander

Colwell (Caldwell), Daniel; Cooper, Lydia; Thomas Williams; 25 Mar 1837; M W Abernathy

Colwell(Caldwell), Daniel; Robinson, Martha; Andrew Colwell (Caldwell); 11 Jul 1849; Robt Williamson

Colwell (Coldwell), John; Eaton, Margaret; Thomas Williams; 23 Dec 1835; M W Abernathy

Colwell (Caldwell), Philip; Cook, Sarah; David Colwell (Caldwell); 2 Oct 1841; L E Thompson

Colwell, Tho x; Martin, Ann; Martin x Cline; 19 Sep 1815; V McBee

Colwell (Coldwell), Thomas; Abernathy, Nancy; John Johnson; 11 Aug 1828; V McBee

Colwell (Coldwell), William; Stiles, Elizabeth; Samuel Painter (Panter); 8 Aug 1830; V McBee

Combest, William M; Knowles, Elizebeth; David Taylor; 5 Sep 1831; Isaac Holland

Compton, William N; Lay, Delilah; William Lay; 9 Dec 1830; Isaac Holland

Compton (or Campton), William N; Lay, Mary; Absalom x Lay; 28 Mar 1837; J G Hand JP

Con (Conn), William; Alexander, Elisabeth; Martain Selyr, William Snider; 6 Dec 1778; Adam Baird

Conar (Coner), Hugh E; Wiatt, Rachel; Aron Dameron (Damern); 4 Mar 1839

Coner (Conner), Britain B x; Norton, Mary; Turner Skidmore; 18 Jul 1823; Saml M'Kee

Conlay (McConly), Neal; Hogin, Caty (or Paty); James Sulavan (Sullivan); 3 Oct 1786; Jo Dickson; Ambiguous

Conley, George x (Freedman); Haines, Mary (Col girl); Jonas C Hoyl (Hoyle); 5 Apl 1866; D A Haines JP; M same date by D A Haines JP

Connel, David; Edwards, Lucy; Gideon Moore; 28 Nov 1844

Connel (or Cormel), William P; Hinkle, Susan; Mathew R Armstrong; 4 Dec 1837; H Cansler

Connelly, John B; Lovsey, Catherine; Samuel P Simpson; 11 Nov 1828; V McBee

33

Connelly (Connolly), Minton A; Rozzell, Mary V; --------; 7 Jul 1857; J A Huss
    Clerk by W R Clark DC; M 8 Jul 1857 by Landy Wood; L and C, no B
Connelly, William of Burke Co; Sherril, Rebecca; Jacob Sherrill (Sherril), of Burke;
    7 Nov 1793
Conner (Connor), Charles D; Linebarger, Mary; Jonas Elmore; 22 Dec 1851; Robt
    Williamson; M 23 Dec 1851 by F J Jetton JP
Conner (Connor), David; Brunton, Nicey; Joseph Carroll; 29 Sep 1837; H Cansler
Conner, Jacob; Swearingin, Masny; John x Beck; 11 Aug 1803
Conner (Connor), Jacob; Jones, Azuba; Jacob Ramsour; 16 Dec 1828; J T Alexander
Conner, James; Swaringame, Delila; John x Conner; 25 Jan 1814; Da'd Warlick
Conner, John x; Swareingame, Eleanor; William Conner; 7 Nov 1816; Saml Wilson
Conner (Connor), Noah D; Eaker, Adline; Andrew x Hoyl (Hoyle); 8 Mar 1859;
    P Carpenter JP; M same date by Philip Carpenter JP
Conner (Connor), Seth; Kendrick, Elizabeth; Jacob Conner (Connor); 27 May 1837;
    M W Abernathy
Conner, Thomas x; Ross, Mary; John Tucker; 6 Feb 1794
Conner, Thomas; Sherrel, Caroline; Perkins Robinson; 5 Apl 1825; V McBee
Conner, William x; Fisher, Susanna; Richard Fisher; 21 Dec 1795; Jno M Dickson
Conner, William W; Anthony, Leah; George Dellinger; 30 Aug 1834; M W Abernathy
Connolly (Connelly), James D; Wells, Wille; Burrel F Wells; 8 May 1827 ; V McBee
Connor, Columbia; Wilkinson, Salina; John W Long; 12 Jan 1841; Wm Long JP
Connor, Harry W; Burton, Mary L; B F Withers; 12 Aug 1856; M 13 Aug 1856 by
    Horatio H Hewitt (MG)
Connor, James; Welmon, Rebeccah; Andrew H Loretz; 13 Oct 1834; M W Abernathy
Connor, John; Turner, Elizabeth; Isaac Erwin (Irvin); 1. Dec 1838; H Cansler
Conor, Fed x; Forney, Elen; William x Huiston; 4 Nov 1866; R Nixon JP; Colored
    Freedmen; M same date by R Nixon JP
Conrad, Daniel; Martin, Hanah; George Willfong; 3 Apl 1801
Conrad, David; Cresemon, Betcy; Elias Jarrett (Jarret); 8 Jan 1825; V McBee
Conrad, John x; Smith, Betcy; Thomas x Coldwell; 24 Jul 1826; V McBee
Conrad, Logan; Coulter, Elizabeth; Maxwell Shuford; 4 Feb 1837; M W Abernathy
Conrad (Cunrad), Peter; Abernathy, Sally; Will Reed; 13 Mar 1810; Danl M Forney
Conrad, Rudolph; Stockinger, Christina; Arthur Graham; 6 Jul 1792
Constable, Thomas x; Winn, Mary; Thomas x Winn; 15 Sep 1785
Cook, Aaron; Jarrett, Anna; John R Dunn; 20 Sep 1831; L McBee
Cook, Abraham x; Burns, Elisabeth; Jacob x Burns; 17 Jul 1823; Mic Cline
Cook, Barryman; Childers, Delpha; Charles Bleckly (Blakeley); 4 Jul 1821; D Rein-
    .hardt, James McGinnas
Cook, Christian x; Wise, Anna; John Cook; 27 Aug 1819; V McBee
Cook, David x; Goodwin, Milley; Christian x Cook; 18 Dec 1820; V McBee
Cook, George x; Brock, Elisabeth; Isaac x Brock; 22 Feb 1796 ; Michl Eaker
Cook, Joseph x; Sepaugh, Poley; Philip x Cook; 19 May 1814; Saml Wilson
Cook, Matthew; Costner, Mary Magdaline; Caleb C Withers (Weathers); 29 Sep 1840;
    Elisha Weathers (?)
Cooke, Aron x; King, Betcy; John x Johnson; 26 Jan 1814; V McBee
Coon, Adam x; Horten, Nancey; Isaac Vanhorn; 5 Mar 1789; John Moore
Coon (Koons), George; Seagle, Elizabeth; John M Jacobs; 21 Mar 1832; L McBee
Coon (Koon), Jacob; Lenhardt, Mary Ann; John x Hallman; 10 Feb 1835; G Hoke
Cooper, Thomas; Chittim, Harett P; William M Grier (Greer); 15 Oct 1827
Cooper, Thomas x; Ingol, Polly; John Keener; 19 Feb 1841
Corbey, David; Lingerfelt, Elizabeth; (Ger) Johannes Brendel; 5 Aug 1800; Ligt
    Williams JP
Cordell, Calven x; Wier, Milly; Daniel x Twigs; 6 Mar 1832; M Hull JP
Cornelius, Austin; Sherrill, Ann J; Robert L Barkley; 23 Feb 1836
Cornelius, Benjamin; Dillin, Jude; Cary Hugens; 28 Nov 1789; And Taylor
Cornelius, William; Asbury, Letty; Henry Asbury; 18 Jul 1820; Jas T Alexander
Cornet, Cullen x; Crays, Sally; Newet x Edwards; 16 Nov 1808; Maxl Chambers
Cornwell, Cage x; McEntire, Liddy; Andrew Parker; 16 Mar 1789
Cornwell (Cornwall), John; Sullivan, Martha A; A B Homesly; 3 Dec 1851; Robt
    Williamson; M 2 Dec 1851 (sic) by F J Jetton JP
Cornwill, James; Weaver, Susan; B M Jetton; 16 Sep 1840; H Cansler
Corzine, Abel; Shinn, Prudence; Eli Sherrill; 28 Sep 1830; J T Alexander
Corzine, Eli; Sherril, Esther; Enos Sherrill; 14 Feb 1791; John Dickson
Costner, Absalom x; Pinion, Fanny; Joseph Costner; 30 Aug 1836; Eli Hoyl
Costner, Ambrose; Quickle, Malinda; Robert Rankin; 18 Mar 1846; Jno M Huffman
Costner, Frederick x; Wise, Fanney; John Fronaberger (Froneberger); 26 Nov 1819;
    Jas T Alexander

Costner, Jacob; Rudessel, Anne; John Rudisail (Rudessel); 10 Dec 1810; H Y Webb
Costner, John; Kiser, Barbary; Joseph Kiser; 2 Oct 1809; Danl M Forney
Costner, Jonas; Huffman, Susanna; Gillam Powers; 15 Jun 1822; D Reinhardt
Costner, Joshua x; Brown, Sarah; William x Brown; 13 Nov 1828; V McBee
Costner, Lawrance x; Gipson, Nancy; Thomas Costner; 3 Dec 1817; James T Alexander
Costner, Levi x; Weir, Elizabeth; John Costner; 26 Nov 1828; V McBee
Costner, Levi x; Gales, Elizabeth; __ William Gales; 15 Jan 1847; Robt Williamson
Costner, Michael H; Rudisill, Lavinia; Levi Plonk; 20 Sep 1844
Costner, Peter; Walters, Luisa; And Hover; __ ____ 1804; Lwn Henderson
Costner, Peter x; Rhyne, Elizabeth; Jonas Cloninger; 11 Dec 1837; H Cansler CC
Costner, Thomas x; Low, Jenny; Jesse x Low; 12 Dec 1809; H Y Webb
Coulter, Daniel; Stilwell, Nancey; Henry x Coulter; 29 Apl 1817; John Willfong
Coulter, Eli S; Fry, Harriet C; Abel Fry; 15 Nov 1841
Coulter, Elkanah P; Wilson, Malinda; Ezekiel Wilson; 5 Jan 1831; J T Alexander
Coulter, Henry x; Rader, Polley; John x Frye; 29 Oct 1814; V McBee
Coulter, J (Jedediah); StJohn, Julia L; John Coulter; 9 Jan 1849; V A McBee
Coulter (Colter), John; Ramsour, Barbara; Jacob Summey Jnr (or Snr); 8 Feb 1813
Courtney, Henry; Dellinger, Elizabeth; James Courtney; 28 Dec 1814; V McBee
Covington, John; Hager, Lucy B; John Hager; 14 May 1836; J D King
Cowan, Richard D; Sides, Hannah; Jacob Hinkle; 28 Jul 1807; Lwn Henderson
Cox, Aaron; Baker, Olly; Absalom Bonham (Bonam); 4 Jan 1787
Cox, Elijah; Huggin, Jane; Elisha Cox; 12 Aug 1796; Jo Dickson
Cox, Elisha; Hollen, Margaret; Thomas Moore; 14 Dec 1793; Ambiguous
Cox, Fleet; Phillips, Rachel; Joseph Wright; 21 Oct 1805; Lwn Henderson
Cox, Green W; Davis, Jane; John Davis; 3 Jan 1829; J T Alexander
Cox, John; Carpinter, Mary; James Sulavan; 27 Jul 1800; John Crouse JP
Cox, John; Clark, Anny; David Smith; 21 Mar 1805; Betsey Henderson
Cox, Morris; Black, Elizabeth; Wallace Alexander; 21 May 1797
Cox, Robert; Louer, Betsy; John x Louer; 27 May 1800; John Crouse JP
Cox, Robert; Vendike, Aney; Adam Hoyl (Hoyle); 22 Apl 1818; David Fite
Cox, William; Stowe, Margaret; Joel Stowe; 5 Dec 1814; James T Alexander
Cox, William x; West, Mary; Ebenezer West; 31 Dec 1829; Eli Hoyl
Cox, William; Shannon, Mary; William Shannon; 12 Dec 1843; Eli Hoyl
Coxe (Cox), James x; Cobb, Sally; Isaiah x Abernathy; 3 Jun 1815; V McBee
Coxe, Vinson x; Webb, Rebeckah; Gray x Bynum; 24 Jan 1823; Wm F Zimerman
Craft, George H; Gilbert, Eliza; F J Jetton; 5 Nov 1840
Craft (Crauft), John P; Conner, Margaret; John Beam; 15 Oct 1824; V McBee
Craft, John P; Neil, Margaret; Hugh x Neil; 15 Sep 1832; J T Alexander
Craft, Moses x; Connor, Hetty; Jonathan M Carroll; 20 Jan 1829; J T Alexander
Craig, S W; Pegram, A M; S N (Set) Stowe (Stow); 28 Jan 1841
Craig (Crage), William; Nelly, Margret; Henry C Duff; 21 May 1836; Isaac Holland
Craige (Crage), Thomas; Right, Leanna; James Wright (Right); 11 Aug 1819; V McBee
Crawford, H P; Courtney, Margaret; M T Bynum; 1 Aug 1855; J A Huss; M same date by F J Jetton JP
Crawford, James; Litton, Nancy; Hiram Litten (Litton); 13 Apl 1818; V McBee
Crego (Crago), John; Lewis, Marget; John Reynolds; 19 Oct 1813; V McBee
Cresman, Abraham x; Ingel, Catharine; John x Shell; 24 Sep 1804; John Dickson
Crites, Danl x; Kinder, Barbara; Jno Lockman; No date (Ashe Governor 1795-8)
Crites, John x; Lorance, Catharina; Jacob Slinkard (Ger Jacob Shlunkad), Devault x Crites; 19 Mar 1799; J Graham
Crites, William x; Dellinger, Barbara; William Conner; 18 Jul 1821; V McBee
Crocker, Rufus M; Beisaner, Issabella; Seburn Crocker; 16 Apl 1865; Elisha Saunders; M same date by Elisha Saunders JP
Crockett, James P; Hunter, Isabella M; Cyrus L Hunter; 14 Apl 1828; B J Thompson
Cronister, Daniel; Duncan, Polley; James x Cronister, Fredrick x Myars; 15 Sep 1808; Hy Conner
Cronkleton, James; Howard, Mary (Mary Ann); Franklin Howard; 1 Mar 1851; Robt Williamson; M 2 Mar 1851 by W W Munday JP
Cronland, C R F; Goodson, Ann; C J Hammarskold; 23 May 1863; M 31 May 1863 by J R Peterson
Crook, A B; Hoke, Sarah E; G Hoke; 14 May 1835; M W Abernathy
Cross, Abraham; Killan (?), Barbara; Adam Wisnant; 14 May 1799
Cross, John; Bull (or Beele), Mary; Solomon x Cross, Moses x Cross; 4 Apl 1797; Jno Dickson

35

Cross, John x; Baker, Sarah; Joseph x Baker; 7 Aug 1802; John Dickson
Cross, Mosis x; Moistala, Polly; John x Cross; 3 Feb 1795; John Dickson
Cross, Zebulon x; Hogue, Easter; Thomas Ramsey; 11 Jul 1825; J Blackwood Esq; "A widow Easter Hogue of South Carolina Now Resideing in this County"
Crotts (Crots), Jacob x; Self, Mimy; Elijah x Self; 1 May 1831; Andrew Dickson JP
Crouse, Benjamine x; Kids, Mary; William x Kids; 20 Apl 1813; James T Alexander
Crouse, David; Rudisill, Mary; Abner Berry; 23 Sep 1820; James T Alexander
Crouse, David; Plonk, Sally; George x Tetherow (Tethero); 25 Oct 1836
Crouse, David E; Sronce, Barbara R; A B Laney; 3 Mar 1864; Elisha Saunders; M same date by Elisha Saunders JP
Crow, James M; Mcarter, Rebecca; Thomas W Crow; 24 Jan 1837; John Dickson
Crow, John; Waggoner, Susanna; Fredrc Sleegal; 20 Aug 1806; Jas McEwin
Crow, John Dimbarr x; McGill, Jane; John x Mauney; 21 Jul 1829; J T Alexander
Crow, Richard x; Abernathy, Francis E; Matthew Collier (Colier); 1 Mar 1841
Crow, Robert x; Collins, Jean; Wilm Collins; 3 Apl 1804; John Dickson
Crow, Robert Armstrong; Weir, Matsey Graham; John Carroll (Carrol); 21 Apl 1833; Wm W Norris
Crow, Thomas x; Blackwood, Elizabeth; John Crow; 13 Sep 1830; J T Alexander
Crowder, Anderson; Wilbourn, Rebecah; Absalom Warlick; 25 Jul 1808; Ab McAfee Esq
Crowder, John x; Havner, Mary; George Coon; 22 Dec 1850; Robt Williamson
Crowder, Paschal P; Speck, Barbara A; R R (Robert) Summy (Summey); 18 Jan 1853; R Williamson
Crowder (Crouder), Ulrick; Barier (Barringer), Barbara; Martin Colter; 9 Dec 1788
Crowder (Crouder), William N; Haines, Didamey; John Michael (Michel); 11 Dec 1853; Daniel A Haines JP
Crowel, Eli; Lourance, M B; David A Coon; 9 Apl 1860; W R Clark; M 10 Apl 1860 by A J Fox MG
Crowell, Churchwell A; Ramsour, Lenney; William J Jackson; 19 Dec 1833; John Schenck; Ambiguous
Crup, Martin x; Sigmon, Catharine; Henry Sigmon (Ger Heinrich Siegmann); 10 Oct 1816; Jo Laurance; Ambiguous
Cruthers, Edmond; Statia, Lucrecie; James x Fairwell; 7 Nov 1789; Jonathan Greaves
Crysel, Andrew x; Bumgarner, Elisabeth; Moses Bumgarner; 22 May 1798; Jno Dickson
Crysell (Crisel), John; Earhart, Amy; Philip Earhart, Andrew Crisel (Ger Andreas Crysel); 2 Feb 1796; J Graham
Crysler (Crissel), George x; Word, Elisabeth; Fredrick x Word; 2 Apl 1801; Benj Dorsey JP
Cunniham (Cunningham), James; Terry, Martha; Featherstun Wells; 30 Aug 1808; Joseph Neel
Curry, Elam A M; Hauss, Frances G; A J Howser (Houser); 18 Apl 1866

Daeter, Jacob; Bysinger, Catharine; George W Motz; 13 Jun 1835; M W Abernathy
Daganhert (Degenhart), Henry; Mosar, Polly; Fredk Hoke (Ju); 23 Jul 1828; Fr Hoke JP
Dagenhart, Peter x; Fox, Maitty; Henry x Dagenhart; 2 Dec 1830; M W Abernathy
Dailey (Daily), Jacob F; Kibler, Jane M; F A Hoke; 18 Aug 1841; H Cansler CC
Dailey, Patrick x; Hunt, Nancy; Enoch x Kelley; 23 Jun 1817; James T Alexander
Daily (Dayly), Ephraim; Duncan, Patsy; Absalom Duncan; 30 Jan 1827; Wm Little
Daily (Dailey), Lawson; Goodson, Mahala; Washington Dailey; 30 May 1838; H Cansler CC
Daliner (Dellinger), John A; Whitener, Lovina P; Moses B Whitener; 3 Jan 1836; Jonas Bost
Dameron (Damron), David; Huson, Sarah; Edward Huson; 9 May 1800; Jonn Greaves
Dameron, Dixon; Weathers, Leusia; Alexander Strain; 27 Apl 1840; And Hoyl JP
Dameron, Edward B; Henry, Elizabeth; Edward Boyd; 20 Sep 1819; V McBee
Dameron, John; Rhyne, Margret E; David Gingles; 20 Dec 1837; I Holland
Dameron, Joseph; Brimer, Mary; Hugh B Hand; 14 Feb 1831
Dameron, Thomas; Huson, Susannah; Edward Huson; 21 Dec 1810; Joseph Neel
Dameron, William; Tucker, Margret; Joseph Dameron; 16 Oct 1828; Isaac Holland
Daniel see O Daniel
Daniel, John x; Colwell, Becky; Henry Clippad (Clippard); 10 Feb 1818; James T Alexander
Danner, Alexander; Sherrall, Susan; David J Sherrill (Sherrall); 5 Oct 1839; J A Ramsour
Darnall (Darnel), Joel; Jinkins, Nancy; Ezekiah x Drake; 28 Dec 1803; Jonathan Greaves

36

Darnall (Darnel), Jordon; Jinkins, Mary; Stephen Senter; 26 Jan 1799; Jonn Greaves
Darr, Henry R; Blackburn, Anna; Charles C Henderson; 12 Jan 1831; L M McBee
Darr (Derr), Valentine; Rutledge, Sarah; Paul Kistler; 8 Feb 1821; V McBee
Darr, Valentine; Morris, Mary; B J Johnson; 25 Jun 1839
Daugherty, John; Whisenhunt, Barbara; Geo Whisenhunt; 2 Apl 1805; Lwn Henderson
Davidson, James; Patterson, Martha; John Patterson; 16 Aug 1791; George Newton
Davidson, John; _____; _____; 25 Mar 1793; Blank Bond; Note fr Saml Givens
    to Clerk date 17 Mar 1793 asks that license issue to Jon Davison to marry Givens's
    daughter Nancy, probably refers to this
Davies, Isaac x; Berry, Hannah; John Berry; no date; endorsement in same hand as
    bonds dated 1801-1803-1804, probably hand of Eliza Greaves
Davis, Alexander x; Fair, Sarah M; Stephen Fisher; 13 Dec 1847; Robt Williamson
Davis, Anderson x; Steward, Caroline; Benjamin Beel (Beal); 19 Dec 1865; A S
    Haynes CCC; M 21 Dec 1865 by Elisha Saunders JP
Davis, Benjamin C; Ewing, Mary B; Wm R Price; 27 Nov 1845; W Reeves JP
Davis, David; Patterson, Jane; Elias Jackson; 15 Nov 1819; V McBee
Davis, Ephraim; Blackwood, Jane; Thomas P McGill; 20 Apl 1819; James T Alexander
Davis, George; Jarret, Hannah; Richard Johnson (Johnston); 6 Apl 1820; V McBee
Davis, George L; Henderson, Fannie A; S P Sherrill; 9 Apl 1867; M same date by
    R N Davis Minister
Davis, J J; Bess, Candies; W C Childers; 22 Jan 1866; A S Haynes CCC; M 1 Feb
    1866 by H A T Harris
Davis, James x; Davis, Sarrah; Johnathen x Henderson; 19 Jan 1842; D Hoffman JP
Davis, James; Dickson, Harriet A; Jasper N Holland; 24 Feb 1845; Isaac Holland
Davis, James L; Killian, Rebecca; Jacob Reel; 26 Dec 1842
Davis, John; Lytle, Elisabeth; Archibald Little (Lytle); 12 Apl 1785
Davis, John; Wingate, Sophia; Albert C Williamson; 3 Mar 1846; V A McBee
Davis, John; Spake, Caroline; John P Cansler; 18 Jan 1853; R Williamson
Davis, John B; Oliver, Jamima; Alfred Linebarger (Leinbarger); 18 Oct 1838
Davis, John W; Mcalister, Lisah; Henry A Dilling; 27 Jul 1841; D Hoffman JP
Davis, Luke L; Ralph, Dianah; Joseph J McKell; 18 Jan 1831; J T Alexander
Davis, Michall; Smith, Elizabeth; Edwin x Mullen; 29 Nov 1841; A J Cansler
Davis, Samuel; Campell, Nancy; James C M'Koun (James M C Koun); 7 Feb 1854;
    Daniel A Haines
Davis, Thomas; Glenn, Elizabeth; Moses Roberts; 17 Jan 1826; J T Alexander
Davis, Thomas x; Stowe, Catherine; G W Hull; 12 Oct 1864; D H Tillett; M 13 Oct
    1864 by G W Hull
Davis, Uriah; Norman, Sebrey; William Moore, Pery G x Reynolds; 5 Nov 1811;
    Saml Wilson Dp Cl
Davis, William; Bigam, Naomi; Saml x Bigam; 4 Feb 1806; J McEwin
Davis, William; Clemmer, Susanah; Eli Clemmer; 28 Dec 1822; Isaac Holland
Davold (Devolt), John x; Dick, Susanah; Abraham Forney; 24 Apl 1782
Day, Haner (Henry); Sherril, Sally L; Carlos Leonard; 3 Sep 1827; Silas L McBee
Dayley (Daily), Abraham; Abernathy, Polly; James Hayns; 10 Mar 1807; Betsey
    Henderson
Deal, Anthony; Huffman, Nancy; Abraham x Yount; 25 Nov 1830; Mic Cline
Deal, Daniel; Rosemond, Ruanna; Jonathan Bost; 24 Sep 1838; Jesse Gantt
Deal, David; Bollinger, Roseannah; Henry Deal; 3 Apl 1830; Mic Cline
Deal, Eli E; Rudesill, Eliza A; Noah C Deal; 24 Oct 1838
Deal, George; Rader, Sally; Anthony Moose; 23 Jun 1828
Deal, George; Bullenger, Betsy; David Deal; 16 Aug 1828; V McBee
Deal, Henry; Frye, Margaret; George Rinck; 10 Jan 1832; L McBee
Deal, Jacob; Ward, Catharine; David Wike; 22 Feb 1829; Mic Cline
Deal, Jacob; Rudisel, Francis; Daniel Sigmon (Sigman); 2 Nov 1840; H Cansler
Deal, Jonas; Fry, Fany; David Herman; 2 Jan 1834; J D Herman
Deal, Mathias; Anders, Nancy; John W Gant; 15 Apl 1829; Mic Cline
Deal, Solomon x; Yount, Sally; Abraham Yount; 29 June 1815; J Lourance
Deal, William; Smyer, Cathrine; John Stine; 10 Aug 1824; Mic Cline
Deal, William; Yount, Susannah; (Ger) Joseph Hunsicker (?); 8 Aug 1827; Miles
    Abernathy
Dealasnider, David x; Oliver, Elizabeth; William Lamerris (Lemeris); 16 May 1815;
    Jo Lourance
Debenport, John x; Long, Elizabeth; Rheubin x Tallant; 8 Mar 1827; M Hull JP
Deck, John; Williams, Mary; John Moore; 1 Feb 1802
Deck, Jonas; Fronebarger, Lavina; Alfred Ramsaur (Ramsour); 14 Feb 1837; M W
    Abernathy

Deck, Peter; Vickers, Louisa; John Vickers; 26 Jan 1846; V A McBee
Decker, Frederick x; Moore, Ruthy Lucinda; David Wike; 16 Jan 1838; John H Robinson
Decker, Michael x; Deal, Christiana; George x Decker, John x Roney; 12 Oct 1798; John Dickson
Defenbach (Tefenbach), John; Martin, Sarah; George Aderholt; 29 Feb 1812; Elizabeth Henderson
Delane, Alvin; Helterbrant, Mrs Sarah; J D Anthony; 27 Sep 1865; A S Haynes CCC; M same date by O B Jinks
Dellinger, A C (Cathey); Kids, Mary Ann; R S Proctor; 28 Feb 1855; G P Keever; M same date or next day by W C Patterson (MG)
Dellinger, Adam x; Fulks, Anny; Philip Fulks; 30 Jan 1810; Danl M Forney
Dellinger, Adam; Blakely, Mary; Valentine Dellinger; 29 Mar 1848; Robt Williamson
Dellinger, Andrew x; Golding, Hanah; Henry x Underwood; 11 Feb 1808; Danl Forney
Dellinger, Andrew; Shelton, Polley; Solomon Dellinger; 29 Mar 1824; V McBee
Dellinger, Charles; Homesly, Jemima; George x Dellinger; 12 Dec 1846; Robt Williamson
Dellinger, Daniel x; Bradshaw, Milley; Washington Sitz; 24 Dec 1827; J T Alexander
Dellinger, Daniel; Bradshaw, Emelia; Samuel Dellinger; 13 Oct 1838; J A Ramsour DC
Dellinger, Daniel; Houser, Fanny; Abram Houser; 25 Feb 1840; A J Cansler
Dellinger, Daniel; Bynum, Susannah; Alfred Dellinger; 12 Sep 1848; Robt Williamson
Dellinger, David; Butts, Sally; Henry Butts; 27 May 1824; Jas T Alexander
Dellinger, David; Hines, Mary Ann; Milton A Smith; 8 Mar 1836
Dellinger, Ephraim x; Robison, Mrs Anny; Daniel Delinger (Dellinger); 12 Sep 1830; Jacob Henry
Dellinger, Franklin; Sanders, Sarah; Edward S Saunders (Sanders); 10 Feb 1840; H Cansler Clk
Dellinger, George x; McKinny, Mary; George Goldman; 7 Apl 1803; John Dickson
Dellinger, Henry; Dellinger, Catherine; Moses Dellinger; 9 Oct 1818; V McBee
Dellinger, Henry; Summerow, Catharine; Lawson A Dellinger; 1 Sep 1860; W R Clark; M 11 Sep 1860 by J Finger (MG)
Dellinger, Henry J; Bradshaw, Matilda; Jacob Reinhardt; 20 Apl 1833; L McBee
Dellinger, Jacob; Setzer, Sarah; ; Henry Sigmon (Ger Heinrich Siegmann); 28 Mar 1818; John Willfong
Dellinger, Jacob; Dellinger, Sarah; Christopher Carpenter; 4 Oct 1831; J T Alexander
Dellinger, John (Ger Johannes Diellienger); Fisher, Barbara; (Ger) Johannes _____; 10 Dec 1792; Joseph Steel
Dellinger, John; Shuford, Elissabeth; John Smyer; 8 (or 9) Sep 1808; John Willfong
Dellinger, John; Hollman, Anny; Valentine Dellinger; 2 Oct 1851; George Coon JP; M same date by George Coon JP
Dellinger, John G x; Goodson, Mary; William x Crites; 1 Jan 1833; L McBee
Dellinger, John W (or A); Plantina, Lovina; George W Kincaid; 24 Dec 1833; Carlos Leonard
Dellinger, Joseph x; Sigman, Margred; Bolsor x Sigman; 21 Feb 1811
Dellinger, Josiah R; Bynum, Melinda; James A Barkley; 3 Jul 1855; J A Huss; M same date by F J Jetton JP
Dellinger, L M; Nixon, Sarah; David Cherry; 13 Oct 1866; W R Clark Cl; M 16 Oct 1866 by J Finger MG
Dellinger, Lorenzo Dow; Macaul, Delia Annabeor; Josiah Allen (Allin); 18 May 1862; R Nixon JP; M same date by Robt Nixon JP
Dellinger, M C; Nance, Harriette R; _____; 23 Apl 1861; W R Clark Clk; M 24 Apl 1861 by R·H Morrison; L and C, no B
Dellinger, Moses; Copeland, Minerva; Henry Hansel; 3 Jul 1822; V McBee
Dellinger (Dillinger), Moses x; Childress, Rachel; John Harriss (Harris); 7 Apl 1825; V McBee
Dellinger, Moses N; Stroup, Mary; Simon Dellinger; 4 Sep 1820; V McBee
Dellinger, Munroe x (Freedman); Nance, Betsy (Freedwoman); P Cody; 25 Aug 1866; D A Lowe; M same date by D A Lowe JP
Dellinger, Noah; Summerow, Margaret; J C Stroup; 6 Jul 1838; H Cansler CC
Dellinger, Peter x; Hains, Peggy; Peter Forney; 27 Oct 1807; Jacob Forney
Dellinger, Philip; Blakely, Sarah Ann; J C Stroup; 21 Mar 1846
Dellinger, Valentine x; Collins, Jane; David Harry; 25 Aug 1836
Dellinner (Dillenger), Philip; Black, Rebeckah; Daniel Deline (Dillenger); 1 Oct 1819; V McBee
Denham, John; Robinson, Ruth; William x Spencer; 20 Jun 1837; D Hoffman JP
Denton, William x; Flowers, Ann; James Cobb; 14 Oct 1837; H Cansler
Derr see Taar and Tarr

Derr, A J (Andrew J); Little, Jane K; Abner Goodson; 9 Jan 1858; M 14 Jan 1858 by R H Morrison
Derr, Andrew; Whitley, Mary; Jacob Reinhardt; 2 Jan 1814; Vardry McBee
Derr, Harbert x; Forney, Marthe; Tyrus x Burton; 2 Dec 1866; R Nixon JP; Endorsed "Colored Freedman"; M same date by R Nixon JP
Derr, John H; Sifford, V N (V A); J C Rudisill; 6 Mar 1866; M 13 Mar 1866 by R H Morrison
Derr (Darr), Valentine; Lee, Silvia; James M Smith; 23 Feb 1858; H Asbury; M same date by H Asbury
Deshaser, Hardy x; Smith, Polly; Jacob x Tommy; 23 Jul 1801; John Dickson
Dethrow, Jonathan x; Clemmer, Louisa; Solomon x Srum; 28 Mar 1823; V McBee
Detter, Albert W; Cannon, Emily; Z A Moss; 27 Apl 1856; Robt Williamson; M 8 May 1856 by J T Alexander JP
Detter, Andrew; Falls, Sarah; David M'Cullouch (McColloch); 23 Aug 1822; V McBee
Detter, Daniel; McCasland, Polly; John Zimmerman; 6 Jul 1811; Danl M Forney
Detter, Frederick (Ger Dater or Deter); Cline; Lavina; Henry Eckerd; 25 Nov 1837; H Cansler CC
Detter, George; Glenn, Margaret S; --------; 27 Jan 1853; M this date by Major Hull JP; R only, no B
Detter, John; Wilson, Martha; Rufus Reed; 23 Jan 1817; James T Alexander
Detter, John; Spake, Vica; John W B Harris; 3 Apl 1840; H Cansler
Detter, John R; Carpenter, S A; W R Edwards; 16 Apl 1862; M 17 Apl 1862 by L M Berry (MG)
Dettor see Ditton
Dettor (Detter), David; Harris, Nancy; Peter Hoyl; 5 Aug 1834; G Hoke
Dettor (Detter), David; Coulter, Harriet; Lawson A Reinhardt; 15 Nov 1838
Deven, Patrick; Conner, Elizebeth; Jacob Conner; 27 Oct 1825; V McBee
Devenport, Abraham; Bohannon, Elizabeth; Wm Featherston; 21 Jul 1797; Jonn Greaves
Devenport, John; Abernathy, Delilah; Edward Boyd; 5 Dec 1805; Lwn Henderson
Devenport, William; Henderson, Issabella; James A Henderson; 10 Feb 1821; V McBee
Dickerson (Dickeson), J L; Herndon, Mary W; Geo L Davis; 10 Jan 1865; M same date by W R Wetmore "Christ's Minister & Rector of St Luke's Church"
Dickey, Alexander; Sinclair, Jane; Samuel M Turner; 27 Feb 1821; V McBee
Dickson, Ezekiel; McKisick, Polley; John Dickson; 25 Sep 1802; Jas McKisick
Dickson, James; Moore, Agness; Wm Moore; 12 Jan 1786; Elizabeth Dickson
Dickson, James; Rine, Susanah; Samuel Cox; 28 Dec 1818; V McBee
Dickson, John; Holland, Mary; Isaac Holland; 12 Dec 1787
Dickson, John; Falls, Nancy; Andrew Harmon, Andrew Falls; 28 Sep 1820; John Falls JP
Dickson, John; Goforth, Pricilla Ann; Preston Goforth; 20 Dec 1838; H Cansler
Dickson, John M; West, Juliet; William Berry; 11 Sep 1816; James T Alexander
Dickson, Joseph of Rutherford Co, Tenn; Rankin, Ellener; --------; 11 Oct 1810
Dickson, Thomas; Falls, Rosana; Andrew Falls; 5 Apl 1791; J Dickson
Dickson, Thos x; Brown, Betsey; Jas G Beatty; 9 Apl 1800
Dickson, William; Martin, Frances; John Dickson, James Martin; 21 Apl 1796; William Martin, J Wilson
Dietz, Daniel; Cline, Mary; James T Alexander; 8 Apl 1830; Jacob R Shuford
Dietz, David; Hoke, Ann; Charles Reinhardt; 23 Aug 1816; V McBee
Dietz, Emanuel; Hawn, Anna M; Chrst (Christian) Hawn (Jr); 2 Oct 1834; Jonas Bost
Dietz, Frederic; Bost, Catharina; George Huffman; 12 Aug 1809; Mic Cline
Dietz, Israel; Sommit, Anna; Michael x Yoder; 12 Nov 1837
Dietz, Jacob; Ash, Nancy; David Killian; 12 Oct 1822; Mic Cline
Dietz (Deitz), Lazarus; Harman, Mary; Solomon x Deitz; 3 Nov 1836; Henry Cline
Dietz, Solomon; Huffman, Elisabeth; --------; 26 Apl 1797
Dietz, Solomon; Dietz, Elizabeth; Joseph x Fisher; 31 Mar 1816; Mic Cline
Dillenger (Dellinger), Frederick; Dellinger, Polly; James Carrol; 19 Jan 1830; J T Alexander
Dilliner (Dellinger), George; Anthony, Barbara; Daniel x Anthony; 23 Dec 1828; B J Thompson
Dilling, Henry A; Bradley, Elisabeth; John W Davis; 30 Nov 1841; Dnl Hoffman JP
Dilling, William x; Houten, Hester; Samuel Hawkins; 5 Aug 1842; __ Reeves JP
Dillinger, George (Ger Georg Dellinger); Stroup, Barbara; Phillip x Stroup; 25 Oct 1782
Dillinger, Henry; Link, Susanah; Henry x Link; 8 Aug 1826; V McBee
Dillinger, John; Sides, Hannah; Alexr Moore; 4 Oct 1804
Dillinger, Lewis; Hyne, Elizabeth; Daniel Shuford (Shufford); 12 Feb 1827; Charles L Torrence

Dillinger, Michael; Wills, Christiana; Jacob Dillinger; 15 Jul 1788
Dillinger, Philip x; Stroup, Katherine; John x Hovis; 23 Sep 1790; Jas Dickson
Dillingham, Vachel; Beatty, Betsey; Solomon Beeson (Beason); 21 Mar 1797
Dillon (Dillin), Edmond; McAnear, Nancey; Benjamin Cornelus (Cornelius); 5 Aug
1795; Jo Dickson
Dillon (Dillion), Henry; Gibbs, Susanna; J Wilkinson; 15 Aug 1805; Thos Wheeler
Dilner (Dellinger), Daniel x; Masegee (Massagee), Caroline; John Farmer; 28 Nov
1858; L H Hill JP; M same date by L H Hill JP
Dinwiddie, James; Robertson, Jean; John Dinwodey (Dinwiddie); 22 Sep 1790;
Jas Dickson
Ditton (or Dettor), Nicholas; Heedick, Mary; Henry Hoke; 10 May 1787
Dobson, William; Ford, Minty; Milton Berry; 1 Dec 1823; Isaac Holland
Doggett, John R; Shuford, Francis; I Martin Roberts; 19 Jan 1835; M W Abernathy
Dormire, Peter x; Bridges, Elisabeth; David x Bridges; 20 Feb 1794; Joseph Steel
Dormire, Samuel Jr x; Cook, Eve; Saml x Dormire Sr; 22 Feb 1785; Joseph Steel
Dormyer, David x (of Iredell); Grisenbery, Mary; Henry Trit (of Iredell) (Ger
Heinrich Tritt); 27 Jul 1797; Michael Cline
Dorsey (Dawsey), Benjamin; Short, Joan (Jean); Isaac Robinson; 28 Dec 1784;
Joseph Steel
Dorsey (Dawsey), Elishe; Ashe, Delilah; Benjamin Dorsey (Dawsey); 3 Nov 1793;
Joseph Steel
Dorsey, Joseph; Barr, Margaret; Elias Ferguson; 25 Dec 1797
Dorty, Henry x; Glenn, Adline; Peter Bess; 6 Oct 1865; A S Haynes CCC, H A Chap-
man; M 10 (or 7) Oct 1865 by O B Jenks JP
Doss, Joel; Penny, Mary; William Penny; 27 Oct 1796; John Dickson
Dougherty, Bernard; Swenson, Lydicia; William Rutledge; 16 Mar 1822; V McBee
Douglas, William; Dehebough, Peggy; Ab (Abram) Laurance (Lorance); 18 Oct 1819;
V McBee
Douglass (Duglas), David; Gant, Avaline; William Dugles (Douglass); 4 May 1828;
Mic Cline
Douglass (Douglas), John; Dickson, Mary; Thomas Dickson; 12 Sep 1791; Jo Dickson
Downey, Patrick; Cox, Lucey; Vincent x Cox Jr; 2 Mar 1802; Jos Dickson
Drum, Eli; Grice, Ann E; Lawson H Abernathy; 10 Jul 1838; H Cansler CC
Drum, John; Linebarger, Susanah; George Drum; 13 Aug 1822; V McBee
Drum, John; Shook, Barbara; Peter Drum; 4 Dec 1825; David Henkel
Drum, Joseph; Huffman, Sally; Barnet x Moser; 21 Mar 1833; Miles W Abernathy
Drum, Peter x; Hefner, Elizabeth; Archibald Ray; 18 Sep 1828; Mi W Abernathy JP
Drum, Philip; Horse, Mary; John Drum; 29 Dec 1784; Joseph Steel
Drum, Phillip; Marshall, Elizabeth; John L Grise (Grice); 15 Mar 1842; H Cansler
Drum, William; Mays, Patsy; I W (or J W) Gabriel (Wilson Gabriel); 5 May 1835;
M W Abernathy
Drumm, John; Isahower, Mayry; George x Isahower; 31 May 1798; Peter Little
Duck, Ezekiel; Shelton, Matisha; Samuel Shelton; 8 Mar 1828; Beverly J Thompson
Ducker, Frederick; Earnest, Hanah; Christopher x Decker; 26 Aug 1798
Duckworth, Abel Hkns ("hankins"); Carathers, Mary; Robert Caruthers (Corrithers);
10 Jun 1783; James Freeman; "Abel hnks Duckworth and Robert Corrithers the
one of Mecklinburgh and the other of the County of Lincoln"
Duckworth, Robert A; Hager, Mary A; Simon C Hager; 7 Oct 1849; R E Burch
Duckworth, William x; Drake, Margaret; Abel H Duckworth (Hankin Duckworth);
13 Sep 1808; H Y Webb
Duderow, Michael x; Srum, Barbara; Lewis Clemmer; 24 Dec 1798; Jno Dickson
Duff, Denis; Morris, Elizabeth; James x Morris; 31 Mar 1778; Jonathan Hampton
Duffy, Robert; Fountain, Elizabeth; Demsey Fountain; 22 Apl 1819; V McBee
Dugless (Douglas), Isaac; Fish, Dolly; William Dugless (Douglas); 21 Nov 1820;
Zachariah Stacy
Dugless (Duclis), James; Wike, Febe; Elias Smyer; 23 Jan 1825; Mic Cline
Dunbar, John A; Leonhardt, Rosannah; J G Rudisill; 23 Dec 1858; W R Clark;
M same date by Wm J Hoke JP
Dunbar, Joseph A; Barkly, Rebeckah C; Henry Barkley (Barkly); 21 Nov 1821;
V McBee
Duncan, Absalom; Bynam, Patsy; Ephraim Daily; 30 Jan 1827; Wm Little
Duncan, Andrew; Earley, Nancey; John Duncin (Duncan); 24 May 1816; John Allen
Duncan, Carter; Bradshaw, Judy; Isaac Lowe; 23 Aug 1819; V McBee
Duncan, George; Edwards, Patience; Daniel Asbury, Peter Dunkin (Duncan);
9 Oct 1793
Duncan, John; James, Polly; John Duncan; 20 Aug 1807; Thos Wheeler
Duncan, John; Killon, Youley; Absalom Duncan; 1 Oct 1807; Thos Wheeler

Duncan, Turner; Crites, Fanny; Owen Clark; 14 Apl 1813
Duncan, Turner; Williams, Rebecca; Nedham x Kincaid; 29 Jul 1844; R Williamson Jr
Dunken (Danken), Ephram; Rodgers, Nancy; Smith Sherill (Sherrill); 21 May 1842;
    Wm Long JP
Dunkin (Duncan), Nathan; Linebarger, Lovina; William x Duncan; 22 Mar 1819;
    V McBee
Dunn, James x; Wells, Rachel; Thomas Oates; 8 Aug 1816; V McBee
Dunn, James; Cox, Elisabeth; George Reed; 1 Feb 1823; Saml M'Kee
Dunn, Joseph; Long, Jane; William Dunn, William Long; 17 Feb 1778
Dunn, Moses M x; Wells, Elizabeth; Samuel Wells; 16 Mar 1818
Dunn, Simon; Wells, Peggy; Felix Kennedy (Canady); 5 May 1821; I'Holland
Dunn, Thomas; Hamilton, Ellender; William Beatey; 29 Dec 1810; H Y Webb
Dunn, William M; Spencer, Isabella; William Featherston; __th Jul 1823
Dusenberry, E La Fayette; Summey, Caroline Amanda; L P Henderson; 18 May 1852;
    Robt Williamson; M same date by Rev R N Davis
Dutrow, Soloman x; Jenkins, Elizabeth; John Shrum; 5 Jun 1815; James T Alexander
Duty, Rusell; Aker, Afee; William Whit (Whitt); 3 Jul 1818; James T Alexander
Dyer, Elisha; _____ _____; Daniel Speck; 10 Nov 1825; V McBee
Dyer, George; Detherow, Barbary; John Shrum; 28 May 1814; Ja T Alexander
Dyer, John; Johnson, Catharine; John Jonson (Johnson); 5 Feb 1832; M Hull JP

Eaby (Abey), Andrew; Wehon, Catherine; Daniel Hoke; 1 May 1809; Danl M Forney
Eake (Aker), Peter; McClerd, Catherine; James McClurg (McClerd); 16 Apl 1816;
    V McBee
Eaker (Aker), Abraham; Hugins, Mary; Noah Mauny (Mauney); 13 Jun 1833;
    J T Alexander
Eaker, Abram x; Cody, Sarah; Jacob x Havner; 17 Feb 1857; W R Clark; M 18 Feb
    1857 by David Bailey JP
Eaker, Christian; Rudisel, Salley; William Aderhod (Aderhold); 21 Apl 1821
Eaker (Aker), Christian; Carrol, Martha; James Lacky, James Hill; 1 Nov 1826
Eaker, Daniel; McCarty, Sarah; _____; 30 Apl 1802
Eaker (Aker), Daniel; Carpenter, Fanny; (Ger) Peter Eker; 25 Mar 1808; Danl Forney
Eaker, Daniel; Kizer, Ann; Peter Eaker; 9 Nov 1835; M W Abernathy
Eaker, Daniel; Eaker, Elvira; John Eaker; 22 Dec 1859; W R Clark; M same date
    by R H Abernathy JP
Eaker (Aker), Henry; Mauney, Catharine; John C Rutledge; 19 Jul 1831; J T
    Alexander
Eaker, Jacob; Moore, Anna; John Clemmer; 18 Sep 1826; J T Alexander
Eaker (Aker), Jesse; Baker, Elizabeth; Samuel x Huttel; 6 Dec 1830; L M McBee
Eaker, Jesse; Workman, Nancy A; Daniel Eaker; 9 Mar 1866; W R Clark; M 14 Mar
    1866 by H A T Harris
Eaker (Acre), John; Kiser, Barbary; Daniel Eaker (Acre); 4 Feb 1809; H Y Webb
Eaker (Aker), John; Best, Nancy; James Eaker (Aker); 9 Jul 1816; James T Alexander
Eaker, John; Baker, Margaret; George Seller; 15 Jul 1822; Samuel M Turner
Eaker, John; Baker, Ann Catharine; Willie Baker; 27 Apl 1844; Robt Williamson Jr
Eaker, John; McFalls, Martha; James Eaker; 18 Dec 1857; W R Clark; M 24 Dec
    1857 by David Crouse (JP)
Eaker, Joseph x; Helms, Visey; Martin x Hafner; 30 Nov 1859; V A McBee;
    M 2 Dec 1859 by P Carpenter JP
Eaker (Aker), Michael; Keykindall, Ruth; Samuel Carbinder (Carpenter); 2 Jan 1787
Eaker, Peter (Ger Peter Eker); Hambright, Sarah; 14 Nov 1798; Jno Dickson
Eaker, Peter; Warlick, Mary Ann; John Rutledge; 16 May 1836; John B Harry
Eakerd, Solomon x; Millar, Prasila; Elkanah Flouers; 4 Apl 1841; J Yount JP
Earley, Charles x; Ward, Ruth; Thos James; 1 Aug 1818; John Allen
Early, John; Rudisell, Dolly; Jacob Linck (Ger same); 13 Jan 1798; Jno Dickson
Earnest, Daniel; Cline, Elisa; Andrew Arnst; 6 Jan 1797
Earney see Arney
Earney, Henry; Mosteller, Elizabeth; James T Alexander; 12 Apl 1821
Earney, Henry x; Carpenter, Elizabeth; Jonas x Carpenter; 20 Jan 1842; J A
    Ramsour DC
Earney (Arney), John; Mosteller, Ann C; George Mosteller; 8 Apl 1841
Earny, Lafayette x; Sherrill, Nancy; Lee Johnson; 4 Mar 1867; M 5 Mar 1867 by
    R H Abernethy JP
Earny (Arney), Martin; Deal, Lydia; John x Earney (Arney); 6 Oct 1835; G Hoke
Earny (Earney), William L; Robinson, Caroline C; Alexander H Robison (Robin-
    son); 7 May 1844; H Cansler

Earp, Philip; Ward, Francess; Alexander Lowe; 15 Jan 1827; J T Alexander
Earwood, Frederick x; Haskins, Jenny; William x Earwood; no date (Ashe Governor 1795-8)
Earwood (Erwood), Thomas; Creesman, Mary; Peter Smith; 25 Aug 1830
Earwood, William x; Haskins, Susanah; John x Shutley; 18 Nov 1794; Jo Dickson
Eaton, Adam x; Taylor, Nancy; George Keener; 21 Oct 1859; Elisha Saunders; M 23 Oct 1859 by Elisha Saunders JP
Eaton, George; Sherril, Polly; Jno Turbyfill, John Allen; 6 Oct 1806; Lwn Henderson
Eaton, John x; Whitney, Elizabeth; Branson x Whitney; 30 Nov 1840; H Cansler CC
Eaton, Jonathan x; Palmer, Sarah; Jonathan x Long; 18 Dec 1813
Eatris (Atris), John; Duncan, Nancy; John H Long; 23 Nov 1829; V McBee
Eaves, Burrel; Malone, Izza; Graves Eaves, William Eaves; 1 Oct 1778; Jonathan Hampton
Eberhard, Charles T; Ballard, Mary A; John H Ballard; 22 Oct 1861; W R Clark; M 23 Oct 1859 by J A Huggins Min M P C
Ecker see Aker and Acer
Ecker, Jacob x; Creesmore, Catherine; John Baker (Ger Johannes B____); 5 May 1807; Phil Whitener JP
Eckerd, George (Ger Gorg Eckerd); Rouch, Peggy; (Ger) Martin Eckerd; 19 Feb 1818; Mic Cline
Eckerd, George (Ger Iorg Eckerd); Probst, Mary; Philip Miller; 2 Mar 1826; Mic Cline
Eckerd, Jonathan x; Simmon, Addy Celena; Martin Huffman; 7 Apl 1837; Henry Cline
Eddleman, Bostian x; Gualtney (Gwaltney), Susanna; Nathan Gwaltny (Gualtney); 19 Sep 1797
Eddleman (Eddleman), David F; Summerrow, Louisa F; W S Edwards; 14 Jan 1857; J A Huss; M 28 Jan 1857 by Landy Wood
Edgen, James x; Adams, Nancy; William x Foster; no date (Turner Governor 1802-5); ____ Williamson
Edgin, Moses; Burpo, Mary; James x Edgin; 29 May 1813; Vardry McBee
Edgin, Samuel; Sronce, Nancy; John x Sronce; 23 Feb 1813; V McBee
Edgin (Edgins), Samuel; Harthorn, Polley; Jacob Tommy (Tommey); 16 Jul 1816; V McBee
Edleman, David; Adams, Elisabeth; Jacob Stroup (Ger Jacob Straub); 24 Nov 1795; Jo Dickson
Edleman (Eddleman), Henry; Hager, Mary; Michael Seitz; 3 Nov 1813; James T Alexander
Edleman, Jacob x; Henkle, Nancy; Moses Abernathy; 28 May 1813; V McBee
Edleman (Eddleman), Peter; Cleppard, Dica; John White; 25 Mar 1830; J T Alexander
Edmond, Francis M x; Simms, Sarah; Joshua Lore; 20 Feb 1865; S P Sherrill
Edward (Edwards), Nathaniel; Asbury, Martha; Jonathan x Long; 25 Jul 1794; John Dickson; Ambiguous
Edwards, Alexander; _____ _____; Jas M Litten; 15 Dec 1837
Edwards, Amos; Nixon, Betsey; William Nixon; 25 Mar 1823
Edwards, Benjamin; Williams, Saly; Morris Williams; 21 Oct 1809; Danl M Forney
Edwards, Charles; Litten, Ruth; James x Litten; 28 Apl 1812; Elizabeth Henderson
Edwards, Charles; Call, Ann; Alexander Jones; 15 Apl 1830; J T Alexander
Edwards, David L; Clark, Susan M; Samuel Edwards; 21 Jan 1839; H Cansler CC
Edwards, Edmond; Hill, Jane; John x Finison; 6 Mar 1821; V McBee
Edwards, Ephraim S; Randleman, Isabella C; Peter S Kistler; 4 Jan 1849; Robt Williamson
Edwards, James x; Reynolds, Anna; Leonard Long; 27 Feb 1800; Jno Dickson
Edwards, James; Loftin, Elizabeth; John Edwards; 26 Feb 1828; Electious Conner JP
Edwards, John; Ettleman, Eve; William Maskal (Baskell); 4 May 1789
Edwards, John; Loftin, Mary; Obed Edwards; 7 Apl 1828; Electious Conner JP
Edwards, John H; Little, Harriot; Wm P Burch; 1 Apl 1858; J D King; M same date by J D King JP
Edwards, Joseph; Hager, Barbara; George Jarrett; 1 Nov 1831; L McBee
Edwards, Lewis; Goodin, Abby; Peter Forney, Robert Luckey; 7 Jan 1784; Jo Henry
Edwards, Lewis x; Clipperd, Sophiah; David Connel (Connell); 22 Aug 1843; H Cansler
Edwards, Lewis; Little, Elizabeth; Hezekiah C Barkley; 21 Apl 1848; Robt Williamson
Edwards, Mark; Hammentree, Nancy; John Fulenwider; 1 Nov 1788
Edwards, Mathew; Steasy, Elizabeth; Joseph Stevenson; 19 Jul 1814; James T Alexander
Edwards, Moses x; Johnson, Peggy; John Mabery; 26 Dec 1815; V McBee
Edwards, Robert; Hansell, Sarah; Osburn Henkle; 31 Mar 1838; H Cansler

Edwards, Samuel; Miller, Roxanna; John Edwards; no date, end 1834
Edwards, Starling; Cobb, Selina; Clizby Cobb; 26 Mar 1793; Joseph Steel
Edwards, Stephen; Shelton, Mititia; Freeman Shelton; 6 Feb 1811; Danl M Forney
Edwards, William x; Clifton, Polley; Richard Cowen; 6 Feb 1808; Jacob Forney
Edwards, William x; Shrantz, Polly; William Cobb; 11 Sep 1810; H Y Webb
Edwards, William L; Coventon, Harriot; S C Hager; 10 Sep 1858; J D King; M same
    date by J D King JP
Edwards, William R; Detter, Eliza E; Benj H Sumner; 23 Dec 1864; M same date
    by E G Gage
Edwards, William R Jr; Dettor, Sarah; Adolphus H Kibler; 6 May 1843; H Cansler
Eikerd see Ikerd and Ichard
Eisenhower see Isenhower
Ekard (Eckherd), Joseph; Mull, Sarah; Jacob Hunsicker (Hunsucker); 16 Oct 1842;
    Jonas Bost
Ekeart (Eckerd), David; Williams, Elizabeth; Martin Huffman; 24 Oct 1832; Mic
    Cline
Eker (Ecre), Cornelius x; Eker, Barery; Peter x Srum; 29 Jan 1784; James Dickson
Elders, Thomas; Wilson, Betey; John Wilson; 24 Jan 1829; V McBee
Elliotte (Eliott), Andrew; Ewing, Kevreenah; Hugh Ewing; 10 Apl 1793; John
    Dickson; Ambiguous
Ellis, Stanford; Warlick, Catharine; Martin Quin (Quinn); 18 Apl 1835; G Hoke
Ellmore (Elmore), Lewis; Avery, Anna; Philip x Avery; 23 Nov 1858; W R Clark;
    M same date by G L Hunt MG
Ellmore, William x (Randall's son); Cloninger, Elizabeth; William x Ellmore (Edward's
    son); 28 Apl 1827; J T Alexander
Elmore, David x; White, Nancey W; Eli Clemer (Clemmer); 20 Jun 1838; Jacob
    Plonk JP; Ambiguous
Elmore, Edward x; Smith, Betsy; John Smith; 21 Dec 1804; Polly D Greaves
Elmore, Ephraim; Bess, Mrs Eliza; John Carpenter; 29 Oct 1850; Robt Williamson
Elmore, James; Costner, Anne; David Friday; 21 Mar 1829; V McBee
Elmore (Ellmer), Jesse x; Wright, Elenor; George Clemmer; 1 Apl 1833; J T Alexander
Elmore, Jonas; Davis, Cyntha; Ephraim Kizer; 19 Mar 1857; M 20 Mar 1857 by
    David Crouse JP
Elmore, Lewis; Farmer, Nancy; Michal x Ellmore (Elmore); 8 Aug 1865; A S
    Haynes CCC, William M Thompson; M same date by S P Sherrill JP
Elmore, Wm x; Yount, Elizer; Wm R Edwards; 29 Oct 1864; S P Sherrill; M same
    date by B S Johnson JP
Emerson (Emberson), James; Moore, Margaret; William T Emerson (Emberson);
    12 Oct 1791; Jo Dickson
Endsley, Archibald; Collins, Mary; Alexander Endsley; 7 Dec 1813; Da'd Warlick JP
Endsley, William; Roberts, Nancy C; Joseph Lusk; 10 Aug 1837; Joseph Carroll
Engle, Andrew x; Srum, Barbara; Peter x Srum; 18 Apl 1815; V McBee
Engle, Daniel; Keener, Polley; John Keener; 9 Apl 1832; V McBee
Engle, John x; Panter, Salley; Henry Keever (or Keener); 15 Jul 1826; V McBee
Engle, John x; Martin, Sarah Ann; William x Williams; 14 Oct 1848; Robt Williams
Engle, Martin x; Church, Nancy; John Bumgarner (Bomgarner); 10 Feb 1824;
    V McBee
Engle, Michael x; Bell, Elizabeth; Michael x Keener; 24 Nov 1828; V McBee
Eply, W J; Shrum, Mary; A S Haynes; 8 Jan 1867; W R Clark CC; M 10 Jan 1867
    by J R Peterson
Epply (Apley), Jacob x; Crisel (Crysel), Susanna; John Crysell; 5 Jan 1796; J Dickson
Epply, Peter x; Schrum, Susannah; Henry Carpenter; 27 Mar 1801; John Dickson
Erson, E; Avent, S J; J F Reinhardt; 2 Feb 1866; M 4 Feb 1866 by J R Peterson
Ervin see Irvin
Erwin (or Irwin), Alexander; Smith, Martha; Isaac Erwin; 5 Feb 1817; James T
    Alexander
Erwin, Arthur R; Maclean, Mary M; Samuel Leitch; 3 Mar 1834; Isaac Holland
Erwin, Isaac; Genglis (or Gingles), Peggy; Adlai Genglys (Genglis); 3 Jan 1818;
    V McBee
Espie, John; Oats, Jeane; John Oates (Oats); Saml Espey (Espie); 26 (or 20) Aug
    1811; John Carruth
Etris, Henry x; Teavebaugh, Catharine; Philip x Teavebaugh; 10 Aug 1802; John
    Dickson
Etters, Jacob; Earls, Trathena; John H Harry; 15 Mar 1831; L M McBee
Eudy, M J; Helderman, Julia C; W A Morton; 20 Jan 1864; W R Clark
Evans, Edward K; Ballard, Mollie; N H Pixley; 20 Mar 1865; M 26 Mar 1865 by
    Peyton G Bowman Methodist Minister

Evans, Moses; Murphy, Elizabeth; Philip x Speck (Seck); 3 Jan 1826; V McBee
Evens (Evans), John; Barns, Patience; Anthony Graves (Graff); 18 Feb 1788; Joseph
   Steel
Ewing, Hugh; Armstrong, Sarah; Joseph Henry; 27 Jan 1786; Elizabeth Dickson
Ewing, Robert A; Wells, Nancy; Burrel F Wells; 3 Sep 1825; J T Alexander
Ewing, Samuel; Patrick, Rachel; Jonathan Beaty; 13 Mar 1818; V McBee

Fairies (Feires), Elias M; Wells, Sarah; Burrel F Wells; 8 Feb 1844; Isaac Holland
Falls, Andrew; Ferguson, Mary H; James T Alexander; 8 Feb 1832
Falls, Andrew; Mendinghall, Sarah Louisa; John Falls; 2 Feb 1838; Daniel Hoffman
Falls, And N; Quin, Margaret E; John Falls, James Quin; 2 Apl 1835; Wm J Wilson
Falls, David; Falls, Rosanah; James Falls; 2 Nov 1820 (end 1821)
Falls, David E; Falls, Rosanah; --------; 28 Nov 182--; Vardry McBee; L only,
   no B
Falls, George L; Williams, Catharine; W Lander; 25 Nov 1845; R Williamson
Falls, James; Ferguson, Mary; John Ferguson; 12 Aug 1788
Falls, John; Jerrill, Susanna; George Falls; 25 Nov 1828; Wm J Wilson
Falls, William; Falls, Esther; John Falls; 13 Nov 1806; James Beaty JP
Falls, William; Falls, Rebecca; David L Falls; 15 Dec 1831; J T Alexander
Faris, Osker A; Mauney, Elizabeth; Robert B W Faris; 15 Jul 1844; R Williamson Jr
Farmer, Absalom; Plonk (Plunk), Nancy; --------; 22 Sep 1857; J A Huss Clerk
   by W R Clark DC; M 24 Sep 1857 by Philip Carpenter JP; L and C, no B
Farmer, Caleb x; Wacaser, Mahala; S P Sherrill; 14 Jul 1858; W R Clark; M 17 Jul
   1858 by Joshua Pendleton (JP)
Farmer, David; Woods, Nancy; Bosten Best; 19 Mar 1834; Miles W Abernathy
Farmer, John; Helms, Anna; David Farmer; 22 Jul 1839; J T Alexander
Farmer, John H; Havner, Martha J; --------; 20 Jul 1859; W R Clark Clk;
   M 21 Jul 1859 by G L Hunt MG; L and C, no B
Farrar, Aaaron; Farrar, Margaret; M B Abernathy; 14 Dec 1822; S McBee
Farrar (Farrow), John; Abernathy, Betsey; Joseph Blackwell; 3 May 1783
Farrar, William; Bynum, Lotte; Jones Abernathy; 27 Oct 1807; Danl Forney
Farrell (Farewell), Aaron; Abernathy, Mary; Chas B x Abernathy; 26 Aug 1848;
   Robt Williamson
Faulkner (Falkner), John N; Dellinger, Zenith; Lewis D H Abrams; 11 Jul 1857;
   R Williamson
Faulkner, Vincent A; Carpenter, Susanah; George Carpenter; 5 May 1824; V McBee
Featherston, Jasper; Rhyne, Elizabeth; Adam Cloninger; 2 Feb 1846; V A McBee
Featherston, William; Spencer, Caty; John Spencer; 24 Apl 1809
Felker, Michael (Ger Michel Felcher); Earheart, Molly; George x Delinger; 23 Nov 1787
Felker, Peter x; Stockininger, Elisabeth; Abraham x Fox; 7 Oct 1800; Jno Dickson
Felmet, C F; Spratt, Margaret; J L Spratt; 10 Sep 1866; W R Clark; M 18 Sep
   1866 by H A T Harris
Felmet, Hugh Mc (or McFelmet, Hugh); Carpenter, Sarah; Jacob Conner; 19 Jan
   1818; V McBee
Felps, Samuel; Vines, Susannah; George Winfree (Winfray); 13 Feb 1782; Jas McEwin
Ferguson, James; Barnet, Sarah; Charles McLean, Samuel Barnet; 10 Mar 1789;
   James Henery, John Wilson
Ferguson, James; Neil, Polley; Samuel B Ferguson; 14 Sep 1820; V McBee
Ferguson, James; Fronebarger, Susan; Caleb Fronabarger; 29 Jan 1839; H Cansler CC
Ferguson, John; Falls, Sarah; William Ferguson; 18 Sep 1820; V McBee
Ferguson, Robert; Falls, Rachel; Aaron Ferguson; 2 Feb 1819; V McBee
Ferguson, Thomas Jr; Wright, Salley; Thomas Ferguson (Sr); 18 Apl 1820; V McBee
Ferguson, William; Carrol, Susanah D; Clizby Cobb; 16 Jul 1839; J A Ramsour
Fevours, William; Vines, Agness; Essix Capshaw, Robert Taylor; 4 Feb 1779; ------
   Miller
Fewell, Henry; Armstrong, Agness B; John x Brimer; 30 Jan 1827; Isaac Holland
Fey (Fye, Fie), Jacob; Killion, Mary; Abraham Killion (Ger same); 20 Sep 1791;
   Joseph Steel
Fie, Jacob x; Luts, Betty; Jacob Lutes (Luts); 13 Apl 1819; John Willfong
Figh, Phillip x; Earns, Ann; Christian Eaker; 5 May 1794; Michl Eaker
Finger, Daniel (Ger same); Sumerow, Catherine; Jacob Reinhardt; 28 Jan 1809
Finger, David x; Sumerour, Mary; Daniel x Finger; 9 Feb 1813; V McBee
Finger, Henry; Killian, Mary; Robert Blackburn; 6 Oct 1823; V McBee
Finger, Henry Jr x; Houser, Molly; Henry Finger Sr (Ger Henrich Finger); 2 Apl 1805
Finger, Jacob x; Troutman, Susanah; John Finger (Ger Johannes Finger); 26 Nov
   1810; HY Webb

Finger, John x; Troutman, Polly; Henry x Troutman; 7 Nov 1801; Jno Dickson
Finger, John; McCasland, Polley; Daniel Detter; 7 Jun 1813; V McBee
Finger, John x; Moos, Tena; Daniel x Ornts; 7 Nov 1840
Finger, John x; Earney, Ann (Jane); John Linch; 12 Jan 1857; W R Clark; M 28
 (24) Jan 1857 by F J Jetton JP
Finger, Jonas x; Sumerour, Susanah; Jacob Reinhardt; 26 Apl 1818; V McBee
Finger, Jonas x; Arntz (or Hintz), Elz; Lauson Propst (Probst); 6 Dec 1841
Finger, Joseph; Keestler, Nancy; John Cansler; 25 Aug 1828; B J Thompson
Finger, Michael; Warlick, Rachel; Franklin D Reinhardt; 7 Feb 1834; Miles W
 Abernathy
Finger, Michael; Killian, Elizabeth C; P S Kistler; 26 Jan 1849; Robt Williamson
Finger, Moses W; Carpenter, Caroline; Daniel Finger; 7 Jan 1848; Robt Williamson
Finger, Peter x; Holler, Anne; Jacob x Engle; 27 Sep 1805; Wm Scott
Finger, Peter; Warlick, Catharine; Joseph Finger; 21 Jan 1836; M W Abernathy
Finison (Finnison, Tinnison), John x; Hill, Fanny; Lewis x Edwards; 2 Jul 1820;
 Edmon Edwards, Jno Turbyfill JP
Finison, John x; Low, Margaret; Thomas G Williamson; 11 Jul 1842; A J Cansler
Finley, Alexander; Gingles, Melissa J; Thomas S Neely; 25 Mar 1839
Finley, John; Marchel, Catharine S; Milton H M Gullick; 15 Mar 1830
Finley (Findley), Robert; Brian, Nancy; John McClure; 14 Jan 1808; Joseph Neel
Finn, Jesse x; Stroud, Fanny; Leonard x Webb; 30 May 1776; And Neel
Fish, Briant x; Belk, Ebby; Isaac Dugless (Dougless); 21 Apl 1823; V McBee
Fish, James x; Henderson, Sarah; Thomas Ward; 3 Jul 1828; Alexander Ward
Fish, John; Abernathy, Susanah; Isaac Dugles (Douglas); 15 Oct 1825; J T Alexander
Fish, William; Kale, Sarah; Barnet Snider; 7 Mar 1803; John Dickson
Fisher see Tucker
Fisher, Benjamin x; Turbefield, Elvira; Rufus Fisher; 5 Mar 1839; L E Thompson
Fisher, David; Litton, Betsey; Uriah Fisher; 19 Jan 1830; J T Alexander
Fisher, David; Kirksey, Elizabeth; _____; 21 Apl 1857; J A Huss Clerk; M 25 Apl
 1857 by Robt Blackburn JP; L and C, no B
Fisher, James; Gilleland, Polly; Stephen Fisher; 14 Mar 1812; Lwn Henderson
Fisher, James E; Steward, Mary A; Benjamin Bel (Beal); 19 Dec 1865; A S
 Haynes CCC
Fisher, John; Hohnau (?), Elizabeth; Joseph H Moore (Moor); 7 Oct 1837;
 H Cansler
Fisher, Joseph; Holman, Sahra; Henry Hollman (Holman); 21 Aug 1800; John
 Willfong
Fisher, Joseph x; Whitener, Susanna; Benjamin x Whitener; 26 May 1808; Phil
 Whitener JP
Fisher, Joseph x; Weaver, Sallema; Jacob Yount; 25 Mar 1824; Phil Whitener JP
Fisher, Lawson x; Lafever, Sarah Jane; John Kistler; 26 Oct 1852; V A McBee
Fisher, Lawson x; Hoyle, Martha L; John Kistler; 6 June 1854; J A Huss; M 8 Jun
 1854 by Danl Siegel JP
Fisher, Reuben; Fisher, Mary; Mason Harwell; 10 Mar 1822; Jas T Alexander
Fisher, Richd; Harwell, Anna; Wm x Conner; 1 Oct 1798; Jno Dickson
Fisher, Rufus; Turbyfill, Anna; William Allen; 15 Apl 1834; M W Abernathy
Fisher, Samuel x; Partin, Elizabeth; James Beatty (Beaty); 15 Jul 1824; Wm Little JP
Fisher, Stephen; Gilleland, Elizabeth; William Gilleland; 6 Oct 1806
Fisher, Stephen G; Fisher, Fanny; Uriah Fisher; 2 Dec 1830; J T Alexander
Fisher, Stephen G x; Fisher, Arminda A; R R Templeton; 18 Jan 1848; Robt
 Williamson
Fisher, William; Harwell, Jenny; William Connor; 20 Jun 1796; Jo Dickson
Fisher, William G; Howard, Mary M; J H Fisher (Joal or Joab H Fisher); 6 Mar 1866
Fite (Fight), Jacob; Wells, Nancy; Peter Fite; 13 Feb 1806; Lwn Henderson
Fite, John W; Brandon, Margaret, of York District S C; Robt Rankin; 25 Feb 1845;
 And Hoyl JP
Fite, Joseph; Beaty, Jane; Moses H Rhyne; 21 Oct 1834
Fite, Pleasent x; Armstrong, Polly; John x Armstrong; 6 Sep 1824; Isaac Holland
Fite, Robt H; Cansler, Barbara S; H Nims; 27 Feb 1861; W R Clark; M 28 Feb
 1861 by L M Berry MG
Fite, Solomon; Wells, Mrs Fanny; Adam Hoyl; 6 May 1816; Daniel McPhaill
Fite, Solomon (Jr) x; Capps, Permelah; Eneas Campbell; 24 Oct 1831; Isaac Holland
Fitzjarold (Fitzjerral), Mylas (Miles); Proctor, Eliza; Thomas O Proctor; 11 Apl 1836
Fitzpatrick, James; Bryan, Sarah; John Wasson; 3 Nov 1796
Flanigan, Jacob x; Wise, Clara; George Sumerow (Sumrow); 16 Jul 1856; J A Huss;
 M 20 Jul 1856 by George Coon JP

45

Flanigin, Jacob x; Gilbert, Polley; Daniel x Sumrow; 27 Jul 1821; V McBee
Fleming, Anderson; Barkley, Sarah; Moses M Sherrill; 20 Apl 1839; H Cansler CC
Fleming, Archa; Thompson, Martha; Archibald Fleming; 6 Aug 1807; Thos Wheeler
Fleming, Archibald; Cherry, Matilda; James Lucky; 14 Jan 1850; S A Burch
Fleming, George; Sherrill, Jane; Aaron F Sherrill; 20 Oct 1843; H Cansler
Fleming, John; Anderson, Mary; Robert Cherry (Chirry); 8 May 1797
Fleming (Flemming); Robert; Hill, Polly; Archibald C Barkley; 25 Jan 1821; John
    Turbyfill JP
Flemming, Archibald; Cherry, Elizabeth; James Cherry; 3 Oct 1834; Jno D Graham
Flonabarger, John x; Hostetler, Barbara; Nicholas x Drum (Srum); 26 Jun 1784;
    James Dickson
Flours (Flowars), Darlin x; Petty, Margarett; Henery x Flours (Flowars); 20 Aug
    1844; Willis Reeves JP
Flowers, Adam; Lanier, Sarah; Joseph Flowers (Ger Joseph Flauers); 27 Jul 1819;
    Joseph Fisher
Flowers, Andrew x; Seabold, Sally; Joseph Flowers (Ger Flouers); 29 Sep 1821;
    Mic Cline
Flowers, Joseph x; Herman, Elizabeth; Simeon Barger Jr; 18 Feb 1830; Henry Cline
Flowers, Lewis x; Long, Harriet; John Roberts; 26 Jun 1833; S McBee
Flowers, Peter x; Seabold, Molly; Christofal x Flowers; 30 Oct 1821 (end 1822);
    Mic Cline
Floyd, Andrew; Shannon, Esther; Henry Houser; 9 Feb 1828; V McBee
Floyd, Robert; Baird, Elizabeth; John Baird; 30 Dec 1805; Lwn Henderson
Floyd, Robert; Carpenter, Sarah; Peter Carpenter; 28 Feb 1834; Miles W Abernathy
Foley (?), Washington Green L; Greyhcm, Catey; Abner McAfee; 14 Nov 1805
Forbes, John H; Thornbury, Cathern; Moses Thornbery (Thornbury); 17 Jan 1842
Ford, Alberry R; Hill, Frances I (or J); Alfred Linebarger (Lineberger); 6 Oct
    1838; Isaac Holland
Ford, Amzi; Ragon, Ellen; Isom Ford; 25 Mar 1830; Isaac Holland
Ford, Andrew; Kizer, Mary; John C Rutledge; 5 Mar 1834; Carlos Leonard
Ford (Fourd), Asberry; Montgemery, Martha; Wm Reese, John Ford; 3 Mar 1812;
    Joseph Neel
Ford, Daniel; Irby, Mary; Samuel Cox; 13 Oct 1816; James T Alexander
Ford, Eli M; Lewis, Mary A; Jacob Linebarger; 8 Jan 1844
Ford, Frederick; Beaty, Sarah S; Peter Titman; 4 Apl 1827; Isaac Holland
Ford, George L; Gastin Mary; A H S Neagle; 10 Aug 1837; Isaac Holland
Ford, Hugh M; Hill, Salina; David L Davis; 27 May 1835; J G Hand JP
Ford, James M; Hill, Elerna; Eli M Ford; 30 Dec 1841; And Hoyl
Ford, John; McKee, Peggy S; Levi Ward; 13 Mar 1820; I Holland for Vardry
    McBee Clk
Ford, John; Gilam, Lucasa; Milton Ford; 16 Nov 1835; J G Hand JP
Ford, Jno N; Ward, Margaret L; Jas M Ford; 16 May 1841; Eli Hoyl
Ford, Lawson; Hill, Mary; James D Hill; 15 Jul 1820; I Holland
Ford, Manuel; Baird, Mary; Isom Ford; 7 Feb 1837; Wm J Wilson
Ford, Nathaniel; Huson, Elizabeth; Jacob Stow; 1792; (N)
Ford, Robert F; Fite, Mary Isabella; John W Fite; 13 Oct 1842; Eli Hoyl
Ford, Tapley M; Massey, Talitha C; Milton McCarver; 13 Jan 1835; J G Hand JP
Ford, William; Berry, Elizebeth; Milton Ford; 7 Feb 1832; Isaac Holland
Fore (Ford), Isom; Baird, Arixney; Levi Ward; 12 Jan 1819; James T Alexander
Forney, A E; Lucky, Jane C; --------; 13 Jan 1857; J A Huss Clerk by W R
    Clark DC; M 18 Jan 1857 by J D King JP; L and C, no B
Forney, Abrm (Abraham); Grabel, Rachel; Henry Pinter (?); 27 Feb 1803; Thos
    Wheeler
Forney, Abraham E; Linebarger, Polley; Reuben x Ballard; 30 Nov 1825; J T
    Alexander
Forney, Abram E; Reggin, Diadame; Charles G Regan; 2 Sep 1831; V McBee
Forney, D J; Ramsour, Sarah C; Wm H Michal; 15 Jun 1859
Forney, Daniel M; Brevard, Harriet; Jacob Ramsour; 18 Oct 1817; V McBee
Forney, Hiram A; Shrum, Sarah; J F (Franklin) Bynum; 27 Jan 1853; R William-
    son; M 10 Feb 1853 by Rev David Crooks
Forney, Jacob; Hoke, Sarah; Jacob Ramsour; 5 Mar 1817; James T Alexander
Forney, Peter; Abernathy, Nancey; Joseph Henry; 27 Feb 1783; John Carruth
Forney, Temple x; Burton, Duley; J C Rudisill; 6 Aug 1866; M same date by R H
    Abernethy JP
Foster, Cornelious x; Frisle, Rachel; Jacob x Frisle; 1 Oct 1793; Joseph Steel
Foster, T M; Bess, Mary F; Hiram Kiser; 14 Dec 1866; W R Clark; M 18 Dec
    1866 by Rev J W Naylor

46

Fox, David x; Cosnar, Elizabeth; Moses Fox; 14 Oct 1830; Fr Hoke JP
Fox, Elisha x; Harmon, Sarah; Elijah Price; 25 Feb 1827; M W Abernathy for
  V McBee
Fox, Hugh x; Hooke, Sally; Moses Fox; 2 Jan 1842; J Yount JP; Ambiguous
Fox, Jacob; Horse, Catharine; Joseph Morris; 8 May 1797
Fox, James x; Rhom, Susanah; Thomas Black; 6 Oct 1825; V McBee
Fox, Patrick; Rabb, Hannah; John H Harry; 28 Apl 1835; M W Abernathy
Foy, James; Spain, Nancy; James Altun (Altom); 4 Jan 1827; George Willkie;
  Ambiguous
Foy, Jesse; Parker, Lovina; Peter Mauny (Mauney); 18 Apl 1820; V McBee
Fraley, Stephen x; Herron, Abagil; John Webster; 24 Feb 1840; Eli Hoyl
Francis, Ruben; Long, Polley; John Turbyfill; 5 May 1828; V McBee
Frazer (Frazier), Alexander; Smyer, Margaret M; Adolphus H Kibler; 2 Aug 1841;
  H Cansler
Freeman, Jesse x; Price, Fanny; Philip x Price; 1 Feb 1797
Freeman, John B; Little, Sarah; William Fulenwider; 20 Mar 1833; J T Alexander
Freytag (Friday), Martin; Rudisel, _____; Robt McCasland, Wm x Tankersly; 22 Oct
  1777; Andr Neel
Friday (Fryday), Andrew; Hoyle, Elizabeth; Joseph Henry; 16 Oct 1792
Friday, David; Jenkins, Susannah; Ephraim Friday; 12 Jan 1836; M W Abernathy
Friday, Ephraim; Holland, M E; L H Kistler; 27 Feb 1841
Friday, Jacob W; Carpenter, Susan Catharine; Jacob (?) F Plonk; 3 Sep 1855; J A
  Huss; M 4 Sep 1855 by A J Fox
Friday, John N; Fronabarger, Sarah; David Friday; 18 Aug 1835; G Hoke
Friday (Fryday), Jonas; Costner, Elizabeth; Joseph Henry; 12 Mar 1790; Joseph
  Henry
Friday, Jonas; Hovis, Mary M; Daniel Loretz; 18 Apl 1825; V McBee
Friday, Martin; Carpenter, Peggy; Joseph Henry; 9 Oct 1783
Frisbie, Samuel; Slade, Elizabeth A; Z A Moss; 24 Oct 1854; Robt Williamson;
  Certificate: marriage of Samuel Frisbie of Montgomery, Ala and Elizabeth A Slate
  of Lincolnton, 25 Oct 1854, signed R N Davis
Frisl (Frisle), Jacob x; Philips, Betsey; Peter x Philips; 24 Dec 1793; Joseph Steel
Fronabargar (Froneberger), Jacob; Linebarger, Elisabeth; Fredrick Leinberger (Line-
  barger); 7 Sep 1813; Ezekiel Abernathy
Fronabarger, Ambrose; Wells (or Wills), Catharine; Peter Beam; 14 Sep 1838;
  H Cansler CC
Fronabarger (Froneberger), Daniel W; Beam, Margaret C; Jonas Deck; 28 Aug 1835;
  M W Abernathy
Fronabarger, David; Mooney, Nancy; Jonas Deck; 13 Sep 1836; M W Abernathy CC
Fronabarger (Froneberger); John; Sellers, Caty; William Fronaberger (Froneberger);
  11 May 1809; Danl M Forney; Ambiguous
Fronabarger, Philip; Kizer, Cynthia; Felix Sellers; 20 June 1835; Carlos Leonard
Fronabarger, William; Plonk, Catharine; Emanuel Aderhold (Arderholdt); 18 Jan
  1843; H Cansler
Fronaberger (Fronaberger), John; Blackwood, Anna; Jacob Fronaberger (Frone-
  barger); 20 Jul 1824; Jas T Alexander
Fronaberger (Froneberger), William; Rhine, Barbara; Jacob Plonk (Plunk) (Jr);
  8 Jan 1812; Lwn Henderson
Fronaberger (Froneberger), William; Jenkins, Peggy; Christopher x Kizer; 7 Mar
  1820; V McBee
Froneberger, A L; Baxter, Sarah; H A Chapman; 21 Jan 1867; W R Clark; M 23 Jan
  1867 by Wade Hill
Froneberger, William; Carpenter, Sally; Henry Carpenter; 11 Oct 1817; V McBee
Fronsher (Frencher), Lewis; Janes, Sally; (Ger) Henrich Schintt, John Lusk; 22 Apl
  1821; Jacob Carpenter JP
Frontis, Stephen; Dews, Martha; Patrick J Sparrow; 29 Jan 1830; V McBee
Frost, James; Hager, Sally; William Featherston; 15 May 1806; Lwn Henderson
Frost, Robert (Jr); Jenkins, Sarah; John Moore; 7 Mar 1801; John Dickson
Froy, David x; Zimmerman, Elisebeth; John Smith; 30 Oct 1827; Phil Whitener JP
Froy, David x; Scarlet, Jemyme; John Link; 14 Nov 1828; Phil Whitener JP
Frush, Jacob x; Froneberger, Salley; John x Froneberger; 29 Oct 1813; Vardry McBee
Frushaur, Christian x; Bird, Polley; Elisha Sanders; 8 May 1824; V McBee
Fry, Absolum; McGee, Peggy; Lewis Rees; 22 Dec 1833; Henry Cline
Fry, Conrad; Bost, Nency; Jacob Fry (Ger Jacob Fr__); 26 Aug 1823; Mic Cline
Fry, Daniel; Smith, Magdalin; George x Fry; 25 Jul 1813; John Smith
Fry, Daniel; Herman, Helena; Joseph Burns; 8 Nov 1827; Mic Cline

47

Fry, Henry x; Eikerd, Sally; George x Fry, John Ikerd (Eikerd); 5 Jun 1813; Mic Cline
Fry, Henry; Ward, Elizabeth; John Holler; 29 Dec 1834; G Hoke
Fry (Frye), Jacob; Cline, Fanny; Jesse Bost; 26 Sep 1825; V McBee
Fry, John (Ger Johannes Frey); Reader, Elisabeth; Adam Reader (Ger R-d-r); 5 Jan 1805; John Willfong
Fry, Jonas; Gross, Etty; Philip Fry; 18 Jun 1823; Mic Cline
Fry, Moses; Bost, Leah; Silas Bost; 18 Mar 1836; M W Abernathy
Fry, Peter (Ger Peter Frey); Bowman, Maria; George Whisenhaunt (Ger Georg Wiesnand); 6 Nov 1800
Fry, Philip (Ger Philib Frey—); Stark (?), Elissabeth; George x Fry; 16 Oct 1808; John Willfong
Fry, Philip (Jr); Bysinger, Polly; Philip x Fry Sr; 6 Jul 1816; Ambiguous
Fry (Frye), Philip; McGee, Polly; Jacob Bolch (Bolick); 15 Oct 1829; Mic Cline
Fulbright, Barnet; Eisenhower, Marey; Jacob Fulbright; 5 Mar 1812; Peter Little
Fulbright, Daniel x; Porter, Cyrena; Peter x Fulbright; 25 Jun 1837; P Stamey JP
Fulbright, George; Settlemier, Sally; John Jones (Jonas); 19 Aug 1824; M Hull JP
Fulbright, George E; Knipe, Sarah C; Jacob H Rhodes; 27 Mar 1866; W R Clark; M 29 Mar 1866 by A J Fox MG
Fulbright, Henry; Mingers, Susannah; Jacob Reinhardt; 10 Dec 1814; V McBee
Fulbright, Peter; Cline, Sally; John Fulbright; 3 Feb 1818; James Graham
Fulbright (Fullbright), William; Sigman, Regena; Nicholas Carpenter (Ger Nicklus Zimmerman); 5 Nov 1829; Miles W Abernathy
Fulbrite (Fulbright), Daniel x; Money, Elitha (Mauney, Eliza); John A Roberts; 9 Feb 1851; M same date by Max Warlick JP
Fulenwider (Fullenwider), Eli H; Lander, Martha; John M Richardson; 23 Feb 1854; John F Miller; M 28 Feb 1854 by Wm I Langdon
Fulenwider, Henry (Henry E); Ramsour, Ann; John D Hoke; 7 Jun 1827; R H Norris
Fulenwider, Jacob; Hoyle, Polley; Jacob Summey Jr; 16 Mar 1813; V McBee
Fulenwider, John; Forney, Lovina; Robert H Burton; 7 Mar 1820; V McBee
Fulenwider, William; Hays, Martha E; Henry Fulenwider; 18 Sep 1826; William Vickers
Fullbright, Andrew x (of Arkansas); Moser, Eliza; William x Fullbright; 29 Jan 1833; M W Abernathy
Fullbright, John x; Sane, Sidney; Jonas Bost; 3 Jul 1834; M W Abernathy
Fullenwider, David; Fullenwider, Sug; --------; 30 Aug 1866; W T McCoy JP; Acknowledgment by former slaves
Fulmauten see Auten

Gabrel (Grabel), Abraham; Abernathy, Anney; John Abernathy; 30 Jan 1806
Gabriel, Jacob F; Robinson, Nancy; Rubin Perkins; 10 May 1834; G Hoke
Gabriel, John W; Sigman, Harriett C; Thomas Slade; 10 Dec 1840; H Cansler
Gabriel, Joseph M; Robinson, Rebecker; Eli S Sherrill; 6 Feb 1842; Wm Long JP
Gaines, Henry; Featherston, Susana; Rolley Harwell; 1 Jul 1797; Note signed by Henry Gaines and Susana Featherston dated 9 Jun 1797 addressed to John Dickson, Clarke of Lincoln Court
Gaines, Robert; ------ ------; Lewis Featherston; no date; Ambiguous; Blank except for signatures, printed form (this form was used in 1799, 1800, and 1801)
Gales, Briant (Bryant); Long, Nancy; Lanson Long; 28 Apl 1830; Peregrine Roberts
Gales, Jacob A; Greenhill, Sarah; Lawson Greenhill; 12 Aug 1858; Joshua Pendleton Esq
Gales, William; Carpenter, Fanney; Samuel Gales; 16 Nov 1826; J T Alexander
Gamble, John; Ferguson, Mary; John Falls; 31 Mar 1835; Wm J Wilson
Gamble, Joseph; Servis, Mary; Thomas Servis; 15 Jan 1839; Daniel Hoffman JP
Gant, Giles; Armstrong (?), Elisabeth; Thomas Little (Lytle); 17 Jan 1783
Gant, James x; Johnson, Sarah E; J H Hager; 31 Oct 1861; R Nixon JP; M same date by Robt Nixon JP
Gant (Gantt), Jefferson; Little, Amanda; James F Crawford; 13 Jan 1850; Robt Williamson
Gant, Jesse; Cloninger, Christina; Jonathan Bost; 22 Oct 1840; Jn Yount JP; Ambiguous
Gant, John H (or W); Deal, Eliza; Jesse Gantt (Gant); 27 Apr 1827; M M Abernathy
Gant, Lewis; Armstrong, Mary; William Gant, John Thompson; 10 Jan 1783; Tho White
Gant, Martin L; Fry, Lenny; Paul Cline; 2 Dec 1836; Abs Miller
Gant, Sherrod; Jones, Sarah; Henry x Gant; 6 Mar 1818; V McBee

Gant, Tiry (Tyra); Hoyle, Rhoda; Willard Boyden; 25 Nov 1833; M W Abernathy

Gant, Willis; Lee, Nancy; Sherod Gant; 22 Oct 1822; Jas T Alexander

Gantt (Gant), Henry; Walls, Betsey; Nathaniel Edwards; 8 Sep 1814; Jesse Perkins; M this date

Gantt, James x; Eaton, Mary; William Stacy; 27 Dec 1822; Joel Dyer

Gantt (Gant), Jesse; Sherrill, Debitha; James Pettillo; 17 Jul 1814; Jesse Perkins; M this date

Gardiner, Andrew; Vickers, Alice; William Vickers; 10 Apl 1811; Danl M Forney

Gardiner (Garner), John; Vickars, Mary; Andrew Gardiner (Garner); 28 Feb 1821; V McBee

Garison, Alfred x; Hawkins, Elmina (Elmira); Ivy H Laney; 21 Oct 1860; Jonas W Derr; M same date by Jonas W Derr JP

Garman, George; Lollar, Rachel; Td Ward; 12 Dec 1791; Joseph Steel

Garner, Lewis; Kendrick, Polly; Spencer x Vaughan; 28 Feb 1825; Jas T Alexander

Garrison, Henry; Rudisil, Martha A; _____; 23 Sep 1857; M this date by D Crooks; C only, no B

Garrison, John; Johnson, Elizabeth; Henry Shrum; 24 Nov 1804; Betsy Henderson

Garrison, John; Hinson, Elizabeth; Philip Hovis; 18 May 1838; L E Thompson

Garrison, William x; Bell, Dicy; Logan x Perkins; 12 Jan 1829; B J Thompson

Gaston, H N; Joy (or Joyce), Mary S; James Quinn; 29 Apl 1842; H Cansler

Gaston, James A; Wells, Mary; Robert Rankin; 10 Mar 1846; And Hoyl

Gaston, Robert H; Moore, Mary M; Larkin B Gaston; 26 Aug 1843; R Williamson Jr

Gates, M Wilson; Rhyne, Nancy; Levi Baker; 6 Nov 1860; W R Clark; M 14 Nov 1860 by Robert G Ramsey (JP)

Gates, William; Norman, Betsy; Wilson Norman; 27 Sep 1839

Gaudelok (Gaudelock), James; Elliott, Agatha Y; Thomas F Elliott; 12 Dec 1832; J T Alexander

Geanes see Janes

Gerald, Adam; Queen, Margaret; Squire x Towery; 26 Sep 1846; Robt Williamson

Gerding, Gerard George; Fingers, Catharine; Conrad Cancellor (Ger illegible); 14 Mar 1804

Gevin, George x; Wheeler, Ann; Thomas Wheeler; 23 Feb 1789; Jo Dickson

Ghent (Gant), John; Purkins, Honora; Augustus Perkins (Purkins); 29 Dec 1789; Joseph Steel

Gibbs, Aoris; Abernathy, Jancy; James Wilkinson; 21 Dec 1816; V McBee

Gibbs, James; Abernathy, Jane; Thomas L Mayes (Mays); 23 Oct 1821; James T Alexander

Gibbs, James; Morgan, Elizebeth; Martin Linebarger (Lingbergh); 7 Mar 1842; Nath Edwards JP; Ambiguous

Gibbs, John; Abernathy, Lucy; Avris Gibbs; 3 Jul 1821; D Reinhardt, Silas McBee

Gibbs, Willy (Wiley); Abernathy, Susannah; Isaac H Ward; 20 Jul 1830; J T Alexander

Gibson, George x; Queen, Elizabeth; George Carpenter; 25 Oct 1838; L E Thompson

Gibson, James x; Huffstotler, Mary; Henry x Huffstotler; 25 Apl 1815; James T Alexander

Gibson, James x; Jinken, Nancey; Aron Jenkins (Jinken); 14 Oct 1824; And Hoyl JP

Gibson, Joseph x; Estrige (?), Polley; James Boyd; 31 Jan 1826; V McBee

Gilbert, Alfred; Smith, C Catharine (Cynthy C); Allen Gilbert, David G Smith; 28 Mar 1853; R Williamson; M 29 Mar 1853 by Maxll Warlick JP

Gilbert, Andrew x; Tronbierg, Rachel; Philip Rudisill (Rudisel); 16 Jul 1825; V McBee

Gilbert, Daniel x; Havner, Jane (Hafner, Jane C); William Leonard; 26 Dec 1853; Robt Williamson; M 29 Dec 1853 by George Coon JP

Gilbert, George x; Holman, Anne; Daniel x Sumrow; 17 May 1824; V McBee

Gilbert, J M x; Wise, Catharine A; A N Wise; 7 Feb 1857; W R Clark; M 12 Feb 1857 by George Coon JP

Gilbert, John F; Summerow, Sarah; V A McBee; 5 Mar 1849; Robt Williamson

Gilbert, Robert x; Leonard, Mary; William Leonard; 26 Jan 1852; Robt Williamson; Uncertain; groom may be William Leonard; M 29 Jan 1852 by George Coon JP

Gileland (Gilliland), Joab; Bridges, Patsy; John Bridges; 6 May 1830

Giles see Piles

Gillam (Gillum), John; Lowe, Nancy; Obed Parrish; 29 Jan 1833; V McBee

Gilleland, Allen; White, Jane; Silas Littlejohn; 16 Jun 1821; V McBee

Gilleland, George; Kale, Nancy; James Fisher; 26 Jan 1821; V McBee

Gilleland, Henderson; Jones, Lavina; John Litten; 28 Nov 1835; M W Abernathy

Gilleland, O; Norwood, Sarah L C; J (or I) W Litton; 31 Aug 1857; W R Clark

Gilleland, Thomas; Parish, Mehala; Stephen Fisher; 11 Aug 1824; V McBee

Gilleland, Thomas; Kale, Elizabeth; Silas Littlejohn; 17 Sep 1825; V McBee

Gilleland, William; Fisher, Elizabeth; James Lofton; 11 Oct 1805

Gillespie, John; Starrett, Elisabeth; William Starrett; 11 Apl 1787

Gilliland, James; Pelmer, Elizabeth; John Turbyfill; 8 Oct 1808

Gillim, Mason x; Brown, Charity; William Massey; 5 May 1801

Gillum, Winfield x; Martin, Penthy; Lawson Hoffstetler; 15 Aug 1833; Vardry McBee

Gingles, Adlai; Caldwell, Charlotte; Wm McKee; 21 Jul 1845

Gingles, David; Rhyne, Mary; John Robinson; 8 May 1830; W D Hannah

Gingles, Thomas H; Ewing, Peggy B; Lawson Henderson; 28 Dec 1816; James T Henderson

Givens, John; Reed, Mary; John Reed; 2 Apl 1785

Gladen, Aaron; Spurlin, Polley; Andrew Gladen; 19 Aug 1831; V McBee

Gladen, Andrew; Wier (or Weer), Martha; James Wier (or Weer); 27 Dec 1831; L McBee

Gladen (Gladden), John; Willis, Dolly; John Whisenat (Whisenheach); 7 Dec 1816; Ligt Williams JP

Gladen, Joseph; Beason, Amy; --------; 15 Nov 1807; D M Forney

Gladin, Moses; Hambleton, Sarah; Joseph Gladin; 14 May 1795

Glance, Charles; Cross, Caty; Michael Best (Ger same); 14 May 1792

Glanton, F H B; Clark, Mary; H D Rutter; 8 Nov 1865; A S Haynes Cty Ct Clk; M same date by R N Davis Minister

Glenn, Alexander; Griggs, Fanny; John Glenn; 10 Oct 1815; James T Alexander

Glenn, David; Grissim, Elizabeth; --------; 1809; (N)

Glenn, David N; Dameron, Cinthey; John B Glenn; 30 Aug 1839; Isaac Holland

Glenn, Enos B; Wallice, Juliet C; John F Glenn; 5 Oct 1842

Glenn, John; Grissim, Mary; --------; 27 May 1797

Glenn, John; Runnels, Nancy; Robert x Ramsey; 1800; (N)

Glenn, Milton; Kendrick, Mary A E; Newton B Craig (Creig); 18 Feb 1837; I Holland

Glenn, Robert; Gregory, Frances; William Gregory; 20 Dec 1808; Joseph Neel

Glenn, Samuel; Falls, Rachael; Robert G Ramsay; 7 Mar 1829; B J Tohmpson

Glenn, Stanhope (H); Glenn, Nancy; Enos B Glenn; 8 Aug 1842

Glover, J B; Brumly (or Brumby), A E; Jno H Glover; 21 Jun 1865; M same date by R N Davis Minister

Goble, Absolum x; Little, Chatarina, wi; Henry x Mossar; 18 Dec 1825; Fr Hoke JP

Goble, Corban x; Robinson, Elizabeth; Andrew Greene Robinson; 8 June 1793; John Willfong

Goble, Henry; Deel, Freny; Andrew x Goble, John x Mosar, Jacob x Hancks; 17 Dec 1818; Fr Hoke; Ambiguous

Goble, John; Cook, Shusanah; Cornelious x Cryder; 24 Dec 1788; Joseph Steel

Goble, Lewis; Hefnar, Evi; Noah x Hefnar; 30 Jun 1839; Fr Hoke JP

Goforth, Andrew; Falls, Margaret; James A Falls; 18 Aug 1841; James Ferguson

Goforth, Preston; Berry. Elizabeth; Robert Berry (?); 26 Dec 1831; L McBee

Goforth, William C; Goforth, Sally; John Goforth; 17 Dec 1835; Miles W Abernathy CC

Gofourth, Johnson; Falls, Anable; George x Gofourth; 12 Feb 1836; John Dickson

Going (Goings), Wiley; Gooldman, Anna; Daniel Smith; 26 Jan 1839; H Cansler CC

Goings (Goins), Arren; Leonard, Ann; Elisha W Roderick; 10 Jan 1837; M W Abernathy

Goins, James x; Kincaid, Mary A; William Dunn; 4 Aug 1836; M W Abernathy

Goins, John (or John M); Clippard, Polly; Phillip Kelly; 5 Oct 1833; J T Alexander

Goins, Philip P; Smith, Elisabeth; Daniel Reinhardt; 29 Mar 1866; M same date by Daniel Siegle JP

Goins (Gowens), Wiley; Clippard, Elizabeth; William Roderick; 3 Mar 1829; B J Thompson

Goldman, Martin; Link, Sally; Lemuel Saunders; 7 Jan 1805

Goode, B F; Hull, Eliza; F M Abernathy; 7 Dec 1859; N A G Goode; M same date by E D Elliott MG

Goode, John T; Warlick. Barbara; Joseph Jay; 12 Jun 1834; G Hoke

Gooden, Aaron; Grosse, Elizabeth; David Cook; 20 Jan 1825; M Hull JP

Goodman, John; Seagle (Siegel), Barbara L; James F Siegle (Seagle); 30 Aug 1851; Robt Williamson; M 4 ____ 1851 by Rev P C Henkle

Goodson, Aaron; Cansler, Margaret; Valentine Derr (Darr); 13 May 1833; L McBee

Goodson, Abner; Seits, Lucrecy; John D Graham; 1 Dec 1815; V McBee

Goodson, Champion x; Buff, Barbary; Michael x Stroup; 22 Oct 1810; Danl M Forney

Goodson, Ephraim; Regins, Elizabeth; Samuel Dellinger; 4 Oct 1833; S McBee

Goodson, Ephraim; Rudisell, Luiza; Starling x Parker; 15 Sep 1834; M W Abernathy

Goodson, George W x; Dellinger, Rebeccah; Charles C Henderson; 6 Feb 1833; V McBee

Goodson, George Wm; Lehmons, Catharine; John Goodson; 19 Nov 1858; W R Clark; M 2 Dec 1858 by Elisha Saunders JP

Goodson, H M; Hallman, Mrs B K; J F Reinhardt; 17 Jan 1866; A S Haynes CCC; M 18 Jan 1866 by J Finger MG

Goodson, Jacob; Goodson, Rebecca; Moses Bisanar (Bisinger); 22 Sep 1838; H Cansler

Goodson, Jeremiah; Keener, Malinda; B M Jetton; 4 Aug 1856; J A Huss; M 6 Aug 1856 by Elisha Saunders JP

Goodson, Joel x; Brotherton, Elizabeth; L E x Brotherton; __ Aug 1840

Goodson, John; Beal, Frances; Joel x Goodson; 11 Apl 1804; John Dickson

Goodson, John F x; Abernathy, Eliza; Isaiah x Abernathy; 10 Oct 1833; J T Alexander

Goodson, Milton; Falls, Jane; Jacob Painter; 25 Dec 1837; H Cansler

Goodson, Milton; Loftin, Martha; Benjamin Beel; 22 Nov 1852; R Williamson; M 28 Nov 1852 by Elisha Saunders JP

Goodson, Milton A; Keener (or Keever), Mary; Calvin x Taylor; 16 Feb 1866; W R Clark

Goodson, Rufus L; Childres, Martha H; H C Regan (Rigins); 7 Dec 1866; D A Lowe; M same date by D A Lowe JP

Goodson, William; Goodson, Rebekah; James Graham; 30 Sep 1805; Betsey Henderson

Goodson, William; Baker, Anna; Milton x Goodson; 20 Aug 1835; M W Abernathy

Goolman, Jacob x; Weahon, Catharine; William x Weahon; 2 Mar 1808; Maxl Chambers

Gordan, John x; Sigman, Dorethea; Jacob x Setser; 19 Nov 1789; Joseph Steel

Gordon, Henry; Jonston, Mary; Samuel Gordon, John Gordon; 10 Sep 1778; Adam Baird

Gordon, Hugh; Patterson, Sarah; David Elder; 22 Jan 1787

Gordon, James; Moore, Susanna; Moses Moore; 15 Oct 1804; J McEwin for Lwn Henderson Clk

Gordon, John; Witherspoon, Ruth; James S Witherspoon; 9 Mar 1813; V McBee

Gosnell, Joshua x; Belew, Judith; Zachariah Spencer; 28 May 1788

Gosnell, Necles (Nicolas); Senter, Kezia; Stephen Senter; 12 Apl 1787

Gosnell, Peter; Wyett, Nancey; Charles Gosnell; 4 Feb 1788

Graham, Archibald; Beaty, Jane; James Little (Lytle); 21 Aug 1782; Hugh Torrence

Graham, Ephraim; Nixon, Jane; --------; 25 Aug 1866; R Nixon JP; Acknowledgment, not a B

Graham, Ephraim x (Freedman); Sherrel, Martha (Freedwoman); Peter x Wingate (Freedman); 14 Feb 1867; J M Smith; M same date by J M Smith JP

Graham, John; Caruth, Polly; Max Chambers; 4 Dec 1808; H Y Webb

Graham, John; Little, Bridget; Rufus Reid (Read); 11 Nov 1834; R R Williamson

Graham, John D; Johnston, Jane E; Wm Williamson; 30 Oct 1840

Graham, Thomas; Bennick, Pheby; Thomas Dickson; 30 Sep 1823; M Hull JP

Grant, Charles; Wyatte, Sarah; John Smith; no date (Samuel Ashe Governor, 1795-8)

Graves, Anthoney; Young, Katrine; Love Evins (Evans); 5 Aug 1784; Joseph Steel

Greaves, Philip; Felps, Rachel; William Sloan; 5 Apl 1792

Green, David x; Green, Nancy; Elkanah x Cline; 25 Aug 1837; M W Abernathy

Green, Jacob; Aker, Fanney; Samuel Carbender (Carpenter); 3 Apl 1787

Green, John H; Costner, Catharine; Peter x Cosner (Costner); 20 Sep 1836; Jacob Plonk

Green, Joseph; Greyham, Margaret; Ab McAfee; 22 Jul 1812

Green, Oliver C; Smoyer, Percidia; Willard Boyden; 18 May 1833; J T Alexander

Green, Pleasant x; Clifton, Eliza; John Cline; 17 Jan 1831; L M McBee

Green, Samuel; Roberts, Sally; Charles Y Doggett; 31 Jul 1820; Joshua Roberts

Green, William B; McMurtry, Zarian; A J Burnett (Orsburn J Burnett), William x Cockram; 20 Dec 1832; J T Alexander

Greenhill, Philip; Pollard, Elizabeth; Hurier (Uriah) Pollard; 13 Nov 1815; V McBee

Greenhill, Philip x; Havner, Sally; Joseph Linhart; 28 Mar 1817; V McBee

Greer, Andrew; Hoyl, Salama; Eli Hoyl; 24 Feb 1824; And Hoyl, Jno W Harris

Greer, William M; Hayes, Minerva; Larkin Stowe; 14 Oct 1827; Isaac Holland

Gregory, James J; Gibson, Ruth; William T Gregory; 21 Oct 1831; Isaac Holland

Gregory, William T; Dameron, Anny; Allen x Pinner; 12 Jan 1829; Isaac Holland

Grice, William M (John M); Grice, Martha C; David Drum; 18 Jul 1842; A J Cansler

Griffin, Peter; Dyer, Sally; John Huggins; 14 Apl 1814; V McBee

Griffith, Jonathan; Lumly, Sarah; William Griffith; 25 Nov 1810; Jacob Ramsour

Grigg, Abner; Oneal, Honour; Burrel Grigg; 14 Jul 1819; V McBee

Grigg, B F; McCoy, Mary J; W M Reinhardt; 1 Jan 1863; W R Clark; M same date by R N Davis Minister

Grigg, Berry P; Spratt, Jane; Daniel Seagle; 21 Sep 1839

Grigg, Burrel; Oneil, Malinda; Jacob Ramsour; 5 Jun 1820; Jas T Alexander
Grigg (Grig), Edward; Carpenter, Susannah; Jacob Carpenter; 10 Apl 1828; M Hull JP
Grigg, Jesse; Taylor, Susanah; John x Carpenter; 4 Nov 1817; V McBee
Grigg, Wes'y J; Davis, Sarah; Edwin Mullin; 11 Oct 1838; B S Johnson
Grise (Grice), Henry F; Jones, Thusy; Fergus H Reynolds; 7 May 1842; A J Cansler
Grise (Grice), John; Ballard, Lizer; Thomas Beaty; 17 May 1825; Wm Little
Grise (Grice), John; Jones, Tempey; James M Daniel; 21 Dec 1837; John D King
Grise (Grist), John; Caldwell, Sarah; F J Jetton; 21 Sep 1842; H Cansler Clk
Grissim, Martin; Gregory, Elizabeth; Hosea Gregory, Den _____ (illegible); 17 Mar 1812; Jas Baird JP
Grissom, Benjamin; Bell, Mrs Jamimah; Thomas Grissom, Wm Featherston; 18 Aug 1808; And Hoyl JP
Grissom, I F (Isaac F); Cox, Margaret M; E E (Eli) Cox; 2 Dec 1846; Robt Rankin
Grissom, Milton W; Slate, Nancey; William W Jackson; 30 Oct 1827; Isaac Holland
Grissom, Moses; Slate, Elizabeth; John Bennet (Bennit); 21 Dec 1815; Isaac Holland for Vardry McBee CCC
Grose, Henry (Jr); Abernathy, Sarah; Nathan Abernathy; 15 Dec 1808; Phil Whitener JP
Grose (Gross), Philip; Robinson, Prissy; Jacob Reinhardt; 9 Jan 1811; Danl M Forney
Gross, Adam; McHaffey, Rody; John R Stamey; 2 Mar 1840
Gross, Christian; Bery, Ruth; John x Whisenhunt; 27 Sep 1806; Ligt Williams JP
Gross, David x; Wood, Sally; Henry Bangle; 24 Nov 1823; Jas T Alexander
Gross, Henry; Johnson, Sary; Daniel x Gross; 14 Aug 1810; Ligt Williams JP
Gross, John x; Overwinters, Margret; James Johnson; 3 Jun 1806; Ligt Williams JP
Groves, John x; Robinson, Melinda; Henry x Jonston; 27 Dec 1836; Isaac Holland
Groves, Thomas; Drake, Milberry; Hezekiah x Drake; 14 Aug 1806; Lwn Henderson
Guffey, John; Reed, Elisabeth; John Reed; 21 Feb 1795; Jo Dickson
Guffy, John S; Fleming, Nancy; David Cherry; 26 Mar 1829; Wm Little
Guinn see Mann
Guion, B S; Caldwell, C C; V A McBee; 26 Oct 1864; M same date by W R Wetmore Rector St Luke's Church
Gullick, Benaiah; Gingles, Elizabeth; John H Spencer; 2 Nov 1814; James T Alexander
Gullick, John; Craig, Nancy; Jonn Gullick; 10 Sep 1804; Jonn Greaves
Gullick, Jonathan; Berry, Nancy; John Gullick; 25 Oct 1803; Eze'l Dickson
Gullick, Milton H M; Marchal, Rebeckah; Thomas F Sugg; 27 Mar 1826; Isaac Holland
Gunn, Alexander C; Blackwood, Margaret; David Moose; 12 Sep 1827; J T Alexander
Guthrey (Guthrie), Carter; Beal, Barbara; Moses Abernathy; 15 Aug 1800
Guthrey (Guttery), Madison; Proctor, Elizabeth; Orrsbern Proctor; 27 Jul 1832; V McBee
Guthrie, James x; Bynum, Nancy; Jacob Hinkle; 1 Apl 1799; Jno Dickson
Guttrey, Nelson; Lowe, Catherine; Carter Guttrey; 3 Apl 1808; Jacob Forney
Guyton (Gidon), Abram J (or S); Warlick, Levica; _____ Quin, Judson Warlick; __ Jan 1838; Dvd Warlick
Gwaltney, Abraham; Richard, Elizabeth; (Ger) Johannes Schlunker (?); 16 Jul 1812; Jesse Perkins
Gwaltney, Isaac; Loller, Margret; James x Faith; 6 Jul 1779

Haas, John; Clay, Barbara; David Hass (Haas); 28 Jul 1829; Luther M McBee
Haase (Hause), David; Shereman, Ann; Ezekiel Sullivan; 7 Feb 1831; V McBee
Haeffer (Hafer), Lewis; Oaves (?), Hanah; Frederick Hoke; 5 Oct 1810; H Y Webb
Haffner see Huffman
Hafner (Havner), Abraham (Jr); Pringle, Betcy; Abraham Hallman (Holman); 23 Apl 1825; V McBee
Hafner (Havner), Alfred; Crowell, Adaline; John x Waters; 30 Dec 1850
Hafner, Franklin x; Fox, Prudence; Edward x Cobb; 21 Aug 1866; W R Clark CC; M 22 Aug 1866 by L A Fox MG
Hafner (Havner), Frederick; Haus, Martha; Vardry A McBee; 12 Jun 1847
Hafner, Jacob (Ger Heffner); Plunk, Catherine; Jacob Plunk; 14 Sep 1812; Lwn Henderson
Hafner (Heafner), John; Rudisil, Susanah; David Crouse; 17 Nov 1817; Andrew Loretz
Hafner (Havner), Levi; Huss, Margaret; Laurence Black; 30 Nov 184__; George Coon JP; Printed form 184__; Ambiguous
Hafner (Havener), Nicholas x; Shitle, Christiana; Martin Shitle (Ger Martin Schötle); 6 Feb 1789; Eliza Dickson

Hafner (Havner), Stephen; Havner, Mary; James Long; 30 Jan 1839; J T Alexander
Hagar, Frederick x; Aker, Mary; James Frost; No date (end 1807); R Williamson
Hagar, Henry; Nixon, Nancy; --------; 26 Feb 1854; M this date by R E Burch JP; C only, no B
Hager, A M; Hager, M L; Jos (or Jas) T Norwood; 24 Dec 1857; Robert Nixon JP
Hager, Aron; Steely, Lurany; John Abernathy; 20 Jan 1825; V McBee
Hager, Benjamin; King, Nancy; David Blaylock (Blalock); 28 Aug 1819; V McBee
Hager, Daniel; Stroup, Elizabeth; Moses x Stroup; 26 Oct 1824; V McBee
Hager, David x; Clifton, Jane; Jacob Reinhardt; 5 Jul 1825; V McBee
Hager, David B; Black, Elizabeth; Joseph Barnett; 4 Aug 1853; A.exr J Cansler; M 4 ____ 1853 by Rev A J Cansler
Hager, Franklin F; Coventon, Eliza Ann; Robert H Robinson; 15 Mar 1848; J D King
Hager, Frederick x; Miller, Betsey; William Heaker; 14 Oct 1809; Danl M Forney
Hager, Frederick x; Hinkle, Margaret; John Petree (Ger Johannes Petrie); 27 Nov 1818; James T Alexander
Hager, G W; Hager, Mary Jane; S C Hager; 3 Jun 1866; R Nixon JP; M same date by R Nixon JP
Hager, George; Thompson, Mary; Thos McGee (?); 7 Aug 1799; Jno Dickson
Hager, George; Hager, Betsy; James Bryant; 12 Dec 1812; James T Alexander
Hager, George; Fry, Mary Ann; Moses T Abernathy; 3 Mar 1840
Hager, Henry x; Hager, Ann; Simon H Hager; 22 Nov 1833; Miles W Abernathy
Hager, Henry x; Tucker, Matilda Ann; William J Cashion; 26 Oct 1863; R Nixon JP; M same date by R Nixon JP
Hager, J M; Hager, Racheal H; Wm P Burch; 11 Mar 1858; J D King; M same date by J D King JP
Hager, James; Norwood, Mary; John Davis; 24 Dec 1844; J __ King
Hager, James; Nixon, Nancy; Conner S (Sam C) Little; 9 Nov 1859; J D King; M same date by John D King JP
Hager, John; Hawn, Jenny; Hy Conner, Lwn Henderson; 27 Mar 1805
Hager, John x; Martin, Nancy; James Bryan; 30 Dec 1822; Joel Dyer
Hager, John; Weathers, Frances M; David x Smith; 15 Oct 1836; M W Abernathy
Hager, John E; Nixson, Sally; Richard Burch, Wm Nixson; 6 Dec 1835; John D King
Hager, John H; Hager, Rebecca A; Starling x Wamac; 9 Sep 1862; R Nixon JP; M same date by R Nixon JP
Hager, Jonathan; White, Sarah; Peter Dec (Deck); 2 Oct 1834; M W Abernathy
Hager, Michael; Nixon, Catherine; Frederick x Hager; 28 Feb 1821; V McBee
Hager, Robt N (M); Benton, Mary M; E G Gage; 12 Aug 1865; A S Haynes CCC; M 13 Aug 1865 by E G Gage
Hager, Sherod H x; Armestrong, Sarah; S J Connel; 16 Jan 1867; D A Lowe; M same date by D A Lowe JP
Hager, Simon; Hager, Mary M; David Davis; 9 Oct 1842
Hager, Simon S; Lawing, Nancy L; Solomon Sifford; 16 Feb 1847; Robt Williamson
Hager, Solomon; Wier, Margaret; J A Ramsour; 27 Sep 1838; H Cansler
Hager, William; Deck, Catherine; John Hoenig; 24 Mar 1810; Danl M Forney Cl
Hager, William; Hager, Betcy; Wm Heaker (Hager); 1 Aug 1818; V McBee
Hager, William; McDannel, Catharine; Christian Eaker (Aker); 26 Dec 1820; Jas T Alexander
Hager, William; Robison, Frankey; Green Abernathy; 28 (or 27 or 29) Mar 1824; Jas T Alexander
Haggin, Randolph x; Bennett, Esther; John x Bennett; 9 Aug 1832; William Berry
Hain (Hains), Philip; Lindsey, Mary; Jacob Reinhardt; 20 Dec 1812; V McBee for Hain
Haines, James x; Goodwin, Tempe; Philip Hines; 8 Apl 1807; Lwn Henderson
Haines, Robert S (Haynes, Robert G); Carpenter, Elizabeth; John W Bevin (Bevins); 25 Nov 1830; L M McBee
Hains, James H x; Dellinger, Elizabeth; William Haynes (Hains); 4 Aug 1837; M W Abernathy
Hains (Hain), Lenord x; Hermon, Barbra; Joseph Henry; 5 Jul 1786; Thos Wheeler
Hains, Matthew x; Seitz, Fanny; John Size (Seitz); 13 Mar 1814; V McBee
Haker, William; Little, Salley (?); Henry Conner, Alexander Reed; ------ 1812; Illegible, taken from (N)
Hakins (Hawkins), William P x; Laney, Martha Ann; E M Lynch; 6 Oct 1860; Elisha Saunders; M 7 Oct 1860 by Elisha Saunders JP
Hale, William; Moore, Henryetta; Willard Boyden; 22 Oct 1832; J T Alexander
Hall, Fergus A; --------; Josiah Q Hall; 12 Aug 1836; M W Abernathy
Hall, Josiah Q; Sherrill, Darcus E; Elihu D Sherrill; 30 May 1831; L McBee

Hallman, Alfred; Killian, Mary A; Andrew Hallman; 17 Feb 1852; Robt Williamson
Hallman, Ambrose; Henry, Margaret; Henry Sumerowe (Summerour); 14 Jan 1842
Hallman, Andrew; Hallman, Mary S; Jonas G Rudisill; 13 Sep 1859; W R Clark;
    M 15 Sep 1859 by P Carpenter JP
Hallman, Anthony; Bolinger, Susannah; William Rudisill; 18 Mar 1837
Hallman, Daniel x; Stroup, Esther; James x Hallman; 26 Feb 1867; W R Clark
Hallman (Hollman), David; Wheon (or Whion), Susannah; Peter C Hoyl; 14 Oct
    1840; H Cansler
Hallman (Holman), Henry (Henrig); Warlick, Rachel; Daniel Warlick; 4 July 17__
    (torn), (Ashe Governor, 1795-8)
Hallman (Holland), Isaac; Anthony, Mary; Henry Smith; 13 Jul 1811; Danl M
    Forney CC
Hallman (Hollman), Jacob; Lantz, Betcy; John Blackburn; 13 Aug 1808; Maxl
    Chambers
Hallman, Jacob x; Hoyl, Maria Louisa C; John P Anthony; 2 Jul 1845; R Williamson
Hallman, Jacob x; Sumrour, Margarett E; John F Hill; 22 Apl 1858; Logan H
    Lowrance; M same date by Logan H Lowrance JP
Hallman (Holman), John; Loretz, Barbara; Samuel x Dietz; 21 Mar 1814
Hallman, Michael; Dellinger, C L; P M Hauss (Huss); 21 Feb 1863; W R Clark;
    M 26 Feb 1863 by A J Fox MG
Hallmon, John x; Linhardt, Harriet; John Smith; 29 Feb 1836
Hallmon, Oliver x; Moony (Mauny), Mary Matilda; John Lusk; 14 Apl 1864;
    M 14 Apl 1864 by Alfred Black JP
Hallmon (Hallman), W M; Dellinger, Belzora K; A S Haynes; 13 Dec 1858
Halman, Daniel x; Cline, Sally; Thomas Smith; 29 Nov 1818; James T Alexander
Hambright, Christian; Williams, Anna; John Cook; 15 Dec 1821; Jas T Alexander
Hambright, Franklin; Nance, Mary S; Wesley Williams; 2 Oct 1851; Robt Williamson
Hambright, Fredk; Dover, Mary; David Dickey; 17 Jul 1781; end Colo Hambright
Hambright, Frederick; Eker, Mary; John Sudduth (Suddith): 3 Nov 1787; Eliz
    Dickson
Hamby, Allen; Schenck, Barbara; Samuel Lander (Landres); 26 Feb 1834; M W
    Abernathy CC
Hamilton, Alexander; Macaver, Mary; John M'Caver (Macaver); 29' Nov 1786; Jas
    Dickson
Hamilton (Hambleton), Drury; Bridges, Elizabeth; Reuben Hamilton (Hambleton);
    14 May 1825; V McBee
Hamilton (Hambleton), Drury; Little, Mary; Lewis Little; 29 Jul 1829; V McBee
Hamilton, James W; Law, Lavina L; Reuben Hamilton; 4 Aug 1841; H Cansler
Hamilton (Hambleton), John; Welch, Polley; John M'Caver (McCarver); 12 Apl
    1813; V McBee
Hamilton (Hambleton), Ninian; Wilfong, Mary M; Drury Hamilton (Hambleton);
    20 Aug 1824; V McBee
Hamilton, Reuben; Colliers, Sally; Jacob Lollar; 10 Jan 1800; Jno Dickson
Hamilton, Thomas Jefferson; Blakely, Delphia R; Miles W Abernathy; 16 Nov 1833;
    A__ Hoyle
Hamilton, William; Simmons, Susana; Lwn Henderson; 16 Jun 1802; William
    M'Callister
Hammontree, Jeremiah; Holloway, Sarah; Andrew Friday; No date (Ashe Governor,
    1795-8)
Hamontree, John x; Hawkins, Sally; Samuel x Hawkins; No date (watermark same as
    on bond dated 1798)
Hampton, David; Robinson, Harriet; William Hager; 28 Oct 1828; J T Alexander
Hampton, John x; Kerril, Nancy; William Kerril; 25 Aug 1789; Joseph Steel
Hampton, John; Sherrell, Levina; Thomas Hampton; 26 Nov 1826; J T Alexander
Hampton, William x; Armstrong, Sally; Joel Hampton; 1 May 1809; Danl M Forney
Hamton, William; Bolin, Rody; John Sloan; 20 Jan 1789
Hand (Hann), Aaron; Henry, Rebecka; Jonathan Gullick; 27 Sep 1798
Hand, John Conrad x; Caldwell, Rebecka; Henry x Caldwell; 18 Nov 1788
Hand, Jonathan; Brimer, Ruth; Edward B Dameron; 14 Nov 1820; I Holland
Hand, Moses H; Henry, Narcissa; Wm M Holland; 17 Mar 1842; Eli Hoyl
Hand, William P; Gaskins, Jane; Samuel x Brimer; 8 Oct 1822; I Holland
Hanes (Hayne), Daniel A; Cansler, Polly; Miles A Sanders (Saunders); 3 May 1836
Hanes, Jesse x; Ward, Betcy; James Sronce; 22 Sep 1833; V McBee
Hanks, David; Hoyl, Elizabeth; Frederick x Bess; 31 Oct 1793; John Dickson;
    Ambiguous
Hanks, Ezekiel; Huffman, Mary; William Hanks; 12 May 1831; Bitheai Cross

54

Hanks, James; Starriat (Starrett), Mary; William Sterret (Starriat); 26 Aug 1779; John Brown Skrimshire

Hanks, John; Weathers, Elizabeth; John Weathers; (14 or) 16 Aug 1810

Hanks, Joshua; Renwick, Mary; Richard x Hanks; 13 Feb 1812; Joseph Neel

Hanks, Richard x; Young, Levina; Samuel L Ewing; 1 Mar 1821; Saml McKee

Hanks, William; Gasten, Lucy Jane; Alfred Linebarger; 28 Apl 1835; J G Hand JP

Hannah, John; Wells, Mary; Joseph Baxter; 24 Jul 1821; V McBee

Hannah, Thomas; Martin, Elisabeth; Joseph Spencer (?); 1 Mar 1797

Hannah, Thomas; Martin, Jean; Robert Curry; 27 Feb 1808

Hannah, Thomas M; Weathers, Margaret R; Samuel Martin; 14 Mar 1835; J G Hand JP

Hannah, William D; Bell, Hannah C; Alfred Linebarger; 23 Sep 1830; Isaac Holland

Hansel, Henry; Coble, Jane; Turner Edwards; 7 Jul 1827; V McBee

Hansel, Henry; Hansel, Mary; Drury G Abernathy; 26 Nov 1827; V McBee

Hansel (or Hausel), Hubbard x; Murray, Elizabeth; Obed Parrish; 23 Jul 1833; L McBee

Hansel (Hansyl), William; McGinnis, Elisabeth; Drury Kimbal; 1 May 1799

Hansell, John P x; Armstrong, Nancy Lemarius; Robert Edwards; 19 Mar 1850; Robt Williamson

Hansil, William J; Riley, Dovey; Milton A Smith; 20 Nov 1844

Hansill (Hansyl), James; Sadler, Susanna; Zachariah x Sadler; 10 Feb 1804; John Dickson

Happoldt, John M; Williamson, Sarah; Wm Williamson; 2 Jan 1843; V A McBee

Harberson, Rufus x; Bolick, Mary; George T Harberson; 4 Mar 1830; Miles W Abernathy JP

Harbeson, Hiram; Bumgarner, Nancy; Thomas x Bumgarner; 6 Oct 1816; G Milligan

Harbison, Alberto x; Starns, Nancy; John Lowrance (Lorance); 23 Mar 1826; V McBee

Harden, Ruben; Garel, Elender; Reuben Collins; 16 Oct 1836; John Dickson

Hardy (Hardie), James A; Matthews, Mary; Isaac W Carpenter; 14 Nov 1839; H Cansler

Hargrove (Hartgrove), Benjamin; Rankin, Jean; Samuel Rankin; 21 Sep 1792; Robert Dickson

Harman, Henry x; Miller, Fanny; Joseph x Flowers; 30 Dec 1831; V McBee

Harman, Marcus M x; Martin, Mary; B P G Hicks; 24 Aug 1855; M 26 Aug 1855 by David Crouse JP

Harman, Michael (Ger same); Rudisell, Catharine; Casper Bolick (Ger Caspar Bolch); 26 Aug 1825; Jas T Alexander.

Harman, Moses; Hunsicker, Mary; Henry Bolch; 4 Oct 1837 (or 1827); Mic Cline

Harman, Presten x; Harman, Elizabeth; Ab McAfee; 24 Sep 1818

Harmen, George x; Winbargner, Lidda; William Herman (Harmen); 14 Jan 1841; J Yount JP

Harmon, David; Moore, Betsey; Michl Eaker; 5 Oct 1797; Jo Dickson

Harmon, George (Ger Georg Herman); Eslinger, Elisabeth; Adam Bolick (Ger Johan Adam Bolch); 31 Dec 1791; John Willfong

Harmon, Haywood; Branton, Mary; John Harmon; 5 Sep 1831; J T Alexander

Harmon (Hermon), John G; Cobb, Rachel; _____ Collins; 12 Jan 1837; John Dickson

Harmon, Peter Jr (Ger Peter Hermunn); Simon, Lidia; John x Simon; 10 Mar 1811

Harmon, Robert C; Harmon, Ruannah; James Boggs; 15 Jul 1836; M W Abernathy

Harper, Benjamin x; Moore, Hanah; Aaron Harper; 28 Nov 1808; H Y Webb

Harrell (Harrel), Hugh H; Wilfong, Catherine; John Smyer; 24 Mar 1819; V McBee

Harrelson, William x; Buff, Sarah; John Harriss; 28 Feb 1818; James T Alexander

Harrill, Abraham G; Cauble, Adaline; Andrew O'Brien (Obrian); 16 Feb 1843; H Cansler

Harris, H A T; Bess, Mary A F; L J Barker; 25 Apl 1860; W R Clark Clk

Harris, James x; Hafner, Mary; Jacob Havner (Hafner); 17 Jul 1822; Joshua Roberts

Harris, James A; Hanks, Mary; William Hanks; 18 Apl 1825; Isaac Holland

Harris, John; Gingles, Margaret; Isaac Gullick; 6 Sep 1815; James T Alexander

Harris, John F; Ballard, Martha L; Henry Alexander; 14 Mar 1857; W R Clark; M 15 Mar 1857 by David Bailey JP

Harris, John W B; Coulter, Emmily Elizabeth; David Dettor; 15 Oct 1839

Harris, Sidney J; Hayes, Jane J; Middleton Dougherty (Doeherty); 18 Oct 1825; V McBee

Harris, Tarlton x; Swaringgame, Mary; Druriah x Swaringgame, Richard x Walker; 2 Jun 1808; (Ger) Peter Eker

Harris, Valentine x; Weaver, Eve; James McClurg; 26 Oct 1830; J T Alexander

Harris, Wilie (Willie); _____, Nancy; John Roberts; 26 Jul 1809; Danl M Forney CC

Harrison (Harison), Richard; Dawsey, Rachel; Isaac Robinson (Robertson); 13 Feb 1786; Joseph Steel

Harriss (Harris), John; Roberts, Unity; John Brown; 6 Jan 1818; V McBee

Harriss (Harris), Robt T; Lamasters, Mary; Christopher x Reynolds; 23 Feb 1858; WR Clark; M 25 Feb 1858 by David Crouse JP

Harriss, Wm; Ward, Nancy; Melger x Ward; 30 Aug 1810; Jesse Perkins

Harrup (Harp), Arthur; Moreland, Phebe; Francis Moreland; 1 Sep 1789

Harry, John H; Tucker, Sophia; Nicholas I (or J) Tucker; 19 Nov 1828 (end 1831); John B Harry

Harry, John H; McCullock, Sarah F; A R Porter; 6 Dec 1837

Hart see Horl

Hart, James; McCarver, Mary; Jacob Stow; 12 Jan 1826; Isaac Holland

Hartgrove (Hargrave), Benjamin; Anthony, Mary K; Paul Anthony; 3 Mar 1830; V McBee

Hartley, Tilman; Harden, Susannah; Michel Pearson (Person); 10 Mar 1812; Ligt Williams JP

Hartman, Wilie x; Norman, Thane; Joseph x Wise; 9 Jan 1832; V McBee

Hartness, Hiram; Linch, Elizabeth; T L Painter; 3 May 1837; M W Abernathy

Hartse (Hartshog), Abel; Huntly, Seliah; Daniel Hoover; 25 Dec 1839; H Cansler

Hartsec (Hartsoke), David; Wion, Sally; George Reinhardt; 10 Dec 1832; L McBee

Hartsock, Emanuel x; Sanders, Polly C; Henry Finger; 16 Jul 1837

Hartsog (Hartzog), John; Summey, Catherine; Daniel Probst (Propst); 8 Aug 1822; V McBee

Hartsoge, Elias x; Reece (or Royce), Sally; J____ Boyd; 10 Jan 1833; L McBee

Hartt, John; Lindsay, Violet W; John D Maclean; 25 Mar 1835; Isaac Holland

Hartzog, John; Jarrett, Mary; Jacob Jarrett; 19 Jan 1830; J T Alexander •

Hartzoge, Danl M x; Hallman, Martha E; Henry Huss; 16 Aug 1865; A S Haynes CCC; M 17 Aug 1865 by P Carpenter JP

Hartzoke (Hartzoch, Hartsoph), William A; Hartzoch (Hardtsoph), Caroline; William J Nantz; 28 Dec 1854; J A Huss; M same date by Max Warlick JP

Harvel, Nathaniel x; Fisher, Catharine; Eli Sherrill; 14 May 1821; James T Alexander

Harvey, Thomas; Sadler, Anny; Thomas Sadler; 19 Aug 1815; Thos McGee

Harvill, Nelson; Abernathy, Mary; L B Lindsey (Linzy); 6 Feb 1826; Wm Little

Harwell, Buckner (by John Turbyfill); Westmoreland, Rhoda; John Turbyfill; 30 Apl 1828; V McBee

Harwell, Gardner; Featherston, Nancy; John Allen, Rolly Harwell; 6 Jul 1802; John Dickson

Harwell, James; Sherrell, Epsey M; Elisha Sherrill; 15 Sep 1829; J T Alexander

Harwell, John H x; Abernathy, Polly; Benjamin x Fisher; 6 Feb 1839; H Cansler CC

Harwell, Mason; Linebarger, Peggy; Frederic Harwell; 13 Aug 1813; V McBee

Harwell, Rolley; Fetherston, Sally; Harbird x Abernathy; 29 Nov 1790

Harwell, Rolly; Garnie, Susannah; --------; No date; (N)

Harwell, Thomas; --------; Fredk x Harwell, Jesse Perkins; 20 Feb 1810; Danl M Forney Cl; Doubtful

Harwood, Ely; Philips, Polley; James Fillips; 24 Apl 1814; Jesse Perkins; M this date

Harwood, William; Robinson, Fanny; Aaron O Bumgardner (Bumgarner); 7 Jun 1847; Robt Williamson

Haskins, Robert; Ewert, Betsey; Fredk Earwood; 5 Jul 1796; Jno Dickson

Hasley, Richard R x; Stowe, Marthew; James A x Branon; 6 Jan 1841; D Hoffman JP

Hass, Peter (Ger same); Houser, Liddy; John Havener (Havner); 14 Sep 1818; James T Alexander

Hass, Robert M; Killian, Luiza S; Solomon Sumerow (Summerrow); 23 Jan 1854; J A Huss; M 26 Jan 1854 by J R Peterson (MG)

Haun (Hawn), David; Treffelstad, Susanna; Jacob Bolick (Ger Bolch); 13 Mar 1823; Mic Cline

Haun, Sampson; Whitener, Hannah; Cristain x Haun; 3 Jan 1822; Phil Whitener JP

Haus (Hass), John H; Cline, Fanny; Jesse Cline; 9 Dec 1842; Wm Herman JP

Hause (Hauss), Andrew J; Mullens, Mary; John E Hoke; 26 Feb 1845

Hause, Andrew J; Ramsey, J B; J L Wilkie (Wilkey); 16 Mar 1867; M 17 Mar 1867 by S Lander

Hause, David x; Trout, Nelly; William Trout; 29 Mar 1809; Maxl Chambers

Hause (Haus), David; Clay, Elizabeth; Jacob Hause (Haus); 10 (or 13) Oct 1842; A J Cansler

Hause, Henry (Ger Hennrich Hass); Plunk, Catherine; John Weaver; 4 Dec 1810; H Y Webb

Hause (Haus), Jacob; Clay, Eliza; Franklin Taylor; 18 Nov 1846; R Williamson

Hause (Haus), John F; Jinks. Amanda S; Adam Whisnant (Whisenant; 4 Nov 1846
Hause. Simon x; Burns (or Barns), Anna; David Hass (Hause); 16 May 1833;
  V McBee
Hauser, Jacob x: Hafner, Catharine; (Ger) Peter Hauser; 18 Jan 1806; Js McEwin
Hauser, Jacob (Ger same); Cook, Mary; Philip x Cook; 15 Jun 1813; Saml Wilson
Hauser (Houser), John T; Phifer, Sarah L; V A McBee; 12 Oct 1846; Robt
  Williamson
Hauser, Joseph x; Spangler, Barbara; Frederick Spangler (Ger. Friedrich Spengler);
  14 Dec 1819; V McBee
Hauss, Andrew; Ramsey, Mary N (V); M C Clay; 23 Nov 1861; M 24 Nov 1861
  by G W Ivy (MG)
Hauss (Horse), David; Holmon, Sarah; Andrew x Dellinger; 8 May 1830; Peregrine
  Roberts
Hauss, J C; Smith, Malinda; Philip C Weaver; 10 Apl 1854; M __ Apl 1854 by
  George Coon JP
Hauss (Haus), Jacob; Shell. Susan E; Joshua Roberts; 14 Aug 1847; Robt Williamson
Hauss, John R; Sullivan, Nancy M; M C (Caleb) Clay; 17 Oct 1857; W R Clark;
  M 18 Oct 1857 by F J Jetton JP
Hauss (Hause), Peter; Hauser, Barbara; Abram Howser; 14 Mar 1831; V McBee
Havener, John; Hause. Catharine; Peter Houser (Ger Hauser); 17 Feb 1814; V McBee
Havener, John (John Havner, J Son); Lambus, Nancy; Abner Berry; 7 Oct 1819;
  V McBee
Havener, Walter (Hefner, W H); Helton, Mary; Emanuel Shuford; 3 Dec 1842;
  H Cansler
Havner (Hafner), A A; Johnson, Sarah A; John W Carpenter; 10 May 1866; W B
  McCaslin; M 13 May 1866 by Rev Alex Stamey
Havner (Hafner), David; Reinhardt, Elizabeth; Felix Abernathy; 19 Feb 1836;
  J A Ramsour DC
Havner, David x; Moore, Esther; Wilkinson x Moore; 9 Mar 1847; Robt Williamson
Havner, David x; Moore, Catharine; George Avery; 17 Dec 1857; Robt Williamson
Havner, George F; McFalls, Harriet; Alvin (Albane) Delane; 2 Jan 1854; J A Huss;
  M 4 Jan 1854 by David Crouse JP
Havner, George H; Havner, Eliza E; Isaac Hause (Houser); 23 Jan 1854; J A Huss
Havner (Hafner), Jacob x; Brown, Martha A; Jacob J Brown; 10 Feb 1859; W R
  Clark; M 17 Feb 1859 by G L Hunt MG
Havner (Havener), John; Homer, Betcy; Charles Reinhardt; 17 May 1819; V McBee
Havner, Joseph; Moore, Polley; Samuel x Moore; 31 Mar 1821; V McBee
Havner, Lawson x; Harris, Malinda; Jonas Brown; 27 Oct 1855; R Williamson;
  M 23 (or 28) Oct 1855 by David Crouse JP
Havner, Levi Jr; Leonhardt, Clarissa; Noah x Kistler; 6 Sep 1845; R Williamson
Havner, Martin x; Cross, Edy; Joseph Black; 30 Oct 1818; V McBee
Havner, Michael x; Moore, Polly; George F Havner; 11 Mar 1857; W R Clark;
  M same date by David Bailey Esqr
Havner, Nicholas x; Werble, Senna; Solomon Tutherow (Totherow); 7 Sep 1844
Havner, Peter;' Kistler, Pricilla; Felix W Reinhardt; 25 Dec 1837; H Cansler
Havner, Philip x; Mauney, Mary; Wilkensen x Moore; 5 Feb 1830; V McBee
Havner, Valentine; Shitle, Elizabeth; Henry Shitle; 5 Apl 1827; J T Alexander
Hawkins, Burwell; Houston, Mary; Edward Huson; 11 Apl 1809
Hawkins, Elisha; Hovis, Charity; Tilman x Jenkins; 7 Feb 1831 (end 1832); And
  Hoyl JP
Hawkins, J R; Haynes, Caroline; R H Abernathy; 5 Jan 1861; M 7 Jan 1861 by
  R H Abernathy JP
Hawkins, James; Little, Rachel; Archibald Hamilton; 6 Apl 1789
Hawkins, John x; O'Nell, Ann; John x Turbyfill; 28 Jul 1828; B J Thompson
Hawkins, Pinkney C x; Nance, Sarah; John Thomas; 24 Oct 1832; Isaac Holland
Hawkins, Samuel; Weathers, Polly; Elisha Weathers; No date, watermark same as
  on bond dated 1798
Hawkins, Samuel; West, Amey; James A Weathers; 23 Nov 1828; Isaac Holland
Hawkins, Samuel; Cathey, Ellin; David Jenkins; 26 Jan 1833; B T Kirby; Ambiguous
Hawkins, William; Maclean, Margaret; John McKee; 5 Jun 1805; Lwn Henderson
Hawkins, William Pressley x; Bell, Sarah; William Hawkins; 29 Oct 1839; And
  Hoyl JP
Hawkins, Woodliff x; Rhodes, Sarah; William D Hannah; 31 Dec 1840; Eli Hoyl
Hawn, Christian; Hawn, Anna; Absalom Miller; 11 Mar 1831; L M McBee
Hawn, Daniel; Sides, Ann; Andrew M Whitener (Whitner); 11 Sep 1841; H
  Cansler CC

Hawn, David; Miller, Julianne; John Whitener; 17 Feb 1825; Mic Cline
Hawn, David; Sides, Sarah; Andrew M Whitener; 28 Jun 1842; A J Cansler
Hawn, Henry; Seitz, Levina; Darius D Seitz; __ Dec 1837; L E Thompson
Hawn, Jacob x; Trefelstatt, Sally; David Hawn; 6 Jan 1830; Mic Cline
Hawn, John; Whitener, Susannah; David Link; 18 Jan 1831; J T Alexander
Hawn (or Haun), John; Miller, Margaret; Christian Hawn (or Haun); 2 Mar 1833; Vardry McBee
Hawn, Samuel; Conrad, Polley; Henry W Robinson (Robison); 13 Sep 1819; V McBee
Hawn, Samuel; Dellinger, Barbara; Frederick Hawn (Ger Friederich Hahn); 29 Jan 1821; V McBee
Hayes (Hays), John; Johnston, Catharine; Robert Johnston; 1 Oct 1803; John Dickson
Haynes (Hains), James; Holland, Elizabeth; Joseph x Smith; 2 Feb 1814; V McBee
Haynes, James C x; Haynes, Mary Jane; William W Haynes; 16 May 1856; J A Huss; M 18 May 1856 by David Crouse JP
Haynes, James H; Hause, Eliza S; A P Cansler; 1 Sep 1855; M 13 Sep 1855 by W C Patterson MG
Haynes, John F; Hartzog, F B; A S Haynes; 12 Oct 1866; M 14 Oct 1866 by J Finger MG
Haynes, L D; Leonhardt, Frances; W W Ramsey; 13 Feb 1866; M 16 (?) Feb 1866 by Rev Alex Stamey
Haynes, R M x; Blalock, Mary Jane; S D Lowe; 25 Oct 1865; A S Haynes CCC, J M Abernethy
Haynes, William; Morrison, Margaret; David x Kincaid; 6 Jan 1837; M W Abernathy
Haynes, William H; Cody, Frances; _____; 9 Feb 1856; J A Huss Clerk; M 17 Feb 1856 by R B Jones MG; L and C, no B
Hays (Hayes), William; Falls, Esther; Am Neel (?); 7 Oct 1819; Jno Falls
Hazlet, John; Spencer, Nancy; Wm Featherston; 31 Oct 1806
Head, A S (Spence); Stroup, Elisabeth; Jacob Stroup; 15 Feb 1800; Jno' Dickson
Head, John; Hewet, Salley; Joseph Huet (Hewet); 27 Mar 1819; V McBee
Heaker (Hager), Christian; Beele, Elisabeth; John Robinson; 28 Dec 1790; Jno Dickson
Heaker (Heger), John; Statia, Sally; John x Beel; 25 Aug 1788; Eliza Dickson
Heaker (Hager), John; Bynum, Lucy; George x Little; 22 Dec 1814; V McBee
Heaker (Heager), Robert; Robertson, Anne; Herit Hunt; 29 Sep 1807; Thos Wheeler
Heaker (Hager), William; Blaylock, Ann; _____; 30 Apl 1785; Jas Dickson
Healms (Helms), Joshua T; Hovis, Susan; J F Plonk; 15 Mar 1858; W R Clark; M 22 Mar 1858 by J R Peterson
Heart (Hart), Sollomon; Gant, Mary; Jeames Gant; 13 Apl 1828; Wm Little
Heavner (Havner), Daniel M; Yoder, Eliza C; W M Reinhardt; 23 Feb 1861; V A McBee DC; M 7 Mar 1861 by Danl Siegel JP
Heavner (Hafner), Henry P; Hill, Eliza E; George H Heafner (Hafner); 31 Oct 1866; M 1 Nov 1866 by L A Fox MG
Heavner (Havner), Julius A; Coon, Mary Ann; William F Wise; 16 Mar 1857; George Coon JP; M 19 Mar 1857 by A J Fox MG
Heavner (Havner), Levi; Mauney, Elizabeth; Abram Howser (Houser); 9 Dec 1829; Luther M McBee
Heavner, M L; Hill, Fannie E; George H Heafner (Heavner); 19 Nov 1865; A S Haynes CCC; M 23 Nov 1865 by A J Fox MG
Heavner (Havner), Martin x; Eaker, Olly L; Peter Bess; 20 Dec 1864; S P Sherrill; M 22 Dec 1864 by G L Hunt MG
Hedgcock, Thomas x; Edwards, Betsy; Charles x Thompson; 3 Jan 1811; David Warlick JP
Hedgspeth (Hedspeth), George x; Beel, Lavinia; Christopher Beel; 14 Dec 1849; Robt Williamson
Hedick, George; Abernathy, Caroline W; P S Kistler; 11 May 1853; Robt Williamson; M 12 May 1853 by P C Henkel
Hedick, John; Canseller, Barbara; Andrew Ramsaur; 7 Dec 1819; V McBee
Hedrick, Joseph x; Hefner, Catherine; Michael x Hefner; 13 Dec 1834; J D Herman
Hedrick, Peter x; Deal, Fanny; Philip Hetrick (Hedrick); 31 Aug 1834; J D Herman
Hedrick, Solomon x; Null, Margred; Daniel Hoke; 23 May 1821; Fr Hoke
Heedick (Hedick), David; Ramsour, Barbara; Henry Beenick (Benick); 15 Dec 1831; L McBee
Heedick (Headick), Jacob; Roberts, Unity; Michael Carpenter; 21 Mar 1835; M W Abernathy
Heedick, Jonas; Ramsaur, Barbara; Daniel Shufford (Ger Schuffert); 4 Dec 1792; John Willfong JP
Heffenner, Noah x; Bolick, Elizabeth; Geo T (?) Wilkie; 27 Oct 1842; J Yount JP

Heffner, Henry x; Isenhour, Susannah; Jacob x Heffner; 21 Dec 1830 (end 1831)

Hefnar, Elias x; Null, Sarah; John x Brower (or Brown); 26 Oct 1824; Fr Hoke JP

Hefnar, Jacob x; Baker, Mary, wido; John x Hefnar; 18 Oct 1831; Fr Hoke

Hefnar, John x; Kegle, Catharina; Jacob x Hefnar; 19 Apl 1829; Fr Hoke JP

Hefner, Daniel x; Baker, Barbara; Joseph Drum; 1 Jul 1832; M W Abernathy JP

Hefner, George (Ger Höffner); Moretz, Rachael; Martin Icenhour (Isenhour); 24 Dec 1833; J D Herman

Hefner (Hevner), George; Smith, Cleresa; George Heafner (?); 26 Apl 1859; M 29 Apl 1859 by P Carpenter Esqr

Hefner (Havner), Martin; Lootz (or Lootey), Margaret; Alfred Havner; 12 Feb 1828; J T Alexander

Hefner, Philip x; Bolick, Elisabeth; Casper x Bolick; 14 Mar 1822; Mic Cline

Heger, David x; Self, Elizabeth; William Heaker (Heger); 15 Jan 1788

Heldabrand (Heltebrand), Henry; Kiser, Barbara; Conrad Heltabrand (Heltebrand); 18 Sep 1819; Jas T Alexander

Helderman, David; Saunders, Lenny; Thos Sifford; 12 Mar 1836

Helderman, George Franklin; Sronce (or Scronce), Elizabeth Catharine; James Monroe x Armstrong; 30 Nov 1859; V A McBee; M 4 Dec 1859 by Elisha Saunders JP

Helderman, J F; Arents, A S; Jacob A Miller; 29 Dec 1854; J A Huss

Helderman, Jacob; Richards, Catherine; Valentine Richards; 13 Aug 1824; V McBee

Helderman, Valentine; Blalock, Harriet M; Daniel Delliner (Dillinger); 4 Dec 1833; Carlos Leonard

Helderman, Valentine; Forney, Sarah D; John F Helderman; 14 May 1865; M same date by J Helderman

Helms, Alexr x; Anthony, Elizabeth; Caleb Miller; 12 Feb 1863; W R Clark; M same date by Alfred Black JP

Helms, Eli x; Mauney, Sarah; Joseph D Hallman; 27 Mar 1861; David Bailey; M 28 Mar 1861 by David Bailey (JP)

Helms, Hiram x; Rhyne, Susannah; John Farmer; 3 Mar 1839; M Hull JP

Helms, Jacob x; Reymer, May; John x Helms; 11 Nov 1809; Danl M Forney

Helms, Jacob x; Massagee, Martha; Isaac Houser; 13 Mar 1862; W R Clark

Helms, John; .Throneberg, Matilda; Moses Harman (Herman); 16 Mar 1842; Wm Herman JP

Helms, John x; Cope, Mary; Harmon x Campbell; 7 Mar 1862

Helms, Peter x; Penatton, Nancy; Jacob x Helms; 22 Aug 1815; James T Alexander

Helms, Pinckney x; Hauss, Catharine; John Houser; 8 Aug 1854; J A Huss; M 10 Aug 1854 by F J Jetton JP

Helms (Hellums), William; Wacaser, Mary Ann; Henry L Bangle; 27 Oct 1848; Robt Williamson

Helton (or Holton), Andrew M; Black, Malinda; James M Leonard, John D Hoke; 13 Jun 1829; J T Alexander

Helton, Jessy x; Williams, Tempe; Philip G x Bomgarner; 18 Mar 1833

Helton, Joel x; Hawn, Molly; Abram Cook; 22 Jan 1835; Henry Cline

Helton, John x; Wallis, Ruthey; Tilmon Jinkins; 25 Sep 1832; Bolen T Kirby; Ambiguous

Helton, John L x; Lawing, Louisa; Parsons Naylor; 23 May 1866; M same date by R H Abernethy JP

Helton, Robert; Perkins, Epsey; Henry Cobb; 26 Oct 1839; J A Ramsour DC

Helton, William; Stamey, Lucinda; Joseph W Morris; 19 Jan 1853; R Williamson

Henderson, Ahira; Chitham, Rachel; Thomas Chittim (Chitham); 23 ____ 1815; V McBee

Henderson, James A; Abernathy, Lena; James T Alexander; 6 Feb 1830; Luther McBee

Henderson, Joseph; McCormack, Elisabeth; Thomas x McCormack; 29 May 1783; Joseph Henry

Henderson, Lawson; Carruth, Elisabeth; John Dickson; 25 Jul 1798

Henderson, Logan; Johnston, Peggy; Lwn Henderson; 4 Jun 1806

Henderson, W M F; Burch, Epps N; David Kincaid; 18 Dec 1866; R E Burch; M same date by R H Morrison

Henderson, William; Boldredge, Nancy; Benjamin Wilson; 12 Sep 1797

Henderson, William; Abernathy, Betsy; David Abernathy; 29 Dec 1797; Jo Dickson

Henderson, Wm; Mendenhall, Mary; Wm M Holland; 3 Nov 1834; Isaac Holland

Hendricks, Tiberius; Wallace, Elisabeth D; James x Wallace; 12 Jan 1804

Henkel, Ambrose; Hoke, Catherine; Frederick Hoke; 29 Sep 1812; Philip Henkel

Henkel, Ambrose; Hoyle, Veronica; John N Stirewalt; 3 Oct 1827; J T Alexander

Henkel, David; Hoyle, Catharine; Peter Hoyle; 17 May 1814; Philip Henkle

Henkle, John x; Keever, Nancy; Daniel x Reel; 2 May 1815; V McBee

59

Henry, Isaac; Wells, Mary; Thomas Henry; 23 Oct 1830; Polly Holland
Henry, Israel W; Porter, Martha; E Milton Berry; 12 Nov 1839
Henry, Jacob see Baker, Henry
Henry, James; Patterson, Esther; Robert Campbell; 10 Sep 1798
Henry, John; Hill, Polly; Francis Henry; 25 Jul 1799; Jno Dickson
Henry, John; Brison, Margaret N; George R Brison; 11 Jan 1838
Henry, John x; Harrelson, Elizabeth; Joshua Pendleton; 19 Mar 1838; H Cansler CC
Henry, Lawson x; Loretz, Mary H; John Michal (Michael); 1 Apl 1835; M W
    Abernathy
Henry, Malcolm; Gordon, Elinor; William Henry, Hugh Gordon; 30 Mar 1779
Henry, Melcom; Moore, Ann; Jacob Summey; 26 Oct 1808; Danl M Forney
Henry, Thomas; Campbell, Nurcissa; Isaac Henry; 10 May 1830; I Holland JP
Henry, William; Gullick, Nancy; William Gullick; 23 Mar 1803
Henry, William; Pannel, Mary; James Wells; 16 Jan 1805
Henry, William x; Mcalister, Elizabeth; Alexander Smith; 31 Aug 1837; Eli Hoyl
Herman (Harmon), Andrew; _____, Savina; William x Vandyke; 13 Apl 1835; M W
    Abernathy
Herman, Daniel; Killian, Polly; Peter Herman (Ger same); 31 Aug 1820; Mic Cline
Herman, Daniel x; Trit, Sally; Daniel Herman; 14 Jan 1830; Henry Cline
Herman, David; Fry, Susannah; Jonas Deal; 4 Jan 1838; Mic Cline
Herman, George; Deal, Cathrine; Peter Herman (Ger same); 22 Jun 1820; Mic Cline
Herman, George; Hunsucker, Barbara; Peter Herman (Ger same); 21 Jan 1833;
    V McBee
Herman, Henry; McGee, Mary; George Herman; 9 Dec 1830; Henry Cline
Herman, John x; Killian, Elizabeth; Peter Herman (Ger Petrus Herman); 4 Oct 1829;
    Mic Cline
Herman, Matthias; Peterson, Anna; Peter Herman Sr (Ger Peter Herman); 29 Jan
    1839; Wm Herman JP
Herman, William; Killian, Elisabeth; John Gross; 21 Dec 1813; Mic Cline
Herman, William; Hunsicker, Elisabeth; Mathias Bovey; 23 May 1824; Mic Cline
Hermon (Harmon), Daniel; Sulvent, Sary; Moses Moore; 4 Sep 1800; John Crouse JP
Hern, John; Duckworth, Sarah; James Gordon; 9 Oct 1769; Ezekiel Polk
Herndon, Joseph; Graham, Sophia N; Thomas N Herndon; 28 Nov 1839; H Cansler
Herndon (Hearndon), Thomas N; Henderson, Mary G; Geo W Motz; 31 Mar 1835;
    M W Abernathy
Heron, Samuel H; Nelson, Mary; William Owens; 17 Oct 1816; Joseph Neel
Herren, Moses; Fronebarger, Mary; John Allen; 9 ____ 1803; Lwn Henderson
Herrington, Whitmel (by Jno Dickson); Hall, Susana; John Dickson; 20 Mar 1807;
    Lwn Henderson
Herron (Herrin), Isaac; Martin, Polly; Samuel M'Kee; 9 Jul 1822; James W McKee
Herron, Joshua; Gunn, Jane; Lawson Hofsteteler (Hufstutler); 18 Jan 1831; Jno
    Blackwood JP
Heslep, Ezekiel x; McCarver, Margaret; James McArver (McCarver); 29 Mar 1798
Heslet, Ezekiel; Cogle (or Cegle), Martha; Samuel Givens; 28 May 1789
Heslet (Hazlet), Ezekiel; Rutherford, Nancy; James Rutherford; 16 Feb 1803;
    Lwn Henderson
Hetrick (Hedrick), Philip; Yount, Catherine; George P x Somhenor; 21 Dec 1813;
    Philip Henkel
Hettrick (Hedrick), Conrad; White, Ann; George Sigman (Ger Georg Siegmann);
    27 Jan 1829; Miles W Abernathy
Hevner (Havner), Henry; Coon, Betcy; Henry Houser; 11 Dec 1827; V McBee
Heyard, Lewis (Ger Lu__ Heyhard); Reather, Fanny; Jacob Starr; 14 Dec 1787;
    Joseph Steel
Hickman, James; Sanger, Mary Ann; William Turner; 24 Oct 1832; Mic Cline
Hicks, Albert; Childers, Dovy; David x Hicks; 23 Dec 1854; J A Huss; M 24 Dec
    1854 by Elisha Saunders JP
Hicks, David x; Ingle, Mary; Adam Ingle; 12 Jun 1856; J A Huss; M 22 Jul 1856 by
    Elisha Saunders JP
Hicks, Miles x; Sanders, Louisa; Isaac x Lynch; 24 Dec 1827; J T Alexander
Hicks, Samuel; Bynum, Sarah J; _____; 24 Jun 1866; M this date by Elisha
    Saunders JP; C only, no B
Hifner (or Hefner), Frederick x; Moser, Elvira; Jacob Isaacs; 23 May 1833; M W
    Abernathy
Hildebrand (Helderbrand), Marcus V; Wood, Sarah; A P Cansler; 29 Jul 1858;
    W R Clark
Hildrman, John; Ward, Rebecky B; Fredrick x Myars, Gatlop v Hildrman; 13 Sep
    1808; Hy Conner JP

Hill, Alexander M; Jackson, Louisa; John R Dunn; 10 Nov 1830; L M McBee

Hill, Andrew; Campbell, Juliet; Solomon Hill; 3 Jan 1808

Hill, Daniel H (Maj USA); Morrison, Isabella S; Wm W Morrison; 30 Oct 1848; Robt Williamson

Hill, Isaac L; Fisher, Sarah C; A B Little; 18 Jun 1859; M 21 Jun 1859 by Elisha Saunders JP

Hill, James; Robinson, Anne; Thomas Barkly (Berkley); 6 Mar 1786; Elizabeth Dickson

Hill, James; Robinson, Jean; James Robinson; 28 Jul 1789

Hill, James D; Massey, Jane; Lawson A Henry; 18 Dec 1821; I Holland for Vardry McBee

Hill, James H; Carpenter, Sarah; John F Asbury; 26 Nov 1845; R Williamson

Hill, Jeremiah; Little, Jane; Robert Bartley; 17 Nov 1789

Hill, John; Paterson, Sarah; William Berry; 13 Nov 1816; James T Alexander

Hill, John F; Carpenter, Francis; Solomon Carpenter; 28 Nov 1839; L E Thompson

Hill, John W; Kistler, Margaret C; James C Jenkins; 31 Oct 1846; Robt Williamson

Hill, Lawson H; Hoyl, Elizabeth; John F Hill; 2 Oct 1838; J A Ramsour DC

Hill, Thos; Eward, Sarah; William Baldrige; 13 Dec 1786

Hill, Thomas; --------; Robert Williamson; ------ 1804; Js McEwin; Ambiguous

Hill, Thomas x; Clark, Lettis; James Martin; 26 Aug 1823; Wm Little

Hill, Wm B; Lyttle, Sarah E; J C Jenkins; 20 Oct 1865; A S Haynes CCC; M 26 Oct 1865 by E W Thompson

Hillebrand, Peter; Houser, Julia A; J C Jenkins; 6 Aug 1866; M 7 Aug 1866 by R N Davis Minister

Hilton, Randolph x; Neale, Elizabeth; Henry x Cobb; 21 Dec 1839; L E Thompson

Hine (Hines), John G; Bullinger, Mary M; Daniel Shuford; 8 Mar 1834; Carlos Leonard

Hines, Bryan; Hoyl, Elmina C; William Roberts; 11 Sep 1837; Eli Hoyl

Hines, Daniel; Hovis, Susan; Charles x Leonard; 18 Mar 1836; M W Abernathy

Hines, Philip (Ger Bhililib Heun or Huun); Shuford, Polly; Jno Hoke; 18 Mar 1803; Ja McKisick

Hinkell (Hinkle), Lewis; Joins, Mary Ann; Carlos Leonard; 10 Feb 1838; H Cansler CC

Hinkle, Anthony; Sides, Barbary; John Seitz (Sides); 2 Nov 1791; Robert Dickson

Hinkle, Cyrus; Nixon, Elisabeth; Albert M Nixon; 2 Oct 1861; Robert Nixon JP; M same date by Robert Nixon JP

Hinkle, Isaac; Lockman, Rachael; Wm P Connel (or Cormel); 26 Dec 1838; H Cansler

Hinkle, Jacob; Sides, Susanna; John Flatt; 1 Feb 1788

Hinkle, Jacob; Wills, Barbay; Conrad Wills; 22 Jan 1808; Jacob Forney

Hinkle, John; Hinkle, Elisabeth; Jacob Hinkel; 6 Dec 1785; Jo Dickson; Ambiguous

Hinkle, John L; Nixon, Catherine; Osburn Hinkle; 28 Nov 1865; A S Haynes; M 29 Nov 1865 by R H Morrison

Hinson, Aaron x; Bynum, Elizabeth; James P Mullen; 25 Jul 1851; Robt Williamson; M 27 Jul 1851 by Elisha Saunders JP

Hinson, Lazarus; Low, Elizabeth; George x Low; 26 Jun 1815; James T Alexander

Hix, Marcus W x; Ballard, Harriet; Adam Ingle; 4 Jul 1857; Elisha Saunders; M 5 Jul 1857 by Elisha Saunders JP

Hix, Miles x; Childers, Susannah; Andrew x Blaylock; 21 Nov 1848

Hix, Queen x; Bird, Charlot; Daniel x Humphreys; 28 ____ 1833; Miles W Abernathy

Hix (Hicks), William; Robinson, Polly; Miles x Hicks; 7 Jan 1830; J T Alexander

Hoan, Jacob (Ger Jacob Hahn); Burns, Elisabeth; Martin x Gortner; 5 Nov 1788; Joseph Steel

Hobbs, Nathaniel (of Iredell Co); Creatheres, Sarah; John Abernathy, James White; 19 Apl 1813; Henry Conner

Hobbs, William C; Hobbs, Mary; Jos B J H Mayhew; 13 Dec 1854; W B Withers JP; M same date by W W Munday Esq

Hodge, William x; Kale, Anne; William Walker; 10 Jun 1822; D Reinhardt

Hoffman (Hufman), David; Jenkins, Leanna; John F Canon (Cannon); 19 Mar 1846; And Hoyl

Hoffman, Frederick; Smith, Mary J (or I); Peter Kistler; 5 Oct 1841; R Williamson Jr

Hoffman, J____ x; Miller, Cathrine; Samuel (?) Smyer; 25 Sep 1831; Mic Cline

Hoffman (Huffman), Jonas; Rhyne, Sarah; Jonas R Linebarger; 16 Apl 1842; And Hoyl

Hoffman (Hufman), Miles; Rhyne, Fanny; David Hoffman (Hufman); 9 Oct 1845

Hoffman (Hufman), Peter; Berry, Ann; Geo W McAllister; 10 Dec 1832; Eli Hoyl

Hoffstetele (Huffstitler), Lawson; Heron (?), Elizabeth; Levi x Huffstetter (Huffstitler); 13 Jan 1824; Jas T Alexander

Hoffstiler (Huffstotler), David; Huffstotler, Charity; John Vickers (Vicars); 8 Feb 1823; V McBee

61

Hofman, Eli; Hamilton, Martha; Jacob Linebarger; 18 Jan 1836; J G Hand JP
Hofman (Huffman), Jacob; Rhine, Margaret; Alexander Smith; 3 Feb 1829; V McBee
Hogan (Huggins), John; Bennet, Betsey; Samuel Ramsey; 8 Apl 1800
Hogins, John R; Bradshew, Susanna; Josiah Bradshaw (Bradshew); 8 Nov 1791;
    Robert Dickson
Hoil (Hoyl, Hoyle), Jonas C; Taylor, Mary; John W Linhardt; 28 Jul 1853; J F
    Mullens; M 4 Aug 1853 by D Williams JP
Hoke, A L; Cline, Nancy C; Thos T Slade; 15 Dec 1841; R Williamson Jr
Hoke, Alfred; Abernathy, Susan; F A Hoke; 27 Sep 1837; H Cansler
Hoke, Andrew; Coulter, Elizebeth; Lewis Hafer (Hefar); 18 May 1820; Fr Hoke
Hoke, Daniel; Smith, Sally; Lewis Hafer; 20 Jan 1818; V McBee
Hoke, Daniel; Rudisill, Susannah; Jacob Mosteller; 10 Nov 1836; Miles W Abernathy
Hoke, David; Burns, Nancy; Willard Boyden; 7 Feb 1832; L McBee
Hoke, F E; Baker, Catharine; John P Cansler; 23 Nov 1854; J A Huss; M same
    date by David Crouse JP
Hoke, Franklin A; Zimmerman, Mary A; Elam Caldwell; 24 Jan 1838; L E Thompson
Hoke, Frederick; Smith, Cathrine; John Smith; 5 Nov 1816; Mic Cline
Hoke, Frederick; Lourance, Elizabeth; Alexander Lourance; 11 May 1817; Peter
    Little JP
Hoke, Frederick; Kiblar, Rebeca; Peter Little; 7 Feb 1839; J Yount JP
Hoke, Frederick (si); Stierwalt, Elizebeth; Daniel Hoke; 4 Aug 1833
Hoke, Frederick L (F); Carpenter, Frances C; John F Alexander; 7 Sep 1847; Robt
    Williamson
Hoke, George M; Maclean, V R J; Wm J Hoke; 9 Nov 1864; M same date by
    R N Davis Minister
Hoke, Henry; Ramsour, Catey; Jos Henry; 4 Oct 1785; Joseph Henry
Hoke, Henry; Smith, Mary; Lewis Hafer (Hefar); 27 Apl 1823
Hoke, Henry; Ramsour, Susannah; John F Loretz; 1 Jul 1826; J T Alexander
Hoke, Henr.'; Hunsecker, Susannah; Frederick Hoke; 10 Mar 1829
Hoke, Jacob; Sheremon, Barbara; David Wise; 29 Oct 1833
Hoke, John; Quigle, Barbary; Jacob Summey; 9 Jan 1808; D M Forney
Hoke, John; Killian, Nancy; John Smith; 7 Apl 1825; Daniel Moser
Hoke, John E; Sullivan, Nancy J; Lawson H Lenhart (Leonhardt); 27 May 1845
Hoke, Michael; Burton, Francis; L M McBee; 6 May 1833; J T Alexander
Hoke, William J; Sumner, Georgiana T; Augustus W Burton, Henry W Burton;
    17 Jun 1851; Robt Williamson; M 18 Jun 1851 by Joseph C Huske Rector St Luke's
Holdbrooks, John F x; Johnson, Hazeltine; Joshua x Holdbrooks; 23 Nov 1859;
    M 24 Nov 1859 by A J Fox MG
Holdsclaw, Lewis; Robinson, Jane; Elisha Sherrill (Sherril); 23 Jul 1823; V McBee
Holdsclaw, Lewis; Hager, Martha; Silas S Scarbrough (Scarborough); 17 Jan 1832;
    J T Alexander
Holdtree, Joseph (Ger Johann Joseph __); Smith, Margaret; Jacob Setser; 3 Feb 1789;
    Joseph Steel
Holebrooks, Joshua x; Strutt, Mahala; D L Hoke; 17 Oct 1854; J A Huss; M 19 Oct
    1854 by George Coon JP
Holland, Daniel; Hawkins, Ruth; Samuel x Hawkins; 17 Mar 1798; Eliza Greaves
Holland, Franklin H; Quinn, Mary A; W F (Washington) Holland; ____ ____ 1838;
    Isaac Holland
Holland, Franklin H; Wilson, Priscilla R; William R Holland; 13 Dec 1843; Isaac
    Holland
Holland, Henery (Henry); Nolen, Penelipy; Oliver W Holland; 8 Jul 1820
Holland, Isaac; Graves, Polly D; Joseph D Graves; 1807; (N)
Holland, Jasper N; Quinn, Sarah E; William R Holland; 14 Feb 1846; Isaac Holland
Holland, John; Huggins, Elisabeth; James Huggins; 26 Mar 1782
Holland, Judas; Gaskins, Mary Ann; Francis Gascin (Gaskins), Saml Kuykendall;
    8 Mar 1784
Holland, Julius; Rhyne, Mary; Robert Holland; 3 Jan 1833; B T Kirby; Ambiguous
Holland, O W Jun; Martin, Elisabeth J; W F Holland; 15 Apl 1842; I H (or J H)
    Holland
Holland, Oliver Wily; Moore, Poley; Joseph D Greaves (Graves); 4 Sep 1807; D M
    Forney
Holland, Robert; Rhyne, Eliza; Jonathan Rhyne; 27 Aug 1830; Bolin T Kirby
Holland, Washington Frenau; Queen, Nancy C; Jas W Reid; 11 Nov 1845; Isaac
    Holland
Holland, William; Best, Levica; Mathew x Holland; 28 May 1811; Jacob Ramsour
Holler (Hollar), Andrew; Miller, Lavina; Daniel Miller; 12 Feb 1839; H Cansler

Holler, Daniel; Isenhour, Lavina; Daniel Miller, Andrew Holler; 12 Feb 1839;
H Cansler; Doubtful, endorsed "Daniel Miller's Marriage Bond"

Holler, Israel; Lennier, Anna; Adam Flowers (Flower); 27 Mar 1838; Wm Herman JP

Holler, John; Ward, Sally; Mathias Setser; 13 Dec 1827; Mic Cline

Holler (Hollar), Lawson x; Millar, Anny; Daniel Miller (Millar); 30 Sep 1841;
J Yount JP

Holler (Hollar), Peter; Townsend, Elizabeth; Henry x Hollar; 5 Dec 1830; Henry
Cline

Hollman, Daniel; Loretz, Polley; Daniel (Jacob) x Hollman; 5 Feb 1824; V McBee

Hollman (Holman), Wile; Sumrow, Barbara; Jacob Hallman (Holman); 25 Mar 1823;
V McBee

Holloman, Moses; Low (or Law), Caroline; James M Daniel; 4 Nov 1837

Holloway, Barnes; Magill, Sarah; Peter Winfree; 1 Apl 1800; Betsey Henderson

Holloway (Holoway), Billey; Senter, Anne; And Hoyl; 23 Jan 1809

Holly, Daniel; Reinhardt, Susannah; William Ramsey; 28 Feb 1837; M Hull JP

Holly, John; Fish, Sarah; Caleb Miller; 23 Jan 1828; V McBee

Holly, M A; Hoyle, Frances C; J W Lloyd; 21 Jun 1865; W R Clark; M 29 Jun
1865 by E G Gage Minister

Homer, John x; Cornelius, Rebecca; William Little (Lytle); 25 Feb 1793; Jo Dickson

Homesley (Homesly), Moses G; McGinnas, Sarah; W W McGinnas; 16 Apl 1840;
A J Cansler

Homesley (Homesly), Stephen; Roberts, Ester; Joseph Homesley (Homesly); 13 Feb
1809; H Y Webb

Honesley (Homesly), A B; Cornwell, Mary; Ephraim Black; 1 Feb 1845; R Williamson Jr

Hooper, Edley (Adly); Wilkerson, Milly; Thomas x Wilkerson; 4 Oct 1835; M W
Abernathy

Hooper, Elias; Hoyle, Salley; John Michal; 10 Mar 1825; John D Hoke

Hooper, John x; Hooper, Eliza; Jas A Ramsour (Jacob Ramsour), Michael Hoke;
16 Jun 1828; B J Thompson

Hooper, John; Sherrell, Elitha; Willis Hooper; 30 Oct 1830; V McBee

Hoover, Absalom; Jerret, Melline; Samuel Jarrett (Jarret); 30 Dec 1829; Luther McBee

Hoover, Alexander (Danl A); Fullbright, Elizabeth; Ephraim Lutz; 21 Nov 1859;
W R Clark; M 1 Dec 1859 by Danl Siegel JP

Hoover, Daniel; Mooney, Sarah; Jeremiah Mosteller; 26 May 1838

Hoover, Daniel x; Bynum, Polley; James F Bynum; 1 Sep 1842; J Helderman

Hoover, David x; Hoyle, Mary; Valentine Lore; 7 Dec 1841

Hoover, Edney; Dellinger, Mary C; Daniel M Heavner (Hafner); 1 Jan 1861; W R
Clark; M 10 Jan 1861 by L H Hill JP

Hoover, Ephraim; Willson, Minervy; David Clay; 27 Jan 1829; J_-- Seagle JP

Hoover (Hover), Ephraim; Wion, Christeener; David M Isendhawer (Ichour); 19 Feb
1835; M Hull JP

Hoover, Franklin x; Roderick, Eliza; Joshua Lore; 16 Nov 1852; Robt Williamson;
M 25 Nov 1852 by Daniel Siegel Sen JP

Hoover (Huver), Henry Jr; Myers, Elizabeth; Henry Hoover Sr (Ger Heinrich Huver);
24 Mar 1817; V McBee

Hoover, John; Lantz, Barbara; John x Hoover; 26 Sep 1832; J T Alexander

Hoover, John; Mosteller, Juliana C; Samuel Jarrett; 27 Jul 1835; G Hoke

Hoover, Thomas x; Hamilton, Jane; William D (or J) Caldwell; 28 Jan 1841; Eli Hoyl

Hoover, Warlick x; Lutz, Elizabeth; Samuel Jarrett; 6 Jan 1834; G Hoke

Hope, Christian; Cross, Prudence; William x Richards; 8 Apl 1832; V McBee

Hope, Christon (Christian); Johnson, Polley; William Low; 19 May 1813; V McBee

Hope, Henry; Johnson, Phoeby; David x Thornbury; 2 May 1818; V McBee

Hope, Henry; Smith, Hariet E; John A Parker; 14 Sep 1842

Hope, William x; Engle, Margaret; John Keener; 26 Nov 1846; Robt Williamson

Hopkins, John; Sadler, Salley; David Jones (Johns); 4 Oct 1808; Hy Conner

Hopkins, Richard; Penick, Phebe; Adam x Penick; 17 Jul 1809; Danl M Forney

Hopper (Hoper), John Alexander; Harry, Julian; Thomas Bridges; 20 Apl 1837

Hoppes (Hoppis), Adam; Link, Catherine; Jacob Link; 3 Dec 1810; H Y Webb

Hoppes, John; Sullivan, Sally; Ezekiel Sullivan; 10 Jan 1826 ; J T Alexander

Horl (or Hart), Rooben x; Brown, Maryam; Peter Eaker (Ger Peter Eker); 14 Feb 1793

Horse, John x; James, Elizabeth; David Shuford; 7 Jul 1801; Lwn Henderson

Horton, George x; Golden, Betsey; William x King; 9 Feb 1803; Eliza D Greaves

Horton, George x; Haines, Nancy; Sandford x Horton; 7 Apl 1851; Robt Williamson

Horton, Nimrod; Wells, Susannah; William x Wyatt; 27 Nov 1803; Eliza Greaves

Houghstetlar, Michael x; Hullet, Elizabeth; Peter Acre (Ger Peter Eker); 5 May 1812;
Elizabeth Henderson

63

Houk, Leander; Link, Anna Catharine; John Sides; 11 Oct 1842
Houser (Howser), Elias; Delinger, Mieranna; Joseph Hoser (Howser); 25 Dec 1836; M Hull JP
Houser, Emmanuel; Leonhardt, Emily Adaline; Henry Havner (?); 2 Jan 1851; Ambiguous
Houser, Franklin A; Lingafelt, Sarah; Allen Alexander; 21 Sep 1850; Robt Williamson
Houser, Henry (Ger Henrich Hauser); Bullinger, Susanah; Peter Houser (Ger Huser); 22 Oct 1823; V McBee
Houser, Henry; Kistler, Sarah Caroline; John Houser; 29 Mar 1856; J A Huss; M 30 Mar 1856 by Logan H Lowrance JP
Houser, Isaac; Smith, Catherine; H H Thompson; 31 Jul 1839; H Cansler
Houser, John x; Seine, Caty; (Ger) Henrich Lang; 17 Jan 1809; Danl M Forney
Houser (Howser), John; Bess, Mary E; Joshua P Carpenter; 3 Sep 1856; Logan H Lowrance; M 4 Sep 1856 by Logan H Lowrance JP
Houser, Jonas; Robeson, Martha; Benjamin Hull; 11 May 1858; D Williams JP; M same date by David Williams JP; B and C as above, R shows groom Jonas Rhine
Houser, Jonason x; Sain, Sarah; Jacob Houser; 9 Nov 1818; V McBee
Houser, Joseph x; Spangler, Susanah; Frederick Spengler (Ger Friederich Spengler); 14 May 1817; V McBee
Houser, Joseph; Haus, Mary; William Robinson; 27 Sep 1830; Jno D Hoke
Houser, Joseph; Shull, Martha A; Philip A Shull; 16 Sep 1865; J C Jenkins; M 21 (or 20) Sep 1865 by James H Postell
Houser, Lawson; Hoke, Cammilla; Wm H (Henry) Shell; 12 Feb 1866
Houser, Peter (Ger Peter Hauser); Hafner, Sarah; Jacob Aderholt; 7 Feb 1803; John Dickson
Houser, Peter; Connor, Susan E; Daniel Warlick; 16 Oct 1839; J A Ramsour DC
Houston, Joel B; McCorkle, Elizabeth L; John McCorkle; 4 Sep 1826; J T Alexander
Houston, John; Wilson, Martha; Jno A Wilson; 23 Oct 1802
Houston, John; Patton, Jane; John A Wilson; 28 Oct 1805
Houston (Hueston), Joseph; Byers, Pagy; John x Mattiss (?); 20 Feb 1809; Mic Cline
Houston, Robert; Isenhour, Mahala; Lawson Douglass (Dougless); 9 Nov 1837
Hover (Huver), Philip; Fite, Polley; Jacob Brem; 27 Jul 1812; Vardry McBee CC
Hoves (Hovis), George (Jr); Cloninger, Eve; William Rankin; 3 Feb 1800
Hovis, Adam; Rhyne, Anny; Moses Hovis; 7 Aug 1826; Isaac Holland
Hovis, Caleb x; Hovis, Susan; Daniel Hovis; 2 Mar 1855; J A Huss
Hovis, Daniel x; Parker, Hanah; George x Weathers; 23 Mar 1820; I Holland
Hovis, David x; Stroup, Sarah Ann; Jacob Stroup; 2 Jan 1826; V McBee
Hovis, Elias; Weatherspoon, Eliza; Moses Hovis; 3 Jan 1824; Isaac Holland
Hovis, Frederick; Rudicill, Polly; George Cathey; 5 Feb 1793; Jo Dickson
Hovis, George; Carpenter, Catherine; John Hoke; 17 Mar 1825; V McBee
Hovis, George; Carpenter, Mary; John Michal; 17 Feb 1838; H Cansler CC
Hovis, Henry; Cathey, Nancy; George W McCallister; 13 Sep 1825; Isaac Holland
Hovis, Henry x; Sauls, Caroline; Allen Alexander; 6 Nov 1860; W R Clark; M 8 Nov 1860 by R H Abernathy JP
Hovis, Henry M; Dellinger, Lucretia L; Israel B Stroup; 5 Mar 1853; R Williamson; M 9 Mar 1853 by Elisha Saunders JP
Hovis, Jacob see Rudisel, Jacob
Hovis, Jacob; Rudissale, Susana; Thomas Cloninger; 12 Mar 1810
Hovis, Jacob; Carpenter, Anna; Emanuel Carpenter; 30 Apl 1831; J T Alexander
Hovis, John; Carpenter ,Elizabeth; Levi Rudasele (Rudisel); 10 Aug 1826; V McBee
Hovis, John P; Bradshaw, Susannah; John A McGinnas (Meginnis); 29 Oct 1833; Miles W Abernathy
Hovis, John P; Brown, Mary M; Michael Cloninger; 16 Feb 1839; H Cline JP; Doubtful, end Michael Cloninger's MB
Hovis, Joseph; Givens, Sarah L; Washington F Holland; 19 Mar 1841
Hovis, Levi x; Tucker, Rebecca; Elam A Curry; 18 Jun 1863; W R Clark; M 25 Jun 1863 by R H Abernathy JP
Hovis, Michael R; Cline, Nancy E; Malchi Hovis; 16 Oct 1865; A S Haynes CCC; M 19 Oct 1865 by S P Sherrill JP
Hovis, Michel; Reid, Charlotte; George W McCallister; 15 Dec 1827
Hovis, Moses; Rhyne, Elizabeth; David Summey; 27 Feb 1823; V McBee
Hovis, Moses; Carpenter, Louisa; James x Nantz; 7 May 1856; J A Huss; M 15 May 1856 by J R Peterson (MG)
Hovis, Philip; Carpenter, Sarah; Milton A Smith; Aug 26 1830; J T Alexander
Hovis, Philip; Stroup, Delaney; George Carpenter; 6 Jul 1833; J T Alexander
Hovis, Sidney J x; Bynum, Sarah Ann; Benjamin Beel (Beal); 9 Jan 1860; M 22 Jan 1860 by Elisha Saunders JP

Hovis, Solomon; Carpanter, Anna; Philip Hovis; 15 Sep 1831; J T Alexander
Hovis, Solomon; Summey, Ann; A J Hovis; 8 Mar 1845; C L Hunter
Hovis, Wesley Hartwel (Hartwell W); Richards, Mary; John Bradshaw; 10 Jan 1853;
    R Williamson; M 18 Jan 1853 by Jacob Helderman JP
Howard, Benjamin; Rocket, Salley; Joseph Howard; 3 Mar 1814; Phil Whitener JP
Howard, Edmon M; Lockman, Sarah Jane; Freeman M Shelton; 23 Jan 1857; W B
    Withers JP; M 29 Jan 1857 by J Lowe JP
Howard, Francis R; _____; Allen Howard; 20 Aug 1829; Wm Little
Howard, Franklin; Howard, Catharine; John A Lockman; 24 Apl 1852
Howard, Freeman; Brotherton, Susanah; David x Lockman; 26 Apl 1831; V McBee
Howard, George; Lantz, Sarah; Freeman Howard; 1 Jan 1842; R Williamson Jr
Howard, Henry x; Ballard, Charlotte; John Little; 19 Nov 1813; V McBee
Howard, Henry x; Burton, Charlotte; Cathey White; 1 Dec 1825; J T Alexander
Howard, Henry; Caldwell, Elizabeth; Robert L (or E) x Barkly; 16 Nov 1833
Howard, Jackson A; Howard, Rachael E; William H Brotherton; 14 Apl 1866;
    H Asbury Mst; M 15 Apl 1866 by J Lowe JP
Howard, John x; Caldwell, Rebecca; John H x Barkley; 3 Sep 1838; N M Reinhardt
Howard, John; Robeson, Sarah Jane; Joseph Gabriel; 2 Mar 1841; H Cansler
Howard, Joseph; Hyde, Elisabeth; John Hide (Hyde); 24 Jul 1785; Danl McKisick
Howard, Joshua Loyd x; Deal, Mary Magdelene; Henry Bolch; 6 Mar 1836; John
    Kayler
Howard, Warner x; Nixon, Tabitha; William Nixson (Nixon); 9 Oct 1817; V McBee
Howard, William x; Blalock, Anne; Horace x Roby; 7 Oct 1816; V McBee
Howard, William; Childers, Nancy; William H Howard; 24 Dec 1826; Wm Little
Howard, William; Edwards, Elizabeth; _____; 16 Feb 1858; W R Clark Clk;
    M 18 Feb 1858 by J Lowe JP; L and C, no B
Howard, William H; Waggoner, Rachel; James Cashion; 16 Dec 1822; V McBee
Howard, Worner; McMinn, Ann; William Childress; 6 Aug 1814; V McBee
Howel, Joshua (Jr); Hoyle, Margaret; Joshua Howel (Sr); 2 Mar 1839; H Cansler CC
Howser, John x; _____, Elizabeth; Benjamin x Hull; 17 May 1840; M Hull JP;
    Ambiguous
Howser (Hauser), John; Stamey, Eliza; Isaac Reinhardt; 22 May 1847; Danl Siegel JP
Hoyl (Hoyle), Burril W; Rhyne, Anna; Valentine Costner; 25 Oct 1827; J T Alexander
Hoyl, Eli; Ramsour, Cynthia L; Zenas A Grier; 5 Jan 1830; Jno F Tomkies
Hoyl, Eli; Burton, Elizabeth; Caleb W Hoyl; 26 Sep 1841
Hoyl (Hoyle), John; Wells, Dolly; Lwn Henderson; 4 Nov 1805
Hoyl (Hoyle), John A; Houser, Eliza; Franklin A Houser; 7 Mar 1857; Danl
    Siegel JP; M same date by Daniel Siegel JP
Hoyl (Hoyle), L W; Boggs, Rebecca; Wm J Hoke; 12 Apl 1859; W R Clark; M same
    date by Wm J Hoke JP
Hoyl, Martin; Carpenter, Mary; Samuel Bigham; 22 Feb 1816; Saml Wilson
Hoyl, Nathen M; Wells, Martha; Jacob Fite; 1 Feb 1823; Isaac Holland
Hoyl (Heyel), Peter; Hovis, Sosana; Frederick Hovis; 23 Jun 1792; Jo Dickson
Hoyl (Hoyle), Peter C; Hull, Elizabeth; W R Clark; 2 Jan 1849; Robt Williamson
Hoyl, Samuel Smith; Hovis, Cathrine; And Hoyl; 10 Mar 1813; I Holland
Hoyl (Hoyle), Solomon; Summey, Anne; Jacob Reinhardt; 14 Jan 1814
Hoyle, Abel; Moorman, Nancy H V; Willard Boyden; 7 Jun 1831; L McBee
Hoyle, Andrew x; Saine, Mary C; Jonas W Paysour; 21 Aug 1865; A S Haynes CCC,
    __ H Bisaner; M 27 Aug 1865 by O B Jenks
Hoyle, David R; Hoke, Barbara; George Coon; 1 Oct 1831; L McBee
Hoyle, David R; Carpenter, Elizabeth; John Hoyle Jr; 26 Aug 1835; M W Abernathy
Hoyle, Humphrey H; Dickson, Elizabeth; Daniel B P Moorman; 4 Jun 1845; R
    Williamson
Hoyle (Hoyl), Jacob; Summy, Catharine; Jacob Rinehart; 9 May 1803; John Dickson
Hoyle, Jacob; Robeson, Leah; Jacob Reinhardt; 6 Aug 1811
Hoyle, Jacob; Rhodes, Elizabeth; Michael Schenck (Ger Shenck); 29 Jan 1834;
    Miles W Abernathy
Hoyle, Jacob x; Hill, Rachel L; Jacob x Hallman; 9 Nov 1848; Robt Williamson
Hoyle, John; Holman, Catherine; Jacob Reinhardt; 15 Oct 1823; V McBee
Hoyle, John Samuel x; Carpenter, Martha; W C Taylor; 20 Dec 1860; Wm J Hoke;
    M 1 Jan 1861 by G W Hull (JP)
Hoyle, Laban A; Henderson, Mary Helen; Robt Williamson; 23 Sep 1858; W R Clark;
    M same date by J T Alexander JP
Hoyle, Noah; Shuford, Elizabeth; George W Shuford; 24 Sep 1829; Danl Conrad JP
Hoyle, Peter x; Bailey, Elizabeth; Samuel C Bailey; 4 Oct 1856; M 7 Oct 1856 by
    Logan H Lowrance JP

Hoyle, Reuben; Whitener, Sarah M; E B Torrence; 17 Jul 1838; H Cansler

Hubard (Hubbard), Isaac; Kiser, Sarah; John Huggins; 1 Mar 1842

Hubbard, Charles W; Propst (Props), Ann; William A Neal; 9 Apl 1857; M same date by D A Haines JP

Hubbard, Lemuel Alexander x; Canipe, Anna Eliza; Noah Boiles; 15 Feb 1866; M same date by David Boiles JP

Hubberd, David; Wise, Elizabeth; --------; 21 Feb 1852; M this date by, Daniel Siegel JP; R only, no B

Hubburd, Kearby; --------; --------; No date; Joseph Steel; Incomplete and doubtful

Huddleston, James; Flemming, Agnias; John Fleming (Flemming); 2 Feb 1811; Daniel M Forney Clk

Hudgpeth, Thos A x; Goodson, Mary A; James E Fisher; 11 Apl 1867; M same date by B S Johnson JP

Hudson, Daniel (Jr); Gross, Catharine; Henry Stamey (Stamy); 14 Oct 1800; Ligt Williams

Hudson, Enoch; Sullivan, Harriet C; Solomon Ramsey; 24 Oct 1833; P Stamey JP

Hudson, Ephraim; Speck, Barbara; Alexander Hudson; 7 Jan 1830; Luther M McBee

Hudspath (Hedgspeth), John T; Sherrill, Eliza; A C Robison (Alexander Robinson); 24 Dec 1848; Robt Williamson

Hudspeth (Hedgpeth), Ayres; Hoke, Sarah E; Martin H Shuford; 26 Jul 1866; M same date by A J Fox MG

Hudspeth, John T; Kirksey, Mary; Airs x Hudspeth; 3 Mar 1853; R Williamson; M 6 Mar 1853 by Ambrose Costner JP

Hudspeth (Hedgpeth), Wesley; Sumrow (Summerow), Elmira; Daniel Sumrow; 16 Feb 1856; M 19 Feb 1856 by David Crooks MG

Huell (Hull), Abner; Parker, Elizabeth; Benjamin Moore; 2 Sep 1795; Michl Eaker JP

Huffman (or Haffner), Alferd; Simons, Melinda; Jonathan Eaker (or Eakerd); 23 (?) May 1840; J Yount (?) JP

Huffman, Daniel; Linebarger, Susannah; Christian Rhodes; 22 Apl 1817; James T Alexander

Huffman, David; Naugle, Sally; James Sims; 4 Jan 1830; Jonas Bost

Huffman, David x; Killian, Sarah; Abraham x Yount; 18 Oct 1832; Miles W Abernathy

Huffman, Eli x; Shook, Nancy; Frederick x Shook; 8 Jul 1830; Miles W Abernathy JP

Huffman, Elijah; Bullinger, Leah; Jacob Cline; 1 Nov 1831; V McBee

Huffman, George; Hunsecker, Polly; Elijah Huffman; 11 Nov 1834

Huffman, Henry x; Bolch, Polly; Jacob Miller; 24 Dec 1833; Henry Cline

Huffman, Henry W; Cook, Rachel; William Turner; 14 Jul 1833; Henry Cline

Huffman, Jackson; Miller, Polly; Henry W Huffman; 31 Mar 1836; Henry Cline

Huffman, Jacob; Shook, Susannah; John Drumm (Drum); 20 Sep 1827; M W Abernathy

Huffman, Jacob; Linebarger, Elizabeth; Jacob H Rhyne; 2 Feb 1839; And Hoyl

Huffman, Joseph; Sigman, Delilah; Casper Bolick (Ger Bolch); 20 May 1828; Mic Cline

Huffman, Langdon; Miller, Ammy; Henry Miller; 25 Nov 1841; Epm Yount JP

Huffman, Levi; Rhyne, Rebeckah; Henry Linebarger; 14 May 1835; Isaac Holland

Huffman, Martin; Eikerd (or Eckerd), Sarah; Daniel Denmon; 1 Sep 1825; Mic Cline

Huffman (Hoffman), Martin J; Hovis, Elizabeth; Harrison Houk; 17 Apl 1845; R Williamson DC

Huffman, Peter x; Shepherd, Becky; David x Huffman; 8 May 1834; Henry Cline

Huffman, Samuel; Haines, Martha J; John M Michael (Micheal); 9 Aug 1854; Daniel A Haines

Huffman, William; Drum, Anny; Christopher x Huffman; 6 Jan 1828; M W Abernathy for V McBee

Huffstetelr (Huffstetler), Eli; Pasour, Annie; Felix Paysour (Pasour); 20 Oct 1841; L E Thompson

Huffstetler (Hoffstetler), Caleb A; Smith, Sarah; Jimison F Torrence (Torrance); 22 Apl 1845; Isaac Holland

Huffstetler (Hoffstutler), Ephraim M; Baker, Louisa; N R Stamey; 7 Apl 1856; A P Cansler; M same date by A P Cansler JP

Huffstetler, Jonas; Jenkins, Martha; Drury Jenkins; 20 Dec 1824; Jas T Alexander

Huffstetler, Michael x; Costner, Mary Ann; John x Costner; 16 Jan 1828; B J Thompson

Huffstetler, Michael; Fronebarger, Elizabeth; Lawson Huffstetler; 13 Aug 1829; J T Alexander

Huffstetsler (Huffstetler), Logan; Weir, Sally; Andrew Niell (Neel); 27 Dec 1828; J T Alexander

Huffsticklar (Huffstidtler), Daniel; Weer, Peggy; Charles D____; 16 Jun 1833; A F Niel JP; "Peggy Weer daughter of David Weer"

Huffstickler (Huffstutler), David; Harmon, Julian (Julia Ann); Newton V Chaneller (Chandler); 28 Mar 1864; W R Clark; M same date by R H Abernathy JP

Huffstotler, Adam x; Davis, Susana; George x Huffstotler; 20 Jul 1813; V McBee

Hufman, Geo; Hook, Susanna; Mic Cline, Jacob Cline; 12 Jan 1801

Hufman (Huffman), John; Lineberger, Polly; Peter Rhyne (Ryne); 2 Feb 1811; Danl M Forney

Hufman, Joseph; Weathers, Sarah; John N Friday; 13 Nov 1824; Isaac Holland

Hufmon (Huffman), Jonas; Cosner, Anna M; Isaac Jones; 4 Apl 1814; V McBee

Hufstatler, John; Brown, Elisabeth; Jno Fulenwider, John Moore; 4 Feb 1802

Hufstatler, Peter x; Lemons, Hannah; Elias x Ferguson; 7 Jan 1800

Hufstetler (Huffstotler), Jacob; Summy, Polly; Jacob ·Carpenter; 16 Jan 1806; Lwn Henderson

Hufstetler, John; Mooney, Jane; Samuel P Wilson; __ Oct 1833

Huggin (Hoggins), John A; Fisher, Catharine; Stephen Fisher; 21 Dec 1839; H Cansler

Huggins (Hugins), James; Bennet, Mariah; Stacey Liming (?); 5 Feb 1807; Betsey Henderson

Huggins, M H; Stroup, Nancy Jane; J A Kids; 9 Sep 1866; Philip Ballard; M same date by James M Kids JP

Huggins, William; Gilleland, Frances; John Henderson; 14 Jun 1796

Huggins, William; Espie, Martha; Logan Henderson; 28 Aug 1806; Lwn Henderson

Huit (Hewet), David; Summit, Nancy; Lewis Hewet (Ger Lutwig Hiut); 20 Feb 1830; V McBee

Huit (Hewit), Henry; Summet, Catherine; Lewis Hewet (Ger Lutwig Huet); 21 Oct 1817; V McBee

Huit (Hewet or Huvet), Joseph; Gross, Tenea; Jacob Reinhardt; 4 Mar 1822; V McBee

Huit (Hewit), Lewis (Jr); Lutz, Sally; Lewis Hewit Sr (Ger Lutwig Huit, or Heuit); 13 Jan 1814; V McBee

Huit, Moses M; Fry, Rhody; Absalom Miller; 12 Sep 1837; M W Abernathy

Huit (Hewet), Solomon; Berry, Barbara; Daniel Diets (Dietz); 16 Dec 1829; Luther M McBee

Huitt, Lewis (Ger Lutwig Huit); Deits, Margarett; John Hoke; 19 Nov 1816; James T Alexander

Hulbard (Hubbard), Isaac; Wowicks (?), Susanah; James Rhonay; 12 Mar 1825; Jas T Alexander

Hulbert (Hubard), Mathew x; Brilhart, Elizabeth; James Rhonay; 5 May 1825; M Hull JP

Hull, Benjamin (Jr) x; Williams, Amy; Abner Hull; 8 May 1812; Lwn Henderson

Hull, Benjamin x; Stacia (?), Selina; George x Wacaster; 23 Sep 1823; M Hull JP

Hull, Comoder (Comadore) P x; Gilbert, Mary Ann; John F Coon; 9 Mar 1858; W R Clark; M 16 Mar 1858 by Logan H Lowrance JP

Hull, Daniel x; Helms, Barbara; John x Stamey; 20 Jul 1824; Jas T Alexander

Hull, Daniel x; Farmer, Sarah; William Leonard, Comadore x Hull; 17 Sep 1858; W R Clark; M 18 Sep 1858 by Logan H Lowrance JP

Hull, E M; Pendleton, Margaret; B M Massagee; 27 Oct 1865; A S Haynes CCC; M 29 Oct 1865 by _____

Hull, John; Smith, Margaret; P W Carpenter; 31 Oct 1865; A S Haynes Cty Ct Clk; M 2 Nov 1865 by P Carpenter JP

Hull (or Hall), Levi x; Reinhardt, Sally; George Coon (Koon); 1 Nov 1834; G Hoke

Hull, M M; Hafner, Caroline C; W M Hull; 13 Feb 1867; W R Clark CC; M 14 Feb 1867 by H A T Harris

Hull, Major; Gross, Margaret; Jacob Ramsour; 9 Feb 1824; V McBee

Hull, Major; Smith, Margarett; George H Heafner (Heavner); 15 Oct 1858; Logan H Lowrance; M same date by Logan H Lowrance JP

Hull, Miles O; Carpenter, Mary; Elias Hull; 31 Jan 1860; W R Clark; M 3 Feb 1860 by J P Carpenter Esquire

Hull, Richard; Jeams, Catherine; John x Horse; 2 Nov 1805; Wm Scott·

Hull, William; Cline, Catherine; Benjamin x Hull; 8 Nov 1814; Saml Wilson

Hull, William; James, Barbary; Abram Wacaster; 31 Mar 1832; Vardry McBee

Hull, William x; Davis, Rachel; John Williams; 25 Feb 1864; David Boiles JP; M same date by David Boiles JP

Hullender (Hullander), Christopher; Kizer, Rebeccah; (Ger) Heinrich Kaiser; 28 Feb 1837

Hullet, Calep x; Brown, Marget; Peter Beam; 11 Mar 1845; David Crouse, John Gardiner

67

Hullet, John x; Dyer, Polley; David Eaker; 2 Nov 1825; V McBee

Hullet, Moses; Smith, Barbra; _____; 11 Dec 1856; J A Huss Clerk; M same date by David Williams JP; L and C, no B

Hullit (Hullet), Peter x; Morrison, Mary; William Gales (or Giles); 9 Jun 1842; David Crouse

Humphrey, Daniel x; Cistler, Malinda; James E Witherspoon; 27 Mar 1836; Jonathan Bost; Ambiguous

Humphreys, Daniel x; Long, Elizabeth; Pelham x Yarboro; 21 Jul 1835; M W Abernathy

Humphreys, James x; Pope, Julia; William x Humphreys; 18 Feb 1867; "Freed Men"; M 26 Feb 1867 by R N Davis Minister

Humphreys, Richard R x; Wallace, Ann; Isaac M'Kee; 1 Nov 1821; Saml M'Kee

Humphry, William; Beard, Harriet; William Murrel (Murrill); 10 Dec 1842; H Cansler

Hunley, P F; Johnston, M A (M E); James F Johnston; 5 Nov 1859; M 8 Nov 1859 by R H Morrison (MG)

Hunley, Richard R; Johnston, Martha; Robert E Johnston; 10 Jul 1847; Robt Williamson

Hunly (Hunley), Ransom G; Forney, Caroline M; John D Hoke; 21 Oct 1824; Al____ Brevard

Hunsecker, David; Barringer, Polly; Miles W Abernathy; 29 May 1835

Hunsecker (Hunsucker), Jacob; Killian, Salley M; John Butts; 18 Sep 1820; V McBee

Hunsicker, John (Ger Johannes Hun_____); Sigman, Polly; Jacob Hunsicker; 11 Apl 1824; Fr Hoke JP

Hunsicker, Joseph (Ger same); Yont, Polly; John Yount (Yont); 14 Mar 1824; Fr Hoke

Hunsuker (Hunsecker), John; Gross, Lydia; Electious Conner (Connor); 15 Jan 1829

Hunt, George L; Carpenter, Sarah Ann; _____; 1 Dec 1853; J A Huss; M 3 Dec 1853 by David Crouse JP

Hunt, John x; Rouse, Catherine; Wm (?) Wilson; 9 Jun 1812; Saml Wilson Dp C

Hunt, Noah; Reinhardt, Anna; William _____; 15 Feb 1832; L McBee

Hunter, Cyrus L; Forney, Sophia G; Sydney J Harris; 15 Jan 1834 .

Hunter, Cyrus L (Dr); Lyman, Catharine F; J F Johnston; 19 May 1851; M 20 May 1851 by R H Morrison

Hunter, George R; Ferguson, Ann; Charles L Torrence; 4 Aug 1826; V McBee

Hunter, Michael; Turpin, Delphy Taylor; Isaac Henry; 4 Jul 1808; Danl Forney; endorsed "Henry Hunter M Bond"

Huntley, Haywood x; Ikerd, Saly; David x Killian; 31 Jul 1836; Abel H Shuford

Huntley (Huntly), Isaac; Bailey, Nancy; Miles Abernathy; 25 Oct 1825; V McBee

Hurbenson (Harberson), George T; Yount, Elizabeth; Henry Miller; 8 Apl 1830; Miles W Abernathy

Huskins, Robert x; Plott, Katharine; James x Abernathy; 23 Sep 1823; Jas T Alexander

Huskins, William x; Club, Elizabeth; David x Club; 15 Jan 1823; V McBee

Husky, Jesse x; Champin, Polley; John x Wood; 16 Feb 1811; Da__d Warlick

Huson, George x; Skidmore, Ann; _____; 1818; (N)

Huson, John; Damron, Nancy; David Dameron (Damron); 22 Sep 1803; Jonn Greaves DCC

Huss, Henry; Houser, Mary E; Henry Houser; 7 Oct 1865; A S Haynes CCC; M 11 Oct 1865 by P Carpenter JP

Huss, John A; McLerd (McClurd), Mary A; H C Hamilton; 23 Dec 1856; W R Clark; M same date by F J Jetton

Huss, P M; Wilson, E M; J P Anthony; 28 Nov 1866; W R Clark CC; M 1 Dec 1866 by H A T Harris

Hussey, Josiah; Garner, Rebecca; Budde Wheeler; 13 Apl 1797

Hutchason (Hutchinson), John; Roberts, Susannah; George Kiser (Kyser); 10 May 1836; John B Harry

Hutchison, James; Hill, P C; Jos D Shull; 22 Dec 1859; W R Clark .

Hutchison, Thomas L; Negle, Esther; Matthew Neagle; 31 Mar 1829; Isaac Holland

Hutson, Daniel; Rocket, Jane; John Mosteller; 18 Apl 1834; Miles W Abernathy

Hutson (Hudson), Matthew; Cline, Catharine; John Mosteller (Mausteller); 8 Mar 1832; J T Alexander

Huver (Hoover), Levi; Lutz, Sally; David Warlick; 5 Dec 1826; J T Alexander

Huver (Hoover), Philip; Gross, Margaret; Joseph Clay; 12 Sep 1833; V McBee

Iceenhour, John x; Baley, Sarah; George Snider; 3 Feb 1811; Jesse Perkins; Uncertain

Ikerd, Anthony; Finger, Anna; Silas Bost; 30 Dec 1835; M W Abernathy

Ikerd, Daniel x; Nail, Barbara; John Hed; 1 Dec 1820; V McBee

Ikerd, David x; Bysinger, Sarah; John Henry Bisener (Bysinger); 14 Dec 1812
Ikerd, George A; Finger, Susanah; Jacob Seapaugh (Seaback); 8 Apl 1829; V McBee
Ikerd (Eikerd), Henry; Miller, Elisabeth; Henry Yount; 19 Jul 1823; Mic Cline
Ikerd (Eikerd), Phillip; Lutz, Susy; (Ger) Jonnes Eigardt; 21 Nov 1809
Ingle, Adam; Keener, Sally; Daniel Goodson; 4 May 1857; Elisha Saunders; M 9 Jun
    1857 by Elisha Saunders JP
Ingle, David x; Abernathy, Caroline; A G Harrill (Harrell); 18 Oct 1856; W R Clark;
    M 19 Oct 1856 by F J Jetton JP
Ingle, Ephraim x; Clemmer, Martha; Levi Baker; 15 Mar 1861; W R Clark; M 17 Mar
    1861 by L D Childs JP
Ingle, Jacob x; Childers, Fanny; Gilbert Milligan; 22 Apl 1828; J T Alexander
Ingle, Levi x; Liggins (Leggins), Mary; John Lefever; 24 Jul 1857; W R Clark;
    M 24 (or 29) Jul 1857 by F J Jetton JP
Ingle, Martin x; Troutman, Elisabeth; Samuel Zimmerman (?); 5 Sep 1798
Ingle, Michael; Troughbach, Betcy; Andrew x Ingle; 20 Dec 1812; Vardry McBee
Ingle, Michael x (son of Martin); Stiles, Rebeckah; Green x Burk; 6 May 1824;
    V McBee
Ingle, Michael x; Sronce, Sarah; John Kistler; 26 Oct 1852; V A McBee
Ingol, Peter x; Wilson, Margaret; John x Baker; 3 (or 30 or 31) Dec 1843; A J Cansler
Ingold, Henry; Henkel, Leah; J A (Anthony) Mose; 26 Feb 1833; M W Abernathy
Ingold, Jonathan; Michael, Mary; Daniel Blackburn; 13 Jan 1824; Jas T Alexander
Ingram, John x; Fronabarger, Lydia; Hiram W Abernathy; 6 Jun 1846; R Williamson
Irby, Joshua M; Jones, Mary H; Thomas W Price; 5 Jul 1821; I Holland JP
Irvin (Ervin), David; White, Sarah ; Elias White; 19 Jan 1809; Joseph Fisher
Irwin see Erwin
Irwin, James P; Morrison, Harriet; S Nye Hutchison (Hutchinson); 21 Nov 1849;
    Sam J Lewis (?)
Isaac, Jacob x; Shook, Nancy; A H S Shuford (Andrew Shuford); 20 Mar 1836;
    Fr Hoke JP
Isacks, Jacob x; Deal, Barbary; Peter x Deal; 24 Aug 1815; Jo Lourance for Vardry
    McBee
Iseler, Adam x; Cills, Martha; John x Miller; 2 Sep 1793; Joseph Steel
Isenhower (Eisenhower), Henry; Stine, Sally; Timothy Moser (Mossar); 2 Nov 1840;
    Fr Hoke JP
Isenhower, Jacob; Hunsuker, Elizabeth; Peter Little; 26 Sep 1839; John Yount JP
Isenhower, Martin; Moratz, Margred; Davold Grund; 22 Aug 1831; Fr Hoke JP
Ivester, Hugh x; Lingerfelt, Eve; Jacob Lingerfelt (Ger Lingenfeld); 30 Nov 1820;
    V McBee
Ivester, John x; Helms, Elizabeth; John x Helms; 14 Jul 1817; V McBee
Ivins, David; _____; Andrew Bomgarner; 12 Apl 1821; Jas Hanes JP

Jack, Joseph; Ewart, Margaret; John Hill, James Johnston; 24 Oct 1774; John
    Kirkconnell
Jackson, Abner (sig by R P); Hill, Jane; Robert Patterson; 25 Feb 1812; Lwn
    Henderson
Jackson, Elias M; Patterson, Polly; James D Hill; 7 Sep 1820; I Holland for
    V McBee CCC
Jackson, John; Vanhorn, Sary; Isaac Vanhorn; 18 May 1809; Ligt Williams JP
Jackson, T J (Maj); Morrison, Mary Anna; Wm W Morrison; 14 Jul 1857; M 16 Jul
    1857 by Drury Lacy
Jacobes, Adam x; Sebach, Elisebeth; (Ger) Peter Jacobs; 24 Apl 1804; Peter Hoyl JP
Jacobs, Daniel M; Johnson, Martha M; W R Edwards; 19 Apl 1855; J A Huss;
    M 22 Apl 1855 by Samuel Lander (MG)
Jacobs, Michael; Havner, Nancy; James Spratt; 31 May 1823; Jas T Alexander
James, Augustus P; McCulloh, Margaret; Warren Gheen; 11 Jun 1852; Robt William-
    son; M 13 Jun 1852 by Rev R N Davis
James, Benjamin; Devebaugh, Uly; James James; 27 Dec 1814; V McBee
James, James (Jimmey); Tritt, Molley; Henrey Tritt (Ger Henrich Tritt); 14 Jul
    1811; Peter Little
James, James; Stewinter, Margaret; William x Bird; 20 Apl 1819; James T Alexander
James, Thomas; Allen, Rachel; John Allen; 10 Mar 1807; Lwn Henderson
James, William x; Airwood, Ann; James x James; 2 Dec 1784; Joseph Steel
Janes, John P; Boggs, Rebecca J; William Boggs; 3 Dec 1840; M Hull JP
Janes (Geanes), Thomas; Baggs, Beackey, Clark; James Baggs; 27 Jan 1814; Saml
    Wilson

69

Jarmon, William; Scott, Mary D; Robert Johnston; 9 Jul 1823; Jas T Alexander
Jarret, Absalom; Sherman (or Shereman), Polly; Jacob Seagle; 26 Feb 1827; V McBee
Jarret, Jonas; Jarret, Catherine; George Loer (Ger Georg Lehr or Lohr); 3 Sep 1819
Jarrett, Daniel; Whitner, Anna M; John J Reinhardt (Jacob Reinhardt); 20 Apl 1841;
L E Thompson
Jarrett, Elias; Launby (?), Fanny; James T Alexander; 6 Mar 1827; Charles __
Torrence
Jarrett, (or Jarrell), George; Zimmerman, Elizabeth; John Schenck; 12 Jan 1832;
L McBee
Jarrett, Jacob; Mauney, Mary; Wm H Michal; 17 May 1841; H Cansler
Jarrett, John; Shufford, Claressy; Solomon Warlick; 15 Aug 1817; V McBee
Jarrett, John; Heltebrand, Elizabeth; George Lowe (Ger Georg Lohr); 26 Jul 1819;
V McBee
Jarrett, Samuel; Zimmerman, Clary L; John Motz; 8 Oct 1834; M W Abernathy
Jeffres, Thomas x; Helms, Anne; John x Helms; 14 Jul 1817; V McBee
Jenkins, Aron; Jenkins, Mary; David Jenkins; 30 Jun 1821; V McBee
Jenkins, Ben J x; Rhodes, Fanny; Berryman x Jenkins; 27 May 1837; M W Abernathy
Jenkins, Benjamin x; Helton (or Hilton), Sarah Ann; Eli Clemmer; 27 Nov 1824
Jenkins (Jinkins), Benjamin; Rhyne, Anny; Reuben Jenkins (Jinkins); 4 Aug 1825
Jenkins, Benjamin; Cathey, Margaret; Sedrach Jenkins; 24 Jul 1832; B T Kirby;
Ambiguous
Jenkins, Berryman x; Clemor, Salena; Lewis x Cloninger; 25 Jul 1837; Jacob Plonk JP
Jenkins, David; Carpenter, Nancy; Abraham Mauney; 7 Oct 1811; Lwn Henderson
Jenkins, David x; Hogans, Elizabeth; Solomon ·x Totherow; 19 Feb 1819; James T
Alexander
Jenkins, David; Perkins, Susannah; Jonathan Rhyne; 4 Oct 1830; Eli Hoyl
Jenkins, Edward x; Smith (?), Peggy; Benjamin Ravan (Revan), 12 Aug 1797
Jenkins, Harison; Kizer, Sally; Benjamin Jenkins; 22 Jul 1822; I Holland for
Vardry McBee
Jenkins (Jinkins), Hugh; Campbell, Jenny; Joseph B Campbell; 1 Nov 1809; Danl M
Forney
Jenkins, Hugh; Rhyne, Margaret; Lewis Clemmer; 20 Apl 1813;· James T Alexander
Jenkins (Jinkins), Hugh; Best, Susana; Christen Best; 25 Jun 1829; Jno Blackwood Esq
Jenkins, James; Huffman, Susanah; William McAlister (McCollister); 30 Aug 1817
Jenkins (Jinkins), James C; Schenck, Barbara; W H Alexander; 20 Dec 1848; Robt
Williamson
Jenkins (Jinkins), John; Whiteside, Kathrine; Benjamin Jenkins (Jinkins); 7 Sep
1831; Jno Blackwood Esqr
Jenkins, Joseph; Mauney, Margaret; David Wells; 30 Jul 1816; V McBee
Jenkins (Jenkings), Joseph M; Mooney, Anna; Allen x Baker; 24 Oct 1836; J A
Ramsour DCC
Jenkins, Reuben (Jr); Holland, Margret; Reuben Jenkins Sr; 5 Nov 1827; Isaac
Holland
Jenkins, Samuel; Frost, Ica; Robert x Frost; 17 Dec 1801; Jno Dickson
Jenkins, Smith; Huffstetler, Margret; Eli Clemmer; 22 Jan 1825; Isaac Holland
Jenkins (Jinkens), Tilman x; Clemmer, Margred; Aron Jenkins; 17 Apl 1834; Jacob
Plonk JP
Jenkins, William; Ross, Mary; Elias Blott (Plott); 23 Jul 1812; Jesse Perkins JP
Jenkins, William; Eaker, Lavinia; Jacob Mauney; 1 Jan 1842; Eli Hoyl
Jenks, O B; Hull, Mary Ann; W A Thompson; 14 Jan 1858; M 21 Jan 1858 by
Wade Hill (MG)
Jetton, B M; Hoke, Anthea; Jacob F Dailey; 12 Feb 1840; H Cansler
Jetton, F J; Seagle, Sarah Ann; Alexander Moore; 5 Apl 1843; H Cansler
Jinkens (Jinkins), Wiatt (Wyatt); Smith, Elizabeth; John Jinkins; 1 Mar 1799;
Jonn Greaves
Jinkins, Benjamin; Miller, Nancy; Edward Baker; 12 Sep 1818; V McBee
Jinkins, Edward; Hamilton, Lucy; William Perkins; 16 Jan 1798; Jonn Greaves
Jinkins, Elijah; Wells, Polly; James Wells; 25 May 1795; Joseph Dickson
Jinkins, James; Massey, Polley; John Massey; 4 Apl 1811; Thos Ferguson
Jinkins, Jesse x; Revan, Milley; Benjamin Reeven; 30 Nov 1796
Jinkins, Jinkey (Jinkin); Beam, Anna; Joseph x Baker; 1 Oct 1800; John Crouse JP
Jinkins (Jenkins), Jinkey; Wells, Nancy; Joel Darnall (Darnell); 4 May 1815;
I Holland for Vardry McBee CCC
Jinkins, Tilman x; Francis, Lucinda; Robert Clark; 26 Dec 1832; B T Kirby;
Ambiguous
Jinkins, William x; Mauney. Catherine; Peter Eaker (Ger Peter Eker); 7 Jul 1801

70

Johnson, A L; Abernathy, Elizabeth; Geo F Johnson; 22 Apl 1839; L E Thompson
Johnson, Alexander; Scott, Nancey; _____; 16 Aug 1784
Johnson, Alexander x (Freedman); Sherrill, Nancy (Freedwoman); Frank x Bird
   (Freedman); 24 Dec 1866; H Asbury for W R Clark Cl Cty
Johnson, Allen; Aker, Hannah; John Hostetter (Mausteller); 14 Apl 1829; J T
   Alexander
Johnson, Andrew; Rutledge, Salley; George Rutledge; 23 Sep 1811; Lwn Henderson
Johnson, Benjamin; Johnston, Sarah A; Moses J B Hayes; 26 Nov 1828; V McBee
Johnson (Johnston), Benjamin S; Dettor, Barbara; Joseph E Bell; 19 Apl 1825
Johnson, Daniel P; Moore, Selina; B M Collins; 23 Jan 1835; ____ Collins
Johnson (Johnston), David; Orr, Rachel; Jesse _____, Jacob Shuf____; _____ 1804;
   · Peter Hoyl
Johnson, Eli; Bandy, Catherine; William Putman; 14 Apl 1833; V McBee
Johnson (Jonson), Henry; Yong, Mary C; A A Tallant (And Talent); 6 Feb 1859;
   David Williams; M same date by David Williams JP; L shows groom Henry
   Thompson
Johnson, Hiram; Johnson, Elizabeth; James Johnson; 28 Mar 1836; John B Harry
Johnson, John; Alexander, Peggy; Joshua x Roberts; 6 Jul 1784
Johnson, John x; Dellinger, Peggy; Joseph x Dellinger; 16 Feb 1815; V McBee
Johnson, John; Martin, Mary; Solomon Speegle (Speagle); 14 Dec 1837; H Cansler
Johnson (Johnston), Joseph; Boyls, Hannah; John Brindal (Ger Johannes Brendel);
   29 May 1810
Johnson, Joseph; Loois, Patsey; Richard x Johnson; 25 Dec 1817; Daniel Lutz JP
Johnson (Johnston), Joseph; Hutson, Ibby; Joseph Johnson (Johnston); 26 Dec
   1823; Jas T Alexander
Johnson (Johnston), Joseph; Hedrick, Susannah; Timothy Moser; 4 Mar 1843;
   Wm Herman JP
Johnson, Joseph x; Rankin, Susan; Alexander x Graham; 26 Dec 1866; R Nixon JP;
   M same date by R Nixon JP; "Colored Man and Woman"
Johnson, Leander R (of Iredell Co); Sigman, Polly; Henry Sigman; 27 Sep 1837;
   Mic Cline
Johnson, Richard x; Akerd, Elizabeth; John Mosteller (Moseteller); 17 Jan 1833;
   Abel Shuford
Johnson (Johnston), Robert; Moore, Anna; Joseph Johnson (Johnston); 13 Nov 1788;
   Joseph Steel
Johnson, Sankey T; Jones, Rebecca P; Hugh I Johnson; 22 Nov 1825; J T Alexander
Johnson, William x; Gilbert, Barbara; Conrad x Gilbert; 8 Oct 1805; Lwn Henderson
Johnson, William; Alexander, Nancy; _____; 22 Aug 1866; R Nixon JP; Acknowl-
   edgment of marriage as of 24 Dec 1857
Johnson, William B; Carpenter, Elizabeth; Peter x Carpenter; 30 Jun 1834; Miles W
   Abernathy Clk
Johnston, Alexander; Wethers, Leeanna; John Wethers; 16 Aug 1779; Adam Baird
Johnston, Elijah; Hide, Margret; Joseph Johnson; No date (end 1801); Ligt
   Williams JP
Johnston, G H (Johnson, Henry); Kincaid, Martha S; James L (James F) Clark;
   23 Nov 1843
Johnston (Jonston), Henry; Groves, Sarah; William Groves; 24 Nov 1831; Isaac
   Holland
Johnston, James; Martin, Rachel; James Martin; 18 Mar 1805; Lwn Henderson
Johnston, Jesse x; Brown, Annie; James x Johnston, Josiah Bradshaw (Bradshe),
   John x Parr; 18 Sep 1798; J Graham
Johnston, John; Thompson, Rachel; John Thompson; 22 Jan 1787
Johnston (Jonston), John; Groves, Elizebeth; John Glenn (Glen); 24 Nov 1831;
   Isaac Holland
Johnston, John C; Baldwin, Winney Perry; Sqire x Baldwin; 3 Jan 1840; Daniel
   Hoffman JP
Johnston, Lewis; Brown, Sareth; Isaac Justice, George x Miller; 11 Jun 1798
Johnston, Richard x; Davis, Sary; Elijah Johnson (Johnston); 4 Mar 1800; Ligt
   Williams JP
Johnston, Richard; Abernathy, Susana; James Johnson (Johnston); 5 Sep 1805;
   Phil Whitener
Johnston, Robert; McCord, Mary; Robert McCord; 29 Aug 1785; Elizabeth Dickson
Johnston, Robert; Reed, Mary; David Ramsour; 21 Apl 1807; M Chambers
Johnston (Johnson), Robert; Abernathy, Dicey; Lawson Henderson; 31 Jul 1827;
   S L McBee
Johnston, Robert E; Shuford, M Caroline; J R Johnston; 26 Jul 1853; M 27 Jul
   1853 by R N Davis (MG)

Johnston, Sidney X (or H); Connor, Harriet K; William (Wm W) Williamson; 9 Sep 1835; Miles W Abernathy
Johnston, Wilis x (freedman); Suford, Jane I (freedwoman); Middleton x Shuford (freedman); 3 Oct 1867; M same date by J Finger
Johnston, William; Forney, Nancy; Rufus Reid; 3 Oct 1820
Jonas, Abel; Sane, Catharine; Joseph Boggs; 15 Feb 1838; M Hull JP
Jonas, Daniel; Hanks, Adaline; Vincent Avery; 20 Feb 1849; Robt Williamson
Jonas, Henry; Bangle, Elizabeth; Wm Hull; 31 Jan 1839; M Hull JP
Jonas, John x; Loore, Fanney; George Siegel (Seagel); 30 Aug 1810; Ligt Williams JP
Jones, Alexander; Robinson, Leah; Philip Bennick; 6 Sep 1831; J T Alexander
Jones, Allen; Lee, Jincy; Hiram Jones; 20 Apl 1830; V McBee
Jones, Charles; Horton, Elisabeth; John x Weathers; 7 Nov 1797; Jo Dickson
Jones, Elisha; Perkins, Betsey; George Cathey; 5 Dec 1794; Jo Dickson
Jones, Hiram; Kale, Martha; George Broun; 27 Jul 1827; V McBee
Jones, Isaac; Spencer, Eliza Clark; John Bynum; 31 Aug 1814; Jas Taylor Alexander
Jones, Isom I (or J); Hill, Mary C; Alexander __ Hill; 12 Oct 1845; Wm J Wilson; M 23 Oct 1845
Jones, James; Robinson, Elizabeth; Mitchel Sherrill; 15 Jul 1833; L McBee
Jones, Miles; _____; John Litten; ____ 183__
Jones(James), Strawden; Edwards, Susana; Hensy (Henasey) Gant; 19 Feb 1835; Nath Edwards
Jones, Talbert; Mellon, Jane M; George E Mellon; 17 Dec 1822; Isaac Holland
Jones, William x; Copeland, Lucy; Daniel x Copeland; 22 Sep 1798; Jno Dickson
Jones, William; White, Anna; Charles Edwards; 20 Jul 1825; J T Alexander
Jonston (Johnson), Larkin; Marritt, Polley; William Childers; 28 Apl 1814; Jesse Perkins; M same date
Jonston, William x; Grisom, Martha F; William R Gaston (Gastin); 7 Jan 1836; J G Hand
Jordan, Harry H (S); Martin, Elizabeth; J W Martin; 1 Mar 1860; W R Clark
Jordan, Robert; Alexander, Mary; William Alexander; 30 Aug 1796; Jno M Dickson
Jordon (Jorden), Jesse; Havener, Elizabeth; Charles Bennett; 13 May 1817; V McBee
Julian, Baily F; Sherrill, Roana E; Philip Ramsaur (Ramsour); 15 Nov 1832; J T Alexander
Justice, Abraham; Holly, Anna; Joshua Robinson, Jesse Robinson; 5 Aug 1809; Mic Cline
Justice, Alex; Green, Sidney E; B S Guion; 10 May 1864; M 11 May 1864 by W R Wetmore Rector St Luke's Ch
Justice, Moses x; Tritt, Elizebeth; Henry x Tritt, Andrew x Shook; 27 Mar 1814; Peter Little
Justice, Peter; Dasey, Nancy; Griffith Williams; 28 Dec 1786; Joseph Steel

Kale, Absalom; Edwards, Sally; George Gilleland; 22 Dec 1825; J T Alexander
Kale, Lanson; Janes, Levina; Absalom Kale; 24 Aug 1839; J T Alexander
Kale, Polser x; Edwards, Ruth; Jacob Fry; 30 Oct 1827; Miles W Abernathy JP
Kannedy (Kanneday), Gilbert; Dickson, Elizabeth; Jas Wright; __ Dec 1810; Robt Winter
Karr (Kerr), Robert; Like, Suckey; _____; 30 Apl 1798
Kayler, Eli; Howard, Elizabeth; J D Herman; 6 Aug 1838; Wm Herman JP
Kayler, Levi A; Burch, Melvina L (A); ____ (I W?) Moore; 15 Oct 1857; __ Asbury; M same date by H Asbury MG
Kayler, Peter C; Martin, Mahala; Henry Benfield; 31 Dec 1835; Mic Cline
Keen, Aldridge; Parish, Elizabeth; Wilson x Turbyfill; 5 Feb 1823; V McBee
Keen, James; Hooper, Annie M; Lindsey C Weaver; 2 May 1827; Philip Weaver
Keene, James x; Baker, Elisabeth; Abner x Baker; 13 Mar 1787; Joseph Steel
Keene, James x; Matthews, Sarah; John x Matthews; No date; Joseph Steel
Keener, Abraham; Justice, Anna; Michael x Keener; 6 May 1818; V McBee
Keener (Keaner), Abraham; Ingle, Catharine; Peter Srum; 13 Jan 1834; M W Abernathy
Keener, Adam x; Finger, Mary; John x Keener; 2 Aug 1806; Jas McEwin
Keener, Andrew x; Abernathy, Charity; John D Hoke; 11 May 1832; L McBee
Keener, Cephas; Hallman, Isabella; Benjamin Beel (Beal); 23 Feb 1858; W R Clark; M 25 Feb 1858 by D Crooks (MG)
Keener, Daniel; Sulivan, Mariah; Lyman Woodford; 21 Aug 1837; J A Ramsour DC
Keener, David x; Bomgarner, Betcy; Michael x Keener; 27 Jan 1817; V McBee
Keener, David x; Beal, Elizabeth J; Daniel Shrum; 8 Oct 1866; W R Clark CC; M 11 Nov 1866 by H A T Harris

72

Keener, Ephraim; Keever (Keener), Harriet; George Keener; 22 Jan 1852; Elisha Saunders; M same date by Elisha Saunders JP
Keener, Henry; Sraunce, Elizabeth; Jacob x Keener; 10 Feb 1818; James T Alexander
Keener, Henry; Keener, Linny; Ephraim Keener; 29 Dec 1850; Elisha Saunders
Keener, Jacob x; Troutman, Nancy; Nancy x Engle; 2 Sep 1805; Wm Scott
Keener, John x; Keller (or Killen), Elizabeth; Michael x Keener; 2 Dec 1805; Wm Scott
Keener, John x; Engle, Barbera; David x Keener; 20 Nov 1827; V McBee
Keener, John; Ingle, Frances; Marcus Beel; 2 Jan 1840; H Cansler
Keener, John Jr x; Ingle, Hannah; John x Keener Sr; 15 Feb 1808; Max Chambers
Keener, Lawson W; Goodson, Winny; Henry Keener; 27 Jul 1853; Elisha Saunders; M same date by Elisha Saunders JP
Keener, Levi; Keener, Elizabeth; P S Kistler; 19 Mar 1850; Robt Williamson
Keener, Lewis; Summerow, Ann; Daniel Keener; 26 Sep 1840; H Cansler
Keener, Martin x; Barnes, Sarah; (Ger) Johannes Ebli; 2 Jan 1802; Jno Dickson
Keener, Martin x; Tetherro, Hannah; Martin x Keener; 18 Sep 1804; John Dickson
Keener, Martin x (son Jno); Panter, Patsy; Abraham Keener; 28 Jan 1827; V McBee
Keener, Michael x; Bains (Barns), Mary; John x Keener; 24 Mar 1805; Wm Scott
Keener, Michael x; Srum, Catharine; Daniel x Srum; 20 Nov 1819; Jas T Alexander
Keener, Michael; Ingle, Mary; David _____ (torn); 6 Feb 1832; L McBee
Keener (Kener), Moses; Drum, Elisabeth; Jacob x Kener; 18 May 1826
Keener, Peter; Keener, Fanny; Michael Keener; 7 Mar 1848; Robt Williamson
Keener, Simon; Weathers, Sarah Ann; Milton Goodson; 13 Jul 1861; Elisha Saunders; M 21 Jul 1861 by Elisha Saunders JP
Keepers, William; Seeford (or Suford), Caty; Benjamin x Bell (Beele); 26 Nov 1800; Ambiguous
Keever, David; Goodson, Milly; John A Thompson; 22 Sep 1858; W R Clark; M 23 Sep 1858 by H Asbury Mns
Keever, George x; White, Fanny; James Nance; 18 Nov 1830; Wm Little
Keever, Henry; Clippard, Sally; Henry Clippard; 22 Sep 1823; Jas T Alexander
Keever, Henry x; Stroup, Dinny; Benjamin Stroup; 9 (or 6) May 1831; L McBee
Keever (Keaver), Henry; Bradshaw, Melinda; B F Withers; 28 Feb 1854; W B Withers JP; M 29 Feb 1854 by J Lowe JP
Keever, Henry; Bynum, Belzora; Lauson Keener; 9 Jun 1860; W R Clark; M 10 Jun 1860 by Elisha Saunders JP
Keever (Keaver), James; Bradshaw, Mary; Matthew Fitzgarald; 25 Mar 1837; M W Abernathy
Keever, James; Goodson, Caroline; Emanuel Sifford; 6 May 1848; J Helderman
Keever, Lawson; Johnston, Malinda E; A L Ramsour; 28 Dec 1841
Keever, Thomas; Reel, Nancy; Daniel Gwaltney (Gaulteny); 20 Mar 1807; Lwn Henderson
Keever, Thomas; Lynch, Susan; John Rabb; 28 Aug 1849; Robt Williamson
Keever, William x; Pool, Anna M; William Pool; 14 Mar 1866; W R Clark; M 18 Mar 1866 by Jephthae Clark
Kellar, Alford x; Isenhower, Christeni; John x Kellar; 20 Mar 1837; Fr Hoke JP
Keller, Christian; Keller, Shusanah; Rudolph Conrad; 6 May 1788
Keller, Enuck; Clubb, Anney; John x Clubb; 16 Mar 1809; Jacob Forney; Ambiguous
Keller, James x; Dunbar, Rebecca; Isaiah x Abernathy; 6 Sep 1831; J T Alexander
Keller, Joseph x; Bently, Phoebe; Aquiller Keller; 12 Apl 1837
Kelley (Kelly), Charles; Mabray, Martha; John E Kelley (Kelly); 13 Nov 1826; Charles L Torrence
Kelley, Robert C; Davis, Patsey; Jacob Sronce (Scronce); 20 Jul 1824; Jas T Alexander
Kelly, Enoch x; Law, Dumeris; James x Kincaid; 12 Nov 1833; Miles W Abernathy
Kelly, Jackson (Andrew J); Mendenhall, Ann R; Charles B Kelley; 18 Apl 1840; H Cansler
Kelly, Wm F (Freeman); Howard, Rebecca; Thomas Thompson; 13 Apl 1852; Robt Williamson
Keneday, Isaac x; Seine, Elizabeth; Nathl Mechum; 7 Jul 1807; D M Forney
Kenedy, Robert x; Baldwin, Ann; Elisha Jones (Jr); 30 Mar 1837; Daniel Hoffman JP
Kenedy, Robert x; Hovis, Elenor; Elisha Jones; 23 Jan 1840; Daniel Hoffman JP
Kenipe, Jacob x; Blevins (or Beevins), Lowery (?); Joseph Brindal (Brindel); 5 Jul 1821; D Lutz JP
Kennedy (Keneday), Robert; Eaton, Polly; Ewarte (?) (Edward) Carral; 11 Nov 1809; Danl M Forney
Kennedy (Kenada), Thomas H (or W); Jenkins, Polley; Robert Adams; 25 Oct 1814; V McBee
Kennipe, John M x; Linn, Tempy; Jacob Smith; 14 Jul 1865; J C Jenkins; M 17 Jul 1865 by D A Haines JP

Kerk, William x; White, Bega; Cornelious x Conly; 9 (?) Jul 1794; Michl Eaker
Kerns, Washington x; Totherow, Christina; H D Rutter; 23 Sep 1865; A S Haynes CCC,
    J A Bisaner; M 24 Sep 1865 by R N Davis Minister
Kerr, James; Rozzel, Mary; John Little; 11 Jan 1830; Luther M McBee
Kerr, John; Martin, Margt; Joseph Martin; 8 Nov 1806; Jas McEwin
Kerr, Robert; Warlick, Barbara; James T Alexander; 7 May 1817; James M Erwin
Kerr, Robert B; Murphy, Sarah; William Martin; 31 Oct 1826; V McBee
Kerr, William; Dickson, Jain; David Dixon (Dickson); 20 Dec 1790; Jo Dickson
Keys, Hugh; Ernest (Earnest), Elisabeth; Frederick x Diker (Decker); 19 Apl 1803;
    John Moore
Kibler, Jacob; Wilson, Rebekah; John Butts; 2 Aug 1806; Js McEwin
Kids, Rufus; Delliner, Mary Ann; G P (J P) Keever; 6 Aug 1855
Kids, William; Childers, Mary; John x Kids; 26 Jun 1820; Jas T Alexander
Kiestler, Abram (Kistler, Abraham); Larnse, Margret; Peter Stamey; 21 Jun 1827;
    M Hull JP
Kiestler (Kistler), Joseph; Kistler, Elizabeth; J M Jacobs; 23 Nov 1835; Miles W
    Abernathy
Kilain (Killian), Jesse; Yoder, Lavina; Babel Whitener (Whitner); 3 Apl 1840;
    H Cansler
Kilian (Killian), Fedrick (Frederick); Richards, Polley; Valentine Richards; 11 Feb
    1817; V McBee
Killen, Robert x; McCorey, Betsey; Thomas x Parker; 10 Mar 1789
Killen, William x; Goodwin, Mary; Robert x Killen; 28 Aug 1788
Killian, Abel; Frye, Lavina; Paul Settlemyer; 9 Jan 1836; Mic Cline
Killian, Abram; Davis, Eleanor; Solomon x Shrum; 6 Nov 1834; G Hoke
Killian, Andrew; Moody, Susanah; Robert Blackburn; 9 Sep 1823; Jas T Alexander
Killian, Andrew x; Reece, Sophia; George Rees (Reece); 2 Jul 1837
Killian, Daniel; Baker, Osley; Samuel Killian; 15 Jan 1787
Killian, Daniel x; Gwaltney, Elizabeth; Nathan Galtney (Gwaltney); 28 Oct 1815;
    V McBee
Killian, David; Cline, Catharine; William Bost; 10 Jan 1809; Mic Cline
Killian, David x; Eikerd, Polly; John Killian (part Ger Johannes Killian); 18 Feb
    1817; Mic Cline
Killian, David x; Miller, Rachel; Henry Whitener; 27 Jan 1822; Mic Cline; "Rachel
    Miller formerly Rachel Whitener"
Killian, Ephraim; Killian, Mary; John Cody; 20 Aug 1835; M W Abernathy
Killian, Frederick; Gross, Anne (or Anie or Ame); Daniel Herman; 7 Sep 1822;
    Mic Cline
Killian, Frederick; Lutz, Cathrine; Elias Senter; 18 Dec 1826; Mic Cline
Killian, Henry; Rudissel, Polly; Lewis Haeffer (Hafer); 31 Jan 1809; H Y Webb
Killian, Henry; Clay, Juda; James T Alexander; 19 Feb 1842
Killian, Jacob B; Wells, Elizabeth; A A Brown; 13 Oct 1858; W R Clark; M same
    date by Saml Lander
Killian, John; Brown, Elizabeth; Michael Summerew; 3 Nov 1818; V McBee
Killian, John; Wingate, Martha M; H Asbury; 27 Aug 1858; Thomas H Asbury;
    M same date by H Asbury Mns
Killian, John A; Rudisill, Carrie; Cyrus J Frazer; 11 Sep 1860; W R Clark; M 13 Sep
    1860 by A J Fox MG
Killian, Joseph; Bolick, Regina; Casper Bolck (Bolick); 24 Feb 1824; Mic Cline
Killian, Levi E; Wilkerson, Ibby; Jacob Bisaner (Bysinger); 4 Jun 1836; M W
    Abernathy
Killian, Samuel; Hegar, Barbara; William x Hegar; 1784; Joseph Henry
Killian, Simon; Davis, Mary; Michael Finger; 29 Sep 1832; J T Alexander
Killian, William; Beal, Weaney; Jacob Shutley (Ger Jacob Schötle); 2 Jan 1787
Killian, William; Bost, Elizabeth; John Gross; 26 Dec 1816; Mic Cline
Killion (Kilyand), Jacob; Carpenter, Catherine; John x Smith; 24 Dec 1808; Jacob
    Reinhardt JP
Kimball, Green x; Cornelius, Judey; William Little (Lytle); 22 Jan 1800
Kincad(Kincaid), James x; Moody, Nancy; Jesse Wingate; 8 Jul 1815; James T
    Alexander
Kincad (Kinkaid), John; Black, Mary Ann; Robert Kincad (Kinkaid); 28 Apl 1787;
    Jos Henry
Kincaid (Kinkaid), David; Vaughen, Patsey; John Kincaid (Kinkaid); 30 Nov 1801;
    Jos Dickson
Kincaid, David; Pryor, Golsey; Isaac Lowe; 14 Nov 1827; V McBee
Kincaid, George W; Davis, Ann; John A (John W) Dellinger; 24 Dec 1833; Carlos
    Leonard

Kincaid, George W; Davis, Barbara; R E Burch; 2 Jan 1846

Kincaid (Kinkaid), Thomas; Hood, Jaine; Robt Kincaid; 21 Oct 1796; Jo Dickson

Kincaid, William; Davis, Elisabeth; G W Kincaid; 11 Jan 1853; John Davis; M same date (reads 1852) by R E Birch JP

Kincaide, David x; Hansel, Winey; J A Ramsour; 11 Jan 1855; J A Huss

Kinder, John; Abernathy, Eliza T; F M Abernathy; 21 Mar 1836; M W Abernathy

Kinder, Pcter; Crites, Elisabeth; Andw Hoyl, John Kinder; 20 Nov 1804; Jno Dickson

King, Adolphus E; Shrum (Srum), Caroline V; Edward Beatty; 2 May 1865; M same date by Elisha Saunders JP

King, Elijah; Deel, Catharina; William Deel (Ger Diehl); 4 May 1823; Fr Hoke

King, J C; Hull, M L; H A Chapman; 11 May 1866; M 14 May 1866 by David Boiles JP

King, John x; Duncan, Mary; John Buchanan (Bohannon); 10 Jul 1786; Jo Dickson

King, John D; Scarborough, Elizabeth; Jephthah Shaw; 31 May 1809; Maxl Chambers

King, William; Goldman, Hannah; Boston Best (Ger Bastian Best); 17 Sep 1789

King, William x; Hawkins (?), Elizabeth; Thomas x Wyett; 11 Feb 1799; William G Dickson

King, William x; Tetherow, Mary; Martin x Best; 14 Jun 1800; Jonn Greaves

King, William; McCorkle, Rebeckah; Thomas Wheeler; 7 Apl 1807

King, William; Proctor, Fanny; Philip H Bennick; 14 ____ 1832; V McBee

King, Wm; Litle (Lytle), Sarah; S A Burch; 14 Aug 1853; M same date by R E Birch JP

King, Wm O; Howard, Millie L; M L Hager; 22 Mar 1861; W R Clark; M 24 Mar 1861 by G W Ivy (MG)

Kingcade, David x; Hansell, B; Thomas Little; 29 Oct 1840

Kingery, Daniel; Harman, Elizabeth; Anthony Harman; 19 Apl 1780; Andw Neel CC

Kinters (or Winters), Saml E; Adams, Mary C; Joseph W Adams; 16 May 1837; John Dickson

Kirby, Augustus H; Durant, Mary E; H H Durant; 21 Sep 1852; M same date evening by Rev H H Durant

Kirby, Bolden T; Jones, Patsey; Elisha Jones; 7 Dec 1826

Kirksey, Albert; Keener, Isabella; P S Beal; 21 Mar 1867; W R Clark CC; M 24 Mar 1867 by Robt Blackburn JP

Kirksey, Franklin; Bandy, Eliza; William Miller; 21 Dec 1836; M Kirksey

Kirksey, William x; Beal, Elizabeth; Benjamin Beel (Benjamin Beal Jr); 18 Sep 1841

Kirksy (Kirksey), Matthew; Abernathy, Sarah; J F Crawford; 30 Aug 1855; J A Huss; M 6 Sep 1855 by J Helderman JP

Kirton, Joseph P; Norton, M; Allen Hamby; 9 Dec 1839

Kiser, Christopher x; Lingerfeldt, Sally; Daniel x Costner; 21 Jun 1821; James T Alexander

Kiser (or Kizer), Ephraim; Havner, Mary; E J Alexander; 11 Oct 1859; W R Clark; M same date by Philip Plonk

Kiser (Kizer), George; Wilson, Rebecca K; Ephraim Wilson; 24 Feb 1827; J T Alexander

Kiser, Henry x; Parker, Mary; William McClurg; 16 Jul 1808; Danl Forney

Kiser, John; Mosteller, Margaret; Michael Kiser; 11 Dec 1865; A S Haynes CCC; M 14 Dec 1865 by G L Hunt MG

Kiser (Kizer), Jonas; Dillen, Fanny; Caleb W Hoyl; 16 Jun 1835; Eli Hoyl

Kiser, Joseph x; Arley, Hanah; John x Kiser; 14 Apl 1808

Kiser (Kizer), Joseph x; Parker, Sally; Christy x Parker; 4 Feb 1810; Danl M Forney Cl

Kiser, Joseph x; Fronebarger, Anna; William Whitt; 10 Nov 1827; J T Alexander

Kiser (Kizer), Levi; Mauney, Mary; Isaac Kiser (Kizer); 7 Nov 1845

Kiser, Martin x; Ryne, Fanny; Samuel Kiser; 26 Feb 1825; Jas T Alexander

Kiser, Peter; Carpenter, Anna; James McKee; 29 Sep 1841; R Williamson

Kiser, Philip; Carpenter, Hannah; Martin Carpenter; 26 Oct 1830; J T Alexander

Kiser (Kizer), Philip; Carpenter, Louiza; John Carpenter; 2 Aug 1835; M W Abernathy

Kiser (Kizer), Samuel; Carpenter, Susanah; John Hooper; 10 Aug 1826; V McBee

Kistler, Aaron x; Shuford, Adaline; D Mullen (Mullins); 22 Sep 1852; V A McBee; M 23 (or 25) Sep 1852 by George Coon JP

Kistler, Elias x; Summet, Sarah; Joseph Houser; 22 Feb 1839; E Mauney

Kistler, J L; McCaslin, F A R; M Turbyfill; 21 Mar 1863; M 22 Mar 1863 by A J Fox MG

Kistler (Keistler), Jacob; Blackburn, Susannah; Samuel Lantz; 8 Feb 1809; Danl M Forney

75

Kistler, Jacob; Hiltebrand, Salley; Samuel Lantz; 7 Dec 1829; V McBee

Kistler, Jacob; Hoover, Elizabeth; Abel Hoyle; 2 Oct 1834; M W Abernathy

Kistler, Jacob x; Whetstone, Salina; John F Leonhardt (Lenhardt); 3 Jan 1842; H Cansler Clk

Kistler, James; Finger, Frances; Absalom Miller; 4 Feb 1836; M W Abernathy

Kistler, Noah x; Summit, Barbara; Joseph Kiestler (Kistler); 18 Sep 1841; R Williamson Jr DC

Kistler, Noah x; Leonhardt, Caroline; Levi Havner Jr; 10 May 1845; R Williamson Jr

Kistler (Keistler), Paul; Smith, Anny; Jacob Ramsour; 12 Jul 1810; Danl M Forney

Kistler, Peter S; Alexander, M J; W Williamson; 15 May 1855; J A Huss; M same date by Paul F Kistler MG

Kistler, Robert A; Johnston, Sarah Rose; C O Conley; 20 Mar 1854; J A Huss; M 28 Mar 1854 by P F Kistler MG

Kistler, Wm H; Seagle, Sarah J; P A Summey; 22 Jan 1867; P A Summey DC; M 23 Jan 1867 by A J Fox MG

Kizer, Christy x; Rutledge, Nancy; John x Kizer; 10 May 1832; L McBee

Kizer, Ezekias; Wier, Mary A; David Fronabarger; 22 Oct 1832; L McBee

Kizer (Kiser), George; Baxter, Susanah; Lawson Carpenter; 3 Oct 1836; J A Ramsour DC

Kizer, Henry (Ger Hennrich Kaiser); Carpenter, Peggy; John (Johnas) Carpenter; 28 Oct 1811; Elizabeth Henderson

Kizer, James; Carpenter, Catherine; Noah Carpenter; 25 Jan 1828; Luther McBee

Kizer, John x; Pasour, Polley; Henry Carpenter; 1 Jan 1822; V McBee

Kline (Cline), John; Moll, Catharine Jr; Henry Mull (Moll); 19 Sep 1816; Ligt Williams JP

Knight, John F; Chittam, Mary; William Ryndles; 19 Jan 1808; Joseph Neel

Knipe, Adam x; Bivings, Sally; Joseph x Bivings; 19 Jul 1820; James T Alexander, B James

Knipe, Christian x; Reinhardt, Polley; Jacob x Helm; 10 Nov 1816; V McBee

Knipe, Henry x; Hager, Sarah Caroline; John Bangle (Pangle); ____ 1833; Vardry McBee

Knipe, John x; Fulbright, Polly; George x Fulbright; 5 Jan 1832; P Stamey JP

Knipe, Joseph x; Massigee, Harriet; Joseph Houser; 27 Sep 1845; R Williamson

Knipe, Miles x; Jones, Ealizabeth; Daniel x Knipe; 28 Apl 1853; George Coon JP; M same date by George Coon JP

Knop, Mathew x; Benfield, Barbara; Henry Whitener; 17 Aug 1820; Phil Whitener JP

Knox, John; Bell, Jane; John McConnel (McConnor); 18 Sep 1827; J T Alexander

Knox, Robert; Wattson, Peggy B; Robert Finley; 8 Sep 1818; V McBee

Koons see Coon

Kruse (Kruise), Herman; Beckler, Mrs Catharine; John Hoke; 16 Sep 1842; H Cansler Clk

Kugan, John; Charlton, Agness; Thomas M'Gill; 28 Feb 1786 (or 1784); Jas Dickson

Kuykandall (Kuykendal), John; Hagarty, Nancey; Jacob x Shipman; 19 Jan 1779; Andrew Neel

Kuykendall (Kirkendall), Abram; Vinsant, Elisabeth; Jacob Vansant (Vinsant); 3 Jun 1790

Kuykendall, Jesse, Capt; Hall, Jeane; Nicholus x Chapman; 27 Jun 1802

Kuykendall, Samuel; Harris, Susanah; Thomas Hanks; 12 Feb 1791; Jo Dickson

Kyser, Christian x; Hullet, Susanna; Peter Eaker (Ger Peter ____); 14 Aug 1802

Kyser, John x; Arney, Caty; Joseph x Kyser; 31 Jul 1802; John Dickson

Kyser, Larans x; McKracken, Ruth; James Shearwood; 14 Jul 1793; Michael Eaker

Kysor, John x; Hullet, Sarah; Moses Wilson; 7 Jul 1803

Kysor, Philip x; McClurg, Ruth; Andrew x McClurg; 13 Aug 1804; John Dickson

Lackey, David; Boggs, Mary; Samuel x Lackey; 29 Aug 1843; H Cansler Clk

Lackey, Edward x; Gladen, Mary Ann; J A Ramsour; 18 Mar 1840; H Cansler

Lackey, James; Reep, Mary; N C Oliphant; 22 Sep 1845; R Williamson

Lackey, John; Wilson, Ann; B S Johnson; 21 Sep 1847; Robt Williamson

Lackey, Samuel x; Boggs, Elizabeth; Solomon Tuthuerrow (Tutherow); 8 May 1846; R Williamson C

Lackey, T O; Bess, S J; _____; 19 Mar 1867; W R Clark Clerk; M 20 Mar 1867 by H A T Harris; L and C, no B

Lackey, Thomas; Espey, Margaret; David Williams; 17 Jun 1835; M W Abernathy

Lackey, Wm; Gladden, Martha; Martin Zimmerman; 23 Jan 1835; Ambiguous

Lacky (Lackey), David; Taylor, Sarah; Thos W Lindsay (Lindsey); 6 Oct 1866; M 15 Nov 1866 by C A Pickens

Lafon, Daniel x; Heffner, Rachel; Philip x Heffner; 7 May 1829; Henry Cline
Lagle, George; Longcrier, Polly; Jacob x Long; 24 Dec 1842
Lagle, Jacob x; Coons, Susannah; George x Lagle; 11 Oct 1835; Henry Cline
Lagle, John; Hedrick, Leah; Jacob Null; 27 Aug 1835; Henry Cline
Lambert, Peter (Ger ____); --------; Casper Culp (Ger ____); 1 May 1769; Ezekiel
    Polk CC
Lander, Samuel Jr; McPherson, Laura Ann; John M Richardson; 20 Dec 1853;
    William S Hamby, D Schenck; M same date by Samuel Lander Sr
Laney, Archibald B; Robeson, Seina; Morgan x Robeson; 1 Jun 1839; Elisha Saunders
Langdon, Wm I; Lander, Margaret I; Wm H Michal; 17 Dec 1844
Lanier, Edmun; Bolch, ____nna; Adam Flowers; __ __ber 1832; Henry Cline; Uncertain
Lanning (Lemons), William; Rosamon, Rachina; Jacob x Rosamon; 5 Sep 1813;
    J Lourance
Lantz, Jacob; Hoke, Sarah; Jno Hoke; 21 Aug 1806; Js McEwin
Lasley, Samuel; Falls, Sarah; William Price; 22 Jan 1817; James T Alexander
Latta, James; Knox, Jain; James Johnston; 12 Apl 1796
Lattimore (Latimore), Joseph; Roberson, Luisa; Samuel Lattimore (Latimore); 13 Jan
    1841; H Cansler C
Laurance (Lorance), Nicholas; Harbison, Mira; Thomas Weatherspoon (Wetherspoon);
    27 Feb 1818; V McBee
Laurence (Lourance), William; Taylor, Susanah; Andrew x Cline; 6 Jan 1814; Jesse
    Perkins; M same date
Lavender, Joseph x; Lowe, Nancy; John Buck; 18 Jul 1818; V McBee
Law, Henry; Clark, Ann; Cornelius Clark; 23 Dec 1819; Wm Little
Lawing, Andrew; Phillips, Elizabeth; Thomas McGee; 26 Mar 1813
Lawing, David; Sides, Anny; Simon x Hager; 30 May 1809; Danl M Forney
Lawing, John M; Beel, Elizabeth; Oliver W Weathers; 17 Sep 1860; Elisha Saunders;
    M 18 Sep 1860 by Elisha Saunders JP
Lawing, John S; Beal, Rhoda C; T J Saunders (Sanders); 6 Apl 1867; M 7 Apl
    1867 by Elisha Saunders JP
Lawing, Joseph; Moore, Mary; William Riley; 29 Dec 1840; Eli Hoyl
Lawing, William; Beal (Beel), Ann; Milton Goodson; 21 Jan 1860; W R Clark;
    M 22 Jan 1860 by Elisha Saunders JP
Lay, James H (Harry); Ballard, Sarah; Philip Ballard; 26 Apl 1863; R Nixon JP;
    M same date by R Nixon JP
Lay, Jesse; Browing, Lasina; Robeson Compton; 27 Apl 1846; A B Cox
Lay, R (Rudesel); Baldwin, Ann; William B (?) Lay; 10 Dec 1837; Isaac Holland
Lay, William B; Weathers, Eliza; Caleb C Withers (Caleb Weathers); 18 Sep 1839;
    Eli Hoyl
Laypole, John x; Bartley, Betcy; Henry Hause (Ger Henrich Hasz); 17 Aug 1814;
    V McBee
Leadford (Ledford), John; Buff, Susanah; Champion Goodson; 10 Aug 1816; V McBee
Leak, John; Moreland, Catharine; Thomas Keepes (Keepys), Wm White; 4 Apl 1797
Leatherman, Rudolph x; Rayfel, Harriett; Joseph Stamey; 20 Jun 1839; P Stamey JP
Leatherman, Solomon x; Williams, Nancy; John Gardiner (Gardner); 23 Mar 1840;
    L E Thompson
Leathermon, John; Abernathey, Eliza; Thomas Davis; 14 Feb 1842; A J Cansler
Leathers see Seathers
Ledford, James x; Baily, Ann; W B Sloan; 7 Jun 1858; W R Clark; M 8 Jun 1858
    by Logan H Lowrance JP
Ledford, Jesse; Self (or Selt), Hanna; William x Self (or Selt); 1 Nov 1829; M
    Hull JP
Ledford, William x; Hasley, Jean; Thomas x Parker; 15 Sep 1789
Lee, Alexander x; Bradsha, Mecky; Frederick Williams; 13 Jan 1802; Jos Dickson
Lee, James; Turbyfill, Elisabeth; William Alexander; 4 Apl 1797
Lee (Lea), Jesse; Abernathy, Nancy; Turner Abernathy; 28 Jul 1834; M W Abernathy
Lee, Lawson x; Fisher, Nelly; Smith Abernathy; 30 Dec 1829; Luther M McBee
Lee, Orsbun; Sherrale, Clarinda; Young Shelton; 18 Jul 1839; J A Ramsour
Lee, William; Abernathy, Susannah; Wm Alexander; 12 Aug 1803; Jas McKisick
Lee, William; Keener (Keaver), Amy; Milton Goodson; 28 Jan 1854; Robt William-
    son; M 29 Jan 1854 by Elisha Saunders JP
Leeper, Andrew; Mellon (or Milton), Mary; J G Hand; 6 Sep 1837; H Cansler Clk
Leeper (Leaper), Andrew; Armstrong, Margaret; John N Ford; 29 Apl 1843
Leeper, James x; --------; Jacob x Hinkle; 25 Mar 1793; Joseph Dickson; Ambiguous
Leeper, James; Henry, Margaret; Jos Henry; 4 Mar 1795
Leeper (Leaper), James; Armstrong, Naomi; Matthew Armstrong; 1 Apl 1816; James T
    Alexander

77

Leeper, James; Armstrong, Naomi; Jacob R Stowe; 15 Feb 1845; C L Hunter

Leeper, Matthew; Henry, Jane; Joseph Henry; 18 Mar 1782

Lefever, Isaac x; Flanigin, Salley; Henry Fulenwider; 24 Jun 1828; V McBee

Lefever, Isaac; Rhodes, Catharine; --------; 12 Mar 1856; J A Huss Clerk; M 13 Mar 1856 by Danl Siegel JP; L and C, no B

Lefever, John; Peacock, Susan; Robert G Haines (Hayne); 9 Nov 1830; J T Alexander; Signature of "Lefever" is apparently "Leverts" or "Feverts"

Lefever, John; Ingle, Elizabeth; Lyman Woodford; 21 Feb 1835; M W Abernathy

Lefever, John; Dellinger, Sarah; William x Lafever; 11 Sep 1860; F J Jetton; M same date by F J Jetton JP

Lefsey, Shederick x; Hovis, Rosannah; Peter Best (Ger Peter ____); 5 Oct 1830; J T Alexander; Name appears also Shadrack Luffey and Frederick Lovsey

Legle, John x; Lewis, Catharina; George x Legle; 17 Oct 1822; Fr Hoke JP

Lehman, Francis J (Ger Frantz J Lehman); Abernathy, Susanah; Isaiah x Abernathy; 18 Dec 1824; V McBee

Lehmans (Lehmon), Francis J; Goodson, Susan; David J Clarke (Clark); 29 Sep 1861; M 29 Sep 1861 (reads 1862) by Jonas W Derr JP

Lehmans (Lehmons), William M; Troutmon, Adaline; Valentine Helderman; 28 Feb 1864; Elisha Saunders; M same date by Elisha Saunders JP

Lemaster, John W x; Cobb, Frances; Parsons Naylor; 6 Feb 1866; W R Clark; M same date by R H Abernethy JP

Lenhardt (Leanhardt), Jacob; Bess, Martha Jane; Noah Childers; 19 Jan 1854; Danl Siegel; M same date by Danl Siegel JP

Lenhardt (Leonhardt), John W; Shell, Sarah C; Samuel C Bailey; 9 Jan 1856; J A Huss; M 10 Jan 1856 by George Coon JP

Lenoir, William A; Derr, Jane K; A C Williamson; 14 Dec 1847; Robt Williamson

Leonard, Andrew; Rhodes, Catherine; Paul Anthony; 25 Feb 1822; V McBee

Leonard, Charles x; Groce, Catharine; Jacob Reinhardt; 17 Mar 1809; Maxl Chambers

Leonard, Charles x; Hoyle, Barbara; Maxwell Shuford; 3 Apl 1834; Miles W Abernathy

Leonard, Daniel; Blackburn, Betcy; Jacob Leonard; 1 Jul 1826; V McBee

Leonard, Franklin; Havener, Barbara; Henry Havner; 11 Jan 1848; Robt Williamson

Leonard, George; Stamey, Eliza; Lawson A Stamey; 20 Feb 1827; V McBee

Leonard, Jacob; Shuford, Anna; James Bivings; 21 Mar 1821; James T Alexander

Leonard, Jacob; Saypaugh, Margarett; Daniel Seagle (Esq); 25 Dec 1827; J T Alexander

Leonard, James M; Ferrell, Eliza O; John R Williamson; 10 Feb 1831; J T Alexander

Leonard, William see Gilbert Robert x

Leonard, William; Gilbert, Catharine; B M Jetton; 4 Nov 1851; Robt Williamson; M 6 Nov 1851 by Ambrose Costner JP

Leonhardt, Jacob M; Havener, Sarah A; Andrew Hauss; 7 Mar 1853; R Williamson; M 10 Mar 1853 by George Coon JP

Leonhardt, Jacob M; Hafner, Eliza E; J P Cansler; 27 Oct 1856; W R Clark; M 28 Oct 1856 by George Coon JP

Leonhardt (Lenhardt), John F; Havner, Sarah; Absalom Houser; 22 Feb 1839; H Cansler CC

Leonhardt, Lawrance; Cody, Rachel; David P Hauss; 6 Apl 1864; M 7 Apl 1864 by G L Hunt MG

Leonhardt, Lourance; Kistler, Anna; Levi Havner Jr; 15 Mar 1845; R Williamson Jr

Lethca (or Lethco), Pinkney; Burd, Jane; --------; 4 Aug 1856; M this date by F J Jetton JP; C only, no B

Letherman (Leatherman), Jonas; Temple, Elisabeth; Solomon Letherman (Leatherman); 1 Jan 1837; P Stamey JP

Levain, Isaac; Rosimond, Mary; Cornelious Cryder; 5 Feb 1789; Joseph Steel

Levan, William x; Wyatt, Susanah; Peter x Gosnel; 1 Apl 1795

Lewis, C P x; Harriss, Adaline; Aaron Boggs; 8 Oct 1866; M same date by R H Abernethy JP

Lewis, Edward; Hoyle, Mrs Nancy H V; Andrew Roseman; 27 Dec 1848; Robt Williamson

Lewis (Luis), George x; Dickson, Jean; James Collins (or Collier); 4 Dec 1810; Robt Pinter __

Lewis, James; Witherspoon, Anne; James McCaerver (McCarver); 24 Jan 1812; Lwn Henderson

Lewis, James; Clemmer, Susanna; Jonas Huffman (Hufman); 26 Dec 1840; And Hoyl JP

Lewis, John x; Dauherty, Cerease (?); George Wright; __ ____ 1832; Andrew Dickson JP

Lewis, John; Lufcey, Martha; Thomas Lufcy (Lufcey); 13 Jan 1840; Eli Hoyl
Lewis, Richmd; Mathus, Susanah; John Yount; 14 Dec 1828; Fr Hoke JP
Lewis, Simon Jr x; Deem, Polley; Daniel Yoder; 27 Mar 1808; John Willfong
Liddell, John G; Neagle, Mary; Andrew Neagle; 23 Jan 1824; V McBee
Ligal (Legle), Henry; Sommet, Sally; George x Legle); 27 ____ 1832; Fr Hoke
Like (or Luke), Joseph; Broher, Susana; Christen x Like (or Luke) ,(Ger) Johannes
   Braucher; 22 May 1806; Hy Conner JP
Liles, Henry x; Self, Elizabeth; William Self; 8 Jul 1823; Joseph Willis
Liming (Lemons), Isaiah; Frost, Drusilla; Robert Fost; 16 Dec 1805; Js McEwin
Liming (Limming), Samuel; Cratz, Cathrine; Robert x Watts; 16 Aug 1810; Jacob
   Reinhardt
Liming, Stacey; Cross, Anne; Michael Shenck (Ger same); 27 Jul 1819; V McBee
Lin, Daniel; Mitchem, Jamima; Jacob Probst; 2 Feb 1840; P Stamey JP
Lin (Lynn), John W; Propst, Elizabeth; Logan Mitchem; 5 Nov 1831; L McBee
Lin (Linn), William P; Lutes, Catharine L; Vincent Avery; 31 Jan 1849; Robt
   Williamson
Linbarger (Linebery), Daniel; Wilkerson, Patsey; Michael Linbarger; 29 Nov 1810;
   Jesse Perkins
Linbarger (Linebargar), Jonas R; Cannon, Sarah Ann; David Hoffman (Hufman);
   12 Feb 1845; And Hoyl JP
Linch (Lynch), John; Bradshaw, Nancy; David Lockman; 14 May 1838; L E
   Thompson
Lindsay, Samuel W; Maclean, Vilet W; Richard D S McLean (Maclean); 22 Feb
   1820; V McBee
Lindsay, Thos W; Adams, Carrie; Jonas G Rudisill; 8 May 1861; M same date by
   R N Davis Minister
Lindsey, James; Wright, Isabela; Henry Wright; 8 Mar 1814; Saml Wilson
Lindsey, Samuel; Wilson, Elaner Jr; James Graham; 25 Sep 1790
Lindsey, William H; Edwards, Sally Ann; W Gabriel (Wilson I [or J] Gabriel);
   __ ____ 183__ (end 1834)
Linebarger, A P; Wingate, Jane; J A Killian; 8 Dec 1862; M 16 Dec 1862 by L M
   Berry MG
Linebarger, Caleb; Rhodes, Mary M; Frederick Hoffman; 5 Oct 1841; R Williamson Jr
Linebarger, Caleb; Hufman, Susan; Lawson A Mason; 11 Mar 1843; Eli Hoyl
Linebarger, Daniel x; Cook, Mary; Robert Murrel (Murrell); 11 Jun 1821; Jas T
   Alexander
Linebarger, David; Jinkins, Elizabeth; William Smith; 25 Oct 1814; James Taylor
   Alexander
Linebarger, David; Kincaid, Catherine; Drury Abernathy; 2 Sep 1826; V McBee
Linebarger, Eli; Rutledge, Lema; Isaac H Holland; 5 Oct 1840
Linebarger, Frederick; Wilkison, Nancy; John Linebarger (Ger Johannes Leinberger);
   7 Sep 1826; Wm Little
Linebarger, Fredrick; Hovis, Mary; James Rutledge; 24 Mar 1829; And Hoyl JP
Linebarger, Frederick H; Connor, Amia; Osburn Henkle; 19 Aug 1839; Eli Hoyl
Linebarger, Hosea (Hosa H); Sherrill, Susan M; J (or I) W Gabriel (Wilson
   Gabriel); 17 Oct 1840; H Cansler CC
Linebarger, Jacob; Cryseller, Sally; David x Linebarger; 4 Nov 1817; V McBee
Linebarger (Leinbarger), Jacob; Lewis, Sarah P; James H Dickson; 14 Jun 1838;
   S C Robinson
Linebarger, James; Kincaid, Isabella; John Sigman; 12 Feb 1830; L M McBee
Linebarger, John; Costner, Betsey; Fredrick Leinberger; 15 Jan 1799; Jo Dickson
Linebarger, John; Best, Betsy; John Rhyne; 11 Aug 1809; Danl M Forney
Linebarger, John; Marshall, Mary Maria; John x Marshall, William x Allen; 12 Jun
   1834; G Hoke
Linebarger, John x; Hobbs,. Nancy; Z A Moss (Motz); 24 Jul 1856; J A Huss;
   M same date by F J Jetton JP
Linebarger, Lewis; Peasour, Elizabeth; Michael Linebarger; 20 Aug 1829; And
   Hoyl JP
Linebarger, Lewis (Jr); Rhyne, Fanny; Falty Clemmer (Valintine Clemmer); 8 Mar
   1827; Eli Hoyl
Linebarger, Martin; Wilkinson, Effy; John Linebarger (Ger Johannes Linberger);
   4 Apl 1825; Jas T Alexander
Linebarger, Michael; Perkins, Anne; John Linebarger; 2 Dec 1819; V McBee
Linebarger (Linbarger), Michael; Hovis, Cathrine; Jacob Rhyne; 13 Jul 1822; Isaac
   Holland
Linebarger, Michael; ____ninger, ____; Len____ Linebargar; 2 Nov 1833

Linebarger, Peter; Cloninger, Elizabeth; Daniel Rhyne; 2 Sep 1836; And Hoyl JP
Linebarger, Solomon; Morris, Margaret; Caleb Linebarger; 2 Mar 1838; And Hoyl JP
Lines, Charles L; Beam, Ann; A Ramsour (A A Ramsour); 19 Mar 1853; R Williamson; M 31 Mar 1853 by J R Peterson (Rev)
Lingafelt, Daniel x; Gilbert, Frances J; Comadore x Hull; 27 Mar 1861; W R Clark; M 28 Mar 1861 by G L Hunt MG
Lingafelt, David x; Pendleton, Martha A; John Butts; 7 Apl 1852; Robt Williamson; M 8 Apl 1852 by Esli Rhyne Esq
Lingafelt, John; Lutes, Anna; William P Lin (Lean); 12 Sep 1848; Robt Williamson
Lingerfelt, Daniel (Ger Lingenfeld); Brindle, Rosanna; Henry Brendle (Brindle); 3 Apl 1811; Ligt Williams JP
Lingerfelt, Daniel; Houser, Mary; Franklin A Houser; 19 Aug 1850; V A McBee
Lingerfelt, David x; Wion (or Weon), Barbara; John x Lingerfelt; 10 Jan 1818; V McBee
Lingerfelt, Jacob (Ger Jacob Lingerfeld); Slagle, Peggy; Daniel Hoke; 11 Mar 1820; V McBee
Lingerfelt, John x; Brindle, Rachel; Jacob Reinhardt; 1 Dec 1808; H Y Webb
Lingerfelter, Jacob x; Long, Mary; John x Bivens, John x Debenporte; 21 Aug 1831; M Hull JP
Lingerfelter, John x; Kiser, Rebeckey; Daniel x Lingerfelter; 13 Oct 1831; M Hull JP
Linhardt (Lenhart), Jacob; Letherman, Susannah; Lorents Lienhard (Lorance Lenhart); 8 Jul 1827; M Hull JP
Linhardt, Joseph; Hause, Susanah; David Bailey; 30 Apl 1814; V McBee
Linhardt, Lawson H; Carpenter, Catharine; George Coon; 1 Aug 1847; V A McBee; Ambiguous
Linhart, Daniel; Bailey, Biddy; Joseph Linhart; 30 Jan 1819; V McBee
Linhart (Lenhardt), John x; Kistler, Susana; Joseph Linhart;; 24 Mar 1816; V McBee
Link, David; Seagle, Polly; Jacob A Ramsour; 6 Jan 1832; L McBee
Link, Henry W; Rough, Catherine; Henry R Darr (Tarr); 3 Dec 1828; VMcBee
Link, Jacob (Ger Jacob Linck); Rudisail, Catharine; Frederic x Link; 15 Jun 1789
Link, Jacob; Shuford, Sarah; Michael Link; 9 Feb 1819; Phil Whitener JP
Link, Jacob; Friday, Margaret; Drury Clanton; 11 Feb 1823; V McBee
Link, John; Warlick, Barbara; Daniel Seagle (Seegle); 10 Apl 1823; V McBee
Link (Linck), Michael; Whitener, Sally; Turner Abernathy; 15 Jun 1816; Mic Cline
Link, Moses; White, Achsah; Michael Summerow (Sumerow); 15 Nov 1819; V McBee
Linkhorn, Thomas x; Rhodes, Susy; Adam Shetly; 22 Apl 1808; Danl Forney
Linn, Archibald; Rudesail, Marget; 3 Apl 1857; J A Huss Clerk; M same date by D A Haines JP; L and C, no B
Linn, William; Boyd, Nancey; James Shannon; 4 Dec 1797; Jonn Greaves
Linster, A J x; Williams, Margaret; I H (or J H) Holland; 27 Feb 1844; __ Keener (or Keever) JP; Ambiguous
Lippard (or Sifford) (Leopard), Solomon; Minges, Elizabeth C; Joseph x Minges; 2 Aug 1829; Miles W Abernathy JP
Litten (Litton), Gilbert; Summit, Levina; John Sumit (Summit); 16 Jan 1827; J T Alexander
Litten (Litton), Hiram; Sherril, Alis; Charles Beatty (Beaty); 30 Sep 1819; V McBee
Litten, Isaac; Bridges, Anna; Henry Andras (Andrass); 17 Mar 1810; Dal M Forney
Litten (Litton), James; Edwards, Nancy; George x Jones; 20 Oct 1812; Vardry McBee
Litten (Lytton), Joel; Bridges, Sarah; Isaac Litten (Lytton); 1 Oct 1823; Jas T Alexander
Litten (Littlen), Michael; Jones, Mary; Benjamin Taylor; 11 Jul 1807; D M Forney
Litten (Litton), Samuel; Proctor, Elizabeth; John Sherrill (Sherril); 25 Nov 1813
Litten, Thomas; Whitson, Margaret; Price x Williams; 20 Oct 1784
Litten (Litton), William; Sherril, Eliza; David Day; 20 Jul 1824; V McBee
Little, Alexander; Abernathy, Fanny; James Little, John Abernathy; 30 Aug 1810; Hy Conner
Little, Davolt; Bostian, Catharina; John Yount (Yont); 6 Nov 1823; Fr Hoke JP
Little, George; Beaty, Betcy C; John x Wilkinson; 27 Mar 1824; V McBee
Little, George; Peed, Nancy; Eli Sherrill (Sherril); 15 Sep 1826; V McBee
Little, George; Beatie, Margaret A; Lewis E Brotherton; 30 (or 20) Aug 1842
Little, George; King, Martha; --------; 13 Sep 1858; W R Clark Clk; M 14 Sep 1858 by R H Morrison; L and C, no B
Little, George x; Hambright, Mary; A A Maclean (McLean); 20 Oct 1862; M 23 Oct 1862 by R H Morrison
Little, James; Duncan, Martha; Carter Duncan; 17 Dec 1818; V McBee
Little (Lytle), John; Nixon, Agness; William Beal; 17 Nov 1794; Jo Dickson

Little (Lytle), John; Baldrige, Jane; Henry Hen__ry; 7 Feb 1798; Jno Dickson

Little, John x; Duncan, Elizabeth; James Sherrill (Sherril); 7 Apl 1815; V McBee

Little, John F; Lockman, Lucinda C; J M M Houston; 22 Dec 1855; W B Withers JP; M 24 Dec 1855 by Wm W Munday Esqr

Little, L W; Finger, Margaret E; A S Haynes; 10 Aug 1858; W R Clark; M 12 Aug 1858 by L M Little

Little, Peter; Conner, Malina; Cyrus J Frazier (Frazer); 24 Jul 1841; J Yount JP

Little, Robert; Little, Mary; --------; 17 Aug 1859; M this date by J D King JP; R only, no B

Little (Lytle), Samuel C; Edwards, Vashti (Vestia); H____ Brotherton; 24 Jan 1852; Robt Williamson; M 29 Jan 1852 by J Lowe JP

Little (Lytle), Thomas; Petillo, Susana; Litleton Petillo; 17 Jan 1783

Little, Thomas; Mauney, Eliza; H W Burton; 20 Dec 1842; A J Cansler

Little, Thomas J; Fisher, Matilda; Hosea Linebarger; 23 Jan 1836; M W Abernathy

Little (Littel), William; Cox, Bede; John Allen; 19 Jun 1806

Little, William; Springs, Mary L; John Skelly (or Shelly or Shelby); 23 Oct 1837; H Cansler

Little, William; Little, Jane; Albert F Derr; 12 Apl 1842; R Williamson Jr

Little, William; Cronkleton, Martha Ann; Thos J Little; 29 Oct 1842; H Cansler

Little, Wm P; Sifford, Mariah; Robt D Whitley; 28 Dec 1854; S Sifford

Littlejohn, Robertson; Gastin, Darius; William Nolen; 10 Jul 1824; Isaac Holland

Litljohn (Littlejohn), Silas; Gillenger, Peggy; Dempsey Perkins; 30 Mar 1821; V McBee

Litton (Litten), Isaac; Lytle, Frances; William Little (Lytle); 8 Dec 1795

Litton, Lawson H; Shuford, Barbara; Elam Lewis; 13 Sep 1830; J T Alexander

Litton (Litten), Logan C; Sherill, Nancy C; Uriah Long; 25 (or 20) Jan 1837

Litton, Samuel; Robeson, Rachel; Silas Littlejohn; 16 Jun 1821; V McBee

Litton (Litten), Wesley; Thompson, Ann; James Allen; No date; Joseph Steel

Lloyd, J W; Killian, E C; S P Sherrill; 13 Jul 1865; J C Jenkins; M 16 Jul 1865 by A J Fox MG

Loar, George (Ger Georg Lohr); Hosselbarger, Susana; George Siegel (Siggel); 10 Dec 1806; Lwn Henderson

Lockman, David; Duncan, Sarah; William Little; 24 Nov 1797; Jno Dickson

Lockman, David; Little, Elisabeth; Wm W Munday (Wesly W Monday); 15 May 1837; M L Hoke

Lockman, Elihu; Thompson, Betsy; David Lockman, John Lockman; 4 Oct 1821; Wm Little JP

Lockman, John; Barkly, Polly; Osburn Munday (Monday); 24 Nov 1833; M W Abernathy

Lockman, Levi; Saunders, Nancy; John x Saunders; 30 Mar 1824; V McBee

Lockman, Levy x; McMin, Rachel A; John Lockman; 21 Dec 1818; James T Alexander

Loftin, Edmund; Newman, Dovey; Smith Abernathy; 3 Sep 1837; H Cansler

Loftin, Eldridge (Edward); Sherril, Mary; Eli Sherrill (Sherril); 19 Dec 1808; H Y Webb

Loftin, Henderson; Edwards, Catharine; William x Newmon; 8 Apl 1828; M W Abernathy JP for Els Connor JP

Loftin, James; Sherrill, Susanah; Nicolas Sherrill; 27 Dec 1796

Loftin (Loften), John; Edwards, Polley; Joshua Sherrill (Sherrel); 19 Sep 1825; Jas Holdsclaw Jr

Loftin, Lafayett; Weathers, Mary; Starling x Parker; 23 Aug 1853; Robt Williamson; M 25 Aug 1853 by Elisha Saunders JP

Loftin, Martin; Lemons, Mary; Thomas Keever; 20 Mar 1849; Robt Williamson

Loftin, Thomas; Baty, Viney; William Long; 22 Apl 1821; Eldridge Loftin

Logan, Drury; Moor, Serah; Joseph Henry; 27 Feb 1783; John Carruth

Logan, Drury; Bias, Polley; Abner Massee; 19 Nov 1805

Logan, James x; Deel, Catharine; Mathias Deel; 3 May 1832; Z Stacy JP

Login, Thomas x; Garden, Matty; Abner McAfee; 6 Aug 1803

Lollar, Jacob; Hamilton, Margaret; William x Earwood; No date (Ashe Governor 1795-8); John Dickson

Lollar, Jesse; Bridges, Lydia; John Null; 23 Feb 1830; Endorsed "John Lollar's Marriage L Bond"

Loller, Henry; Sherrill, Margaret; Ephraim Kale (Cail); 13 Nov 1817; Andrew Loretz

London, A J; Hobbs, Sarah; E J Alexander; 26 Dec 1854; J A Huss; Certificate, M 26 Dec 1854, signed F J Jetton JP

London, Henry x; Sane, Sarah; Andrew x Sane; 8 Dec 1856; Robt Williamson; M 11 Dec 1856 by Logan H Lowrance JP

Lonergan, Patrick; Leeper, Margaret S; W F Holland; 26 Nov 1845; A B Cox
Long, Alfred; Gales, Barbara; William Gales; 27 Apl 1836; John B Harry
Long, Henry; Tallent, Malinda; R C Lowrance (Lorance); 1 Jan 1857; W R Clark;
   M 8 Jan 1857 by David Williams JP
Long, Henry H; Sauls, Mary A; James A x McLoud; 21 Sep 1860; W R Clark;
   M 23 Sep 1860 by Philip Plonk JP
Long, J L; King, Ellen E; Alfred Nixon; 28 Sep 1866; W R Clark; M 2 Oct 1866
   by J Finger MG
Long, James; Havner (?), Catharine (?); Peter Havner (?); 3 Jan 1833
Long, John; Beaty, Ann; Donald (Daniel) Cambell; 17 Dec 1783; Elisabeth Dickson
Long, John; Turbyfield, Nancy; John Turbyfill (Turbyfield); 26 Oct 1812
Long, Jonathan; Woods, Nancy; Smith Abernathy; 24 Jul 1830; V McBee
Long, L S (Lanson S); Crawley, Elizabeth; Thomas Reed (Reid); 5 Aug 1832;
   J T Alexander
Long, Lawson; Edwards, Matilda; Jacob Williams; 30 Mar 1850; V A McBee
Long, Leonard; Edwards, Sarah; Jonathan x Long; 22 Aug 1799; Jno Dickson
Long, Robt x; Johnston, Caroline; Christopher Mauney; 18 Nov 1856; W R Clark;
   M 22 Nov 1856 by G W Hull
Long, Thomas; Sherril, Rebecca; Richard Hunter; 18 Sep 1807
Long, Uriah; Sherrill, Sarah E; John S Robinson; 30 Dec 1839; Wm Long JP
Long, Wiley x; Lingerfelter, Molly; John Devenport (Debenport); 25 Nov 1838;
   M Hull JP
Long, Wm; Roberson, Rachel E; Henry Asbury; 22 Jan 1834
Long, Wm T; Cherry, Matilda Ann; Leroy M Dellinger; 20 Sep 1865; A S Haynes
   CCC; M 26 Sep 1865 by R H Morrison
Longcrier, Elias x; Setzer, Catherine; Jacob x Longcrier; 21 Dec 1837; Henry Cline
Longcryer, Jacob x; Bolick, Caty; Adam Bolick (Ger Adam Bolch); 29 Jan 1814;
   Mic Cline
Lore, John; Pringel, Letty; Adam Segel; 30 Jun 1811; Ligt Williams JP
Lore (Loar), John; Hedick, Sarah; John J (Jacob), Reinhardt; 12 May 1840;
   A J Cansler
Lore (Loar), Joshua; Reinharte, Rachel; Daniel Holly; 7 Nov 1833; M Hull JP
Lore, Joshua; Edmund (Edmunds), Emeline; James F Siegle (Seigle); 22 Nov 1859;
   W R Clark; M 24 Nov 1859 by Danl Siegel JP
Loretz, Andrew H; Ramsour, Elizabeth; H Cansler; 1 May 1822; V McBee
Loretz, Daniel; Reinhardt, Eliza; Andrew H Loretz; 23 Oct 1828; V McBee
Loretz, John F; Ramsour, Polley; Daniel Seagle; 21 Aug 1827; J T Alexander
Lourance, Alxr; _____; Moses Abernathy; No date (probably 1803)
Lourance (Lorance), Daniel; Messey, Prieilla; David Lourance (Lorance); 30 Sep
   1789; Joseph Steel
Lourance (Lowrance), Joseph; Sherril, ____; _____; 21 Jul 1809; Danl M Forney
Lourance (Lowrance), Lawson; Witherspoon, Emeline; Jacob Bolch (Bolick); 3 Jan
   1826; Mic Cline
Lourance (Lowrance), Martin; Sherrill, Ruannah; Jo Lourance; 14 ____ 1806; Js
   McEwin
Love, Andrew; Willson, Mary; Samuel Wilson; 13 Mar 1832; J T Alexander
Love, William; Gamble, Lucinda; Andrew Love; 10 Aug 1843; Calvin Ferguson
Lovey (Lovecy), Thomas; Torrance, Martha S; Robert Mendenhall; 23 Feb 1843
Low (Lowe), Alexander; Kincaid, Susanah; Isaac Low (Lowe); 17 Feb 1824; V McBee
Low, George x; Dellinger, Barbara; Isaiah x Abernathy; 8 Oct 1816; James T
   Alexander
Low (Lowe), Isaac; Kincade, Nancy; Alexander Low (Lowe); 27 Mar 1824; V McBee
Low (Lowe), James W; Shelton, Abigail; Wm W Munday (Monday); 20 Apl 1830;
   Jno Coulter
Low, Jesse x; Cresman, Nancy; Conrad x Cresman; 30 Aug 1803
Low (Lowe), John; Saunders, Betcy; David Dillinger (David Linebarger); 4 Feb
   1828; V McBee
Low (Lowe), Rufus; Helderman, Susannah; J W Low (Lowe); 6 Dec 1842
Low, William; Hope, Betcy; Henry Hope; 5 Sep 1812; V McBee
Lowe, Franklin; Monday, Martha; Wm Wesley Munday (Monday); 28 Apl 1829;
   And Derr
Lowe, Green; White, Elvarna; Philip B Whitener; 24 Jan 1829
Lowe (Low), John A; Baxter, Luvsa Ann; R W Falls; 30 Sep 1858; M same date
   by Joshua Pendleton JP
Lowman, Martin x; Howard, Elisebeth; Benjamin Howard; 7 Nov 1815; Phil
   Whitener JP

Lowrance (Lourance), Cany M; Cansler, Mary M; S N Lowrance (Lourance); 27 Feb 1843; V A McBee

Lowrance, Hiram A; Abernathy, Martha T; Jno B Davis; 4 Aug 1830; V McBee

Lowrance (Lourance), Isaac (Jr); Witherspoon, Anna; Thomas Witherspoon (Weatherspoon); 14 Feb 1814; J Lourance

Lowrance (Lorance), Jacob; Frisset, Betsy; David Lowrance; 10 Aug 1797

Lowrance, Logan H; Hill, Margery N; M W Abernathy; 29 Dec 1834

Lowrance, Martin C; Ferguson, Jane; James Mt'gomery (McGummery); 7 Már 1843; A J Cansler

Lowrance (Lourance), Newton; Jones, Rachel; James Jones (James); 22 Jul 1831; J T Alexander

Lowrance (Lourance), Peter; Ikerd, Elizabeth; Abraham Lowrance (Lourance); 15 Aug 1815; Jo Lourance

Lowrance, Robert F; Hoke, Susannah; Miles W Abernathy; 5 Jun 1823; George Smith

Lowrance, Rufus; Cobb, Sarah; David x Smith; 10 Jul 1841; A J Cansler

Lowrey (Lowry), William; McGill, Nancy S; Levi W Ferguson; 19 Dec 1825; J T Alexander

Lowrie, Samuel; _____; Robt Alexander; 25 Dec 1788

Lowry, Dobbins; Garrison, Mima; Thomas Bell; 14 Dec 1850; Robt Williamson

Lowry (Lowrey), John; Cline, Shusanah; William x Frizle; 8 Nov 1785; Joseph Steel

Loyd, William x; Adams, Margaret; Urbane Ashanbranner (Orband Ashabrand); 12 Jun 1782

Lucas, Isaac; Thompson, Elizabeth; William Thompson; 20 Jul 1814; James T Alexander

Luckey, Hugh; Bond, Dinah; Thomas McGee; 18 Feb 1794

Luckey, John x; Cherry, Mary; Emper x Luckey; 2 Feb 1867; R Nixon JP; M same date by R Nixon JP

Lucky (Luckey), Archibald C; Jetton, Rachael M; B M Jetton; 12 Nov 1855; M 13 Nov 1855 by W C Patterson MG

Lucky, David; Stillwell, Theresa; John Lucky; 13 Dec 1860; J D King; Certificate of Marriage of John Lucky and Theresa Stillwell, 13 Dec 1860 by J D King JP

Lucky, John; Black, Isabeller; Henry Hager; 5 Apl 1857; R E Burch JP; M same date by R E Burch JP

Lucky (Luckey), William; Hager, Dilly Ann; James T (James G) Nixon; 15 Dec 1845

Lufsey, John x; Bradshaw, Mary; Cyrus Cathey; 20 Jun 1829; And Hoyl JP

Lufsey, Levi; Smith, Mary; Green Massey; 3 Dec 1822; Saml M'Kee

Lusk, Lucius Y; Hoyle, Margaret E; E S Barrett; 20 Nov 1852; L Y Lusk of New Orleans and Margaret E Hoyle of Gaston County; M 22 Nov 1852 by David Crooks

Lusk, Salomon x; Mosar, Elizabeth; Fredk Hoke (yu); 1 Jun 1835

Lutes, George (Ger Georg Lutz); Lorance, Elisabeth; George Lorance; 14 Feb 1791; Joseph Steel

Lutes (Lutz), John; Frye, Sally; Jonathan Bost; 16 Nov 1824; Mic Cline

Lutes, Laben; Naugle, Adaline; Paul Settlemyer (Settlemire); 2 Mar 1843; Wm Herman JP

Luts, Eli; Black, Elizabeth; Alfred Black; 17 Nov 1864; M same date by Alfred Black Esqr

Lutz, Alexander x; Martin, Mary; John Harmon; 16 Feb 1830; L M McBee

Lutz, Daniel; Bost, Susannah C; James T Alexander; 10 Oct 1842; A J Cansler

Lutz (Lutes), Daniel; Lytle, Mary Ann; E H Fulenwider; 16 Dec 1854; R Williamson; M 21 Dec 1854 by D Williams JP

Lutz (Luts), Daniel; Whise (Wise), Rhody C; Henry Rhodes; 6 Oct 1857; M same date by D A Haines (JP)

Lutz, David; Ikerd, Catherine; Elias x Clodfelter; 25 Dec 1818

Lutz, David; Bandy, Catherine; George x Lutz; 4 Jul 1820; V McBee

Lutz, Eli; Bandy, Mehala; Samuel Yount; 1 Jul 1825; V McBee

Lutz, Eli; Bandy, __sannah; Daniel Lutz; __ May 1833; M Hull JP

Lutz, Elias; Miller, Elizabeth; John Starr; 10 Oct 1820; Mic Cline

Lutz, Ephraim; Jarrett, Lusina; Daniel Lutz; 1 Nov 1832; L McBee

Lutz, Ephraim H; Mull, Anna; Henry Rhodes; 29 Mar 1855; D A Haines JP

Lutz, George x; Brown, Mary M; Daniel Clodfelter; 29 Aug 1815; V McBee

Lutz, Jacob x; Keller, Polly; David Zimmerman (Ger same); 31 Aug 1812; Vardry McBee

Lutz, Jacob; Mehaffy, Harriet R; John M Jacobs; 6 Feb 1832; L McBee

Lutz, M Luther; Williams, Vicey M; W T Williams; 3 Nov 1859; M same date by D Williams

Lutz, M M; Sain, M J; G P Sain; 15 Dec 1866; W R Clark; M 16 Dec 1866 by
Daniel Siegel JP
Lynck (or Lynch), L L; Wilson, Lavina; Hiram Hartss (Hartness); 21 Jan 1840
Lyons, William x; West, Hanah; Robert x West; 2 Jan 1786; Joseph Steel
Lytle, James H; Reinhardt, Jane H; Franklin A Hoke; 31 Oct 1839; H Cansler

Mabry (Maberry), Jesse; Sadler, Disey; Zachariah x Sadler; 27 Mar 1813; V McBee
Mabury (Maberry), John; Huskins, Mary; Bartholomew Thompson; 25 Oct 1814;
V McBee
Maby, W H (Mayberry, William); Barr, Margaret; John Schenck (Shank); 24 Sep
1833; J T Alexander
McAfee(McKafee), Lemuel Austin; Fulenwider, Frances C; James M Forney; 18 Apl
1840; And Hoyl JP
McAlister, James; Dellinger, Jane; Jacob Stroup; 26 (or 20) Aug 1843; Eli Hoyl
McAlister (McCollister), Joseph; Spencer, Jane; Benjamin x Jenkins; 25 Apl 1820;
James T Alexander
McAlister, William S x; McAlister, Susan; James McAlister; 25 Feb 1843; Eli Hoyl
McAllister (McCallister), Cornelius; Davis, Salley; Elisha Weathers (Wethers); 13 Aug
1798; Jonn Greaves
McAllister (Mcalister), George W; Plonk, Elizabeth; Peter Hoffman; 10 Dec 1832;
Eli Hoyl
McAllister (McAlister), Joseph; Spencer, Eliza; H W Reeves; 11 Feb 1846; Willis
Reeves JP
McArthur (McCarty), John; Roberts, Susanna; Ab McAfee; 22 Dec 1814
McArver (McCarver), Alexander; Baldwin, Sarah; Joseph L Vandyke (Vandike);
26 Dec 1823; Isaac Holland
M'Ashlin (McCaslin), William; Waist, Mary; Joseph Morris; 8 Apl 1805
Macaslin (McCasland), Robert; Haynes, Sophia; Daniel Carpenter; 19 Jul 1831;
L M McBee
McBee, Vardry A; Sumner, M E; Aug W Burton, T T Slade; 15 Dec 1847; Robt
Williamson
McCafee(McAfee), Wm; Beaty, Jane; Jacob Forney; 19 Aug 1816; V McBee
M'Cald (Macall), Archebil; Allison, Nancy; Joseph Martin; 27 Apl 1807; Maxl
Chambers
McCall, James A x; Fite, Martha; Abram Fite; 6 Feb 1843; Eli Hoyl
McCall, John; Howard, Ann; --------; 2 Apl 1851; M this date by E Edwards JP;
R only, no B
M'Call (McCaul), Robert; Lovsey, Polley; Colal (Colonel) Buchanan; 7 Jul 1818;
V McBee
M'Callister, John; Hamilton, Patsey; George M'Callister; 11 Sep 1794; John Dickson;
Ambiguous
McCarta, Jacob; Clark, Nancy; John x Brown; 3 Jan 1822; V McBee
M'Carter, Caleb R; Clark, Francis; Andrew J Falls; 23 Feb 1843
McCarter, Michael; Weir, Elizabeth M; Ramsour; 15 Mar 1843
McCartey, Jacob x; Jenkins, Judah; Peter x Gosnell; 28 Mar 1791; Jo Dickson
McCarty see McArthur
McCarty, Cornelius x; Bell, Jemima; John Baker; 1 Dec 1821; James T Alexander
M'carty (McCarta), Cornelius; Jenkins, Polley; Michael Rhyne (Rhine); 17 Mar
1824; V McBee
McCarver, David; McCall, Elizabeth; John McCarver; 29 Aug 1803; Jonn Greaves
McCarver, Ephraim; Bradley, Jane; Joseph L Vandyke (Vandike); 25 Mar 1825;
Isaac Holland
McCarver (McArver), James; Lewis, Peggy; George Witherspoon; 6 (3) Oct ----
(probably 1801-4); Eliza Greaves
McCarver, James; Rhoades, Carey; Joseph McAllister (McCallister); 15 Feb 1832;
Bolen T Kirby
McCarver, John M x; Jackson, Jane; James McCarver; 27 Dec 1835; E Hanks JP
McCarver, Wm H; Spencer, Anne B; Joseph Miller; 7 Mar 1818; V McBee
McCasland see Caslin
McCaslin, Alfred C; Carpenter, Frances A; Henry Pharr; 26 Dec 1856; M 30 Dec
1856 by JR Peterson (MG)
McCaslin, William; Killian, Susan; Carlos Leonard; 31 Mar 1834; M W Abernathy
McCaul, James; Jinkins, Susana; Robert Johnson; 15 Sep 1801; Jos Dickson
McCaul, John; Brotherton, Polly; Meacon Shelton; 5 Jan 1839; H Cansler CC
M'Caul (Mcall), Robert; Buckhannon, Patsey; Jas M'Caul; 10 Feb 1807; Betsey
Henderson

84

M'Caver (McCarver), James; Hamilton, Patsey; Alexander McIntosh; 11 Jan 1811; Danl M Forney

McCaver, John; Hamilton, Mary; William Hamilton; 19 Dec 1787

McClain, Edward; Yates, Nancy; Thos Beatty, Wiley Ballard; 9 May 1805; Thos Wheeler

McClellan (McClelin), Elias; Collins, Susanah; Isaac Collins; 7 Mar 1819; John B Harry

McClelland (or McLelland), Ezekiel; Mauney, Marian; David Butts; 26 Dec 1832; Vardry McBee

McCloud, James A x; LeMarsters, Martha; John T Russel; 15 Aug 1856; F J Jetton; M same date by F J Jetton JP

McClurd (McLurd), Wiley A; Chody (Cody), Margaret; Daniel x Gilbert; 13 Mar 1859; M same date by L H Hull JP

McClure, James H; Irby, Mary H; William Lander; 4 Apl 1843; H Cansler

McClure, John; Henry, Rachel; Joseph Henry; 20 Dec 1792; John Dickson; Ambiguous

McClure, William; Clark, Elisabeth; Anthony Clark, John McClure; 16 Feb 1797; John Watterson, J Wilson

McClurg (McClurd), James; Carrol, Susanah; William Carroll (Carrol); 27 Feb 1819; V McBee

McClurg, John x; Gross, Rebeca; David Ramsey; 4 Oct 1838; P Stamey JP

McClurg, William; Blackburn, Mary; John Dickson; 10 Apl 1802; James Blackburn

M'Colister (McCollister), William; Huffman, Mary; James Jenkins; 30 Aug 1817

McCombs see Combest

McCombs, J J (or I I); Smith, Mary R; Pinckny Lowe; 12 Dec 1846

McCombs, James; Mitchel, Amy; F J (Joseph) Jetton; 25 Jul 1840; H Cansler CC

McComes, Robert; Jonstone, Leamah; Robert Ionson (Jonstone); 19 Dec 1792; Robert Dickson

McConly see Conlav

McConnell, T A; Howard, Rachel R (Rechaba R); Joel H Howard; 6 Jan 1862; W R Clark; M 9 Jan 1862 by J Lowe JP

McCord, John; Hyet, Else; Wm McCord; ____ 1783; James Dickson

McCord, Robert; Black, Fanney; James Witherspoon; 15 May 1787; Jo Dickson

McCord, William; Moore, Jane ; William Moore; 17 May 1790; Jo Dickson

McCorkle, Frans (Francis); Abernathy, Betcy; Matthew McCorkle; 4 Jan 1813; V McBee

McCorkle, Richard; Sherril, Agness; Absalom Sherrill (Sherril); 9 Apl 1814; V McBee

McCorkle, Richard A; Fisher, Jane A; Robert x Barkley; 3 Jan 1857; Elisha Saunders; M 4 Jan 1857 by Elisha Saunders JP

McCorkle, Stephen; Martin, Mary; William Martin; 7 Nov 1795; Jo Dickson

McCorkle, Thomas; Sherril, Casy; Charles Beatty (Beaty);; 26 Dec 1818 V McBee

McCormack (McCormick), John x; Keener, Elisabeth; Martin x Keener; 2 Oct 1804; John Dickson

McCormick (McKormack), John S; Singleton, Seussanah; William x Singleton; 30 May 1822; Saml M'Kee

McCoy (McKoy), Abner; Wilson, Sarah A; Blair M Jenkins; 25 Oct 1836; M W Abernathy

McCoy, James; Henderson, Patsey; Lawson Henderson; 22 Aug 1796; John Dickson

McCoy, William T; West, Amanda; Joseph Saunders (Sanders); 22 Dec 1852; M 24 Dec 1852 by David Crouse JP

McCulloch, Robert; Falls, Rachal; William D Hannah; 13 Oct 1823; Isaac Holland

M'Cullouch (McCulloch), David; Falls, Synthey; Alexander McArver (McCarver); 21 Mar 1821

McCully (McCulley), Thomas M; Patterson, Eliza; John B Patterson; 2 Jan 1824; Jas T Alexander

McCurry, J T M; Sane, Mary; Franklin x Wise; 19 Jul 1865; A S Haynes CCC, Leonard T Ramsaur; M same date by S P Sherrill JP

McDaniel, Daniel G; Shenck, Elizabeth; H Spain (Hartnal Spain); 7 Feb 1833; L McBee

McDougle, Thomas; Brown, Margaret; Archibald Little; 23 Feb 1792

McElrath, J J; Jones, Ann; C C Henderson; 2 Oct 1838

McElroy (Mugelry), David; Stamay, Sallay; Isaac Johnson; 23 Apl 1820; D Lutz JP

McEntire, Alexander; Wright, Agness; Henry Wright; 10 May 1814; Saml Wilson

McEntire, Alexander x; Rippy, Rhodah; Ab McAfee; 17 May 1814

McEntire, John; Wright, Else; Henry Wright; 19 Oct 1813; Da'd Warlick JP

McEntosh, William; Hager, Pricilla; Benjamin Heaker (Hager); 14 Jan 1817; V McBee

McFalls, Leander x; Dellinger, Cinthia; Josiah B (or R) Dellinger; 29 Mar 1855; J A Huss; M same date by J Helderman JP

McFarland, James Jr; Endsley, Marg; Caleb Miller; 15 Nov 1822; Joel Dyer

McFarlin (McFarland), Wylie; Bookout, Jane; Willis Putman; 7 Jul 1838; Wm W Morris (?) JP

McFarson see McPherson

McFelmet see Felmet

McGalliard, William; Wilson, Jane; Samuel Wilson; 22 Dec 1830; Peregrine Roberts

McGaughey, John; Bickerstaff, Mary; Phillip Null; 3 Oct 1786; Jo Dickson

McGee, Thomas; Abernathy, Louisa; George A Reel (Reed); 22 Sep 1826; V McBee

McGill, John; Lowry, Elizabeth J; Levi W Ferguson; 19 Dec 1825; J T Alexander

McGill, Thomas P; Dickey, Martha; Gabriel Batey (Beaty); 17 Jul 1821; Jas T Alexander

McGill (Magill), William; McClain, Agles; Thomas Maclean (McClain); 20 Mar 1792; Robert Dickson

McGiness (McGinnas), John J; Huss, N J; J M McGinnas; 22 Jan 1866; A S Haynes CCC; M 23 Jan 1866 by P Carpenter JP

McGinnas (McGinness), James; Gillam, Hesther; Christopher Carpenter; 28 Jul 1824; V McBee

McGinnas, John Al (McGinnis, John A L); Rutledge, Amy; John Michal; 3 Mar 1834; Carlos Leonard

McGinnas, Lawson; Carpenter, Barbara; John McGinnas; 23 Apl 1825; V McBee

McGinnas, Lawson; Taylor, Sally; Matthew Stroup; 29 Aug 1827; J T Alexander

McGinnas, Sydney A x; Davis, Sophia S; Albert x McGinnas; 18 Dec 1851; Robt Williamson; M same date at house of Polly Davis by Wm J Hoke JP

McGinnas (Meginnis), Wiley W; Holmesly, Jane; Albert R Homesley (Holmesley); 6 Mar 1835; M W Abernathy

McGinnas (McGinness), William; Capenter, Catherine; John B Harry; 12 May 1824; V McBee

McGinnis, Larkin; Anthoney, Peggy; John Anthony; 6 Mar 1828

McGrath, Edward; Huffstetler, Betsy; Andrew x Ingle; 21 Jul 1830; J T Alexander

McIlwain, David; Costner, Mary; Lawrence x Costner; 16 Apl 1816; James T Alexander

Mcintosh, Alexander; Siffert, Belinda; Amos Morris; 7 Feb 1846; And Hoyl

McKee, George; Oliver, Margaret; John McKee; 6 Aug 1821; Saml M'Kee

McKee, Isaac; Slown, Margaret; Mathew Armstrong; 26 (?) Sep 1793; Joseph Dickson

McKee, James; Carpenter, Margaret; Peter Kiser; 29 Sep 1841; R Williamson

McKee, James (Jr); Underwood, Betcy; Henry Underwood; 27 Mar 1817; V McBee

McKee, John; Allison, Susanah; William McKee; 29 Jul 1823; Saml McKee

McKee, John x; Carpenter, Susan; Noah Alexander; 4 Mar 1850; Robt Williamson

McKee, Peter C; Summey, Catharine Elmina; John Blackwood; 15 Mar 1845

McKee, Richard W; Carpenter, Fanny; John Zimmerman; 23 Mar 1818; V McBee

McKee, William; Allison, Mary; John M'Kee; 20 Aug 1821; Saml M'Kee

McKeirnan, Owen; Berry, Lucy; Moses L Whiteside (Whitesides); 30 Nov 1826; J T Alexander

McKenzie (McKenzea), David U; Nolen, Rebecca G; Thomas L Brandon; 10 Feb 1844; "David U McKenzea and Thomas L Brandon of South Carolina"

McKinney, Thomas x; Barns, Cunney (or Anney); Martin x Keener; 12 Jan 1786; Danl McKisick

McKinzie, James; Moore, Jane; Wm D Hannah; 27 Feb 1827; I Holland JP

McKisick, James x; Huggins, Eliza; Jacob Reinhardt; 25 Jan 1827; V McBee

Maclain, William B; Graham, Jane; George Litle; 14 Dec 1858; M 15 Dec 1858 by R H Morrison

Maclean (McLean), A A; Schenck, C L; J B Summey; 4 Feb 1841; H Cansler

McLean, Alexander; Hais, Ann; James Cunningham; 1 Apl 1782

McLean, Jno D (Dr); McLean, Mary D; Andrew Roseman; 8 Nov 1865; A S Haynes CCC; M 9 Nov 1865 by R N Davis Minister

Maclean, T B; Salmon, Almira M; Danl T Pegram; 27 Mar 1844; I Holland

Maclean (McLane), Thomas; Lewis, Peggy; Isaac O Lewis; 10 Oct 1796; Jo Dickson

Mcleroy (Muckleroy), James; Rinehart, Elisebeth; Robinson Johnson (Jhonston); 2 (?) Nov 1819; Phil Whitener JP

McLurd, John C; Carpenter, Mary M; Ephraim Kizer; 28 Feb 1856; Robt Williamson; M same date by George Coon JP

McLurd, Robinson L; Summerow, Adaline E; Jacob J Carpenter; 13 Jul 1860; W R Clark; M 24 (13) Jul 1860 by J Finger

McLure, James; Dellinger, Caroline; ⌐_____; 2 Apl 1857; John A Huss by W R Clark DC; M same date by B S Johnson JP; L and C, no B

McLure, James H; Armstrong (Stroup), Miriam; D A Lowe; 23 Oct 1860; M 25 Oct 1860 by Elisha Saunders JP

McLure, John D; Beattie, Esther H; James H McLure; 12 Mar 1845; John Hill

McMin, Daniel; Howard, Betsy; Michael Beam; 27 Dec 1817; V McBee

McMin, John; Howard, Polly; Jacob Arents; 18 Oct 1814; James Taylor Alexander

McMin, Samuel; Derr, Barbara; Jacob Summey; 16 Mar 1814; V McBee

McMin, William __; Whealer, Reachel; Michael Schanck; 21 Dec 1810; Jacob Summey Jnr

McMurry, Edward x; Hanna, Sarah; John Jordan, William Brady (Bready); 25 Aug 1769; Ezekiel Polk

McNair, James; Arawood, Sarah; James x Davis; 3 Jan 1843; D Hoffman JP

McNeely, James; Cowen, Catharine; James Cowen; 10 Jun 1801; John Dickson

M'Nighten (Nighten, McKnight), Alexr (Alex M); Brown, Feby; John Gibson; 5 Aug 1811; Lwn Henderson

McPherson (McFarson), Angus; Schenck, Lovina; John Schenck; 23 Oct 1832; V McBee

McRaven (McCravan), David (Rawn, David M); Nance, Amanda; Rufus Williams; 20 Nov 1854; J Lowe JP; M 23 Nov 1854 by R H Morrison

McWhorter, Robert; Cherrey, Elisabeth; Robert Chirry; 27 Aug 1796

Magginnas (Meginas), John x; Starrit, Elezebeth; Shadrick x Cobb; 26 Nov 1810; Jacob Summey Jnr

Maginnes (McGinnis), William; Cobb, Charlotte; Peter Evans (Evins); 30 Apl 1816; V McBee

Magness, Joseph; Twitty, Abella; William Magness; 3 Aug 1787

Magness, Morgan; Elliott, Kizia Ann; William Roberts; 14 May 1827; J T Alexander

Mahew (Mehue), Aaron; Gowing, Nancey; Edmond Dillion, Abner Cornelius; 30 Jan 1792

Mahu (Mayhew), John; Hunnicut (Hunycutt), Elizabeth; --------; 27 Mar 1853; M this date by Wm W Munday Esq; C only, no B

Mann, Thomas (Guinn, Thomas); Guinn, Betcey; Ashman Guin (Guinn); 3 Jan 1814; Vardry McBee; Endorsed Thomas Man's Marriage L Bond

Maples, Thomas x; Taylor, Rachel; Jacob Reinhardt; 9 Jun 1813

Marks, Richard; Border, Rebecca; Samuel Dormire (Ger S D____); 17 Nov 1784; Joseph Steel

Maroney, Mathew; Mosteller, Sarah; Melvin Rash; 14 Apl 1860; W R Clark; M 15 Apl 1860 by L D Childs JP

Martin, Adam M; Henderson, Elizabeth; David B Martin; 6 Apl 1825; V McBee

Martin, Alfred; Bumgarner, Catharine; Daniel x Campbell (Cammell); 5 Oct 1826; J T Alexander

Martin, Barnet (Martin, Barnett Hill); Caldwell, Beckey; Thomas x Caldwell; 17 Aug 1825

Martin, George x; Willis, Mary; Daniel Willis; 12 Jul 1838; M Hull JP

Martin, J B; Jetton, M E; Oliver Wells; 16 Oct 1866; W R Clark; M 17 Oct 1866 by J Finger MG

Martin, Jacob x; Pluming, Mary; Robt x Johnston; 27 Jun 1787; Joseph Steel

Martin, James x; McCoy, Elisabeth; Jacob Miller; 29 Sep 1784; Joseph Steel

Martin, James; Alexander, Lilly; Samuel Lowrie (Lowry); 22 Oct 1792; Jo Dickson

Martin, James; Adams, Polley; Ab McAfee; 13 Aug 1815; Ab McAfee

Martin, James; Glenn, Elizabeth; James Holland; 26 Oct 1818; V McBee

Martin, James; Clark, Nancy; David Cherry; 15 Feb 1821; Jno Turbyfill JP

Martin, John Jr; Hutson, Jene; John x Martin (Sr); 17 Jan 1805

Martin, John Sr x; McCoy, Sary; George Whisenhunt (Ger Georg Wiesnand); 20 Feb 1808; Ligt Williams JP

Martin, Joseph; Rutledge, Jean; James Rutledge; 21 Jul 1807; Danl M Forney

Martin, Moses; Bulinger, Matilda; Andrew Holshouser; 9 Aug 1830; J T Alexander

Martin, Philip x; Staymey, Maria; Jacob x Martin, Henry x Staymey; 24 May 1792; John Willfong JP

Martin, Richard x; Carpenter, Ann; Abraham Carpenter; 27 Feb 1813; V McBee

Martin, Richard C; Conner, Sarah; Hugh M C Felmet (Hugh Felmet); 11 Sep 1821; V McBee

Martin, Samuel; Moore, Margaret; Cyrus Stinson (Stincen); 23 Dec 1835; J G Hand

Martin, William; Reynolds, Polly; Jacob Reinhardt; 10 Jul 1810; Danl M Forney

Martin, William; Sample, Hannah; John Sample; 13 Aug 1834; And Hoyl

Martin, William S; Hannah, Ann L; William D Hannah; 4 Feb 1831; Isaac Holland

Martin, William S; Caneda, Ellen; Jonas R Linebarger; 1 Sep 1845; Benj Smith JP

Martin, Zadok; Holland, Jane; B W (Westly) Hill; 25 Apl 1828

Maskal, William; Hansel, Elizabeth; Robert Moreland; 24 Nov 1789; Jonathan Greaves
Maskal (Maskil), William; Clifton, Mary; William Heaker (Heager); 21 Apl 1794;
John Dickson; Ambiguous
Mason, L A; Linebarger, Catherine; Drewry Jenkins; 28 Sep 1843; J Webster JP
Mason, Thomas; Evins, Hannah; John D Abernathy; 18 Jan 1814; James T Alexander
Mason, William H; Hawkins, Lucy; John x Browning; 18 Oct 1822; I Holland
Massagee, Abner x; Leonard, Elizabeth; Martin Smith; 5 Jan 1848; Robt Williamson
Massagee, Abner x; Gilbert, Barbara; F J Jetton; 27 Oct 1862; M 6 Nov 1862 by
G L Hunt M Gospel   --
Massagee, Benj M; Hauss, Mrs Linna; Elias Hull; 15 Jan 1859; W R Clark;
M 16 Jan 1859 by R H Abernathy JP
Massagee, John x; Hull, Nancy; John Huggin (Huggins); 15 Aug 1821; V McBee
Massey, Green; McCosough (?), Reachel; Robert McCall; 7 Feb 1811
Massey, John; Berry, Sidley; William Robinson; 25 Apl 1825; Isaac Holland
Massey, Mary; Duck (?), Betsey; John Massey, Moses Darnell (Darnald); 18 Feb
1794; Jo Dickson
Massey, William; M'Cullick, Mary; James D Hill; 8 May 1832; John Massey
Master, John; Stroup, Elizabeth; Moses x Stroup; 13 Mar 1822; V McBee
Matheson (Mattheson), Eli; Best, Anna; Henry Fulenwider; 5 May 1827; V McBee
Mathias, Samuel x; Hare, Charlotte; William Bird; 4 Oct 1810; Ligt Williams JP
Mathus, Peter x; Yarboro, Elizbeth; George Sigman; 24 Dec 1840; Fr Hoke JP
Matthews (Mathews), Nathan; Davis, Nancy; William x Bird; 26 Dec 1815; Ligt
Williams
Mauney, Abraham; Rudisill, Margaret; K B Price; 1 Nov 1845; R Williamson
Mauney, Christian; Rine, Susanah; Michel Mauney; 19 Sep 1815; V McBee
Mauney, Christian x; Mauney, Margaret; Joseph Kiser (Kizer); 15 Sep 1826;
V McBee
Mauney, Christian (Jr); Swarengame, Hannah; Michal Mauney; 3 Sep 1817; V McBee
Mauney, Christopher; Self, Elizabeth; John Harriss; 4 Mar 1820; Jas T Alexander
Mauney, David; Carpenter, Fanny; John Mauney; 9 May 1838; H Cansler
Mauney, Eli x; Carpenter, Eliza; Mexull Mauny; 10 Jul 1847; Robt Williamson
Mauney, George; Hansel, Lavina; Saml Black; 13 Feb 1837; M W Abernathy
Mauney, Isaac; Rush, Sarah; David Crouse; 29 Sep 1814; James Taylor Alexander
Mauney, John; Ikerd, Elizabeth; James Bleckley (Blakely); 17 Jan 1824; V McBee
Mauney (Mooney), John x; Crow, Betcey L; John Dimbarr x Crow; 21 ____ 1829;
J T Alexander
Mauney, John; Clark, Mary L; John Rudasill (Rudisill); 25 Dec 1844; R William-
son Jr
Mauney, Livingston; Cathey, Jane; Abram Howser (Houser); 21 Aug 1829; J T
Alexander
Mauney, Mark; Dellinger, Eve; Peter Mauney; 19 Jan 1824; Jas T Alexander
Mauney, Michael; Havner, Margaret; Jacob Sellers; 2 Feb 1816; James T Alexander
Mauney, Michael; Sullivan, Mary E; P P Hoke; 9 Oct 1848; Robt Williamson
Mauney, Michal; Black, Jemima; Peter Mauney; 2 Mar 1812; Lwn Henderson
Mauney, Noah H; Bailey, Margaret; John A Carpenter; 7 Aug 1857; J A Huss;
M 13 Aug 1857 by Philip Carpenter JP
Mauney, Peter x; Havener, Barbara; John Eaker; 3 Dec 1810; H Y Webb
Mauney, Peter; Sullivan, Mary Ann; Abraham Mauny (Mauney); 26 Oct 1846
Mauney, Peter x; Page, Elizabeth; George W Mooney (Mauney); 23 Nov 1853; J A
Huss; M 26 Nov 1853 by G W Hull (JP)
Mauny (Mauney), Abraham; Carpenter, Marget; John Carpenter; 3 Apl 1813;
V McBee
Mauny (Mauney), Jonas; Hullet, Janey; Wylie Black; 11 Jan 1831; Vardry A McBee
Mauny (Mauney), Maxvill (Maxwell); Hauss, Mary; Valentine Mauny; 13 May
1837; M W Abernathy
Mauny (Mauney), Maxwill; Haus, Anna; Samuel Black; 7 Jun 1845; R William-
son Jr
Mauny (Mooney), Noah; Huggins, Cynthia; Abraham Eaker (Aker); 1_th Jul 1833;
J T Alexander
Mauny (Money), Vallentine; Brook, Maryan; Vallentine Mauny Sr (?); 30 Apl 1793;
Michail Eaker
Maxwell, John; Julian, Margaret; Luke S Davis; 22 May 1833; J T Alexander
Maxwell, S D; Thomas, Anna; Israel Fink; 10 Nov 1866; W R Clark; M same
date by Wm J Hoke JP
Mayberry see Maby
Mayhew, J B J H; Hobbs, Eliza; Thomas B Withers; 1 Aug 1855; W B Withers JP;
M same date by W R Withers JP

Mayhew (Mayhue), James; Conner, Mariah; Henson Conner; 21 May 1825; James T Alexander

Mays, James L; Drumfield, Patcy; John Turbyfill Jr; 28 Sep 1812; Vardry McBee

Medlin, Columbus; Williams, Margaret; Millinton Williams; 25 Nov 1857; Danl Siegel JP; M same date by Danl Siegel JP

Megee (McGee), Jacob; Sigman, Mary A; Absolum Fry; 7 Aug 1838; Wm Herman JP

Meginness, Ambrose x; Cobb, Judith; Joshua Abernathy; 23 Jun 1813

Mehafey (Mehaffee), Joseph, of Rowan Co; Steel, Ann; Samuel Steel; 26 Dec 1786; Joseph Steel

Mehaffey, Joseph; Puntch, Elizabeth; William Puntch; 28 Aug 1814; Mic Cline

Mehaffey, Thomas A; Eckhart, Leah; Wm L Mehaffey; 10 Nov 1836; Jonas Bost

Mehaffey, William L; Bost, Jemima M; Jonas Cline; 6 Aug 1841

Melton, Marvel; Roberts, Catherine: David Reinhardt; 22 Mar 1832; L McBee

Mendenhall, Eli; Rhyne, Jane C; W F Holland; 9 Aug 1842; I H (or J H) Holland

Mendenhall, Joseph H; Rudisell, Rebeccah; Edwin B Torrence; 27 May 1834; Miles W Abernathy

Mendenhall (Mendingall), Robert; Hoyl, Anne; James Wilson; 22 Sep 1804; Polly Greaves

Mendenhull (Mendinall), Nathan; Torrence, Mary B; Edwin B Torrence; 28 Mar 1834; Carlos Leonard

Merit (Meredeth), Thomas; Wallis, Polly; William Spencer; 19 Jan 1830; Mary Holland

Metcalf, Augustus D; Eaker, Sarah; John Carpenter; 12 May 1852; Robt Williamson; M 14 May 1852 by David Crouse JP

Meuray (Murray), Leonard; Bird, Elizabeth; H N Ward; 6 Apl 1842

Miares (Myers), Elias; Downy, Polly; Henry x Hoover; 21 Sep 1821; V McBee

Miarse (Myers), Henry; ------ ------; John Myers (Ger Meyers); 1 Nov 1814; Wm Nesbitt JP

Miarse (Miars), Jacob; Downey, Ibby; Elias Miars; 8 Jun 1830

Michael, Daniel; Benick, Polley; Charles Reinhardt; 12 Apl 1823; V McBee

Michael, George W; Heedick, Belzora; --------; 20 Sep 1857; M this date by A J Fox MG; C only, no B

Michael, Jacob x; Loretz, Anne; Daniel Michael; 13 Nov 1820; V McBee

Michael (Michal), John M; Goodson, Mary E; W 'H Motz; 19 May 1855; W R Clark; M 22 May 1855 by Robt Blackburn JP

Michal (Michael), Jacob; Ramsour, Catherine; Jacob Summey Jnr; 10 May 1815; V McBee

Michal, John; Matthews, Sarah; John D Hoke; 9 May 1825; J E Bell

Middlekauff, Solomon S; Ramsour, Mary A E; Jno F Ramsour; 12 Sep 1843; R Williamson Jr

Miles, Daniell x; Twitty, Charlott; Archibald Graham; 26 May 1791

Millard (Miller), William; Ferguson, Eliza; Benjamin Millard (Miller); 30 May 1822; D Reinhardt

Miller, R C; Abernathy, Lucy K; E A Perkins; 4 Nov 1849

Miller, Absalom; Whitener, Mary; Caleb Miller; 24 Oct 1826; J T Alexander

Miller (Millar), Adam; Rudisill, Ann Mary; Daniel Hoke; 22 Aug 1829; Fr Hoke JP

Miller, Adam; Roberts, Susan; Wm H Michal; 4 Aug 1857; M same date by David Crouse JP

Miller, Ambrose; Bovey, Mandy; P H (Philip) Bennick (Benick); 28 Sep 1839; Alex J Cansler

Miller, Andrew; Lowe, Delilah; John A Parker; 14 Dec 1842

Miller, Caleb; Whitener, Rachel; Jas T Alexander; 24 Apl 1819

Miller, Caleb; Shuford, Sarah; James M Erwin; 24 Dec 1822; Joel Dyer

Miller, Daniel see Holler, Daniel

Miller, Ephraim W; Miller, Amy; Daniel Miller; 2 Mar 1840

Miller, George x; Warren, Margaret; Peter Hoke; 18 Mar 1827; M W Abernathy JP

Miller, George x; Bowers, Polly; Archibald Ray; 14 Jul 1829

Miller, George; Clay, Harriet S; David Hauss; 30 Jun 1853; George Coon JP; M same date by George Coon JP

Miller, Henry (Ger Heinrich Miller); Willhight, Barbara; Daniel x Sipe; 16 Jul 1798; Peter Little

Miller, Henry; Bolch, Mehala; Hiram Bolch; 8 Jan 1843; Epm Yount JP

Miller, Jacob; Whiteley, Elisabeth; --------; 13 May 1794; John Willfong JP

Miller, Jacob; Yount, Sarah; Henry Yount; 31 Mar 1820; Jas T Alexander

Miller, Jacob x; Fulbright (Fullbright), Elizabeth; George Yount; 8 Aug 1826; M W Abernathy JP

Miller, Jacob; Whitener, Polly; Absalom Miller; 11 May 1830; Jonas Bost
Miller, John; Abernathy, Nancy; Philip Shuford; 27 Jul 1806; Phil Whitener JP
Miller, John x (of Burke Co); Starr, Ester, widow; Jacob Lutes (Lutz); 28 Oct 1809; Mic Cline
Miller, John x; Spangler, Mary; Peter x Spangler Sr; 15 (or 18 or 19) Apl 1815; Saml Wilson
Miller, John; Haun, Sarah; Jacob Miller; 18 Sep 1819; Jas T Alexander
Miller, John x; Weaver, Susanna; William x Cline; 5 May 1825; Mic Cline
Miller, John; Hefner, Eliza; Jacob Moser; 29 Mar 1829
Miller, John T; Haus, Susan; Peter S (or T or G) Rush; 3 Aug 1846; R Williamson
Miller, Jonathan; Coulter, Eliza; Silas Bost; 20 Sep 1835; Mic Cline
Miller, Joseph x; Mull, Margaret; John Shell; 15 Jan 1825; Mic Cline
Miller, Michael x; Cresemon (or Cresemore), Barbara; David Conrad; 29 Nov 1824; V McBee
Miller, Moses; Eikerd, Elizabeth; Elias Lutz; 3 Mar 1825; Mic Cline
Miller, Nicholas; Drum, Mary Magdaline; Philip Drum; no date; Joseph Steel
Miller, Philip (Jr); Eikerd, Cathrina; Philip x Miller Sr; 22 Aug 1820; Mic Cline
Miller, Robert Johnston (Rev); Perkins, Mary; Jno Perkins; 5 Mar 1787; Jo Dickson
Miller, Samuel; Smith, Betcy; John Miller, David Miller, (Ger) Heinrich Schmitt; 12 Jul 1817; V McBee
Miller, W J T (or W I T); Fulenwider, Elizabeth; William Slade; 4 ____ 1833; V McBee
Miller, Washington; Beal, Polley; Ephraim Goodson; 21 Aug 1832; V McBee
Miller, William; Henderson, Martha; James Henderson; 14 Sep 1836; Isaac Holland
Miller, Willington F; Richard, Sally Dovina; Charles Beel (?); 22 Apl 1841; J Helderman
Millican, James; Lewis, Pheby; Benjamin Newton; 17 Apl 1779
Milligan (Milican), Gilbert; McCorkle, Rebekah; H Bollinger; 16 Oct 1806; Thos Wheeler
Milligan, William; Carpenter, Mary; Henry Carpenter (son of Jacob); 1 Feb 1823; V McBee
Milling, Alexander; Robinson, Eliza; Archibald Henderson; 25 Apl 1838; S C Robinson
Mills, Daniel; Harrell, Malinda; Wm R Clark; 13 Jul 1839; J T Alexander
Mincy, Moses x; Harmon, Harriet; J L x Thornburg; 10 May 1856; Robt Williamson; M 11 May 1856 by P S Kistler JP
Mingus, Conrad x; Sigman, Maria; George Sigman (Ger Georg Siegman); 17 May 1796; John Willfong JP
Mingus, George; Baker, Sary; Abraham x Mingus; 7 Dec 1809
Miraile, Lorance x; Hair, Margaret; Rudolph Conrad; 1 Nov 1785; Joseph Steel
Mitchael, Jacob; Shulahr (?), Rosie; Thomas Fisher; 29 Oct 1788; Joseph Steel
Mitcham (Mitchell, Michell), Joshua; Williams, Amia; Jacob Probst (Propst); 20 Jan 1825; Jas T Alexander
Mitcham, Logan; Best, Lueser; Ezekiel Hanks (Hancks); 22 Jan 1829; J__ Seagle JP
Mitchell see Mitcham
Mitchell, John; Baird, Nancy; Samuel Gingles; 6 Oct 1808; Joseph Neel
Mitchell, William L; Revels, Mrs Mary; H R Revels; 20 Feb 1845; R Williamson Jr
Mitchem, Banks x; Wise, Sussana; Isaac x Leatherman; 7 Dec 1831; P Stamey JP
Mitchem, Nathaniel; Rannals, Mimy; Isaac x Kenady; 20 Oct 1801
Moll, Daniel; Sites, Anny; Jhon x Moll; 3 Feb 1806; Phil Whitener JP
Moll, Jhon x (Jr); Ring, Mary; Abraham Seitz (Sitz); 29 Dec 1807; Phil Whitener JP
Monday, Francis; Drue (?), Lucie; Christopher Monday, John Carruth; 7 Jan 1783
Montgomery see Mtgomery
Moody, David x; Berry, Margaret; John x Johnson; 6 Feb 1833; J T Alexander
Moody, John x; Abernathy, Polly; Adam Carruth; 21 Dec 1794
Moody, John; Rankin, Margaret; Hiram Hartness; 22 Nov 1842; H Cansler
Moon (or Moore), A A; Henderson, Jane AA; Marcus F Alexander; 8 Nov 1843; R M Alexander JP
Mooney (Mauney), A J; Stamey, Mary M; Levi Baker; 24 Dec 1860; M 25 Dec 1860 by L D Childs JP
Mooney, Jacob x; Carpenter, Anna; John D Hoke; 25 (or 20) Apl 1835; G Hoke
Mooney (Mauney), John; Norman, Betsy; Wilson Norman; 2 Sep 1818; V McBee
Mooney (Mauney), Lawson; Neil, Polly; William Arrowood; 20 Apl 1837
Mooney, Philip M x; Abernathy, C; Abram x Mooney; 3 Oct 1865; A S Haynes CCC, D Falls; M 5 Oct 1865 by S P Sherrill JP
Moor (Moore), Edward; McClure, Margaret; John McClure; 31 May 1799; Jonn Greaves DCC

Moor (More), Abraham (of Rowan Co); Pitts, Maryan; Jacob Bolick (Ger Jacob Bolch); 30 Nov 1787; Joseph Steel

Moore, Adolphus; Linebarger, Dovey; E J Alexander; 16 Jul 1857; J A Huss; M 18 Jul 1857 by P S Kistler JP

Moore, Adolphus x; Mooney, Milly Ann; P S Rush; 3 Jun 1863; W R Clark; M same date by F J Jetton JP

Moore, Alexander; Rhyne, Anna; Daniel Rhyne; 17 Dec 1817; James T Alexander

Moore, Alexander; Butts, Susan C; J C Jenkins; 10 Mar 1845

Moore, Alfred; Hause, Elizabeth; Moses Moore, John Bartly; 15 Sep 1809; Danl M Forney

Moore, Andrew F; Beal (Bell), Mary; William A Lawing; 12 Aug 1860; Elisha Saunders; M same date by Elisha Saunders JP

Moore, Aron (Aaron); Smith, Nancy; Patrick x Mullen; 30 Jul 1829; Luther McBee

Moore, Arthur x; Mucklewreath, Polly; Thomas Witherspoon; 28 Sep 1811; Lwn Henderson

Moore, Elisha x; Skrimshire, Elisabeth; John McGaughey; 5 Jun 1787

Moore, Ezekiel; Hazlet, Elizabeth; John McClure; 14 Aug 1806; Lwn Henderson

Moore, Franklin B; Null, Catharine A; David Clark; 12 Nov 1842; L E Thompson

Moore, James; Cathey, Margaret; John Cathy; 10 Feb 1825; James T Alexander

Moore, James x; Stamey, Peggy; O C Green; 19 Jul 1836; John B Harry

Moore, James; Mauney, Rosannah; Jonas Elmore; 30 Jul 1851; Robt Williamson; M 5 Jul 1851 (sic) by Allen Alexander JP

Moore, John; Goodwin, Polly; Thomas x Moore; 4 Aug 1797; John Dickson

Moore, John; Scott, Mary; Daniel Hoke; 26 Jul 1816; V McBee

Moore, John x; Slagle, Mary; Abner Berry; 3 Dec 1816; James T Alexander

Moore, John x; Mathis, Mary; Samuel x Moser; 28 Jul 1828; Mi W Abernathy JP

Moore, John; Shrum, Mary; George Wm Goodson; 5 Apl 1858; W R Clark; M 14 Apl 1858 by Robt Blackburn JP

Moore, John (Jr); Reid, Jean; William Reed (or Reid); 22 Aug 1808; Danl M Forney

Moore, Joseph H; Killian, Sarah; Thomas C Payne; 22 Dec 1837; L E Thompson

Moore, Lee A; Cozens, Martha C; Eli Hoyl; 29 Feb 1840; And Hoyl

Moore, Moses; Cox, Nancey; Robert Weer (Wier); 29 Jul 1785; Jno Moore

Moore, Moses; Sullivan, Catherine; Thomas R Shuford (Shufford); 4 Nov 1826; V McBee

Moore, Philetus x; Miller, Polly S; Allen Alexander; 28 Jan 1858; W R Clark; M same date by P S Kistler JP

Moore, Samuel x; Sullivan, Betsey; Moses Moore; 21 Apl 1821; V McBee

Moore, Simeon x; Parish, Lucinda; John R Dunn; 22 Nov 1831; L McBee

Moore, Thomas x; Bynum, Elizabeth; Benjamin Beel; 31 Mar 1849; Robt Williamson Clk

Moore, Wesley x; Cobb, Minty; Wm S Turbyfill; 31 Dec 1831; J T Alexander

Moore, Wilk x; Havner, Susanah; Moses Moore; 7 Aug 1821; V McBee

Moore, William; Patterson, Elizabeth; William G Dickson; 11 May 1799; Jonn Greaves

Moore, William T; Graham, Elizabeth E; John H Harry; 26 Dec 1835; M W Abernathy CC

Moore, Wright; Moore, Elsey; _____; 31 Aug 1866; W T McCoy JP; Acknowledgment by former slaves

Moorman, Daniel B P; Kerr, Jane S; Wm H Michal (Michael); 27 Jan 1841

Moose, Andrew x; Summit, Eliza; John x Moose; 2 Nov 1832; L McBee

Moose, Frederick (Ger Fridrich Mussgenug); Carba, Christina; John Moose; 19 Dec 1808; H Y Webb

Moose, Frederick (Ger Fridrich Mussgenug); Loots, Elizabeth; Jesse Robinson; 14 Dec 1826; J T Alexander

Moose, George; Boovey, Druzy; William R Hass (Hause); 7 Dec 1840

Moose, George; Keener, Mary; John Keener; 6 Jan 1859; W R Clark; M same date by Wm J Hoke JP

Moreland, John; _____; Samuel Fisher; 14 Oct 1785

Moretz (Morris), Daniel; Bolick, Catherine; Daniel x Bolick; 17 Jan 1832; Henry Cline

Moretz, John; Hefnar, Catharina; John x Hefnar; 2 Nov 1826; Fr Hoke JP

Morgan, John; Cathy, Nancy; John Carruth; 23 Jan 1817; V McBee

Morison (Morrison), Moses; Wise, Elisebeth; Henry Wise (Ger Weiss), Isaac x Holman; 8 Sep 1823; Peter Hoyle, Abraham Hevner; Ambiguous

Morris see Moretz

Morris, Amos; Davenport, Mary E; A W Davenport; 4 Mar 1846

Morris, Benjamin; Holland, Rebecca; Willard Boylen (?); 10 Mar 1831; J T Alexander

Morris, Benjamin; Rankin, Sarah C; W Williamson; 28 Aug 1843; R Williamson Jr

Morris, John J; Carpenter, Polly; Henry Schenck; 29 Sep 1824; Jas T Alexander

Morris, Joseph; Havner, Catherine; --------; 3 May 1829; V McBee

Morris, Joseph W; Howell, Mary; J A Ramsour; 3 Aug 1854; J A Huss; M same date by FJ Jetton JP

Morris, Stephen; Sifford, Maxamelia; David A Abernathy; 22 Jul 1840

Morris, Vinson; Allison, Sarah; Eli Hoyl; 22 Sep 1840; And Hoyl

Morris, William W; Graham, Jane; John B Harry; 28 Nov 1829; W Graham

Morrison, Abner; Runolds, Rachael; Wilie (Willie) Harris; 6 Feb 1810; Danl M Forney

Morrison, George; Linhardt, Susana; Maxwell x Morrison; 6 Jul 1829; V McBee

Morrison, John x; Hains, Rosanah; George Mauney; 2 Jun 1815

Morrison, John x; Smith, Ellen; Abe x McDowel; 22 Mar 1867; D A Lowe; M same date by D A Lowe JP

Morrison, Joshua x; Rhaume, Catharine; Peter Mauny (Mauney); 8 Dec 1813; James Taylor Alexander

Morrison, Maxwell; Kistler, Sarah; Robert H Brown; 17 Oct 1834; M W Abernathy

Morrison, Maxwell; Eaker, Elizabeth; Peter Eaker; 13 Apl 1836; John B Harry

Morrison, R H; Graham, Mary; David T Caldwell; 23 Apl 1824; V McBee

Morrison, Robert; Hauss, Barbara; Jacob Hauss; 16 May 1842; L E Thompson

Morrison, Thos; Sumpter, Anne; S Lourie; 8 Jan 180__ (1800)

Morrison, William; Prevet, Asceneth; Wm W McGinnas; 30 Jul 1834; M W Abernathy

Morrow, William; Bryan, Jane; James Fitzpatrick; 14 Feb 1797; Jno M Dickson

Moser, John; Hefner, _____; William Abernathy; 1 Aug 1832; _____ Abernathy

Moser, Marcus M; Peterson, Mary M; Benjamin Massagee; 24 Feb 1851; Robt Williamson; M 27 Feb 1851 by P C Henkel

Moser, Peter; Baly, Molly; Francis x Moser; 17 Sep 1812; Philip Hinkel

Moser, Timothy; Hedick, Margaret Malinda; Anderson A Brown; 31 Aug 1848; Robt Williamson

Moser, Tobias; Sigman, Catharina; John W Richards; 10 Mar 1829; Fr Hoke JP

Moss, Willis x; Garrison, Lancy; R__ F Dickson; 10 Feb 1852; Robt Williamson

Moss, Z A; Slade, Virginia B; --------; 25 May 1852; M this date by Rev H H Durant M E Church; R only, no B

Mostellar (Mosteller), Israel; Leonhardt, Barbara; John Rhyne; 30 Aug 1848; Robt Williamson

Mosteller, Eli; Havner, Lavina (Laviree); Pierson Shull; 28 May 1861; W R Clark; M 30 May 1861 by Philip Plonk (JP)

Mosteller, John (Ger Johannes Mosteller); Arney, Betsey; Peter x Mostiller; 15 Mar 1803; John Dickson

Mosteller, John Jr; Rudisel, Eve; John Mosteller Sr (Ger Johannes Masteller); 15 Dec 1818; V McBee

Mosteller, Jonas; Carpenter, Margaret; Peter x Mosteller, Solomon Ramsy; 7 Dec 1806; Lwn Henderson

Mosteller, Michael x; Lutz, Mary; Jacob Reinhardt; 8 Oct 1818; V McBee

Mosteller, Peter x; Rudisil, Polley; Christian x Parker; 14 Apl 1813; V McBee

Mosteller, Peter; Mull, Saraha; L A Stamey (Losson Stamey); 5 Mar 1831; Vardry McBee Jr

Mostetler (or Mosteller), John; Mull, Catharine; John Mull; 27 Apl 1839; H Cansler CC

Mostillar (Mausteller), Daniel; Carpenter, Catharine; William S Rush; 18 Jan 1831; J T Alexander

Mostiller, Peter Jr (Ger Peter Masteller); Dellinger, Mary; David Mosteller; 1 Dec 1798

Motz, John; Loretz, Catharine; Philip Henckel; 16 Nov 1809; Andrew Loretz

Motz, Wade H; Johnson, Jane; W M Reinhardt; 20 Nov 1854; J A Huss

Mousar, George x; Smith, Mary; Henry Smith (Ger Heinrich Schmidt); 27 Apl 1794; Joseph Steel

Mowser, Frederick; Rogers, Fanny; John Spencer; 27 Aug 1829; Henry Cline

Moyers (Myes), Lyas; Burch, Mary; Lyas x Raisone, Thomas Bury; 4 Jan 1809; Jacob Forney; Ambiguous

Moystiller, George (Ger Georg Masteller); Moll, Elizabeth; Peter x Moystiller; 1 May 1806; Ligt Williams

Mozur (Mosar), Jacob; Little, Barbera; Daniel Hoke; 25 Jun 1828; Fr Hoke

Mtgomery (Montgomery), John; Ferguson, Mary S; Martin C Lourance; 23 Jul 1843; H Cansler

Muckelvein, Calep x; Williams, Mary; Aron Low (Lowe); 24 Dec 1839; D Hoffman JP

Muckleroy (Mucelroy), John; Ramsy, Polly; Robinson Johnson; 7 Nov 1822; Phil Whitener JP

Mulens, D (Mullin, Durell); Davis, Elizabeth; Jonas W Paysour; 8 Sep 1849; V A McBee

Mull, Abraham; Suttlemyer, Sally; Lawson H Seitz; 26 Aug 1830; Henry Cline

Mull, Abram; Fisher, Mary; John Fisher; 11 Oct 1791; Joseph Steel

Mull, Harison; Mostiller, Anny; John Mull; 4 Feb 1841; M Hull JP

Mull (Moll), Henry; Hull, Mary; John Moll; 9 Feb 1809; Ligt Williams JP

Mull, John; Mull, Margret; Philip Martin; 30 Nov 1841; M Hull JP

Mullen (Mullins), Alfred E; Carpenter, Sarah A; J C Cobb; 28 Oct 1857; M 28 Oct 1857 by G L Hunt MG

Mullen, James; Low, Emily; Levi T Saunders; 28 Dec 1850; Elisha Saunders

Mullen, Patrick x; Keever, Mary; Benjamin Millend (?) (Miller); 27 Dec 1824; Jas T Alexander

Mullenax, Brison; Berry, Sarah; Robert Berry; 17 Apl 1836; John Dickson

Mullens (Mullen), Davrell; Eaker, Nancy; Edwin B Torrence; 15 Mar 1836; M W Abernathy

Mullens (Mullins), Durell; Elmore, Jane ; --------; 26 Apl 1862; W R Clark Clerk; M 27 Apl 1862 by Philip Plonk (JP); L and C, no B

Mullens (Mullins), Jas H; Leonhardt, Catharine; A E Mullens (Mullins); 26 Nov 1857; W R Clark; M 27 Nov 1857 by Robert G Ramsey (JP)

Mullens (Mullins), John F; Hauss, Nancey G; M C (Caleb) Clay; 15 Feb 1858; M 16 Feb 1858 by Robert G Ramsey (JP)

Mullens, William; Kincaid, Mary; David x Kincaid; 1 Mar 1853; V A McBee; M 4 Mar 1853 by David Crouse JP

Mullin (or Muller), Alexander; ------ ------; Barney West; 29 Jan (or Feb) 1813

Munday (Monday), J A; Robeson, July Ann; Lee A Lockman; 11 May 1867; R Nixon JP; M 12 May 1867 by J Finger MG

Munday, James A; Parks, Amanda; S T Thompson; 4 Oct 1863; W R Clark

Munday (Monday), Joseph M; M'Call, Mary Ann M; John M Rankin; 26 Sep 1826; Wm Little

Munday, Osburn (Monday, Osborn); Crunkelton, Eliza; David x Lockman; 28 Dec 1833; Carlos Leonard

Munday (Monday), Spencer; Shelton, Susan; David x Lockman; 14 Dec 1836; John B Harry

Munday (Monday), William W; Shelton, Lucinda; David Lockman; 15 May 1837; M L Hoke

Munson, William x; Gill, Levicee; Joseph Westcott (Waistcoat); 17 Aug 1781; Jas McEwin

Murphey, John; McNamare, Hanah; Phillip Null; 6 Oct 1786; Jo Dickson

Murphey (Murphy), Moses x; Jinkins, Genney; Wm Wilson; 7 Mar 1811; Saml Wilson

Murphy (Murphrey), John x; Jenkins, Mary; Robt M Wilson, Moses x Murphrey; 18 Nov 1813; David Warlick JP

Murrel, Isaac; Shearman, Letty; Jacob Ramsour; 9 Dec 1817; V McBee

Murrell (Murrel), Edmond; Bomgarner, Nancy; David x Linebarger; 9 Oct 1821; V McBee

Myers see Miares, etc

Nail (or Neil), David; Fye, Catherine; Elijah Sulivan (Sullivan); 8 Jan 1819; V McBee

Nance, Daniel; Baldridge, Nancy; Wm ------; -- Mar 1808; Thos Wheeler; "the first Satday in March 1808"

Nance, David L; Hovis, Frances; G H & Stroup; 28 Dec 1864; S P Sherrill; M same date (reads 1860) by R H Abernethy JP

Nance, J C; Little, Bettie; P Cody; 16 May 1867; D A Lowe; M 21 May 1867 by R H Morrison

Nance, James; White, Betsy; David Smith; 1 Oct 1817; V McBee

Nance, James x; Hovis, Martha; J B Smith; 28 Dec 1853; J A Huss; M 8 Jan 1854 by P C Henkle MG

Nance, James A (Albert); Reed, Julier; William Reed; 29 May 1859; R A McConnel; M same date by Wm W Munday Esq

Nance, John x; Barnet, Mary; Israel R Stroup; 24 Dec 1850; Robt Williamson

Nance, John C; Jones, Anne H; Andrew Dellinger (Delliner); 28 Jan 1851; John Kiestler; M same date by John D King JP

Nance, Lawson x; Stroup, Ann; Moses Cloninger; 25 Oct 1821; V McBee

Nance, William; Johnston, Mary; John Little; 21 Jul 1819; Jas T Alexander
Nance, William x; Pryor, Martha Ann; Spencer Munday; 21 Dec 1841
Nance, William; Saddler, Mary; David Davis; 5 Sep 1843
Nantz, Levi x; Dellinger, Malinda; Josiah R Dellinger; 25 Jun 1855; J A Huss
Naugle, Henry x; Whitener, Elizabeth; John Whitener; 27 Apl 1826; Mic Cline
Naylor, Parson; McCorkle, Rosanah; Jesse D Williford; 8 Aug 1832
Neagle, Andrew; Leeper, Maria Jane; Andrew Leeper; 25 Apl 1831; L McBee
Neagle, John; Leeper, Margaret; Wm Maclean; 2 Oct 1786
Neal, Adam; Brown, Rachel; John Neill (Neal), John Crouse); 10 Nov 1804
Neal, Hugh x; Acre, Catharine; David Eaker (Acre); 8 Mar 1828; Beverly J
 Thompson
Neal (Neall, Niell), William; Crow, Jane; James Niell (Niele); 11 Nov 1833; Wm W
 Morris JP
Nearns, Jesse x; Brindle, Mary; John Brindle (Ger Johannes Brendel); 27 Jan 1801;
 Ligt Williams
Neel, Moses x; Huffstotler, Susanah; David x Aker; 7 Mar 1832; V McBee
Neill (Neal), Alexander; Falls, Sarah; Jeremiah Sadler (Saddler); 14 Mar 1817;
 G Milligan
Neill, John; Stevenson, Myra; Jas K Thomas; 22 Jul 1818; James T Alexander
Neill (Neil), William; Neil, Elizabeth; Alexander Neill (Neil); 29 Nov 1809; H Y
 Webb
Nelson, James; Lamly (?), Betsy; Jonathan Griffith; 26 Dec 1808
Nelson, James x; Reynolds, Nancy; Jesse Reynolds; 26 May 1810; Danl M Forney
Nesmith (Neasmith), William; Craig, Jane; John Finley (Findly); 2 Feb 1795
Newton, Ebenezer; Retherford, Rachel; Alexander McCarver (McCavee); 8 Apl 1795;
 Jo Dickson
Newton, Ebenezer; Rutherford, Ellener; William Rutherford; 23 Mar 1803; Jonn
 Greaves
Newton, George; McCaule, Mary; Jo Dickson; 19 Mar 1794
Newton, Maridy N x; Dellinger, Mary Ann; John N Faulkner; 13 Feb 1855; M same
 date by P S Kistler JP
Nichols, John x; Stowe, Mary; Robert K Graham; 12 Oct 1840; Daniel Hoffman JP
Nickelson (Nicolson), John; Morris, Catherine; Moses Bigger; 19 Sep 1786; Danl
 McKisick
Nickles, John; Wright, Mary; John Wright; 8 Dec 1828; Isaac Holland
Niel (Neel), Andrew; Smith, Barbara; John Niel (Neel); 30 Oct 1823; V McBee
Niel (Neil), Andrew; Martin, Patsy A; Samuel Martin; 29 Nov 1828; V McBee
Niel (Niell, Nell), John (Jr); Mauney, Susannah; Ephraim Mauney; 27 Jul 1832;
 V McBee
Niell (Neel), Adam; Mauney, Anna M; George Mauny (Mauney); 18 Sep 1824;
 Jas T Alexander
Niell (Neel); Adam; Oates, Sarah; Charles H Oates; 31 Mar 1830; J T Alexander
Niell (Neel), Alexander; _____ _____; Jas Beaty; 3 Jan 1808; D M Forney
Niell, George x; Money, Sarah; John Oates; 5 Sep 1834
Niell, Green Berry; Mauny, Barbury N, wid; John Niel (Niell); 22 Sep 1840;
 Christopher Stroup JP
Niell (Neil), James; Costner, Elizabeth; John Costner; 11 Jul 1827; B Y Johnson
Niell, Thomas; Ray, Jean; Thomas Dickson; 27 May 1819; Jacob Carpenter JP
Nile (Neel), William; Winter, Mary; James Beaty; 4 Jul 1815; V McBee
Nixon, Albert M; Hager, Rachael A; Simon R Hager; 5 May 1867; M 6 May 1867
 by J Finger MG
Nixon, Archibald; Norwood, Susanah; Robert Nixon; 21 Feb 1850; R H Abernathy JP
Nixon, Franklin; Rankin, Catharine; Bartlet Nixon; 1 Dec 1856; W B Withers JP;
 M 2 Dec 1856 by R H Morrison
Nixon, James; Proctor, Mary A; Jos H King; 30 Jul 1864; M 2 Aug 1864 by R H
 Morrison
Nixon, Robert; Womac, Milly; Alfred Nixon; 24 Apl 1855; R H Abernathy; M same
 date, R H Abernathy
Nixon, Sidney; Downs, Elizabeth; _____; 17 Oct 1852; M this date by R E Birch
 JP; R only, no B
Nixon, William; Runels, Susan E; John C Reyondls (sic three times); 22 May 1866;
 R Nixon JP; M same date by R Nixon JP
Nixson (Nixon), James; Beel, Salley; Hugh Luckey; 18 Oct 1790; Jo Dickson
Nixson (Nixon), John; Bonn (?), Sarah; Joel Williams; ...th Sep 1787
Nixson (Nixon), William; Reed, Mary; John Little; 22 Aug 1796; Jo Dickson
Nixson (Nixon), William; Luckey, Mitilda; Robert Lucky (Luckey); 17 Nov 1812;
 V McBee

Nixson (Nixon), William; Tucker, Rebecah; Isaac Nixson (Nixon); 11 Aug 1815; V McBee

Nolen, Daniel x; Lind, Nancey; Thomas Buchanan; 5 Apl 1821; I Holland

Nolen, John; Moore, Myre; Felix W Henry; 10 Jan 1818; V McBee

Nolen, William; Irby, Nancey; Samuel Cox; 2 Oct 1819; I Holland

Nolin (Knowlen), David; Ward, Nancy; Burnet Grigg (Grig); 6 Apl 1833; V McBee

Norman, James; Ledford, Barbara G; Noah Boiles ((Biles); 5 Jan 1850; Robt Williamson

Norman, James S; Gardener, Martha J; John Gardener; 31 Mar 1841; H Cansler

Norman, Robert x; Walker, Susan; George W x Stockton; 27 Jun 1850; Robt Williamson

Norman, William; McAllon, Hannah; John Creg____; 29 May 1802; John Dickson

Norman, Wilson; Willis, Nancy; Catey (Catherine) Norman; 14 Sep 1814; V McBee

Norton, James; Penny, Abigail; Leonard Fite; 1 Mar 1823; Saml M'Kee

Norton, William x; Clark, Jennet; Cornelius x Clark; 21 Jun 1783; Jas Freeman

Norwood, James T; Hager, Sarah L; Ezekiel Duck; 2 Mar 1840

Nowland, Charles x; Nowland, Sarah; John Nolan (Nowland); 5 Feb 1814; James T Alexander

Nowlin, Hardin; Dickson, Elizabeth; Thomas Dickson (Sr); 28 Sep 1824; M Hull JP

Noyes, Horatio; Elmore, Polley; James Keen; 12 Nov 1825; V McBee

Null, George; Sigman, Peggy; Henry Hoke; 7 Sep 1798

Null, Jacob; Hedrick, Magtelena; Johan Noll (John Null); 26 May 1825; Fr Hoke

Null, John; Ward, Nancy; John J Perkins; 21 Apl 1837; J A Ramsour DC

Oates, Charles H; McGill, Rebecca; Adam Niell (Neel); Mar 31 1830; J T Alexander

Oates (Oats), James; White, Lucy; Samuel McKee; 18 Jul 1815; V McBee

Oates (Oats), James P; Beaty, Jane H; Wm F Beaty; 14 Oct 1844

Oates (Oats), William; Aspie, Elisabeth; Jacob Summey; 13 Sep 1806; Js McEwin

Oates (Oats), William; Smith, Sarah; Wm F (?) Zimerman; 21 Oct 1823; Robt Kerr

Oats, Franklin; Abernathy, Sina; Marcus L Hoke; 26 Nov 1836; M W Abernathy

Oats, John; Blackwood, Mary; Thomas McGill; 15 Dec 1782; Jas McEwin

Oats, John; McClure, Elizabeth Reid; James Wright; 15 Apl 1811; Danl M Forney

Oats, John; Espey, Mary; Adam Neel; 9 Nov 1835; M W Abernathy

Oats (Oates), John; Montgomery, Hannah; William Ferguson; 7 Mar 1842; H Cansler CC

Oats (Oates), John; Reep, Susan; N G Long; 17 Jan 1861; M same date by David Boiles (Esqr)

Oats, Robert; White, Lillis; _____; 20 Nov 1816

Oats (Oates), Saml R; Tucker, Belsora A; W H Alexander; 5 Feb 1850; Robt Williamson

Odam, George; Howerd, Jane; Jacob Bolch (Bolick); 19 Mar 1831; Mic Cline

O'Daniel, Joseph (or Daniel, Joseph O); Armstrong, Esther L; LeRoy Stowe; 10 Apl 1837

Odell, H S; Edwards, Martha E; Allen Alexander; 28 Sep 1862; M same date by L M Berry MG

Odom, William x; Yount, Sarey; George Yount (Ger Georg Jund); 20 Aug 1809; Peter Little JP

Oel (Ayle), Frederick; Shook, Catharine; Paul Carethers (?); 17 Sep 1804; John Dickson

Ogle, William B; Hoover, Sarah Ann; David Hoover; 16 Apl 1858; Robt Williamson; M 21 Apl 1858 by D Crooks

Oglesby, Albert A; Abernathy, Agnas B; M (McCagah) Oglesby; 16 Oct 1837; H Cansler

Oliver, George; McKee, Abigail; Andrew Armstrong; 21 Jul 1819; James T Alexander

Oliver, John; Abernathy, Amey; Richard Nantz (Nance); 5 May 1800

Oliver, John; Smith, Rachel; Edward Boyd; 26 Feb 1817; V McBee

Oliver, Pleasant; Hoover, Elminah; James M Ford; 6 Feb 1840; W F Holland for Isaac Holland

Oliver, William; Cathy, Frances; John Henry; 27 Mar 1815; James T Alexander

Ormand (Orman), Benjamin; Dixon, Nancy; Jacob Ramsour; 29 Dec 1823; Jas T Alexander

Ormand, Zenas S; Pinion, Mrs Malinda; Peter Hoke; 25 Nov 1848; Robt Williamson

Ornd, Daniel x; Moose, Beggy; F A Hoke; 19 Dec 1835; M W Abernathy CC

Ornt (Ornd), Henry; Townsend, Sally A; James Townsen (Townsend); 26 May 1837; Henry Cline

Ornts (Ornt), Fredrick; Robison, Holly; Valintine Darr (Derr); 26 Oct 1820; V McBee
Otter see Auter
Owens, William; Chorum, Salley; Abner Berry; 12 Jun 1816; V McBee
Oxford, William; Ichard, Barbara; James Goodall; 19 Nov 1790

Padgett (Pagget), Mansfield; Speck (or Spock), Mary Ann; P S Rush; 27 Dec 1862;
    M same date by R H Abernethy JP
Page, James Matison x; Temples, Sufiar; David x Lutz; 26 Jan 1842; M Hull JP
Pain, Isaac E; Sherrill, Sarah C; Robert x Pain; 2 Aug 1838; H Cansler CC
Pain, John F; Burch, Elizabeth R; S A Burch; 17 Oct 1855; R E Burch JP; M 18 Oct
    1855 by H Asbury Mnst
Paine, Robert x; Fronebarger, Mary; F M Abernathy; 23 Jan 1839; L E Thompson
Painter, Elisha S; Hope, Louisa; Paulson Cannon; 1 Feb 1841; L E Thompson
Painter, John; Money, Froncia; Simon Hager; 3 Feb 1795
Painter, John x; Kirksey, Martha; John Smith; 18 Apl 1848; Robt Williamson
Painter, Samuel; Styles, Polley; Abraham Keener; 5 Feb 1823; V McBee
Palmer, Jacob; Wethers, Ebby; Michael Rhyne (Rhine); 23 Feb 1813; V McBee
Palmer, Jesse; Hufman, Elisabeth; John Hufman; 21 Sep 1785; Ibbey Dickson
Pamer, John x; King, Reliance; William x King; 2 Feb 1795; Joseph Dickson
Pangle see Bengle
Park (Parks), Patrick; Smith, Sarah; Saml Caldwell (Calwell); 23 Feb 1784
Parker, Albertus x; Leatherman, Sarah; Saml x Edmonds; 21 Oct 1857; W R Clark Clk
Parker, Christian x; Rudicil, Elisabeth; John x Helms; ____ 1805; Js McEwin
Parker, David x; Gabriel, Sarah; James Lollar; 12 Dec 1797; Jno Dickson
Parker, David x; Richards, Susanah; James x Bynum; 30 Dec 1826; V McBee
Parker, Ezekiel; Earley, Susannah; Levy x Parker; 28 Aug 1817; Saml Wilson
Parker, Hosea; Bynum, Jane; J R Dellinger; 31 Dec 1861; W R Clark; M 7 Jan
    1862 by Jonas W Derr JP
Parker, John; Edwards, Jane; Wilson x Parker; 4 Mar 1828; J T Alexander
Parker, John; McCarver, Jane; William Hanks; 15 Feb 1831;' Bolin T Kirby
Parker, Jonathan; Yarber, Elisebeth; Christy Carpenter; 16 Apl 1826; Jacob Car-
    penter JP
Parker, Levi x; Parker, Rody; John Wilson; 2 Jan 1808; D M Forney
Parker, Nicholas x; Whienand (or Whisnand), Caty; Jonathan Parker; 22 May 1819;
    Jacob Carpenter JP
Parker, Nicholas; Gauldney, Mayry; Absalom x Duncan; 8 Apl 1827
Parker, Peter x; Williams, Lizur; Frederick x Ward; 10 Mar 1825; Johnson Jones
Parker, Solomon; McCarty, Elizabeth; John x Williams; 5 Dec 1817; James T
    Alexander
Parker, Starling x; Beal, Salley; John Goodson; 2 Dec 1822; V McBee
Parker, Thomas; Davis, Prudence; Henry Dillon; 30 Dec 1804
Parker, Wm x; Homest (?), Ana; Thomas x Parker; 25 Aug 1793
Parker, William x; Bishop, Mary; Mathew x Goodson, Beal x Bishop, Wm Bishop;
    1 Nov 1796; J Graham
Parker, William; Beaty, Mary; Frederick Ford; 2 Jul 1829; Isaac Holland
Parker, Wilson; Sronce, Peggy; Valentine Darr (Derr); 13 Dec 1817; V McBee
Parks, George D (Rev); McLean, Mary M; Wm B Maclean (McLean); 25 Apl 1859;
    M 3 May 1859 by R H Morrison
Parrish, Johnston; Deshaser, Abby; Danl x Critez, Geo x Club_____; 5 Jan 1802
Parsons, Robert; Ford, Mary; Colonan Buchhannon (Buchannan); 28 Mar 1827; Isaac
    Holland
Partin, Henry; Green, Elisabeth; John Stiles; no date (Sam Ashe Governor 1795-8)
Partlow, James M; Wright, Lucinda; Henry Wright; 30 Oct 1839; Isaac Holland
Pasour, Samuel; Huffstotler, Mary; 11 Jan 1831; V McBee
Pate (Porter), J M; Leonhardt, Abarilla; W C Taylor; 29 Dec 1851; V A McBee;
    M 30 Dec 1851 by Esli Rhyne JP
Paterson (Peterson), Thomas; Peterson, Martha; David Elder; 9 Apl 1787; Jo Dickson
Patrick, Isaac; McNear, Sarah; Enoch McNair (McNear); 2 Dec 1841
Patrick, James; Fronebargar, Leah; Felix Sellers; 23 Jul 1833; J T Alexander
Patrick, Robert; Leeper, Elisabeth; James Leeper; 4 Sep 1792; Jo Dickson
Patrick, Robert M; Froneberger, Margaret; Philip Sellers; ____d Jan 1832; J T
    Alexander
Patterson, Alexander; Wells, Sarah; Aaron Hand (Hann); 30 Jul 1798; Jonn Greaves
Patterson, Alfred; Ferguson, Eliza M; James __ Ferguson; 31 Oct 1838; J A
    Ramsour DC

96

Patterson, Arthur Jr; Price, Eleanor; Thomas Price; 11 Feb 1794; Thos Price Jr, J Wilson

Patterson, Francis; Moore, Elisabeth; Wm Moore; 17 Aug 1797

Patterson (Pattison), James A; Thompson, Sarah A; Joseph B Shelton; 8 May 1855; H Asbury; M 10 May 1855 by H Asbury Mnst

Patterson (Peterson), John; Henderson, Mary; James Henderson; 28 Mar 1785; Jo Henry

Patterson, John M; Goforth, Rachel; George Goforth; 22 Dec 1835

Patterson, Richard, of York·Co S C; Barnett, Martha; Samuel Barnet (Barnett); 22 Jan 1793; J Wilson

Patterson, Robert; Barber, Isabellah; Alexander Patterson; 11 Nov 1793; Joseph Dickson; Ambiguous

Patterson, Samuel B; Goforth, Elizabeth; George Goforth; 30 Oct 1830; V McBee

Patterson, Thomas; Dickson, Narcissa; Benjamin Ormand (Orman); 27 Oct 1829; J T Alexander

Patterson, William; Cunningham, Anne; William Alexander; 26 Dec 1786

Patton, David (of York Co S C); Wilson, Agness (or Nancy); James Wilson; 23 May 1793; Joseph Steel

Payne, J W A; Smith, Eugenia B; R A Smith; 1 Dec 1859; V A McBee; M 6 Dec 1859 by R H Morrison (MG)

Paysaur (Paysour), Jonas W; Smith, Harriet; John Earney; 4 Jan 1845; R Williamson

Paysoar (Payshour), Jacob; Kizer, Peggy; Joseph x Kizer; 24 Oct 1810; Danl M Forney

Paysour, Caleb; Jinken, Eliza Jane; David Hoffman (Hufman); 14 Apl 1845; And Hoyl JP

Paysour (Pasour), Daniel; Kizer, Susanah; Jonas Friday; 25 Aug 1814; V McBee

Paysour (Pasour), David; Rine, Hannah; Jonas Carpenter; 23 Apl 1822; H Cansler

Paysour, Ephraim; Rhyne, Barbara; John Hefman (Hufman); 19 Sep 1846; And Hoyl

Paysour (Pasour), Felix; Reinhardt, Balinda; Eli Huffstetler; 20 Oct 1841; L E Thompson

Paysour, George; Wise, Elizabeth; Jonas Friday; 29 Feb 1816; James T Alexander

Paysour, George J; Garrison, Emma (Emeline); J A Ramsour; 21 Jun 1856; Robt Williamson; M 24 Jun 1856 by J R Peterson

Paysour (Pasour), John; Rhyne, Elizabeth; Samuel Paysour (Pasour); 30 Sep 1826; Jacob Plonk

Paysour, Manasseh; Thornbery, Mary; David Paysour; 22 Sep 1835; M W Abernathy

Peck, Willis; Zimmerman, Ann E; Martin Zimmerman; 12 Nov 1834; M W Abernathy

Pee, George; Dearment, Sarah; Nathl x Aldrige; 9 Jul 1779; And Neel

Peeler, Antony (Ger And____ Bohler); Carbinder, Ann; John Carpender (Carbinder); 15 Apl 1800; John Crouse

Pegram, Winchester; Stowe, Mary; _____; 1818; (N)

Pendleton, Hiream x; Smith, Elizabeth; John x Pollard; 4 Aug 1818; V McBee

Pendleton, John; Shitle, Anny; Martin Shitle; 5 Aug 1851; George Coon JP; M same date by George Coon JP

Pendleton, Joshua; Rhyne, Peggy; John x Pollard; 5 Aug 1828; B J Thompson

Pendleton, William; Williams, Laura; Elias M Hull; 3 Feb 1866; M 6 Feb 1866 by Rev A Stamey

Penion (Pinion), George W; Bird, Malinda G; Michael x McCarty; __ Jan 1843; A J Cansler

Penny, Cullen; Seitz, Darcus; Drury G Abernathy; 15 Jan 1830; Luther M McBee

Penny, Frank x; Brown, Harriet; Eli B Revels; 26 Oct 1839; J A Ramsour DC

Penny, William; Bryant, Abigail; Jno Dickson; 8 May 1798; Eliza Greaves

Penny (Penney), William; Sadler, Polley; Stephen x Cobb; 21 Apl 1821; V McBee

Peny (Penny), Richmond; Martin (or Marlin), Oliss; John Sadler; 9 Feb 1822; V McBee

Perkins, Avery x; Hoover, Catharine; William Bynum (Bynam); 26 Sep 1821; James T Alexander

Perkins, Elisha; Sherrill, Elizabeth L; W F Thomas; 28 Jan 1828; M W Abernathy JP

Perkins, Ephraim; Abernathy, Elisabeth; Peter Forney; 1 Feb 1796; Jo Dickson

Perkins, Isaac x; Summy, Katharine; John Barnes; 14 Oct 1830; J Blackwood

Perkins, James; Hamilton, Rebeca; Ninian Hamilton; __ 9 (or 9 __) 1838; H Cansler CC

Perkins, James S x; Keever, Margaret; James Mullen (Mullins); 6 Apl 1858; W R Clark; M 8 Apl 1858 by Elisha Saunders JP

Perkins, Jesse; Fish, Mary; Wallace Alexander; 31 Oct 1797; Jno M Dickson

Perkins, John; Abernathy, Nancy; Jacob F Abernathy; 26 Jun 1817; V McBee
Perkins, John x; Hover, Polly; Henry x Hoover (Hover); 23 Jan 1824; Jas T Alexander
Perkins, John x; Keever, Rebecca; Areny (?) x Perkins; 25 Nov 1830; L M McBee
Perkins, John Jr; Norris, Elizabeth; Michael Kibler, B Shipp; 12 Dec 1833; M W Abernathy
Perkins, Leander x; Bynum, Sophia; R B Stroup; 28 Mar 1864; M 29 Mar 1864 by J W Derr Esqr
Perkins, Logan x; Carpenter, Fanny; David Jenkins; 6 Feb 1829; V McBee
Perkins, Reuben; Relf, Susan W; John Hutcheson; 31 Jan 1836; M W Abernathy
Perkins, William x; Jenkins, Polly; Jenkins x Jenkins; 25 Apl 1797
Perkins, William Jr; Bullinger, Katrine; William Perkins Sr; 1 Apl 1788; Joseph Steel
Person, Alfred x; Robinson, Elender; Miles O Litton; 25 Sep 1838; H Cansler
Peters, Francis; Whisenhunt, Unica; John Whisenant (Whisenhunt); 29 Oct 1832
Peterson, C J; Hoyle, Sarah A; John P Cansler; 5 Oct 1854; J A Huss; M 8 Oct 1854 by P C Henkel (MG)
Peterson, Daniel; Mull, Elizabeth; Abraham Mull (Ger Moll); 12 Aug 1815; Mic Cline
Peterson, Henry; Slagle, Susannah; Samuel Peterson; 27 Jun 1820; Jas T Alexander
Peterson, Jesse R; Dettor, Mary; John E Hoke; 11 Mar 1842; H Cansler Clk
Peterson, John; Brown, Fanne; Peter Peterson; 30 Nov. 1786; Joseph Steel
Peterson, Matthias; Rominger, Ketren; George Fink (Ger Georg Fink ?); 29 Sep 1779
Peterson, Samuel; Jarret, Petcy; Samuel Jarrett (Jarret); 28 Jul 1818; V McBee
Petray, Lawson x; Cobb, Mary; John x Smith; 4 Oct 1835; M W Abernathy
Petre, Henry x; ------ ------; Robert Blackburn; 23 Apl 1825; V McBee
Petree, John x; Martin, Amanda; Henry Tevepaugh; 14 Feb 1829; J T Alexander
Petree, John x; Smith, Polly; Lindsey C Weaver; 8 Nov 1832; J T Alexander
Petry, William x; Turbyfield, Elizabeth; Robert Helton (Hilton); 29 Sep 1837
Pettillo, James; ------ ------; Choonrod Ward; __ Jan 1808
Pettre, John x; Butts, Barbara; Samuel Zimmerman; 7 Jan 1802 (17 Jun 1802); John Dickson
Phifer, Caleb; Ramsour, M A; Henry Fulenwider; 10 Jan 1838; W H Phifer
Phifer, George; Fullenwider, Saley; Jacob Fulenwider (Fullenwider); 25 Apl 1808; Danl Forney
Phifer, John; Fullenwider, Esther; G____ Phifer; 27 Aug 1805; Betsey Henderson
Phifer, John F; Ramsour, Elizabeth C; Caleb Phifer; 5 Jun 1839; Henry Fulenwider
Phifer, Martin Jr; Ramsour, Eliza; Henry Fulenwider; 19 May 1835; R A Burton
Phifer, Martin C; Brem, Caroline; Charles Reinhardt; 18 Feb 1819; James T Alexander
Philips, Joseph x; Tompson, Polly; Robert Cobb; 29 Nov 1817; James T Alexander
Philips, Joseph T (or F) x; Laning, Elizabeth; Marcus F Alexander; 31 Jan 1843; R M Alexander
Philips, S H; Stroup, Joannah; Daniel Hoover; 14 Sep 1840; H Cansler
Phillips, David; Smith, Anne; Robert Cobb; 17 Jul 1821; V McBee
Phillips (Philips), Greenbury x; Hampton, Elizabeth; Thomas Hampton; 16 Aug 1827; Miles W Abernathy
Phillups (Phillips), James; Phillips, Martha; Fleet Cox; 3 Aug 1819; V McBee
Pigg, John; Spurling, Rebeca; John W B Harris; 10 Mar 1840
Piles (Giles), John x; Nearns (?), Mary; Leonard x Giles; 29 Apl 1800; Ligt Williams
Pinner, Demsy; Witt, Jane; Silas Witt; 25 Sep 1819; I Holland
Pinner (Piner), Loady B; Law, Faney C; W F Holland; __ Feb 1842; D Hoffman JP
Pinner, Noah B; Law, Mary Ann; Andrew C Fulenwider; 11 Sep 1843; Eli Hoyl
Pinner, William; Shearer, Sarah; John x Pinner; 13 Feb 1797; Michael Moore
Pirkins, Elija; Jinkins, Serah; Edward Jenkins; 10 Jul 1821
Pirkins, Henrey x; Childers, Nancy; John x Ballard; 8 Mar 1849
Pirkins, John x; Allen, Elisabth; John Hoover; 12 May 1847; J Helderman JP
Pirkins, Richard x; Wilians, Mary T; Jep Sherrill; 23 Sep 1841; Wm Long JP
Pitts (?), Henry; Carigen, Mere An; Ben x Stells (Stel), Owen Conner; 14 Dec 1810; Henry Conner
Pixley, N H; West, Dulcina; John x Baker; 20 Oct 1863
Pixley, Noah H; Stamey, Sarah A; Edward D Ramsey; 14 Feb 1859; W R Clark; M same date by R G Ramsey (JP)
Plonk, David; Rudisill, Mary M; John A Hafner; 29 Dec 1841; R Williamson Jr
Plonk (Plunk), Jacob; Cosner, Cathrine; John Weaver; 24 Dec 1812; V McBee

Plonk (Plunk), Joseph; Rudisel, Barbara; John Hafner (Havner); 28 Sep 1816; James T Alexander

Plonk, Philip; Beam, Mary Jane; Robison Crouse; 14 May 1851; Robt Williamson

Plot (Plott), Elias; Conrad, Charity; John Campbell; 24 Jan 1801; Jno Dickson

Plott, E W; Jacobs, Mary A; H P Crawford; 15 Dec 1856; W R Clark; M 23 Dec 1856 by A J Fox MG

Plott, Elias; Kelly, Margaret; Robert C Kelly; 10 Apl 1835; M W Abernathy

Plunk, Jacob; Tethrow, Salley; Jacob x Havner; 17 Dec 1824; V McBee

Pollard, Hiram x; Shitle, Malinda; John Carpenter; 17 Mar 1853; V A McBee; M 22 Mar 1853 by George Coon JP

Pollard, James; Bigham, Susannah (or Rosannah); Martin Hoyle; 5 (or 15) Jul 1830 (endorsed 1831); M Hull JP

Pollard, John x; Pendleton, Milley; Hereman x Pendleton; 26 Mar 1813; V McBee

Pollard, Uriah; Dameron, Sarah W; Joseph x Dameron; 13 Jan 1822; V McBee

Pollard, William x; Dameron, Nancy; Uriah Pollard; 8 Oct 1828; B J Thompson

Ponder, John; Peerson, Betsey; Jesse (or Sam) Ponder, John Person; 30 Jan 1812

Ponder, Silas; Spurlin, Elizabeth; Jehu Ponder; 27 Aug 1833; V McBee

Pope, Daniel; Deal, Polly; John K Gant; 11 Oct 1827; Miles W Abernathy

Pope, Lawson x; Samson, Carolna; Jonathan Bost; ____ Jan 1841 (endorsed 1840); J Yount JP

Popst (Propst), Amos x; Hedrick, Lise; Simon x Deel; 17 Dec 1835; Fr Hoke JP

Popst, George x; Deal, Fanny; John x Mosar; 29 Dec 1825; Fr Hoke JP

Porter, James L; Beaty, Nancy H; William Beaty; 18 May 1840; And Hoyl

Porter, James M; Titmon (or Tetmon), Mary M; John Smith; 18 Feb 1840; Isaac Holland

Porter, James M; Titman, Violet; John Armstrong; 11 Mar 1846; R M Alexander

Porter, Samuel G; Whisnant, Martha; George x Whisnant; 18 Apl 1824; Dvd Warlick for Vardrey McBee Clark

Posten, Daniel x; Stroup, Hannah; John Smith; 27 Feb 1788; Eliz Dickson

Poston, John (Jr, of Rowan Co); Boldrige, Rebekah; John Poston (Sr, of Rowan Co); 24 Apl 1782; Ambiguous

Poston, Samuel; King, Rachael; Adam Stroup; 12 Jan 1790; Jo Dickson

Potter, William; Massey, Betsey; Matthew Holland; 27 Jan 1794; Jo Dickson

Powel, Charles x; Bookout, Sarah; John Bookout; 25 Aug 1822; V McBee

Powel, Wm x; Williams, Susanna; Wm Collins; 13 Jun 1811

Powell (Powel), Philip (of Burke Co); Hermon, Elizabeth; Michael Hermon (Ger same); 26 Apl 1821; Mic Cline

Powell, Smith L A; Willson, Eliza; N A Powell; 7 Feb 1838; Jesse Gantt

Powell, William; Moore, Sally; David Harry; 27 Jul 1833

Powers see Bowers

Prather, Hamilton; Lambeth, Mary; William Aruin (Erwin); 17 May 1825

Prece (Price), Isaac; Vickers, Peggy; John Vickers; 15 Apl 1818; V McBee

Prevett (Prevet), Matthew; _____ _____; Thomas Bell; ____ Dec 1807

Previtt, Andrew R x; Aderholt, Catherine; Abraham Aderhold (Aderholt); 25 Oct 1828; V McBee

Price, Aron x; Coldwell, Ruth; Thomas x Coldwell; 17 Aug 1820; V McBee

Price, Ezekial; Graham, Betsey; John Ramsey; 24 Oct 1810; Danl M Forney

Price, George x; Coldwell, Salley; Thomas x Coldwell; 4 Mar 1822; V McBee

Price, James; Woods, Mary; William Kinkead; 27 Oct 1795

Price, John; Barber, Anna; Wm J Wilson; 12 Nov 1810; Danl M Forney

Price, John J; Neely, Martha J; Henry N Knox; 5 Aug 1843; Isaac Holland

Price, Jonathan; Ewert, Elisabeth; James Dickson; 15 Feb 1790; William Dickson

Price, Thos B; Neagle, Margaret E; Thos B Maclean; 9 Aug 1839; Isaac Holland

Price, Thomas W; Falls, Nancy S; Alexander Robinson; 11 Nov 1836; Samuel C Robinson

Prim, George x; Nixon, Elizabeth; I W Moore; 27 Apl 1848; R E Burch JP

Prim, William x; Black, Ann; John M Nixon; 9 Apl 1860; R E Burch; M same date by R E Burch JP

Privet, James; Aderholt, Elizabeth; Alfred Hoke; 18 Sep 1833; V McBee

Probst, Abel J; Hallman, Delila; Jesa Cline; 26 Mar 1835

Probst (Propts), Daniel; Bysinger, Elizabeth; David x Ikerd; 25 Feb 1822; V McBee

Probst (Propst), Henry; Bowman, Polly; John Bolick; 7 Jan 1829; J T Alexander

Probst (Propst), John; Deitz, Christina; Jacob Cline; 9 Jan 1802

Proctor, Benjamin x; Shelton, Anny; David Blalock; 15 Feb 1808; Maxl Chambers

Proctor (Procter), H S; Edwards, Jane; Thos O Proctor (Procter); 4 (or 11) Sep 1840; A J Cansler

Proctor, Joseph; Proctor, Elizabeth; Thomas Blalock; 18 Dec 1842; R Williamson Jr
Proctor, Richard; Spain, Patcy; Randolph Barnet (Randel Barnett); 4 Apl 1808; Max Chambers
Proctor, Thomas O; Guthrey, Elizabeth; Matthew Fitzgarald; 11 Jul 1836; M W Abernathy
Propst (Propest), Avey (Avery); Setzer, Nancy E; John Mauny (Mauney); 19 Sep 1840; E Mauney
Propst, Daniel; Ikerd, Sarah; Lorance Ikerd (Ger Eigerdt); 18 Dec 1812
Propst, Daniel; ------ ------; Young Shelton; 4 May 1835
Propst, Daniel A; Linn Sarah; John H Propst; 3 Aug 1841; H Cansler
Propst, Jacob; McCulloh, Mary; John D Hoke; 1 Apl 1828; Daniel Hoke
Propst, John; Peacock, Susannah; Eli Johnson; 1 Jul 1831; J T Alexander
Propst (Probst), John M; Propst, Susan C; Joseph x Sain; 2 Apl 1859; Danl Siegel JP; M 3 Apl 1859 by Danl Siegel JP
Propst (Probts), Josiah A; Grosse, Margret; Absalom Angel (Angle), Jacob Probts (Probst); 30 Nov 1828; M Hull JP
Propst, Larsen (Lawson); Earney, Malina; Martin (F) Earney; 14 May 1839; H Cansler CC
Propst, William x; Causby, Hannah; Tilman x Stilwell; 8 Jun 1829; Vardry McBee
Propst, Wilson; White, Rebecca; Leroy M Shelton; 14 Feb 1839
Pryor, Burton x; Kincaid, Catherine; John M Jacobs; 8 Jul 1827; V McBee
Pryor, David †J; Shelton, Jinsey Janet; George W Kincaid; 23 Mar 1832; L McBee
Pryor, Samuel; Howard, Jane; Daniel Carpenter; 4 Jun 1841; John D King JP
Pryor, Stuart L; Haynes, Susan C; William Crow; 7 Aug 1844
Pryor, Thos J (Thomas Prior); Tucker, Polly; Daniel Tucker; 20 Oct 1817; V McBee
Pryor (Prior), Wiley; Tucker, Patsy A; Wilson Tucker; 18 Sep 1821; V McBee
Punch, Wm F; Huffman, Amy; Langdon Huffman; 16 Oct 1840; H Cansler
Puntch, A (Archable); Killian, Jude; Abraham Killian (Ger same); 29 Jan 1818; Joseph Fisher
Puntch (Punch), Thomas; Killian, Salley; A (Archibald) Puntch (Punch); 2 Oct 1818; V McBee
Puntch, William; Hally, Mary; Joseph Mehaffey; 20 Oct 1821; Mic Cline
Purkins, John F x; Buynem, Violet C; Francis J Lehmans (Lemons Jr); 4 Apl 1861; J W Derr; M same date by Jonas W Derr JP
Purkins, Joshua; Sherril, Rebeca; Jacob Sheril; 13 Dec 1795
Purvians, James; Sherrill, Deborough; Nicolas Sherrill; 21 Oct 1794; John Dickson; Ambiguous
Putman, Elias W; Gilleland, Margaret J; J W Wyckoff; 19 Dec 1855; M same date by F J Jetton JP
Putman, James L; Mauney, Harriet; Thomas Branton; 25 Jan 1855; J A Huss; M same date by George Coon JP

Quals, John x; Moore, Sally; Mathias Deal; 3 Oct 1839; Wm Herman JP
Queen, Berry x; Richards, Julia; Elam A Curry; 8 Feb 1864; M 9 Feb 1864 by F M Reinhardt JP
Queen (Quin), Joshua x; Richards, Malinda; John B Smith; 30 Jul 1859; W R Clark; M 4 Aug 1859 by J B Smith JP
Queen, Laban; Newton, Mary Ann; Maraday (Meredith) Queen; 23 Dec 1845; R Williamson
Queen, Maraday (Merida); Summey, Lavina; Solomon Hovis; 25 Sep 1843; H Cansler
Queen, William x; Kelly, Margaret; John Bradshaw; 10 Apl 1851; Robt Williamson; M same date by J T Alexander JP
Queen, William x; Fuss, Sophia; Albert Hawkins; 1 Sep 1860; W R Clark; M 4 Sep 1860 by J B Smith JP
Quickel, Cephas; Killian, Sarah R; Albert C Williamson; 16 May 1840; H Cansler
Quickel, Michael (Jr); Hoke, Elisabeth; Philip Henckel; 1 Mar 1810; Frederick Hoke
Quin (Quinn), Henry; Greyham, Elisabeth; Ab McAfee; 29 Jan 1812; Joseph Green
Quin (Quinn), Richard; Greyham, Polley; Ab McAfee Esqer; 3 Jan 1810
Quin (Quinn), Robert; McArthur, Isabella; Jas Quinn; 24 Nov 1846; Wm J Wilson
Quin, William x; Hutchinson, Catherina; George x Quin; 16 Apl 1836; John B Harry
Quinn, James x; Kelly, Martha; Jacob Carpenter; 1 Jul 1856; J A Huss; M 5 Jul 1856 by J Helderman JP
Quinn, James E; Killian, Julian E; Henry Pharr; 28 Mar 1859; W R Clark; M 5 Apl 1859 by A J Fox MG
Quinn, John R; Dickson, Mary E; W F Holland; 26 Mar 1842; Isaac Holland
Quinn, Merideth; Chapman, Susannah; Peter Williams; 27 Jan 1842; R Williamson Jr

Rabb, James x; Keever, Hannah; John x Hinkle (Hink), Jacob Forney; 8 May 1817; V McBee
Rabb, John; Keener, Rebecca; Michael Keener; 4 Aug 1839; Elisha Saunders
Rabb, Wm A; Shitle, Rebeca; G W Toury; 1 Sep 1858; Logan H Lowrance; M same date by Logan H Lowrance JP
Raby, Robert x; Huffman, Fanny; David x Huffman; 15 Apl 1830; Jonas Bost
Rader, Daniel; Deal, Fanny; Jonas Rader; 15 Jan 1829; Mic Cline
Ragan, Daniel F; Glenn, Frances H; Edward M Berry; 23 Jun 1842
Ragan (Regon), Morgan; Ford, Ibby; Milton Ford; 22 Sep 1833; I Holland
Ragan (Rigon), Washington; Marchel, Eliza J; Morgan Ragan Sr (Rigon); 24 Feb 1831; Isaac Holland
Ramer, Peter x; Cook, Sally; Matthias x Whetstone; 19 Dec 1812; James T Alexander
Ramsaur (Ramsour), Andrew; Ramsour, Sarah; Jonas Ramsour; 11 Mar 1822; V McBee
Ramsaur (Ramsour), David; Wilfong, Sarah; John Hoke; 12 Jul 1805
Ramsaur, David; Loretz, Mary; Jacob Summey Jr; 15 Sep 1814
Ramsaur (Ramsour), David A; Wilfong, Anna; Daniel Conrad; 22 Jan 1828; J T Alexander
Ramsaur, Eli; Warlick, Sarah; Daniel Loritz; 23 Nov 1825; V McBee
Ramsaur (Ramsour), Henry F; Shuford, Sarah E; F J Jetton; 6 Jun 1858; H Cansler
Ramsaur (Ramsour), John (Jr); Summey, Susannah; John Heedick (Hedick); 17 Dec 1813; V McBee
Ramsaur, Philip; Summy, Salley; Jacob Summey (Summy); 26 Apl 1808
Ramsaur, Philip; Rhodes, Mary; David A Ramsaur; 19 Mar 1833; Hugh Quin V D M
Ramsey, Allen; Johnson, Elisabeth; Terrill G Cloud; 9 May 1830; P Stamey JP
Ramsey, Andrew; Neill, Margret; John Neill; 29 Jul 1817; Jo Lourance
Ramsey, D L; Johnson, Eveline; J F Hutson; 2 Aug 1865; A S Haynes CCC; M 3 Aug 1865 by D A Haines JP
Ramsey, E D; Hauss, Jane; W W Ramsey; 2 Oct 1866; M same date by R N Davis Minister
Ramsey, James; Hutson, Ruth; David Ramsey; 11 Feb 1790; John Moore
Ramsey, James; Mull, Salley; John Muckleroy; 26 Oct 1819; V McBee
Ramsey, John x; Black, Martha; --------; 11 Nov 1785
Ramsey, John; Rill, Rachel; James Duff; 18 Dec 1793; John Dickson
Ramsey, John M; West, Sophia; C P Johnson; 27 Jun 1863; W R Clark
Ramsey, Rhodolphus M; Beaty, Rosa E; Andrew Hauss; 19 Nov 1865; A S Haynes Cty Ct Clk; M 21 Nov 1865 by S P Sherrill JP
Ramsey, Robert G; Davis, Elizabeth; James Keen; 6 Dec 1826
Ramsey, Rodolphus M; Blackburn, Frances C; Andrew Hauss; 27 Sep 1860; W R Clark; M same date by J Finger (MG)
Ramsey, Samuel; Hugens, Rebecka; Paul Cox; 23 Nov 1797; Jon Dickson
Ramsey, Solomon; Glenn, Agness; Paul Kistler; 31 Jul 1816; V McBee
Ramsey, Thomas x; McAslen, Marget; John Orr (Oar); 8 Oct 1794
Ramsey, Thomas; Dinwiddie, Esther; John Dinwode (Dinwiddie); 11 Jun 1795; J Wilson
Ramsey, Thomas; Summey, Catharine; Samuel x Dyer; 23 Jul 1812; Vardry McBee
Ramsey, W W; Sumy (Summey), M J; Andrew Hauss (Hause); 20 Feb 1867; M 21 Feb 1867 by S Lander
Ramsey, William; Cox, Polly; Arnold Bonham; 15 Aug 1804; John Dickson
Ramsour, Caleb H; Ramsour, Julia A E; F S Ramsour; 8 Apl 1852; V A McBee; M same date by Rev David Crooks
Ramsour, David; Summy, Betsey; Danl Reinhart (Rinehart); 20 Jul 1803; Jno Dickson
Ramsour, David; Duckworth, Jane; George S Ramsour; 17 Nov 1841; R Williamson
Ramsour (or Ramsaur), Elisha J; Finger, Eliza; Jno F (Franklin) Ramsour; 7 Jan 1843; V A McBee
Ramsour, F S; Ramsour, H C; Solomon Ramsour; 28 Mar 1839; Max Wilson JP
Ramsour, George S; Warlick, Eliza; George A Leopold; 9 Dec 1839; H Cansler
Ramsour, Jacob; Summy, Barbara; Jacob Summey Jr; 10 Sep 1811; Lwn Henderson
Ramsour, Jacob; Ramsour, Mary; Jonas Ramsour; 16 Nov 1825; J E Bell
Ramsour, Jacob H; White, Sarah H; John Boyd; 10 Apl 1840; H Cansler
Ramsour, Jonas; Shuford, Eve; Andrew Ramsour; 15 Nov 1817; Andrew Loretz
Ramsour, Solomon; Warlick, Elizabeth; Andrew Ramsour; 20 Sep 1820; James T Alexander
Ramsour, Vardry M; Ramsour, Nancy C; Allen Alexander; 13 May 1850; Robt Williamson
Ramsour, William; Ramsour, Martha A; R E Johnston; 7 Jun 1852; Robt Williamson

101

Ramsour, William; Ramsour, Ann; _____; 25 Aug 1866; W T McCoy JP; Acknowledgment by former slaves

Ramsy, Robert x; Glen, Margrat; Saml x Ramsy; 9 Feb ____ (probably 1793-6); (Drafted by Michl Eaker)

Randleman, Henry; Dellinger, Mary; Daniel Reell (Reel); 31 May 1824; V McBee

Rankin, A V; McCoy, Elizabeth; A G Halyburton (Halliburton); 24 Mar 1863; W R Clark; M same date by R N Davis Minister

Rankin, Alexander; Moore, Elizabeth; _____; 1804 (?); Not a bond; account of property received by Alexander Rankin from Alexander and Elisabeth Moore parents of his wife Elisabeth

Rankin, Alexander; Jenkins, Nancy A; Dallas Williamson; 25 Mar 1840

Rankin, Denny; McMin, Sarah; Samuel McMin; 4 Jan 1803

Rankin, James; Johnson, Polly; John Meroney; 26 Aug 1812

Rankin, James (of Iredell Co); Little, Patsey; David Lockman; 17 Mar 1858; M same date by J Lowe JP

Rankin, James R; Jenkins, Mary; Daniel McGee; 24 Jan 1839; H Cansler CC

Rankin, John D; Johnson, Nancy; Tho H Jones; 7 Jun 1825

Rankin, John D; Jenkins, Salenia K; Blair M Jenkins; 5 Sep 1837; H Cansler Clk

Rankin, John M; Nixon, Catharine; James Nixon; 5 Jan 1859; R Nixon JP; M same date by R H Morrison

Rankin, Joseph M; Linebarger, Mary; Daniel McGee; 2 Nov 1837; Eli Hoyl

Rankin, N A; Hand, Rebecca C; William Murrell; 26 Oct 1844; C L Hunter

Rankin, Robert; Witherow, Mary; James Witherow; 7 Nov 1769; Ezekiel Polk

Rankin, Robert; McCallister, Sarah; John M'Callister; 15 Dec 1800; Jonn Greaves

Rankin, William; Camble, Mary; Thomas Rhine (Ger Rein ?); 15 Apl 1791

Rankin, William; Lourance, Mary; William Nesbitt; 17 Jan 1810; Danl M Forney Cl

Rankin, William R; Capps, May Ame (or Ann); Joseph N Fite; 19 Dec 1842; R M Alexander JP

Ransom, Demse (Demese) x; _____ _____; _____; 28 Dec 1810; Not a bond; a note from Alexr Brevard to the Clerk Bride is a "free black woman"

Ratchford, John; Henry, Isabella; Robert Alexander; 3 Apl 1823; Saml M'Kee

Ratchford, Moses; Henry, Nancy M; Joseph L Vandyke (Vandike); 23 Mar 1822; Saml M'Kee

Ratchford, Robert C; Martin, Ann; Adlai Gingles; 10 Aug 1822; Saml M'Kee

Ratcliff, Benjamin x; Bradshaw, Beckey; David Williams; 3 Jul 1784; Joseph Henry

Ray see Wray

Ray (Rhea), George W; Smith, Rosannah; John x Gilbert; 9 Feb 1832; Eli Hoyl, And Hoyl

Raynalls (Runnels), Calib x; Shull, Mary; Valentine Dellinger; 7 Oct 1851; George Coon JP; M 8 Oct 1851 by George Coon JP

Reas(Reese), Paul A; Saunders, Polley; Saml Saunders; 22 Feb 1821; V McBee

Reather, William x; Sharpe, Katrine; Hophel Cline (Ger Christoffel Klein); 25 May 1785; Joseph Steel

Rector, John; Williams, Judith; Charles Williams; 7 Jan 1819; Peter Hoyle, Heny Banick (?)

Rector, Silas; Grice, Agness; Aaron Sherrill (Shirrill); 3 Oct 1822; Wm Little

Redman, Saml x; Rhyne, Ann; Jonathan x Tronbarger; 26 Aug 1829; Eli Hoyl

Redmon, James A x; Yarber, Martha; Elihu Moffit; 6 Aug 1832; Vardry McBee

Reed, Alexander; Litle, Martha; John Litle; 18 Dec 1798

Reed, Alexander; Little, Peggy; Anderson Nunneley (Nunely); 27 Aug 1805; Hy Conner JP

Reed, George A; Coxe, Eliner L; David Cox (Coxe); 13 Dec 1827; V McBee

Reed, Jacob; Sigman, Sarah, widow; Gasper Bolick (Ger Caspar Bolch); 14 Nov 1826; V McBee

Reed, James; Beatey, Margaret; Richard Rankin; 14 Feb 1793

Reed, William; Linebarger, Susannah; Wm Allen; 15 Apl 1834

Reedey (Reedy), William; Cashing, Hanna; Abel H Duckworth, Alexander McCorkle; 15 Feb 1806; Hy Conner JP

Reel, Daniel; Moody, Elizabeth; Jacob Forney; 17 Feb 1817; James T Alexander

Reel, George; Stroup, Mary; Philip Stroup; 24 Jul 1784

Reel, Jacob B; Helderman, Mary; James C Jenkins; 7 Feb 1849; Robt Williamson

Reel, Spaight M; Clemmer, E M; John A Brown; 8 Aug 1866; W R Clark; M 12 Aug 1866 by Elisha Saunders JP

Reep, Daniel; Sebaugh, Betsey; Peter Seabah (Sabaughe); 24 Jul 1819; James T Alexander

Reep, Daniel x; Engle, Sarah; David Hauss (Haas); 4 Dec 1841

Reep, Daniel; Johnson, Mary Ann; _____; 26 Jul 1863; M this date by D Williams JP; R only, no B
Reep, David x; Yoder, Barbera; Jacob Weaver (Ger Jacob Weber); 20 Mar 1828; Phil Whitener JP
Reep, Emanuel; Howser, Elizabeth; Peter Hoyl; 22 Oct 1835; M Hull JP
Reep, Henry; Saine, Mary Ann; John Sain; 3 Jan 1832; L McBee
Reep, Henry x; Rayfield, Jane; Samuel x Reep; 10 Nov 1839; M Hull JP
Reep, Jonas; Stamey, Sufroney Matilda; William R Self; 1 Apl 1858; D Williams JP; M same date by D Williams JP
Reep, Peter x; Houser, Mary; Peter Houser (Ger Peter Hauser); 29 Apl 1803; John Dickson
Reep (Reap), Philip; Haus, Susannah; Jonas Reap; 19 Nov 1833; M W Abernathy
Reep, Samuel x; Spake, Mary; Thomas Williams; 21 Oct 1832; M Hull JP
Rees, James x; West, Fereby; Stephen x West; 24 Jan 1797
Rees (Reese), John; Lorance, Henry Ette; Jacob Rees (Reese); 22 Oct 1821; V McBee
Rees, Lewis; Fry, Anna; Peter Rees; 2 Apl 1831; Mic Cline
Reeves, Jennings R; Titman, Eliza; William E Reeves; 22 Nov 1836; Samuel C Robinson
Reeves, John N; Armstrong, Sarah; Jeremiah L McCarver; 3 Apl 1834; J G Hand JP
Regan (Reggen), Charles; Linebarger, Mary; William A Robey (Roby); 1 May 1824; V McBee
Regan (Reagan), Henry C; Dellinger, Fany R; Sidney A Burch; 5 May 1867; R Nixon JP; M on same date by R Nixon JP
Reid, Allen; Gastin, Elisa; Robert Gastin; 9 Sep 1823; Saml M'Kee
Reid, James W; Ratchford, Mary D; Isaac H Holland (Jr); 2 Jan 1847; Isaac Holland
Reid, Thomas; Calloway, Mary E; _____; 6 Mar 1857; M this date by W W Munday JP; R only, no B
Reid, William; Rankin, Nancy; John Rankin; 27 Jul 1812; Vardry McBee CC
Reinhardt, Abram; Warlick, Julia; _____; 19 Mar 1856; J A Huss Clerk; M 20 Mar 1856 by Danl Siegel JP; L and C, no B
Reinhardt, Alfred x; Saine, Susan; W M Reinhardt; 14 Aug 1856; M same date by Danl Siegel JP
Reinhardt, Charles; Loutz (or Loretz), Betcy; _____; 6 Oct 1812; Vardry McBee
Reinhardt (Rinehart), Christian Jr; Forney, Polly; David Ramsour; 25 Jan 1803
Reinhardt, Daniel; Parker, M J; Jno A Roberts; 4 Jan 1866; A S Haynes CCC
Reinhardt, David; Mason, Mary; John Jonas; 25 Aug 1825; M Hull JP
Reinhardt, Felix; Havener, Mary; Joseph Shuford; 23 Sep 1835; M W Abernathy
Reinhardt, Franklin D; Perkins, Martha J (or I or S); Benjamin Norris; 30 Oct 1838; J A Ramsour DC
Reinhardt, Franklin M; Smith, Sarah M; Ethel H Porter; 11 Jan 1834; M W Abernathy
Reinhardt, Isaac x; Bird, Rebeckah; William x Bird; 30 Dec 1814
Reinhardt, Isaac; Wyant, Elizabeth; Joshua Lore; 6 May 1847; Danl Siegel JP
Reinhardt, Isaac; Rudisill, Sarah; David Rudisill; 28 Mar 1858; W R Clark; M same date by F J Jetton JP
Reinhardt (Rinehart), Jacob; Hoyle, Margaret; Danl Reinhardt (Rinehart); 18 Oct 1804
Reinhardt (Rhinehard), Jacob; Michel, Mayry; Daniel Michael (Michel); 9 Apl 1820; D Lutz JP
Reinhardt, Jacob; Keen, Elizabeth A; Henry Cansler; 16 Aug 1838
Reinhardt, Joseph x; Byrd, Jane; William x Byrd (Bird); 6 Oct 1808; D M Forney CC
Reinhardt, Lawson A; Shuford, Susan; Thos Young; 16 Sep 1837; H Cansler
Reinhardt, Michael; Moore, Polley; Jacob Reinhardt; 27 Oct 1812
Reinhardt, Michael; Allyn, Maria; John D Hoke; 20 Oct 1829; B J Thompson
Reinhardt, Robt P; Ramsour, Susan B; And Roseman; 30 Jun 1862; W R Clark
Reinhardt, Rudolph x; Bragg, Frances A; William B Bragg; 8 Nov 1827; V McBee
Reinhardt, Wallace M; Johnson, Frances Ann; J C Jenkins (Jinkins); 13 Oct 1845; R Williamson
Reinhart (Rinehart), John; Moore, Anna; John Dickson; 19 Mar 1798
Reinharte, John x; Saine, Sally; Jacob x Saine; 5 Aug 1828; M Hull JP
Reinheardt (Reinhardt), Henry; Finger, Elizabeth; Henry I (or J) Anthony; 14 Dec 1839; H Cansler
Relph, John W x; Smith, Sarah; Michael x Petray; 1 Aug 1835; M W Abernathy; Ambiguous
Rendelmon, Sisarow x; Brevard, Marey Ann; Stephen x Brevard; 2 Mar 1866; Freedmen and Freedwoman; M same date by J Helderman JP

Rendleman, Lawrence O; Abernathy, Ann Catharine A; --------; 7 Apl 1852; M this
    date by Rev P C Hinkel; R only, no B
Reynolds, Anson; Buff, Mary; James x Nealson; 6 Jan 1814; Saml Wilson
Reynolds, Fergus H; Grice, Mary; Hugh Wilson x Marshal; 30 Aug 1842
Reynolds, Jesse; Moses, Nancy; William Baxter; 9 Mar 1824; Jas T Alexander
Reynolds, John; Creags (?), Agness; James x Nealson; 20 Nov 1811; Saml Wilson Dp C
Reynolds, John x; McGinnas, Louisa; John McGinnas; 14 Aug 1827; J T Alexander
Reynolds, Josiah (Joseph); Eaker, Catharine; John Eaker; 13 Jun 1815; James T
    Alexander
Reynolds, Reuben H; Devibach (?), Lydia; John Huggins; 28 Dec 1819; V McBee
Reynolds, Thomas; Titerbeam, ------; Robert Weear; 10 Apl 1788
Reynolds, Thomas x; Mauney, Sally; William Martin; 17 Nov 1819; V McBee
Reynolds, Uell; King, Patsy; William Baxter; 26 Dec 1818; V McBee
Reynolds, Wiley W; Elmore, Susan; Francis B Jones; 3 Mar 1855; J A Huss;
    M 5 Mar 1855 by David Crouse JP
Reyonalds (Reyonelds), Elias x; Mostiller, Margret; Nethaniel x Mitchum; 14 Apl
    1830; M Hull JP
Rhine (Rhyne), Daniel W; Setzer, Nancy; Jonas R Linebarger; 21 Nov 1840;
    H Cansler
Rhine, John x; Kizer, Anne; Abraham Mauney; 22 Jan 1812; Lwn Henderson
Rhine, Jonas see Houser, Jonas
Rhine, Martin; Freeman, Jain; Jacob Rhine; 14 Apl 1797
Rhoads (Rhodes), Bennet; Smith, Esbel; Nicholas x Dillan; 20 Dec 1813; V McBee
Rhoads, Daniel x; Hofstatler, Matty; Tilmon Jinkens (Jenkins); 14 Jun 1837; Daniel
    Hoffman JP
Rhoads, David; Nance, Caroline; Henry A Dilling; 2 May 1837; Daniel Hoffman JP
Rhoads, Jacob x; Weathers, Sarah; John x Weathers; 12 Aug 1782; Ja McEwin
Rhodes, Caleb; Huffman, Myra; John Cansler; 14 Aug 1840; H Cansler
Rhodes (Roads), Christian; Rhyne, Mary; Jacob Link; 28 Feb 1818; James T
    Alexander
Rhodes, David x; Wial, Nancy; Peter Hufman; 26 Oct 1830; J T Alexander
Rhodes, Henry; Carpenter, Catharine; Philip Reep; 16 Apl 1829; J T Alexander
Rhodes, Henry; Rhyne, Barbara; Ephraim S Weathers; 16 Jul 1833; J T Alexander
Rhodes, Henry; Stamey, Luiza; Wm H Michal; 20 May 1853; R Williamson;
    M 26 May 1853 by Daniel Siegel JP
Rhodes, Jacob H; Hoke, Rosanna E; Ambrose Costner; 15 Mar 1858; W R Clark;
    M 18 Mar 1858 by A J Fox JP
Rhodes, Melchi; Killian, Caroline; B A Dye; 19 Mar 1855; M 3 Apl 1855 by J R
    Peterson (MG)
Rhodes, Peter x; Pack, Betsy; Edward Atkinson; 27 Dec 1785; Jas Dickson
Rhonay (Roaney), James; Gilbert, Anna; Daniel Sumerour; 9 Aug 1813; V McBee
Rhyne, Absalom; Mosteller, Elizabeth; George Mosteller; 15 Sep 1838; H Cansler
Rhyne, Adam A; Wethers, Jane; James W Reed (Reid); 30 Jan 1838; Eli Hoyl
Rhyne, Christian; Clemer, Elizabeth; George Clemmer (Clemer); 28 Sep 1830; J T
    Alexander
Rhyne (Ryne), Daniel; Huffman, Katharine; John Linebarger; 18 Mar 1808; Jacob
    Forney
Rhyne, Daniel; McGee, Louisa; Thomas H Jones; 31 Dec 1823; Jas T Alexander
Rhyne, Daniel; Hovis, Elizabeth; Joseph W Rhyne; 19 Jan 1847
Rhyne, David x; Carpenter, Anna; Joseph McAlister; 16 Jul 1816; James T Alexander
Rhyne, David; Fite, Malinde S; Samuel W Craig; __ Jan 1839; And Hoyl JP
Rhyne, Emanuel; Weathers, Polly; Alfred Lineberger (Linebarger); 3 Sep 1833;
    Isaac Holland
Rhyne, Esli; Plonk, Margaret; Jno A Parker; 19 Dec 1843; H Cansler
Rhyne, George; Dellinger, Mirey A; Wm H (Henry) Shell; 20 Dec 1860 (endorsed
    1862); W A Carpenter; M same date by P Carpenter JP
Rhyne (Rine), Jacob; Huffman, Elizabeth; Martin Rhine (Rine); 20 Jan 1800;
    Jonn Greaves
Rhyne (Rhine), Jacob; Stroup, Caty; Michael Rhyne (Rhine); 28 Dec 1810; H Y
    Webb
Rhyne, Jacob; Rhyne, Elizabeth; Robert Thomas; 22 Oct 1822; Jas T Alexander
Rhyne, Jacob; Smith, Nancey; Oliver Smith; 29 Mar 1836; Isaac Holland
Rhyne, Jacob; Clemmer, Anney; Christy (Cristian) Rhyne; 10 Apl 1838
Rhyne, Jacob; Best, Margaret; Caleb Linebarger; 3 Nov 1840; Eli Hoyl
Rhyne, Jacob; Costner, Barbara; F A Hoke; 30 Dec 1844; R Williamson

Rhyne, John x; Lefener (or Lefever), Nelly; Bastin (Boston) Best (Bess); 19 Apl 1808; Jacob Forney
Rhyne, John; Shuford, Sally; Martin Shuford; 2 Feb 1810; Danl M Forney
Rhyne, Jonas x; Ransom, Elisabeth; James H Wall; 4 Sep 1846; Robt Rankin
Rhyne, Jonathan; Huffman, Rebeca; Morgan x Weathers; 8 Feb 1831; Bolen T Kirby
Rhyne, Joseph K; Plonk, Susan C; Esli Rhyne; 12 Oct 1840; H Cansler
Rhyne, Joseph W; Cloningar, Viney; John Franklin Cannon; 19 Jan 1844
Rhyne, Lauson; Houser, Margaret C; Andrew x Hoyle (Hoyl); 3 Jan 1857; Robt Williamson; M 8 (or 18) Jan 1857 by Maxwell Warlick JP
Rhyne (Rine), Michael; Huffman, Catarine; John Hofman (Huffman); 3 Dec 1798; William G Dickson
Rhyne (Rhine), Michael; Weathers, Barbara; Allen Weathers; 15 Feb 1809; H Y Webb
Rhyne, Michael; Mauney, Polly; John Rhyne; 6 Dec 1822; V McBee
Rhyne, Michael: Hoyle, Margaret; Jonas Rudisill; 27 Jun 1827; J T Alexander
Rhyne, Michael; Jenkins, Lewsi; John Beeson; 1 Jun 1830; Jno Blackwood Esq; Ambiguous
Rhyne, Moses H; Huffman, Margrat L; Levi Hoffman; 13 Jan 1835; Isaac Holland
Rhyne, Peter; Bess, Catharine; David Linebarger (Lineberry); 16 Apl 1811; D M Forney
Rhyne (Rhine), Peter; Williams, Catherine; Henry Hope; 12 Mar 1824; V McBee
Rhyne, Simon; Lay, Nancy; Elisha Jones (Junr); 10 Feb 1834; Eli Hoyl
Rhyne, Simon; Houser, Mary; Moses Carpenter; 18 Oct 1848; Robt Williamson
Rhyne, Simon P; Rhyne, Elizabeth; D H Rhine; 10 Aug 1841; Eli Hoyl
Rhyne (Rhine), Solomon; Huffman, Betsey; David Linebarger; 21 Mar 1812; Lwn Henderson
Rhyne, Solomon; Carpenter, Catharine; Samuel Carpenter; 26 Sep 1838; H Cansler
Rhyne, Solomon H; Fronabarger, Cathrine; Michael H Costner; 8 Oct 1842; And Hoyl JP
Rhyne, Thomas x; Rudisel, Catharine; Joseph Miller; 5 Nov 1814; James T Alexander
Rice, James L; Sanders, Nancy J; Thomas J Saunders (Sanders); 8 Jun 1859; W R Clark; M same date by J T Alexander JP
Richards, A P x; Hovis, Mary C; M Hovis; 3 Mar 1866
Richards, Fealty; Clipard, Elizabeth; Joseph x Beal; 1 Jan 1816; V McBee
Richards, James x; Murphy, Fanney; Robt McM (McN?) Wilson, John Norman; 11 Apl 1809; Saml Wilson JP
Richards, Jno; Vence, Christiana; (Ger) Johannes Schlenker, Jeremiah x Bishop; 29 Sep 1796; Doubtful
Richards, John B x; Goodson, Michel; Jacob Helderman; 28 Jul 1834; M W Abernathy Clk
Richards, William; Cobb, Dycy; Philip Cobb (?); 15 Jun 1805; Lwn Henderson
Richards, William x; Garrison, Louisa; John x Johnson; 22 Aug 1822; V McBee
Richardson (Richeson), James I; Schenck, Catherine; John Schenck; 13 Jan 1832; V McBee
Richardson, John M; Ramsour, Alice M; David Schenck; 21 Dec 1858; M same date by C T Bland Rector St Luke's Church
Richey, Joseph; Allsan, Lucintha C; Jacob Allsan (Allson); 7 Dec 1848; P Stamey JP
Riel, Godfrey x; Cloninger, Catharine; Abraham x Fox; 11 Oct 1800
Riggs, George x; Wallace, Jenny; Benjamin James; 25 Jul 1809; Danl M Forney Cl
Riggs, Israel; Wisnant, Elisabeth; George x Wisnant; 28 Feb 1811; David Warlick
Riley, Andrew; Fite, Mary; William Riley; 26 Nov 1839; Isaac Holland
Riley, William x; Moore, Kissiah; Patrick Broaddaway (Brodaway); 8 Jan 1838; And Hoyl JP
Rily (Riley), James; Prim, Mary Ann; Milton A Smith; 13 Mar 1859; R E Burch JP; M same date by R E Burch JP
Rinck, Ephraim; Dietz, Christina; George Rinck; 24 Mar 1842; Epm Yount JP
Rinck, George; Clodfelter, Elizabeth; Reuben H Reynolds; 3 Nov 1834; G Hoke
Rinck, Jacob x; Seitz, Polly; Andrew Seitz (Ger Andreas Seitz); 25 Dec 1813; Mic Cline
Rinck, Jesse x; Burns, Susan; Andrew Gilbert (Guilbert); 4 May 1841; H Cansler
Rinck, Noah; Clay, Catharine; Wiley x Clay; 22 Feb 1847; Robt Williamson
Rine, Adam x; Best, Peggy; Phillip x Rine; 1 (or 7) Aug 1803; Jonn Greaves
Rippy, Edard (Nead); Martin, Polly; Ab McAfee; 30 May 1810
Ritchey (Richey), John S; Young, Sary (Sarah S); Peter Chapman; 3 Mar 1856; D A Haines; M same date by D A Haines JP
Ritchy (Ritchey), J Thomas x; Stamey, Barbara; Jeremiah x Campbell; 16 Feb 1849; Danl Siegel JP
Rivers, Thomas; Abernathy, Polly; St (?) Abernathy; 9 Jan 1798; Jno Dickson

Roades (Rodes), Jacob; Clemer, Susana; Aron Jenkins (Jinkins); 3 Sep 1829; J Blackwood JP

Roads, James; Pinner, Jeane; Bennet Roads; 29 Oct 1811; Elizabeth Henderson

Roaney, John x; Robison, Jane; Lawson A Rhoney (Roaney); 8 Jan 1842; H Cansler CC

Robards, Thomas x; Collins, Elizabeth; Abner McAfee; 15 Nov 1793

Roberson (Robinson), Thomas M; Munday, Rose A; M A Lowe (Low); 23 Jul 1861; Wm W Munday; M same date by Wm W Munday JP

Roberson (Robison), William x; Earny (or Eaney), Letha Jane; William Murrell; 22 Sep 1843; H Cansler

Roberts, Abel x; McGinnes, Sally; James T Alexander; 28 Mar 1818; V McBee

Roberts, Eli x; Caldwell, Isabella; Chas P Johnson; 15 Mar 1866; M same date by W R Wetmore Rector St Luke's Church

Roberts, John; Black, Elisabeth; Arthur Graham; 15 Nov 1797; John Dickson

Roberts, John; Rudisell, Katy (?); James Beaty; 10 Oct 1807; D M Forney

Roberts, John; Turbyfill, Holly; John R Dunn, Simeon Moore; 25 Oct 1831; L McBee

Roberts, John A (Anderson); Beam, Mary C; John F Alexander; 18 Jan 1848; Robt Williamson

Roberts, Martin; Logan, Drucilla; Abner McAfee; 24 Oct 1827

Roberts, Morris; Adams, Susannah; J T Alexander; 21 Dec 1838

Roberts, Moses; Harris, Elizabeth; Joshua Roberts; 29 Nov 1819; James T Alexander

Roberts, Thomas x; Eker, Mary; Joseph Dickson; 19 Aug 1783; Elisabeth Dickson

Roberts, Thomas x; Glen, Jean; Abraham Collins (Collans); 30 Jun 1791

Roberts, Thomas; Warlick, Eliza; Jas T Alexander; 3 Oct 1820; V McBee

Roberts, William; Fulenwider, Mary M; J (or I) Martin Roberts, J T Alexander; 2 Apl 1839

Robertson, Alexander; _____, Elizabeth; Robert Givens; 18 Sep 1797; Jo Dickson

Robeson, Hugh T; Berry, Jean; William Robeson; 27 Jul 1807; Robert Patterson

Robeson, Isaac x; Sims, Elizabeth; James H Lytle (Little); 9 Jan 1841

Robeson, Jesse; Shell, Salley; Isaac Robeson; 4 Sep 1813; V McBee

Robey, Wm A; Cornelias, Susanah; James Martin; 16 Sep 1824; V McBee

Robinson, A P see Smith, John

Robinson, Aaron; Hoyle, Eliza; Jacob Bost; 21 Dec 1835

Robinson, Adam; Bridges, Nancy; John Gilleland; 21 Aug 1829; J T Alexander

Robinson (Robison), Adam P; Reed, Martha; James Harwell (Harvil); 19 Dec 1825; Wm Little

Robinson, Alexander S; Weathers, Mary S; L H Torrence; 11 Aug 1842

Robinson, Andrew; Dormire, Barbara; Samuel Dormire; 30 Oct 1791; Joseph Steel

Robinson, Andrew x; Summett, Catharine; James Sronce (Sraunce); 13 Jul 1839; J T Alexander

Robinson (Robison), David; White, Betcy; Alexander Robinson (Robison); 1 Nov 1808; Maxl Chambers

Robinson, David; Shuford, Anna; David Shuford; 6 May 1817

Robinson (Robeson), David; Wilson, Rosanah L; Elam Moore; 18 Sep 1821; Jas T Alexander

Robinson, Elam; Davis, Elizebeth; Joshua E Davis; 5 Nov 1823; Isaac Holland

Robinson, Elhanan (W); Denem, Mary Ann; John Dinin (?); 2 Apl 1840

Robinson, Eli J; Fisher, Elizabeth; John Fisher; 29 May 1841; Abner B Payne

Robinson, Elijah; Wilson, Jane; James Wilson, Isaac Robinson; 7 Jan 1797

Robinson, Emanuel; Hetrek (or Hetick), Ann; Daniel Shuford (Shufford); 2 Sep 1833; V McBee

Robinson (Robison), Gideon; Gingles, Patsey; Robt Patterson; 25 Dec 1806; Lwn Henderson

Robinson, Gideon; Cathy, Carolina; Vardry McBee; 18 Jan 1834; J T Alexander

Robinson, Henry C; Warlick, Mary R; D S Hoover; 10 Nov 1849; Robt Williamson

Robinson, Henry I; Leonard, Malinda; Alexander Hudson; 23 Apl 1833; L McBee

Robinson (Robison), Henry W; Wilfong, Polley; David Robinson (Robison); 3 Aug 1819; V McBee

Robinson, Isaac x; Wilson, Polly; James Wilson; 16 Dec 1797; John Dickson

Robinson, J A; Rhodes, Nancy F; Ambrose Costner; 16 Dec 1865; A S Haynes CCC; M 17 Dec 1865 by A J Fox MG

Robinson, J H; King, M E M; A S Haynes; 25 Mar 1867; M 28 Mar 1867 by J Finger MG

Robinson, Jesse; Whitnor, Molliana; David Robinson; 29 May 1787; Joseph Steel

Robinson, Jesse; Moll, Maria; John x Moll; 16 May 1797; John Willfong JP

Robinson (Roberson), Jesse; Sherril, Cassandria; Jacob Reinhardt; 2 Mar 1809; H Y Webb

106

Robinson (Robison), Job; Kendrick, Susana; Is Holland; 20 Aug 1805
Robinson, John; Leeper, Mary; Matthew Leeper; 13 Jan 1783
Robinson, John; Hartwell, Sarah; David Robinson; 21 Nov 1787; Joseph Steel
Robinson, John; Wilson, Peggy; Lawson Henderson; 28 Sep 1815; "John Robinson
  of Madison County in the Illinois Territory"
Robinson, John; White, Martha H; Green Abernathy; 16 Jan 1823; V McBee
Robinson, John; Whitney, Nancy; William Brag (Bragg); 17 Jul 1824; Jno Turbyfill
Robinson, John H; Sherrill, Mary; Joseph Wilson; 2 (or 2__d) Jul 1818; James T
  Alexander
Robinson, John H; Cloninger, Barbara; Alexander Rutlege (Rutledge); 9 Jul 1834;
  And Hoyl
Robinson, John S; Wilkinson, E E; John W Long; 21 Oct 1840; Wm Long JP
Robinson, John W; Clark, Mary; Morgan Ragan (Regon) Jr; 1 Dec 1829; Isaac
  Holland
Robinson, John W; McCullouch, Rosanna; James Ferguson; 18 Jan 1847; A B Cox
Robinson (Robison), Jonathan; Stamey, Barbary; Henry Stamey; 12 Sep 1809; Ligt
  Williams JP
Robinson, Joseph B; Asbury, Julian R; Josiah Asbury; 12 Mar 1861; H Asbury;
  M same date by G W Ivy MG
Robinson, Joshua; Shell, Eave (Eve); James Robinson; 14 Sep 1809; Mic Cline
Robinson, Levi; Hoke, Catharine; Caleb Miller; 31 Jul 1855; Robt Williamson;
  M 2 Aug 1855 by George Coon JP
Robinson, Levi A; M'Calister, Catharine M; Hugh A Torance (Torrance); 29 Apl 1843
Robinson, Marcus L; Kistler, Margaret C; _____; 20 Dec 1859; W R Clark Clk;
  M 22 Dec 1859 by Danl Siegel JP; L and C, no B
Robinson, Morgan x; Linch, Elizabeth; John Slinkard (Ger Johannes Schlenkur);
  22 Oct 1808; Danl M Forney
Robinson, Orsbern; Abernathy, Eliza; Wesley Asbury; 31 Dec 1828; J T Alexander
Robinson (Robertson), Robert H; Plott, Sarah Jane; _____ Kelly; 8 Jul 1856; Landy
  Wood; M 11 Jul 1856 by Landy Wood MG
Robinson, Samuel; Haynes, Marth; J Mason Spainhour (Dr); 23 Dec 1865; A S
  Haynes CCC; M 31 Dec 1865 by Jno Finger MG
Robinson, Samuel C; Torrance, Mary B; Alexander Robinson; 25 Apl 1839; Isaac
  Holland
Robinson, William; Torance, Anna; John Robinson, Hugh Torance; 15 Dec 1778
Robinson, William; Gibson, Elizabeth; John Dickson; 6 Dec 1803; Eliza Greaves
Robinson, William; Wilson, Anne; Lawson Henderson; 28 Sep 1815; "William
  Robinson of the County of Gibson in the Indiana Territory";
Robinson, William; Dews (?), Eliza; John R Dunn; 12 Oct 1830; V McBee
Robinson, Zimri; Torrance, Margaret J I; Alexander Robinson; 23 Aug 1837; S C
  Robinson
Robison (Robinson), Alexander H; Parker, Elizabeth; William J McCoy; 18 Dec 1852;
  R Williamson; M 19 Dec 1852 by Rev Wade Hill Baptist
Robison, John; Lewis, Polly; Isaac S Henderson; 2 Apl 1806; Betsey Henderson
Robison (Roberson), John W; Sherrill, Martha; W M (Merion) Robison (Roberson);
  30 Sep 1860; Wm W Munday; M same date by Wm W Munday JP
Robison, Johnson; Chapman, Elizabeth; George P Shuford; 6 Mar 1843; A J Cansler
Robison (Robinson), William M; Sherrill, Margaret; John W Long; 12 Mar 1842;
  Wm Long JP
Robson (Robeson), James; Murrill, Nancy; Patrick Broaddaway (Brodaway); 5 May
  1837; Eli Hoyl
Roby (Robey), Horace; McCaul, Jane; James Starr (Star); 9 Oct 1819; V McBee
Roby (Robey), John W; Cornelius, Elizabeth; James H M'Caul; 28 Jan 1822; Jas T
  Alexander
Rocket, James; Huntly, Nancy; John Rockett (Rocket); 22 Feb 1826; V McBee
Rocket, Richard; Abernathy, Eleanor; John Abernathy; 15 Sep 1789
Rockett, James; Bandy, Elizabeth; Turner x Abernathy; 2 Jun 1813; James T Alexander
Rockett, John; Abernathy, Sarah; Smith Abernathy; 11 Jan 1787; Edward Hunter
Rockett, John (Jr); Jhonston, Anna; Robinson Johnson (Johnston); 19 Aug 1817;
  Phil Whitener JP
Rockett (Rocket), John R; Rhodes, Mary Ann; Solomon H Rhodes; 15 Apl 1847;
  P Stamey JP
Rockett (Rocket), Richard; Pinkston, Eliner; John Rockett (Rocket); 29 Dec 1825;
  J T Alexander
Roderick (Rhodrick), Elisha W; Smith, Elizabeth; Gilbert Bridges; 19 Dec 1835;
  M W Abernathy CC

Roderick, Nicholas x; Gowins, Julia; Joseph x Northem; 24 Oct 1827; V McBee

Roderik (Roderick), Marcus; Jonas, Amy; John Jonas; 10 Apl 1847; Robt Williamson

Rodes (Rhodes), Christian; Shutley, Sophia; Jacob Shutley (Ger Schötle); 11 Apl 1791

Rodes, Elisha x; Dillen, Rachel; James x Huffman; 23 Aug 1813; Vardry McBee

Rodes, John x; Smith, Sally; John x Pinner; 14 Feb 1807; Lwn Henderson

Rodes (Rhodes), Rudolph; Carpenter, Anne Mary; Paul Anthony; 26 Jan 1820; D Reinhardt

Rodgers, Aaron x; Williams, Sally; Cornelius x Rodgers; 16 Jan 1835; G Hoke

Rogers, Curnelias; Palmer, Martha; Jesse Palmer; 1 Sep 1792; Jo Dickson

Rogers, John B; Collier, Ann S; S S Harris; 11 Jun 1844; C L Hunter

Rogers, Nicles x; Williams, Ellender; Samuel C Panter (Painter); 26 Apl 1835; Andrew Dickson JP

Rogers (Rodg----) ,Thomas; Grissom, Hannah Fininger; Drury D Grisson (Grissam); 30 Sep 1802; Jonn Greaves

Rogers, William x; Norton, Alender; Adam x Whisenhunt; 2 Mar 1820; Jacob Carpenter JP

Rogers, Woodson; Mauney, Sarah; --------; 9 Apl 1857; M this date by F J Jetton JP; C only. no B

Rohm (Rom), Isaac; Woods, Sally; Jacob Reinhardt (Jacob Rom); 29 Jun 1815; V McBee

Romefelt, Abraham; Ginkens, Elizabeth; John Rumfelt, Isaac x Weast Jr; 14 Sep 1813; Henry Conner

Roner (or Rome), Henry x; Huttel, Barbara; Moses Beam; 3 (or 30) Jan 1831; L M McBee

Roney, John; Deaker, Polly; Wm Rankin; 6 Apl 1790; Joseph Dickson

Rooker (Rucker), Daniel; White, Gane; William x Rucker; 28 Aug 1832; Andrew Dickson

Roper, William; Ramsey, Anna; Allen Ramsey; 1 Feb 1830; Luther McBee

Roseman, Andrew; Moorman, Cornelia; Jacob F Heim; 26 Oct 1841; R Williamson Jr

Roseman, Daniel; Hoke, Annah; Daniel Rougch (Rough); 29 May 1828; Daniel Moser

Roseman (Rosaman), Henry; Loretz, Saloma; Charles Reinhardt; 12 Mar 1816

Ross, Aaron x; Ledford, Jane; William x Ledford; 25 Nov 1816; James T Alexander

Ross, Benjamin; Frizel, Saphira; Jacob Frizell (Frizel); 20 Nov 1794; John Willfong JP

Ross, John x; Hedgcock, Eliby; James x Bradley; 23 Dec 1813; Da'd Warlick

Ross, Moses; Bookout, Rachel; John Bookout; 18 Sep 1819; _____ Reinhardt

Roswell, Lewis x; Benge, Susanna; William _____; 14 Jul 1798; Jno Dickson

Rqthrock, Lewis P; Rudisill, Rebecca R; Alexander Ramsour; 11 May 1840; H Cansler

Rouch (Rough), Daniel; Hoke, Elizabeth; Andrew Hoke; 17 Feb 1825; Daniel Moser

Rouch, George; Bost, Mary; Jonas Bost; 10 Mar 1830

Rouche, John x; Kelly, Catherine S; Nicholas x Mosteller; 8 May 1832; L McBee

Rousche, F A; Smith, Eliza; John Skelly (Skelley); 22 Jul 1838; L E Thompson

Routh (Rough), Gilbert P; Rough, Soloma S; Wm L Wycough; 30 Jul 1840; H Cansler

Row, Jacob x; Perkins, Salley; Isaac Duglass (Douglas); 27 Feb 1819; V McBee

Row, John x; Seagle, Chatrena; Henry x Seagle; 21 Aug 1798; Peter Little

Rozell, Richard; Abernathy, Mary; Ber Thompson; 8 Jan 1798; John M Dickson Cl

Rozell, Richard A; Kistler, Elizabeth; Wm T Shipp; 16 Dec 1839; H Cansler

Rozzell, Jake x (Freedman); Bolinger, Martha; Monroe x Abernathy (Freedman); 1 Dec 1866; D A Lowe; M same date by D A Lowe; Bride called Martha Hunter in Certificate

Rudasall (Rudisel), Jonas; Beam, Margaret; David Crouse; 4 Feb 1817; James T Alexander

Rudasile (Rudisill), Willie (Wyly); Carpenter, __ Susan; David Aderhold; 11 Oct 1828; B J Thompson

Rudasill (Rudesil), John; Hager, Mary; John Hill; 20 Dec 1815; V McBee

Ruddock, T G (or T C); Lytle, M J; David Cherry; 22 Jul 1867; R Nixon JP; M 30 Jul 1867 by J Finger MG

Rudesil, John x; Saine, Susana; George Coon (Ger Georg Kuhn); 5 Aug 1812; Lwn Henderson

Rudesill (Rudisill), Jacob; Beam, Mary; Christian Eaker (Aker); 20 Nov 1820; James T Alexander

Rudisail (Rudisel), Henry (Jr); Costner, Betsey; Henry Rudiseal (Rudisel) (Sr); 22 Jul 1809; Danl M Forney

Rudisail (Rudiseal), John; Cline, Sarah; Martin Fritay (Friday); 1 Jan 1811; Jacob Ramsour

Rudisail (Rudicill), Philip; Johnson, Bettey; Robert Johnston; 22 Feb 1788; Jo Dickson

Rudisail (Rudisil), Solomon; Finger, Mary; Madison Smith; 25 Dec 1829; Luther M McBee

Rudiseal (Rudisale), Aaron (of Co of "Ruther"); Clemer, Fany; Moses Wilson; 11 Oct 1825

Rudiseal (Rudecill), Henry; Friday, Catrin; Martin Friday; 16 Jun 1788

Rudiseale (Rudisel), David; Hoviss, Susannah; Valintine Darr; 20 Jun 1818; James T Alexander

Rudisel (Rudisill), David H; Rinharte, Mary; Joshua Lore (Loar); 18 Nov 1841; M Hull JP

Rudisel, Jacob; Hovis, Saloma; Robert Williamson Jr; 14 Aug 1840; H Cansler CC; Doubtful, B reads "Jacob Hovis and Saloma Hovis"

Rudisel, Jonas; Beam, Anne; Paul Anthony Jr; 3 May 1825; V McBee

Rudisel (Rudisel), George; Reinhardt, Sally; John x Rudisel; 29 Jan 1838; H Cansler CC

Rudisell, George x; Mosteller, Elizabeth; Joseph Stamey; 22 Jul 1842; A J Cansler

Rudisell, Levi; Carpenter, Milly; Peter Mauney; 19 Jan 1827; V McBee

Rudisil, John x; Reinhart, Catharine; Jacob x Reinhart; 12 Jan 1815; Ligt Williams JP

Rudisill (Rudesil), Daniel; Bailey (or Railey), Salley; John x Rudesil; 20 Dec 1820; V McBee

Rudisill, David; Carpenter, Barbara; Philip Carpenter; 24 Feb 1827; J T Alexander

Rudisill, George; Rudisill, Dicy; _____; 25 Jan 1865; W R Clark Clk; M 26 Jan 1865 by Rev Alex Stamey; L and C, no B

Rudisill, James C; Alexander, Amanda; James T Alexander; 2 Jul 1831

Rudisill (Rudisel), Jonas; Segel, Polley; Adam Segel; 7 Jul 1812; Ligt Williams JP

Rudisill (Rudisel), Marcus H; Killian, Francis L; Martin L Rudisill (Rudisel); 19 Aug 1839; H Cansler

Rudisill (Rudisele), Michael; Detter, Betsey; Jacob Reinhardt; 23 Jul 1810

Rudisill (Rudisall), Philip; Cansellor, Elisebeth; Philip Henckel; 29 Apl 1810

Rudisill (Rudisel), William; Holman, Fanny; Joseph Barringer (or Berriger); 17 Oct 1832; V McBee

Rudsill, Michael (Rudesel, Michail Jr); Hedick, Catherine; John Hafner (John Havener Martins son); 4 Oct 1817; V McBee

Rumfelt, Hezekiah; Hendricks, Polley; Henry Underwood; 14 Sep 1816; James T Alexander

Rumfelt, Hezekiah W; Maclean, Vilet P; Thomas B Maclean; 29 Nov 1839; Isaac Holland

Rumfelt, Isaac x; Bluford, _____cy; Daniel Bluford; 11 Dec 1832; Eli Hoyl

Rumfelt, John; Belk, Margaret; Robert Rumfelt; 10 Jan 1822; Saml M'Kee

Runce, Nicholas x; Funts (Funce), Sarah; George x Lorance; 16 Mar 1786

Rush, Jacob; Shuford, Clarissa; John B Harry; 3 Jan 1825; J E Bell

Rush, P S; Lefever, Elvira; P S Kistler; 5 Oct 1858; W R Clark; M 6 Oct 1858 by P S Kistler JP

Russ, Samuel x; Mauney, Sally; Joseph Linhardt; 26 Dec 1823; Jas T Alexander

Russell, Peter x (F M); Russell, Elvy; Danl x Holland (F M); 22 Aug 1866; W R Clark CC; M 21 Aug 1866 (sic) by Wm J Hoke JP

Rutledge, Alexander R; Jenkins, Ann C; Sidney H Rankin; 11 Feb 1845; C L Hunter

Rutledge, Charles; Bealk, Sally; William Rankin; 15 Apl 1789; Eliza Dickson

Rutledge, George; Abernathy, Sarah Ann; Blair M'Gee; 1 Sep 1812; Vardry McBee

Rutledge, George; Neel, Barbary Wid; John C Rutledge; 7 Apl 1840; Christopher Stroup JP

Rutledge, James; Rankin, Ann; Jacob Reinhardt (Esqr); 5 Dec 1814; V McBee

Rutledge, James; _____ _____; Peter Hufman; 4 Aug 1831; Isaac Holland; Ambiguous

Rutledge, Robert; Beatty, Martha Jane; W A Gamewell; 24 Feb 1844; R Williamson

Rutledge, William; Bohannon, Peggy; David Wills; 20 Nov 1815; V McBee

Ryne, David x; Weathers, Catharine; John Wethers (Weathers); 23 Sep 1807; Jacob Forney; Ambiguous

Sadler, Alfred; Harrison, Peggy; Isadler, John Sadler; 26 Aug 1818; Henry Conner JP

Sadler (Saddler), Henry; Abernathy, Susan A; Joseph C Cobb; 18 Mar 1846; R Williamson

Sadler (Saddler), J A; Cloninger, Sarah H; Vincent Barnett; 29 Jan 1847; Robt Williamson

Sadler, James x; Parker, Polly; Zachariah x Sadler; 22 Feb 1809; William Gates

Sadler, John; Simmons, Patsy (Martha); William Hambleton (Hamilton); 2 Jan 1804; Polly Greaves

Sadler, John; Arnts, Susannah; Jacob Arnts; 15 Feb 1817; James T Alexander

Sadler, Nathaniel; Moreland, Phebe Tucker; William Sadler (W R Sadler); 24 Mar 1796; John Dickson

Sadler, Thomas; Hill, Rebecca; Spencer Shelton; 30 Sep 1822; Samuel M Turner

Sadler, William Rose; Moreland, Nancey; Peter Forney; 3 May 1791

Sadler, Zachariah x; Mayberry, Elizabeth; Jere Sadler; 1 Sep 1806; Lwn Henderson

Sain, Abraham; Lenhardt, Elizabeth; Peter Sain; 21 Dec 1838; H Cansler CC

Sain, Amanul (Sane, Emanuel); Johnson, Rebecca; Abel Jonas (Johnson); 4 Aug 1840; H Cansler CC

Sain, Barna M (or Barnett); Hoover, Martha; T L Siegle (Siegel); 17 Feb 1853; Danl Siegel; M same date by Daniel Siegel JP

Sain (Saine), Daniel; McClure, Adaline; Levi Sain; 10 Feb 1861; M same date by David Boiles Esq

Sain (Saine), Jacob; Howser, Catharine; John x Howser (Sr); 9 Aug 1836; M Hull JP

Sain, Jacob; Smith, Sally; Abram Houser (Howser); 7 Sep 1841; M Hull JP

Sain, Jacob; Wise, Barbara; Levi Sain; 15 Feb 1849; P Stamey JP

Sain, Jno x; Houser, Elizabeth; Henry x Houser; 20 Nov 1815; V McBee

Sain (Saine), John; Reep, Fanny; Philip Reep; 22 ____ 1832; M Hull

Sain (Sane), Joseph; Howser, Lidia; Michael x Reep; __ Aug 1839; M Hull JP

Sain, Levi; Houser, Margeret; Samuel W x Wyant; 11 Jan 1855; Danl Siegel JP; M same date by Danl Siegel JP

Sain, Noah; Sain, Catharine; Levi Sain; 8 Jan 1862; G W Hull; M same date by G W Hull JP

Sain, Solomon; Hollman, Elmira; Andrew Hallman (Ephraim Hallman); 13 Sep 1852; R Williamson; M 14 Sep 1852 by F J Jetton JP

Sain (Sane), Winehardt; Hollman, Elleanor; John W Linhardt (Leonhardt); 19 Sep 1849; Robt Williamson

Sain, Winhardt; Huss, Fanny; _____; 7 Apl 1861; W R Clark Clk; M same date by P Carpenter JP; L and R, no B

Saine, Daniel x; Brindel, Betsay; Joseph Brandal (Brindel); 12 Dec 1820; D Lutz JP

Saine, Daniel; Reep, Mary; Peter x Saine Jr; 4 Dec 1827; V McBee

Saine, Samuel; Weon, Matleaner; David x Lingerfelter; 2 Feb 1826; M Hull JP

Sample, Robert M; Henderson, Adeline; Levi N Alexander; 25 Mar 1834; Carlos Leonard

Samson (Sampson), James; Ward, Elizabeth; Alfred Bridges; 16 Feb 1820; V McBee

Sanders, Edward x; Goodson, Elizabeth; Mathew x Goodson, John x Link; 25 Aug 1796; J Graham

Sanders, Jesse; Crouse, Elizabeth; Lemuel Saunders (Sanders); 20 Apl 1823; Jas T Alexander

Sanders, John x; McEntire, Jane; Jesse Wingate; 10 Feb 1819; James T Alexander

Sanders(Saunders), Miles A; Goodson, Malinda; Andrew Fry; 19 Nov 1836; M W Abernathy

Sanford(Stanford), John; Fite, Barbara; James Smith; 31 Mar 1838; And Hoyl JP

Sarvies (Service), Joseph; Oats, Anny; Thomas Oats; 26 May 1836; Jno Blackwood

Sarvies (Service), Thomas; Berry, Emaline; Samuel Sarvies (Service); 7 Nov 1844; James Ferguson

Sauls, David x; Ingle, Sarah; Martin x Keener; 14 Nov 1830; Luther M McBee

Saunders, Edward; Bandy, Sarah; Samuel Saunders; 28 Jun 1823; V McBee

Saunders (Sanders), Elisha; Keener, Nancy Levina; David Helderman; 25 Oct 1839; Joshua Wilson

Saunders, Joseph; Lowe, Rachel; Aron x Lowe; 19 Apl 1825; V McBee

Saunders (Sanders), Lemuel; Abernathy, Willey; _____ _____; 28 Mar 1803; Jos Dickson

Saunders, Lemuel x; Duncan, Milley; Edward Saunders; 1 Sep 1820; V McBee

Saunders, Samuel; Miller, Mary; John Miller; 17 Feb 1810; Danl M Forney

Saunders (Sanders), T J; Beal, Nancy L; A F Moore; 14 Sep 1865; A S Haynes CCC; M 17 Sep 1865 by J A Huggins Minister M P Church

Saunders, Thomas; Blackburn, Hanah; Lemuel Saunders; 24 Aug 1790; Jo Dickson

Saunders, Thomas; Earnest, Elisabeth; John Baley; 6 May 1806; Js McEwin

Scarbrough, Robert x; Finnison, Noray; Thos Beatty; 28 Jan 1808

Scarbrough (Scarborough), Silas S; Robinson, Patsey; Robt Abernathy; 5 Apl 1821; Henry Conner

Schenck, David; Ramsour (Ramseur), Sallie W; J C Jenkins; 25 Aug 1859; D W Schenck; M same date by R N Davis PPC

Schenck, David W; Bevens, Susan R; John Schenck; 8 Nov 1832; V McBee

Schenck, Henry; Ramsaur, Sarah; James T Alexander; 7 Jan 1829

Schenck, John; Allyn, Harriet H; James P Henderson; 6 Dec 1831; L M McBee

Scott, James; Alexander, Polly; Abraham Scott; 21 Jul 1803; Jos Dickson
Scott, Moses; South, Rachel; Ambrose x Cobb; 2 Nov 1785
Scott, Wm; Davis, Elizabeth; J Dickson; 1790; (N)
Scronce, James x; Summit, Rebeckah; John x Parker; 6 Jan 1826; V McBee
Seabach, John; Huffman, Tabitha; Legion Bollinger; 24 Jun 1820; Mic Cline
Seaboch (Seabaugh), Peter; Robison, Polly; Jacob x Seabaugh; 1 Jan 1807; Lwn Henderson
Seabolt (Seabold), Solomon; Flowers, Cathrine; Joseph Flowers (Ger Flauers ?); 10 Jun 1824; Mic Cline
Seabouch (Sebough), Joseph; Robison, Sarah; Jacob Sebough (Ger Sebach); 25 ____ 1807; R Williamson
Seagle, Alfred; Mitcham, Narcissa; A S Johnson; 17 Feb 1848; Robt Williamson
Seagle, Andrew; Havner, Ann Elizabeth; James H Oates (Oats); 31 Mar 1856; J A Huss; M 2 Apl 1856 by George Coon JP
Seagle, Daniel; Hoover, Salley; Daniel Seagle; 9 Apl 1821; V McBee; One of above is called Daniel Jr
Seagle (Seegle), Daniel; Hoover, Catherine; John Michal (Michael); 5 Feb 1823; V McBee
Seagle (Seegal), Daniel; Bullinger, Mary; John Michal (Michael); 3 Mar 1824; Jas T Alexander
Seagle, David; Killian, Sarah; Jacob Seagle; 26 Oct 1830; J T Alexander
Seagle, Elam (Elem A); Gilbert, Margret L; Wm F Wise; 17 Jan 1856; George Coon JP; M same date by George Coon JP⁻
Seagle, George; Huver, Melindy; Valentine Lore (Loar); 25 May 1837; M Hull JP
Seagle, John; Coon, Barbary; Lorens Bringle; 1 Dec 1825; M Hull JP
Seagle, Monroe; Hoover, Lina S; F J Jetton; 23 Mar 1861; W R Clark; M 24 Mar 1861 by A J Fox MG
Seapaugh, Jacob; Bost, Eliza; Jesse Bost; 9 Dec 1828; J T Alexander
Seapaugh (Seapagh), Jacob; Fry, Lany; Reuben Setzer; 29 Dec 1836
Seathers (or Leathers), Henry x; Acre, Polly; Michael Rudesel (Ger Rutisiel ?); 25 Nov 1810; H Y Webb
Sechler, Benjamin; Anthony, Elizabeth; Paul Kistler (Kisler); 6 Feb 1834; M W Abernathy CC
Seffret (Sufferet), John; Randles, Mary; Robert Weir; 6 Jan 1786
Seine, Jacob x; Tucker, Nancy; Christy x Parker; 25 Feb 1808; Maxl Chambers
Seitz (Sides), Abel; Whitner, Mary M; Moses B Whitener (Whitner); 3 Mar 1840; Compare Whitener, Moses B
Seitz, Abel; Johnson, Caroline; Emanuel Shuford; 5 Apl 1841
Seitz, Abel; Gross, Catharine; David Haun (Hawn); 1 Nov 1841; R Williamson Jr
Seitz (Sites), Abraham; Moll, Margrate; George x Seitz; 10 Mar 1807; Phil Whitener JP
Seitz, Darius D; Link, Rebecca; Babel Whitener (David Whitner); 7 May 1838; H Cansler
Seitz, George; Hoover, Mary; Jacob Shuford; 20 Mar 1812; Joseph Fisher JP
Seitz (Sides), George L; Johnson, Jane; W R (Rufus) Clark; 27 Feb 1849; V A McBee
Seitz (Sides), Jacob; Master, Susana; Anthony Hinkle; 1 Feb 1792; Jo Dickson
Seitz (Sides), Jacob; Garner, Rebecca; John Seitz (Sides); 3 Jun 1800; Jno Dickson
Seitz, Levi x; Walker, Susanah; Henry x Walker; 27 Nov 1813; V McBee
Seitz, Moses; Gross, Mary; Thomas Seitz; 11 Jul 1811; Mic Cline
Seizen (Sizen), Stephen x; Powell, Elisabeth; James Freeman; 11 Apl 1782; William Rankin
Selevan (Sullivan), Daniel; Boyed, Peggy; Robert Boyd (Boyed); 11 Aug 1809; Danl M Forney CC
Self, Aron; Anthony, Catharine; John x Waters; 18 Nov 1848; Robt Williamson
Self, B (Barest, Barrel); Lackey, Anna; James Lacky (Lackey); 8 Jan 1838; H Cansler CC
Self, Berryman H; Hoover, Susan; Lem J Hoyle; 21 Jan 1861; M 22 Jan 1861 by A J Fox MG
Self, Isaac R; Young, Mary; Rufus x Self; 3 Nov 1865; A S Haynes Cty Ct Clk; M 9 Nov 1865 by O B Jenks JP
Self, Jacob x; Morrison, Jane; Elijah x Self; 4 Nov 1829; M Hull JP
Self, John x; Boman, Clary __; R H (or K H) Brown (Harvy Brown); 26 ____ 1835; Andrew Dickson
Self, Joseph; Baldwin, Abigal; Robert Willis; 5 Mar 1824; Jas T Alexander
Self, Rufus; Summerow, Margaret C; J R Self; 25 Jul 1866; W R Clark; M 9 Aug 1866 by John Lantz MG

111

Self, William x; Gates, Sarah; William Gates; 30 Oct 1839; H Cansler
Self, Williams; Truigs (?), Elizabeth; John x Self; 4 Nov 1830; M Hull JP
Sellers, Alfred B; Baker, Sarah; John Eaker; 14 Jun 1845; F A Hoke
Sellers, Georg; Froneberger, Anna M; John Sellers; 3 Mar 1818; V McBee
Sellers, John; Rush, Mary; Isaac Price; 2 Dec 1818; James T Alexander
Sellers (Cellers), Philip; Fronebarger, Barbara; Jacob Sellers (Cellers); 16 Sep 1815;
    James T Alexander
Selvey, William x; Armstrong, Sally; William x Lewis; 14 Feb 1843; And Hoyl JP
Senter see Center
Senter (Center), Caleb O; Barnett, Frances E; James C Stroup; 29 May 1854;
    M 7 Jun 1854 by Elisha Saunders JP
Senter, Edward x; Mauny, Betsey; William Jinkins; 6 Jun 1811; Danl M Forney
Senter, Joel; Darnel, Sarah; James Massy; 23 Jul 1805
Senter, John; Senter, Agness; Stephen Senter; 13 Jan 1780; Ambiguous
Senter, Stephen; Massey, Winey; James Hanks; 17 Jan 1791; Jo Dickson
Senter, William; Cloninger, Catharine; David Cloninger; 26 Nov 1818; James T
    Alexander
Service see Sarvies
Setlemier,Jacob x (of Burke Co); Phillips, Hanhah; Isaac Ash; 3 Jan 1821; Mic Cline
Setser (Setzer), George; Ward, Betcy A; Charles x Ward; 14 May 1817; V McBee
Setser, John x; Moose, Christina; Frederick Moose (Ger Fridrich Mussgenug); 9 Jun
    1810; Mic Cline
Setser, Mathias; Sigman, Elissabeth; John x Setser; 24 May 1810; John Willfong
Setser, William x; Sigman, Susy; George Herman (Ger same); 4 Oct 1810; Mic Cline
Settlemire (Settlemyer), George; Hawn, Hannah; Paul Settlemire(Settlemyer); 5 Aug
    1834; Henry Cline
Settlemire, Jacob S (Settlemyer, Jacob Sherril); Mauney, Polly; William Bovey; 18 Sep
    1828; Henry Cline
Settlemyer, Henry; Whitener, Sarah; Absalom Miller; 4 Jun 1835; H W Robinson
Settlemyer, Paul; Smith, Clarissa; Michael Bollinger; 26 May 1842; Wm Herman
Settlemyre, James A (C) x; Caldwell, Martha A; John x Whitenburg; 3 Jan 1867;
    W R Clark CC; "Freedman"; M same date by Wm J Hoke JP
Setzer, Andrew x; Cline, Catharine; Wm x Travelstret; 1 Jan 1836; M W Abernathy
Setzer, Christopher x; Bird, Susannah; Henry Clyne (Cline); 25 Apl 1814; Vardry
    McBee
Setzer, Daniel; Wike, Polly; Jacob Wike (Ger Weik); 10 Jan 1813; Philip Henkel
Setzer, David; Sherril, Elinor; Jacob Dellinger; 21 Feb 1822 ; V McBee
Setzer, George; Smyre, Mahala; Jesse R Whitener (Whitner); 3 Jul 1841
Setzer, Henry; Rhyne, Susannah; Caleb W Hoyl; 4 Mar 1837; Eli Hoyl
Setzer, Jacob; Treffelstet, Mary; John Bovay (Pavey); 24 Mar 1810; Danl M Forney
Setzer, Jacob; Deal, Delilah; John Yount; 18 Mar 1829
Setzer, Paul; Gross, Lydia; G D (Daniel) Wilfong; 24 Apl 1827; Luther McBee
Setzer, Paul; Deal, Risa; William Boyden; 25 May 1830; J T Alexander
Setzer, Paul; Simmons, Jemima; Henry Setzer; 5 Feb 1840; H Cansler
Setzer, Reuben; Rhyne, Lavina; Henry Setzer; 1 Feb 1840; Eli Hoyl
Shadden, David; Uton, Rachael; Samuel Rankin; 19 Dec 1785
Shafer (Shaver), John; Haine, Mary; Jacob Reinhardt; 2 Jun 1808; Danl Forney
Shannon, James; Hamilton, Jean; James Moore; 3 Mar 1785; Elizabeth Dickson
Shaw, John D; Henderson, Margaret B; L P Henderson; 2 Nov 1858; M 3 Nov 1858
    by R N Davis Minister
Shaw, Thomas; McKee, Mary; James McEwen; 15 Apl 1782; No signatures; "Thomas
    Shaw and James McEwen of the County of Rowan"
Shelby, Winfield; Bele, Racheal; Clement Nantz (Nance); 6 Dec 1836
Shell, Charles F (Ger Carl Schell); Hahn, Elisabeth; Philip Henkle; 16 Jul 1808;
    Jacob Sala
Shell, David x; Seagle, Margaret; Henry x House; 9 Sep 1824; V McBee
Shell, David x; Hartzoke, Chrisnia; Thos W Lindsay (Lindsey); 2 Mar 1866
Shell, Ephraim; Bovey, Mary Ann; Matthias Bovey; 6 Aug 1835; Mic Cline
Shell, Henry; Huss, Sarah A; John Houser; 13 Oct 1858; W R Clark
Shell, John x; Cressman, Elizabeth; Jacob Fox; 4 Oct 1796; Wallace Alexander
Shell, John x; Ingel (Engel), Betsey; Michl Ingel; 26 Sep 1803; Jno Dickson
Shell, John; Mull, Mary; Martin Huffman; 3 Feb 1821; V McBee
Shell, John x; Hause, Elizabeth; Philip Reep; 6 Jan 1829; James T Alexander
Shell, John x; Cline, Margaret; Jacob Reinhardt; 19 Apl 1833; L McBee
Shell, Samuel; Froy, Mary; (Ger) Nicolaus Fre_____; 18 Jul 1805; Phil Whitener JP
Shell, Solomon; Fry, Nancy; Henry Shell (Ger Henrich Schell); 15 Jun 1811

Shelton, Chrispen; Cresemon, Susan; Spencer Shelton; 26 Dec 1826; V McBee

Shelton, Freeman; Lockman, Susanah; John Lockman; 8 Dec 1815; V McBee

Shelton, Henry; Lowe, Frances; David J Pryor; 29 Aug 1830; J T Alexander

Shelton, Joseph B; Lockman, Elizabeth; William D Thompson; 1 Oct 1849; J D King

Shelton, Meacon; Lockman, Eba; John Lockman; 10 Nov 1817; John Allen

Shelton, Meacon; Sherrill, Nancy; Henry Barkley; 15 Feb 1840; H Cansler

Shelton, Nelson; Sadler, Fanny; Zach x Sadler; 10 Jun 1803; Jos Dickson

Shelton, Samuel T; Caldwell, Perline; James H M'Caul (M'Call); 19 Jan 1829; William Little

Shelton, Spencer; Lockman, Sally; Meacon Shelton; 26 Jul 1823; Jas T Alexander

Shelton, Young; Thompson, Mary M; Wm W Munday (Monday); 15 Feb 1828; V McBee

Shelton, Young; Sherrill, Judith L; Alfred W Thompson; 22 Mar 1837; John B Harry

Shenck, Henry (Ger Henrich Schenck); Dobson, Elizabeth; Maxwell Chambers; 5 Nov 1805; Wm Scott

Shepherd, Edward x; Ingle, Susanah; Andrew x Ingle; 17 Jul 1813; V McBee

Sheril, James F x; Conor, Sarah; Abraham x Sheril; 20 Sep 1866; R Nixon JP; M same date; "Freedman and Woman"

Sherill (Sherril), John; Anderson, Salley; William Williams; 8 Jan 1818; V McBee

Sherill (Sherrill), Nelson; _____ _____; Adam Sherrill; 10 May 1832; Nath Edwards JP

Sherrell (Sherrill), Joseph; Bandy, Mira; Thomas Williams; 18 Jun 1836; M W Abernathy

Sherril, Aron; Parker, Polley; Jep Sherrill (Sherril); 20 Apl 1824

Sherril, Benjamin; Collier, Mary; Jno Dickson; 9 May 1798; Wallace Alexander

Sherril, Enos; McCormick, Elizabeth; Andrew McCormick; 13 Sep 1808

Sherril, Joseph; Jones, Nancy; John Jones; 3 Aug 1807

Sherril (Sherril), Adam; Sherril, Susanah; Elisha Sherrill (Sherril); 9 Aug 1822; V McBee

Sherrill, Alexander; Gabrial, Ruhemer; Moses Sherrill; 24 Jan 1793

Sherrill (Sherrel), Anderson; Drum, Barbara; John Moose (or Moore); 25 Oct 1814; V McBee

Sherrill, Aquilla; Farr, Polly; Aaron Sherrill; 25 Feb 1803; Thos Wheeler

Sherrill, Arerum; Linebarger, Susanah; Joshua Sherrill; 29 Dec 1814

Sherrill, David R; Sherrill, Ann; Gabriel Brown; 22 Jan 1833

Sherrill, E L; Nantz, Julia E; _____; 31 May 1854; M this date by R H Morrison; C only, no B

Sherrill, Eli (Elic); Sherrill, Mira; John Cline; 23 May 1835; Carlos Leonard

Sherrill, Elisha; Milligan, Elizabeth; Francis Sherrill; 16 Dec 1831; L McBee

Sherrill, Evin; Penanton, Kesiah; Moses Sherrill; 29 May 1789

Sherrill, Francis; Little, Polly; Austin Cornelius (Austin Sherrill); 16 Nov 1833

Sherrill, Gabriel; Wilkinson, Dove; John M'Cokle (McCorkle); 13 Apl 1820; V McBee

Sherrill (Sherril), Henry; Sherril, Martha; David Day (Dey); 27 Sep 1825; V McBee

Sherrill (Sherril), Hiram; Sherril, Salley; John Sherrill (Sherril); 11 Aug 1820; V McBee

Sherrill, Hosea; Linebarger, Nancy; William Reed (Reid); 4 Feb 1835

Sherrill (Sherril), Hugh; Litton, Anna; Hiram Litten (Litton); 7 Mar 1818; V McBee

Sherrill, J A; Goodson, Mary L; J D Shelton; 24 Aug 1850; V A McBee

Sherrill, J P; Jetton, Mary; John Robison (Robinson); 16 Feb 1867; W R Clark CC; M 17 Feb 1867 by S Lander

Sherrill (Sherrel), Jacob; Stevenson, Jancey; Jacob Adams; 2 May 1814; V McBee

Sherrill, James M; Mitchell, Martha Ann; Parsons Naylor; 29 Jul 1865; A S Haynes CCC; M 2 Aug 1865 by Elisha Saunders JP

Sherrill (Sherril), Jesse; Eaton, Sarah; Sokr Eiten (?) (or John Eiten); 31 Mar 1808; Jeremiah Munday

Sherrill, John A x; Ingle, Jane; Parsons Naylor; 13 Jul 1865; A S Haynes CCC, S P Sherrill; M same date by S P Sherrill JP

Sherrill (Sherril), Joseph; Sherril, Sally; John Sherrill (Sherril); 1 Jan 1811; H Y Webb

Sherrill, Lawson; Wilkerson, Elizabeth; Anderson Turbyfill; 25 Jul 1828; J T Alexander

Sherrill, Leander B; Hope, Polly; Wm x Hope; 31 Dec 1861; W R Clark; M Evening 5 Jan 1862 by Jonas W Derr JP

Sherrill, Levi; Harwell, Betsey; John Sherrill; 11 Oct 1809; Danl M Forney

Sherrill (Sherrall), Logan; Edwards, Sarah; Bedford Sherrill (Sherrall); 18 Feb 1836; J A Ramsour DC

Sherrill, Mason; Bridges, Margaret; Jacob Adams; 27 Jul 1814; James T Alexander

Sherrill, Michael; Sherrill, Rutha; James Clark; 8 Nov 1804; Thos Wheeler
Sherrill, Miles; Barnes, Mary A; Thomas J Sherrill; 12 Dec 1838; Alexander Ward JP
Sherrill (Sherrall), Moses M; Barcley, Rachel; Anderson Fleming; 14 Apl 1838; J A
   Ramsour D C
Sherrill, Moses W; Little, Matty; Gabriel Brown; 21 Mar 1835; M W Abernathy
Sherrill, Nicolas (Sharell, Nicles); Dilin, Martha; Evin Sherrill (Sherall); 20 Mar 1792
Sherrill, Q A x; Ingle, Elizabeth; A B Laney; 24 __ 1865; W R Clark
Sherrill, Samuel P; Lander, Sarah C; E J Alexander; 8 Dec 1857; W R Clark
Sherrill, Samuel P; Cobb, Mrs B M; James M Abernathy; 2 Jul 1866; M 3 Jul 1866
   by R N Davis Minister
Sherrill (Sherril), Silas; Sherril, Salley; Elisha Sherrill (Sherril); 22 Aug 1822; V McBee
Sherrill, Theo; Milligan, Sally; Thomas Conner; 18 Jan 1825; Jas T Alexander
Sherrill, Theophilus; Robison, Polly; Charles Beatty (Beatie); 10 Jan 1821; James T
   Alexander
Sherrill (Sherril), William; Sherril, Sally; Absalom Sherrill (Sherril); 20 Nov 1811;
   Lwn Henderson
Shetly (Shutley), Robison M; Linebarger, Margaret; Caleb Rhodes; 25 Jul 1840;
   Eli Hoyl
Shikle (Shitle), Henry; Young, Catharine; Jo Stamey; 15 Jan 1829; M Hull JP
Shipp, Bartlett; Forney, Susan; Jacob Ramsour; 29 Nov 1818; V McBee
Shipp, Moses x; Phifer, Adaline; Thomas x Motz; 25 Oct 1866; W R Clark; M same
   date by Wm J Hoke JP
Shipp, William T; Johnston, Harriet; Wm M Shipp; 7 Feb 1842
Shireman, Michael; Shuford, Elizabeth; Jacob Summey Jr; 15 Apl 1807; Lwn
   Henderson
Shires, George W x; Baker, Vicy; Abraham Eaker; 19 Oct 1832; V McBee
Shitel (Shitle), Pinkney; Hoover, Frances E; Robt Williamson; 15 Feb 1855; J A
   Huss; M same date by David Crouse JP
Shitle, Anthony; Reinharte, Christeaner; Thomas Williams; 3 Feb 1833; M Hull JP
Shitle, Charles W; Pollard, Rebecca; Wiley W McGinnas; 23 Aug 1840; George
   Coon JP
Shitle, Henry; Jonas, Caty; Henry Jonas; 15 Nov 1836; M Hull JP
Shitle (Shidle), John; Reep, Sarah; John Cook; 15 May 1826; V McBee
Shitle, Peter x; Gaits, Sally; David x Reep; 20 Oct 1839; M Hull JP
Shitle, Philip; Speagle, Elizabeth; Peter Young; 20 Nov 1831; Major Hull JP
Shittle (Shitle), Jacob x; Umphry, Jane; Alexander Smith; 5 Mar 1840; A J Cansler
Shneider (Snider), Christian; Davis, Mary; Zachariah Spencer; 15 Jun 1799
Sholl, Charles; Hues, Fanny; Alexander Nelson, Absalom Bonham; 9 Apl 1789;
   Jo Dickson
Sholl (Shull), Charles; Antony, Mary Magdelin; Daniel Anthony; 13 Jul 1797
Shook, Adam (Ger Schuk or Schuck); Christopher, Catharina; Henry x Shook; 20 Dec
   1841; J Yount JP
Shook, Andrew; Keiler, Nancy; Frederick x Shook; 6 Sep 1835; Henry Cline
Shook, Daniel x; Woodring, Polly; Frederick x Shook; 27 May 1824; Fr Hoke JP
Shook, Daniel x; Yarbrough, Polly; Daniel Deal (Deel); 3 Aug 1841; J Yount JP
Shook, Fred Jr x; Thronbary, Barbre; Fred x Shook Sr; 10 Mar 1825; Fr Hoke JP
Shook, Henrey x; Dagaharo, Elizabeth; Henry Dagahard (Ger Heinrich Degenhart);
   17 Sep 1812; Peter Little
Shook, John H; Turbyfill, Ann; Joseph I McKell; 18 Sep 1830; J T Alexander
Shook, John Henderson; Petree, Catharine; Lindsey C Weaver; 4 Apl 1825; Jas T
   Alexander
Short, David; Propest, Viney; David Colwell; 13 Oct 1840; E Mauney
Short, John; Arney, Sally; Matthew Wilson; 15 Jan 1827; J T Alexander
Shoup, Gabriel x; Trout, Margret; Abraham x Smith; 9 Apl 1816; Ligt Williams JP
Shronce, Charles; Pitts, Poliey; Wilson x Parker; 8 Jan 1818; V McBee
Shrum, Daniel; Keener, Susanna; Benjamin Beel (Beal); 12 Dec 1857; W R Clark;
   M 16 Dec 1857 by Robt Blackburn JP
Shrum, Henry (Ger _____); Dudro, Susannah; (Ger) Johans D_____; 7 Mar 1797
Shrum, Henry; Forney, Mary M; Enos x Campbell; 18 Jul 1854; J A Huss; M 20 Jul
   1854 by H Asbury Mnst
Shrum, Jacob x; Shetley, Kitty; William Tankersley; 18 Mar 1789
Shrum, Levi; Hollman, Ann; James Summerour; 10 Jan 1847; Robt Williamson
Shrum (Srum), Nickles; Hostotlor, Betsy; Adam x Stroup; 17 Apl 1784; James
   Dickson
Shrum, Solomon; Carpenter, Nancy F; A S Haynes; 30 Jul 1860; W R Clark;
   M 31 Jul 1860 by J Finger (MG)

114

Shuck, David x; Knup, Matilda; Frederick x Shuck; 26 Jun 1839; Wm Herman JP
Shufferd (Shuford), Daniel; Bullinger, Elisabeth; Jno Hoke; 21 Dec 1805; Js McEwin
Shufford, Israel x; Davis, Mary M; George Davis; 25 Oct 1825; V McBee
Shufford, John; Kistler, Elizabeth; Paul Anthony; 26 Dec 1821; V McBee
Shufford (Shuford), Lawson A; Avery, Mary; Abner x Massagee; 21 Aug 1849; Robt Williamson
Shuford, Abel H; King, Elizabeth; Philip W Johnson; 23 Aug 1848; R E Burch
Shuford (Shufford), Daniel (Jr); Robison, Hannah; Andrew Ramsour; 14 Sep 1819; V McBee
Shuford, Daniel; Kistler, Eva Rosannah; Jacob Kistler; 5 Oct 1841; R Williamson Jr
Shuford, David; Coulter, Rody; _____ Coulter; ____ 1812
Shuford (Shufford), Ephraim; Hoyle, Susan; Henry Schenck Jr; 22 Mar 1828; V McBee
Shuford, George P; Baker, Mary; John D Hoke; 3 (or 30) Dec 1831; L McBee
Shuford, George P; Baker, Anna E; Daniel Leonard; 23 Oct 1838; J Stagle
Shuford, Henry; Warlick, Nina; Jacob _____th; 29 Jan 1833; L McBee
Shuford, J S; Hoover, Margaret C; H S Wilson; 8 Jul 1858; W R Clark
Shuford, Jacob; Baker, Catharine; Joseph Barrenger; 13 Oct 1828; B J Thompson
Shuford (Shufford), John; Robison, Elizabeth; Henry Robinson (Robison); 22 Aug 1819; V McBee
Shuford, John M (Martin Jr); Warlick, Margaret; Daniel Hallman (Halman); 23 Feb 1818; James T Alexander
Shuford, John S; Abernathey, Mary; Jacob Reinhardt; 15 Nov 1822; Joel Dyer
Shuford, Joseph; Mauney, Cynthia; Martin Zimmerman; 8 Apl 1835; G Hoke
Shuford, Obed P; Ramsour, Catharine E; George R Bridges; 11 Sep 1847; Robt Williamson
Shuford, Philip; Abernathy, Anna; John Hoke; 9 Feb 1807; Lwn Henderson
Shuford, Philip; Stamey, Sally; Eli R Shuford; 6 Dec 1835; G P Shuford JP
Shuford, Sidney; Rhodes, Clarissa; _____; 19 Feb 1852; M this date by Daniel Siegel JP; R only, no B
Shuford, Thomas R; Butts, Elizabeth; Henry Schenck Jr; 30 May 1827; J T Alexander
Shull, C W x; Hauss, Elizabeth; Henry Huss (Hauss); 3 May 1859; W R Clark; M 5 May 1859 by P Carpenter JP
Shull, Charles x; Dellinger, Elizabeth; Jacob Reinhardt; 30 Jan 1818; Andrew Loretz
Shull, David; Dellinger, Mary; F J (Joseph) Jetton; 12 Feb 1841; A J Cansler
Shull, Joseph D; Hill, Martha A; M C Clay; 5 Oct 1859; W R Clark; M same date by Joseph Parker Minister
Shull, Pearson; Spratt, Nancy; Isaac Erwin; 4 Jan 1835; M W Abernathy
Shull, Philip A; Huss, M A; P S Beal; 6 Apl 1867
Shup, Sonmon (Shoup, Solomon); Lowre, Mary; Peter x Shoup; 1 Mar 1810; Ligt Williams JP
Shutley, John; Wethers, Mary; William Jenkins; 18 Dec 1839; Eli Hoyl
Shutly (Shutley), Alexander; Jenkins, Mary; James H White; 26 Nov 1835; Isaac Holland
Sides see Seitz
Sides, Daniel; Walker, Cena; Osbirn Walker; 2 Feb 1822; V McBee
Sides, Geo W; Rudisill, Mary Jane; Marcus H Smith; 25 Oct 1865; A S Haynes CCC
Sides, Henry x; Bradshaw, Susana; Peter x Sides; 18 Jan 1806; Lwn Henderson
Sides, Peter; Masters, Hannah; Henry Sides; 21 May 1807; Betsey Henderson
Sides, Simon; Walker, Mary; Henry x Walker; 26 Dec 1818; V McBee
Sides, Simon; Henkle, Malinda; Philip Whitener; 22 Jul 1823; Jas T Alexander
Siegle (Seagle), James F; Rhony, Jane; A J Rhoney; 23 Dec 1852; R Williamson; M 30 Dec 1852 by M Hull JP
Sifford see Lippard
Sifford (Shifferd), John; Durr, Elizebeth; John Edwards; 30 Mar 1809; Thos Wheeler
Sifford, Jonas; Asbury, Nancy; Arthur F Barnett; 17 Nov 1851; Robt Williamson; M 20 Nov 1851 by J H Zimmerman JP
Sifford, Lewis x; _____, Charity; (Ger) Johannes Sch_____ (perhaps Schlunker); 15 Apl 1811; Th Wheeler
Sifford, Miles L; Holliman, Elizabeth; Rufus Lowe; 20 Jun 1857; Robt Williamson
Sifford, Solomon; Johnson, Nancy; George Little; 25 Jun 1837; J D King
Sifford, Solomon; Little, Mary; William Little; 22 Jul 1840; H Cansler
Sifford, Thomas; Daily, Mary B; Jonas W Derr (Tarr); 23 Oct 1837; H Cansler CC
Sifford, Wm A; Little, Isabella; Rufus L Low (Lowe); 2 Sep 1862; M 4 Sep 1862 by J M Smith JP

Sigel (Sigle), John; Clay, Susanah; John Segel (Sigle Sr), Abraham Clay; 27 Nov 1792; John Willfong JP

Sigman, Abel; Peterson, Elizabeth; Israel Whitener; 21 Jan 1842

Sigman, Barnet; Eflinger (or Eslinger), Mary; William Sigman; 24 Dec 1789; Joseph Steel

Sigman, Barnet (Ger Siegman, Barnet); Eckerd, Christina; George x Sigman; 25 Sep 1817; Mic Cline

Sigman, Barnet (Jr); Fry, Polly; Matthias Setser; 2 Nov 1819; Mic Cline

Sigman, Barnet; Linebarger, Martha; Archibald Ray; 3 Apl 1828; M W Abernathy JP

Sigman, Cristopher; Whitener, Polly; Daniel Whitener; 28 Sep 1820; Phil Whitener JP

Sigman, Daniel x; Eikert, Fanny; Mathias Bovey; 5 Nov 1816; Mic Cline

Sigman, David; Whitener, Barbara; Daniel Whitener; 30 Apl 1818; Phil Whitener JP

Sigman, Eli; Bost, Rody; Paul Cline; 17 Feb 1840

Sigman, Elias; Lomax, Linny; Alford x Lomax; 5 Jan 1843; Wm Herman JP

Sigman, Ely x; Settlemyer, Elizabeth; Jacob Reinhardt; 22 Jul 1824; V McBee

Sigman, Ely; Smith, Ann; Lawson A Killian; 24 Sep 1835

Sigman, Emanuel; Minges, Perlina; Miles D Minges; 2 Jan 1843; V A McBee

Sigman, George x; Sigman, Elizabeth; William Sigman; 4 Mar 1820; Mic Cline

Sigman, George; Isenhower, Elizebeth A; Isaac Lourance (Lorantz); 20 Dec 1831; Fr Hoke JP

Sigman, George H; Sigman, Mary A; Eli Sigman; 7 Aug 1838; J T Alexander

Sigman, George H; Setzer, Ada; John Smith; 31 Aug 1838; H Cansler CC

Sigman, George Philip; Dellingar, Elizabeth; Andrew Siegman (Sigman); 10 Feb 1831; Fr Hoke JP

Sigman, Henry (Ger Heinrich Sigmann); Dellinger, Barbara; Joseph x Dellinger; 27 May 1813; Phil Whitener JP

Sigman, Henry x; Deal, Sally; Matthias x Bovey; 19 Nov 1813; Mic Cline

Sigman, Henry x; Hewet, Ladecy; James Sims; 9 Mar 1826; V McBee

Sigman, Jacob x; Fye, Elisabeth; Eli Starr; 17 Mar 1836; Mic Cline

Sigman, Jesse x; Cline, Aday; Absalom Miller; 17 May 1838; Mic Cline

Sigman, John x; Bolick, Sally; Jacob Wike (Ger Jacob Weik); __ ____ 1809; Danl M Forney, H Webb

Sigman, John x; Trefenstat, Cathrine; George x Sigman; 10 Apl 1813; Mic Cline JP

Sigman, John x; Rine, Jude; George Eckert (Ger same); 28 May 1827; Fr Hoke JP

Sigman, L H; Miller, Rhoda; Eli Starr; 5 Aug 1840; H Cansler

Sigman, Lawson; Deal, Phoeby Malinda; Jonathan Bost; 28 May 1840; Henry Cline

Sigman, Martin; Minges, Mary; Barnet Sigman (Ger Bernt Siegmnd); 16 Feb 1819; Mic Cline

Sigman, Martin; Linbarger, Susanah; Gilbert Milligan; 21 Jan 1823; V McBee

Sigman, William; Smith, Sabina, widow; Christopher Sigman; 17 Sep 1826; Daniel Moser

Sigman, William; Sigman, Mary; Rufus x Harberson; 8 Mar 1834; M W Abernathy

Sigman, William x; Sumee, Persilla; William Sigman; 22 Sep 1839; John Yount JP

Sigmon (Sigman), Abel; Whitener, Emeline; Z B Whitener; 25 Feb 1842; R Williamson Jr

Simmons, John x; Palmer, Betsy; Martin Friday (Freitag); 9 Nov 1801; Jno Dickson

Simmons, John; Jones, Isabella; James Walls (?); 20 Dec 1804; Lwn Henderson

Simon, John x; Stine, Molly; (Ger) Henrich Stein; 6 Feb 1810; Mic Cline

Simon, Samuel x; Bolick, Caty; Gotfree Bolick (Ger Gottfried Bolch), John Benfield (Ger Benfiel); 20 Nov 1816; Mic Cline

Simonton, W S; Connor, Eliza M; Carlos Leonard; 18 Jul 1826; V McBee

Simpson, S P; Wilfong, Barbara; Jas T Alexander; 17 Nov 1824; V McBee

Simpson, William; Slinkard, Susanah; Andrew Slinkard; 13 Oct 1817; V McBee

Sims, James; Huvet, Catherine; John Head; 23 Oct 1820; V McBee

Sims, John A; Johnson, Sary A; Noah Boiles; 16 Sep 1862; David Boiles Esq; M same date by David Boiles Esq

Sims, Thomas; Sain, Barbara; John Kistler; 5 Sep 1863; W R Clark; M 6 Sep 1863 by David Boiles JP

Sinclair, John; Henry (or Harry), Resign; William Sinclair; 5 Jun 1821; Jno Blackwood Esqr

Singeltun, Starling x; Thonbery, Margerett; William x Singeltun; 13 Jun 1813; Saml (?) Fronabargar, Philip Henkel

Singleton, James; Williams, Susannah; Starling Singleton; 23 Oct 1816; James T Alexander

Sipe, Cicero; Carpenter, Ann E; Tobias Sook (or Shook); 6 Jun 1859; W R Clark; M 9 Jun 1859 by G L Hunt MG

116

Sipe, Daniel, Jur x; Dealasnider (Dealasniger), Catharine; Jacob x Rosamon; 10 Apl 1814; J Lourance
Sipe, Joseph x; Hollar, Lavina; John Yount; 29 Jan 1833
Sipe, Paul; Edwards, Sareth; Daniel Wotring (Woodring); 1 Jul 1798; Peter Little
Sitze (Sides), John; Sides, Ann; Henry x Sides; 9 Aug 1813; V McBee
Skidmor (Skidmore), Turner; Creasman, Jane; Thomas Earwood; 3 Sep 1832; Eli Hoyl
Slade, Squire x; Brooks, Margaret; Alfred Sherril (?); 1 May 1866; W R Clark; M same date by B S Johnson JP
Slagle, John; Shufford, Barbara; Daniel Shuford (Shufford); 5 Dec 1814; V McBee
Slagle, John J; Watson, Mary L; Gilbert Bridges; 27 Nov 1838; H Cansler CC
Slate, Benamin; Grissom, Sarah; Samuel Slate; 19 Feb 1816; I Holland for Vardry McBee CCC
Slegle, George; Marlin, Sally; John Slagal, Henry x Cob; 11 Nov 1794; Jo Dickson
Slinkard, Henry x; Cochran, Susana; H Barkley; 17 Jan 1809; Danl Forney
Slinker, Fredrick (Ger Friedrich Schlunkerd); Grant, Barbarah; Peter Grant (Jr); 1 Apl 1794; Joseph Steel
Sloan (Slone), George; Ewing, Margaret; Hugh Ewing; 10 Feb 1840; I Holland
Sloan, Robert; Beaty, Mary; William McKee; 17 Jul 1835; Isaac Holland
Slone (Sloan), Arthur; Arrowood, Ruth; Abr Forney; 11 Dec 1810; Jesse Perkins
Sloop, Henry; Davis, Elizabeth; Frederick x Ward, (Ger) Heinrich Castner; 12 Dec 1813; Jesse Perkins; M same date
Smere (Snyre), Daniel; Setzer, S M; George Setzer; 15 Mar 1839
Smires, John (Ger Johanes Schmires); Bost, Ottel; William Bost (Ger Wilhelm Bast); 17 May 1785; Joseph Steel
Smith, Abraham; Hallman, _____; Charles Reinhardt; 26 Jan 1810; Danl M Forney
Smith, Abraham x; Rooks, Elizabeth; George Clemmer; 2 Sep 1815; James T Alexander
Smith, Alexander; Rutledge, Mary; James T Alexander; 27 Oct 1829; William H Kistler
Smith, Andrew; Oats, Jane; Samuel Miller; 11 Jan 1820; V McBee
Smith, Andrew; Holland, Martina; Thomas Wells; 23 Dec 1844; R Williamson Jr
Smith, Benjamin; Beaty, Esther; David Linebarger; 11 Dec 1824; V McBee
Smith, Charles W x; Gooden, Sarah; David Cook; 1 Jul 1829; M Hull JP
Smith, Cuddious; Weever, Eve; John Havner (John Havener, Martin's Son); 5 Jun 1813; V McBee
Smith, Daniel; Mooney, Susy; Abraham Mauney (Moony); 12 Aug 1808; Danl M Forney
Smith, Daniel (son of John); Jenkins, Sally; Daniel Smith; 11 Sep 1810; H Y Webb
Smith, David; Sloan, Sarah; Isaac McKee; 19 Apl 1797
Smith, David x; Rodes, Amy; George x Weathers; 30 Oct 1806; Lwn Henderson
Smith, David; Orond, Betsey; John Moore; 27 May 1808; Danl M Forney
Smith, David; Little, Catharine; John Hoke; 16 Jun 1825; Fr Hoke
Smith, David x; Hager, Catharine; Allen x Baker; 13 Jan 1831; L M McBee
Smith, David x; Shoup, Sarah; Absalom Wood; 8 Apl 1836; John B Harry
Smith, David G x; Strutt, Nancy; Peter x Michal; 20 Nov 1848; Robt Williamson
Smith, Ephraim x; Carpenter, Sarah; Vincent Avery; 25 Jun 1861; W R Clark; M 4 Jul 1861 by Daniel Siegel JP
Smith, Frederick; Sigman, Agaline; John Smith Jr; 5 ____ 1834; Ely Sigman
Smith, George; Balley, Batsey; Francis x Bayley; 13 Dec 1810; John Willfong
Smith, George; Hoke, Sally; John Smith; 27 July (?) 1815
Smith, H Hildreth; Hoke, Mary Brent; M L McCorkle; 19 May 1853; R Williamson; M same date by T S W Mott in St Luke's Church
Smith, Henry (Ger Henrich Schmitt); Englefinger, Catherrina; Martin (Martag) Friday; 15 Jun 1800; John Crouse JP
Smith, Henry; Coulter, Anna; Philip x Coulter; 22 Apl 1817; James T Alexander
Smith, Jackson x; Baker, Sarah Ann; S __ Yount (Sylvenus Yount); 30 Jan 1859; Danl Siegel JP; M same date by Danl Siegel JP
Smith, Jacob x; Smith, Sarah; John Linebarger; 11 Apl 1808; Danl M Forney
Smith, James; Beattey, Polly; Robt Martin; 15 Jul 1803; Jos Dickson
Smith, James x; McArver, Mary; John x Mason; 11 Dec 1843; Willis Reeves JP; Ambiguous
Smith, James M; Vickers, Polley; Alex Vickers; 8 May 1817; V McBee
Smith, James M; Rudisill, Hetta; Milton A Smith; 17 Dec 1834; M W Abernathy
Smith, Jeremiah x; Hull, Winney; Jesse Smith; 20 Mar 1817; V McBee
Smith, Jeremiah x; Goings, Sally; Abner Hull; 21 Oct 1825
Smith, Jesse; Moore, Fanny; Aron Moore; 24 Jan 1811; Danl M Forney

Smith, John x; Weathers, Franky; William Holland (Hollin); 1 May 1811
Smith, John; Fry, Mrs Elizabeth; William Ervin; 2 Jul 1816; Ligt Williams
Smith, John x; Tabb, Elizabeth; John Detter; 15 Aug 1816; V McBee
Smith (Smithe), John x; Weathers, Jemima; Elijah x Weathers; 26 Oct 1819;
   James T Alexander
Smith, John; Friday, Elizabeth; John Friday; 9 Dec 1826; J T Alexander
Smith, John; Simon, Catharina; John Hoke; 7 Jan 1829; Fr Hoke JP
Smith, John; Holes Claw, Elizabeth; Adam P Robinson, Henry E Smith (Jacob Smith);
   19 Nov 1836; Wm Little; Doubtful, end "A P Robinson MB"
Smith, John; Seagle, Barbara; David Smith; 25 Dec 1849; Robt Williamson
Smith, John B; Dellinger, Barbara A; P S Kistler; 19 Jul 1854; J A Huss; M 25 Jul
   1854 by R N Davis
Smith, John W; Smith, Lena; Henry Finger; 12 Mar 1834
Smith, Joseph; Holland, Mary; James Holland; 3 Nov 1812
Smith, Joseph x; Fulbright, Elizabeth ; Peter x Fulbright; 11 Jan 1827; M Hull JP
Smith, Joseph; Martin, Hetty; James Carpenter; 15 Mar 1832; J T Alexander
Smith, Joshua J; Leonard, Eve; Jacob Leonard; 7 Dec 1827; V McBee
Smith, Lawson x; Price, Sarah; Thomas W Price (White Price); 26 Jun 1834; J G
   Hand JP
Smith, Martin; Leonard, Eve Catharine; David Haulman (Holman); 25 May 1839;
   L E Thompson
Smith, Milton A; Cobb, Mary N; Martin Zimmerman; 13 Oct 1836; M W Abernathy
Smith, Milton A; Cayhill, Nannie C; Thomas J Eccles; 14 Oct 1851; Robt Williamson
Smith, Moses; Goldman, Hannah; George Seitz (Sitz); 20 Nov 1833; Carlos Leonard
Smith, Oliver (W); Cannon, Mary; James H Dickson; 31 Dec 1834; And Hoyl JP
Smith, Peter; Best, Hannah; Jacob Best; 16 Nov 1784
Smith, Peter; Hope, Margaret; Jacob Hofmon (Huffman); 29 Mar 1830; J T
   Alexander
Smith, Philip; Baker, Nancy; Daniel Killian; 19 Jan 1784; Joseph Steel
Smith, Robert; Baker, Sarah; Martin x Best; 30 Mar 1807; Lwn Henderson
Smith, Robert; Armstrong, Peggy; William Penny; 4 Dec 1828; B J Thompson
Smith, Robert x; Dellinger, Hannah; George W x Goodson; 3 Oct 1833; L McBee
Smith, Robert; Fite, Willie; William Caldwell; 25 Oct 1836; ____ Hanks JP
Smith, Robert; Mauney, Sarah; John Baker; 7 Apl 1846; R Williamson
Smith, Samuel; Godfrey, Maryanne; Gedon Robinson; 24 Jul 1812; Joseph Neel
Smith, Samuel; Marner, Jenny; Joseph Neel; 2 Jul 1818; William McClure
Smith, Solomon; Lingafelt, Nancy; John x Lingafelt; 6 Mar 1862; W R Clark
Smith, Thomas; Holman, Sarah; Jacob Reinhardt; 11 Apl 1812; Lwn Henderson
Smith, Thomas x; McFelmeth, Patsey; Isaac W Carpenter; 22 Oct 1840; H Cansler
Smith, Walter B; Bailey, Mary J; V A McBee; 28 Mar 1853; R Williamson; M same
   date by T S W Mott
Smith, William; Bull, Susanah; Edward Bull, Richard Rankin; 25 Apl 1792; Jo
   Dickson
Smith, William; Mauney, Catharine; Alexander Moore; 19 Jan 1814; James Taylor
   Alexander
Smith, William x; Warran, Martha; Hugh x Warran; 23 Mar 1826; Fr Hoke
Smith, William x; Helms, Mary; John x Massagee; 23 Oct 1833; Vardry McBee
Smith, William L; Price, Polly Minerva; William D Hannah; 21 Mar 1828; Isaac
   Holland
Smoyer (or Smoger), Pinkny x; Taylor, Louisa; Franklin x Smoyer (or Smoger);
   25 Dec 1866; W R Clark; M 1 Jan 1867 by R N Davis Minister
Smyer, Daniel; Frye, Catherine; Philip Frye (Ger Philib Frey); 23 Jan 1822; V McBee
Smyer, David; Bovey, Elizabeth; Henry Cline; 17 Apl 1822; Mic Cline
Smyer, Elias; Smith, Elizabeth; John Smith; __ Mar 1815; Mic Cline
Smyer, Jacob; Bollinger, Sophiah; John Smyer; 30 Nov 1821; Jas T Alexander
Smyer (Smire), John; Shuford, Elissabeth; Wm Bost; 18 May 1809
Smyer, John F; Linebarger, M S; N____ly H Fry; 4 Apl 1846; V A McBee
Smyth (Smith), James; Espey, Jean; James Espey; 6 May 1786; Eliz Dickson
Sneed, Edward; Havener, Ann; Uriah Pollard; 14 Jan 1818; V McBee
Snider, John; Taylor, Elizabeth; Jno Turbyfill, John Allen; 6 Oct 1806; Lwn
   Henderson
Snyre see Smere
Soles, Andrew x; Ingle, Polly; Philip Kelly; 9 Dec 1833; Carlos Leonard
Sommit, Daniel x; Moser, Sally; Francis x Sommit; 3 Dec 1813; Philip Henkel
Sorunts (Sorents), John x; Baker, Rebeca; Nicholas x Sorunts (Sorents); 22 Feb 1790;
   Joseph Steel

Southard, Henry; Piram, Susanna; Mi__ Southard; 25 Sep 1814; Jesse Perkins; M this date

Southard (Suthard), Micajah; Perkins, Martha; Fredrick x Ward; 6 Jan 1795; Jon Greaves ACC

Spact, Henry x; Bailey, Polly; David Bailey; 29 Oct 1816; V McBee

Spact, Philip x; Lewis, Sarah; Henry x Spact; 6 May 1820; V McBee

Spake, Christopher; Craft, Omai; George x Dellinger; 18 Dec 1846; Robt Williamson

Spake, Samuel; Dellinger, Harriet R; Daniel Dellinger; 4 Jul 1840; H Cansler

Spangler, Frederick (Ger Spengler); Howser, Eulia; Jacob Spangler (Ger Spengler); 17 Nov 1814; James T Alexander

Spanuel (Speagle), Emanuel; Roney, Elizabeth; Lawson A Rhoney (Roney); 27 Sep 1842; H Cansler

Spargo, James; Dellinger, Elisabeth S; Valentine Helderman; 3 Feb 1855; J Helderman; M same date by J Helderman JP

Sparrow, Hiram; Dews, Julia; Marcus L Hoke; 19 Feb 1835

Sparrow, Patrick J; Thomas, Mary; James Hains; 28 Apl 1826; V McBee

Speagle, Emanuel see Spanuel, Emanuel

Speagle, Solomon; Angel, Susannah (?); David Robinson; 31 Oct 1833; M W Abernathy

Speck, John F; Wells, Julia A; J H Boyd; 20 May 1862; W R Clark; M 21 May 1862 by G W Ivy (MG)

Spect, George x; Lewis, Elizabeth; Simeon x Lewis; 10 Dec 1812; V McBee

Speegle, John (Ger Johannes Spiegel); Lence, Mary; Davald Spigel (Speegle); 18 Aug 1805; Phil Whitener JP

Speegle (Speagle), Martin; Hudson, Elizabeth; Solomon Speegle (Speagle); 30 Jan 1829; B J Thompson

Speegle, Solomon; Hudson, Sally; Martin Speegle; 29 Aug 1825; J T Alexander

Spegle (Speegle), David; Grose, Marimacdalene; Daniel Hudson (Hutson); 27 Jul 1819; Phil Whitener JP

Spegle (Speagle), Edward; Kistler, Mary; W Lander; 3 Jan 1848; Robt Williamson

Spencer, Absalom; Abernathy, Amy; Nathan Abernathy; 19 Jan 1809; Ligt Williams

Spencer, Benjamin x; Rinck, Susannah; Jacob x Rinck; 14 Oct 1815; Mic Cline

Spencer, Benjamin x; Winkler, Mary; Joseph x Winkler, of Burke Co; 29 Mar 1827; Mic Cline

Spencer, Docter x (of Burke Co); Shell, Mary; Joshua Robinson; 21 May 1818; Mic Cline

Spencer, Eli; Mowser, Lucinda; Frederick Mowser; 19 Aug 1841; Epm Yount JP

Spencer, Ganaway; Spencer, Jemimay; Thomas Spencer; 3 May 1814

Spencer, George; Best, Elizabeth; William x Spencer; 4 Aug 1798; Jonn Greaves

Spencer, Grisiam; Harmon, Mary Ann; Ephraim x Harmon; 2 Feb 1843; A J Cansler

Spencer, Israel; Sigman, Betty An; Abel Bollinger; 11 Feb 1837; Henry Cline

Spencer, John; Huffman, Anna; George McCallister; 3 Oct 1818; V McBee

Spencer, John; Vaughan, Harriet; H (Hiempsal) Vaughan; 29 Nov 1819; James T Alexander

Spencer, John H; Gullick, Mary; Benaiah Gullick; 2 Nov 1814; James T Alexander

Spencer, Joshua x, of Burke Co; Shell, Leah; James Robinson; 10 Apl 1817; Mic Cline

Spencer, Joshua x, of Burke Co; Robinson, Sally, widow; Doctor Spencer, Ganaway Spencer; 24 Jan 1819; Mic Cline

Spencer, Thomas; Senter, Betsey; Absalom Spencer; 28 Jan 1812; Lwn Henderson

Spencer, William x; Taylor, Jane; George Cathy; 30 Mar 1796

Spencer, William; Wallis, _____; Joseph McAlester (M'Callister); 4 Jul 1826; Isaac Holland

Spencer, William; Jenkins, Catharine; H W Reeves; 8 Jan 1846; W Reeves JP

Spencer, Zachariah; Bird, Mary; David Cobbs; 31 Aug 1785; Peter King

Spenser, John; Bonham, Rebecca; Jacob Ramsour; 19 Jan 1811

Spiegel, John C x; Carpenter, Martha M; Jacob Smith; 8 Aug 1857; Danl Siegel JP; M 9 Aug 1857 by Danl Siegel JP

Spiegel (Speegel), Moses; Ashebrener, Cathrine; Abraham x Ashebrener; 19 Feb 1815; Phil Whitener JP

Spigel (Speegle), Davald; Lentz, Hannah; Danl Conrad; 1 Aug 1803; John Dickson

Spigle, Martin x; Shook, Molly; Henry Huver (Huber); 29 Aug 1809; Philip Henckel

Spratt, J L; Sullivan, Margaret; J F x Spratt; 23 Feb 1867

Spratt (Sprat), James; Devebaugh, Anna; Benjamin James; 13 Aug 1823; V McBee

Spratt, Thomas; Cline, Nancy; John Killian; 27 Apl 1838; H Cansler

Spratt, William; Hause, Sarah; Elijah Sulivan; 12 Feb 1831; V McBee

Springs, Elias A; Rhyne, Sarah S; Caleb W Hoyl; 28 Nov 1842; Eli Hoyl

Sronce, Abel x; Brown, Mrs Sarah; A P James; 3 Jul 1865; J A Bisaner; M 8 Jul 1865 by W H Alexander JP

Sronce, Charles F; Ingle, Margaret; --------; 26 Feb 1856; M this date by Elisha Saunders JP; C only, no B

Sronce, Hailey x; Lee, Elener; Isaac x Lafever; 2 Feb 1842; H Cansler Clk

Sronce (Srounce), Jacob; Summey, Susanah; John Parker; 9 Jun 1825; Jas T Alexander

Sronce, Jacob; Ingle, Mary C; Ephr x Dellinger; 29 Dec 1866; W R Clark CC; M 13 Jan 1867 by Elisha Saunders JP

Sronce (Srons), John (Jr); Edwards, Ebbe; Robert Boyd; 25 May 1820; V McBee

Srons, John x; Sauls (?), Barbara; John Parker; 19 Feb 1828; V McBee

Srum, Andrew x; Huffman, Margaret; Christian Rhodes (Rods); 22 Jul 1817; James T Alexander

Srum, Daniel x; Finger, Mary; John x Srum; 4 Oct 1818; V McBee

Srum, David x; Garner, Becky; Peter x Kinder; 11 Jan 1809; Danl M Forney

Srum (Shrum), David; Keener, Elizabeth; Peter Srum (Shrum); 19 Oct 1830; Jno D Hoke

Srum (Shrum), John; Finger, Catharine; Jonas x Finger; 12 Jan 1824; Jas T Alexander

Srum (Shrum), John; Fox, Margaret; Ambrose x Michal; 11 Oct 1851; Robt Williamson; "Margaret Fox of Catawba Co"; M 14 Oct 1851 by D Crooks MG

Srum, Peter; Panter, Nancy; David Srum; 27 Mar 1830; J T Alexander

Srum, Solomon x; Srum, Poly; John Srum; 16 May 1825

Stacy, Elisha x; Williams, Polly; William x Blalock; 26 May 1797; Jno Dickson

Stacy (Stacey), Jeremiah; Southard, Nancy; Zachy (Zachariah) Stacy (Stacey); 28 Nov 1812

Stacy, T F__ (F F); McCaul, Martha Jane; F J Jetton; 3 Aug 1854; M 8 (?) Aug • 1854 by H Asbury MG

Stacy, William; Hanes, Sarah; Richard Lee; 3 Oct 1811; Jesse Perkins

Stacy, Zachary (Zachariah); Whitener, Catherine; John Stacy; 19 Mar 1814; V McBee

Stallcup (Stalcup), Wm (Jr) of Macon Co; Killian, Avaline; Wm Stallcup (Stalcup) Sr; 16 Dec 1838; Wm Herman JP

Stamey, Alexander; Haynes, Belsora; Dr Charles Brendle (Brindle); 12 Jul 1847; Robt Williamson

Stamey, Enoch x; Kener, Polly; David Srum (Shrum); 4 Oct 1833; S McBee

Stamey, John x; Hudson, Elizabeth; Isaac x Reinhardt; 24 Dec 1814

Stamey, John R; Williams, Nelley; Daniel Michael; 28 Mar 1822; Peter Hoyle JP

Stamey, Lawson x; Ramsey, Jane; Joseph Stamey; 26 Feb 1832; P Stamey JP

Stamey, W R; Elmore, Catharine; W W Reynolds; 9 Apl 1856; J A Huss; M 10 Apl 1856 by A P Cansler JP

Stamy, John; Huggins, Sarah; John Dickson; 30 Mar 1801; Margaret Dickson

Stamy, Peter; Rudisell, Elisa; Samuel Ramsey; 9 May 1797

Stanford see Sanford

Stanford, Ezekiel x; Cobb, Ellener; Aron x Stroup; 5 Feb 1841; And Hoyl

Stanford, Lyman x; Starret, Dinny Adeline; Aron x Stroup; 5 Feb 1841; And Hoyl

Stansbury (Stansby), Solomon; Lewing, Jain; George Lawing (Lewing); 22 Feb 1791; Jo Dickson

Staret (Starret), John; McCallister, Elloner; James McCallister; 12 Feb 1793

Starnes, John F; Hovis, Lucinda; --------; 19 Jan 1862; W R Clark Clerk; M same date by Jonas W Derr JP; L and C, no B

Starnes, William x; Hovis, Mary; William Troutman; 21 Jul 1866; W R Clark; M 22 Jul 1866 by J A Huggins Minister of the gospel M P Church

Starns, Columbus x; Purkins, Elisabeth; James Mullen; 30 Dec 1860; Jonas W Derr; M same date by Jonas W Derr (JP)

Starr (Star), Eli; Frye, Elizabeth; David Wilson; 15 Aug 1822; V McBee

Starr (Star), John; Bost, Sally; Jacob Seapaugh (Seabaugh); 23 Aug 1825; Mic Cline

Starret, Alexander; Garner, Jane; William Armstrong; 1 Sep 1824; Wm Little

Stearnes (Starns), John; Caruth, Nancy; Joseph Green; 23 Nov 1820; James T Alexander

Steel, Calvin; Mosteller, Susan; John Earney; 14 Apl 1845; R Williamson Jr

Steely, John x; Price, Ana; Thomas x Ramsey; 21 Sep 1795; Michl Eaker

Steely, Lovick; Hager, Marey; Wm Black, Simon Hagger; 10 Feb 1806; Hy Conner JP

Stemey, John; Ramsey, Saley (?); John Mull, John Summerer (Sumroar); 25 May 1817; Peter Hoyle

Stephenson (Stevenson), John; Clark, Jane; William Moore; 25 Jul 1815; V McBee

Sterret (Starret), Alexander; Gillespie, Mary; James Hanks; 9 Feb 1789
Stevenson, Hugh B; Kelly, Pricilla; Robert C Kelley (Kelly); 17 Feb 1823; V McBee
Stevenson, James N; Gibson, Jane; William Gibson; 3 Nov 1826; Isaac Holland
Steward, Thos W x; Williams, Elizabeth M; Waldin x Hart; 4 Feb 1862; W R Clark;
    M 6 Feb 1862 by F M Reinhardt JP
Stewart see Sturd
Stiles, Benjamin x; McCabe (?), Katherine; John x Stiles; 9 Jan 1794; Jas Dickson
Stiles, Benjamin x; Conner, Susannah; John Allen; 5 Apl 1803; Jas McKisick
Stiles, Carter x; Caldwell, Ann; Samuel Painter; 4 Dec 1832; Vardry McBee
Stiles, Henry x; Eaton, Elizabeth; Samuel Painter; 14 Jan 1834; M W Abernathy;
    Ambiguous
Stiles, Henry; Caldwell, Christina; William Colwell (Caldwell); 12 Mar 1836; M W
    Abernathy
Stiles, John; Fisher, Saley; William Colwell; 20 Jan 1837; Miles W Abernathy
Stiles, William; Cook, Matilda; Andrew Colwell (Caldwell); 6 Apl 1829
Stiller, George; Painter, Susan; John Clippard; 18 Nov 1865; A S Haynes Cty Ct Clk;
    M 20 Nov 1865 by A B Laney JP
Stillwell, Samuel x; Conner, Hannah; Jacob Conner; 22 Oct 1815; Da'd Warlick
Stilwell, Nimrod x; Serratt (or Sernatt), Phebe; Daniel Coulter; 24 Nov 1829; Jonas
    Bost
Stine, Abraham; Bridges, Emily; Isaac Anderson; 29 Aug 1827; S L McBee
Stine, Daniel; Gross, Suey (or Lucy); Philip Gross; 12 Feb 1818; Mic Cline
Stine, John; Deal, Cathrine; Jacob Bolch (Bolick); 1 Jul 1824; Mic Cline
Stine, John; Isonhower, Sarah; J H (Henry) Isenhower (Isonhower); 2 Jan 1843;
    Wm Herman JP
Stinson, Cyrus; Martin, Mary A L; Alberry Ford; 9 Feb 1836; Isaac Holland
Stinson, William x; Parish, Malinda; Wilson x Turbyfill; 9 Mar 1824; Jas T Alexander
Stirewalt (Stierwalt), Michael; Hoke, Jamime; Daniel Roseman; 7 Jul 1834; Fr
    Hoke JP
Stirewalt, Valentine; Hampton, Sarah Ann; Jacob Rush; 17 Jan 1849; R Williamson
Stockston, George W x; Normon, Mary Y; John S Self; 10 Nov 1839; M Hull JP
Stone, James; Eaton, Agatha; William Colwell (Caldwell); 23 Jan 1834; Carlos
    Leonard
Stone, James; Ballard, Willie; John Stone; 14 Nov 1837; John D King
Stone, John x; Nixson, Martha; Thomas x Bumgardner; 23 Jan 1839; J A Ramsour DC
Stone, William x; Knipe, Elizabeth; Aaron Gaza (Gasa); 7 Aug 1813; Vardry McBee
Stoner, Isaac x; Thompson, Ann; Jacob x Collins; 3 Apl 1840; H Cansler
Stowe, Allen R x; Hull, Catharine; Isaac Houser; 4 Jan 1862; W R Clark; M 5 Jan
    1862 by Wm J Hoke JP
Stowe, Decatur (of Gaston Co); Abernathy, Margaret W; --------; 9 Oct 1851;
    M this date by Rev J O Daniel; R only, no B
Stowe, Jacob; Merriner, Sally; William McLean; 12 Jul 1831; I Holland JP
Stowe, James F x; Pinner, Minty K; Jesse H Penny (Penney); 9 Nov 1840; H Cansler
Stowe, Joel A x; Blalock, Maria S; Valentine Helderman; 6 Dec 1847; Robt Williamson
Stowe, Littleberry; Gullick, Jane Caldwell; Jas C Gullick; 1812; (N)
Stowe, Samuel N; Holland, Margaret M; --------; 1843; (N)
Stowe, William; Smith, Sarah; Lemuel Stowe; 8 Sep 1831; Isaac Holland
Strain, Alexander; Weathers, Sousee (or Missousee); Dixon (Dickson) Dameron;
    27 Apl 1840; And Hoyl JP
Strain (Strane), William; Bandy, Eliz; Noah Ferguson; 8 Feb 1842; A J Cansler
Street (or Strut), George x; Gilbert, Susanah; James Rhonay (Roany); 19 Aug 1815;
    V McBee
Stricker, Daniel (Ger same); Whetston, Susana; Henry Hoke; 29 Dec 1818; Peter
    Hoyle
Stroder, Alexander x; Wills, Catharine; Moses Jenkins; 30 Mar 1799; Jno Dickson
Stroder, William x; Scarborough, Dorcas; David H Scarbrough; 21 Jan 1799; Jno
    Dickson
Stroud, John; Ramsey, Elisabeth; Daniel Johnston; 30 Nov 1784; James Dickson
Stroup, Abner; Baker, Lidia; Jacob F Dailey (Daily); 2 Jan 1842; H Cansler Clk
Stroup, Andrew; Link, Caty; Alexander S Head; 19 Feb 1803; John Dickson
Stroup, Andrew J; Bird, Martha Ann; Wesley Stroup; 6 Nov 1854; J A Huss;
    M 9 Nov 1854 at Mostellers Paper Mills by Robt B Jones Pastor Salem Baptist
Stroup, Benjamin; White, Cynthia Winslow; Henry x Keever; 21 Nov 1831; L McBee
Stroup, Champion; McCollister, Elizabeth; Matthew Stroup; 26 Dec 1831; V McBee
Stroup, Christopher; Hallmon, Elizabeth; Matthew Stroup; 20 Dec 1836; M W
    Abernathy

Stroup, Daniel x; Goodson, Polly; Alexander S Head; 19 Feb 1803; John Dickson
Stroup, David; Goodson, Hannah; Jacob Stroup; 14 Apl 1803
Stroup, David; Inglefinger, Peggy; Alexander S Head, Lwn Henderson; 8 Jan 1806
Stroup, David x; Cloninger, Ann; Moses Cloninger; 14 Sep 1821; V McBee
Stroup, David x; Shutley, Levina; James Moore; 16 Nov 1824; Jas T Alexander
Stroup, Eli x; Shetly, Elizabeth; Drury G Abernathy; 15 Feb 1830; V McBee
Stroup, Elisha x; McGinnas, Jane M; Moses Stroup; 11 Feb 1830; Luther M McBee
Stroup, Israel R; Rudisell, Elizabeth S; D R Rudisael (Rudisell); 29 Sep 1854; J A
    Huss; M 4 Oct 1854 by David Crooks (MG)
Stroup, J C; Dellinger, Barbara; W W McGinnas; 18 Oct 1838; L E Thompson
Stroup, Jacob (Ger Jacob Straub); Dillinger, Betsy; William x Goodson; 25 Aug
    1790; Jas Dickson
Stroup, Jacob; Rhyne, Hannah; Alexander S Head; 13 Mar 1809; Jacob Forney
Stroup, Jacob; Stroup, Nancy; Champion x Stroup; 8 Jun 1826; Vardry McBee
Stroup, Jessee x; White, Susannah; R x Kincaid; 10 Jan 1834 (endorsed 1835);
    Ambiguous
Stroup, John x; Master, Barbary; George x Reel; 1 Aug 1796; Jo Dickson
Stroup, John; Rudisel, Ann; Moses Cloninger; 17 Jan 1823; V McBee
Stroup, Jonas; Cloninger, Rebeckah; Moses Cloninger; 25 Nov 1821; V McBee
Stroup, Joseph x; Creasman, Catharine; Danl x Reel; 14 Sep 1798; Jno Dickson
Stroup, Joseph D x; Long, Rebecckah; Levi Stroup; 8 Nov 1836
Stroup, Joseph F; Moore, Eliza; Moses Cloninger; 29 Jan 1838; Eli Hoyl
Stroup, Matthew; Wilson, Elizabeth; John A McGinnas; 21 Apl 1829; J T Alexander
Stroup, Matthew; Black, Barbara; Abner Stroup; 21 Sep 1846; Robt Williamson
Stroup, Michael x; Goodson, Jean; Michael Pentorff; 29 Mar 1800   .
Stroup, Moses; Masters, Susanah; John x Stroup; 26 Nov 1813; Vardry McBee
Stroup, Moses; Clarke, Ginsey Mary; Daniel Hager; 14 Oct 1826; Silas L McBee
Stroup, Phillip; Adtleman, Molly; Boston Adtleman (Adleman); 9 May 1789; Jo
    Dickson
Stroup, Phillip x; Masters, Catherine; Daniel Hoke; 9 Mar 1811; H Y Webb
Stroup, Phillip; McLure, Nancy J; A S Haynes; 12 Oct 1860; W R Clark; M 16 Oct
    1860 by J R Peterson (MG)
Stroup, Robert B; Bisaner, Rachel; Isaac C x Williams; 26 Mar 1864; M 27 Mar
    1864 by Elisha Saunders JP
Stroup, Solomon; Haskins, Nancy; William Head; 3 May 1816; V McBee
Stroup, William x; Earwood, Salley; William Earwood; 15 Dec 1824; V McBee
Stroupe, George x; Attleman, Elisabeth; Boston x Ettleman (Attleman); 20 May 1793;
    Jo Dickson
Strutt, Logan A; Dellinger, Margaret; Gilbert Presnell; 24 Feb 1844; R Williamson Jr
Stuard (Steward), Leander S; Robinson, Mahala; Thomas x Steward; 14 Mar 1842
Stubbs, Elbridge W; Jetton, Sarah; F J Jetton; 3 Jun 1857; H Wells; M same date
    by Landy Wood
Sturd (Stewart), N T; Robison, Jane C; Jonathan Bost; 4 Sep 1837; H Cansler Clk
Sudduth, John x; Gray, Nancy; John x Walker; 27 Dec 1784; John Dickson
Sugg, George; Ward, Sarah; Isaac Erwin; 5 Sep 1811; Joseph Neel
Suggs, A J; Kendrick, Martha A; William S Dickson; 11 Aug 1837; I Holland JP
Suggs, Isaac; Chittem, Margaret M; Joseph Chittam (Chittem); 24 Apl 1820; V McBee
Suggs, Levi H; Grissom, Mary S; John Dameron; 13 Nov 1837; And Hoyl JP
Sulavan (Sullivan), Samuel; Borland, Mary; Moses Moore; 14 Aug 1800; Wallace
    Alexander
Sulivan (Sullivan), Elijah; Cathey, Jane; Henry Clyne (Cline); 3 Aug 1814; V McBee
Sulivan, Owen; McCollister, Fanny; Aron Moore; 26 Dec 1810; H Y Webb
Sullivan, Charles C; Leonhardt, Martha E F; M C Clay; 22 Sep 1858; W R Clark;
    M same date by Logan H Lowrance JP
Sullivan, Elijah; Sprat, Katey; Philip Reep; 23 Dec 1826; V McBee
Sullivan, Ezekiel; Mauney, Salley; John D Hoke; 15 Jan 1828; V McBee
Sullivan, Ezekiel M; Hauss, Clara Anna; M C (Caleb) Clay; 17 Sep 1856; W R
    Clark; M 18 Sep 1856 by George Coon JP
Sullivan, George L (Logan); Haus, Mary Adaline; W Williamson; 24 Dec 1844
Sullivan, James x; McCallister, Jane; Alexander McCarver; 27 Oct 1806
Sullivan, Jerry x; Mooney (Mauney), Catharine; (Dr) M L Brown; 2 Dec 1862;
    M 15 Dec 1862 by Alfred Black JP
Sullivan, Noah; Cambell, Mary; Robert Boyd; 1 Dec 1829; Luther M McBee
Sullivan, Samuel; Summett, Polly; John Zimmerman; 18 Feb 1830; J T Alexander
Sulliven, John x; Miller, Pollay; John Muckleroy (Muckelroy); 8 Feb 1821; D Lutz JP
Sult, Lafayette; Clark, Harriet C; F H B Glanton; 31 Oct 1865; A S Haynes;
    M same date by R N Davis Minister

Sumeroua (Summerough), Jacob; Turner, Zelpha; Jacob Huver (Hoover); 25 Sep 1830
Sumerow, Henry; Whitner, Betsey; John Dellinger; 8 Oct 1784
Sumerow (Summerrow), Henry; Henry, Barbra; Robert Mullen (Mullin); 11 Aug 1840
Summer (Sumro), Jacob; Hallman, Barbara; Jacob Hallman; 7 Mar 1821; James T
    Alexander
Summer, John (Ger Johannes Somer); Loughbam, Margrad; John Smith, John x Setzer;
    19 Feb 1801; John Willfong JP
Summerour (Sumrour), Henry; Sides, Sarah; David Ramsour; 31 Jul 1809; Maxl
    Chambers
Summerour (Sumerour), John; Berry, Beggy; Jacob Carpenter; 22 Dec 1817; V McBee
Summerow (Sumrow), David; Rudisill, Susannah; James T Alexander; 7 Jun 1828
Summerow, James; Carpenter, Eliza; Daniel Sumerow (Daniel Summerow Jr); 9 Feb
    1839; H Cansler CC
Summerow (Summerour), Noah; Loretz, Ann E; George Hedick; 17 Dec 1850; Robt
    Williamson
Summerow, Peter; Ramsour, Elmina; John J Reinhardt; 16 Mar 1840; H Cansler
Summerrour (Summerour), James; Hollman, Susan; Levi Shrum; 10 Jan 1848; Robt
    Williamson
Summey, David; Hovis, Anna; Jacob Summey; 26 Nov 1823; Jas T Alexander
Summey, George x; Ramsey, Jane; Philip Gantzler (Ger same); 24 Jan 1820; V McBee
Summey, George x; Englefinger, Barbara; John x Summey; 18 Jul 1826; J T Alexander
Summey, Jacob; Norris, Lenna; Jacob Ramsour; 24 Dec 1822; Joel Dyer
Summey, Jonas; Rhyne, Margaret; Ambrose Costner; 2 Sep 1843; Eli Hoyl
Summey, Michael; Friday, Elizabeth; Jonas Costner; 30 Mar 1818
Summey, Peter; Dobson, Harriet; Jacob Forney; 4 Aug 1816; V McBee
Summey (Summy), Peter; Wallice, Katharine; Michael Rhyne; 8 Oct 1833; Jno
    Blackwood
Summey, Peter A; Roberts, Jane; B M Edney; 13 Dec 1836; E Caldwell
Summey, Peter W; Hoke, Catherine; Charles Slagle; 9 Sep 1818; V McBee
Summey, Robert R; Mullin, Elizabeth; William Cobb; 9 Nov 1842; A J Cansler
Summey, William; Abernathy, Betcy; Isaiah x Summey; 28 Aug 1826; V McBee
Summit, Christian x; Link, Catharine; Charles x Abernathy; 6 Apl 1802; Jno Dickson
Summit, Christian x; Master, Elizabeth; Jacob Master (Ger Jacob Meister); 9 Jun
    1803; Jonn Greaves
Summit, Daniel; Knipe, Sarah M; Joseph Houser; 27 Sep 1845; R Williamson
Summit, Francis x; Shook, Elisabeth; (Ger) Christian Summit; 19 Jan 1809; Danl M
    Forney
Summit, Frederick; Paysour, Catharina; Levi Plonk; 7 Jan 1837
Summit, Henry x; Mayors (or Moyers), Catharine; John Cloninger; 26 Dec 1815;
    V McBee
Summit, Henry; Lenhardt, Susan; Joseph Houser; 5 Jan 1842; V A McBee
Summit (Summet), Jacob; Clonenger, Polly; Danl Forney; 25 Dec 1805; Lwn
    Henderson
Summitt, John x; Robison, Rebecca; Joseph x Summitt; 29 Jul 1830; Peregrine
    Roberts
Summner, Daniel; Summner, Ann; --------; 28 Aug 1866; W T McCoy JP; Ac-
    knowledgment by former slaves
Summy (Summey), Jacob; Shuford, Eve; --------; 26 Jul 1785 (or 1784)
Summy (Summey), Jacob; Friday, Mary; Christopher x Summey; 19 Sep 1815;
    V McBee
Summy, John x; Hufstutler, Sally; Thomas x Ramsey; 6 Jan 1825; J Blackwood Esq
Summy (Summey), John B; Kizer, Nancy; Henry Tritt; 25 Jan 1846; R Williamson
Summy, Michael x; Jenkins, Susan; J R Reeves; 4 Dec 1842; ____ Reeves
Sumner, Benj H; Ramsour, Myra A; Benj S Guion; 8 Jun 1852; Robt Williamson
Sumrow, Daniel x; Gilbert, Elizabeth; John Blackburn; 12 Feb 1809; H Y Webb
Sumter, John; Alexander, Ann; Robert Alexander; 20 Jul 1785
Sumy (Summy), Michal x; Hostatler, Margaret; Mike (Michal) x Sumy (Summy);
    2 Aug 1783
Sunter, James; Jinkins, Nancy; James Sunter; 26 Jan 1780; Adam Baird
Surrat, James x; Bradshaw, Anne; Hiram Brotherton; 4 Mar 1817; V McBee
Sutherlie (Sutherly), Thomas; Haskins, Mary; Jonas Bratcher (Beachy); 14 Feb 1785;
    Ibby Dickson
Sutten, James x; Brindle, Mary; William Boyles; 21 Nov 1832; M Hull JP
Suttlemyer (Settlemere), David; Sherril, Theney; Martin x Settlemere; 6 (or 5) Jan
    1808; D M Forney
Suttlemyer, Henry H (Settlemyer, Hallmon H); Killian, Mary M; Henry Killian;
    31 Dec 1835; M W Abernathy

Sutton, William; Bragg, Mary K; John Bynum; 16 Nov 1818; James T Alexander

Swaim (Swim), William; Prim, Dovy; S D Lowe; 2 Dec 1852; R E Burch; M same date by R E Birch JP

Swan, Isaac; Hanks, Polly; Burrel Wells; 18 Aug 1804; Lwn Henderson

Swan (Swann), James; Starret, Ruth; Moses Staret (Starret); 19 Mar 1800; Jno Dickson

Swaringham, Saml x; Hunt, Ellen; Saml Ramsey; 20 May 1805

Taar, Adam (Ger Adam Der); Sigman, Katrine; Barnet Sigman (Siegman); 15 Sep 1789; Joseph Steel

Tallant, A A (Aaron); Jonson, Patsey; Henry Johnson; 13 Sep 1855; D A Haines JP

Tankerslay (Tankersly), George; Linkhorn, Elizabeth; Christyan Roads; 16 Sep 1805; Betsey Henderson

Tarr (Derr), David L; Linebarger, Nancy; Edward Saunders; 29 Nov 1822; V McBee

Tate, Joseph; Beatey, Sarah; Samuel Carman; 7 Jan 1796; Jo Dickson

Tate, William; Beatty, Martha; Wm Beatty; 5 Feb 1798; John Dickson

Tayler, Fredrick x; Baker, Margreate; Cornlous x Grider; 10 Mar 1798; Peter Little JP

Taylor, Absalom; Crouse, Katy; David Henning; 1 May 1810; Danl M Forney

Taylor, Andrew J; Plonk, Margaret C; Ezekiel M Sullivan; 6 Feb 1854; J A Huss

Taylor, Calvin x; Keener, Catharine; Milton Goodson; 26 Jul 1853; R Williamson; M 28 Jul 1853 by Elisha Saunders JP

Taylor, Franklin; Williams, Barbara; Jackson x Taylor; 26 Jan 1850; Robt Williamson

Taylor, Isaac; Bumgarner, Nancy; John Bumgarner, Wm Jas Taylor; 29 Apl 1811; Jesse Perkins

Taylor, Jacob; Drum, Barbray; Benja Taylor; 1 Jan 1807; Thos Wheeler

Taylor, James; Martin, Elizabeth; Abner McAfee; 10 Jan 1804

Taylor, James; Sullivan, Nancy; Peter Sullivan; 18 Jan 1812; Lwn Henderson

Taylor, James x; Wilson, Polly; Abram Howser (Houser); 15 Sep 1829; J·T Alexander

Taylor, James (Jr); Brown, Elisabeth; James x Brown (Sr); 31 Oct 1833; Jno Blackwood Esq

Taylor, John; Holmesly, Lena; Thomas Little; 14 Aug 1837

Taylor, William x; Hull, Caroline; J C King; 2 Mar 1867

Temples, Daniel x; Wise, Salley; Henry Wise (Ger Weiss); 21 Mar 1823; Peter Hoyle, _____ Zimerman

Temples, Needham x; Speck, Polly; Daniel Speck; 13 May 1826; P Stamey JP

Templeton, R R; McPherson, Frances L; William Williamson; 21 Jan 1854; M 22 Jan 1854 by Henry H Durant MG

Tetherrow, John (Ger Johannes Doderro); Glammer, Eliza; Georg Glemmer; No date; Endorsement in same hand as on bond of 1803

Tethro, Jacob x; Weathers, Nancy; Thomas x Weathers; 9 Jul 1814; V McBee

Thomas, Aaron; Hope, Mary; Willis x Bell; 28 Aug 1834; Carlos Leonard

Thomas, James; Young, Martha; John Thomas; 15 Dec 1784; Joseph Steel

Thomas, John; .Bradley, Abagail; Joseph Bradley; 28 Mar 1823; Isaac Holland

Thomas, Lewis W; McCulloch, Nancy; Jacob Propst; 25 Jan 1831; J T Alexander

Thomas, Moses x; Ingle, Elizabeth; Ephraim x Ingle; 20 May 1858; W R Clark; M same date by J T Alexander JP

Thomas, Robert; Gamble, Rebeckah; William D Hannah; 29 Jul 1828; Isaac Holland

Thomas, Thomas; ' Rutledge, Jean; John Patterson; 28 Apl 1784; James Dickson

Thomas, Zebulon J (or I); Rush, Lidda; John M (N) Thomas; 17 Nov 1818; James T Alexander

Thompson see Johnson

Thompson, Alfred W; McKee, Harriett A; Charles Kelly; 24 Nov 1843; H Cansler

Thompson, Bat; Mayberry, Mary; Moses Abernathy; 11 Aug 1798

Thompson, Daniel G; Asbury, Mary E; Julious A Munday (Monday); 18 Dec 1866; H Asbury for W R Clark Clk; M 20 Dec 1866 by Elisha Saunders JP

Thompson, E W; Low (or Love), Jane C; J C Jenkins; 27 Dec 1858; A W Burton; M 28 Dec 1858 by J S Nelson

Thompson, Ephraim; McKee, Caroline; Alfred Thompson; 3 Mar 1832; Vardry McBee

Thompson, Henry; Williams, Ann; William Clark (Clerk); 18 Sep 1807; D M Forney

Thompson, Hezekiah H; Robinson, Nersissa; Elhanan Robinson; 6 Nov 1839

Thompson, Isom x; Engle, Susanna; Miles x Hix; 12 Jul 1834; Elisha Saunders JP

Thompson, Jacob L; Rozzell, Elizabeth; I (or J) Lowe; 20 Jan 1836

Thompson, James; Abernathy, Martha; Robert Curry; 27 Jun 1796

Thompson, John; Wright, Betcy; David Ramsour; 18 Oct 1816; V McBee

Thompson, John; Hardy, Mary T; William Garner; 3 Feb 1825; M Hull JP
Thompson, John; Wilkinson, Emala; David J Pryor; 3 Nov 1829
Thompson, John T; Howard, Mary; Thomas Thompson; 20 Mar 1855; H Asbury; M same date by H Asbury Mnst
Thompson, L E; Ramsour, Harriet L; William Slade; 16 Nov 1841; Rob Williamson Jr
Thompson, Monroe; Henderson, Amanda; _____; 16 Sep 1865; A S Haynes Clerk; "The same being persons of color"; M 19 Sep 1865 by Henry C Lay; L and C, no B
Thompson, Nathan; Black, Esther; William Killen (Killian); 19 Aug 1785; John Moore
Thompson, Samuel T; Asbury, L Melvina; Jas A Munday (Monday); 13 Oct 1863; H Asbury; M same date by O A Darby MG
Thompson, Thomas J; Shelton, Frances; Samuel T Shelton; 9 Sep 1828; B J Thompson
Thompson, Thomas J; Forney, Elizabeth R; B M Jetton; 25 Nov 1853; J A Huss; M 27 Nov 1853 by H Asbury Mstr
Thompson, W A; Jinks, Sarah F; J F Hause (Franklin Hauss); 28 Oct 1851; Robt Williamson
Thompson, William x; Williamson, Elizabeth; Turner x Abernathy; 8 Apl 1788
Thompson, William D; Lockman, Nancy G; Benjamin F Withers; 4 Jan 1854; W B Withers JP; M 12 Jan 1854 by H Asbury Mnst
Thompson, William F; Wiley, Elinor; Jacob Forney; 27 Jun 1823; Jas T Alexander
Thomson (Thompson), Horatio; Quickel, Ann; Wm H Michal; 17 Sep 1846
Thomson (Thompson), Isom; Childers, Betsey; (Ger) Johannes Leinberger; 2 Mar 1814; Jesse Perkins; M this date
Thomson, John; Dun, Martha; Moses Scott; 14 Feb 1785; Elizabeth Dickson
Thorn, Daniel; Detter, Roxanna; H D Rutter; 27 Nov 1865; A S Haynes CCC; M same date by R N Davis Minister
Thornbargar, James x; Ballard, Nancy; Matthew N Leeper; 29 Jan 1846; And Hoyl JP
Thornberg (Throneberg), Jacob; Clonninger, Mary; Frederick Summit (Sumit); 30 (or 3) Nov 1836; Jacob Plonk JP
Thornburg, William x; Jenkins, Polly; A L Johnson; 22 Oct 1838; L E Thompson
Thornburgh, Jacob M (Jacob Tronbargar); Wiatt, Susanna; Joseph x Costner; 24 Aug 1835; And Hoyl JP
Thornbury, David x; Summit, Betsey; John Thornbury (Ger Johannis Tronberg); 17 Feb 1810; Danl M Forney
Thorpe (Tharpe), Robert W; Upchurch, Clement; Gilbert Presnell; 14 Nov 1844; R Williamson Jr
Thronbarg, Jacob (Ger Dronberg, Jacob); Summit, Magdlin; Francis Summat (Ger Johannes Franciss Samet); 25 Jul 1813; Philip Henkel
Thronburgh (Troneberg), George; Starr, Polly; Eli Starr; 23 May 1822; Mic Cline
Thronebargh (Thronburg), William; Sigman, Catherine; Eli Sigman; 7 Jun 1840
Throngbary, John (Ger Johannis Tronberg); Justice, Nancey; Matthew Wilson; 24 Oct 1810; Danl M Forney
Throrneburgh (Throneberg), Eli; Tounsen, Cathrine; Jacob x Townsen; 5 Nov 1837; John Moretz JP
Tiddy, William; Rudisill, Martha AA; H C Hamilton; 6 Apl 1860; W R Clark; M 18 Apl 1860 by R N Davis Minister
Tillet, Richard x; Ramsour, Mahala; James x Humphrys; 20 Jan 1866 (probably 1867); W R Clark CC; M 22 Jan 1867 by Francis B Moore Elder
Tilley, Jacob x; Caldwell, Rebecca; James Culwell, Henry x Caldwell; 23 Aug 1786; Wm Harbeson
Tinnison see Finison
Tipps, Thomas x; Tucker, Mary; Nathaniel Michum (Mitchum); 24 Apl 1815; V McBee
Tipps, William; Whitner, Linna; Logan Conrad; 17 Dec 1836; G P Shuford JP
Titman (Tytman), Anthony; Ford, Milley; Frederick Ford; 14 Oct 1811
Titmon, Peter; Pollard, Sally; Anthony Titmon; 3 Mar 1831; Isaac Holland
Todd, George A; Boyd, Rhoda; Lyman Woodford; 31 Oct 1838
Tolbert, William x; Goodson, Nancy; John Slinkard (Ger Johannes Schlenkerd); 27 Feb 1797; Wallace Alexander
Toler, William; Hendrix, Elizabeth; James Appleton; 6 Aug 1822; V McBee
Tomkies, John F; Hoyl, Margaret M; Eli Hoyl; 10 Nov 1825; W C Penick, And Hoyl
Tommy, Jacob x; Bradshaw, Tempe; Moses x Earhart; 18 Feb 1799
Tompson, Hugh x; Lockman, Caroline; Elihu Lockman; 20 Sep 1838; H Cansler
Tomson, Robert x; Shirrill, Adline; Peter Drum; 10 Sep 1833; Fr Hoke JP
Torrance, Hugh A; Robinson, Miriam; Thomas Lovcy (Lovecy); 22 Dec 1841

Torrance, John; Linch, Jane; Samuel A Torrance; 22 Feb 1831; Isaac Holland
Torrance (Torrence), Mathew; Wilson, Nancy; James Wilson; 13 Jul 1803; Jonn Greaves
Torrance, Robert; Falls, Delilah; John Torrance; 13 Feb 1830; Isaac Holland
Torrance, Samuel A; White, Erixene; Ephraim Torrence (Torrance); 30 Oct 1832; Isaac Holland
Torrence, Charles L; Hays, Elizabeth L; Robert G Allison; 27 Mar 1839; H Cansler CC
Torrence, Ephraim; Wilson, Mary; Henry Cansler; 23 Mar 1838
Torrence, John C; Smith, Mary; Edwin B Torrence; 13 Feb 1836; M W Abernathy
Torrence, Lawson H; Roberson, Jane H; Edwin B Torrence; 7 Feb 1837; Ephraim Torrence
Torrence, William W; Wilson, Sarah A; Ephraim Torrence; 27 Feb 1834; Edwin B Torrence
Totherow, Eli x; Hope, Katharine; Jonathan x Totherow; 21 Apl 1818; James T Alexander
Towery, Adam x; Connor, Eliza; Moses x Dellinger; 9 Jan 1841; H Cansler CC
Towery, Adam x; Taylor, Martha; Lewis Ledford; 30 Jun 1847; Robt Williamson; Ambiguous
Townsen, Lewis x; Ekert, Barbara; James Townsin (Townsen); 29 Dec 1833; J D Herman; Ambiguous
Townsen, Peter x; Mitchel, Sally; Jacob x Townsen; 27 May 1827; Henry Cline
Townsend, Andrew x; Hollar, Nancy; James Townsin (Townsend); 21 Oct 1832; Henry Cline
Townsin, Jacob x; Cline, Lusindy; James Townsin; 16 Feb 1837; John Moretz
Towry (Towery), William; Shitle, Rebecca; David Craft; 25 Jun 1849; V A McBee
Traffanstatt (Trefelstat), Peter; Hawn, Hanna; Peter Traffanstatt (?) (Trefelstat) (Sr); 23 Nov 1824; Mic Cline
Tramel (Trammel), James; Helms, Eliza; Wm Towery; 1 Nov 1865; A S Haynes CCC; M 2 Nov 1865 by H A T Harris
Travelstedt, William x; Wilson, Milissa; Daniel Treffanstedt (Travelstedt); 23 Sep 1834; Jno D Hoke
Travelstreet, William; Anthony, Katrine; Peter Deal; 8 Dec 1793; Joseph Steel
Traylor, Wells B; Penny, Luceda; Daniel McGee; 19 Sep 1829; V McBee
Treffanstet (Trefenstet), Daniel; Winebarger, Katherine; Peter Trefenstet Sr (Ger Peder Tfnstett); 25 Jul 1827; Zachary Stacy; Uncertain
Treffanstett, Daniel; Benfield, Elizabeth; Daniel Bollinger; 11 Jul 1820; James T Alexander
Trimmer, Obadiah; McAfee, Polley; Abner McAfee; 1 Feb 1823
Triplett, James; Dellinger, J H (or I H); B M Jetton; 22 Sep 1843; H Cansler
Trobaugh, John x; Wise, Mary; Henry x Wise; 29 Sep 1817; V McBee
Tronberry, Jonathan x; Low, Mary; Lewis Tronberry (Ger Ludwig Tronberg); 26 Jun 1819; James T Alexander
Trout, Michael x; Lorance, Rachael; (Ger) Nicolaus Huns (?); 11 Mar 1797
Trout, William; Haun (?), Sally; Jacob Reinhardt; 29 Oct 1807; Max Chambers
Troutman, David x; Burk, Anne; Aron x Bumgarner; 1 Dec 1815; V McBee
Troutman, Henry x; Canceller, Barbara; Martin x Keener; 15 Feb 1802; John Dickson
Troutman, Jacob; West, Barbara __; Joseph Johnson; 18 Dec (or Nov) 1832; And Hoyl
Troutman, Joseph; Abernathy, Ursula; Jesse Sanders; 21 Jan 1839
Tucker, Butler x; Williams, Elizabeth; Martin x Cline; 5 Dec 1815; V McBee
Tucker, Clinton; Munday, Rebeckah; George Tucker; 5 Jan 1819; V McBee
Tucker, George; Cline, Peggy; Elias Blott (Plott); 25 Apl 1810; Danl M Forney
Tucker, John x; Prithardt (or Prichardt), Catherine; Wiley H x Hartman; 16 Apl 1829; V McBee
Tucker, John x; McCarter, Metilda; James W (or M) Clark; 22 Dec 1834; Jno Blackwood
Tucker, John C; Little, Nancy; Thomas Barnett (Bernett); 23 Feb 1860 (endorsed 1859); J D King; M 23 Feb 1860 by John D King JP
Tucker, Joseph x; Knipe, Polly; John x Knipe (Tucker); 15 Aug 1817; V McBee
Tucker, Levi x; Hallman, Amey; James H Haynes; 30 Mar 1855; J A Huss; M 1 Apl 1855 by D Crooks
Tucker, Nicholas J; Dickson, Rosannah; Teter Beam; 23 Oct 1821; James T Alexander
Tucker, Robert A; Little, Nancy E; George Nixon; 29 Sep 1858; R Nixon JP; M same date by R Nixon JP
Tucker, Samuel x; Leatherman, Elizabeth; John x Rudisill; 21 Sep 1828; M Hull JP
Tucker, Sterling x; Gabriel, Agness; Edward Williams; 8 Jul 1797

Tucker, Wiley S; Clark, Martha A; S W Stubbs; 21 Jan 1856; M same date by F J Jetton JP
Tucker (or Fisher), William x; Hincle, Catharine; Hugh Spratt; 8 Jan 1805
Tucker, William; Friddle, Christina Adeline; John Leatherman; 8 Jun 1854; Danl Siegel JP; M same date by Danl Siegel JP
Tugue (or Teigue), Josiah x; Pierce, Tabitha; Wallis Mcdonale (Wallace McDaniel); 9 Aug 1816; V McBee
Tumberson (Tumbleson, Tumbleston), Joseph; Johnson, Elisabeth; Joseph Johnson; 4 Oct 1797; Jo Dickson
Turbyfill (Turbyfield), Anderson; Linebarger, Sophia; Francis Asbury; 10 Oct 1812; V McBee
Turbyfill, Anderson; Sherrill, Polly; James Bivings; 19 Jun 1821; V McBee
Turbyfill, John; Francis, Polley; John Henderson Shook; 16 Nov 1830; J T Alexander
Turbyfill, M; Seagle, Julia A R; J L Kistler; 21 Mar 1863; M 22 Mar 1863 by A J Fox MG
Turbyfill, Sidney H; McHarg, Betsey; John x Petree; 10 Nov 1832; J T Alexander
Turbyfill (Turbyfield), Sidney H; Briden (or Bridenbe), Lavira; John A Parker (Parke); 10 Jun 1842; A J Cansler
Turbyfill, Spencer x; Linbarger, Susanah; Anderson Turbyfill; 4 Jul 1825; V McBee
Turbyfill, William S; Petree, Polly; John H Sook (Shook); 30 Jun 1832; J T Alexander
Turbyfill (Turbifield), Wilson; Cobb, Malissa; Henry x Cobb; 12 Oct 1839; J A Ramsour D C
Turner, Fielden; _____ _____; Lauson Ward; No date (printed form 183__)
Turner, Gabriel H; Huffman, Lucinda; Daniel Miller; 18 Nov 1838; Wm Herman JP
Turner, George; Spencer, Elizabeth; Benjamin x Spencer; 29 Mar 1808; Joseph Fisher JP
Turner, James; Mellon, Jane C; Daniel F Ragan; 1 Oct 1834; J G Hand JP
Turner, John x; Fish, Polley; Silathian x Fish; 21 Sep 1814
Turner, William; Bolick, Lavina; Andrew Bolch (Bolick); M W Abernathy; Ambiguous
Tuthero, George; Plunk, Susana; Jacob Costner; 12 Nov 1811; Lwn Henderson
Tutherow, Jacob x; Crouse, Barbara; Jacob Plonk (Plunk); 30 Mar 1812; Lwn Henderson
Tutherow, John; Keever, Mary Ann; Franklin A Houser; 12 Jan 1850; Robt Williamson
Tutherow (Tetherrow), Solomon; Moore, Faney; Nicholas x Hevner; 15 Aug 1840
Tutherow (Totherow), Solomon; Hauss, Sarah; Christy Carpenter; 4 Jul 1850; Robt Williamson
Tutherro (Tutherow), George x; Bromfield, Mattie; Mike x Summy; 30 Jan 1867; M 31 Jan 1867 by W T McCoy JP
Tuttle, William x; Turbyfield, Sally; Joab Moore; 1 May 1843; H Cansler
Twigs, Henry; Mauney, Mary; Robert Willis; 23 Dec 1815
Twigse (Twiges), David x; Hoiles, Barbery; Williams Self; 2 Oct 1834; Andrew Dickson Esq

Umphrey, William; Shetley, Mary; John H Robison; 3 Mar 1840
Underwood, Henry; Philips, Jane; Jacob Forney; 18 Mar 1824
Underwood, Jacob; Moore, Elizabeth; Blair McGee; 2 Sep 1833
Underwood, Reuben x; Club, Elizabeth; Peter x Club, John x Club, George x Club, Peter Forney; 20 Sep 1796
Underwood, Samuel; Bradshaw, Elizabeth; William Penny; 16 May 1828; Luther M McBee
Underwood, Willis (W); Lufsey, Izabella; Reuben Underwood; 8 Nov 1841; H Cansler

Vanata (Vannutto ?), Peter; Starret, Rebecca; William Newton; 31 Jul 1793; Jo Dickson
Vance, David, of Mecklenburg Co; Penney, Cattey; Wm Hendri____; 18 Apl 1801; Jos Dickson
Vance, James; Barnett, Polly; Arthur Patterson; 21 May 1792
Vance, Samuel; Rocket, Elisabeth; Smith Abernathy; __ Jul 1807; Phil Whitener JP
Vandike (Vendike), James; Clark, Dolley; Jacob Sellors (Sellers); 18 Dec 1815; V McBee
Vandike, Joseph; _____; Samuel Ramsey; 3 Apl 1798
Vandike (Vandyke), Joshua; Moany, Peggie; Mason x Gillem; 21 Jan 1801

Vandike (Vandyke), Joshua; Carpenter, Catharine; Aron Dameron; 28 Jul 1846
Van Dike, William x; Herman, Sally; Henry Kayler (Kayley); 15 Mar 1829; Mic Cline
Vandyke, Joseph L; Bird, Meriah; Alexander S Dickson; 23 Dec 1829; Isaac Holland
Vanhorn, Isaac; Bouland, Christina; Henry Staney; 4 Apl 1797
Varner, Albert x; Dellinger, Martha; Noah x Dellinger; 22 Dec 1863; W R Clark
Varner, Wm A x; Mullen, Ann; Levi Saunders; 12 Feb 1853; Elisha Saunders; M 13 Feb 1853 by Elisha Saunders JP
Vaughan, W B (Vaun, Washington); Stroup, Eve; Henry Underwood; 12 Mar 1833; L McBee
Vaughn, Hempsel; Spencer, Mary; John Spencer; 16 Jan 1821; V McBee
Veitch, Henry F; Costner, Barbara; James H White; 26 Jun 1834; Jno Blackwood Esq
Vickers, John; Deck, Mary M; Jonas Deck; 18 Oct 1827; V McBee

Wacaser, Abraham x; Hull, Elizabeth; Levi N Alexander; 29 Oct 1833; Miles W Abernathy
Wacaser, George W; Schnider, Frances; --------; 17 Aug 1859; W R Clark Clk; M same date by Joshua Pendleton JP; L and C, no B
Wacaster, John (Jr); Hull, Sally; John Wacaster (Sr); 1 Aug 1824; M Hull JP; Ambiguous
Waddel (Waddle), James; Hill, Peggy; Thomas Hill; 16 Mar 1798; Jno Dickson
Waggoner, Andrew; Cashon, Caty; William H Howard; 6 Dec 1826; Wm Little
Waggoner, Conrad x; Baker, Shusanah; Wm x Reather; 28 Apl 1789; Joseph Steel
Waggoner, John x; Froy, Cristeena; John x Berry; 14 Jul 1816; Phil Whitener JP
Wagner (Waggoner), Peter; Eckerd, Susanna; William Herman; 20 Dec 1827; Henry Cline
Wagner, Randolph; Wright, Jane S (or L); Allen Alexander; 8 Oct 1866; W R Clark CC; M same date by R H Abernathy JP
Waldrip, Elihu x; Flanegan, Catharine; Daniel x Cammell; 11 Mar 1826; James T Alexander
Walker, Benjamin; Cathey, Margery; Johnston Clark; No date (Martin Governor 1782-4 and 1789-92)
Walker, Henry x; Sides, Susanna; Simon Sides; 2 Mar 1816
Walker, Osbirn W; Henkle, Christina; Simon Sides (Seitz); 13 Dec 1822; V McBee
Wallace (Walis), David H; Williams, Nancy; Thomas Wallace (Walis); 28 Oct 1839; D Hoffman JP
Wallace, John Allen; Palmer, Leanan; Daniel x Gray; 24 Jul 1783
Wallace, Samuel; Butler, Polley; Isaac Wyckoff (Wycoff); 14 Nov 1812; V McBee
Wallace, William; Rice, Mary; William Rice; 16 Feb 1809; Joseph Neel
Wallis, David x; Hawkins, Sarah; H W Reeves; 20 Nov 1844; Willis Reeves JP
Wallis, Joseph N; Thorman, Mary; Andrew B Cox; 28 Sep 1840; Isaac Holland
Walls, Alexander x; Humphrys, C Susannah; Christopher Beel (Beal); 21 Jan 1847; Robt Williamson
Wamac, Starling x; Tucker, Nancy; Levi A Kayler (Kaylor); 13 Feb 1866; M 15 Feb 1866 by R Nixon JP
Wamac, William; Forney, Margaret L; --------; 1 Oct 1854 (or 185--); M this date by R H Abernathy JP; R only, no B
Ward, Alexander; Wycough, Margaret; Thomas Ward; 10 Sep 1829; V McBee
Ward, And J; Lourance, C L; Jonas Cline; 10 ---- 1842
Ward, Charles x; Ward, Sally; Thomas Ward; 20 Jul 1819; James T Alexander
Ward, Conard; Lee, Luizur; William x Harris; 3 Mar 1825; Henry Grose
Ward, David; Weathers, Minerva; Carlos Leonard; 19 Dec 1836; M W Abernathy
Ward, Fedrick x; Fikes, Rachal; Alexander Ward; 7 Sep 1835; Nath Edwards JP
Ward, Franklin B; Peed, Mary; James Perkins; 19 Jun 1837; M L Hoke
Ward, General; Mingus, Betcy; George Setser (Setzer); 17 Sep 1819; V McBee
Ward, H N; Pegram, M H C; John E Boger; 2 Nov 1843; R Williamson Jr
Ward, Hasten x; Martin, Nancy; Jacob Hollar; 4 Aug 1816; V McBee
Ward, Isaac x; Hope, Susannah; Jonas Bradshaw; 12 Jan 1825; V McBee
Ward, Isaac H; Abernathy, Marranda; Wiley Gibbs; 12 Jan 1828; J T Alexander
Ward, J W; Dellinger, M C; L H Lowrance; 18 Sep 1860; W R Clark; M same date by A J Fox MG
Ward, John; Whitener, Barbara; Paul Setzer; 12 Oct 1829; V McBee
Ward, Josiah; Childress, Michel; Charles x Early; 22 Sep 1825; V McBee
Ward, Lawson; Turner, Betsey; John Fish; 11 Jun 1825; Jas T Alexander
Ward, Levi; M'Kee, Ann; Saml M'Kee; 13 Jun 1822; Polly McKee

Ward, Thomas; Sherrill, Nancy; James Pettillo (Petty), (Ger) Henrich Castner; 22 Jun 1812; Jesse Perkins .
Ward, Thomas (Captain); Wycoff, Polly; Isaac Dugless (Douglass); 26 Apl 1821; James T Alexander
Ward, William; Turner, Sarah; John J Shuford; 20 Jun 1839; Alexander Ward JP
Warlick, Absalom; Lutz, Salley; Eli R Shuford (Eli Shufford); 28 Aug 1824; V McBee
Warlick, Daniel; Ramsour, Marget; John Reinhart; __th Jan 1794; Michl Eaker
Warlick, Daniel; Smith, Catherine; Paul Kistler; 28 Oct 1812; V McBee
Warlick, David; Rudesille, Catherina; David W Schenck; 23 Apl 1836; John B Harry
Warlick, David E; Sides, Rachel; Absalom Warlick; 10 Dec 1827; V McBee
Warlick, Eli A (H); Seagle, Catharine M; Wm S Ramsaur (Ramsour); 8 Jun 1855; J A Huss; M 12 Jun 1855 by A J Fox MG
Warlick, Eli A; Dusenbury, C A; P A Summey; 12 Dec 1866; M same date by R N Davis Minister
Warlick, Franklin D; Carpenter, Catharine; Henry Schenck; 2 Oct 1839; Spencer M Grigg
Warlick, Jack x; Martson, Anna; Nixon x Ramsour; 24 Dec 1866; W R Clark; M 25 Dec 1866 by Wm J Hoke JP
Warlick, James M; Sain, Anna · Elizabeth; James F Siegle (Siegel); 29 Oct 1857; Danl Siegel JP; M same date by Danl Siegel JP
Warlick, John; Davis, Mary; Michael Schenck (Ger same); 22 Nov 1814; James T Alexander
Warlick, John; Baker, Elizabeth; John M Shuford (Martin Shufford); 30 Apl 1819; V McBee
Warlick, John; Reynolds, Lydia; Michael Shenck (Ger Shenck); 14 Feb 1828; V McBee
Warlick, John; Baggs, Jane Colwell; William Baggs (Jr or Sr); 2 Aug 1832; M Hull JP
Warlick, Lawson; Black, Jemima; Micheal Beam; 11 Jan 1847; Robt Williamson Clk
Warlick, Maxwell; Coulter, Catharine M; A L Ramsour; 7 Aug 1837; M W Abernathy
Warlick, Noah; Kistler, Mary; Peregrine Roberts; 7 Jul 1834; Miles W Abernathy
Warlick, Peter; Shufford, Catherine; Daniel Seagle; 6 Jan 1826; V McBee
Warlick, Philip; Baker, Sally; Abel H Shuford; 21 Oct 1823; James T Alexander
Warlick, Philip; Norris, Nancy; Jno D Hoke; 17 Jan 1828; V McBee
Warlick, Solomon; Warlick, Barbara; John Jarrett (Jaret); 15 Aug 1817; V McBee
Warren (Worran), Elijah; Goble, Sally; Corbin x Goble; 6 Jan 1825; Fr Hoke
Warren, Robert x; Carpenter, Sarah; Daniel Carpenter; 7 Aug 1846; R Williamson
Warren, William; Melton (or Mellon), Matilda; William Campbell; 5 Apl 1821; I Holland
Wasson, William; Delp, Salley; James Wilson; 1 Dec 1815; V McBee
Waters, John M x; Self, Sarah; William Lander; 29 Aug 1842; H Cansler Clk
Waterson (Watterson), John; Taylor, Polly; Wm J Wilson; 18 Oct 1808; Danl Forney
Waterson, John x; Waterson, Jenny; Wm J Wilson; 27 Aug 1811; Lwn Henderson
Wats, Enoch x; Web, Peggey; James Holdsclaw, James Martin; 25 Feb 1827; H____ Little
Wats (Watts), Richard; Limming, Elizabeth; Robert x Watts; 31 Mar 1813; V McBee
Watson, John; Martin, Martha; James Finley; 5 Mar 1804; Polly D Greaves
Watts, Robert x; Lemming, Sarah; George Aderhold (Adderhold); 23 Dec 1809; Jacob Reinhardt JP
Weather, Elisha; Gaskins, Sarah; Julius Holland; 9 Feb 1784; Elisabeth Dickson
Weathers, Allen (Elen); Senter, Betsey; Jesse Holland; 19 Feb 1808
Weathers, Elisha (Jr); Costner, Susan; Isaac Weathers; 2 Jan 1834; And Hoyl JP
Weathers, Ephraim S; Berry, Sarah; Felix M Abernathy; 12 Dec 1835; M W Abernathy
Weathers, George x; Smith, Martha; Isaac x Hawkins; 16 Dec 1807; Danl Forney
Weathers, James A; Shrom, Margaret; Ephraim S Weathers; 22 Feb 1834; And Hoyl
Weathers, John; Irwin, Nancy; Elisha Weathers; 29 Sep 1806; Lwn Henderson
Weathers, John A; Hoyle, Lucinda; John Goodson; 25 May 1861; W R Clark; M 26 May 1861 by Elisha Saunders JP
Weathers, Laban; Keener, Adaline; W R Clark; 6 Sep 1850; Robt Williamson
Weathers, Martin R x; Rhyne, Sarah Lavina; Eli H Weathers; 22 Jun 1844; And Hoyl
Weathers, Michael H; Clippard, Betsey Ann (Belza A); J F (Franklin) Bynum; 15 Jan 1853; R Williamson; M 16 Jan 1853 by Jacob Helderman JP
Weathers, Morgan x; Cox, Sarah; Jonathan Rhyne; 8 Feb 1831; Bolen T Kirby
Weathers, Oliver W; Shrum, Sarah; W Williamson; 4 Nov 1850; Robt Williamson
Weathers, Oliver W; Beel, Amy; James Mullen; 14 Apl 1861; Elisha Saunders; M same date by Elisha Saunders JP
Weathers, Samuel; Rhyne, Sally; Elisha Weathers; 23 Jan 1812; Lwn Henderson

Weathers, Simpson F; Weathers, Margaret A; Dixon Dameron; 23 Sep 1844

Weathers, Thomas x; Wells, Peggy; Elisha Weathers; 19 Apl 1808; Danl Forney

Weathers, William x; Smith, Mary; Oliver Smith; 19 Nov 1838 (possibly 1834); And Hoyl JP

Weatherspoon, Elisha; Lourance, Catharine; Thos Watherspoon (Wetherspoon); 4 Jan 1816; Jo Lourance for McBee

Weaver, Conrad x; Weston, Nancy; John N (or U) Vogler; 19 Sep 1837; M W Abernathy

Weaver, Ephraim; Hawn, Polly; David B Whitener; 1 Apl 1836; M W Abernathy; Ambiguous

Weaver, Jacob (Ger Jacob Weber); Yoder, Cristeena; John Whitener; 21 Dec 1823; Phil Whitener JP

Weaver, Jacob (John J); Fisher, Fanny; Ephraim Weaver; 18 Jan 1837; M W Abernathy

Weaver, John; Plunk, Sarah; (Ger) Jacob Heffner; 12 Jul 1811; Danl M Forney

Weaver, Levi; Carpenter, Mary; James Keen; 2 Apl 1827; V McBee

Weaver, Lindsey C; Martin, Ann; John D Hoke; 6 Jul 1825; V McBee

Weaver, Noah x; Ashabranner, Lavina; David x Ashabraner (Ashabranner); 20 Aug 1840

Weaver, Philip; Jenkins, Adaline; John Cornwell (Cornwall); 17 Apl 1849; Robt Williamson

Webb, David; Leeper, Esther; John D Leeper; 10 Nov 1820; V McBee

Webb, Henry Y; Forney, Eliza; Jacob Summey Jr; 29 Dec 1812

Weber (Webber), John; Sanders, Ann; William Slade; 15 Apl 1835

Weer (Wear), Thomas; Dicky, Catherane; John Weer; 8 Jan 1811; Robt Winter

Weer, William; Beaty, Mary; Alexander Berrey (Berry); 20 Jan 1842

Wehunt, Caleb; Lackey, Sarah; B M Massagee; 21 Jul 1859; W R Clark Clk; M 27 Jul 1859 by D Williams JP

Wehunt, John; Hoyle, Polly; Elias Jarrett; 22 Mar 1833; L McBee

Wehunt, John; Shitle, Sarah Ann; Trusvant x Rayfield; 8 Oct 1845; R Williamson

Weir, Alexander; Oates, Martha; John Oats (Oates); 2 Mar 1832; J T Alexander

Weir, John D; Gofourth, Elizabeth; Johnson Goforth (Gofourth); 12 May 1836; John B Harry

Weir, William; Falls, Ruth; Robert Ferguson, William H W Price; 10 Aug 1832; V McBee

Welch, John x; Randels, Christian; Nicolas x Welch; 14 Feb 1792

Welch, John; Bradsha, Nancy; John x Club, Josiah Bradsha; 28 Jan 1808; Henry Conner JP

Welch, William; Cronister, Eve; Robert Wier, John Barber; 10 Mar 1783; John Weer

Welker, George William (Rev); Mason, Abagail; Andrew Ramsaur (Ramsour); 6 Apl 1843; L E Thompson

Wells, Anderson x; Mattox, Nancey; Edward x Robinson; 13 Jan 1795; Jonn Greaves

Wells, David; Mauney, Salley; Joseph Miller; 15 Feb 1814; V McBee

Wells, Henry W; Thompson, Martha Ann; Josiah Asbury; 2 Oct 1857; H Asbury; M same date by H Asbury Mnst

Wells, James; Munday, Polly; Clinton Tucker; 10 Apl 1821; (N)

Wells, John x; Gordon, Torethey; George Sigman (Ger Georg Siegmann), John x Lutz; 29 Dec 1795; John Willfong JP

Wells, Robert; Price, Jemima; Samuel Collins; 1800; (N)

Wells, Thomas; Jinkins, Emeline; Richard x Walker; 1 Jan 1846; R Williamson

Wells, William S; Reinhardt, Susan Adaline; Allen Alexander; 24 Sep 1833; J T Alexander

Welmon (Welman), Wilkins (Wilkey); Wilson, Mary; Jno Wilson; 12 Nov 1811; Saml Wilson Dep C

Welsh, David; Wesson, Rose; E J Alexander; 24 Jan 1853; R Williamson; M same date by Rev H H Durant

West, Abner x; Belck, Levine; John x West; 28 Feb 1794; John Dickson; Ambiguous

West, Allen x; Belk, Polly; Stephen x Belk; 12 Oct 1822; Saml M'Kee

West, Barney (Barnabas); Wallace, Sally; William McEwen; 2 May 1787

West, Barny x; Rumfelt, Barbary; Isaac x West; 2 Sep 1807; D M Forney

West, Ebenezer; Wills, Dinna Adaline; William x Cox; 29 Jan 1830; And Hoyl

West, Ephraim; Kail, Margt; Elisha Kale (Kail); 8 Nov 1802; Jno Dickson

West, Isaac; Armstrong, Betsey; Jonathan West, Hugh Jenkins; 11 May 1822; Saml M'Kee

West, Isaac; Cox, Elizabeth; John H Robeson; 20 Jan 1829; D Linebarger

West, Isaac Jr x; Rumfelt, Catherine; William x West; 26 Jun 1804; Lwn Henderson

West, Isaac W P; Price, Mary D; George Goforth; 2 Jul 1836; M W Abernathy
West, James x; Robeson, Eliz'th; Ebenezer West; 7 Jan 1830; Eli Hoyl
West, Jonathan; Armstrong, Precilla; Edward Boyd; 20 Mar 1816; V McBee
West, Joseph x; Bird, Catharine; David Short; 18 Jul 1838; N M Reinhardt
West, Michael; Sauls, Mary; Ross Nisbitt; 8 Oct 1806; Lwn Henderson
West, Reuben x; Belk, Susanna; Moses Jenkins; No date (Spaight Governor 1792-5)
West, W B; Harding, A A (A N); G R Harding; 28 Dec 1863; W R Clark;
    M same date by O A Darby Minister of Gospel
West, William; Lewis, Elitha; Chas West; 19 Oct 1795; (N)
Wethers (Weathers), Benj E; Pinner, Peggy; Allen Weathers; 15 May 1823; Isaac
    Holland
Wethers (Weathers), Caleb C; Leonard, Margaret; William B Lay; 4 Oct 1841; Eli Hoyl
Wethers, Joel x; Best, Delilah; Jacob Palmer; 13 Mar 1814; V McBee
Wethers, Valentine x; Atkins, Sarah; Jacob x Rodes; 2 Jun 1784 (or 1782); James
    Dickson
Weylie (Wiley), Benjamin; Sherril, Ruana; David Sherrill (Sherril); 26 Jun 1797;
    Jno M Dickson
Wheelar (Wheeler), William; Freeman, Mary; Vincent Cox; 29 Oct 1781
Whetstine, D M; Hull, Mary Ann; Miles Hull; 21 Dec 1865; A S Haynes CCC;
    M 28 Dec 1865 by P Carpenter JP
Whetstine, David; Hull, Rebeckah; John x Massagee; 26 Oct 1826; V McBee
Whetstone, John x; Raymer, Susanna; Christy x Parker; 7 May 1810
Whiseant (Whisenhunt), David; Gladen, Elizabeth; Andrew Gladen; 20 Aug 1832;
    V McBee
Whisenant (Whisnant), John; Copelin, Elizabeth; Nicholas Whisenant (Whisnant);
    25 Aug 1814; Da'd Warlick
Whisenhant (Wisnant), Daniel; Dellinger, Susana; David Abernathy; 6 Feb 1823;
    Phil Whitener JP
Whisenhant (Whistenhunt), Lauson H; Yarberough, Sally; Abner Berry; 4 Mar 1826;
    Jas T Alexander
Whisenhunt, Philip; Abernathy, Polly; Moses Whitner; __ __1835; Abel H Shuford JP
Whisnant (Whisenant), Adam; Fronebarger, Susanah; John Fronaberger (Frone-
    barger); 4 Feb 1820; V McBee
Whisnant, David; Koon, Maryan; John Hause; 14 Feb 1821; V McBee
Whisnant (Whisenhunt), John; Carpenter, Elizabeth; John Hafner (Havener); 10 Jul
    1813; V McBee
White see Wright
White, Hugh; Long, Evaline; George Gilleland; 7 Mar 1823; Jas T Alexander
White, Isaac; Givens, Jain; --------; 8 Jan 1782
White, Isaac; Falls, Polley; Andrew Gardner (Garner); 25 Jul 1820; V McBee
White, James; Brown, Milly; James Litten (Litton); 28 Oct 1824; V McBee
White, James; White, Mary C; David Fronabarger; 10 Nov 1831; L McBee
White, James E (or C); Dixon, Margaret; William Neill; __ __ 1834; Ambiguous
White, James H; Jenkins, Margret; Alexander Shutly (Shutley); 3 Jul 1834; Isaac
    Holland
White, Joabert; Mowser, Sally; Frederick Mowser; 24 Jan 1829; J T Alexander
White, John; Baird, Polly; Wm J Wilson; 3 Jan 1804; Jas McKisick
White, Joseph P G; Spencer, Sally; Philip Whitener; 14 Sep 1824; Jas T Alexander
White, Samuel; Ormand, Cyntha; Benjamin Ormand; 18 Sep 1819; Jas T Alexander
White, Thomas; McCL_____, Rebeca; Isaac White; 9 Jan 1783
White, Thomas; Barber, Mary; Josias Martin; 5 Jul 1787; Jno Wilson
White, Wesley; Stine, Mary; Joshua White; 19 Aug 1830; J T Alexander
White, William; Moore, Margaret; Joseph Collans; 4 Jan 1791
White, Wm; Gates, Nancy; W R Edwards; 13 Jan 1862; M 14 Jan 1862 by F J
    Jetton (JP)
Whitener, Daniel; Robinson, Polley; John Whitener; 28 Dec 1809; John Willfong
Whitener, Daniel; Sigman, Catherine; George x Sigman; 3 Jun 1815; Phil Whitener JP
Whitener, David; Abernathy, Annie; Solomon Warlick; 20 Feb 1812
Whitener, David; Stilwell, Sarah; Daniel Coulter; 24 Dec 1829; Jonas Bost
Whitener, David B; Haun, Cathrina; Daniel Whitener; 11 Apl 1822; Phil Whitener JP
Whitener, Eli; Wisenhunt, Sarah; Abel Hoyle; 18 Feb 1834; M W Abernathy
Whitener, Ephraim; Probst, Delila; Turner Abernathy; 27 Mar 1823; Micll Eaker
Whitener, George; Dellinger, Margarett; Jacob Dellinger; 23 Sep 1824; Mic Cline
Whitener, Henry; Sherrill, Margret; David Robinson (Robertson); 2 Feb 1815; Joseph
    Fisher
Whitener, Henry; Hoyle, Margaret E; G D Wilfong; 10 Sep 1835; Jonas Bost

Whitener (Whitner), Jesse; Link, Elizabeth E; Z B (Babel) Whitener (Whitner); 11 Feb 1843; H Cansler
Whitener, John; Weaver, Sarah; Jacob Wever (Weaver); 6 Feb 1814; Phil Whitener JP
Whitener, Joseph; Cline, Polly; George Wisnand (Wisanand); 27 Apl 1824; Mic Cline
Whitener (Whitner), Moses B; Whitner, Mary M; Abel Seitz (Sides); 3 Mar 1840; H Cansler; Compare Seitz, Abel
Whitener, Philip; Gross, Malinda; Alexander M'Corkle; 17 Oct 1835; M W Abernathy; Ambiguous
Whitener, Philip B; Gutrey, Nancy; Daniel Seagle; 4 Sep 1826; J T Alexander
Whitener, Z B; Arntz, Mary; Jacob Sigmon (Sigman); 14 Aug 1847; Robt Williamson
Whiteside, Edward; Walker, Rachel; Moses Wilson; 2 Oct 1810; Saml Wilson
Whiteside, Joseph; M'Kee, Elisabeth; John M'Kee; 1 Apl 1822; Saml M'Kee
Whitesides, Edward N (Edward M); Gamble, Salley; W F Holland; 11 Jan 1842
Whitesides, James; Wilson, Catherine; William Whitesides; 12 Mar 1844; John Webster JP
Whitesides, Wallaes; Hagar, Peneleth (or Perreleth); Edward Whitesides; 18 Aug 1842; D Hoffman JP; Ambiguous
Whitner, George; Fry, Salley; Mic Cline; 12 Nov 1805
Whitney, Branson x; Finison, Sarah; F J Jetton; 7 Aug 1838; H Cansler CC
Whitney, David; Gant, Elizabeth; Henry Minges; 30 Oct 1825; Mic Cline
Whitney, Zeno; Hawn, Fanny; Jacob Bolch (Bolick); 14 Dec 1835; Abs Miller
Whitnor, Michael x; Fry, Elisabeth; Philip x Fry; 22 May 1787; Joseph Steel
Whitstone, Daniel x; Rudesiele, Sussana; Jacob x Helmes; 28 Dec 1820; D Lutz JP
Whitt (Whit), Wm; Frieshour (or Frushour), Polley; John x Huffstotler; 22 Mar 1819; V McBee
Whitte (White), Thomas P; Mahaffy, Polly; Thomas Sloan; 1 Sep 1807; Maxl Chambers
Whitworth, John; Kendrick, Margaret; Jacob Ramsour; 27 Feb 1823; V McBee
Whitworth, Southerland; Hood, Marey; Wm Temple Coles; 3 Jan 1792
Whitworth, Thomas; Craft, Mary A; John P Craft; 12 Dec 1825; J T Alexander
Wiatt, Abrihan x; Wells, Caty; Barnes Holloway; 9 (?) Dec 180__ (Turner Governor 1802-5); Betsey Henderson
Wiatt, Caleb; Swearingame, Malinda; Samuel W Craig; 10 Oct 1838; Eli Hoyl
Wiatt, James; Swearingham, Jane; James Wells; 22 Jan 1833; Ja Ferguson; Ambiguous
Wiells (or Wells), William x; Barns, Ealsey; Thomas x McKenny; 11 Dec 1787; Joseph Steel
Wier, John Abel; Neel, Mary Ann; John Carroll (Carrol); 12 Feb 1833; L McBee
Wihont (Wihon), William; Lingerfelt, Fanney; Peter Aby (Abey); 4 Apl 1815; Ligt Williams
Wike, David; Deal, Polly; John Deal (Ger Johannes Diel); 9 Jan 1823; Mic Cline
Wike, David; Andrews, Lila (or Lela); Thomas x Bomgarner; 15 Nov 1839; H Cansler
Wike, Jacob x; Cline, Elizabeth; Henry Bollinger (Ballinger); 21 Mar 1813; Mic Cline
Wilbanks, Warren S; Sadler, Lucy; Jacob Brem; 10 Aug 1815; V McBee
Wilfong (Willfong), David; Jaratt, Kissia; George Wisnant (Ger George Weisnd); 13 Apl 1819; Phil Whitener JP
Wilfong (Willfong), David; Hutson, Nancy; William Bandy; 18 Apl 1833; Dd L Tarr
Wilfong, G D (David); Ramsour, Anna; David Ramsour; 27 Nov 1815
Wilfong, G Danl; Ramsour, Ann; Jonas Ramsour; 30 Aug 1824; V McBee
Wilfong, George; Surratt, Susannah; Jno Earwood; 1803; (N)
Wilfong, John Jr; Summey, Lovena; Charles L Torrence; 24 May 1826; V McBee
Wilfong, Martin; Gross, Mary; James Robinson; 17 Aug 1809; Jacob Reinhardt
Wilkerson, Francis; Linebarger, Elizabeth E; F J Jetton; 14 Jun 1836; M W Abernathy
Wilkins, Anderson S; Warlick, Levina; Peter P Wilkins; 17 Apl 1833; J T Alexander
Wilkinson (Wilkeson), Franklin; Wilson, Mariah C; Elisha Cook; 8 Jan 1841; H Cansler
Wilkinson, James; Asbury, Susanah L; James T Asbury; 8 Nov 1817; V McBee
Wilkinson (Wilkason), James; Stiles, Nancy; James x Surrat; 27 Aug 1818; Jno D Graham JP; Note from Jno D Graham to Clerk
Wilkinson, Thomas; Loretz, N_____; Francis Wilkinson; 25 Jun 1835
Wilkinson, William; Duncan, Susanah; James Wilkinson; 10 Sep 1807; Thos Wheeler
Wilkison (or Wilkinson), Marcus L; Shelton, Mary M; Jacob D Shelton; 23 Sep 1850; V A McBee
Williams, Alexander; Hoard, Rebecca A; F M Dellinger; 21 Aug 1861; W R Clark; M 28 (25) Aug 1861 by David Boiles (JP)
Williams, Benjamin; McCollister, Sarah; James McCollister; 15 Sep 1813; V McBee
Williams, Billey; Bradshaw, Judy; Thomas McGee; 10 Sep 1783

Williams, C (Calbind); Puntch, Jaine; H B Witherspoon; 20 Oct 1842; J Yount JP
Williams, C R; Monday, Martha Ann; W T Williams; 13 Mar 1861; R Nixon JP;
    M same date by H Asbury (Minister)
Williams, Charles; Bradsha, Elizabeth; Billey Williams, Jonah Bradsha; 24 Nov 1795
Williams, Charles; Morrison, Peggy; William Williams; 28 Aug 1802; Jos Dickson
Williams, Charles; Williams, Elisabeth; Benjamin x Hulle (Hull); 30 Jul 1817; Saml
    Wilson
Williams, D F; Houser, Cathrine; Jonas x Houser; 26 Feb 1857; Danl Siegel JP;
    M 27 Feb 1857 by Daniel Siegel JP
Williams, Daniel x; Robinson, Susannah; Thos x Moore; 17 Jul 1833; J T Alexander
Williams, David; Cooper, Anna; Joel Williams, Hugh McGee; 22 Apl 1790
Williams, David; Lacky, Susanna; James Lacky; 2 Feb (?) 1832; Andrew Dickson;
    Uncertain
Williams, David; Freeman, Catharine L; ‑‑‑‑‑‑‑‑; 20 Feb 1851; M this date by
    R H Morrison; R only, no B
Williams, Hartwell Spain; Yount, Leah (Sarah); James x Codey; 9 Nov 1852; Robt
    Williamson; M 11 Nov 1852 by Daniel Siegel Sen JP
Williams, Isaiah x; Williams, Polly; Stephen Homesley; 18 Jan 1825; Jas T Alexander
Williams, Jacob; Edwards, Mehala; Alfred L Hobbs; 17 Sep 1843; Carlos Leonard
Williams, Jacob; Wise, Mary L; N T (Thomas) Steward; 12 Nov 1849
Williams, James x; Gladden, Lina; Wm x Powell; 6 Aug 1833
Williams, Joel; McGee, Margaret; ‑‑‑‑‑‑‑‑; 7 Aug 1790; Jo Dickson
Williams, Joel; Horse, Elizabeth; Henry Banick (Beanack); 8 Apl 1824; M Hull JP
Williams, John x; Morland, Amy; Jacob Painter; 17 Feb 1796; Michl Eaker
Williams, John x; Reep, Polly; John x Hauser (Howser); 12 Aug 1834; M Hull JP‑
Williams, Joseph x; Thompson, Polley; Elias Clodfelter; 17 Feb 1820; V McBee
Williams, Laban; Drum, Delila; John Drum; 9 Sep 1830; J T Alexander
Williams, Marcus; Carpenter, Fanny; John A Hoyl (Hoyle); 4 Aug 1857; Joshua
    Pendleton JP
Williams, Miles; Lackey, Mary; James Lackey; 16 Jan 1838; H Cans'er CC
Williams, Millinton; Williams, Sarah; Peter Reepe (Reep); 3 Sep 1852; Robt Wil-
    liamson; M 21 Sep 1852 by Amos Hilderbrand
Williams, Nelson x; Delinger, Rebeckey; Jonathan Eaton; 6 Nov 1826; M Hull JP
Williams, Nelson G x; Delinger, Sally; Charley x Bayles; 10 Jan 1837; M Hull JP
Williams, Ransom (Ramsour); Boiles, Mary; L E Thompson; 2 Dec 1852; M 9 Dec
    1852 by Daniel Siegel Sen JP
Williams, Reuben x; Bell, Nancy; John x Jhonson; 6 Feb 1833; J T Alexander
Williams, Samuel; ‑‑‑‑‑‑ ‑‑‑‑‑‑; William Owens, James McKee (James C McKee Jr);
    9 Apl 1814; Jas McKee
Williams, Silas; Ensley, Deborah; Marcus L Hoke; 11 Jul 1835; G Hoke
Williams, Thomas; Caldwell, Michel; John Colwell (Caldwell); 20 Oct 1834; Miles W
    Abernathy
Williams, Thomas; Hoover, Myra; J C Jenkins (Jinkins); 16 Jun 1847; R Williamson
Williams, W H; Finger, M S; R W Boyd; 3 Oct 1866
Williams, William; Morrison, Polly; Charles Williams; 28 Aug 1802; Jos Dickson
Williams, William; Parker, Peggy; Sterling x Parker; 6 Apl 1820
Williams, William x; Wheton (?), Polley; Aaron Sherrill; 23 Apl 1822; V McBee
Williams, William x; Bomgarner, Tempy; Abraham Gabriel; 25 Jul 1822; Thos Ward
Williams, William x; Hause, Catherine; Thomas Williams; 25 Mar 1823; V McBee
Williams, William T; Williams, Mary; David Williams; 2 Dec 1857; W R Clark;
    M 8 (or 3) Dec 1857 by G W Hull (JP)
Williamson, Robert; Reed, Elizabeth G; Lwn Henderson; 22 Nov 1806
Williamson, Seth; Ewing, Patsy; Featherstun Wells; 25 Oct 1816; V McBee
Williman, Christopher; McMin, Esther; Samuel McMin; 23 Nov 1809; Thos Wheeler
Willims (Williams), Isaac; Smith, Barbara; Henry x Srum; 19 Aug 1815; V McBee
Willis, Daniel; Boyles, Lucy; William Jones; 12 Feb 1831; V McBee
Willis, Henry x; Spangler, Sarah; Solomon Willis; 6 Nov 1836; M Hull JP
Willis, J F; Huggins, Mary; J R Willis; 3 May 1859; W R Clark; M same date
    by J W Naylor
Willis, Joseph x; Boyles, Sarah; Wiley x Hartman; 19 Nov 1831; L McBee
Willis, Joseph; Towery, Mime; Solomon Young; 15 Feb 1833; Andrew Dickson
Willis, R H; Coon, Sarah; W P Bingham; 20 Mar 1866; M 22 Mar 1866 by A J
    Fox MG
Willis, Robert; Young, Elizabeth; James x Back; 27 Jul 1816; V McBee
Willis, Solomon; Glenn, Elizabeth; M L (Luther) Killian; 3 Nov 1851; R William-
    son; M 6 Nov 1851 by M Hull JP

Willis, William; Norman, Prethean (?); Pery G x Reynolds, William Moore; 5 Nov 1811; Saml Wilson Dpt Cl

Willkie, George J (of Rutherford Co); Whitener, Anna; John Whitener; 28 Sep 1826; Mic Cline

Willkie (Wilkie), James L; Hauss, C C; Martin P Miller; 24 May 1859; W R Clark; M same date by L M Berry MG

Wills, John; Best, Ann; Thomas Cloninger; 30 Sep 1809; Jacob Reinhardt

Willson, Andrew; Steel, Rosanah; Joseph Steel; ____ 178__

Wilson, Alexander; Lutz, Amy; Jacob A Ramsour; 2 Jun 1834; M W Abernathy

Wilson, Andrew; Harbison, Sally M; Thomas x Maples; 29 Dec 1818; V McBee

Wilson, Andrew; Taylor, Catherine; Marmaduke Maples; 22 Jan 1822; V McBee

Wilson, Andrew; Maxwel, Sarrah Greg (?); Samuel Simpson; 3 Mar 1823; Saml M'Kee

Wilson, Asaph; Maheffey, Elizabeth; Maxwell Wilson; 6 Oct 1814; Mic Cline

Wilson, C L G; Huss, M S; M A Stroup; 19 Jan 1867; P A Summey DC; M 24 Jan 1867 by Rev J W Naylor

Wilson, David; Setlemier, Polly; Frederick Killian; 27 Aug 1822; Mic Cline

Wilson, Edwin; Ferguson, Elizebeth; Alexander M Hill; 6 Apl 1829; Isaac Holland

Wilson, Ephraim; Huffstettler, Mary Magdelene; Absalom Wilson; 8 Sep 1827; Silas L Mc Bee

Wilson, Ezra B; Hill, Anna; John McArthur (McCarthur); 19 Feb 1828; V McBee

Wilson, Hugh L; McCaul, Delia B; David Chirry (Cherry); 11 Apl 1826; V McBee

Wilson, Isaac; Maclean, R I (or R J); T' B Maclean; 2 Sep 1846; Isaac Holland

Wilson, James; Gevins, Sarrah; Samuel Givens (Givings); 18 Apl 1791; Jno Moore

Wilson, James; Maclure, Mary; John McClure; 1 Mar 1803

Wilson, James; Campbell, Mary; John Campbell; 12 Jul 1813; V McBee

Wilson, James; Falls, Elizabeth; John Wilson; 13 Feb 1829; B J Thompson

Wilson, James; Bird, Starey; George F Johnson; 27 Dec 1836; John B Harry

Wilson, James A; Norman, Sarah; James Norman; 23 Feb 1850; Robt Williamson

Wilson, John; Murphey, Joannah; Thomas Graham; 30 Nov 1804; Js McEwin

Wilson, John; Miller, Polley; Martin Keller; 8 Jul 1809; Danl M Forney

Wilson, John; Walker, Janet; Thos Wilson; 5 Mar 1811; Saml Wilson

Wilson, John; Stacy, Nelly; Matthew Wilson; 4 May 1819; V McBee

Wilson, John Jr; Drew, Jane; Thomas Whitesides; 28 Jan 1796; J Wilson

Wilson, John M; Gasten, Miram; William P Hand; 15 Dec 1828; Isaac Holland

Wilson, Joseph; Debter (Deter), Catharine; David Robinson; __ Dec 1816; Michael Cline

Wilson, Joseph; Robison, Catherine; John H Robinson (Robison); 5 May 1819; V McBee

Wilson, Joseph C; Thronburg, Cloah M; Fields x Thronburg; 17 Mar 1842; Eli Hoyl

Wilson, Joshua; Wilson, Rebeca; William Willson (Wilson); 22 Nov 1791; Joseph Steel

Wilson, Joshua; Wilson, Priscilla; Nathaniel Wilson; 11 Jun 1829; J T Alexander

Wilson, Lafayette; Baley, Susan E; _____; 18 Mar 1856; M this date by Logan H Lowrance JP; C only, no B

Wilson, M M; Setzer, Mary Ann; Lawson Fry; 7 Sep 1842; H Cansler

Wilson, Matthew; Arney, Juliana; Jacob Arney; 21 Jan 1813; V McBee

Wilson, Maxwell; Coulter, Catharine; James T Alexander; 28 Feb 1826

Wilson, Maxwell; Connor, Jane; Enoch Welmon (Wellmon); 7 Nov 1840; H Cansler

Wilson, Moses; Costner, Barbara; James Graham; No date (watermark J Honig & Zoonen appears on two other bonds dated Dec 1788 and Feb 1789); Doubtful

Wilson, Moses; Mastello, Margaret; Jonas Deck (Dick); 3 Mar 1827; Charles __ Torrence

Wilson, Munford (Muntfort, Mumford); Battle, Angelico; Scroop Egerton; 26 May (Sep?) 1778; Jonathan Hampton

Wilson, Philip x; Reinhardt, Violet; Nicholas x Ranson; 1 Sep 1866; W R Clark Cl; M same date by R H Abernethy (?) JP

Wilson, Robert (McN); Murphy, Anney; John Wilson, John Norman; 12 Oct 1809; Saml Wilson

Wilson, Robert; Falls, Rachel; John Wilson; 17 Jul 1823; Wm J Wilson

Wilson, Samuel; Glenn, Jane; James Glenn (Glen); 11 Feb 1808; Max Chambers

Wilson, Samuel; Wilson, Lettitia; John Michal (Michael); 10 Oct 1837; H Cansler

Wilson, Samuel P; Holmesly (?), Sarah; John Huffstetler; __ Oct 1833

Wilson, Solomon x; Martin, Delpha; William A Norwood; 15 Oct 1832; V McBee

Wilson, Thomas; Whiteside, Jean; Thomas Servies; 2 Oct 1810; Saml Wilson

Wilson, Thomas; Williams, Rebecca; Thomas Williams; 22 Mar 1828; J T Alexander

Wilson, William; Graham, Isabella; John Oats, Samuel Lindsey; 20 Sep 1792; __ Wilson, Ephrm McLean

Wilson, William J; Beard, Sarah; Wallace Alexander; 16 Oct 1799
Wilsone (Wilson), John A; Davis, Violet P; John Dickson; 21 Dec 1803; Jas McKisick
Winebargar, Jacob x; Null, Christine; Cunrad x Winebargar; 16 Dec 1827; Daniel Moser
Winebargar, William x; Null, Marry; Cunrod x Winebargar; 28 Nov 1822; Fr Hoke JP
Winebarier, Conrad (Ger Wejnberger); Wiells (?), Katrine; George Winebarier (Ger Georg Wejnberger); No date; Joseph Steel
Wineberger, Conrad; Hedrick, Susannah; George x Wineberger; 13 Dec 1832; Daniel Herman
Wingate, Jesse; Low, Elizabeth; _____; 3 Jan 1820; James T Alexander
Wingate, Norris A; Summerow, Salome A; J D Lowe; 27 Dec 1851; Robt Williamson; M 1 Jan 1852 by Henry Asbury
Wingate, Peter; Hansel, Elizabeth; R x Kincaid; 1 Mar 1837
Wingate, Peter x (F M C); Brown, Lucinda; Daniel Goodson; 4 Aug 1866; M same date by R H Abernethy JP
Wingate, Risdon; Wingate, Mary; David Kincaid, Jesse ·Wingate; 8 Apl 1821; Wm Little JP
Winget (Wingate), Thomas; Nance, Hanner S; William Robinson (Roberson), Thos J Pryor; 17 Apl 1831; John D King
Winkler, Abraham; Pitts, Susannah; Joseph Winkler; 22 Dec 1831; Henry Cline
Winkler, Joseph; Ash, Emaline; Simeon Barger Jr; 7 Jan 1830; Henry Cline
Winters, John; Harwell, Cynthia; A B Honesley (Homesley); 5 Dec 1845; R Williamson
Wion, Peter; Jarvett, Hannah; David Boils (Boyles); 12 Sep 1839; M Hull JP
Wise, Absalom; Rhyne, Polly A; J P Armstrong; 28 Sep 1866; W R Clark; M 30 Sep 1866 by A J Fox MG
Wise, Andrew N; Hoover, Catharine E; Andrew Hauss; 21 Dec 1858; W R Clark; M 23 Dec 1858 by A J Fox MG
Wise, David; Gilbert, Sarah; Daniel Shireman; 1 Jun 1835; M W Abernathy
Wise, Frederick x; Farmer, Peggy; Jacob Leonard; 21 Nov 1828; B J Thompson
Wise, George; Wood, Maryann; J A (Jacob) Ramsour; 15 Feb 1834; M W Abernathy
Wise, George W x; Williams, Mary Ann; Luther Yount; 24 Aug 1861; Danl Siegel JP; M 25 Aug 1861 by David Boiles (JP)
Wise, Henry; Havner, Anna; Joseph x Wise; 25 Feb 1824; Jas T Alexander
Wise, Henry (Ger Heinrich Weiss); Lingerfeldt, Mary; Jacob Lingerfeldt (Ger Lingerfeld); 11 Mar 1824; Jas T Alexander
Wise, Jacob; Houser, Ann C; John Houser; 19 Oct 1834; M W Abernathy
Wise, John x; Brindle, Margaret; Henry Rhodes; 10 Dec 1835; M W Abernathy
Wise, Joseph x; Reep, Susanah; John Havner; 26 Sep 1826; V McBee
Wise, Levi x; Cadell, Elisebeth; Henry Rhodes; 6 Sep 1857; M same date by D A Haines JP
Wise, William F; Thompson, Elizabeth E; John M Richardson; 9 Jun 1857; W R Clark; M same date by A J Fox MG
Wisenhunt, Philip (Ger Philip Viesnand); Helms, Ann; George Wisenhunt (Ger Georg Viesnand), Robert Wear (Wier); 10 Apl 1788
Wisom (Wysom), John; Simmons, Elisabeth; William Featherston; 11 Oct 1796
Withers (Weathers), Logan; Spencer, Nanny; Isaac E Withers (Weathers); 14 Nov 1828; Isaac Holland
Witherspoon, Calvin A (Calvin E); Mahaffy, Adaline; Cany M Lowrance; 19 Feb 1842
Witherspoon, George; McClure, Patsey; William McClure; 24 Sep 1806; Betsey Henderson
Witherspoon, H B; Costner, Mary; Joshua B Little; __ ____ 1842; J Yount JP
Witherspoon, John R; Graham, Sophia; John D Graham; 1 May 1815; V McBee
Witherspoon, Miles R; Aderholdt, Sarah; Emanuel Aderholdt; 11 Nov 1844
Witherspoon (Weatherspoon), Nelson; Clotfelter, Malinda; Noah Cloninger; 26 Oct 1840; Henry Cline
Witherspoon, Thos; Rankin, Peggy; Joseph Stevenson (Stephenson); 6 Jul 1801; Lwn Henderson
Withespoon (Whetherspoon), James; Setser, Elizabeth; Jacob Setzor (Setser); 26 Apl 1829; Mic Cline
Withrow, James; McGee, Elisabeth; Richard x McGee; 8 Aug 1786; Danl McKisick, Jas Wilson
Witt (Whitt), Charles; Blufort, Elizabeth; John Rumfelt; 20 Jul 1819; V McBee
Witt, John; Acock, Mary A; George J Thorneburgh (Throneburgh); 4 Oct 1841

Wittenberg, Henry x; Shell, Barbary; John Wittenberg (Ger Johannes Wittenberg); 5 Nov 1808; Ambiguous

Wittenberg (Whittenburg), Peter; Settlemire, Agness; Joseph C Newland; 7 Apl 1841; Jacob Moore

Wolwer, John x; Robeson, Betcy; John Loften; 30 Apl 1825; V McBee

Womack (Wammuck), Abner; Reid, Agness; John Reed; 24 Sep 1787; Jo Dickson

Womack, Starling; Lawing, Mary A E; S S Hager; 6 Feb 1855

Wood, Absalom; Shoup, Catharine; _____; 30 Dec 1836; M W Abernathy

Wood, John H; Best, Catharine; Felix M Abernathy; 2 Nov 1835; M W Abernathy

Wood, Vincent; Sheets, Barbara; John x Horse; 30 Oct 1805; Wm Scott

Wood, William; Spencer, Ann; Zacariah x Spencer; 5 Feb 1782

Wood, William x; Goodson, Polly; George Cristle; 21 Dec 1809; H Y Webb

Woodford, Lyman; Boyd, Jane; Alson Hugley (Higley); 20 Feb 1821; V McBee

Woodford, Lyman; Wycough, Sarah; A A (Andrew A) Loretz, Taylor Alexander; 17 May 1833; L McBee

Woodring, Daniel; Rector, Carline; Jacob x Hefner; 30 Jun 1838; Wm Herman JP

Workman, Henry x; Goins, Sarah; Daniel x Workman; 28 Aug 1847; Robt Williamson

Workman, Marten x; Kiser, Catherina; Michael Shrum (Srum); 14 Aug 1838; Jacob Plonk; Ambiguous

Workmon (Workman), Jacob L K; Helms, Nancy A F; Andrew Hauss; 1 Oct 1859; M 6 Oct 1859 by D Williams JP

Wray (Ray), William; Warlick, Sally; Andrew Dickson; 3 May 1825

Wray, William; Ramsour, Amelia C; O A Ramsaur (Ramsour); 31 Jul 1866; M same date by J Ingold Minister

Wright, Benjamin x; Self, Elizabeth; James Wright; 4 Feb 1820; V McBee

Wright, J M (James M); Cox, Catherine; R A (Robert A) Ewing; 22 Dec 1819; V McBee

Wright, Joseph; Cox, Sally; William Cox; 9 Oct 1797; Jo Dickson

Wright, Richard; Alexander, Nancy; Newan (Newman) Alexander; 3 Mar 1845; R Williamson Jr

Wright (White), Robert; Self, Patsey; John Self; 20 Jan 1825; M Hull JP

Wright, Samuel; Shitle, Mary; _____; 28 Oct 1852; M this date by Esli Rhyne JP; R only, no B

Wright, Solomon; Wishon, Mary; Henry Whitener, Joseph x Dellinger; 8 Dec 1818; Mic Cline

Wright, Thomas; McGill, Elisabeth; John Oats, Robert Ferguson; 11 Mar 1794; William McGill, J Wilson

Wright, W H; Lackey, Effie J; E Hamrick (Hambric); 21 Nov 1865; A S Haynes CCC; M 23 Nov 1865 by O B Jenks JP

Wyant, Peter; Rudesale, Susana; George x Rudesale; 11 Aug 1842; P Stamey JP

Wyant, S Washington x; Gross, Nancy; Benjamin Friddle; 26 Feb 1859; Danl Siegel JP; M 27 Feb 1859 by Danl Siegel JP

Wyant, Samuel W x; Sain, Rosanna; Samuel x Sain; 12 Apl 1855; Danl Siegel JP

Wyatt, James x; Wyrim, Mary; James Senter; 19 Mar 1787; Ambiguous

Wyatt, William x; Holleway, Jean; Barnes Hollway (Holleway); 13 Jan 1804; Jonn Greaves

Wycough, S B; _____ _____; H R Spainhower; No date (printed form 182__)

Wyette, Thomas x; Horton, Agy; Peter x Gosnel (Gausnel); 6 Mar 1793; John Dickson; Ambiguous

Wyont (Whyon), Daniel; Hover, Sarah Ann; Peter C Hoyl; 1 Sep 1842; H Cansler Clk

Wyont, Noah __; Slagle, Elizabeth; Joseph Stamey; 22 Nov 1838

Yearwood, William; Cetser (or Celser), Polley; Michel Cloer; 22 May 1806; Thos Wheeler

Yelton, Charles; Brooks, Margaret; _____; 15 Jul 1856; J A Huss Clerk; M same date by P S Kistler JP; L and C, no B

Yelton, James; Havner, Eliza; George F (Franklin) Havner; 17 Aug 1857; W R Clark; M same date by Wm J Hoke JP

Yoakley, John; Wilson, Eliza; Jesse Bost; 30 Jun 1835; M W Abernathy

Yoder, Andrew; Kistler, Ann; Henry Reinhardt; 1 Aug 1837; M W Abernathy

Yoder, David; Wilson, Ruth; Solomon Yoder; 16 Jan 1827; Luther McBee

Yoder, Eli; Detter, Elizabeth; David Isenbhoure (Isenhour); 15 Jul 1834; M W Abernathy

Yoder, Jacob; Haun, Cathrina; Jacob Weaver (Ger Jacob Weber); 6 Jun 1824; Phil Whitener JP

Yoder, John Jr; Whitener, Sarah; Daniel Whitener; 15 May 1819; Phil Whitener JP
Yoder, John A; Jarrett, Elizabeth; Robert L Abernathy; 22 Mar 1841
Yoder, Micheal; Dietz, Polly; Jacob Weaver (Ger Weber); 10 Nov 1825; Phil Whitener JP
Yoder, Peter x; Hawn, Rachael; David B Whitener; 8 May 1832; L McBee
Yoder, Solomon; Seagle, Sarah; Joseph Clay; 25 Sep 1832; V McBee
Yonce, Wm x; Bently (?), Margat; Christian Eaker; 25 Sep 1794; Michl Eaker
Yother, Daniel x; Davis, Elender; Richard Johnson (Johnston); 24 Feb 1807; Ligt Williams JP
Yound (Yount), Samuel; Lutz, Catherine; Daniel Lutz; 5 May 1814; (Ger) Johannes Jund
Young, Danl x; Layman, Meryber; Martin Friday; 11 May 1808; Danl Forney
Young, John; Boggs, Sarah; Martin C Phifer; 2 Oct 1834; M W Abernathy
Young, John A; Graham, Malvina S; Joel A Huggins; 20 May 1840; J F Alexander
Young, Peter; Carpenter, Mary; Jno D Hoke; 3 Jan 1834; Carlos Leonard
Young, Phillip x; Abernathy, Charity; Moses Abernathy; 12 Oct 1802; Jos Dickson
Young, Solomon; Rithey (Ritchey), Poley An; Sidney Shuford; 13 Oct 1859; M same date by D A Haines JP
Young, Solomon; Robinson, Nancy M; David Boiles; 19 Sep 1866; W R Clark; M 22 Sep 1866 by D Boiles JP
Yount, Abraham x; Kuffman, Fanny; John Cloninger; 22 Mar 1829; Mic Cline
Yount, Andrew; Hamilton, Elizabeth; James Perkins; 29 Sep 1837; H Cansler
Yount (Yond), Daniel; Odam, Nancy; George x Yond; 19 Nov 1820; Fr Hoke
Yount, Ephraim; Miller, Catharine; John Miller (Ger Hannes Miller); 15 Jan 1821; James T Alexander
Yount, Franklin; Cline, Jamima; James Cline; 13 Feb 1840; J Yount JP
Yount, G D L (Lafayett); Crouse, Catharine; Joshua P Carpenter; 8 Oct 1857; W R Clark; M 13 Oct 1857 by A J Fox MG
Yount, George (George Yond, Yount, Jr); Fulbright, Polly; George Yond Sr (Ger Georg Jund); 2 Oct 1819; Fr Hoke
Yount, Henry; Miller, Salley; _____; 27 Feb 1819; V McBee
Yount (Yont), Henry; Miller, Sarah; David Miller (Ger same); 6 Sep 1819; V McBee
Yount, Jacob; Dellinger, Polly; Jacob Miller; 5 Mar 1823; Jas T Alexander
Yount, John; Whitener, Elisabeth; David Hohn (Ger David Hahn); 30 Mar 1818; Daniel Moser
Yount (Yont), John; Little, Elizabeth; John Hoke; 14 Sep 1822; V McBee
Yount, Jonathan; Goble, Susana; George Thronburgh, Andrew Yount (Ger Jund); 26 Jan 1826; Zachary Stacy
Yount, Joseph (Jr) x; Little, Polly; John Yount; 3 Mar 1824; Jno Coulter
Yount, Noah; Jarret, Mary Mariah; Ephraim H Lutz; 3 Nov 1838
Yount, Samuel (Jr); Young, Elizabeth E; Wm J Hoke; 19 Jan 1861; M 31 Jan 1861 by D Williams JP
Yount, William A; Dellinger, Lovina; M M (Marcus) Smith; 8 Oct 1842; Wm Herman JP

Zimmerman, Samuel; Butts, Elisabeth; David Zimmerman; 3 Oct 1796

Cross-Index

Abernathey, Eliza—Leathermon, John
Abernathey, Mary—Shuford, John S
Abernathy, Agnas B—Oglesby, Albert A
Abernathy, Amey—Oliver, John
Abernathy, Amy—Spencer, Absalom
Abernathy, Ann Catharine A—Rendleman, Lawrence O
Abernathy, Anna—Shuford, Philip
Abernathy, Anney—Gabrel, Abraham
Abernathy, Annie—Whitener, David
Abernathy, Betcy—McCorkle, Frans
Abernathy, Betcy—Summey, William
Abernathy, Betsey—Farrar, John
Abernathy, Betsy—Henderson, William
Abernathy, Betsy—Cline, Philip
Abernathy, C—Mooney, Philip M
Abernathy, Caroline—Ingle, David
Abernathy, Caroline W—Hedick, George
Abernathy, Charity—Young, Phillip
Abernathy, Charity—Keener, Andrew
Abernathy, Delilah—Devenport, John
Abernathy, Dicey—Johnston, Robert
Abernathy, Disey—Abernathy, Turner
Abernathy, Eleanor—Rocket, Richard
Abernathy, Elisabeth—Perkins, Ephraim
Abernathy, Eliza—Robinson, Orsbern
Abernathy, Eliza—Goodson, John F
Abernathy, Eliza T—Kinder, John
Abernathy, Elizabeth—Campbell, James
Abernathy, Elizabeth—Johnson, A L
Abernathy, Fanny—Little, Alexander
Abernathy, Frances—Abernathy, Miles
Abernathy, Francis E—Crow, Richard
Abernathy, Franky—Bird, Francis
Abernathy, Franky—Abernathy, Daniel A
Abernathy, Glaffira—Abernathy, Joseph
Abernathy, Jancy—Gibbs, Aoris
Abernathy, Jane—Gibbs, James
Abernathy, Katherine—Clotfelter, John
Abernathy, Lena—Henderson, James A
Abernathy, Letty—Bandy, Rufus
Abernathy, Louisa—McGee, Thomas
Abernathy, Lucy—Gibbs, John
Abernathy, Lucy K—Millen, R C
Abernathy, Margaret W—Stowe, Decatur
Abernathy, Marranda—Ward, Isaac H
Abernathy, Martha—Thompson, James
Abernathy, Martha T—Lowrance, Hiram A
Abernathy, Mary—Rozell, Richard
Abernathy, Mary—Harvill, Nelson
Abernathy, Mary—Bumgarner, John A
Abernathy, Mary—Farrell, Aaron
Abernathy, Mary M—Bynum, Albert A
Abernathy, Milla—Berry, Adam
Abernathy, Nancey—Forney, Peter
Abernathy, Nancy—Miller, John
Abernathy, Nancy—Perkins, John
Abernathy, Nancy—Colwell, Thomas
Abernathy, Nancy—Lee, Jesse
Abernathy, Polly—Moody, John
Abernathy, Polly—Rivers, Thomas
Abernathy, Polly—Dayley, Abraham
Abernathy, Polly—Whisenhunt, Philip

Abernathy, Polly—Harwell, John H
Abernathy, Ritty—Abernathy, James
Abernathy, Sally—Conrad, Peter
Abernathy, Sarah—Rockett, John
Abernathy, Sarah—Grose, Henry (Jr)
Abernathy, Sarah—Kirksy, Matthew
Abernathy, Sarah A—Brown, H H
Abernathy, Sarah Ann—Rutledge, George
Abernathy, Sina—Oats, Franklin
Abernathy, Susan—Hoke, Alfred
Abernathy, Susan A—Sadler, Henry
Abernathy, Susana—Johnston, Richard
Abernathy, Susanah—Lehman, Francis J
Abernathy, Susanah—Fish, John
Abernathy, Susannah—Lee, William
Abernathy, Susannah—Cline, Miles
Abernathy, Susannah—Asbury, Wesley
Abernathy, Susannah—Gibbs, Willy
Abernathy, Ursula—Troutman, Joseph
Abernathy, Willey—Saunders, Lemuel
Acock, Harriot—Berry, Ebizur M
Acock, Mary A—Witt, John
Acre, Catharine—Neal, Hugh
Acre, Polly—Seathers, Henry
Adams, Carrie—Lindsay, Thos W
Adams, Elisabeth—Edleman, David
Adams, Margaret—Loyd, William
Adams, Margaret—Beam, Andrew
Adams, Mary C—Kinters, Saml E
Adams, Nancy—Edgen, James
Adams, Polley—Martin, James
Adams, Susannah—Roberts, Morris
Aderholdt, Sarah—Witherspoon, Miles R
Aderholt, Catherine—Previtt, Andrew R
Aderholt, Elizabeth—Privet, James
Adtleman, Molly—Stroup, Phillip
Airwood, Ann—James, William
Aker, Afee—Duty, Rusell
Aker, Fanny—Green, Jacob
Aker, Hannah—Johnson, Allen
Aker, Mary—Hagar, Frederick
Akerd, Elizabeth—Johnson, Richard
Alexander, Amanda—Rudisill, James C
Alexander, Ann—Sumter, John
Alexander, Elisa—Chittim, Thomas
Alexander, Elisabeth—Con, William
Alexander, Lilly—Martin, James
Alexander, M J—Kistler, Peter S
Alexander, Mary—Jordan, Robert
Alexander, Nancy—Wright, Richard
Alexander, Nancy—Johnson, William
Alexander, Nancy C—Bennett, William T
Alexander, Peggy—Johnson, John
Alexander, Polly—Scott, James
Allen, Elisabth—Pirkins, John
Allen, Margaret—Black, Joseph
Allen, Rachel—James, Thomas
Allen, Stanly—Black, Autison
Allen, Susanna—Black, James
Allison, Mary—McKee, William
Allison, Nancy—M'Cald, Archebil
Allison, Sarah—Morris, Vinson
Allison, Susanah H—McKee, John

Allsan, Lucintha C—Richey, Joseph
Allyn, Harriet H—Schenck, John
Allyn, Maria—Reinhardt, Michael
Amburn, Sally—Cline, Solomon
Amburn, Susanah—Cline, Michael
Anders, Nancy—Deal, Mathias
Anderson, Jean—Belew, James
Anderson, Mary—Fleming, John
Anderson, Salley—Sherill, John
Andrews, Lila—Wike, David
Angel, Susannah—Speagle, Solomon
Anthoney, Peggy—McGinnis, Larkin
Anthony, Barbara—Dilliner, George
Anthony, Catharine—Self, Aron
Anthony, Elizabeth—Sechler, Benjamin
Anthony, Elizabeth—Helms, Alexr
Anthony, Katrine—Travelstreet, William
Anthony, Leah—Conner, William W
Anthony, Mary—Hallman, Isaac
Anthony, Mary K Hartgrove, Benjamin
Antoney, Salley—Brown, James
Antony, Mary Magdelin—Sholl, Charles
Arawood, Caroline—Beel, Richard
Arawood, Sarah—McNair, James
Arents, A S—Helderman, J F
Arley, Hanah—Kiser, Joseph
Armestrong, Sarah—Hager, Sherod H
Armstrong, Agness B—Fewell, Henry
Armstrong, Ann—Alexander, James
Armstrong, Betsey—West, Isaac
Armstrong, Elisabeth—Gant, Giles
Armstrong, Esther—Clouney, Samuel
Armstrong, Esther L—O'Daniel, Joseph
Armstrong, Margaret—Leeper, Andrew
Armstrong, Mary—Blaylock, William
Armstrong, Mary—Gant, Lewis
Armstrong, Mary C—Barnwell, James A
Armstrong, Miriam—McLure, James H
Armstrong, Nancy Lemarius—Hansell, John P
Armstrong, Naomi—Leeper, James
Armstrong, Naomi—Leeper, James
Armstrong, Peggy—Smith, Robert
Armstrong, Polly—Fite, Pleasent
Armstrong, Precilla—West, Jonathan
Armstrong, Sally—Hampton, William
Armstrong, Sally—Selvey, William
Armstrong, Sarah—Benton, Calvin
Armstrong, Sarah—Ewing, Hugh
Armstrong, Sarah—Reeves, John N
Arney, Betsey—Mosteller, John
Arney, Caty—Kyser, John
Arney, Juliana—Wilson, Matthew
Arney, Sally—Short, John
Arnts, Susannah—Sadler, John
Arntz, Elz—Finger, Jonas
Arntz, Mary—Whitener, Z B
Arrawood, Dacey—Arawood, Lawed
Arrowood, Anna—Arowood, Zachariah
Arrowood, Ruth—Slone, Arthur
Asbury, Julian R—Robinson, Joseph B
Asbury, L Melvina—Thompson, Samuel T
Asbury, Letty—Cornelius, William
Asbury, Martha—Edward, Nathaniel
Asbury, Mary E—Thompson, Daniel G
Asbury, Nancy—Sifford, Jonas
Asbury, Rebecca—Bisaner, Wm H

Asbury, Susanah L—Wilkinson, James
Ash, Emaline—Winkler, Joseph
Ash, Nancy—Dietz, Jacob
Ashabranner, Lavina—Weaver, Noah
Ashe, Delilah—Dorsey, Elishe
Ashebrener, Cathrine—Spiegel, Moses
Aspie, Elisabeth—Oates, William
Atkins, Sarah—Wethers, Valentine
Attleman, Elisabeth—Stroupe, George
Avent, S J—Erson, E
Avery, Anna—Ellmore, Lewis
Avery, Mary—Shufford, Lawson A

Baggs, Beackey Clark—Janes, Thomas
Baggs, Jane Colwell—Warlick, John
Baggs, Sally—Bess, Noah
Bailey, Biddy—Linhart, Daniel
Bailey, Elizabeth—Hoyle, Peter
Bailey, Margaret—Mauney, Noah H
Bailey, Mary J—Smith, Walter B
Bailey, Nancy—Huntley, Isaac
Bailey, Polly—Spact, Henry
Bailey, Salley—Rudisill, Daniel
Baily, Ann—Ledford, James
Baily, Elizabeth—Cathcart, John
Baily, Sarah L—Brendel, Joseph H
Bains, Mary—Keener, Michael
Baird, Arixney—Fore, Isom
Baird, Betsy—Adams, James
Baird, Elizabeth—Floyd, Robert
Baird, Mary—Ford, Manuel
Baird, Nancy—Mitchell, John
Baird, Polly—White, John
Baker, Anna—Goodson, William
Baker, Anna E—Shuford, George P
Baker, Ann Catharine—Eaker, John
Baker, Barbara—Hefner, Daniel
Baker, Hetty—Carpenter, John
Baker, Catharine—Shuford, Jacob
Baker, Catharine—Hoke, F E
Baker, Elisabeth—Keene, James
Baker, Elizabeth—Warlick, John
Baker, Elizabeth—Eaker, Jesse
Baker, Elizabeth—Capenter, William
Baker, Lidia—Stroup, Abner
Baker, Louisa—Huffstetler, Ephraim M
Baker, Margaret—Barret, Isaac
Baker, Margaret—Eaker, John
Baker, Margreate—Tayler, Fredrick
Baker, Mary—Hefnar, Jacob
Baker, Mary—Shuford, George P
Baker, Nancy—Smith, Philip
Baker, Olly—Cox, Aaron
Baker, Olly—Carpenter, John
Baker, Osley—Killian, Daniel
Baker, Rebeca—Sorunts, John
Baker, Sally—Warlick, Philip
Baker, Sarah—Cross, John
Baker, Sarah—Smith, Robert
Baker, Sarah—Sellers, Alfred B
Baker, Sarah Ann—Smith, Jackson
Baker, Sary—Mingus, George
Baker, Sary Delany—Carroll, John
Baker, Shusanah—Waggoner, Conrad
Baker, Vicy—Shires, George W
Baldridge, Nancy—Nance, Daniel

Baldrige, Jane—Little, John
Baldwin, Abigal—Self, Joseph
Baldwin, Ann—Kenedy, Robert
Baldwin, Ann—Lay, R
Baldwin, Patsey—Black, Samuel
Baldwin, Sarah—McArver, Alexander
Baldwin, Winney Perry—Johnston, John C
Baley, Sarah—Iceenhour, John
Baley, Susan E—Wilson, Lafayette
Ballard, Charlotte—Howard, Henry
Ballard, Harriet—Hix, Marcus W
Ballard, Lizer—Grise, John
Ballard, Martha L—Harris, John F
Ballard, Mary A—Eberhard, Charles T
Ballard, Mollie—Evans, Edward K
Ballard, Nancy—Thornbargar, James
Ballard, Sarah—Lay, James H
Ballard, Willie—Stone, James
Balley, Batsey—Smith, George
Baly, Molly—Moser, Peter
Bandy, __sannah—Lutz, Eli
Bandy, Catherine—Lutz, David
Bandy, Catherine—Johnson, Eli
Bandy, Eliz—Strain, William
Bandy, Eliza—Kirksey, Franklin
Bandy, Elizabeth—Rockett, James
Bandy, Mehala—Lutz, Eli
Bandy, Mira—Sherrell, Joseph
Bandy, Nancy—Bumgarner, Andrew
Bandy, Sarah—Saunders, Edward
Bangle, Elizabeth—Jonas, Henry
Bangle, Salley—Clay, Jacob
Bangle, Sarah—Anthony, Daniel
Barber, Anna—Price, John
Barber, Isabellah—Patterson, Robert
Barber, Jane—Adams, Robert
Barber, Mary—White, Thomas
Barcley, Rachel—Sherrill, Moses M
Barey, Catey—Cloninger, Daniel
Barger, Jemima—Burns, Jacob
Barier, Barbra—Crowder, Ulrick
Baringer, Mary—Clifton, Warren
Barkley, Sarah—Fleming, Anderson
Barkly, Letty L—Boyd, Moses
Barkly, Nancy C—Bell, Thomas M
Barkly, Polly—Lockman, John
Barkly, Rebeckah C—Dunbar, Joseph A
Barnes, Mary A—Sherrill, Miles
Barnes, Sarah—Keener, Martin
Barnet, Mary—Nance, John
Barnet, Sarah—Ferguson, James
Barnet, Winiford Balsora—Barnet, Daniel
Barnett, Frances E—Senter, Caleb O
Barnett, Martha—Patterson, Richard
Barnett, Nancey—Bradshaw, Jonas
Barnett, Polly—Vance, James
Barnett, Susan A—Abernathy, George W
Barns, Cunney—McKinney, Thomas
Barns, Ealsey—Wiells, William
Barns, Patience—Evens, John
Barr, Margaret—Dorsey, Joseph
Barr, Margaret—Maby, W H
Barringer, Betsy—Carpenter, Jacob
Barringer, Polly—Hunsecker, David
Bartley, Betcy—Laypole, John
Battle, Angelico—Wilson, Munford
Baty, Viney—Loftin, Thomas

Baxter, Luvsa Ann—Lowe, John A
Baxter, Sarah—Baxter, Peter
Baxter, Sarah—Fronebarger, A L
Baxter, Susanah—Kizer, George
Bayley, Margret—Cathcart, Allen
Beach, Sarah—Cobb, James
Beal, Ann—Lawing, William
Beal, Barbara—Guthrey, Carter
Beal, Elizabeth—Kirksey, William
Beal, Elizabeth J—Keener, David
Beal, Frances—Goodson, John
Beal, Mary—Armstrong, William
Beal, Mary—Moore, Andrew F
Beal, Nancey—Belk, Chamberlain
Beal, Nancy L—Saunders, T J
Beal, Polley—Miller, Washington
Beal, Rhoda C—Lawing, John S
Beal, Salley—Parker, Starling
Beal, Salley—Burk, Yancy
Beal, Weaney—Killian, William
Beale, Betsy—Bynum, James
Beale, Mary—Abernathy, Battee
Bealk, Nancy—Beal, Turner
Bealk, Sally—Rutledge, Charles
Beam—see also Titerbeam
Beam, Ann—Lines, Charles L
Beam, Anna—Jinkins, Jinkey
Beam, Anne—Rudisel, Jonas
Beam, Barbara C—Carpenter, Joshua P
Beam, Catherine—Bess, Lawson
Beam, Elizabeth—Anthony, Jacob
Beam, Mrs Elizabeth—Baker, Edward
Beam, Margaret—Rudasall, Jonas
Beam, Margaret C—Fronabarger, Daniel W
Beam, Mary—Rudesill, Jacob
Beam, Mary Ann M—Alexander, John F
Beam, Mary C—Roberts, John A
Beam, Mary Jane—Plonk, Philip
Beam, Sarah—Best, Peter
Beard, Harriet—Humphry, William
Beard, Sarah—Wilson, William J
Beard, Sarah—Armstrong, Andrew
Beason, Amy—Gladen, Joseph
Beatey, Margaret—Reed, James
Beatey, Sarah—Tate, Joseph
Beatie, Margaret A—Little, George
Beatie, Mary—Buckhannon, John N
Beattey, Polly—Smith, James
Beattie, Charlotte R—Blalock, Thomas R
Beattie, Esther H—McLure, John D
Beatty, Betsey—Dillingham, Vachel
Beatty, Dovey B—Blalock, Winslow F
Beatty, Martha—Tate, William
Beatty, Martha Jane—Rutledge, Robert
Beaty, _____a—Cathey, James
Beaty, Ann—Long, John
Beaty, Betcy C—Little, George
Beaty, Esther—Smith, Benjamin
Beaty, Jane—Graham, Archibald
Beaty, Jane—McCafee, Wm
Beaty, Jane—Fite, Joseph
Beaty, Jane H—Oates, James P
Beaty, Mary—Parker, William
Beaty, Mary—Sloan, Robert
Beaty, Mary—Weer, William
Beaty, Nancy—Cathey, William
Beaty, Nancy H—Porter, James L

Beaty, Rosa E—Ramsey, Rhodolphus M
Beaty, Sarah S—Ford, Frederick
Beaty, Susannah—Allen, John
Beckler, Mrs Catharine—Kruse, Herman
Beel, Amy—Weathers, Oliver W
Beel, Elizabeth—Lawing, John M
Beel, Lavinia—Hedgspeth, George
Beel, Salley—Nixson, James
Beele, Elisabeth—Heaker, Christian
Beisaner, Issabella—Crocker, Rufus M
Belck, Levine—West, Abner
Bele, Racheal—Shelby, Winfield
Belew, Judith—Gosnell, Joshua
Belk, Ebby—Fish, Briant
Beik, Margaret—Rumfelt, John
Belk, Polly—West, Allen
Belk, Susanna—West, Reuben
Bell, Dicy—Garrison, William
Bell, Elizabeth—Engle, Michael
Bell, Hannah C—Hannah, William D
Bell, Mrs Jamimah—Grissom, Benjamin
Bell, Jane—Knox, John
Bell, Jemima—McCarty, Cornelius
Bell, Nancy—Williams, Reuben
Bell, Sarah—Hawkins, William Pressley
Benfield, Barbara—Knop, Mathew
Benfield, Elizabeth—Treffanstett, Daniel
Benfiele, Catherine—Collins, William
Benge, Susanna—Roswell, Lewis
Benick, Polley—Michael, Daniel
Bennet, Betsey—Hogan, John
Bennet, Mariah—Huggins, James
Bennett, Esther—Haggin, Randolph
Bennick, Pheby—Graham, Thomas
Bently, Margat—Yonce, Wm
Bently, Phoebe—Keller, Joseph
Benton, Dulsinea—Brawner, Lewis
Benton, Mary M—Hager, Robt N
Berry, Ann—Hoffman, Peter
Berry, Barbara—Huit, Solomon
Berry, Beggy—Summerour, John
Berry, Elizabeth—Goforth, Preston
Berry, Elizebeth—Ford, William
Berry, Emaline—Sarvies, Thomas
Berry, Hannah—Davies, Isaac
Berry, Jean—Robeson, Hugh T
Berry, Lucy—McKeirnan, Owen
Berry, Margaret—Moody, David
Berry, Mary—Cloninger, Henry
Berry, Nancy—Gullick, Jonathan
Berry, Nancy—Aprey, Joseph
Berry, Sarah—Weathers, Ephraim S
Berry, Sarah—Mullenax, Brison
Berry, Sidley—Massey, John
Bery, Ruth—Gross, Christian
Bess, Candies—Davis, J J
Bess, Catharine—Rhyne, Peter
Bess, Mrs Eliza—Elmore, Ephraim
Bess, Euphemia—Baxter, Thos H
Bess, Jane Catharine—Carpenter, J M
Bess, Martha Jane—Lenhardt, Jacob
Bess, Mary—Carpenter, Joseph
Bess, Mary A F—Harris, H A T
Bess, Mary Ann—Baily, Samuel C
Bess, Mary E—Houser, John
Bess, Mary F—Foster, T M
Bess, S J—Lackey, T O

Bess, Susannah—Beam, David F
Best, Ann—Wills, John
Best, Anna—Matheson, Eli
Best, Betsy—Linebarger, John
Best, Catharine—Wood, John H
Best, Delilah—Wethers, Joel
Best, Elizabeth—Spencer, George
Best, Hannah—Smith, Peter
Best, Levica—Holland, William
Best, Lueser—Mitcham, Logan
Best, Margaret—Rhyne, Jacob
Best, Nancy—Eaker, John
Best, Peggy—Rine, Adam
Best, Sally—Boggs, David
Best, Susana—Jenkins, Hugh
Bevens, Susan R—Schenck, David W
Bias, Polley—Logan, Drury
Bickerstaff, Mary—McGaughey, John
Bigam, Naomi—Davis, William
Bigham, Jane—Clark, James
Bigham, Susannah—Pollard, James
Bird, Catharine—West, Joseph
Bird, Charlot—Hix, Queen
Bird, Elizabeth—Meuray, Leonard
Bird, Kitty—Cobb, David
Bird, Malinda G—Penion, George W
Bird, Martha Ann—Stroup, Andrew J
Bird, Mary—Spencer, Zachariah
Bird, Meriah—Vandyke, Joseph L
Bird, Polley—Frushaur, Christian
Bird, Rebeckah—Reinhardt, Isaac
Bird, Starey—Wilson, James
Bird, Susannah—Setzer, Christopher
Bisaner, Rachel—Stroup, Robert B
Bishop, Mary—Parker, William
Bivens, Mary—Brendle, Henry
Bivings, Sally—Knipe, Adam
Black, Ann—Prim, William
Black, Barbara—Stroup, Matthew
Black, Elisabeth—Roberts, John
Black, Elizabeth—Cox, Morris
Black, Elizabeth—Beaty, John
Black, Elizabeth—Bell. Hugh
Black, Elizabeth—Hager, David B
Black, Elizabeth—Luts, Eli
Black, Esther—Thompson, Nathan
Black, Fanney—McCord, Robert
Black, Isabeller—Lucky, John
Black, Jemima—Mauney, Michal
Black, Jemima—Warlick, Lawson
Black, Malinda—Helton, Andrew M
Black, Martha—Ramsey, John
Black, Mary Ann—Kincad, John
Black, Rachael—Cobb, Ambrose
Black, Rebeckah—Dellinner, Philip
Blackburn, Anna—Darr, Henry R
Blackburn, Betcy—Leonard. Daniel
Blackburn, Elizabeth M—Carpenter, Henry
Blackburn, Frances C—Ramsey,
    Rodolphus M
Blackburn, Hanah—Saunders, Thomas
Blackburn, Mary—McClurg, William
Blackburn, Susannah—Kistler, Jacob
Blackwood, Anna—Fronaberger, John
Blackwood, Elizabeth—Crow. Thomas
Blackwood, Jane—Davis, Ephraim
Blackwood, Margaret—Gunn, Alexander C

Blackwood, Mary—Oats, John
Blackwood, Polly—Clark, James W
Blakely, Delphia R—Hamilton,
 Thomas Jefferson
Blakely, Mary—Dellinger, Adam
Blakely, Sarah Ann—Dellinger, Philip
Blalock, Anne—Howard, William
Blalock, Harriet M—Helderman, Valentine
Blalock, Maria S—Stowe, Joel A
Blalock, Mary Jane—Haynes, R M
Blanton, Bazilla—Berrey, John
Blaylock, Ann—Heaker, William
Blevins, Lowery—Kenipe, Jacob
Bluford, _____cy—Rumfelt, Isaac
Blufort, Elizabeth—Witt, Charles
Boggs, Elizabeth—Lackey, Samuel
Boggs, Jien—Caldwell, James
Boggs, Mary—Baldridge, Dornton
Boggs, Mary—Lackey, David
Boggs, Rebecca—Hoyl, L W
Boggs, Rebecca J—Janes, John P
Boggs, Sarah—Young, John
Bohannon, Elizabeth—Devenport, Abraham
Bohannon, Peggy—Rutledge, William
Boiles, Abygail—Brindle, David
Boiles, Mary—Williams, Ransom
Bolch, ____nna—Lanier, Edmun
Bolch, Catherine—Bolch, Sebastian
Bolch, Elizabeth—Barger, Isaac
Bolch, Mehala—Miller, Henry
Bolch, Polly—Huffman, Henry
Bolch, Suannah—Cloninger, Henry
Boldredge, Nancy—Henderson, William
Boldrige, Rebekah—Poston, John
Bolick, Catherine—Moretz, Daniel
Bolick, Caty—Longcryer, Jacob
Bolick, Caty—Simon, Samuel
Bolick, Elisabeth—Hefner, Philip
Bolick, Elissabeth—Bauman, Henry
Bolick, Elizabeth—Bolch, Solomon
Bolick, Elizabeth—Heffenner, Noah
Bolick, Fanny—Benfield, Henry
Bolick, Lavina—Turner, William
Bolick, Liney—Cline, Amen
Bolick, Margarate—Benfield, John
Bolick, Mary—Harberson, Rufus
Bolick, Mary—Bovey, Joseph
Bolick, Rachel—Barger, John
Bolick, Regina—Killian, Joseph
Bolick, Regina—Bumgarner, Thomas
Bolick, Sally—Sigman, John
Bolick, Sally—Austin, Samuel
Bolick, Sarah—Bolch, Jonas
Bolin, Rody—Hamton, William
Bolinger, Catharine—Cloninger, Moses
Bolinger, Martha—Rozzell, Jake
Bolinger, Susannah—Hallman, Anthony
Bollinger, _____—Bolch, Andrew
Bollinger, Ann—Bowman, John
Bollinger, Polly—Bolch, Joseph
Bollinger, Roseannah—Deal, David
Bollinger, Sophiah—Smyer, Jacob
Boman, Clary—Self, John
Bomgarner, Betcy—Keener, David
Bomgarner, Michel—Boyd, John
Bomgarner, Nancy—Murrell, Edmond
Bomgarner, Nancy—Abernathy, Miles

Bomgarner, Sarah—Cobb, John
Bomgarner, Tempy—Williams, William
Bond, Dinah—Luckey, Hugh
Bond, Mary—Armstrong, John
Bonham, Rebecca—Spenser, John
Bonim, Eliza—Auter, Fulcard
Bonn, Sarah—Nixson, John
Bookout, Jane—McFarlin, Wylie
Bookout, Rachel—Ross, Moses
Bookout, Sarah—Powel, Charles
Boovey, Druzy—Moose, George
Boovey, Sally—Cline, Henry
Border, Rebecca—Marks, Richard
Borland, Mary—Sulavan, Samuel
Bost, Catharina—Dietz, Frederic
Bost, Catharine E—Brown, Martin L
Bost, Eliza—Seapaugh, Jacob
Bost, Elizabeth—Killian, William
Bost, Elizabeth E—Burns, Philip
Bost, Jemima M—Mehaffey, William L
Bost, Leah ᴸ—Fry, Moses
Bost, Mary—Rouch, George
Bost, Nency—Fry, Conrad
Bost, Ottell—Smires, John
Bost, Polly—Bost, Joseph
Bost, Rody—Sigman, Eli
Bost, Sally—Starr, John
Bost, Selina—Cline, Paul
Bost, Susannah C—Lutz, Daniel
Bostian, Catharina—Little, Davolt
Bouland, Christina—Vanhorn, Isaac
Bovey, Elizabeth—Smyer, David
Bovey, Mandy—Miller, Ambrose
Bovey, Mary Ann—Shell, Ephraim
Bowers, Polly—Miller, George
Bowman, Maria—Fry, Peter
Bowman, Polly—Probst, Henry
Boyd, _____—Beaty, James U
Boyd, Jane—Woodford, Lyman
Boyd, Nancey—Linn, William
Boyd, Rhoda—Todd, George A
Boyed, Peggy—Selevan, Daniel
Boyles, Lucy—Willis, Daniel
Boyles, Sarah—Willis, Joseph
Boyls, Hannah—Johnson, Joseph
Bracher, Usley—Abernathy, Miles
Bradley, Abagail—Thomas, John
Bradley, Elisabeth—Dilling, Henry A
Bradley, Jane—McCarver, Ephraim
Bradsha, Elizabeth—Williams, Charles
Bradsha, Mecky—Lee, Alexander
Bradsha, Nancy—Welch, John
Bradshaw, Anne—Surrat, James
Bradshaw, Beckey—Ratcliff, Benjamin
Bradshaw, Catharine—Bynum, Wm L
Bradshaw, Elizabeth—Underwood, Samuel
Bradshaw, Elizabeth—Abernathy, Seth
Bradshaw, Emelia—Dellinger, Daniel
Bradshaw, Emily—Asbury, Henry
Bradshaw, Frances—Bradshaw, John
Bradshaw, Judy—Williams, Billey
Bradshaw, Judy—Duncan, Carter
Bradshaw, Mary—Lufsey, John
Bradshaw, Mary—Keever, James
Bradshaw, Matilda—Dellinger, Henry J
Bradshaw, Melinda—Keever, Henry
Bradshaw, Milley—Dellinger, Daniel

Bradshaw, Nancy—Linch, John
Bradshaw, Susan—Clifton, Jacob
Bradshaw, Susana—Sides, Henry
Bradshaw, Susannah—Hovis, John P
Bradshaw, Tempe—Tommy, Jacob
Bradshew, Susanna—Hogins, John R
Bragg, Frances A—Reinhardt, Rudolph
Bragg, Mary K—Sutton, William
Brandon, Margaret—Fite, John W
Branton, Mary—Harmon, Haywood
Brem, Caroline—Phifer, Martin C
Brendle, Margret—Beavin, Joseph
Brevard, Harriet—Forney, Daniel M
Brevard, Marey Ann—Rendelmon, Sisarow
Brevard, Mary M—Brumby, Richard T
Brevard, Nancy—Anderson, Matison
Brian, Nancy—Finley, Robert
Briden, Lavira—Turbyfill, Sidney H
Bridges, Anna—Litten, Isaac
Bridges, Dycy—Anderson, Isaac
Bridges, Elisabeth—Dormire, Peter
Bridges, Elizabeth—Hamilton, Drury
Bridges, Emily—Stine, Abraham
Bridges, Lydia—Lollar, Jesse
Bridges, Margaret—Sherrill, Mason
Bridges, Nancy—Robinson, Adam
Bridges, Patsy—Gileland, Joab
Bridges, Sarah—Litten, Joel
Brilhart, Elizabeth—Hulbert, Mathew
Brillhardt, Catharine—Bevins, John
Brimer, Mary—Armstrong, Francis
Brimer, Mary—Dameron, Joseph
Brimer, Ruth—Hand, Jonathan
Brindel, Betsay—Saine, Daniel
Brindle, Margaret—Wise, John
Brindle, Mary—Nearns, Jesse
Brindle, Mary—Sutten, James
Brindle, Rachel—Lingerfelt, John
Brindle, Rosanna—Lingerfelt, Daniel
Brindle, Viney—Boiles, Joseph
Brison, Margaret N—Henry, John
Brock, Elisabeth—Cook, George
Broher, Susana—Like, Joseph
Bromfield, Mattie—Tutherro, George
Brook, Maryan—Mauny, Vallentine
Brooks, Margaret—Yelton, Charles
Brooks, Margaret—Slade, Squire
Brotherton, Eliz—Barkly, Henry
Brotherton, Elizabeth—Goodson, Joel
Brotherton, Martha—Brotherton, Thomas
Brotherton, Nancy—Brotherton, William H
Brotherton, Polly—McCaul, John
Brotherton, Susanah—Howard, Freeman
Browing, Lasina—Lay, Jesse
Brown, Annie—Johnston, Jesse
Brown, Betsey—Dickson, Thos
Brown, Charity—Gillim, Mason
Brown, Elisabeth—Brown, Amos
Brown, Elisabeth—Hufstatler, John
Brown, Elisabeth—Taylor, James
Brown, Elizabeth—Killian, John
Brown. Elizabeth—Black, Stephen
Brown, Fanne—Peterson, John
Brown, Feby—M'Nighten, Alexr
Brown, Harriet—Penny, Frank
Brown, Lucinda—Wingate, Peter
Brown, Margaret—McDougle, Thomas

Brown, Marget—Hullet, Calep
Brown, Martha A—Havner, Jacob
Brown, Marthew—Childers, William
Brown, Maryam—Horl, Rooben
Brown, Mary M—Lutz, George
Brown, Mary M—Hovis, John P
Brown, Milly—White, James
Brown, Polly—Carter, John
Brown, Polly—Carpenter, Samuel
Brown, Rachel—Neal, Adam
Brown, Rebecca E—Aderholdt, Emanuel M
Brown, Sarah—Costner, Joshua
Brown, Mrs Sarah—Sronce, Abel
Brown, Sareth—Johnston, Lewis
Brown, Synthia—Cansler, John
Brumly, A E—Glover, J B
Brunton, Nicey—Conner, David
Bryan, Jane—Morrow, William
Bryan, Sarah—Fitzpatrick, James
Bryant, Abigail—Penny, William
Buckhannon, Patsey—M'Caul, Robert
Buff, Barbary—Goodson, Champion
Buff, Elizabeth—Clay, Andrew
Buff, Mary—Reynolds, Anson
Buff, Sarah—Harrelson, William
Buff, Susanah—Leadford, John
Bulinger, Matilda—Martin, Moses
Bull, Mary—Cross, John
Bull, Susanah—Smith, William
Bullenger, Betsy—Deal, George
Bullinger, Elisabeth—Shufferd, Daniel
Bullinger, Katrine—Perkins, William Jr
Bullinger, Leah—Huffman, Elijah
Bullinger, Mary—Seagle, Daniel
Bullinger, Mary M—Hine, John G
Bullinger, Susanah—Houser, Henry
Bullinger, Susanna—Barringer, Matthias
Bumgar, Elizabeth—Campbell, John
Bumgarner, Catharine—Martin, Alfred
Bumgarner, Elisabeth—Crysel, Andrew
Bumgarner, Nancy—Taylor, Isaac
Bumgarner, Nancy—Harbeson, Hiram
Bumgarner, Rebecca—Clipard, Andrew
Bumgarner, Rutha—Berry, Henry
Burch, Elizabeth R—Pain, John F
Burch, Epps N—Henderson, W M F
Burch, Mary—Moyers, Lyas
Burch, Melvina A (L)—Kayler, Levi A
Burd, Jane—Lethca, Pinkney
Burk, Anne—Troutman, David
Burk, Emeline—Abernathy, Nathan
Burns, Anna—Hause, Simon
Burns, Elisabeth—Hoan, Jacob
Burns, Elisabeth—Cook, Abraham
Burns, Nancy—Hoke, David
Burns, Polly—Berrey, Richard
Burns, Susan—Rinck, Jesse
Burpo, Mary—Edgin, Moses
Burton, Charlotte—Howard, Henry
Burton, Duley—Forney, Temple
Burton, Eliza—Adams, James
Burton, Elizabeth—Hoyl, Eli
Burton, Francis—Hoke, Michael
Burton, Mary L—Conner, Harry W
Butler, Polley—Wallace, Samuel
Butts, Barbara—Pettre, John
Butts, Elisabeth—Zimmerman, Samuel

Butts, Elizabeth—Shuford, Thomas R
Butts, Margaret E—Cobb, Joseph C
Butts, Sally—Dellinger, David
Butts, Susan C—Moore, Alexander
Butz, Mary—Baker, Edward
Buynem, Violet C—Purkins, John F
Byers, Pagy—Houston, Joseph
Byianm, Dice—Abernathy, Robert
Bynam, Patsy—Duncan, Absalom
Bynum, Barbara—Barnet, Randolph
Bynum, Belzora—Keever, Henry
Bynum, Elizabeth—Hinson, Aaron
Bynum, Elizabeth—Moore, Thomas
Bynum, Jane—Parker, Hosea
Bynum, Lotte—Farrar, William
Bynum, Lucy—Heaker, John
Bynum, Melinda—Dellinger, Josiah R
Bynum, Nancy—Guthrie, James
Bynum, Polley—Hoover, Daniel
Bynum, Sarah—Baker, William
Bynum, Sarah Ann—Hovis, Sidney J
Bynum, Sarah J—Hicks, Samuel
Bynum, Sophia—Perkins, Leander
Bynum, Susana—Abernathy, Moses
Bynum, Susannah—Dellinger, Daniel
Byrd, Jane—Reinhardt, Joseph
Bysinger, Catharine—Daeter, Jacob
Bysinger, Elizabeth—Probst, Daniel
Bysinger, Polly—Fry, Philip
Bysinger, Sarah—Ikerd, David
Bysinger, Susanna—Aurends, John

Cadell, Elisebeth—Wise, Levi
Caldwell, Ann—Stiles, Carter
Caldwell, Beckey—Martin, Barnet
Caldwell, C C—Guion, B S
Caldwell, Charlotte—Gingles, Adlai
Caldwell, Christina—Stiles, Henry
Caldwell, Elizabeth—Howard, Henry
Caldwell, Isabella—Roberts, Eli
Caldwell, Martha A—Settlemyre, James A
Caldwell, Michel—Williams, Thomas
Caldwell, Perline—Shelton, Samuel T
Caldwell, Rebecca—Tilley, Jacob
Caldwell, Rebecca—Howard, John
Caldwell, Rebecka—Hand, John Conrad
Caldwell, Sarah—Grise, John
Call, Ann—Edwards, Charles
Calloway, Mary E—Reid, Thomas
Cambell, Mary—Sullivan, Noah
Camble, Mary—Rankin, William
Camble, Rachael—Caldwell, Samuel
Campbel, Elizabeth—Caldwell, William
Campbell, Jenny—Jenkins, Hugh
Campbell, Juliet—Hill, Andrew
Campbell, Mary—Wilson, James
Campbell, Nurcissa—Henry, Thomas
Campell, Nancy—Davis, Samuel
Canceller, Barbara—Troutman, Henry
Caneda, Ellen—Martin, William S
Canipe, Anna Eliza—Hubbard,
    Lemuel Alexander
Cannon, Emily—Detter, Albert W
Cannon, Mary—Smith, Oliver
Cannon, Sarah Ann—Linbarger, Jonas R
Canon, Nancy—Clemor, David

Canseller, Barbara—Hedick, John
Cansellor, Elisebeth—Rudisill, Philip
Cansler, Barbara S—Fite, Robt H
Cansler, Margaret—Goodson, Aaron
Cansler, Mary M—Lowrance, Cany M
Cansler, Polly—Hanes, Daniel A
Capenter, Catherine—McGinnas, William
Capps, May Ame—Rankin, William R
Capps, Permelah—Fite, Solomon
Carathers, Mary—Duckworth, Abel Hkns
Carba, Christina—Moose, Frederick
Carbinder, Ann—Peeler, Antony
Carigen, Mere An—Pitts, Henry
Carpanter, Anna—Hovis, Solomon
Carpanter, Mary—Carpanter, Peter
Carpanter, Sally—Carpenter, Philip
Carpenter, Ann—Martin, Richard
Carpenter, Ann—Black, Samuel
Carpenter, Ann E—Sipe, Cicero
Carpenter, Anna—Rhyne, David
Carpenter, Anna—Carpenter, Martin
Carpenter, Anna—Hovis, Jacob
Carpenter, Anna—Carpenter, Christopher
Carpenter, Anna—Mooney, Jacob
Carpenter, Anna—Kiser, Peter
Carpenter, Anne Mary—Rodes, Rudolph
Carpenter, Barbara—McGinnas, Lawson
Carpenter, Barbara—Carpenter, George
Carpenter, Barbara—Rudisill, David
Carpenter, Barbary—Bigam, Samuel
Carpenter, Caroline—Finger, Moses W
Carpenter, Catharine—Rhodes, Henry
Carpenter, Catharine—Mostillar, Daniel
Carpenter, Catharine—Rhyne, Solomon
Carpenter, Catharine—Warlick, Franklin D
Carpenter, Catharine—Vandike, Joshua
Carpenter, Catharine—Linhardt, Lawson H
Carpenter, Catherine—Killion, Jacob
Carpenter, Catherine—Alexander, Newman
Carpenter, Catherine—Hovis, George
Carpenter, Catherine—Kizer, James
Carpenter, Elisabeth—Cline, Henry
Carpenter, Elithabeth—Carpenter, Michael
Carpenter, Eliza—Summerow, James
Carpenter, Eliza—Mauney, Eli
Carpenter, Elizabeth—Whisnant, John
Carpenter, Elizabeth—Carpenter, Joseph
Carpenter, Elizabeth—Hovis, John
Carpenter, Elizabeth—Haines, Robert S
Carpenter, Elizabeth—Johnson, William B
Carpenter, Elizabeth—Hoyle, David R
Carpenter, Elizabeth—Carpenter, Samuel
Carpenter, Elizabeth—Earney, Henry
Carpenter, Fanney—Gales, William
Carpenter, Fanny—Eaker, Daniel
Carpenter, Fanny—McKee, Richard W
Carpenter, Fanny—Perkins, Logan
Carpenter, Fanny—Mauney, David
Carpenter, Fanny—Williams, Marcus
Carpenter, Frances—Cauble, E H
Carpenter, Frances A—McCaslin, Alfred C
Carpenter, Frances C—Hoke, Frederick L
Carpenter, Francis—Hill, John F
Carpenter, Hannah—Kiser, Philip
Carpenter, Lavina—Blackburn, Ephraim
Carpenter, Leanah—Beam, John
Carpenter, Louisa—Hovis, Moses

Carpenter, Louiza—Kiser, Philip
Carpenter, Margaret—Mosteller, Jonas
Carpenter, Margaret—McKee, James
Carpenter, Marget—Mauny, Abraham
Carpenter, Martha—Hoyle, John Samuel
Carpenter, Martha M—Spiegel, John C
Carpenter, Mary—Carpenter, John
Carpenter, Mary—Hoyl, Martin
Carpenter, Mary—Beam, John
Carpenter, Mary—Milligan, William
Carpenter, Mary—Weaver, Levi
Carpenter, Mary—Young, Peter
Carpenter, Mary—Hovis, George
Carpenter, Mary—Hull, Miles O
Carpenter, Mary A—Avery, John
Carpenter, Mary Ann—Carpenter, H F
Carpenter, Mary M—McLurd, John C
Carpenter, Milly—Rudisell, Levi
Carpenter, Nancy—Jenkins, David
Carpenter, Nancy F—Shrum, Solomon
Carpenter, Peggy—Friday, Martin
Carpenter, Peggy—Kizer, Henry
Carpenter, Polly—Best, Bosten
Carpenter, Polly—Morris, John J
Carpenter, Rebeccah—Carpenter, Michael
Carpenter, Rebeckah—Carpenter, John
Carpenter, S A—Detter, John R
Carpenter, Salley—Baxter, William
Carpenter, Sally—Fronebarger, William
Carpenter, Sally Salina—Carpenter,
  Solomon
Carpenter, Sarah—Felmet, Hugh Mc
Carpenter, Sarah—Hovis, Philip
Carpenter, Sarah—Floyd, Robert
Carpenter, Sarah—Hill, James H
Carpenter, Sarah—Warren, Robert
Carpenter, Sarah—Smith, Ephraim
Carpenter, Sarah A—Mullen, Alfred E
Carpenter, Sarah Ann—Hunt, George L
Carpenter, Susan—Rudasile, Willie
Carpenter, Susan—McKee, John
Carpenter, Susan Catharine—Friday,
  Jacob W
Carpenter, Susanah—Faulkner, Vincent A
Carpenter, Susanah—Kiser, Samuel
Carpenter, Susannah—Grigg, Edward
Carpinter, Mary—Cox, John
Carrol, Esther—Aderholt, William
Carrol, Martha—Eaker, Christian
Carrol, Susanah—McClurg, James
Carrol, Susanah D—Ferguson, William
Carruth, Elisabeth—Henderson, Lawson
Carson, Martha—Anthony, John
Caruth, Nancy—Stearnes, John
Caruth, Polly—Graham, John
Cashing, Hanna—Reedey, William
Cashon, Caty—Waggoner, Andrew
Cashon, Martha—Clifton, Robert
Cathey, Ellin—Hawkins, Samuel
Cathey, Jane—Sulivan, Elijah
Cathey, Jane—Mauney, Livingston
Cathey, Margaret—Moore, James
Cathey, Margaret—Jenkins, Benjamin
Cathey, Margery—Walker, Benjamin
Cathey, Nancy—Hovis, Henry
Cathy, Betcy—Clyne, John
Cathy, Carolina—Robinson, Gideon

Cathy, Frances—Oliver, William
Cathy, Nancy—Morgan, John
Cauble, Adaline—Harrill, Abraham G
Causby, Hannah—Propst, William
Cayhill, Nannie C—Smith, Milton A
Centre, Susanna—Cloninger, David
Cetser, Polley—Yearwood, William
Champin, Polley—Husky, Jesse
Chapman, Elizabeth—Robison, Johnson
Chapman, Susannah—Quinn, Merideth
Charlton, Agness—Kugan, John
Cherrey, Elisabeth—McWhorter, Robert
Cherry, ------—Boggs, William
Cherry, Elizabeth—Flemming, Archibald
Cherry, Jane—Black, Samuel
Cherry, Mary—Luckey, John
Cherry, Matilda—Fleming, Archibald
Cherry, Matilda Ann—Long, Wm T
Chetham, Peggy—Beaty, Jonathan
Childers, Betsey—Thomson, Isom
Childers, Delpha—Cook, Barryman
Childers, Dovy—Hicks, Albert
Childers, Fanny—Ingle, Jacob
Childers, Mary—Bishop, Beal
Childers, Mary—Kids, William
Childers, Nancy—Howard, William
Childers, Nancy—Pirkins, Henrey
Childers, Susannah—Hix, Miles
Childres, Martha H—Goodson, Rufus L
Childress, Michel—Ward, Josiah
Childress, Rachel—Dellinger, Moses
Childress, Rosanah—Carpenter, David
Childress, Salley—Ballard, Jno
Chitham, Rachel—Henderson, Ahira
Chittam, Mary—Knight, John F
Chittem, Margaret M—Suggs, Isaac
Chittim, Harett P—Cooper, Thomas
Chody, Margaret—McClurd, Wiley A
Chorum, Salley—Owens, William
Christopher, Catharina—Shook, Adam
Church, Nancy—Engle, Martin
Cills, Martha—Iseler, Adam
Cistler, Malinda—Humphrey, Daniel
Clark, Ann—Law, Henry
Clark, Ann—Cashion, James
Clark, Anny—Cox, John
Clark, Dolley—Vandike, James
Clark, Elisabeth—McClure, William
Clark, Francis—M'Carter, Caleb R
Clark, Harriet C—Sult, Lafayette
Clark, Harriet E—Brison, George R
Clark, Jane—Stephenson, John
Clark, Jennet—Norton, William
Clark, Lettis—Hill, Thomas
Clark, Margret—Bigham, Robert
Clark, Martha—Carrigan, John
Clark, Martha A—Tucker, Wiley S
Clark, Mary—Robinson, John W
Clark, Mary—Glanton, F H B
Clark, Mary L—Mauney, John
Clark, Nancy—Martin, James
Clark, Nancy—McCarta, Jacob
Clark, Sally—Black, Robert
Clark, Susan M—Edwards, David L
Clarke, Ginsey Mary—Stroup, Moses
Clay, Anna—Carpenter, Jonathan
Clay, Barbara—Haas, John

Clay, Catharine—Rinck, Noah
Clay, Eliza—Hause, Jacob
Clay, Elizabeth—Hause, David
Clay, Harriet S—Miller, George
Clay, Juda—Killian, Henry
Clay, Susanah—Sigel, John
Clemer, Elizabeth—Rhyne, Christian
Clemer, Fany—Rudiseal, Aaron
Clemer, Susana—Roades, Jacob
Clemer, Susanah—Cloninger, Adam
Clemmer, Anney—Rhyne, Jacob
Clemmer, E M—Reel, Spaight M
Clemmer, Louisa—Dethrow, Jonathan
Clemmer, Margred—Jenkins, Tilman
Clemmer, Martha—Ingle, Ephraim
Clemmer, Susanah—Davis, William
Clemmer, Susanna—Lewis, James
Clemmon, Elizabeth—Cloninger, Jacob
Clemor, Salena—Jenkins, Berryman
Cleppard, Dica—Edleman, Peter
Cleppard, Lovina—Beel, Giles
Clifton, Edey—Broadway, Alen
Clifton, Eliza—Green, Pleasant
Clifton, Jane—Hager, David
Clifton, Mary—Maskal, William
Clifton, Polley—Edwards, William
Cline, Aday—Sigman, Jesse
Cline, Anna Barbara—Bost, Daniel
Cline, Catharine—Killian, David
Cline, Catharine—Hutson, Matthew
Cline, Catharine—Setzer, Andrew
Cline, Catherine—Hull, William
Cline, Charity—Butts, Henry
Cline, Elisa—Earnest, Daniel
Cline, Elizabeth—Wike, Jacob
Cline, Eve—Abernathy, Nathen
Cline, Fanny—Fry, Jacob
Cline, Fanny—Haus, John H
Cline, Harriet—Ballew, W A
Cline, Jamima—Yount, Franklin
Cline, Lavina—Detter, Frederick
Cline, Lusindy—Townsin, Jacob
Cline, Margaret—Shell, John
Cline, Margaret A—Cobb, William W
Cline, Mary—Dietz, Daniel
Cline, Nancy—Spratt, Thomas
Cline, Nancy C—Hoke, A L
Cline, Nancy E—Hovis, Michael R
Cline, Peggy—Tucker, George
Cline, Polly—Abernathy, Seth
Cline, Polly—Whitener, Joseph
Cline, Sally—Fulbright, Peter
Cline, Sally—Halman, Daniel
Cline, Sarah—Rudisail, John
Cline, Shusanah—Lowry, John
Clipard, Elizabeth—Richards, Fealty
Clippard, Betsey Ann—Weathers, Michael H
Clippard, Elizabeth—Goins, Wiley
Clippard, Nancy—Burns, James
Clippard, Polly—Goins, John
Clippard, Sally—Keever, Henry
Clipperd, Sarah—Asbury, Daniel M
Clipperd, Sophiah—Edwards, Lewis
Clipperd, Susanah—Cloninger, Henry
Clodfelter, Elizabeth—Rinck, George
Clodfelter, Fanny—Abernathy, James

Cloer, Nancey—Bradshaw, Field
Clonenger, Polly—Summit, Jacob
Clonger, Susanah—Bell, John
Cloningar, Viney—Rhyne, Joseph W
Cloninger, Ann—Stroup, David
Cloninger, Barbara—Robinson, John H
Cloninger, Catharine—Riel, Godfrey
Cloninger, Catharine—Senter, William
Cloninger, Christina—Gant, Jesse
Cloninger, Elizabeth—Ellmore, William
Cloninger, Elizabeth—Linebarger, Peter
Cloninger, Eve—Hoves, George
Cloninger, Mary—Byrum, Upton
Cloninger, Nancy—Carpenter, Emmanuel
Cloninger, Rebeckah—Stroup, Jonas
Cloninger, Sarah H—Sadler, J A
Clonninger, Mary—Thornberg, Jacob
Clore, Elisabeth—Abernathy, James
Clotfelter, Hannah L—Clotfelter, David A
Clotfelter, Malinda—Witherspoon, Nelson
Club, Elizabeth—Underwood, Reuben
Club, Elizabeth—Huskins, William
Clubb, Anney—Keller, Enuck
Cobb, Mrs B M—Sherrill, Samuel P
Cobb, Barbary—Abernathy, Charles
Cobb, Charlotte—Maginnes, William
Cobb, Dycy—Richards, William
Cobb, Ellener—Stanford, Ekekiel
Cobb, Frances—Lemaster, John W
Cobb, Judith—Meginness, Ambrose
Cobb, Kessy—Clubb, George
Cobb, Malissa—Turbyfill, Wilson
Cobb, Mary—Petray, Lawson
Cobb, Mary N—Smith, Milton A
Cobb, Minty—Moore, Wesley
Cobb, Nancey—Abernathy, Miles
Cobb, Rachel—Harmon, John G
Cobb, Sally—Coxe, James
Cobb, Sarah—Lowrance, Rufus
Cobb, Selina—Edwards, Starling
Coble, Jane—Hansel, Henry
Cochran, Susana—Slinkard, Henry
Cock, Rebacka—Bonham, Absalom
Cockran, Elizabeth—Cline, John
Cody, Frances—Haynes, William H
Cody, Nancy—Black, John
Cody, Rachel—Leonhardt, Lawrance
Cody, Sarah—Eaker, Abram
Coffey, Milley—Bell, Lewis
Cogle, Martha—Heslet, Ezekiel
Coldwell, Elizabeth—Abernathy, Valentine
Coldwell, Ruth—Price, Aron
Coldwell, Salley—Price, George
Collance, Polly—Barger, Isaac
Collier, Ann S—Rogers, John B
Collier, Mary—Sherril, Benjamin
Colliers, Sally—Hamilton, Reuben
Collins, Elizabeth—Robards, Thomas
Collins, Jane—Dellinger, Valentine
Collins, Jean—Crow, Robert
Collins, Mary—Endsley, Archibald
Collins, Susan—Brian, James
Collins, Susanah—McClellan, Elias
Colwell, Becky—Daniel, John
Commins, Elisabeth—Arrowwood, Zacharias
Conner, Eliza M—Simonton, W S

Conner, Elizebeth—Deven, Patrick
Conner, Hannah—Stillwell, Samuel
Conner, Malina—Little, Peter
Conner, Margaret—Craft, John P
Conner, Mariah—Mayhew, James
Conner, Mary—Carpenter, Michael
Conner, Sarah—Martin, Richard C
Conner, Susannah—Stiles, Bejamin
Connor, Amia—Linebarger, Frederick H
Connor, Eliza—Towery, Adam
Connor, Epsey C—Cloninger, John
Connor, Harriet K—Johnston, Sidney X
Connor, Hetty—Craft, Moses
Connor, Jane—Wilson, Maxwell
Connor, Susan E—Houser, Peter
Conor, Sarah—Sheril, James F
Conrad, Charity—Plot, Elias
Conrad, Polley—Hawn, Samuel
Cook, Ann—Cody, Murphia
Cook, Anne—Bleckley, Charles
Cook, Eve—Dormire, Samuel Jr
Cook, Mary—Hauser, Jacob
Cook, Mary—Linebarger, Daniel
Cook, Matilda—Stiles, William
Cook, Rachel—Huffman, Henry W
Cook, Sally—Ramer, Peter
Cook, Sarah—Colwell, Philip
Cook, Shusanah—Goble, John
Coon, Barbary—Seagle, John
Coon, Betcy—Hevner, Henry
Coon, Mary Ann—Heavner, Julius A
Coon, Sarah—Willis, R H
Coons, Susannah—Lagle, Jacob
Cooper, Anna—Williams, David
Cooper, Lydia—Colwell, Daniel
Cooper, Margaret—Brown, Daniel
Cope, Nancy—Helms, John
Copeland, Lucy—Jones, William
Copeland, Minerva—Dellinger, Moses
Copelin, Elizabeth—Whisenant, John
Cornelias, Nancy—Beaty, Thomas
Cornelias, Susanah—Robey, Wm A
Cornelius, Elizabeth—Roby, John W
Cornelius, Judey—Kimball, Green
Cornelius, Rebecca—Homer, John
Cornwell, Mary—Honesley, A B
Cosnar, Elizabeth—Fox, David
Cosner, Anna M—Hufmon, Jonas
Cosner, Catharine—Brown, Logan
Cosner, Cathrine—Plonk, Jacob
Costner, Abatine—Carpenter, Moses
Costner, Anne—Elmore, James
Costner, Barbara—Wilson, Moses
Costner, Barbara—Veitch, Henry F
Costner, Barbara—Rhyne, Jacob
Costner, Betsey—Linebarger, John
Costner, Betsey—Rudisail, Henry
Costner, Catharine—Green, John H
Costner, Elizabeth—Friday, Jonas
Costner, Elizabeth—Niell, James
Costner, Fanny—Best, Michael
Costner, Mary—McIlwain, David
Costner, Mary—Witherspoon, H B
Costner, Mary Ann—Huffstetler, Michael
Costner, Mary Magdaline—Cook, Matthew
Costner, Susan—Weathers, Elisha
Coulter, Anna—Smith, Henry

Coulter, Catharine—Wilson, Maxwell
Coulter, Catharine M—Warlick, Maxwell
Coulter, Eliza—Miller, Jonathan
Coulter, Elizabeth—Conrad, Logan
Coulter, Elizbeth—Hoke, Andrew
Coulter, Emmily Elizabeth—Harris, John W B
Coulter, Harriet—Dettor, David
Coulter, Rody—Shuford, David
Courtney, Margaret—Crawford, H P
Coventon, Eliza Ann—Hager, Franklin F
Coventon, Harriot—Edwards, William L
Cowen, Catharine—McNeely, James
Cox, Bede—Little, William
Cox, Catherine—Wright, J M
Cox, Elisabeth—Bynum, Gray
Cox, Elisabeth—Dunn, James
Cox, Elizabeth—West, Isaac
Cox, Esabella—Cobb, Waulter
Cox, Hexxey—Adams, John
Cox, Lucey—Downey, Patrick
Cox, Lucinda—Cathy, Robert F
Cox, Margaret M—Grissom, I F
Cox, Nancey—Moore, Moses
Cox, Peggy M—Berry, Wm
Cox, Polly—Ramsey, William
Cox, Rachael—Carson, Peter
Cox, Sally—Wright, Joseph
Cox, Sarah—Beach, Benjamin
Cox, Sarah—Weathers, Morgan
Coxe, Eliner L—Reed, George A
Coxe, Margt—Bennett, Jacob
Cozens, Martha C—Moore, Lee A
Craft, Mary A—Whitworth, Thomas
Craft, Omai—Spake, Christopher
Craig, Jane—Nesmith, William
Craig, Nancy—Gullick, John
Cratz, Cathrine—Liming, Samuel
Crawley, Elizabeth—Long, L S
Crays, Sally—Cornet, Cullen
Creags, Agness—Reynolds, John
Creasman, Catharine—Stroup, Joseph
Creasman, Jane—Skidmor, Turner
Creatheres, Sarah—Hobbs, Nathaniel
Creesman, Mary—Earwood, Thomas
Creesmore, Catherine—Ecker, Jacob
Cresemon, Barbara—Miller, Michael
Cresemon, Betcy—Conrad, David
Cresemon, Susan—Shelton, Chrispen
Creesmore, Salley—Cloninger, Michal Jr
Cresman, Nancy—Low, Jesse
Cressman, Elizabeth—Shell, John
Crisel, Susanna—Epply, Jacob
Crismore, Mary—Braneman, Christen
Crites, Elisabeth—Kinder, Peter
Crites, Fanny—Duncan, Turner
Cronester, Rachael—Burk, Monroe
Crongleton, Margaret—Brotherton, James
Cronister, Eve—Welch, William
Cronkleton, Martha Ann—Little, William
Cross, Anne—Liming, Stacey
Cross, Caty—Glance, Charles
Cross, Edy—Havner, Martin
Cross, Prudence—Hope, Christian
Crouse, Barbara—Tutherow, Jacob
Crouse, Barbara A—Aderholdt, John A F
Crouse, Catharine—Yount, G D L

Crouse, Elizabeth—Sanders, Jesse
Crouse, Katy—Taylor, Absalom
Crouse, Margaret—Burnett, A Jenkins
Crow, Betcey L—Mauney, John
Crow, Jane—Neal, William
Crowell, Adaline—Hafner, Alfred
Crunkelton, Eliza—Munday, Osburn
Cryseller, Sally—Linebarger, Jacob
Cunningham, Anne—Patterson, William
Curtis, Sarah—Anderson, Isaac

Dagahard, Elizabeth—Shook, Henrey
Dailey, Jane M—Campbell, James A
Daily, Mary B—Sifford, Thomas
Daily, Sarah K—Ballard, William
Dameron, Anny—Gregory, William T
Dameron, Cinthey—Glenn, David N
Dameron, Nancy—Pollard, William
Dameron, Sarah W—Pollard, Uriah
Damron, Nancy—Huson, John
Danizeln, Elizabeth—Chambers, John J
Darnel, Sarah—Senter, Joel
Darte,Biddy—Cody, Perry
Dasey, Nancy—Justice, Peter
Dauherty, Cerease—Lewis, John
Davenport, Elizabeth C—Abernathy,
  Sidney T
Davenport, Mary E—Morris, Amos
Davies, Dealph—Allen, John Y
Davis, Ann—Kincaid, George W
Davis, Barbara—Kincaid, George W
Davis, Cyntha—Elmore, Jonas
Davis, Eleanor—Killian, Abram
Davis,Elender—Yother, Daniel
Davis, Elisabeth—Kincaid, William
Davis, Elizabeth—Scott, Wm
Davis, Elizabeth—Sloop, Henry
Davis, Elizabeth—Ramsey, Robert G
Davis, Elizabeth—Mulens, D
Davis, Elizebeth—Robinson, Elam
Davis, Esther M—Blackburn, William
Davis, Jane—Cox, Green W
Davis, Mary—Shneider, Christian
Davis, Mary—Brown, William
Davis, Mary—Warlick, John
Davis, Mary—Killian, Simon
Davis, Mary M—Shufford, Isarel
Davis, Nancy—Matthews, Nathan
Davis, Patsey—Kelley, Robert C
Davis, Polley—Barber, Thomas
Davis, Prudence—Parker, Thomas
Davis, R C—Brown, A A
Davis, Rachel—Hull, William
Davis, Salley—McAllister, Cornelius
Davis, Sarah—Grigg, Wesly J
Davis, Sarrah—Davis, James
Davis, Sary—Johnston, Richard
Davis, Sophia S—McGinnas, Sydney A
Davis,Susana—Huffstotler, Adam
Davis, Violet P—Wilsone, John A
Dawsey, Rachel—Harrison, Richard
Deaker, Polly—Roney, John
Deal, Barbary—Isacks, Jacob
Deal, Cathrine—Herman, George
Deal, Cathrine—Stine, John
Deal, Christiana—Decker, Michael

Deal, Delilah—Setzer, Jacob
Deal, Eliza—Gant, John H
Deal, Fanny—Popst, George
Deal, Fanny—Rader, Daniel
Deal, Fanny—Hedrick, Peter
Deal, Lydia—Earny, Martin
Deal, Mary Magdelene—Howard,
  Joshua Loyd
Deal, Phoeby Malinda—Sigman, Lawson
Deal, Polly—Pope, Daniel
Deal, Polly—Wike, David
Deal, Risa—Setzer, Paul
Deal, Rosanna—Bolch, Andrew
Deal, Sally—Sigman, Henry
Deal, Sally—Bumgarner, Thomas G
Dealasnider, Catharine—Sipe, Daniel, Jur
Dearment, Sarah—Pee, George
Debter, Catharine—Wilson, Joseph
Deck, Catherine—Hager, William
Deck, Mary M—Vickers, John
Deel, Catharina—King, Elijah
Deel, Catharine—Logan, James
Deel, Freny—Goble, Henry
Deem, Polley—Lewis, Simion Jr
Dehebough, Peggy—Douglas, William
Deits, Margarett—Huitt, Lewis
Deitz, Christina—Probst, John
Delane, Mary A—Bolton, Wm M
Delinger, Elisabeth—Clemmer, John M L
Delinger, Mieranna—Houser, Elias
Delinger, Rebeckey—Williams, Nelson
Delinger, Sally—Williams, Nelson G
Delliner, Mary Ann—Kids, Rufus
Dellingar, Elizabéth—Sigman,
  George Philip
Dellinger, Barbara—Sigman, Henry
Dellinger, Barbara—Low, George
Dellinger, Barbara—Hawn, Samuel
Dellinger, Barbara—Crites, William
Dellinger, Barbara—Stroup, J C
Dellinger, Barbara A—Smith, John B
Dellinger, Belzora K—Hallmon, W M
Dellinger, Betcy—Butz, Michael
Dellinger, Betcy—Brown, John
Dellinger, C L—Hallman, Michael
Dellinger, Caroline—McLure, James
Dellinger, Catherine—Dellinger, Henry
Dellinger, Cinthia—McFalls, Leander
Dellinger, Elisabeth S—Spargo, James
Dellinger, Elizabeth—Courtney, Henry
Dellinger, Elizabeth—Shull, Charles
Dellinger, Elizabeth—Haines, James H
Dellinger, Elvira—Anthony, Philip
Dellinger, Eve—Mauney, Mark
Dellinger, Fany R—Regan, Henry C
Dellinger, Hannah—Smith, Robert
Dellinger, Harriett R—Spake, Samuel
Dellinger, J H—Triplett, James
Dellinger, Jane—McAlister, James
Dellinger, Lavinia C—Blackburn, John H
Dellinger, Lovina—Yount, William A
Dellinger, Lucretia L—Hovis, Henry M
Dellinger, M C—Ward, J W
Dellinger, Malinda—Nantz, Levi
Dellinger, Margaret—Strutt, Logan A
Dellinger, Margarett—Whitener, George
Dellinger, Martha—Varner, Albert

Dellinger, Mary—Mostiller, Peter Jr
Dellinger, Mary—Randleman, Henry
Dellinger, Mary—Browan, Samuel
Dellinger, Mary—Shull, David
Dellinger, Mary Ann—Newton, Maridy N
Dellinger, Mary C—Hoover, Edney
Dellinger, Mary E—Carpenter, Christopher
Dellinger, Mary M—Brown, Arthur
Dellinger, Mirey A—Rhyne, George
Dellinger, Nancy—Blaylock, Hubbard
Dellinger, Peggy—Johnson, John
Dellinger, Polly—Yount, Jacob
Dellinger, Polly—Dillenger, Frederick
Dellinger, Rebeccah—Goodson, George W
Dellinger, Rosannah—Carpenter,
    William A I
Dellinger, Sarah—Dellinger, Jacob
Dellinger, Sarah—Lefever, John
Dellinger, Susana—Whisenhant, Daniel
Dellinger, Zenith—Faulkner, John N
Delp, Salley—Wasson, William
Denem, Mary Ann—Robinson, Elhanan
Denham, Margaret D—Barnes, Jasper N
Derr, Barbara—McMin, Samuel
Derr, Dinah—Arents, Wesley
Derr, Jane K—Lenoir, William A
Derr, Sally—Arney, Jacob
Deshaser, Abby—Parrish, Johnston
Detherow, Barbary—Dyer, George
Detter, Betsey—Rudisill, Michael
Detter, Eliza E—Edwards, William R
Detter, Elizabeth—Yoder, Eli
Detter, Roxanna—Thorn, Daniel
Dettor, Barbara—Johnson, Benjamin S
Dettor, Mary—Peterson, Jesse R
Dettor, Sarah—Edwards, William R Jr
Devebaugh, Anna—Spratt, James
Devebaugh, Uly—James, Benjamin
Devenport, Sally—Beatey, Samuel
Devibach, Lydia—Reynolds, Reuben H
Dews, Eliza—Robinson, William
Dews, Julia—Sparrow, Hiram
Dews, Martha—Frontis, Stephen
Dick, Susanah—Davold, John
Dickey, Martha—McGill, Thomas P
Dickey, Mary M—Clark, James W
Dickson, Elizabeth—Kannedy, Gilbert
Dickson, Elizabeth—Nowlin, Hardin
Dickson, Elizabeth—Hoyle, Humphry H
Dickson, Harriet A—Davis, James
Dickson, Jain—Kerr, William
Dickson, Jean—Lewis, George
Dickson, Jean—Collins, Josiah
Dickson, Letty—Beam, Teter
Dickson, Margaret—Allison, Samuel
Dickson, Mary—Douglass, John
Dickson, Mary E—Quinn, John R
Dickson, Narcissa—Patterson, Thomas
Dickson, Rosannah—Tucker, Nicholas J
Dickson, Sarah—Baggs, William
Dicky, Catherane—Weer, Thomas
Dietz, Barbara—Bolick, Jacob
Dietz, Christina—Rinck, Ephraim
Dietz, Elizabeth—Dietz, Solomon
Dietz, Polly—Yoder, Micheal
Dietz, Sarah—Barger, Moses
Dilin, Martha—Sherrill, Nicolas

Dillen, Fanny—Kiser, Jonas
Dillen, Polly—Adkins, Gervis G
Dillen, Rachel—Rodes, Elisha
Dillin, Jude—Cornelius, Benjamin
Dillinger, Betsy—Stroup, Jacob
Dillon, Susannah—Collins, Richard
Dinkin, Polley—Brotherton, Joseph
Dinwiddie, Esther—Ramsey, Thomas
Dixon, Margaret—White, James E
Dixon, Nancy—Ormand, Benjamin
Dobbins, Mary—Armstrong, John
Dobson, Elizabeth—Shenck, Henry
Dobson, Harriet—Summey, Peter
Doggett, Eveline—Beam, John T
Dohertie, Molly—Bear, Christian
Dormire, Barbara—Robinson, Andrew
Dorsey, Polly—Berry, Wm
Dover, Mary—Hambright, Fredk
Downey, Ibby—Miarse, Jacob
Downs, Elizabeth—Nixon, Sidney
Downs, Mary Ann—Brunt, William R
Downy, Polly—Miares, Elias
Drake, Margaret—Duckworth, William
Drake, Margaret—Bird, John
Drake, Milberry—Groves, Thomas
Drew, Jane—Wilson, John Jr
Drew, Mary T—Asbury, John F
Drue, Lucie—Monday, Francis
Drum, Anne—Bridges, Elisha
Drum, Anny—Huffman, William
Drum, Barbara—Sherrill, Anderson
Drum, Barbray—Taylor, Jacob
Drum, Delila—Williams, Laban
Drum, Elisabeth—Keener, Moses
Drum, Mary Magdaline—Miller, Nicholas
Drum, Sarah—Bradshaw, Larkin
Drumfield, Patcy—Mays, James L
Duck, Betsey—Massey, Mark
Duckworth, Jane—Ramsour, David
Duckworth, Sarah—Hern, John
Dudro, Susannah—Shrum, Henry
Dun, Martha—Thomson, John
Dunbar, Rebecca—Keller, James
Duncan, Effey—Clark, Owen
Duncan, Elizabeth—Little, John
Duncan, Martha—Little, James
Duncan, Mary—King, John
Duncan, Milley—Saunders, Lemuel
Duncan, Nancy—Eatris, John
Duncan, Patsy—Daily, Ephraim
Duncan, Polley—Cronister, Daniel
Duncan, Sarah—Lockman, David
Duncan, Susanah—Wilkinson, William
Dunlap, Sarah—Clark, Anthony
Durant, Mary E—Kirby, Augustus H
Durr, Elizebeth—Sifford, John
Dusenbury, C A—Warlick, Eli A
Dyer, Polley—Hullet, John
Dyer, Sally—Griffin, Peter

Eaker, Adline—Conner, Noah D
Eaker, Catharine—Reynolds, Josiah
Eaker, Elizabeth—Morrison, Maxwell
Eaker, Elvira—Eaker, Daniel
Eaker, Lavinia—Jenkins, William
Eaker, Nancy—Mullens, Davrell

Eaker, Olly L—Heavner, Martin
Eaker, Sally—Carpenter, Christopher
Eaker, Sarah—Metcalf, Augustus D
Eakerd, Margaret—Cline, Sebastian
Earhart, Amy—Crysell, John
Earheart, Molly—Felker, Michael
Earles, Rebekah—Collins, John
Earley, Nancey—Duncan, Andrew
Earley, Susannah—Parker, Ezekiel
Earls, Trathena—Etters, Jacob
Earnest, Elisabeth—Saunders, Thomas
Earnest, Hanah—Ducker, Frederick
Earney, Ann—Finger, John
Earney, Malina—Propst, Larsen
Earney, Mrs Sarah—Carvolt, Richard
Earns, Ann—Figh, Phillip
Earny, Letha Jane—Roberson, William
Earwood, Lucy—Belk, John
Earwood, Salley—Stroup, William
Eaton, Agatha—Stone, James
Eaton, Elizabeth—Stiles, Henry
Eaton, Margaret—Colwell, John
Eaton, Mary—Gantt, James
Eaton, Nancy—Biles, Enoch
Eaton, Polly—Kennedy, Robert
Eaton, Sarah—Sherrill, Jesse
Eckard, Molly—Cline, Jacob
Eckerd, Christina—Sigman, Barnet
Eckerd, Elizabeth—Cline, Henry
Eckerd, Mary—Cline, Ephraim
Eckerd, Susanna—Wagner, Peter
Eckhart, Leah—Mehaffey, Thomas A
Edmund, Emeline—Lore, Joshua
Edwards, Betsy—Hedgcock, Thomas
Edwards, Catharine—Loftin, Henderson
Edwards, Ebbe—Sronce, John
Edwards, Elizabeth—Howard, William
Edwards, Jane—Parker, John
Edwards, Jane—Proctor, H S
Edwards, Lucy—Connel, David
Edwards, Martha E—Odell, H S
Edwards, Matilda—Long, Lawson
Edwards, Mehala—Williams, Jacob
Edwards, Nancy—Litten, James
Edwards, Patience—Duncan, George
Edwards, Polley—Loftin, John
Edwards, Rachel—Brotherton, George
Edwards, Ruth—Kale, Polser
Edwards, Sally—Kale, Absalom
Edwards, Sally Ann—Lindsey, William H
Edwards, Sarah—Long, Leonard
Edwards, Sarah—Sherrill, Logan
Edwards, Sareth—Sipe, Paul
Edwards, Susana—Jones, Strawden
Edwards, Vashti—Little, Samuel C
Edwards, Viry—Allen, Henry H
Eflinger, Mary—Sigman, Barnet
Eikerd, Cathrina—Miller, Philip
Eikerd, Caty—Bolick, William
Eikerd, Elizabeth—Miller, Moses
Eikerd, Polly—Killian, David
Eikerd, Sally—Fry, Henry
Eikerd, Sarah—Huffman, Martin
Eikert, Fanny—Sigman, Daniel
Eisenhower, Marey—Fulbright, Barnet
Eker, Barery—Eker, Cornelius
Eker, Mary—Roberts, Thomas

Eker, Mary—Hambright, Frederick
Ekert, Barbara—Townsen, Lewis
Elliott, Agatha Y—Gaudelok, James
Elliott, Kizia Ann—Magness, Morgan
Ellison, Margaret—Brown, Parker
Ellmore, Anne—Carpenter, Andrew
Elmore, Catharine—Stamey, W R
Elmore, Jane—Mullens, Durell
Elmore, Polley—Noyes, Horatio
Elmore, Susan—Reynolds, Wiley W
Endsley, Elizabeth—Carroll, Joseph M
Endsley, Marey—Collins, William
Endsley, Marg—McFarland, James Jr
Engle—see also Ingle
Engle, Barbera—Keener, John
Engle, Margaret—Hope, William
Engle, Sarah—Reep, Daniel
Engle, Susanna—Thompson, Isom
Englefinger, Barbara—Summey, George
Englefinger, Catherrina—Smith, Henry
Englefinger, Salley—Clanton, Isaac
Englifinger, Anna—Bradshaw, John
Ensley, Deborah—Williams, Silas
Ernest, Elisabeth—Keys, Hugh
Erwin, Margaret—Allison, Henry
Erwine, Maryan—Allison, William M
Eslinger, Elisabeth—Harmon, George
Espey, Jean—Smyth, James
Espey, Margaret—Lackey, Thomas
Espey, Mary—Oats, John
Espie, Martha—Huggins, William
Esterbrook, Ann—Blake, Aaron
Estrige, Polley—Gibson, Joseph
Ettleman, Eve—Edwards, John
Evins, Hannah—Mason, Thomas
Eward, Sarah—Hill, Thos
Ewart, Margaret—Jack, Joseph
Ewert, Betsey—Haskins, Robert
Ewert, Elisabeth—Price, Jonathan
Ewing, ------—Allison, James M
Ewing, Kevreenah—Elliotte, Andrew
Ewing, Margaret—Sloan, George
Ewing, Mary B—Davis, Benjamin C
Ewing, Patsy—Williamson, Seth
Ewing, Peggy B—Gingles, Thomas H

Fair, Sarah M—Davis, Alexander
Falls, Anable—Gofourth, Johnson
Falls, Delilah—Torrance, Robert
Falls, Elizabeth—Wilson, James
Falls, Emaline—Berrey, Alexander
Falls, Esther—Falls, William
Falls, Esther—Hays, William
Falls, Jane—Goodson, Milton
Falls, Margaret—Goforth, Andrew
Falls, Nancy—Dickson, John
Falls, Nancy S—Price, Thomas W
Falls, Polley—White, Isaac
Falls, Rachal—McCulloch, Robert
Falls, Rachael—Glenn, Samuel
Falls, Rachel—Ferguson, Robert
Falls, Rachel—Wilson, Robert
Falls, Rebecca—Falls, William
Falls, Rebeccah—Blackwood, Samuel
Falls, Rosana—Dickson, Thomas
Falls, Rosanah—Falls, David E

Falls, Rosanah—Falls, David
Falls, Ruth—Weir, William
Falls, Sarah—Lasley, Samuel
Falls, Sarah—Neill, Alexander
Falls, Sarah—Ferguson, John
Falls, Sarah—Detter, Andrew
Falls, Synthey—M'Cullouch, David
Farewell, Ebbe—Ballard, Isaah W
Farewell, Polly—Abernathy, John
Farmer, Nancy—Elmore, Lewis
Farmer, Peggy—Wise, Frederick
Farmer, Sarah—Hull, Daniel
Farr, Polly—Sherrill, Aquilla
Farrar, Margaret—Farrar, Aaron
Farwell, Elenor—Beatty, Franklin
Faulkner, Nancy A—Abrams ,Lewis D H
Favell, Elizabeth—Childers, Nelson
Featherston, Nancy—Harwell, Gardner
Featherston, Sarah—Clemmer, Levi
Featherston, Susana—Gaines, Henry
Felps, Rachel—Greaves, Philip
Ferguson, Ann—Hunter, George R
Ferguson, Eliza—Millard, William
Ferguson, Eliza M—Patterson, Alfred
Ferguson, Elizebeth—Wilson, Edwin
Ferguson, Jane—Lowrance, Martin C
Ferguson, Mary—Falls, James
Ferguson, Mary—Gamble, John
Ferguson, Mary H—Falls, Andrew
Ferguson, Mary S—Mtgomery, John
Ferguson, Polly—Alexander, John
Ferguson, S A—Barber, John
Ferrell, Eliza O—Leonard, James M
Fetherston, Sally—Harwell, Rolley
Fikes, Rachal—Ward, Fedrick
Finger, Ann—Arndt, Henry
Finger, Ann—Camel, Abel
Finger, Anna—Ikerd, Anthony
Finger, Barbara—Blackburn, Eli
Finger, Catharine—Srum, John
Finger, Catharine—Arends, David
Finger, Eliza—Ramsour, Elisha J
Finger, Elizabeth—Reinheardt, Henry
Finger, Frances—Kistler, James
Finger, M S—Williams, W H
Finger, Margaret E—Little, L W
Finger, Mary—Keener, Adam
Finger, Mary—Srum, Daniel
Finger, Mary—Rudisail, Solomon
Finger, Sarah A C—Asbury, Josiah
Finger, Susanah—Ikerd, George A
Fingers, Catharine—Gerding,
    Gerard George
Finison, Sarah—Whitney, Branson
Finnison, Noray—Scarbrough, Robert
Fish, Dolly—Dugless, Isaac
Fish, Elisabeth—Alexander, William
Fish, Mary—Perkins, Jesse
Fish, Polley—Turner, John
Fish, Sarah—Holly, John
Fisher, Arminda A—Fisher, Stephen G
Fisher, Barbara—Dellinger, John
Fisher, Catharine—Harvel, Nathaniel
Fisher, Catharine—Huggin, John A
Fisher, Catherine—Barns, Eli
Fisher, Elizabeth—Gilleland, William
Fisher, Elizabeth—Robinson, Eli J

Fisher, Fanny—Fisher, Stephen G
Fisher, Fanny—Weaver, Jacob
Fisher, Jane A—McCorkle, Richard A
Fisher, Mary—Mull, Abram
Fisher, Mary—Fisher, Reuben
Fisher, Mary—Abernathy, Enock
Fisher, Matilda—Little, Thomas J
Fisher, Nelly—Lee, Lawson
Fisher, Saley—Stiles, John
Fisher, Sarah C—Hill, Isaac L
Fisher, Susanna—Conner, William
Fitchjerrold, Nancy—Brooks, Samuel
Fite, Barbara—Sanford, John
Fite, Esther—Capps, Franklin
Fite, Malinde S—Rhyne, David
Fite, Martha—McCall, James A
Fite, Mary—Riley, Andrew
Fite, Mary Isabella—Ford, Robert F
Fite, Peggy—Armstrong, John
Fite, Polley—Hover, Philip
Fite, Willie—Smith, Robert
Flanegan, Catharine—Waldrip, Elihu
Flanegen, Susanah—Barnet, Philip
Flanigan, Susan—Blackburn, Robert
Flanigin, Salley—Lefever, Isaac
Fleming, Nancy—Guffy, John S
Flemming, Agnias—Huddleston, James
Flowers, Ann—Denton, William
Flowers, Cathrine—Seabolt, Solomon
Ford, Ibby—Ragan, Morgan
Ford, Mary—Parsons, Robert
Ford, Milley—Titman, Anthony
Ford, Minty—Dobson, William
Ford, Patsy—Cathey, Alexander
Forney, Caroline M—Hunly, Ransom G
Forney, Christina—Abernathy, David
Forney, Elen—Conor, Fed
Forney, Eliza—Webb, Henry Y
Forney, Elizabeth R—Thompson,
    Thomas J
Forney, Lovina—Fulenwider, John
Forney, M C—Beal, John F
Forney, Margaret L—Wamac, William
Forney, Marthe—Derr, Harbert
Forney, Mary M—Shrum, Henry
Forney, Nancy—Johnston, William
Forney, Polly—Reinhardt, Christian Jr
Forney, Sarah D—Helderman, Valentine
Forney, Sophia G—Hunter, Cyrus L
Forney, Susan—Abernathy, John
Forney, Susan—Shipp, Bartlett
Forsyth, Elisabeth—Black, William
Fortner, Mary—Abernathy, Isaac
Fountain, Elizabeth—Duffy, Robert
Fox, Margaret—Srum, John
Fox, Matty—Dagenhart, Peter
Fox, Prudence—Hafner, Franklin
Francis, Lucinda—Jinkins, Tilmon
Francis, Polley—Turbyfill, John
Freeman, Catharine L—Williams, David
Freeman, Jain—Rhine, Martin
Freeman, Mary—Wheelar, William
Fresham, Elizabeth—Cline, Martin
Friday, Catrin—Rudiseal, Henry
Friday, Elizabeth—Summey, Michael
Friday, Elizabeth—Smith, John
Friday, Magdalene—Abernathy, Alfred

Friday, Margaret—Link, Jacob
Friday, Mary—Summy, Jacob
Friddle, Christina Adeline—Tucker,
  William
Frieshour, Polley—Whitt, Wm
Frisle, Rachel—Foster, Cornelious
Frisset, Betsy—Lowrance, Jacob
Frizel, Saphira—Ross, Benjamin
Fronabarger, Cathrine—Rhyne, Solomon H
Fronabarger, Lydia—Ingram, John
Fronabarger, Nancy—Alexander, Moses
Fronabarger, Sarah—Friday, John N
Fronebargar, Leah—Patrick, James
Fronebarger, Anna—Kiser, Joseph
Fronebarger, Barbara—Sellers, Philip
Fronebarger, Barbara—Carpenter, Frederick
Fronebarger, Elizabeth—Huffstetler,
  Michael
Fronebarger, Lavina—Deck, Jonas
Fronebarger, Margaret—Patrick, Robert M
Fronebarger, Mary—Herren, Moses
Fronebarger, Mary—Paine, Robert
Fronebarger, Salley—Frush, Jacob
Fronebarger, Susan—Ferguson, James
Fronebarger, Susanah—Whisnant, Adam
Froneberger, Anna M—Sellers, Georg
Frost, Drusilla—Liming, Isaiah
Frost, Ica—Jenkins, Samuel
Froy, Barbara—Berry, John
Froy, Cathrein—Ashebrener, Daniel
Froy, Cristeena—Waggoner, John
Froy, Elisebeth—Bowman, Drewrey
Froy, Mary—Shell, Samuel
Fry, Anna—Rees, Lewis
Fry, Catharina—Barringer, David
Fry, Elisabeth—Whitnor, Michael
Fry, Mrs Elizabeth—Smith, John
Fry, Fany—Deal, Jonas
Fry, Harriet C—Coulter, Eli S
Fry, Lany—Seapaugh, Jacob
Fry, Lenny—Gant, Martin L
Fry, Mary Ann—Hager, George
Fry, Nancy—Shell, Solomon
Fry, Polly—Sigman, Barnet
Fry, Rhody—Huit, Moses M
Fry, Salley—Whitner, George
Fry, Susannah—Herman, David
Frye, Barbara—Cline, Nathaniel
Frye, Catherine—Smyer, Daniel
Frye, Elizabeth—Starr, Eli
Frye, Lavina—Killian, Abel
Frye, Margaret—Deal, Henry
Frye, Sally—Lutes, John
Fulbright, Elizabeth—Miller, Jacob
Fulbright, Elizabeth—Smith, Joseph
Fulbright, Polly—Yount, George
Fulbright, Polly—Knipe, John
Fulenwider, Elizabeth—Burton, Alfred M
Fulenwider, Elizabeth—Miller, W J T
Fulenwider, Frances C—McAfee,
  Lemuel Austin
Fulenwider, Mary—Burton, Robert H
Fulenwider, Mary M—Roberts, William
Fulks, Anny—Dellinger, Adam
Fullbright, Catharine—Carpenter, William J
Fullbright, Elizabeth—Hoover, Alexander
Fullenwider, Esther—Phifer, John

Fullenwider, Saley—Phifer, George
Fullenwider, Sug—Fullenwider, David
Funts, Sarah—Runce, Nicholas
Fuss, Sophia—Queen, William
Fye, Catherine—Nail, David
Fye, Elisabeth—Sigman, Jacob

Gabrial, Ruhemer—Sherrill, Alexander
Gabrial, Susana—Beatey, John
Gabriel, Agness—Tucker, Sterling
Gabriel, Mary—Beatey, Francis
Gabriel, Sarah—Parker, David
Gadberry, Nancy—Belk, West
Gaits, Sally—Shitle, Peter
Gales, Barbara—Long, Alfred
Gales, Elizabeth—Costner, Levi
Gamble, Lucinda—Love, William
Gamble, Rebeckah—Thomas, Robert
Gamble, Salley—Whitesides, Edward N
Gant, Avaline—Douglass, David
Gant, Elizabeth—Whitney, David
Gant, Mary—Heart, Sollomon
Garden, Matty—Login, Thomas
Gardener, Martha J—Norman, James S
Gardner, Antoinette—Broomhead, John J
Garel, Elender—Harden, Ruben
Garner, Becky—Srum, David
Garner, Jane—Starret, Alexander
Garner, Rebecca—Hussey, Josiah
Garner, Rebecca—Seitz, Jacob
Garnie, Susannah—Harwell, Rolly
Garrison, Emma—Paysour, George J
Garrison, Lancy—Moss, Willis
Garrison, Louisa—Richards, William
Garrison, Mima—Lowry, Dobbins
Garrison, Nancy—Cauble, Robt W
Gaskins, Jane—Hand, William P
Gaskins, Mary Ann—Holland, Judas
Gaskins, Sarah—Weather, Elisha
Gasten, Lucy Jane—Hanks, William
Gasten, Miram—Wilson, John M
Gastin, Darius—Littlejohn, Robertson
Gastin, Elisa—Reid, Allen
Gastin, Mary—Ford, George L
Gates, Nancy—White, Wm
Gates, Sarah—Self, William
Gauldney, Mayry—Parker, Nicholas
Gaultney, Cenith—Bradshaw, Josiah
Genglis, Peggy—Erwin, Isaac
Gevins, Sarrah—Wilson, James
Gibbs, Martha—Bandy, George
Gibbs, Susanna—Dillon, Henry
Gibson, Elizabeth—Robinson, William
Gibson, Elizebeth—Bradley, William D
Gibson, Jane—Stevenson, James N
Gibson, Ruth—Gregory, James J
Gilam, Lucasa—Ford, John
Gilbert, Anna—Rhonay, James
Gilbert, Barbara—Johnson, William
Gilbert, Barbara—Massagee, Abner
Gilbert, Catharine—Leonard, William
Gilbert, Eliza—Craft, George H
Gilbert, Elizabeth—Sumrow, Daniel
Gilbert, Frances J—Lingafelt, Daniel
Gilbert, Margret L—Seagle, Elam
Gilbert, Mary Ann—Hull, Comoder P

Gilbert, Polley—Flanigin, Jacob
Gilbert, Sarah—Wise, David
Gilbert, Susanah—Street, George
Gill, Levicee—Munson, William
Gillam, Hesther—McGinnas, James
Gilleland, Elizabeth—Fisher, Stephen
Gilleland, Frances—Huggins, William
Gilleland, Margaret J—Putman, Elias W
Gilleland, Polly—Fisher, James
Gillenger, Peggy—Litlejohn, Silas
Gillespie, Mary—Sterret, Alexander
Gilliland, Lydia—Clark, Burgess
Gingles, Elizabeth—Gullick, Benaiah
Gingles, Margaret—Harris, John
Gingles, Melissa J—Finley, Alexander
Gingles, Patsey—Robinson, Gideon
Ginkens, Elizabeth—Romefelt, Abraham
Gipson, Nancy—Costner, Lawrance
Givens, Jain—White, Isaac
Givens, Nancy—Davidson, John
Givens, Sarah L—Hovis, Joseph
Gladden, Lina—Williams, James
Gladden, Martha—Lackey, Wm
Gladen, Elizabeth—Whiseant, David
Gladen, Mary Ann—Lackey, Edward
Glammer, Eliza—Tetherrow, John
Glen, Jean—Roberts, Thomas
Glen, Margrat—Ramsy, Robert
Glenn, Adline—Dorty, Henry
Glenn, Agness—Ramsey, Solomon
Glenn, Elizabeth—Martin, James
Glenn, Elizabeth—Davis, Thomas
Glenn, Elizabeth—Willis, Solomon
Glenn, Frances H—Ragan, Daniel F
Glenn, Jane—Wilson, Samuel
Glenn, Margaret S—Detter, George
Glenn, Milley—Brannum, William
Glenn, Nancy—Glenn, Stanhope
Glenn, Rachel—Brown, Elijah P
Goble, Sally—Warren, Elijah
Goble, Susana—Yount, Jonathan
Godfrey, Maryanne—Smith, Samuel
Goforth, Elizabeth—Patterson, Samuel B
Goforth, Pricilla Ann—Dickson, John
Goforth, Rachel—Patterson, John M
Goforth, Sally—Goforth, William C
Gofourth, Elizabeth—Weir, John D
Goings, Sally—Smith, Jeremiah
Goins, Sarah—Workman, Henry
Golden, Betsey—Horton, George
Golding, Hanah—Dellinger, Andrew
Goldman, Hannah—King, William
Goldman, Hannah—Smith, Moses
Gooden, Sarah—Smith, Charles W
Goodin, Abby—Edwards, Lewis
Goodin, Elizabeth—Baxter, Peter
Gooding, Rebecca—Banday, Thomas
Gooding, Susanna—Abernathy, Turner
Goodson, Ann—Cronland, C R F
Goodson, Caroline—Keever, James
Goodson, Elizabeth—Sanders, Edward
Goodson, Hannah—Stroup, David
Goodson, Hetty—Abernathy, C M
Goodson, Holly—Abernathy, George W
Goodson, Jane—Abernathy, Caleb
Goodson, Jean—Stroup, Michael
Goodson, Mahala—Daily, Lawson

Goodson, Malinda—Sanders, Miles A
Goodson, Margaret—Armstrong, John
Goodson, Mary—Dellinger, John G
Goodson, Mary A—Hudgpeth, Thos A
Goodson, Mary E—Michael, John M
Goodson, Mary L—Sherrill, J A
Goodson, Michel—Richards, John B
Goodson, Milly—Keever, David
Goodson, Nancy—Tolbert, William
Goodson, Polly—Stroup, Daniel
Goodson, Polly—Wood, William
Goodson, Rebecca—Goodson, Jacob
Goodson, Rebekah—Goodson, William
Goodson, Susan—Lehmans, Francis J
Goodson, Winny—Keener, Lawson W
Goodwin, Mary—Killen, William
Goodwin, Milley—Cook, David
Goodwin, Polly—Moore, John
Goodwin, Tempe—Haines, James
Gooldman, Anna—Going, Wiley
Gordon, Elinor—Henry, Malcolm
Gordon, Torethey—Wells, John
Gowing, Nancey—Mahew, Aaron
Gowins, Julia—Roderick, Nicholas
Grabel, Rachel—Forney, Abrm
Graham, Betsey—Price, Ezekial
Graham, Elizabeth E—Moore, William T
Graham, Isabella—Wilson, William
Graham, Jane—Morris, William W
Graham, Jane—Maclain, William B
Graham, Malvina S—Young, John A
Graham, Mary—Morrison, R H
Graham, Nancy—Carruth, Adam
Graham, Sophia—Witherspoon, John R
Graham, Sophia N—Herndon, Joseph
Graham, Sophynealy—Bostick, Littleberry
Graham, Vilet W—Alexander, Moses W
Grant, Barbara—Slinker, Fredrick
Graves, Polly D—Holland, Isaac
Gray, Nancy—Sudduth, John
Green, Elisabeth—Partin, Henry
Green, Joanna—Cline, Elkana
Green, Nancy—Green, David
Green, Sidney E—Justice, Alex
Greenhill, Eliza A—Brindle, Wesley
Greenhill, Luiza—Boiles, Joseph
Greenhill, Sarah—Gales, Jacob A
Gregorey, Margret—Carter, Erwin
Gregory, Elizabeth—Grissim, Martin
Gregory, Frances—Glenn, Robert
Gregory, Susan—Branon, William
Greyham, Elisabeth—Quin, Henry
Greyham, Margaret—Green, Joseph
Greyham, Polley—Quin, Richard
Greyhem, Catey—Foley, Washington
Green L
Grice, Agness—Rector, Silas
Grice, Anne E—Drum, Eli
Grice, Martha C—Grice, William M
Grice, Mary—Reynolds, Fergus H
Grigg, Jane—Bess, Noah
Griggs, Fanny—Glenn, Alexander
Grise, Martha E—Bolinger, Abraham A
Grisenbery, Mary—Dormyer, David
Grisom, Martha F—Jonston, William
Grissim, Elizabeth—Glenn, David
Grissim, Mary—Glenn, John

Grissom, Hannah Fininger—Rogers, Thomas
Grissom, Mary S—Suggs, Levi H
Grissom, Sarah—Slate, Benjamin
Grissum, Sopphia—Bell, James
Groce, Catharine—Leonard, Charles
Grose, Marimacdalene—Spegle, David
Grose, Mary—Ashebrener, Abraham
Gross, Anne—Killian, Frederick
Gross, Catharine—Hudson, Daniel
Gross, Catharine—Seitz, Abel
Gross, Etty—Fry, Jonas
Gross, Lydia—Setzer, Paul
Gross, Lydia—Hunsuker, John
Gross, Malinda—Whitener, Philip
Gross, Margaret—Hull, Major
Gross, Margaret—Huver, Philip
Gross, Mary—Wilfong, Martin
Gross, Mary—Seitz, Moses
Gross, Nancy—Wyant, S Washington
Gross, Rebeca—McClurg, John
Gross, Sary—Bengle, Henry
Gross, Suey—Stine, Daniel
Gross, Tenea—Huit, Joseph
Grosse, Elizabeth—Gooden, Aaron
Grosse, Margret—Propst, Josiah A
Groves, Anny—Boldwin, Armsted
Groves, Elizebeth—Johnston, John
Groves, Sarah—Johnston, Henry
Gualtney, Susanna—Eddleman, Bostian
Guinn, Betcey—Mann, Thomas
Gullick, Jane—Berry, James
Gullick, Jane Caldwell—Stowe, Littleberry
Gullick, Mary—Spencer, John H
Gullick, Nancy—Henry, William
Gunn, Jane—Herron, Joshua
Guthrey, Elizabeth—Proctor, Thomas O
Gutrey, Nancy—Whitener, Philip B
Gwaltney, Elizabeth—Killian, Daniel

Hafner, Caroline C—Hull, M M
Hafner, Catharine—Hauser, Jacob
Hafner, Eliza E—Leonhardt, Jacob M
Hafner, Margaret A—Boggs, Andrew N
Hafner, Mary—Harris, James
Hafner, Sarah—Houser, Peter
Hagar, Peneleth—Whitesides, Wallaes
Hagarty, Nancey—Kuykandall, John
Hager, Ann—Hager, Henry
Hager, Ann—Barnett, Joseph
Hager, Anne—Abernathy, Shadrach
Hager, Barbara—Edwards, Joseph
Hager, Betcy—Hager, William
Hager, Betsy—Hager, George
Hager, Catharine—Smith, David
Hager, Dilly Ann—Lucky, William
Hager, Ebby—Bryant, James
Hager, Hannah—Cobb, Thomas
Hager, Isabella—Barnett, Arthur F
Hager, Jane—Cashion, William J
Hager, Lucy B—Covington, John
Hager, M L—Hager, A M
Hager, Marey—Steely, Lovick
Hager, Margaret—Carpenter, Daniel
Hager, Martha—Holdsclaw, Lewis
Hager, Mary—Bryan, John

Hager, Mary—Edleman, Henry
Hager, Mary—Rudasill, John
Hager, Mary A—Duckworth, Robert A
Hager, Mary Jane—Hager, G W
Hager, Mary M—Hager, Simon
Hager, Pricilla—McEntosh, William
Hager, Rachael A—Nixon, Albert M
Hager, Racheal H—Hager, J M
Hager, Rebecca A—Hager, John H
Hager, Salley—Clark, Jonathan
Hager, Sally—Frost, James
Hager, Sarah Caroline—Knipe, Henry
Hager, Sarah L—Norwood, James T
Hahn, Elisabeth—Shell, Charles F
Haine, Mary—Shafer, John
Haines, Didamey—Crowder, William N
Haines, Martha J—Huffman, Samuel
Haines, Mary—Conley, George
Haines, Nancy—Horton, George
Hains, Peggy—Dellinger, Peter
Hains, Rosanah—Morrison, John
Hair, Margaret—Miraile, Lorance
Hais, Ann—McLean, Alexander
Hall, Jeane—Kuykendall, Jesse, Capt
Hall, Susana—Herrington, Whitmel
Hallman, -------—Smith, Abraham
Hallman, Amey—Tucker, Levi
Hallman, Mrs B K—Goodson, H M
Hallman, Barbara—Summer, Jacob
Hallman, Delila—Probst, Abel J
Hallman, Isabella—Keener, Cephas
Hallman, Martha E—Hartzoge, Danl M
Hallman, Mary J—Bolick, Robert
Hallman, Mary S—Hallman, Andrew
Hallmon, Elizabeth—Stroup, Christopher
Halman, Barbara—Cline, Jacob Sr
Halman, Elizabeth—Campbell, John
Hally, Mary—Puntch, William
Hambleton, Ran—Cole, Ephraim
Hambleton, Sarah—Gladin, Moses
Hambright, Mary—Little, George
Hambright, Sarah—Eaker, Peter
Hamilton, Elizabeth—Yount, Andrew
Hamilton, Ellender—Dunn, Thomas
Hamilton, Jane—Hoover, Thomas
Hamilton, Jean—Shannon, James
Hamilton, Lucy—Jinkins, Edward
Hamilton, Margaret—Lollar, Jacob
Hamilton, Martha—Hofman, Eli
Hamilton, Mary—McCaver, John
Hamilton, Patsey—M'Callister, John
Hamilton, Patsey—M'Caver, James
Hamilton, Rebeca—Perkins, James
Hammentree, Nancy—Edwards, Mark
Hampton, Elizabeth—Phillips, Greenbury
Hampton, Sarah Ann—Stirewalt, Valentine
Hamsley, Doshey—Black, Ephraim
Hamsley, Jean—Ledford, William
Hand, Rebecca C—Rankin, N A
Hanes, Sarah—Stacy, William
Hanks, Adaline—Jonas, Daniel
Hanks, Ann—Brown, Luke
Hanks, Mary—Harris, James A
Hanks, Polly—Swan, Isaac
Hanna, Sarah—McMurry, Edward
Hannah, Ann L—Martin, William S
Hansel, Elizabeth—Maskal, William

Hansel, Elizabeth—Wingate, Peter
Hansel, Lavina—Mauney, George
Hansel, Martha—Armstrong, Thomas
Hansel, Mary—Hansel, Henry
Hansel, Sarah S—Black, James G
Hansel, Winey—Kincaide, David
Hansell, B—Kingcade, David
Hansell, Sarah—Edwards, Robert
Harbison, Mira—Laurance, Nicholas
Harbison, Sally M—Wilson, Andrew
Harden, Susannah—Hartley, Tilman
Harding, A A—West, W B
Hardy, Mary T—Thompson, John
Hare, Charlotte—Mathias, Samuel
Harill, Nancy—Abernathy, Samuel
Harman, Elizabeth—Kingery, Daniel
Harman, Elizabeth—Harman, Presten
Harman, Mary—Dietz, Lazarus
Harmon, Harriet—Mincy, Moses
Harmon, Julian—Huffstickler, David
Harmon, Martha—Cobb, William
Harmon, Mary Ann—Spencer, Grisiam
Harmon, Ruannah—Harmon, Robert C
Harmon, Sarah—Fox, Elisha
Harrell, Malinda—Mills, Daniel
Harrelson, Elizabeth—Henry, John
Harris, C A J—Black, C N
Harris, Elisabeth—Baker, V E
Harris, Elizabeth—Roberts, Moses
Harris, Eve—Alexander, Newman
Harris, Malinda—Havner, Lawson
Harris, Nancy—Dettor, David
Harris, Nancy—Cline, Amon
Harris, Susanah—Kuykendall, Samuel
Harrison, Peggy—Sadler, Alfred
Harriss, Adaline—Lewis, C P
Harriss, Sarah—Carpenter, P H
Harry, Ann Elizabeth—Bridges, Thomas
Harry, Julian—Hopper, John Alexander
Harry, Mary Nell—Benton, Buckley K
Hart, Elizabeth—Clark, James
Harthorn, Polley—Edgin, Samuel
Hartwell, Sarah—Robinson, John
Hartzoch, Caroline—Hartzoke, William A
Hartzog, F B—Haynes, John F
Hartzog, Julia Ann—Campbell, Andrew
Hartzog, Mary E—Berrier, Henry J
Hartzoke, Chrisnia—Shell, David
Harvill, Catherine E—Barkley, Thomas J
Harwell, Anna—Fisher, Richd
Harwell, Betsey—Sherrill, Levi
Harwell, Cynthia—Winters, John
Harwell, Jenny—Fisher, William
Harwell, Patsey—Abernathy, Buckner
Haskins, Jenny—Earwood, Frederick
Haskins, Mary—Sutherlin, Thomas
Haskins, Nancy—Stroup, Solomon
Haskins, Susanah—Earwood, William
Haun, Cathrina—Whitener, David B
Haun, Cathrina—Yoder, Jacob
Haun, Sarah—Miller, John
Haun, Sally—Trout, William
Haus, Anna—Mauny, Maxwill
Haus, Martha—Hafner, Frederick
Haus, Mary—Houser, Joseph
Haus, Mary Adaline—Sullivan, George L
Haus, Susan—Miller, John T

Haus, Susannah—Reep, Philip
Hause, Catharine—Havener, John
Hause, Catherine—Williams, William
Hause, Christina—Burns, John
Hause, Eliza S—Haynes, James H
Hause, Elizabeth—Moore, Alfred
Hause, Elizabeth—Blackburn, Daniel
Hause, Elizabeth—Shell, John
Hause, Sarah—Spratt, William
Hause, Susanah—Linhardt, Joseph
Hauser, Barbara—Hauss, Peter
Hauss, Barbara—Morrison, Robert
Hauss, C C—Willkie, James L
Hauss, Catharine—Helms, Pinckney
Hauss, Clara Anna—Sullivan, Ezekiel M
Hauss, Elizabeth—Shull, C W
Hauss, Frances G—Curry, Elam A M
Hauss, Jane—Ramsey, E D
Hauss, Mrs Linna—Massagee, Benj M
Hauss, Margaret—Cline, Jessa
Hauss, Mary—Mauny, Maxvill
Hauss, Nancey C—Mullens, John F
Hauss, Sarah—Tutherow, Solomon
Havener, Ann—Sneed, Edward
Havener, Barbara—Mauney, Peter
Havener, Barbara—Leonard, Franklin
Havener, Elizabeth—Jordon, Jesse
Havener, Mahala—Bridges, Gilbert
Havener, Mary—Reinhardt, Felix
Havener, Polley—Black, Joseph
Havener, Sarah A—Leonhardt, Jacob M
Havner, Ann Elizabeth—Seagle, Andrew
Havner, Anna—Wise, Henry
Havner, Catharine—Long, James
Havner, Catherine—Morris, Joseph
Havner, Eliza—Yelton, James
Havner, Eliza E—Havner, George H
Havner, Jane—Gilbert, Daniel
Havner, Lavina—Mosteller, Eli
Havner, Margaret—Mauney, Michael
Havner, Martha J—Farmer, John H
Havner, Mary—Abernathy, Eli
Havner, Mary—Hafner, Stephen
Havner, Mary—Crowder, John
Havner, Mary—Kiser, Ephraim
Havner, Nancy—Jacobs, Michael
Havner, Sally—Greenhill, Philip
Havner, Sarah—Leonhardt, John F
Havner, Sarah—Brown, George
Havner, Susan—Beam, Joshua
Havner, Susanah—Moore, Wilk
Hawkins, Anna—Anthony, Jonathan
Hawkins, Elizabeth—King, William
Hawkins, Elmina—Garison, Alfred
Hawkins, Lucy—Mason, William H
Hawkins, Ruth—Holland, Daniel
Hawkins, Sally—Hamontree, John
Hawkins, Sarah—Wallis, David
Hawn, Anna—Hawn, Christian
Hawn, Anna M—Dietz, Emanuel
Hawn, Charity—Barger, David
Hawn, Elizabeth—Barger. John
Hawn, Eve—Baldasor, Andrew
Hawn, Fanny—Whitney, Zeno
Hawn, Hanna—Traffanstatt, Peter
Hawn, Hannah—Settlemire, George
Hawn, Jenny—Hager. John

Hawn, Molly—Helton, Joel
Hawn, Polly—Weaver, Ephraim
Hawn, Rachael—Yoder, Peter
Hawn, Sally—Bowman, Solomon
Hayes, Jane J—Harris, Sidney J
Hayes, Margaret J—Adams, William E
Hayes, Minerva—Greer, William M
Haynes, Belsora—Stamey, Alexander
Haynes, Caroline—Hawkins, J R
Haynes, Marth—Robinson, Samuel
Haynes, Mary Jane—Haynes, James C
Haynes, Sophia—Macaslin, Robert
Haynes, Susan C—Pryor, Stuart L
Hays, Elizabeth L—Torrence, Charles L
Hays, Martha E—Fulenwider, William
Hazlet, Elizabeth—Moore, Ezekiel
Heaker, Elizabeth—Bynum, John
Hedgcock, Eliby—Ross, John
Hedgcock, Elisabeth—Brown, Moses
Hedick, Barbara E—Collier, Wm T
Hedick, Catherine—Rudsill, Michael
Hedick, Margaret Malinda—Moser,
     Timothy
Hedick, Polley—Beanack, Henry
Hedick, Sarah—Lore, John
Hedrick, Leah—Lagle, John
Hedrick, Lise—Popst, Amos
Hedrick, Magtelena—Null, Jacob
Hedrick, Susannah—Wineberger, Conrad
Hedrick, Susannah—Johnson, Joseph
Hedspeth, Caroline—Brown, John
Heedick, Belzora—Michael, George W
Heedick, E C—Aderholdt, Marcus
Heedick, Mary—Ditton, Nicholas
Heffner, Rachel—Lafon, Daniel
Hefnar, Catharina—Moretz, John
Hefnar, Catherina—Brower, John
Hefnar, Evi—Goble, Lewis
Hefner,------—Moser, John
Hefner, Catherine—Hedrick, Joseph
Hefner, Eliza—Miller, John
Hefner, Elizabeth—Drum, Peter
Hefner, Sarah—Bowman, Jesse
Hegar, Barbara—Killian, Samuel
Helderman, Fany—Brown, George
Helderman, Julia C—Eudy, M J
Helderman, Mary—Reel, Jacob B
Helderman, Mary Ann C—Black, Milas D
Helderman, S R D—Clippard, D E
Helderman, Susannah—Low, Rufus
Helms, Ann—Wisenhunt, Philip
Helms, Anna—Farmer, John
Helms, Anne—Jeffres, Thomas
Helms, Barbara—Hull, Daniel
Helms, Catharine—Bangle, Henry
Helms, Elisabeth—Bevins, Joseph
Helms, Eliza—Tramel, James
Helms, Elizabeth—Ivester, John
Helms, Mary—Smith, William
Helms, Nancy A F—Workmon, Jacob L K
Helms, Visey—Eaker, Joseph
Heltebrand, Elizabeth—Jarrett, John
Heltebrand, Susanna—Blackburn, James
Heltenbrand, Mary—Clark, James
Helterbrant, Mrs Sarah—Delane, Alvin
Helton, Mary—Havener, Walter
Helton, Sarah Ann—Jenkins, Benjamin

Henderson, Adeline—Sample, Robert M
Henderson, Amanda—Thompson, Monroe
Henderson, Barbara M—Cobb, Bartlett Y
Henderson, Elizabeth—Martin, Adam M
Henderson, Fannie A—Davis, George L
Henderson, Issabella—Devenport, William
Henderson, Jane A A—Moon, A A
Henderson, Margaret B—Shaw, John D
Henderson, Martha—Miller, William
Henderson, Mary—Patterson, John
Henderson, Mary G—Herndon, Thomas N
Henderson, Mary Helen—Hoyle, Laban A
Henderson, Patsey—McCoy, James
Henderson, Sarah—Fish, James
Hendricks, Polley—Rumfelt, Hezekiah
Hendrix, Elizabeth—Toler, William
Henkel, Leah—Ingold, Henry
Henkle, Christina—Walker, Osbirn W
Henkle, Eliza—Burke, Green
Henkle, Malinda—Sides, Simon
Henkle, Nancy—Edleman, Jacob
Henry, Barbra—Sumerow, Henry
Henry, Elizabeth—Dameron, Edward B
Henry, Isabella—Carl, Joseph
Henry, Isabella—Ratchford, John
Henry, Jane—Leeper, Matthew
Henry, Jane—Byars, Edward
Henry, Margaret—Leeper, James
Henry, Margaret—Hallman, Ambrose
Henry, Nancy M—Ratchford, Moses
Henry, Narcissa—Hand, Moses H
Henry, Rachel—McClure, John
Henry, Rebecka—Hand, Aaron
Henry, Resign—Sinclair, John
Henry, Sarah—Anthony, Gideon
Herbeson, Rebecca—Bollinger, David
Herman, Cathrine—Bovy, John
Herman, Elizabeth—Flowers, Joseph
Herman, Helena—Fry, Daniel
Herman, Leah—Barger, Jesse
Herman, Polly—Bovey, Matthias
Herman, Sally—Van Dike, William
Hermon, Barbra—Hains, Lenord
Hermon, Elizabeth—Powell, Philip
Hermon, Nercisis—Beam, John T
Herndon, Mary W—Dickerson, J L
Heron, Elizabeth—Hoffstetele, Lawson
Herron, Abagil—Fraley, Stephen
Hertle, Cathrine—Bolick, Gotfree
Hetrek, Ann—Robinson, Emanuel
Hevener, Haty—Bennett, Abraham
Hewet, Ladecy—Sigman, Henry
Hewet, Salley—Head, John
Hicks, Epsey—Blalock, Andrew A
Hicks, Phebba—Clifton, William
Hide, Margret—Johnston, Elijah
Hill, Anna—Wilson, Ezra B
Hill, Elerna—Ford, James M
Hill, Eliza E—Heavner, Henry P
Hill, Elizabeth—Barkley, Archd C
Hill, Fannie E—Heavner, M L
Hill, Fanny—Finison, John
Hill, Frances I—Ford, Alberry R
Hill, Jane—Jackson, Abner
Hill, Jane—Edwards, Edmond
Hill, Margery N—Lowrance, Logan H
Hill, Martha A—Shull, Joseph D

Hill, Mary—Ford, Lawson
Hill, Mary C—Jones, Isom I
Hill, P C—Hutchison, James
Hill, Peggy—Waddel, James
Hill, Polly—Henry, John
Hill, Polly—Fleming, Robert
Hill, Rachel L—Hoyle, Jacob
Hill, Rebecca—Sadler, Thomas
Hill, Salina—Ford, Hugh M
Hill, Sarah—Clark, Robt H
Hill, Sarah M C—Bevins, John H
Hiltebrand, Salley—Kistler, Jacob
Hilton, Frances—Cobb, James
Hilton, Nancy—Cobb, Henry
Hincle, Catharine—Tucker, William
Hines, Mary Ann—Dellinger, David
Hinkle, Elisabeth—Hinkle, John
Hinkle, Margaret—Hager, Frederick
Hinkle, Susan—Connel, William P
Hinkle, Susana—Benick, Philip
Hinkle, Winnie M—Armstrong, John R
Hinson, Elizabeth—Garrison, John
Hinson, Mary—Canseler, Henry
Hintz—see Arntz
Hoagens, Salley—Bamber, Jurdan
Hoard, Rebeca A—Williams, Alexander
Hobbs, Eliza—Mayhew, J B J H
Hobbs, Mary—Hobbs, William C
Hobbs, Nancy—Cauble, P V
Hobbs, Nancy—Linebarger, John
Hobbs, Sarah—London, A J
Hobbs, Susannah—Anthony, Joseph D
Hofstatler, Matty—Rhoads, Daniel
Hogan, Betsey—Bradshaw, Josiah
Hogans, Elizabeth—Jenkins, David
Hogin, Caty—Conlay, Neal
Hogue, Easter—Cross, Zebulon
Hohnau, Elizabeth—Fisher, John
Hoiles, Barbery—Twigse, David
Hoke, Ann—Dietz, David
Hoke, Ann—Abernathy, Miles W
Hoke, Annah—Roseman, Daniel
Hoke, Anthea—Jetton, B M
Hoke, Barbara—Hoyle, David R
Hoke, Cammilla—Houser, Lawson
Hoke, Catharine—Robinson, Levi
Hoke, Catherine—Henkel, Ambrose
Hoke, Catherine—Summey, Peter W
Hoke, Elisabeth—Quickel, Michael
Hoke, Elizabeth—Rouch, Daniel
Hoke, Euphemia—Beam, Jacob M
Hoke, Jamime—Stirewalt, Michael
Hoke, Mary Brent—Smith, H Hildreth
Hoke, Nancy—Childs, Lysander D
Hoke, Polly—Brady, Albert
Hoke, Rhoda L—Allen, Burrell C
Hoke, Rosanna E—Rhodes, Jacob H
Hoke, Sally—Smith, George
Hoke, Sarah—Lantz, Jacob
Hoke, Sarah—Forney, Jacob
Hoke, Sarah E—Crook, A B
Hoke, Sarah E—Hudspeth, Ayres
Hoke, Susannah—Lowrance, Robert F
Holdbrooks, Ann—Blake, Aaron
Holdbrooks, Catharine A—Ballard,
    Thomas J
Holes Claw, Elizabeth—Smith John

Holland, Anne—Center, Steven
Holland, Elizabeth—Haynes, James
Holland, Jane—Martin, Zadok
Holland, M E—Friday, Ephraim
Holland, Margaret M—Stowe, Samuel N
Holland, Margret—Jenkins, Reuben
Holland, Martina—Smith, Andrew
Holland, Mary—Dickson, John
Holland, Mary—Smith, Joseph
Holland, Rebecca—Morris, Benjamin
Hollar, Christina—Banday, John
Hollar, Lavina—Sipe, Joseph
Hollar, Nancy—Townsend, Andrew
Hollen, Margaret—Cox, Elisha
Holler, Anne—Finger, Peter
Holleway, Jean—Wyatt, William
Holliman, Elizabeth—Sifford, Miles L
Holliman, Ann—Shrum, Levi
Hollman, Anny—Dellinger, John
Hollman, Elleanor—Sain, Winehardt
Hollman, Elmira—Sain, Solomon
Hollman, Mary Catharine—Bridges, John L
Hollman, Susan—Summerrour, James
Holloway, Sarah—Hammontree, Jeremiah
Holly, Anna—Justice, Abraham
Holman, ------—Blackburn, John
Holman, Anne—Gilbert, George
Holman, Barbara—Cline, David
Holman, Catherine—Hoyle, John
Holman, Catherine—Clark, Jephtha
Holman, Fanny—Rudisill, William
Holman, Rachel—Cline, John
Holman, Sahra—Fisher, Joseph
Holman, Sarah—Smith, Thomas
Holmesly, Jane—McGinnas, Wiley W
Holmesly, Lena—Taylor, John
Holmesly, Sarah—Wilson, Samuel P
Holmon, Sarah—Hauss, David
Homer, Betcy—Havner, John
Homesly, Hester—Black, Ephraim
Homesly, Jemima—Dellinger, Charles
Homest, Ana—Parker, Wm
Hood, Jaine—Kincaid, Thomas
Hood, Marey—Whitworth, Southerland
Hook, Susanna—Hufman, Geo
Hooke, Sally—Fox, Hugh
Hooper, Annie M—Keen, James
Hooper, Eletha B—Bleckley, Thomas C
Hooper, Eliza—Hooper, John
Hoover, Catharine—Perkins, Avery
Hoover, Catharine E—Wise, Andrew N
Hoover, Catherine—Seagle, Daniel
Hoover, Elizabeth—Kistler, Jacob
Hoover, Elminah—Oliver, Pleasant
Hoover, Eve—Brem, Jacob
Hoover, Frances E—Shitel, Pinkney
Hoover, Lina S—Seagle, Monroe
Hoover, Margaret C—Shuford, J S
Hoover, Martha—Sain, Barna M
Hoover, Martha Ann—Aderholdt, John A F
Hoover, Mary—Seitz, George
Hoover, Myra—Williams, Thomas
Hoover, Salley—Seagle, Daniel
Hoover, Sarah Ann—Ogle, William B
Hoover, Susan—Self, Berryman H
Hope, Betcy—Low, William
Hope, Eliza Phoebe—Clanton, David F

Hope, Katharine—Totherow, Eli
Hope, Leana—Cobb, Robert
Hope, Louisa—Painter, Elisha S
Hope, Margaret—Smith, Peter
Hope, Mary—Thomas, Aaron
Hope, Polly—Sherrill, Leander B
Hope, Susannah—Ward, Isaac
Horse, Catharine—Fox, Jacob
Horse, Elizabeth—Williams, Joel
Horse, Mary—Drum, Philip
Hortan, Sarah—Colter, John
Horten, Nancey—Coon, Adam
Horton, Agy—Wyette, Thomas
Horton, Elisabeth—Jones, Charles
Hosselbarger, Susana—Loar, George
Hostatler, Margaret—Sumy, Michal
Hostetler, Barbara—Flonabarger, John
Hostotlor, Betsy—Shrum, Nickles
Houser, Ann C—Wise, Jacob
Houser, Cathrine—Williams, D F
Houser, Eliza—Hoyl, John A
Houser, Elizabeth—Sain, Jno
Houser, Elizabeth—Beam, Peter
Houser, Fanny—Dellinger, Daniel
Houser, Harriet S—Clay, M C
Houser, Julia A—Hillebrand, Peter
Houser, Liddy—Hass, Peter
Houser, Margaret C—Rhyne, Lauson
Houser, Margeret—Sain, Levi
Houser, Mary—Reep, Peter
Houser, Mary—Rhyne, Simon
Houser, Mary—Lingerfelt, Daniel
Houser, Mary E—Huss, Henry
Houser, Molly—Finger, Henry Jr
Houser, S A F—Bess, J F
Houston, Easter—Cloer, Elisha
Houston, Jane—Byars, Robert
Houston, Mary—Hawkins, Burwell
Houten, Hester—Dilling, William
Hover, Polly—Perkins, John
Hover, Sarah Ann—Wyont, Daniel
Hovis, Anna—Summey, David
Hovis, Catharine—Cloninger, Michael
Hovis, Cathrine—Hoyl, Samuel Smith
Hovis, Cathrine—Linebarger, Michael
Hovis, Charity—Hawkins, Elisha
Hovis, Elenor—Kenedy, Robert
Hovis, Elizabeth—Huffman, Martin J
Hovis, Elizabeth—Rhyne, Daniel
Hovis, Elizabeth—Cloninger, Moses
Hovis, Fanny—Bynum, John
Hovis, Frances—Nance, David L
Hovis, Lucinda—Starnes, John F
Hovis, Malinda—Andres, James
Hovis, Martha—Nance, James
Hovis, Mary—Linebarger, Fredrick
Hovis, Mary—Starnes, William
Hovis, Mary C—Richards, A P
Hovis, Mary M—Friday, Jonas
Hovis, Rosannah—Lefsey, Shederick
Hovis, Sally—Cloninger, Philip
Hovis, Sally—Carpenter, Joel
Hovis, Saloma—Rudisel, Jacob
Hovis, Sosana—Hoyl, Peter
Hovis, Susan—Hines, Daniel
Hovis, Susan—Hovis, Caleb
Hovis, Susan—Healms, Joshua T

Hoviss, Susannah—Rudiseale, David
Howard, Ann—McCall, John
Howard, Betsy—McMin, Daniel
Howard, Catharine—Howard, Franklin
Howard, Elisebeth—Lowman, Martin
Howard, Elizabeth—Kayler, Eli
Howard, Jane—Pryor, Samuel
Howard, Mary—Cronkleton, James
Howard, Mary—Thompson, John T
Howard, Mary M—Fisher, William G
Howard, Millie L—King, Wm O
Howard, Minerva—Brotherton, John
Howard, Nancy—Childers, John
Howard, Nancy—Brotherton, Thomas
Howard, Patsy—Childers, William
Howard, Polly—McMin, John
Howard, Polly—Allen, Levi
Howard, Racheal E—Howard, Jackson A
Howard Rachel R—McConnell, T A
Howard, Rebecca—Kelly, Wm F
Howell, Mary—Morris, Joseph W
Howerd, Jane—Odam, George
Howerd, Pecky—Cogswell, William
Howser, Anna—Buff, Henry
Howser, Catharine—Sain, Jacob
Howser, Elizabeth—Reep, Emanuel
Howser, Eulia—Spangler, Frederick
Howser, Lidia—Sain, Joseph
Hoyl, Anne—Mendenhall, Robert
Hoyl, Betsey—Best, Christin
Hoyl, Elizabeth—Hanks, David
Hoyl, Elizabeth—Hill, Lawson H
Hoyl, Elmina C—Hines, Bryan
Hoyl, Margaret M—Tomkies, John F
Hoyl, Salama—Greer, Andrew
Hoyl, Violet—Carpenter, Jacob
Hoyle, Anne—Carpenter, Henry
Hoyle, Barbara—Leonard, Charles
Hoyle, Catharine—Henkel, David
Hoyle, Eliza—Robinson, Aaron
Hoyle, Elizabeth—Friday, Andrew
Hoyle, Frances C—Holly, M A
Hoyle, Lucinda—Weathers, John A
Hoyle, Margaret—Reinhardt, Jacob
Hoyle, Margaret—Rhyne, Michael
Hoyle, Margaret—Howel, Joshua
Hoyle, Margaret E—Whitener, Henry
Hoyle, Margaret E—Lusk, Lucius Y
Hoyle, Maria Louisa C—Hallman, Jacob
Hoyle, Martha L—Fisher, Lawson
Hoyle, Mary—Hoover, David
Hoyle, Mary A—Carpenter, Noah C
Hoyle, Mrs Nancy H V—Lewis, Edward
Hoyle, Polley—Fulenwider, Jacob
Hoyle, Polly—Wehunt, John
Hoyle, Rhoda—Gant, Tiry
Hoyle, Salley—Hooper, Elias
Hoyle, Sarah A—Peterson, C J
Hoyle, Susan—Shuford, Ephraim
Hoyle, Veronica—Henkel, Ambrose
Hubard, Luisa—Canipe, Daniel
Hubbard, Eliza—Bevins, Jacob
Huchison, Elizabeth—Cobb, John
Hudson, Elizabeth—Stamey, John
Hudson, Elizabeth—Speegle, Martin
Hudson, Sally—Speegle, Solomon
Hues, Fanny—Sholl, Charles

Huffman, Amy—Punch, Wm F
Huffman, Anna—Spencer, John
Huffman, Betsey—Rhyne, Solomon
Huffman, Catarine—Rhyne, Michael
Huffman, Elisabeth—Dietz, Solomon
Huffman, Elizabeth—Rhyne, Jacob
Huffman, Fanny—Raby, Robert
Huffman, Julianna—Bolch, Casper
Huffman, Katharine—Rhyne, Daniel
Huffman, Lucinda—Turner, Gabriel H
Huffman, Margaret—Srum, Andrew
Huffman, Margrat L—Rhyne, Moses H
Huffman, Mary—M'Colister, William
Huffman, Mary—Hanks, Ezekiel
Huffman, Myra—Rhodes, Caleb
Huffman, Nancy—Deal, Anthony
Huffman, Polly—Cline, William
Huffman, Rebeca—Rhyne, Jonathan
Huffman, Sally—Drum, Joseph
Huffman, Susanah—Jenkins, James
Huffman, Susanna—Costner, Jonas
Huffman, Tabitha—Seabach, John
Huffmon, Catherine—Bolick, Adam
Huffstetler, Betsy—McGrath, Edward
Huffstetler, Elizabeth—Brady, James
Huffstetler, Margret—Jenkins, Smith
Huffstettler, Mary Magdelene—Wilson, Ephraim
Huffstotler, Charity—Hoffstiler, David
Huffstotler, Mary—Gibson, James
Huffstotler, Mary—Pasour, Samuel
Huffstotler, Polley—Bishop, Edmond N
Huffstotler, Susanah—Neel, Moses
Hufman, Elisabeth—Palmer, Jesse
Hufman, Hannah—Clemer, John
Hufman, Susan—Linebarger, Caleb
Hufstutler, Sally—Summy, John
Hugens, Rebecka—Ramsey, Samuel
Huggin, Jane—Cox, Elijah
Huggins, Ann—Armstrong, John
Huggins, Cynthia—Mauny, Noah
Huggins, Elisabeth—Holland, John
Huggins, Eliza—McKisick, James
Huggins, Margarett E—Ballard, Philip
Huggins, Mary—Willis, J F
Huggins, Sarah—Stamy, John
Hugins, Mary—Eaker, Abraham
Hull, Caroline—Taylor, William
Hull, Catharine—Stowe, Allen R
Hull, Eliza—Goode, B F
Hull, Elizabeth—Wacaser, Abraham
Hull, Elizabeth—Hoyl, Peter C
Hull, Hannah—Anthony, John A
Hull, M L—King, J C
Hull, Mary—Mull, Henry
Hull, Mary Ann—Jenks, O B
Hull, Mary Ann—Whetstine, D M
Hull, Nancy—Massagee, John
Hull, Polly—Cody, Curtis
Hull, Rebeckah—Whetstine, David·
Hull, Sally—Wacaster, John
Hull, Winney—Smith, Jeremiah
Hullet, Elizabeth—Houghstetlar, Michael
Hullet, Janey—Mauny, Jonas
Hullet, Martha E—Brown, Robt F
Hullet, Sarah—Kysor, John
Hullet, Susanna—Kyser, Christian

Humphrys, C Susannah—Walls, Alexander
Hunicut, Rhoda—Brotherton, Hiram
Hunnicut, Elizabeth—Mahu, John
Hunsecker, Polly—Huffman, George
Hunsecker, Sally—Bolick, Henry
Hunsecker, Susannah—Hoke, Henry
Hunsicker, Elisabeth—Herman, William
Hunsicker, Mary—Harman, Moses
Hunsucker, Barbara—Herman, George
Hunsuker, Elizabeth—Isenhower, Jacob
Hunt, Ellen—Swaringham, Saml
Hunt, Nancy—Dailey, Patrick
Hunt, Rebecca—Cheser, Wilson
Hunter, Isabella M—Crockett, James P
Hunter, Judith—Barcley, John
Hunter, Lusinda—Anderson, Lewis
Hunter, Martha—see Bolinger, Martha
Huntly, Nancy—Rocket, James
Huntly, Seliah—Hartse, Abel
Huskins, Mary—Mabury, John
Huskins, Rosy—Abernathy, Robert
Huson, Elizabeth—Ford, Nathaniel
Huson, Rebecca—Beaty, Joseph
Huson, Sarah—Dameron, David
Huson, Susannah—Dameron, Thomas
Huss, Catharine—Beam, David C
Huss, Fanny—Sain, Winhardt
Huss, M A—Shull, Philip A
Huss, M S—Wilson. C L G
Huss, Margaret—Hafner, Levi
Huss, N J—McGiness, John J
Huss. Sarah A—Shell, Henry
Hutchinson, Catherina—Quin, William
Hutson, Ibby—Johnson, Joseph
Hutson, Jene—Martin, John Jr
Hutson, Nancy—Wilfong, David
Hutson, Ruth—Ramsey, James
Huttel, Barbara—Roner, Henry
Huver, Melindy—Seagle, George
Huvet, Catherine—Sims, James
Hyde, Elisabeth—Howard, Joseph
Hyet, Else—McCord, John
Hyne, Elizabeth—Dillinger, Lewis

Ichard, Barbara—Oxford, William
Ichard, Charity—Bumgarner, Moses
Ikerd, Catherine—Lutz, David
Ikerd, Elizabeth—Lowrance, Peter
Ikerd, Elizabeth—Mauney, John
Ikerd, Margaret—Bovey, Matthias
Ikerd, Saly—Huntley, Haywood
Ikerd, Sarah—Propst, Daniel
Ingel, Betsey—Shell, John
Ingel, Catharine—Cresman, Abraham
Ingle—see also Engle
Ingle, Catharine—Keener, Abraham
Ingle, Christena—Baker, Levi
Ingle, Elizabeth—Lefever, John
Ingle, Elizabeth—Thomas, Moses
Ingle, Elizabeth—Sherrill, Q A
Ingle, Frances—Keener, John
Ingle, Hannah—Keener, John Jr
Ingle, Jane—Sherrill, John A
Ingle, Margaret—Sronce, Charles F
Ingle, Mary—Keener, Michael
Ingle, Mary—Hicks, David

Ingle, Mary C—Sronce, Jacob
Ingle, Polly—Soles, Andrew
Ingle, Sarah—Sauls, David
Ingle, Susanah—Shepherd, Edward
Ingle, Susannah—Black, John
Ingle, Viney—Clippard, Henry
Inglefinger, Peggy—Stroup, David
Ingol, Polly—Cooper, Thomas
Irby, Mary—Ford, Daniel
Irby, Mary H—McClure, James H
Irby, Nancey—Nolen, William
Ireland, Elizabeth—Buise, Elisha
Irwin, Nancy—Weathers, John
Isahower, Mayry—Drumm, John
Isenhour, Lavina—Holler, Daniel
Isenhour, Mahala—Houston, Robert
Isenhour, Susannah—Heffner, Henry
Isenhower, Catharina—Bowman, Daniel
Isenhower, Christeni—Kellar, Alford
Isenhower, Elizebeth A—Sigman, George
Isonhower, Sarah—Stine, John

Jackson, Jane—McCarver, John M
Jackson, Louisa—Hill, Alexander M
Jacobs, Harriet L—Blackburn, Wm M S
Jacobs, Mary A—Plott, E W
James, Barbary—Hull, William
James, Delina—Barkley, James
James, Elizabeth—Horse, John
James, Polly—Duncan, John
Janes, Levina—Kale, Lanson
Janes, Sally—Fronsher, Lewis
Jaratt, Kissia—Wilfong, David
Jarret, Catherine—Jarret, Jonas
Jarret, Hannah—Davis, George
Jarret, Mary Mariah—Yount, Noah
Jarret, Petcy—Peterson, Samuel
Jarrett, Anna—Cook, Aaron
Jarrett, Elizabeth—Yoder, John A
Jarrett, Lusina—Lutz, Ephraim
Jarrett, Mary—Hartzog, John
Jarvett, Hannah—Wion, Peter
Jeams, Catherine—Hull, Richard
Jenkins—see also Ginkens
Jenkins, Adaline—Weaver, Philip
Jenkins, Ann C—Rutledge, Alexander R
Jenkins, Anne—Auten, Powell
Jenkins, Catharine—Spencer, William
Jenkins, Elizabeth—Dutrow, Soloman
Jenkins, Jincy O—Clark, Robert
Jenkins, Judah—McCartey, Jacob
Jenkins, Leanna—Campbell, Joseph B
Jenkins, Leanna—Hoffman, David
Jenkins, Lewsi—Rhyne, Michael
Jenkins, Margret—White, James H
Jenkins, Martha—Huffstetler, Jonas
Jenkins, Mary—Murphy, John
Jenkins, Mary—Jenkins, Aron
Jenkins, Mary—Bradley, Joseph W
Jenkins, Mary—Shutly, Alexander
Jenkins, Mary—Rankin, James R
Jenkins, Nancy A—Rankin, Alexander
Jenkins, Peggy—Fronaberger, William
Jenkins, Polley—Kennedy, Thomas H
Jenkins, Polley—Mcarty, Cornelius
Jenkins, Polly—Perkins, William

Jenkins, Polly—Thornburg, William
Jenkins, Salenia K—Rankin, John D
Jenkins, Sally—Smith, Daniel
Jenkins, Sarah—Frost, Robert
Jenkins, Sarah—Baker, John
Jenkins, Susan—Summy,Michael
Jenkins, Susannah—Friday, David
Jerret, Melline—Hoover, Absalom
Jerrill, Susanna—Falls, John
Jetton, M E—Martin, J B
Jetton, Mary—Sherrill, J P
Jetton, Rachael M—Lucky, Archibald C
Jetton, Sarah—Bisaner, Jacob
Jetton, Sarah—Stubbs, Elbridge W
Jhonston, Anna—Rockett, John
Jinken, Eliza Jane—Paysour, Caleb
Jinken, Nancey—Gibson, James
Jinkens, Anne—Carpenter, Jacob
Jinkins, Betsey—Baker, Joseph
Jinkins, Elizabeth—Linebarger, David
Jinkins, Emeline—Wells, Thomas
Jinkins, Genney—Murphey, Moses
Jinkins, Mary—Darnall, Jordon
Jinkins, Nancy—Sunter, James
Jinkins, Nancy—Darnall, Joel
Jinkins, Serah—Pirkins, Elija
Jinkins, Susana—McCaul, James
Jinkins, Susanah—Chism, Daniel
Jinks, Amanda S—Hause, John F
Jinks, Sarah F—Thompson, W A
Johnson, Bettey—Rudisail, Philip
Johnson, Caroline—Seitz, Abel
Johnson, Catharine—Dyer, John
Johnson, Elisabeth—Tumberson, Joseph
Johnson, Elisabeth—Ramsey, Allen
Johnson, Elizabeth—Garrison, John
Johnson, Elizabeth—Johnson, Hiram
Johnson, Elizabeth Ann—Camel, William
Johnson, Eveline—Ramsey, D L
Johnson, Frances Ann—Reinhardt,
    Wallace M
Johnson, Hazeltine—Holdbrooks, John F
Johnson, Jane—Seitz, George L
Johnson, Jane—Motz, Wade H
Johnson, Martha M—Jacobs, Daniel M
Johnson, Mary Ann—Reep, Daniel
Johnson, Nancy—Rankin, John D
Johnson, Nancy—Sifford, Solomon
Johnson, Peggy—Edwards, Moses
Johnson, Phoeby—Hope, Henry
Johnson, Polley—Hope, Christon
Johnson, Polly—Rankin, James
Johnson, Rebecca—Sain, Amanul
Johnson, Sally S—Carpenter, Elias
Johnson, Sarah A—Havner, A A
Johnson, Sarah E—Gant, James
Johnson, Sary—Gross, Henry
Johnson, Sary A—Sims, John A
Johnson, Susanah—Angel, Joseph A
Johnston, Ann—Calloway, Joseph W
Johnston, Caroline—Long, Robt
Johnston, Catharine—Hayes, John
Johnston, Dosey—Biles, William
Johnston, Elisabeth—Black, David
Johnston, Harriet—Shipp, William T
Johnston, Jane E—Graham, John D
Johnston, M A—Hunley, P F

Johnston, Malinda E—Keever, Lawson
Johnston, Martha—Burton, James M
Johnston, Martha—Hunley,Richard R
Johnston, Mary—Nance, William
Johnston, Peggy—Henderson, Logan
Johnston, Rebeckah—Clark, William
Johnston, Sally—Buchanan, James
Johnston, Sarah A—Johnson, Benjamin
Johnston, Sarah Rose—Kistler, Robert A
Joins, Mary Ann—Hinkell, Lewis
Jonas, Amy—Roderik. Marcus
Jonas, Caty—Shitle, Henry
Jones, Ann—McElrath, J J
Jones, Anne H—Nance, John C
Jones, Azuba—Conner, Jacob
Jones, Ealizabeth—Knipe, Miles
Jones. Isabella—Simmons, John
Jones, Lavina—Gilleland. Henderson
Jones, Mary—Clay, Abraham
Jones. Mary—Litten, Michael
Jones, Mary H—Irby, Joshua M
Jones, Nancy—Sherril, Joseph
Jones, Patsey—Kirby, Bolden T
Jones, Rachel—Lowrance, Newton
Jones, Rebecca P—Johnson, Sankey T
Jones, Sarah—Gant, Sherrod
Jones, Tempey—Grise, Joan
Jones, Thusy—Grise, Henry F
Jonstone, Leamah—McComes, Robert
Jonson, Patsey—Tallant, A A
Jonston, Mary—Gordon, Henry
Joy, Mary S—Gaston, H N
Julian, Margaret—Maxwell, John
Justice, Anna—Keener, Abraham
Justice, Nancey—Throngbary, John

Kail, Margt—West, Ephraim
Kale, Anne—Hodge, William
Kale, Elizabeth—Gilleland, Thomas
Kale, Martha—Jones, Hiram
Kale, Nancy—Gilleland, George
Kale, Sarah—Fish, William
Keaner. Molly—Beel. Charles
Keebler, Catherine—Apley, Daniel
Keen, Elizabeth A—Reinhardt, Jacob
Keener, Adaline—Weathers, Laban
Keener, Amy—Lee, William
Keener, Catharine—Taylor, Calvin
Keener, Elisabeth—McCormack, John
Keener, Elizabeth—Srum, David
Keener, Elizabeth—Carpenter, Levi
Keener, Elizabeth—Beel, Marcus
Keener, Elizabeth—Keener, Levi
Keener, Fanny—Keener, Peter
Keener, Hanah—Bradshaw, Fields
Keener, Isabella—Kirksey, Albert
Keener, Linny—Keener, Henry
Keener, Malinda—Goodson, Jeremiah
Keener, Margaret—Carpenter, Jacob
Keener, Mary—Beel, Benjamin
Keener, Mary—Moose, George
Keener, Mary—Carpenter, Joshua
Keener, Mary—Goodson, Milton A
Keener, Nancy Levina—Saunders, Elisha
Keener, Polley—Engle, Daniel
Keener, Rebecca—Rabb, John

Keener, Sally—Ingle, Adam
Keener, Susanna—Shrum, Daniel
Keestler, Nancy—Finger, Joseph
Keever, Hannah—Rabb, James
Keever, Harriet—Keener, Ephraim
Keever, Margaret—Perkins, James S
Keever, Mary—Mullen, Patrick
Keever, Mary Ann—Tutherow, John
Keever, Nancy—Henkle, John
Keever, Rebecca—Perkins, John
Kegle, Catharina—Hefnar, John
Keistler, Catharine—Bailey, David
Keizer, Sarah—Cochrane, William
Keller, Elizabeth—Keener, John
Keller, Nancy—Abernathy, Joseph
Keller, Nancy—Cheser, Wilson
Keller. Nancy—Shook, Andrew
Keller, Polly—Lutz, Jacob
Keller. Shusanah—Keller, Christian
Kelly, Catherine S—Rouche, John
Kelly, Margaret—Plott, Elias
Kelly, Margaret—Queen, William
Kelly, Margaret—Boyd, Perry L F
Kelly, Martha—Quinn, James
Kelly, Pricilla—Stevenson, Hugh B
Kendrick, Elizabeth—Conner, Seth
Kendrick, Margaret—Whitworth, John
Kendrick, Martha A—Suggs, A J
Kendrick, Mary A E—Glenn, Milton
Kendrick, Polly—Garner, Lewis
Kendrick, Susana—Robinson, Job
Kenedy, Janey—Baldwin, Johnathen
Kener, Polly—Stamey, Enoch
Kerr, Jane S—Moorman, Daniel B P
Kerril, Nancy—Hampton, John
Keykindall, Ruth—Eaker, Michael
Kiblar, Rebeca—Hoke, Frederick
Kibler, Jane M—Dailey, Jacob F
Kidd, Catharine—Ballard, Jacob
Kids, Mary—Crouse, Benjamine
Kids, Mary Ann—Dellinger, A C
Killan, Barbara—Cross, Abraham
Killian, Avaline—Stallcup, Wm
Killian, Barbara—Bost, David
Killian, Caroline—Rhodes, Melchi
Killian, E C—Lloyd, J W
Killian, Elisabeth—Herman, William
Killian, Elizabeth—Brown, Absalom
Killian, Elizabeth—Herman, John
Killian, Elizabeth C—Finger, Michael
Killian, Francis L—Rudisill, Marcus H
Killian, Harriat—Bedford, George P
Killian, Jude—Puntch, A
Killian, Julian E—Quinn, James E
Killian, Luiza S—Hass, Robert M
Killian, Mary—Finger, Henry
Killian, Mary—Killian, Ephraim
Killian, Mary A—Hallman, Alfred
Killian, Mary M—Suttlmyer, Henry H
Killian, Nancy—Hoke, John
Killian, Polly—Herman, Daniel
Killian, Rebecca—Davis, James L
Killian, Salley—Puntch, Thomas
Killian, Salley M—Hunsecker, Jacob
Killian, Sarah—Seagle, David
Killian, Sarah—Huffman, David
Killian, Sarah—Moore, Joseph H

161

Killian, Sarah R—Quickel, Cephas
Killian, Susan—McCaslin, William
Killian, Susannah—Bost, Lawson
Killion, Mary—Fey, Jacob
Killon, Youley—Duncan, John
Kimbrel, Winifred—Abernathy, William
Kincade, Nancy—Low, Isaac
Kincaid, Catherine—Linebarger, David
Kincaid, Catherine—Pryor, Burton
Kincaid, Isabella—Linebarger, James
Kincaid, Martha S—Johnston, G H
Kincaid, Mary—Mullens, William
Kincaid, Mary A—Goins, James
Kincaid, Mary C—Burch, R E
Kincaid, Susanah—Low, Alexander
Kinder, Barbara—Crites, Danl
King, Betcy—Cooke, Aron
King, Elisabeth—Burch, Richard
King, Elizabeth—Shuford, Abel H
King, Ellen E—Long, J L
King, M E M—Robinson, J H
King, Martha—Little, George
King, Nancy—Hager, Benjamin
King, Patsy—Reynolds, Uell
King, Rachael—Poston, Samuel
King, Reliance—Pamer, John
King, Sarah—Black, Vincent
Kinton, Mary—Bridges, John
Kirksey, Elizabeth—Fisher, David
Kirksey, Martha—Painter, John
Kirksey, Mary—Hudspeth, John T
Kiser, Barbara—Heldabrand, Henry
Kiser, Barbara—Carpenter, Noah
Kiser, Barbary—Eaker, John
Kiser, Barbary—Costner, John
Kiser, Catherina—Workman, Marten
Kiser, Jean—Acer, Peter
Kiser, Polly—Carpenter, Thomas
Kiser, Rebeckey—Lingerfelter, John
Kiser, Sarah—Hubard, Isaac
Kistler—see also Cistler
Kistler, Ann—Yoder, Andrew
Kistler, Anna—Leonhardt, Lourance
Kistler, Barbara—Carpenter, Jonathan
Kistler, Elizabeth—Shufford, John
Kistler, Elizabeth—Kiestler, Joseph
Kistler, Elizabeth—Rozell, Richard A
Kistler, Eva Rosannah—Shuford, Daniel
Kistler, Margaret C—Hill, John W
Kistler, Margaret C—Robinson, Marcus L
Kistler, Mary—Warlick, Noah
Kistler, Mary—Spegle, Edward
Kistler, Pricilla—Havner, Peter
Kistler, Sarah—Morrison, Maxwell
Kistler, Sarah Caroline—Houser, Henry
Kistler, Susana—Linhart, John
Kizer, Ann—Eaker, Daniel
Kizer, Ann M—Brilhart, Peter
Kizer, Anne—Rhine, John
Kizer, Barbara—Carpenter, William
Kizer, Cynthia—Fronabarger, Philip
Kizer, Jemimah—Clark, Joshua
Kizer, Mary—Carpenter, Jonas
Kizer, Mary—Ford, Andrew
Kizer, Nancy—Summy, John B
Kizer, Narcissa—Carpenter, George
Kizer, Peggy—Paysoar, Jacob

Kizer, Rebeccah——Hullender, Christopher
Kizer, Ruthy—Clark, Washington B
Kizer, Ruthy—Carpenter, Lawson
Kizer, Sally—Jenkins, Harison
Kizer, Sarah—Caustner, Daniel
Kizer, Susanah—Paysour, Daniel
Kline, Rosannah—Buff, Martin
Knipe, Elizabeth—Stone, William
Knipe, Polly—Tucker, Joseph
Knipe, Sarah C—Fulbright, George E
Knipe, Sarah M—Summit, Daniel
Knowles, Elizebeth—Combest, William M
Knox, Jain—Latta, James
Knup, Matilda—Shuck, David
Koon, Maryan—Whisnant, David
Kuffman, Fanny—Yount, Abraham
Kyser, Catharine—Carpenter, Fredk
Kyser, Sarah—Ashabrand, Henry

Lackey, Anna—Self, B
Lackey, Effie J—Wright, W H
Lackey, Effy—Bails, David
Lackey, Mary—Williams, Miles
Lackey, Sarah—Wehunt, Caleb
Lacky, Elizabet—Bess, Boston
Lacky, Susanna—Williams, David
Lafever, Sarah Jane—Fisher, Lawson
Lailors, Nancy—Clipard, John
Lamasters, Elizabeth—Baker, Jos Anderson
Lamasters, Mary—Harriss, Robt T
Lambeth, Mary—Prather, Hamilton
Lambus, Nancy—Havener, John
Lamkin, Jane—Cobbs, Ralph
Lamly, Betsy—Nelson, James
Lander, Margaret I—Langdon, Wm I
Lander, Martha—Fulenwider, John
Lander, Sarah C—Sherrill, Samuel P
Laney, Martha Ann—Hakins, William P
Lanier, Sarah—Flowers, Adam
Laning, Elizabeth—Philips, Joseph T
Lantz, Barbara—Hoover, John
Lantz, Betcy—Hallman, Jacob
Lantz, Linny—Albright, James
Lantz, Sarah—Howard, George
Larnse, Margaret—Kiestler, Abram
Launby, Fanny—Jarrett, Elias
Lavender, Vina—Carpenter, Paul
Law, Dumeris—Kelly, Enoch
Law, Faney C—Pinner, Loady B
Law, Lavina L—Hamilton, James W
Law, Mary Ann—Pinner, Noah B
Law, Nancy—Abernathy, William
Lawing, Louisa—Helton, John L
Lawing, Mary A E—Womack, Starling
Lawing, Nancy L—Hager, Simon S
Lay, Delilah—Compton, William N
Lay, Mary—Compton, William N
Lay, Nancy—Rhyne, Simon
Layman, Meryber—Young, Danl
Laymen, Fanny—Carpenter, Henry
Leatherman, Elizabeth—Tucker, Samuel
Leatherman, Sarah—Parker, Albertus
Ledford, Barbara G—Norman, James
Ledford, Jane—Ross, Aaron
Lee, Elener—Sronce, Hailey
Lee, Elizabeth—Abrams, Joseph

Lee, Jincy—Jones, Allen
Lee, Luizur—Ward, Conrad
Lee, Nancy—Gant, Willis
Lee, Silvia—Derr, Valentine
Leeper, Elisabeth—Patrick, Robert
Leeper, Esther—Webb, David
Leeper, Margarat—Cathey, George
Leeper, Margaret—Neagle, John
Leeper, Margaret S—Lonergan, Patrick
Leeper, Maria Jane—Neagle, Andrew
Leeper, Mary—Robinson, John
Leeper, Mary M—Clark, Archibald M
Leeper, Nancy E—Beaty, Robert A
Leeper, Peggy—Collins, John
Lefener, Nelly—Rhyne, John
Lefever, Elvira—Rush, P S
Lefever, Jemimah—Bumgarner, Wallace
Lehmons, Catharine—Goodson, George Wm
Leinhardt, Sally—Bailey, David
LeMarsters, Martha—McCloud, James A
Lemming, Sarah—Watts, Robert
Lemons, Hannah—Hufstatler, Peter
Lemons, Mary—Loftin, Martin
Lence, Mary—Speegle, John
Lenhardt, Elizabeth—Sain, Abraham
Lenhardt, Mary Ann—Coon, Jacob
Lenhardt, Susan—Summit, Henry
Lenhart, Barbara—Black, Thomas
Lennier, Anna—Holler, Israel
Lentz, Hannah—Spigel, Davald
Leonard, Ann—Goings, Arren
Leonard, Elizabeth—Massagee, Abner
Leonard, Emeline—Cody, D L
Leonard, Eve—Smith, Joshua J
Leonard, Eve Catharine—Smith, Martin
Leonard, Malinda—Robinson, Henry I
Leonard, Margaret—Wethers, Caleb C
Leonard, Mary—Gilbert, Robert
Leonard, Mattie J—Bandy, James M
Leonhardt, Abarilla—Pate, J M
Leonhardt, Barbara—Mostellar, Israel
Leonhardt, Caroline—Kistler, Noah
Leonhardt, Catharine—Mullens, Jas H
Leonhardt, Clarissa—Havner, Levi, Jr
Leonhardt, Ealzabeth—Baxter, Henry
Leonhardt, Emily Adaline—Houser, Emmanuel
Leonhardt, Frances—Haynes, L D
Leonhardt, Louisa—Bess, Thomas
Leonhardt, Martha E F—Sullivan, Charles C
Leonhardt, Rosannah—Dunbar, John A
Leonhardt, Susan—Brendel, David
Leonhardt, Temperance—Boggs, Noah
Letherman, Susannah—Linhardt, Jacob
Lewing, Jain—Stansbury, Solomon
Lewis, Catharina—Legle, John
Lewis, Elitha—West, William
Lewis, Elizabeth—Spect, George
Lewis, Haney—Carouthers, Edmond
Lewis, Louisa R—Brandon, Thomas L
Lewis, Marget—Crego, John
Lewis, Mary A—Ford, Eli M
Lewis, Peggy—Maclean, Thomas
Lewis, Peggy—McCarver, James
Lewis, Pheby—Millican, James
Lewis, Polly—Robison, John

Lewis, Sarah—Spact, Philip
Lewis, Sarah P—Linebarger, Jacob
Liggins, Mary—Ingle, Levi
Like, Suckey—Karr, Robert
Limming, Elizabeth—Wats. Richard
Linbarger, Susanah—Sigman, Martin
Linbarger, Susanah—Turbyfill, Spencer
Linch, Elizabeth—Robinson, Morgan
Linch, Elizabeth—Hartness, Hiram
Linch, Jane—Torrance, John
Linch, Sarah—Boyd, John
Lincoln, Patsey—Berry, George
Lind, Nancey—Nolen, Daniel
Lindsay, Mary D—Adams, R J
Lindsay, Violet W—Hartt, John
Lindsey, Mary—Hain, Philip
Linebarger, Barbara—Clemmer, Fety
Linebarger, Catherine—Mason, L A
Linebarger, Dovey—Moore, Adolphus
Linebarger, Eliner—Cannon, William F
Linebarger, Elisabeth—Fronabargar, Jacob
Linebarger, Elizabeth—Asbury, Francis
Linebarger, Elizabeth—Allen, William
Linebarger, Elizabeth—Huffman, Jacob
Linebarger, Elizabeth E—Wilkerson, Francis
Linebarger, Harriet—Baker, Henry
Linebarger, Lovina—Dunkin, Nathan
Linebarger, M S—Smyer, John F
Linebarger, Margaret—Shetly, Robison M
Linebarger, Margaret E—Cloninger, Jacob
Linebarger, Martha—Sigman, Barnet
Linebarger, Mary—Abernathy, John
Linebarger, Mary—Regan, Charles
Linebarger, Mary—Rankin, Joseph M
Linebarger, Mary—Conner, Charles D
Linebarger, Molly—Ballard, Reuben
Linebarger, Nancy—Brotherton, George
Linebarger, Nancy—Tarr, David L
Linebarger, Nancy—Sherrill, Hosea
Linebarger, Peggy—Harwell, Mason
Linebarger, Polley—Forney, Abraham E
Linebarger, Sophia—Turbyfill, Anderson
Linebarger, Susanah—Sherrill, Arerum
Linebarger, Susanah—Drum, John
Linebarger, Susannah—Huffman, Daniel
Linebarger, Susannah—Clemmer, John
Linebarger, Susannah—Reed, William
Lineberger, Polly—Hufman, John
Lingafelt, Nancy—Smith, Solomon
Lingafelt, Sarah—Houser, Franklin A
Lingerfeldt, Mary—Wise, Henry
Lingerfeldt, Sally—Kiser, Christopher
Lingerfelt, Catharine—Brilhart, Jacob
Lingerfelt, Elizabeth—Corbey, David
Lingerfelt, Eve—Ivester, Hugh
Lingerfelt, Fanney—Wihont. William
Lingerfelter, Molly—Long, Wiley
Lingfelt, Mary—Carpenter, Addolphus
Linhardt, Harriet—Hallmon, John
Linhardt, Susana—Morrison, George
Link, Anna Catharine—Houk. Leander
Link, Catharine—Summit, Christian
Link, Catherine—Hoppes, Adam
Link, Caty—Stroup, Andrew
Link, Elizabeth E—Whitener, Jesse
Link, Rebecca—Seitz, Darius D

Link. Sally—Goldman, Martin
Link. Susanah—Dillinger, Henry
Linkhorn. Elizabeth—Tankerslay, George
Linkhorn. Milley—Berry, Hiram
Linn, Sarah—Propst, Daniel A
Linn. Tempy—Kennipe, John M
Litle, Elizabeth—Clark, Cornelius
Litle. Martha—Reed, Alexander
Litle. Sarah—King, Wm
Litten. Ruth—Edwards, Charles
Litten. Tabitha—Allen, James
Litten. Viney—Brown, George
Little, Amanda—Gant, Jefferson
Little. Barbera—Mozur, Jacob
Little. Bettie—Nance, J C
Little. Bridget—Graham, John
Little, Catharine—Smith, David
Little, Catherina—Allen, Hinchea E
Little, Chatarina—Goble, Absolum
Little, Christina—Cloninger, Moses
Little, Elisabeth—Lockman, David
Little, Elizabeth—Yount, John
Little, Elizabeth—Bowman, Jonas
Little, Elizabeth—Edwards, Lewis
Little, Fanny—Brotherton, Hua
Little, Frances C—Cashion, James H
Little, Harriot—Edwards, John H
Little, Isabella—Sifford, Wm A
Little, Jane—Hill, Jeremiah
Little, Jane—Abernathy, Larkin
Little, Jane—Little, William
Little, Jane K—Derr, A.J
Little, Mary—Hamilton, Drury
Little, Mary—Sifford, Solomon
Little, Mary—Little, Robert
Little, Matty—Sherrill, Moses W
Little, Nancy—Tucker, John C
Little, Nancy E—Tucker, Robert A
Little, Patsey—Rankin, James
Little, Peggy—Reed, Alexander
Little, Polly—Yount, Joseph
Little, Polly—Sherrill, Francis
Little, Rachel—Hawkins, James
Little, Salley—Haker, William
Little, Sarah—Freeman, John B
Little, Sary—Bowman, Joseph
Litton, Anna—Sherrill, Hugh
Litton, Betsey—Fisher, David
Litton, Candis—Bynum, John G
Litton, Nancy—Crawford, James
Litton, Rebecka—Andras, Henry
Lockman, Caroline—Tompson, Hugh
Lockman, Eba—Shelton, Meacon
Lockman, Elizabeth—Shelton, Joseph B
Lockman, Ibby—Beatty, Edmund
Lockman, Lucinda C—Little, John F
Lockman, Mary—Caldwell, Franklin
Lockman, Nancy G—Thompson, William D
Lockman, Rachael—Hinkle, Isaac
Lockman, Sally—Shelton, Spencer
Lockman, Sarah—Caldwell, Thomas
Lockman, Sarah Jane—Howard, Edmon M
Lockman, Susanah—Shelton, Freeman
Loftin, Elizabeth—Edwards, James
Loftin, Martha—Goodson, Milton
Loftin. Mary—Edwards, John
Logan, Drucilla—Roberts, Martin

Login, Frankey—Collins, Isaac
Lollar, Jean—Bodine, Peter
Lollar, Rachel—Garman, George
Loller, Margret—Gwaltney, Isaac
Lomax, Linny—Sigman, Elias
Long, Ann—Cobb, John
Long, Caroline—Clubb, David
Long, Eleanor—Abernathy, Fredrick
Long, Elizabeth—Debenport, John
Long, Elizabeth—Humphreys, Daniel
Long, Evaline—White, Hugh
Long, Fanny—Chandler, John J
Long, Harriet—Flowers, Lewis
Long, Jane—Dunn, Joseph
Long, Mary—Cloninger, Valentine
Long, Mary—Lingerfelter, Jacob
Long, Nancy—Gales, Briant
Long, Polley—Francis, Ruben
Long, Rebeccah—Stroup, Joseph D
Longcrier, Polly—Lagle, George
Loois, Patsey—Johnson, Joseph
Loore, Fanney—Jonas, John
Loots, Elizabeth—Moose, Frederick
Lootz, Margaret—Hefner, Martin
Lorance, Catharina—Crites, John
Lorance, Catharine M—Abernathy, Miles S
Lorance, Elisabeth—Lutes, George
Lorance, Henry Ette—Rees, John
Lorance, Rachel—Trout, Michael
Lorantz, Catharine C—Abernathy, Miles W
Loretz, Ann E—Summerow, Noah
Loretz, Anne—Michael, Jacob
Loretz, Barbara—Hallman, John
Loretz, Catharine—Motz, John
Loretz, Judith—Clay, Joseph
Loretz, Mary—Ramsaur, David
Loretz, Mary—Carpenter, Jacob
Loretz, Mary H—Henry, Lawson
Loretz, Mary J E—Bost, Marcus L
Loretz, N_____, Wilkinson, Thomas
Loretz, Polley—Hollman, Daniel
Loretz, Saloma—Roseman, Henry
Louer, Betsy—Cox, Robert
Loughbam, Margrad—Summer, John
Lourance, C L—Ward, And J
Lourance, Catharine—Weatherspoon, Elisha
Lourance, Elizabeth—Hoke, Frederick
Lourance, Elizabeth—Carpenter, George
Lourance, Elizabeth J—Abernathy, Turner
Lourance, M B—Crowel, Eli
Lourance, Mary—Rankin, William
Loutz, Betcy—Reinhardt, Charles
Lovesey, Elizabeth—Clifton, Jacob
Lovsey, Catherine—Connelly, John B
Lovsey, Polley—M'Call, Robert
Low, Caroline—Holloman, Moses
Low, Elizabeth—Hinson, Lazarus
Low, Elizabeth—Wingate, Jesse
Low, Emily—Mullen, James
Low, Jane C—Thompson, E W
Low, Jenny—Costner, Thomas
Low, Margaret—Finison, John
Low, Mary—Tronberry, Jonathan
Low, Salley—Abernathy, Isaiah
Lowe, Catherine—Guttrey, Nelson
Lowe, Delilah—Miller, Andrew
Lowe, Frances—Shelton, Henry

Lowe, Francess—Bradshaw, John
Lowe, Nancy—Lavender, Joseph
Lowe, Nancy—Gillam, John
Lowe, Rachel—Saunders, Joseph
Lowrance, Elizabeth B—Berriman, James C
Lowre, Mary—Shup, Sonmon
Lowry, Elizabeth J—McGill, John
Luckey, Mitilda—Nixson, William
Lucky, Jane C—Forney, A E
Lufcey, Martha—Lewis, John
Lufsey, Izabella—Underwood, Willis
Lumly, Sarah—Griffith, Jonathan
Lusk, Ann—Carroll, James
Lutes, Anna—Lingafelt, John
Lutes, Catharine L—Lin, William P
Luts, Betty—Fie, Jacob
Lutz, Amy—Wilson, Alexander
Lutz, Catherine—Yound, Samuel
Lutz, Catherine—Bleckley, James
Lutz, Cathrine—Killian, Frederick
Lutz, Elizabeth—Hoover, Warlick
Lutz, Leah—Campbell, Henry
Lutz, Malinda—Abernathy, Miles J
Lutz, Mary—Clodfelter, Daniel
Lutz, Mary—Mosteller, Michael
Lutz, Mary—Canada, Alexander
Lutz, Salley—Warlick, Absalom
Lutz, Sally—Huit, Lewis
Lutz, Sally—Bost, Jonathan
Lutz, Sally—Huver, Levi
Lutz, Susannah—Carpenter, Peter
Lutz, Susy—Ikerd, Phillip
Luvsey, Rosanah Hovis Nore—Carter,
    Daniel Randolph
Lyman, Catharine F—Hunter, Cyrus L
Lynch, Susan—Keever, Thomas
Lytle, Elisabeth—Davis, John
Lytle, Frances—Litton, Isaac
Lytle, Isabella—Baldrige, Michael
Lytle, M J—Ruddock, T G
Lytle, Mary—Clark, William
Lytle, Mary Ann—Lutz, Daniel
Lyttle, Sarah E—Hill, Wm B

Mabray, Martha—Kelley, Charles
McAfee, Polley—Trimmer, Obadiah
Mcalister, Elizabeth—Henry, William
Mcalister, Lisah—Davis, John W
McAlister, Susan—McAlister, William S
McAllon, Hannah—Norman, William
McAlly, Eliza—Adams, John B
McAnear, Nancey—Dillon, Edmond
Mcarter, Rebecca—Crow, James M
McArthur, Isabella—Quin, Robert
McArver, Mary—Smith, James
Mcarver, Sarah—Cathey, John
McAslen, Marget—Ramsey, Thomas
Macaul, Delia Annabeor—Dellinger,
    Lorenzo Dow
Macaver, Mary—Hamilton, Alexander
McBee, Martha A—Carson, Tench C
McCabe, Katherine—Stiles, Benjamin
M'Calister, Catharine M—Robinson, Levi A
McCall, Elizabeth—McCarver, David
M'Call, Mary Ann M—Munday, Joseph M
McCallister, Elloner—Staret, John

McCallister, Jane—Sullivan, James
McCallister, Patsey—Brown, William
McCallister, Sarah—Rankin, Robert
McCarter, Metilda—Tucker, John
McCarty, Barbara—Bird, John
McCarty, Elizabeth—Parker, Solomon
McCarty, Mary—Adams, James
McCarty, Sarah—Eaker, Daniel
McCarver, Jane—Parker, John
McCarver, Margaret—Heslep, Ezekiel
McCarver, Mary—Hart, James
McCarver, Nancy—Brown, James
McCasland, Polley—Finger, John
McCasland, Polly—Detter, Daniel
McCaslin, Angeline—Boils, Alexander
McCaslin, F A R—Kistler, J L
McCaul, Delia B—Wilson, Hugh L
McCaul, Jane—Roby, Horace
McCaul, Martha Jane—Stacy, T F__
McCaule, Mary—Newton, George
McCl____, Rebeca—White, Thomas
McClain, Agles—McGill, William
McClerd, Catherine—Eake, Peter
McClure, Adaline—Sain, Daniel
McClure, Elizabeth Reid—Oats, John
McClure, Jane—Bigham, William
McClure, Margaret—Moor, Edward
McClure, Patsey—Witherspoon, George
McClurg, Ruth—Kysor, Philip
McCollister, Elizabeth—Stroup, Champion
McCollister, Fanny—Sulivan, Owen
McCollister, Sarah—Williams, Benjamin
McCombs, Rosannah—Brown, John P
M'Cord, Martha R—Acock, John H
McCord, Mary—Johnston, Robert
McCord, Sarah—Campbel, James
McCorey, Betsey—Killen, Robert
McCorkle, Charity A—Alexander, Robt J
McCorkle, Elizabeth—Ballard, Wm L
McCorkle, Elizabeth L—Houston, Joel B
McCorkle, Jenny—Alexander, Abraham
McCorkle, Rebeckah—King, William
McCorkle, Rebekah—Milligan, Gilbert
McCorkle, Rosanah—Naylor, Parson
McCormack, Elisabeth—Henderson, Joseph
McCormick, Elizabeth—Sherril, Enos
McCormick, Jane—Carpenter, Samuel
McCosough, Reachel—Massey, Green
McCoy, Elisabeth—Martin, James
McCoy, Elizabeth—Rankin, A V
McCoy, Mary J—Grigg, B F
McCoy, Sary—Martin, John, Sr
M'Cullick, Mary—Massey, William
McCulloch, Nancy—Thomas, Lewis W
McCullock, Sarah F—Harry, John H
McCulloh, Charlotte A—Clark, William R
McCulloh, Margaret—James, Augustus P
McCulloh, Mary—Propst, Jacob
McCullouch, Rosanna—Robinson, John W
McCullow, Harriet E—Boman, Isaac F
McDannel, Catharine—Hager, William
McEntire, Jane—Sanders, John
McEntire, Liddy—Cornwell, Cage
McFalls, Harriet—Havner, George F
McFalls, Martha—Eaker, John
McFelmeth, Patsey—Smith, Thomas
McGee, Elisabeth—Withrow, James

McGee, Louisa—Rhyne, Daniel
McGee, Margaret—Williams, Joel
McGee, Mary—Herman, Henry
McGee, Peggy—Fry, Absolum
McGee, Polly—Fry, Philip
McGill, Elisabeth—Wright, Thomas
McGill, Jane—Crow, John Dimbarr
McGill, Nancy S—Lowrey, William
McGill, Rachel—Boyd, James
McGill, Rebecca—Oates, Charles H
McGinas, Ebby—Cloninger, Moses
McGinnas, Alice E—Cahill, John P
McGinnas, Jane M—Stroup, Elisha
McGinnas, Louisa—Reynolds, John
McGinnas, Patsey—Bradshaw, William
McGinnas, Sarah—Homesley, Moses G
McGinnes, Sally—Roberts, Abel
McGinnis, Elisabeth—Hansel, William
McHaffey, Rody—Gross, Adam
McHarg, Betsey—Turbyfill, Sidney H
McIlvaine, Anna—Butt, Zephaniah
McKee, Abigail—Oliver, George
M'Kee, Ann—Ward, Levi
McKee, Caroline—Thompson, Ephraim
M'Kee, Elisabeth—Whiteside, Joseph
McKee, Harriett A—Thompson, Alfred W
McKee, Mary—Shaw, Thomas
McKee, Peggy S—Ford, John
McKinny, Mary—Dellinger, George
McKisick, Polley—Dickson, Ezekiel
McKracken, Ruth—Kyser, Larans
Maclean, Eliza J—Campbell, William
Maclean, Margaret—Hawkins, William
McLean, Mary D—McLean, Jno D
McLean, Mary M—Parks, George D
Maclean, Mary M—Erwin, Arthur R
Maclean, R I—Wilson, Isaac
Maclean, V R J—Hoke, George M
Maclean, Vilet P—Rumfelt, Hezekiah W
Maclean, Vilet W—Lindsay, Samuel W
McLerd, Mary A—Huss, John A
Maclure, Mary—Wilson, James
McLure, Nancy J—Stroup, Phillip
McMin, Esther—Williman, Christopher
McMin, Rachel A—Lockman, Levy
McMin, Sarah—Rankin, Denny
McMinn, Ann—Howard, Worner
McMinn, Martha—Bynum, Rufus L
McMurry, Poley—Bonham, Arnold
McMurtry, Zarian—Green, William B
McNamare, Hanah—Murphey, John
McNear, Sarah—Patrick, Isaac
McPherson, Frances L—Templeton, R R
McPherson, Laura Ann—Lander,
   Samuel, Jr
Magill, Sarah—Holloway, Barnes
Magness, Levina—Alexander, Frank R
Mahaffy, Adaline—Witherspoon, Calvin A
Mahaffy, Polly—Whitte, Thomas P
Maheffey, Elizabeth—Wilson, Asaph
Maize, Susannah—Clark, Jephthae
Malone, Izza—Eaves, Burrel
Marchal, Rebeckah—Gullick, Milton H M
Marchel, Catharine S—Finley, John
Marchel, Eliza J—Ragan, Washington
Marison, Magaret—Alexander, John
Marlin, Sally—Slegle, George

Marner, Jenny—Smith, Samuel
Marriner, Mary—Armstrong, Matthew
Marritt, Polley—Jonston, Larkin
Marshall, Elizabeth—Drum, Phillip
Marshall, Mary Maria—Linebarger, John
Martin, Abigal—Baird, William
Martin, Amanda—Petree, John
Martin, Ann—Colwell, Tho
Martin, Ann—Ratchford, Robert C
Martin, Ann—Weaver, Lindsey C
Martin, Delpha—Wilson, Solomon
Martin, Elisabeth—Barron, Thomas
Martin, Elisazeth—Hannah, Thomas
Martin, Elisabeth J—Holland, O W, Jun
Martin, Elizabeth—Taylor, James
Martin, Elizabeth—Jordan, Harry H
Martin, Frances—Dickson, William
Martin, Hanah—Conrad, Daniel
Martin, Hetty—Smith, Joseph
Martin, Jean—Hannah, Thomas
Martin, Mahala—Kayler, Peter C
Martin, Margaret—Armstrong, John
Martin, Margt—Kerr, John
Martin, Martha—Watson, John
Martin, Martha S—Armstrong, John M
Martin, Mary—Baxter, David
Martin, Mary—McCorkle, Stephen
Martin, Mary—Lutz, Alexander
Martin, Mary—Johnson, John
Martin, Mary—Harman, Marcus M
Martin, Mary A L—Stinson, Cyrus
Martin, Nancy—Ward, Hasten
Martin, Nancy—Hager, John
Martin, Oliss—Peny, Richmond
Martin, Patsy A—Niel, Andrew
Martin, Penthy—Gillum, Winfield
Martin, Polly—Rippy, Edard
Martin, Polly—Herron, Isaac
Martin, Rachel—Johnston, James
Martin, S J—Cline, Wm A
Martin, Sarah—Defenbach, John
Martin, Sarah Ann—Engle, John
Martson, Anna—Warlick, Jack
Masegee, Caroline—Dilner, Daniel
Mason, Abagail—Welker, George William
Mason, Mary—Reinhardt, David
Massagee, Martha—Helms, Jacob
Massangale, Mary—Atkinson, William
Massey, Betsey—Potter, William
Massey, Jane—Hill, James D
Massey, Polley—Jinkins, James
Massey, Talitha C—Ford, Tapley M
Massey, Winey—Senter, Stephen
Massigee, Harriet—Knipe, Joseph
Mastello, Margaret—Wilson, Moses
Master, Barbary—Stroup, John
Master, Elizabeth—Summit, Christian
Master, Susana—Seitz, Jacob
Masters, Catherine—Stroup, Phillip
Masters, Eave—Clubb, George
Masters, Hannah—Sides, Peter
Masters, Susanah—Stroup, Moses
Mathews, Rachael—Bumgardner, Moses
Mathis, Mary—Moore, Jonn
Mathus, Elizabeth—Baly, John
Mathus, Susanah—Lewis, Richmd
Matthews, Eliza—Carpenter, Isaac W

Matthews, Mary—Hardy, James A
Matthews, Sarah—Keene, James
Matthews, Sarah—Michal, John
Mattox, Nancey—Wells, Anderson
Mauney, Affy—Blackwood, Gideon
Mauney, Anna—Cody, Turner
Mauney, Anna M—Niell, Adam
Mauney, Catharine—Smith, William
Mauney, Catharine—Brown, John
Mauney, Catharine—Carpenter, Samuel
Mauney, Catharine—Eaker, Henry
Mauney, Catharine—Biles, Noah
Mauney, Catherine—Jinkins, William
Mauney, Cynthia—Shuford, Joseph
Mauney, Eliza—Little, Thomas
Mauney, Elizabeth—Heavner, Levi
Mauney, Elizabeth—Butts, John
Mauney, Elizabeth—Faris, Osker A
Mauney, Harriet—Bovey, William
Mauney, Harriet—Putman, James L
Mauney, Margaret—Jenkins, Joseph
Mauney, Margaret—Mauney, Christian
Mauney, Marian—McClelland, Ezekiel
Mauney, Mary—Twigs, Henry
Mauney, Mary—Havner, Philip
Mauney, Mary—Jarrett, Jacob
Mauney, Mary—Kiser, Levi
Mauney, Polly—Rhyne, Michael
Mauney, Polly—Settlemire, Jacob S
Mauney, Rosannah—Moore, James
Mauney, Salley—Wells, David
Mauney, Salley—Sullivan, Ezekiel
Mauney, Sally—Reynolds, Thomas
Mauney, Sally—Russ, Samuel
Mauney, Sarah—Brown, William
Mauney, Sarah—Smith, Robert
Mauney, Sarah—Rogers, Woodson
Mauney, Sarah—Helms, Eli
Mauney, Susannah—Niel, John
Mauny, Barbury N—Niell, Green Berry
Mauny, Betsey—Senter, Edward
Maxwel, Sarrah Greg—Wilson, Andrew
Mayberry, Elizabeth—Sadler, Zachariah
Mayberry, Mary—Thompson, Bat
Mayors, Catharine—Summit, Henry
Mays, Patsy—Drum, William
Mays, Rebeca—Beate, Robert
Mehaffy, Harriet R—Lutz, Jacob
Meheffey, Rosannah—Best, Jonas
Meiers, Caty—Ballard, John
Mellon, Cynthey—Berry, Milton
Mellon, Jane C—Turner, James
Mellon, Jane M—Jones, Talbert
Mellon, Mary—Leeper, Andrew
Melton, Matilda—Warren, William
Mendenhall, Ann R—Kelly, Jackson
Mendenhall, Mary—Henderson, Wm
Mendinghall, Sarah Louisa—Falls, Andrew
Merriner, Sally—Stowe, Jacob
Messey, Katrine—Barrier, Richard
Messey, Pricilla—Lourance, Daniel
Michael, Mary—Ingold, Jonathan
Michal, S J—Clay, G P
Michel, Mayry—Reinhardt, Jacob
Michel, Sussana—Briles, Adam
Middlekauff, Mary A E—Butler, Thornton
Millar, Anny—Holler, Lawson

Millar, Prasila—Eakerd, Solomon
Miller, Ammy—Huffman, Langdon
Miller, Amy—Miller, Ephraim W
Miller, Betsey—Hager, Frederick
Miller, Catharine—Yount, Ephraim
Miller, Catharine—Cauble, Henry
Miller, Cathrine—Hoffman, J----
Miller, Elisabeth—Cobb, Robert
Miller, Elisabeth—Ikerd, Henry
Miller, Elizabeth—Lutz, Elias
Miller, Fanny—Harman, Henry
Miller, Julianne—Hawn, David
Miller, Lavina—Holler, Andrew
Miller, Margaret—Hawn, John
Miller, Mary—Saunders, Samuel
Miller, Mary R—Bradshaw, John F
Miller, Nancy—Jinkins, Benjamin
Miller, Pollay—Sulliven, John
Miller, Polley—Wilson, John
Miller, Polly—Huffman, Jackson
Miller, Polly S—Moore, Philetus
Miller, Rachel—Killian, David
Miller, Rhoda—Sigman, L H
Miller, Roxanna—Edwards, Samuel
Miller, Salley—Yount, Henry
Miller, Sarah—Brown, Andrew
Miller, Sarah—Yount, Henry
Miller, Susannah—Bolch, Hiram
Millican, Jane—Blithe, Stephen
Milligan, Elizabeth—Sherrill, Elisha
Milligan, Sally—Sherrill, Theo
Millon, Sarah—Brandon, Larken P
Mingers, Susannah—Fulbright, Henry
Minges, Elizabeth C—Lippard, Solomon
Minges, Mary—Sigman, Martin
Minges, Perlina—Sigman, Emanuel
Mingis, Betsy—Benfield, Joseph
Mingus, Betcy—Ward, General
Mins, Fanney—Colwell, Andrew
Mires, B—Allen, A G
Mitcham, Narcissa—Seagle, Alfred
Mitchel, Amy—McCombs, James
Mitchel, Elizebeth—Brimer, Moses
Mitchel, Sally—Townsen, Peter
Mitchell, Martha Ann—Sherrill, James M
Mitchem, Jamima—Lin, Daniel
Mitchum, Sally—Cline, Thomas
Moany, Peggie—Vandike, Joshua
Moistala, Polly—Cross, Mosis
Moll, Catharine, Jr—Kline, John
Moll, Elizabeth—Moystiller, George
Moll, Margrate—Seitz, Abraham
Moll, Maria—Robinson, Jesse
Monday, Elizabeth—Bandy, Hugh Q
Monday, Martha—Lowe, Franklin
Monday, Martha Ann—Williams, C R
Money, Elitha—Fulbrite, Daniel
Money, Froncia—Painter, John
Money, Sarah—Niell, George
Montgemery, Martha—Ford, Asberry
Montgomery, Hannah—Oats, John
Moody, Elizabeth—Reel, Daniel
Moody, Nancy—Kincad, James
Moody, Susanah—Killian, Andrew
Mooney, Anna—Jenkins, Joseph M
Mooney, Catharine—Sullivan, Jerry
Mooney, Elizabeth—Beam, Moses

167

Mooney, Jane—Hufstetler, John
Mooney, Milly Ann—Moore, Adolphus
Mooney, Mitilda—Beam, Joshua
Mooney, Nancy—Fronabarger, David
Mooney, Sarah—Hoover, Daniel
Mooney, Susy—Smith, Daniel
Moony, Mary Matilda—Hallmon, Oliver
Moor, Serah—Logan, Drury
Moore, Agness—Dickson, James
Moore, Ann—Henry, Melcom
Moore, Anna—Johnson, Robert
Moore, Anna—Reinhart, John
Moore, Anna—Eaker, Jacob
Moore, Betsey—Harmon, David
Moore, Catharine—Havner, David
Moore, Elisabeth—Patterson, Francis
Moore, Eliza—Stroup, Joseph F
Moore, Elizabeth—Rankin, Alexander
Moore, Elizabeth—Underwood, Jacob
Moore, Elsey,—Moore, Wright
Moore, Esther—Havner, David
Moore, Faney—Tutherow, Solomon
Moore, Fanny—Smith, Jesse
Moore, Hanah—Harper, Benjamin
Moore, Henryetta—Hale, William
Moore, Jane—McCord, William
Moore, Jane—McKinzie, James
Moore, Kissiah—Riley, William
Moore, Levira—Bridenbo, John
Moore, Louisa—Alexander, Robert J
Moore, Margaret—White, William
Moore, Margaret—Emerson, James
Moore, Margaret—Martin, Samuel
Moore, Mary—Lawing, Joseph
Moore, Mary M—Gaston, Robert H
Moore Myre—Nolen, John
Moore, Poley—Holland, Oliver Wily
Moore, Polley—Reinhardt, Michael
Moore, Polley—Havner, Joseph
Moore, Polly—Havner, Michael
Moore, R—Clark, Christopher
Moore, Rosey—Armstrong, Mathew R
Moore, Ruthy Lucinda—Decker, Frederick
Moore, Sally—Powell, William
Moore, Sally—Quals, John
Moore, Sarah F—Cody, James
Moore, Selina—Peterson, Daniel P
Moore, Susanna—Gordon, James
Moorman, Cornelia—Roseman, Andrew
Moorman, Nancy H V—Hoyle, Abel
Moos, Tena—Finger, John
Moose, Beggy—Ornd, Daniel
Moose, Christina—Setser, John
Moose, Sally—Bovey, Conrad
Morason, Mary—Cathy, George
Moratz, Margred—Isenhower, Martin
Moreland, Catharine—Leak, John
Moreland, Nancey—Sadler, William Rose
Moreland, Phebe—Harrup, Arthur
Moreland, Phebe Tucker—Sadler, Nathaniel
Moretz, Rachael—Hefner, George
Morgan, Elizebeth—Gibbs, James
Morison, Mary—Alexander, John
Morland, Amy—Williams, John
Moroson, Sofiah—Bolch, Jacob
Morris, Catherine—Nickelson, John

Morris, Elizabeth—Duff, Denis
Morris, Margaret—Linebarger, Solomon
Morris, Mary—Darr, Valentine
Morris, Nancey—Asberry, Daniel
Morris, Stacy—Abernathy, John R
Morrison, Eugenia E—Barringer, Rufus
Morrison, Harriet—Irwin, James P
Morrison, Isabella S—Hill, Daniel H
Morrison, Jane—Self, Jacob
Morrison, Margaret—Haynes, William
Morrison, Mary—Hullit, Peter
Morrison, Mary Anna—Jackson, T J
Morrison, Nancy—Brown. Philip
Morrison, Peggy—Williams, Charles
Morrison, Polly—Williams, William
Morrison, Susan W—Avery, A C
Mosar, Elizabeth—Lusk, Salomon
Mosar, Polly—Daganhert, Henry
Moser, Barbara—Bauman, Daniel
Moser, Eliza—Fullbright, Andrew
Moser, Elvira—Hifner, Frederick
Moser, Sally—Sommit, Daniel
Moses, Nancy—Reynolds, Jesse
Mosteller, Ann C—Earney, John
Mosteller, Elizabeth—Barnett, William
Mosteller, Elizabeth—Earney, Henry
Mosteller, Elizabeth—Rhyne, Absalom
Mosteller, Elizabeth—Rudisell, George
Mosteller, Frances—Bost, Jacob
Mosteller, Julian C—Hoover, John
Mosteller, Margaret—Kiser, John
Mosteller, Mary A—Cauble, Peter V
Mosteller, Sarah—Maroney, Mathew
Mosteller, Susan—Steel, Calvin
Mostiller, Anny—Mull, Harison
Mostiller, Catharine—Carpenter, Henry
Mostiller, Margret—Reyonalds, Elias
Motz, Caroline R—Cochran, Asa F
Motz, Elizabeth—Caldwell, Elam
Mowser, Catherine—Bolch, Elias
Mowser, Lucinda—Spencer, Eli
Mowser, Polly—Bowman, Boston
Mowser, Sally—White, Joabert
Mucklewreath, Polly—Moore, Arthur
Mull, Anna—Lutz, Ephraim H
Mull, Catharine—Mostetler, John
Mull, Elizabeth—Peterson, Daniel
Mull, Margaret—Miller, Joseph
Mull, Margret—Mull, John
Mull, Mary—Shell, John
Mull, Salley—Ramsey, James
Mull, Sarah—Ekard, Joseph
Mull, Saraha—Mosteller, Peter
Mullen, Ann—Varner, Wm A
Mullens, Mary—Hause, Andrew J
Mullin, Elizabeth—Summey, Robert R
Munday, Polly—Wells, James
Munday, Rebeckah—Tucker, Clinton
Munday, Rose A—Roberson, Thomas M
Murphey, Joannah—Wilson, John
Murphy, Anney—Wilson, Robert
Murphy, Elizabeth—Evans, Moses
Murphy, Fanney—Richards, James
Murphy, Sarah—Kerr, Robert B
Murray, Elizabeth—Hansel, Hubbard
Murrel, Martha—Clanton, William

Murrill, Nancy—Robson, James
Myers, Catharine—Bragg, Benjamin
Myers, Elizabeth—Hoover, Henry, Jr

Nail, Barbara—Ikerd, Daniel
Nance, Amanda—McRaven, David
Nance, Betsy—Anthony, Darling
Nance, Betsy—Dellinger, Munroe
Nance, Caroline—Rhoads, David
Nance, Catey—Abernathy, John
Nance, Francis S—Brindel, Joseph H
Nance, Hanner S—Winget, Thomas
Nance, Harriette R—Dellinger, M C
Nance, Mary—Allran, John
Nance, Mary S—Hambright, Franklin
Nance, Olly—Abernathy, Joseph T
Nance, Polly—Abernathy, Battee
Nance, Sarah—Hawkins, Pinkney C
Nantz, Julia E—Sherrill, E L
Nantz, Martha K—Brotherton, Hugh
Naugle, Adaline—Lutes, Laben
Naugle, Sally—Huffman, David
Neagle, Elizabeth—Anderson, John
Neagle, Margaret E—Price, Thos B
Neagle, Mary—Liddell, John G
Neale, Elizabeth—Hilton, Randolph
Nealey, Rebeca—Barnhill, Samuel S
Nearns, Mary—Piles, John
Nebb, Mary—Clotfelter, Alius
Neel, Anna—Barber, George
Neel, Barbary—Rutledge, George
Neel, Mary Ann—Wier, John Abel
Neel, Rosanna F—Allison, Robert
Neely, Martha J—Price, John J
Negle, Esther—Hutchison, Thomas L
Neil, Elizabeth—Neill, William
Neil, Lucinda—Black, Daniel
Neil, Margaret—Craft, John P
Neil. Polley—Ferguson, James
Neil, Polly—Mooney, Lawson
Neill, Jane—Allison, Thomas J
Neill, Margret—Ramsey, Andrew
Neill, Salley—Bridges, Alfred
Nelly, Margret—Craig, William
Nelson, Mary—Heron, Samuel H
Newman, Dovey—Loftin, Edmund
Newton, Mary—Beaver, William
Newton, Mary Ann—Queen, Laban
Newton, Sarah S—Bradshaw, Pride
Nichademus, Lucinda—Cloninger, Daniel
Nicols, Sarah—Abernathy, Robert
Niell, Poley—Center, James
Nixon, Agness—Little, John
Nixon, Betsey—Edwards, Amos
Nixon, Catharine—Rankin, John M
Nixon, Catherine—Hager, Michael
Nixon, Catherine—Hinkle, John L
Nixon. Elisabeth—Black, William
Nixon, Elisabeth—Hinkle, Cyrus
Nixon, Eliza—Abernathy, David M
Nixon, Elizabeth—Prim, George
Nixon, Isabella—Beal, William
Nixon, Jane—Graham, Ephraim
Nixon, Nancy—Hagar, Henry
Nixon, Nancy—Hager, James
Nixon, Sarah—Dellinger, L M

Nixon, Susan—Abernathy, Milton S
Nixon, Tabitha—Howard, Warner
Nixson, Martha—Stone, John
Nixson, Sally—Hager, John E
Nolen, Penelipy—Holland, Henery
Nolen, Rebecca G—McKenzie, David U
Norman, Betsy—Mooney, John
Norman, Betsy—Gates, William
Norman, Prethean—Willis, William
Norman, Sarah—Wilson, James A
Norman, Sebrey—Davis, Uriah
Norman, Thane—Hartman, Wilie
Normon, Mary Y—Stockston, George W
Norris, Elizabeth—Perkins, John, Jr
Norris, Lenna—Summey, Jacob
Norris, Nancy—Warlick, Philip
Norton, Alender—Rogers, William
Norton, Elizabeth—Belk, Thomas S
Norton, M—Kirton, Joseph P
Norton, Mary—Coner, Britain B
Norwood, Mary—Hager, James
Norwood, Sarah L C—Gilleland, O
Norwood, Susanah—Nixon, Archibald
Nowlan, Nancy—Buchanan, Thomas
Nowland, Sarah—Nowland, Charles
Null, Catharine A—Moore, Franklin B
Null, Christine—Winebargar, Jacob
Null, Elizabeth—Bolick, David
Null, Margred—Hedrick, Solomon
Null, Marry—Winebargar, William
Null, Sarah—Hefnar, Elias

Oates, Martha—Weir, Alexander
Oates, Sarah—Niell, Adam
Oats, Anny—Sarvies, Joseph
Oats, Jane—Smith, Andrew
Oats, Jeane—Espie, John
Oats, Margaret M—Bigham, R H
Oats, Mary—Bell, Alexander
Oats, Mary—Chandler, Milchisedeck
Oaves, Hanah—Haeffer, Lewis
Odam, Elisabeth—Bumgerner, John
Odam, Nancy—Yount, Daniel
Odom, Rebeckah—Bumgarner, Charles
Odum, Delian—Baxter, Burr
Oliver, Elizabeth—Armstrong, Samuel
Oliver, Elizabeth—Dealasnider, David
Oliver, Harriot—Armstrong, Andrew
Oliver, Jamima—Davis, John B
Oliver, Margaret—McKee, George
Oliver, Mary—Bollinger, Abraham
Olliver, Sarah—Boyd, Edward
Oneal, Honour—Grigg Abner
O'Neel, Faney—Burns, Daniel
Oneil, Malinda—Grigg, Burrel
O'Nell, Ann—Hawkins, John
Orents, Polly—Abernathy, Philip
Ormand, Cyntha—White, Samuel
Ormond, Mary—Borland, John
Ornt, Mary—Canseler, Henry
Orond, Betsey—Smith, David
Orr, Rachel—Johnson, David
Overwinters, Margret—Gross, John
Owens, Mary Ann—Cathey, Andrew
Oxford, Katrine—Adams, David

Pack, Betsy—Rhodes, Peter
Page, Elizabeth—Mauney, Peter
Painter, Susan—Stiller, George
Palmer, Anne—Allen, Benjamin
Palmer, Betsy—Simmons, John
Palmer, Leanan—Wallace, John Allen
Palmer, Martha—Rogers, Curnelias
Palmer, Sarah—Eaton, Jonathan
Pannel, Mary—Henry, William
Panter, Nancy—Srum, Peter
Panter, Patsy—Keener, Martin
Panter, Salley—Engle, John
Parish, Elizabeth—Keen, Aldridge
Parish, Lucinda—Moore, Simeon
Parish, Malinda—Stinson, William
Parish, Mehala—Gilleland, Thomas
Parker, Catherine—Bomgarner, Luis
Parker, Elizabeth—Huell, Abner
Parker, Elizabeth—Burns, James
Parker, Elizabeth—Robison, Alexander H
Parker, Hanah—Hovis, Daniel
Parker, Jenny—Bishop, Jeremiah
Parker, Lovina—Foy, Jesse
Parker, M J—Reinhardt, Daniel
Parker, Mary—Kiser, Henry
Parker, Nancy—Bradshaw, Larkin
Parker, Patience—Childers, Isom
Parker, Peggy—Williams, William
Parker, Polley—Sherril, Aron
Parker, Polly—Sadler, James
Parker, Rody—Parker, Levi
Parker, Sally—Kiser, Joseph
Parks, Amanda—Munday, James A
Partin, Elizabeth—Fisher, Samuel
Pasehaur, Betsey—Carpenter, Daniel
Pasour, Annie—Huffstetelr, Eli
Pasour, Polley—Kizer, John
Paterson, Agnes—Alexander, Josiah
Paterson, Sarah—Hill, John
Patrick, Rachel—Ewing, Samuel
Patterson, Catharine—Adams, James
Patterson, Eliza—McCully, Thomas M
Patterson, Elizabeth—Moore, William
Patterson, Esther—Henry, James
Patterson, Jane—Davis, David
Patterson, Lovina—Ballard, John H
Patterson, Martha—Davidson, James
Patterson, Polly—Jackson, Elias M
Patterson, Sarah—Gordon, Hugh
Patton, Jane—Houston, John
Paysaur, Rebeca—Cloneger, David
Paysour, Catharina—Summit, Frederick
Peacock, Susan—Lefever, John
Peacock, Susannah—Propst, John
Peasour, Elizabeth—Linebarger, Lewis
Peed, Mary—Ward,Franklin B
Peed, Nancy—Little, George
Peerson, Betsey—Ponder, John
Pegram, A M—Craig, S W
Pegram, M H C—Ward, H N
Pelmer, Elizabeth—Gilliland, James
Pelt, Margaret A—Bisanar, Moses
Penanton, Kesiah—Sherrill, Evin
Penatton, Nancy—Helms,Peter
Pendleton, Margaret—Hull, E M
Pendleton, Martha A—Lingafelt, David
Pendleton, Milley—Pollard, John

Penick, Phebe—Hopkins, Richard
Penney, Cattey—Vance, David
Penney, Nancy—Cobb, Starling
Penny, Abigail—Norton, James
Penny, Louisa—Cobb, Philip
Penny, Luceda—Traylor, Wells B
Penny, Mary—Doss, Joel
Perkins, Anne—Linebarger, Michael
Perkins, Betsey—Jones, Elisha
Perkins, Eliza T—Adams, Robert E
Perkins, Epsey—Helton, Robert
Perkins, Martha—Southard, Micajah
Perkins, Martha J—Reinhardt, Franklin D
Perkins, Mary—Miller, Robert Johnston
Perkins, Salley—Row, Jacob
Perkins, Salley—Carpenter, Levi
Perkins, Susannah—Jenkins, David
Peterson, Anna—Herman, Matthias
Peterson, Elizabeth—Sigman, Abel
Peterson, Martha—Paterson, Thomas
Peterson, Mary M—Moser, Marcus M
Peterson, Polly—Cline, George
Peterson, Pricilla—Bullinger, Matthias
Petillo, Susana—Little, Thomas
Petree, Catharine—Shook, John Henderson
Petree, Polly—Turbyfill, William S
Petty, Margarett—Flours, Darlin
Phifer, Adaline—Shipp, Moses
Phifer, Sarah L—Hauser, John T
Philips, Abigal—Alexander, Sample
Philips, Betsey—Frisl, Jacob
Philips, Jane—Underwood, Henry
Philips, Polley—Harwood, Ely
Phillips, Barbary—Ashe, Joseph
Phillips, Elenor—Cobb, Robert
Phillips, Elizabeth—Lawing, Andrew
Phillips, Hannah—Setlemier, Jacob
Phillips, Martha—Phillups, James
Phillips, Rachel—Cox, Fleet
Pierce, Tabitha—Tugue, Josiah
Pinion, Fanny—Costner, Absalom
Pinion, Mrs Malinda—Ormand, Zenas S
Pinkston, Eliner—Rockett, Richard
Pinner, Jeane—Roads, James
Pinner, Minty K—Stowe, James F
Pinner, Patience—Baldwin, Armsted
Pinner, Peggy—Wethers, Benj E
Piram, Susanna—Southard, Henry
Pitts, Elisabeth—Benfield, Daniel
Pitts, Fanny—Barger, Simeon, Jr
Pitts, Maryan—Moore, Abraham
Pitts, Polley—Shronce, Charles
Pitts, Susannah—Winkler, Abraham
Plantina, Lovina—Dellinger, John W
Plonk, Catharine—Fronabarger, William
Plonk, Catharine—Avery, Philip
Plonk, Christena—Brown, Jacob J
Plonk, Elizabeth—Cloninger, Adam
Plonk, Elizabeth—McAllister, George W
Plonk, Margaret—Rhyne, Esli
Plonk, Margaret C—Taylor, Andrew J
Plonk, Mary—Bolinger, Daniel J
Plonk, Nancy—Farmer, Absalom
Plonk, Sally—Crouse, David
Plonk, Susan—Avery, George
Plonk, Susan C—Rhyne, Joseph K
Plott, Katharine—Huskins, Robert

Plott, Sarah Jane—Robinson, Robert H
Pluming, Mary—Martin, Jacob
Plunk, Catherine—Hause, Henry
Plunk, Catherine—Hafner, Jacob
Plunk, Cathrine—Carpenter, Nicholas
Plunk, Elizabeth—Baker, Allen
Plunk, Sarah—Weaver, John
Plunk, Susana—Tuthero, George
Pollard, Elizabeth—Greenhill, Philip
Pollard, Rebecca—Shitle, Charles W
Pollard, Sally—Titmon, Peter
Pool, Anna M—Keever, William
Pope, Julia—Humphreys, James
Porter, Cyrena—Fulbright, Daniel
Porter, Martha—Henry, Israel W
Porter, Sally Ann—Brimer, Samuel
Powell, Elisabeth—Seizen, Stephen
Prevet, Asceneth—Morrison, William
Price, Ana—Steely, John
Price, Eleanor—Patterson, Arthur, Jr
Price, Fanny—Freeman, Jesse
Price, Jemima—Wells, Robert
Price, Mary D—West, Isaac W P
Price, Polly Minerva—Smith, William L
Price, Sarah—Smith, Lawson
Prim, Dovy—Swaim, William
Prim, Mary Ann—Rily, James
Pringel, Letty—Lore, John
Pringle, Betcy—Hafner, Abraham
Pritched, Catharine—Barringer, Mathies
Prithardt, Catherine—Tucker, John
Probst, Delila—Whitener, Ephraim
Probst, Mary—Eckerd, George
Probst, Sabina—Bolch, Godfrey
Proctor, Eliza—Fitzjarold, Mylas
Proctor, Elizabeth—Litten, Samuel
Proctor, Elizabeth—Guthrey, Madison
Proctor, Elizabeth—Proctor, Joseph
Proctor, Fanny—King, William
Proctor, Julia—Adams, James P
Proctor, Mary A—Nixon, James
Propest, Viney—Short, David
Propst, Ann—Hubbard, Charles W
Propst, Elizabeth—Lin, John W
Propst, Susan C—Propst, John M
Pryor, Golsey—Kincaid, David
Pryor, Martha Ann—Nance, William
Puntch, Elizabeth—Mehaffey, Joseph
Puntch, Jaine—Williams, C
Purkins, Elisabeth—Starns, Columbus
Purkins, Honora—Ghent, John

Queen, Elizabeth—Gibson, George
Queen, Margaret—Bird, Henry
Queen, Margaret—Gerald, Adam
Queen, Nancy C—Holland,
    Washington Frenau
Quickel, Ann—Thomson, Horatio
Quickiel, Catherine—Carpenter, Jacob
Quickle, Malinda—Costner, Ambrose
Quigle, Barbary—Hoke, John
Quigle, Mary—Cansler, Philip
Quin, Margaret E—Falls, And N
Quinn, Mary A—Holland, Franklin H
Quinn, Sarah E—Holland, Jasper N

Rabb, Hannah—Fox, Patrick
Raden, Lidia—Bowman, John
Raden, Sally—Cline, William
Rader, Charity—Berry, John
Rader, Polley—Coulter, Henry
Rader, Sally—Deal, George
Ragon, Ellen—Ford, Amzi
Railey—see Bailey
Ralph, Dianah—Davis, Luke L
Ramsaur, Barbara—Heedick, Jonas
Ramsaur, Sarah—Schenck, Henry
Ramsey, Anna—Roper, William
Ramsey, Elizabeth—Stroud, John
Ramsey, J B—Hause, Andrew J
Ramsey, Jane—Summey, George
Ramsey, Jane—Stamey, Lawson A
Ramsey, Margret—Carpenter, John
Ramsey, Mary N—Hauss, Andrew
Ramsey, Saley—Stemey, John
Ramsour, Alice M—Richardson, John M
Ramsour, Amelia C—Wray, William
Ramsour, Ann—Wilfong, G Danl
Ramsour, Ann—Fulenwider, Henry
Ramsour, Ann—Ramsour, William
Ramsour, Anna—Wilfong, G D
Ramsour, Barbara—Coulter, John
Ramsour, Barbara—Heedick, David
Ramsour, Catey—Hoke, Henry
Ramsour, Catharine E—Shuford, Obed P
Ramsour, Catherine—Michal, Jacob
Ramsour, Cynthia L—Hoyl, Eli
Ramsour, Eliza—Phifer, Martin, Jr
Ramsour, Elizabeth—Loretz, Andrew H
Ramsour, Elizabeth C—Phifer, John F
Ramsour, Elmina—Summerow, Peter
Ramsour, H C—Ramsour, F S
Ramsour, Harriet L—Thompson, L E
Ramsour, Julia A E—Ramsour, Caleb H
Ramsour, Lenney—Crowell, Churchwell A
Ramsour, Lydia J—Bell, R M
Ramsour, M A—Phifer, Caleb
Ramsour, Mahala—Tillet, Richard
Ramsour, Marget—Warlick, Daniel
Ramsour, Martha A—Ramsour, William
Ramsour, Mary—Carpenter, John
Ramsour, Mary—Ramsour, Jacob
Ramsour, Mary A E—Middlekauff,
    Solomon S
Ramsour, Mary Ann—Boger, John E
Ramsour, Myra A—Sumner, Benj H
Ramsour, Nancy C—Ramsour, Vardry M
Ramsour, Polley—Loretz, John F
Ramsour, Sallie W—Schenck, David
Ramsour, Sally—Bollinger, George F
Ramsour, Sarah—Ramsaur, Andrew
Ramsour, Sarah C—Forney, D J
Ramsour, Susan B—Reinhardt, Robt P
Ramsour, Susannah—Hoke, Henry
Ramsy, Polly—Muckleroy, John
Randels, Christian—Welch, John
Randleman, Isabella C—Edwards,
    Ephraim S
Randles, Mary—Seffret, John
Rankin, Ann—Rutledge, James
Rankin, Catharine—Nixon, Franklin
Rankin, Ellener—Dickson, Joseph
Rankin, Jean—Hargrove, Benjamin

171

Rankin, Margaret—Moody, John
Rankin, Margaret E—Abernathy, Lawson H
Rankin, Nancy—Reid, William
Rankin, Peggy—Witherspoon, Thos
Rankin, Sarah C—Morris, Benjamin
Rankin, Susan—Johnson, Joseph
Rannals, Mimy—Mitchem, Nathaniel
Ransom, Elisabeth—Rhyne, Jonas
Ratchford, Jane C—Carrothers, Ezekiel
Ratchford, Mary D—Reid, James W
Ray, Jean—Niell, Thomas
Rayfel, Harriett—Leatherman, Rudolph
Rayfield, Jane—Reep, Henry
Raymer, Susanna—Whetstone, John
Reader, Elisabeth—Fry, John
Reather, Fanny—Heyard, Lewis
Rector, Carline—Woodring, Daniel
Reder, Margered—Bolick, Jacob
Reece, Sally—Hartsoge, Elias
Reece, Sophia—Killian, Andrew
Reed, Elisabeth—Guffey, John
Reed, Elizabeth—Bradburn, Thomas
Reed, Elizabeth G—Williamson, Robert
Reed, Julier—Nance, James A
Reed, Leteetia—Cochren, Robert
Reed, Martha—Robinson, Adam P
Reed, Mary—Givens, John
Reed, Mary—Nixson, William
Reed, Mary—Johnston, Robert
Reed, Mary—Beatty, John
Reel, Mary—Abernathy, D M
Reel, Nancy—Keever, Thomas
Reel, Susan A—Brown, John A
Reep, Anna Catharine—Bringle, Lorenz
Reep, Barbara—Clay, Daniel
Reep, Fanny—Sain, John
Reep, Mary—Saine, Daniel
Reep, Mary—Lackey, James
Reep, Polly—Williams, John
Reep, Sarah—Shitle, John
Reep, Susan—Oats, John
Reep, Susanah—Wise, Joseph
Reggin, Diadame—Forney, Abram E
Regins, Elizabeth—Goodson, Ephraim
Reid, Agness—Womack, Abner
Reid, Charlotte—Hovis, Michel
Reid, Jean—Moore, John
Reid, Rebecky—Bond, Isaac
Reinhardt, Anna—Hunt, Noah
Reinhardt, Balinda—Paysour, Felix
Reinhardt, Barbara—Abernathy, William I
Reinhardt, Eliza—Loretz, Daniel
Reinhardt, Elizabeth—Havner, David
Reinhardt, Jane H—Lytle, James H
Reinhardt, Katharine—Clapp, Jacob
Reinhardt, Mary—Baker, Eli
Reinhardt, Maryann—Bennick, David R
Reinhardt, Polley—Knipe, Christian
Reinhardt, Sally—Hull, Levi
Reinhardt, Sally—Rudisell, George
Reinhardt, Susan Adaline—Wells, William S
Reinhardt, Susannah—Holly, Daniel
Reinhardt, Violet—Wilson, Philip
Reinhart, Catharine—Rudisil, John
Reinharte, Christeaner—Shitle, Anthony
Reinharte, Rachel—Lore, Joshua
Relf, Susan W—Perkins, Reuben

Renwick, Mary—Hanks, Joshua
Retherford, Rachel—Newton, Ebenezer
Revan, Milley—Jinkins, Jesse
Revels, Mrs Mary—Mitchell, William L
Reymer, May—Helms, Jacob
Reynolds, Anna—Edwards, James
Reynolds, Betcy—Baker, Jose
Reynolds, Lydia—Warlick, John
Reynolds, Nancy—Nelson, James
Reynolds, Polly—Martin, William
Reynolds, Rachael—Brown, Robert H
Reynolds, Sally—Bullenger, Christen
Rhaume, Catharine—Morrison, Joshua
Rheindhart, Anna F—Bird, Frank
Rhine, Barbara—Fronaberger, William
Rhine, Barbara—Bowers, Gillan G
Rhine, Margaret—Hofman, Jacob
Rhine, Mary—Cloninger, Thomas
Rhinehart, Elizabeth—Carpenter, David
Rhoades, Carey—McCarver, James
Rhoads, Cathrine—Clemmer, Eli
Rhoads, Mary—Best, Daniel
Rhodes, Catharine—Lefever, Isaac
Rhodes, Catherine—Leonard, Andrew
Rhodes, Clarissa—Shuford, Sidney
Rhodes, Elizabeth—Hoyle, Jacob
Rhodes, Fanny—Jenkins, Ben J
Rhodes, Magalina—Anthony, Paul
Rhodes, Mary—Ramsaur, Philip
Rhodes, Mary Ann—Rockett, John R
Rhodes, Mary M—Linebarger, Caleb
Rhodes, Nancy F—Robinson, J A
Rhodes, Sarah—Hawkins, Woodliff
Rhodes, Susy—Linkhorn, Thomas
Rhom, Lucinda—Bailey, William
Rhom, Susanah—Fox, James
Rhony, Jane—Siegle, James F
Rhyne, Ann—Redman, Saml
Rhyne, Anna—Moore, Alexander
Rhyne, Anna—Hoyl, Burril W
Rhyne, Anny—Jenkins, Benjamin
Rhyne, Anny—Hovis, Adam
Rhyne, Barbara—Rhodes, Henry
Rhyne, Barbara—Paysour, Ephraim
Rhyne, Eliza—Holland, Robert
Rhyne, Elizabeth—Rhyne, Jacob
Rhyne, Elizabeth—Hovis, Moses
Rhyne, Elizabeth—Paysour, John
Rhyne, Elizabeth—Costner, Peter
Rhyne, Elizabeth—Rhyne, Simon P
Rhyne, Elizabeth—Featherston, Jasper
Rhyne, Elizebeth—Boyd, Robert M
Rhyne, Fany—Best, Michael
Rhyne, Fanny—Linebarger, Lewis
Rhyne, Fanny—Hoffman, Miles
Rhyne, Hannah—Stroup, Jacob
Rhyne, Jane C—Mendenhall, Eli
Rhyne, Lavina—Setzer, Reuben
Rhyne, Louisa—Clemor, Adam
Rhyne, Margaret—Jenkins, Hugh
Rhyne, Margaret—Summey, Jonas
Rhyne, Margret E—Dameron, John
Rhyne, Mary—Rhodes, Christian
Rhyne, Mary—Best, Samuel
Rhyne, Mary—Gingles, David
Rhyne, Mary—Holland, Julius
Rhyne, Marry—Clemmer, Andrew

Rhyne, Nancy—Gates, M Wilson
Rhyne, Peggy—Pendleton, Joshua
Rhyne, Polly A—Wise, Absalom
Rhyne, Rebeckah—Huffman, Levi
Rhyne, Sally—Weathers, Samuel
Rhyne, Sarah—Hoffman, Jonas
Rhyne, Sarah Lavina—Weathers, Martin R
Rhyne, Sarah S—Springs, Elias A
Rhyne, Susannah—Setzer, Henry
Rhyne, Susannah—Helms, Hiram
Rice, Mary—Wallace, William
Richard, Elizabeth—Gwaltney, Abraham
Richard, Sally Dovina—Miller, Willington F
Richards, Catherine—Helderman, Jacob
Richards, Christina—Clipperd, Rufus
Richards, Julia—Queen, Berry
Richards, Malinda—Queen, Joshua
Richards, Margaret—Bynum, William
Richards, Mary—Hovis, Wesley Hartwel
Richards, Polley—Kilian, Fedrick
Richards, Susanah—Parker, David
Richardson, Nancy—Bysinger, John
Right, Leanna—Craige, Thomas
Riley, Dovey—Hansil, William J
Rill, Rachel—Ramsey, John
Rinck, Susannah—Spencer, Benjamin
Rine, Hannah—Boyck, John Henry
Rine, Hannah—Paysour, David
Rine, Jude—Sigman, John
Rine, Susanah—Mauney, Christian
Rine, Susanah—Dickson, James
Rinehardt, Eve—Anthony, Daniel
Rinehart, Elisebeth—Mcleroy, James
Ring, Mary—Moll, Jhon
Rinharte, Mary—Rudisel, David H
Rippy, Rhodah—McEntire, Alexander
Rithey, Poley An—Young, Solomon
Roberson, Jane H—Torrence, Lawson H
Roberson, Leah—Abernathy, William
Roberson, Luisa—Lattimore, Joseph
Roberson, Rachel E—Long, Wm
Roberts, Catherine—Melton, Marvel
Roberts, Ester—Homesley, Stephen
Roberts, Jane—Summey, Peter A
Roberts, Nancy C—Endsley, William
Roberts, Sally—Green, Samuel
Roberts, Sally—Carpenter, Jonas
Roberts, Susan—Miller, Adam
Roberts, Susanna—McArthur, John
Roberts, Susannah—Hutchason, John
Roberts, Unity—Harriss, John
Roberts, Unity—Heedick, Jacob
Robertson, Anne—Heaker, Robert
Robertson, Jean—Dinwiddie, James
Robeson, Betcy—Wolwer, John
Robeson, Elizabeth—Bynum, Vincent
Robeson, Eliz'th—West, James
Robeson, July Ann—Munday, J A
Robeson, Leah—Hoyle, Jacob
Robeson, Martha—Houser, Jonas
Robeson, Rachel—Litton, Samuel
Robeson, Sarah Jane—Howard, John
Robeson, Seina—Laney, Archibald B
Robinson, Anne—Hill, James
Robinson, Caroline C—Earny, William L
Robinson, Elender—Person, Alfred
Robinson, Eliza—Milling, Alexander

Robinson, Eliza—Brown, John
Robinson, Elizabeth—Goble, Corban
Robinson, Elizabeth—Asbury, Henry
Robinson, Elizabeth—Jones, James
Robinson, Fanny—Harwood, William
Robinson, Harriet—Hampton, David
Robinson, Jane—Holdsclaw, Lewis
Robinson, Jean—Hill, James
Robinson, Leah—Jones, Alexander
Robinson, Mahala—Stuard, Leander S
Robinson, Martha—Colwell, Daniel
Robinson, Melinda—Groves, John
Robinson, Miriam—Torrance, Hugh A
Robinson, Nancy—Gabriel, Jacob F
Robinson, Nancy M—Young, Solomon
Robinson, Nersissa—Thompson,
   Hezekiah H
Robinson, Patsey—Scarbrough, Silas S
Robinson, Polley—Whitener, Daniel
Robinson, Polly—Hix, William
Robinson, Prissy—Grose, Philip
Robinson, Rebecker—Gabriel, Joseph M
Robinson, Ruth—Denham, John
Robinson, Sally—Spencer, Joshua
Robinson, Sarah—Clark, James
Robinson, Susannah—Williams, Daniel
Robison, Mrs Anny—Dellinger, Ephraim
Robison, Catherine—Wilson, Joseph
Robison, Elizabeth—Shuford, John
Robison, Frankey—Hager, William
Robison, Hannah—Shuford, Daniel
Robison, Holly—Ornts, Fredrick
Robison, Jane—Roaney, John
Robison, Jane C—Sturd, N T
Robison, Margaret—Armstrong, James
Robison, Polly—Seaboch, Peter
Robison, Polly—Sherrill, Theophilus
Robison, Rebecca—Summitt, John
Robison, Sarah—Seabouch, Joseph
Rocket, Elisabeth—Vance, Samuel
Rocket, Jane—Hutson, Daniel
Rocket, Nancy—Abernathy, Miles
Rocket, Salley—Howard, Benjamin
Rocket, Polly—Abernathy, James
Roderick, Eliza—Hoover, Franklin
Rodes, Amy—Smith, David
Rodgers, Nancy—Dunken, Ephram
Rogers, Adiline—Brodaway, Samuel
Rogers, Fanny—Mowser, Frederick
Rominger, Ketren—Peterson, Matthias
Roney, Elizabeth—Spanuel, Emanuel
Rook, Susey—Barber, Richard
Rooks, Elizabeth—Smith, Abraham
Rosamon, Rachina—Lanning, William
Roseman, Lile—Brown, Levi
Roseman, Nancy—Brown, Levi
Rosemond, Ruanna—Deal, Daniel
Rosimond, Mary—Levain, Isaac
Ross, Mary—Conner, Thomas
Ross, Mary—Jenkins, William
Rouch, Peggy—Eckerd, George
Rough, Catherine—Link, Henry W
Rough, Soloma S—Routh, Gilbert P
Rouse, Catherine—Hunt, John
Rozzel, Mary—Kerr, James
Rozzel, Nancy—Canseler, Peter
Rozzell, Elizabeth—Thompson, Jacob L

Rozzell, Mary V—Connelly, Minton A
Rudesail, Marget—Linn, Archibald
Rudesale, Susana—Wyant, Peter
Rudesell, Elisabeth—Carpenter, Samuel
Rudesiele, Sussana—Whitstone, Daniel
Rudesill, Eliza A—Deal, Eli E
Rudesille, Catherina—Warlick, David
Rudessel, Anne—Costner, Jacob
Rudicell, Milly—Carpenter, William
Rudicil, Elisabeth—Parker, Christian
Rudicill, Polly—Hovis, Frederick
Rudisail, Catharine—Link, Jacob
Rudisel, ------—Freytag, Martin
Rudisel, Ann—Stroup, John
Rudisel, Barbara—Plonk, Joseph
Rudisel, Catharine—Rhyne, Thomas
Rudisel, Eve—Mosteller, John, Jr
Rudisel, Francis—Deal, Jacob
Rudisel, Margaret—Aderhold, Abraham
Rudisel, Mary E—Barringer, Joseph
Rudisel, Salley—Eaker, Christian
Rudisell, Catharine—Harman, Michael
Rudisell, Dolly—Early, John
Rudisell, Elisa—Stamy, Peter
Rudisell, Elizabeth S—Stroup, Israel R
Rudisell, Katy—Roberts, John
Rudisell, Luiza—Goodson, Ephraim
Rudisell, Rebeccah—Mendenhall, Joseph H
Rudisil, Martha A—Garrison, Henry
Rudisil, Polley—Mosteller, Peter
Rudisil, Susanah—Hafner, John
Rudisill, Ann—Bell, Robert H
Rudisill, Ann Mary—Miller, Adam
Rudisill, Betsey—Baker, Allen
Rudisill, Carrie—Killian, John A
Rudisill, Dicy—Rudisill, George
Rudisill, F L—Adams, Wm C
Rudisill, Hetta—Smith, James M
Rudisill, Lavinia—Costner, Michael H
Rudisill, Margaret—Mauney, Abraham
Rudisill, Martha A A—Tiddy, William
Rudisill, Mary—Crouse, David
Rudisill, Mary Jane—Sides, Geo W
Rudisill, Mary M—Plonk, David
Rudisill, Paulina—Coiner, John K
Rudisill, Rebecca R—Rothrock, Lewis P
Rudisill, Sally—Adderholt, David
Rudisill, Sarah—Reinhardt, Isaac
Rudisill, Susannah—Summerow, David
Rudisill, Susannah—Hoke, Daniel
Rudissale, Susana—Hovis, Jacob
Rudissel, Polly—Killian, Henry
Rumfelt, Barbary—West, Barny
Rumfelt, Catherine—West, Isaac, Jr
Runels, Susan E—Nixon, William
Runnels, Nancy—Glenn, John
Runolds, Rachael—Morrison, Abner
Rush, Eliza A—Abernathy, H W
Rush, Lidda—Thomas, Zebulon J
Rush, Mary—Sellers, John
Rush, Sarah—Mauney, Isaac
Russell, Elvy—Russell, Peter
Rutherford, Ellener—Newton, Ebenezer
Rutherford, Nancy—Heslet, Ezekiel
Rutledge, Amy—McGinnas, John Al
Rutledge, Jane—Arent, Jacob
Rutledge, Jean—Thomas, Thomas

Rutledge, Jean—Martin, Joseph
Rutledge, Lema—Linebarger, Eli
Rutledge, Mary—Smith, Alexander
Rutledge, Nancy—Kizer, Christy
Rutledge, Salley—Johnson, Andrew
Rutledge, Sarah—Darr, Valentine
Ryne, Fanny—Kiser, Martin

Saddler, Mary—Nance, William
Sadler, Anny—Harvey, Thomas
Sadler, Assenath—Blalock, James
Sadler, Disey—Mabry, Jesse
Sadler, Fanny—Shelton, Nelson
Sadler, Lucey—Alexander, Isaac
Sadler, Lucy—Wilbanks, Warren S
Sadler, Polley—Penny, William
Sadler, Salley—Hopkins, John
Sadler, Susanna—Hansill, James
Sain, Anna Elizabeth—Warlick, James M
Sain, Barbara—Sims, Thomas
Sain, Catharine—Sain, Noah
Sain, M J—Lutz, M M
Sain, Rosanna—Wyant, Samuel W
Sain, Sarah—Houser, Jonason
Saine, Mary Ann—Reep, Henry
Saine, Mary C—Hoyle, Andrew
Saine, Sally—Reinharte, John
Saine, Susan—Reinhardt, Alfred
Saine, Susana—Rudesil, John
St John, Julia L—Coulter, J
Salmon, Almira M—Maclean, T B
Sample, Hannah—Martin, William
Samson, Carolna—Pope, Lawson
Sanders, Ann—Weber, John
Sanders, Frances—Clanton, Levi
Sanders, Louisa—Hicks, Miles
Sanders, Nancy J—Rice, James L
Sanders, Polly C—Hartsock, Emanuel
Sanders, Sarah—Dellinger, Franklin
Sane, Catharine—Jonas, Abel
Sane, Mary—McCurry, J T M
Sane, Sarah—London, Henry
Sane, Sidney—Fullbright, John
Sanger, Mary Ann—Hickman, James
Sauls, Barbara—Srons, John
Sauls, Caroline—Hovis, Henry
Sauls, Mary—West, Michael
Sauls, Mary A—Long, Henry H
Saunders, Betcy—Low, John
Saunders, Lenny—Helderman, David
Saunders, Nancy—Lockman, Levi
Saunders, Patsey—Beaver, Hezekiah
Saunders, Polley—Reas, Paul A
Saypaugh, Margarett—Leonard, Jacob
Scarborough, Dorcas—Stroder, William
Scarborough, Elizabeth—King, John D
Scarlet, Jemyme—Froy, David
Schenck, Barbara—Hamby, Allen
Schenck, Barbara—Jenkins, James C
Schenck, C L—Maclean, A A
Schenck, Catherine—Richardson, James I
Schenck, Lovina—McPherson, Angus
Schnider, Frances—Wacaser, George W
Schrum, Susannah—Epply, Peter
Scott, Mary—Moore, John
Scott, Mary D—Jarmon, William

Scott, Nancey—Johnson, Alexander
Scott, Nancy—Carns, David B
Scrum, Christina—Clodfelter, Felix
Seabold, Molly—Flowers, Peter
Seabold, Sally—Flowers, Andrew
Seagle, Barbara—Clay, Isaac
Seagle, Barbara—Smith, John
Seagle, Barbara L—Goodman, John
Seagle, Catharine M—Warlick, Eli A
Seagle, Chatrena—Row, John
Seagle, Elizabeth—Coon, George
Sagle, Julia A R—Turbyfill, M
Seagle, Margaret—Shell, David
Seagle, Polly—Link, David
Seagle, Sarah—Yoder, Solomon
Seagle, Sarah Ann—Jetton, F J
Seagle, Sarah J—Kistler, Wm H
Sebach, Elisebeth—Jacobes, Adam
Sebaugh, Betsey—Reep, Daniel
Seeford, Caty—Keepers, William
Segel, Polley—Rudisill, Jonas
Seine, Caty—Houser, John
Seine, Elizabeth—Keneday, Isaac
Seits, Lucrecy—Goodson, Abner
Seitz, Darcus—Penny, Cullen
Seitz, Fanny—Hains, Matthew
Seitz, Levina—Hawn, Henry
Seitz, Polly—Rinck, Jacob
Self, Elizabeth—Heger, David
Self, Elizabeth—Wright, Benjamin
Self, Elizabeth—Mauney, Christopher
Self, Elizabeth—Liles, Henry
Self, Hanna—Ledford, Jesse
Self, Mimy—Crotts, Jacob
Self, Nancy—Brown, Robert H
Self, Patsey—Wright, Robert
Self, Ruthey—Bradly, Willis
Self, Sarah—Waters, John M
Sellars, Betcy—Beever, Henry
Sellers, Caty—Fronabarger, John
Sellers, Margaret—Baker, John
Sellers, Susannah—Baker, Jacob
Senter, Agness—Senter, John
Senter, Anne—Holloway, Billey
Senter, Betsey—Weathers, Allen
Senter, Betsey—Spencer, Thomas
Senter, Judea—Bower, Thomas
Senter, Kezia—Gosnell, Necles
Sepaugh, Poley—Cook, Joseph
Serat, Dorcas—Brotherton, Hiram
Serratt, Phebe—Stilwell, Nimrod
Servis, Mary—Gamble, Joseph
Setlemier, Polly—Wilson, David
Setser, Elizabeth—Withespoon, James
Settlemier, Sally—Fulbright, George
Settlemire, Agness—Wittenberg, Peter
Settlemyer, Elizabeth—Sigman, Ely
Setzer, Ada—Sigman, George H
Setzer, Catherine—Longcrier, Elias
Setzer, Mary Ann—Wilson, M M
Setzer, Nancy—Rhine, Daniel W
Setzer, Nancy E—Propst, Avey
Setzer, S M—Smere, Daniel
Setzer, Sally—Carpenter, Peter
Setzer, Sarah—Dellinger, Jacob
Seury, Mary—Bookout, Silas
Shannon, Esther—Floyd, Andrew

Shannon, Mary—Cox, William
Sharpe, Katrine—Reather, William
Shearer, Sarah—Pinner, William
Shearman, Letty—Murrel, Isaac
Sheets, Barbara—Wood, Vincent
Shell, Barbary—Wittenberg, Henry
Shell, Eave—Robinson, Joshua
Shell, Leah—Spencer, Joshua
Shell, Mary—Spencer, Docter
Shell, Rebecca—Bolick, Ambrose
Shell, Salley—Robeson, Jesse
Shell, Salley—Blackburn, Robert
Shell, Sarah C—Lenhardt, John W
Shell, Susan E—Hauss, Jacob
Shelley, Susannah—Cobb, Enoch
Shelton, Abigail—Low, James W
Shelton, Anny—Proctor, Benjamin
Shelton, Frances—Thompson, Thomas J
Shelton, Jinsey Janet—Pryor, David J
Shelton, Lucinda—Munday, William W
Shelton, Mary M—Wilkison, Marcus L
Shelton, Matisha—Duck, Ezekiel
Shelton, Mititia—Edwards, Stephen
Shelton, Polley—Dellinger, Andrew
Shelton, Susan—Armour, Arthur
Shelton, Susan—Munday, Spencer
Shenck, Elizabeth—McDaniel, Daniel G
Shepherd, Becky—Huffman, Peter
Shereman, Ann—Haase, David
Sheremon, Barbara—Hoke, Jacob
Sherill, Nancy C—Litton, Logan C
Sherman, Polly—Jarret, Absalom
Sherrale, Clarinda—Lee, Orsbun
Sherrall, Susan—Danner, Alexander
Sherrel, Caroline—Conner, Thomas
Sherrel, Margaret R—Carter, Joshua C
Sherrel, Martha—Graham, Ephraim
Sherrel, Sally—Abernathy, Samuel
Sherrell, Elitha—Hooper, John
Sherrell, Epsey M—Harwell, James
Sherrell, Levina—Hampton, John
Sherril, _____—Lourance, Joseph
Sherril, Agness—McCorkle, Richard
Sherril, Alis—Litten, Hiram
Sherril, Cassandria—Robinson, Jesse
Sherril, Casy—McCorkle, Thomas
Sherril, Elinor—Setzer, David
Sherril, Eliza—Litten, William
Sherril, Elizabeth—Barnes, John
Sherril, Esther—Corzine, Eli
Sherril, Mary—Loftin, Eldridge
Sherril, Martha—Sherrill, Henry
Sherril, Polley A—Blackburn, Robert
Sherril, Polly—Eaton, George
Sherril, Polly—Turbyfill, Anderson
Sherril, Rebeca—Purkins, Joshua
Sherril, Rebecca—Connelly, William
Sherril, Rebecca—Long, Thomas
Sherril, Ruana—Weylie, Benjamin
Sherril, Salley—Sherrill, Hiram
Sherril, Salley—Sherrill, Silas
Sherril, Sally—Sherrill, Joseph
Sherril, Sally—Sherrill, William
Sherril, Sally L—Day, Haner
Sherril, Susanah—Sherrill, Adam
Sherril, Theney—Suttlemyer, David
Sherrill, Ann—Sherrill, David R

Sherrill, Ann J—Cornelius, Austin
Sherrill, Darcus E—Hall, Josiah Q
Sherrill, Debitha—Gantt, Jesse
Sherrill, Deborough—Purvians, James
Sherrill, Easter—Clubb, Moses
Sherrill, Eliza—Hudspath, John T
Sherrill, Elizabeth L—Perkins, Elisha
Sherrill, Jane—Fleming, George
Sherrill, Judith—Beatty, Charles
Sherrill, Judith L—Shelton, Young
Sherrill, Margaret—Loller, Henry
Sherrill, Margaret—Robison, William M
Sherrill, Margret—Whitener, Henry
Sherrill, Martha—Robison, John W
Sherrill, Mary—Robison, John H
Sherrill, Mira—Sherrill, Eli
Sherrill, Nancy—Ward, Thomas
Sherrill, Nancy—Shelton, Meacon
Sherrill, Nancy—Johnson, Alexander
Sherrill, Nancy—Earny, Lafayette
Sherrill, Roana E—Julian, Baily F
Sherrill, Ruannah—Lourance, Martin
Sherrill, Rutha—Sherrill, Michael
Sherrill, Sarah C—Pain, Isaac E
Sherrill, Sarah E—Long, Uriah
Sherrill, Susan M—Linebarger, Hosea
Sherrill, Susanah—Loftin, James
Shetley, Kitty—Shrum, Jacob
Shetley, Mary—Umphrey, William
Shetly, Elizabeth—Stroup, Eli
Shidle, Barbara—Beam, David
Shinn, Prudence—Corzine, Abel
Shiphard, Polly—Buchanan, Thomas
Shipp, A E—Bynum, W P
Shirrill, Adline—Tomson, Robert
Shitle, Anny—Pendleton, John
Shitle, Christiana—Hafner, Nicholas
Shitle, Elizabeth—Havner, Valentine
Shitle, Malinda—Pollard, Hiram
Shitle, Martha—Carpenter, Robert C
Shitle, Mary—Wright, Samuel
Shitle, Rebeca—Rabb, Wm A
Shitle, Rebecca—Towry, William
Shitle, Sarah Ann—Wehunt, John
Shitly, Betsy—Cobb, Henry
Shook, Barbara—Drum, John
Shook, Catharine—Oel, Frederick
Shook, Elisabeth—Summit, Francis
Shook, Molly—Spigle, Martin
Shook, Nancy—Huffman, Eli
Shook, Nancy—Isaac, Jacob
Shook, Susannah—Huffman, Jacob
Short, Joan—Dorsey, Benjamin
Short, Polley—Abernathy, Moses
Shoup, Catharine—Wood, Absalom
Shoup, Sarah—Smith, David
Shrantz, Polly—Edwards, William
Shrom, Margaret—Weathers, James A
Shrum, Caroline V—King, Adolphus E
Shrum, Mary—Moore, George
Shrum, Mary—Eply, W J
Shrum, Sarah—Weathers, Oliver W
Shrum, Sarah—Forney, Hiram A
Shuck, Susanna—Arewood, William
Shufford, Barbara—Slagle, John
Shufford, Catherine—Warlick, Peter
Shufford, Claressy—Jarrett, John

Shufford, Elizabeth—Cathy, George
Shufford, Polly—Clay, John
Shufford, Salley—Cline, Jacob
Shuford, Adaline—Kistler, Aaron
Shuford, Anna—Robinson, David
Shuford, Anna—Leonard, Jacob
Shuford, Barbara—Litton, Lawson H
Shuford, Catharine—Carpenter, John J
Shuford, Clarissa—Rush, Jacob
Shuford, Elissabeth—Dellinger, John
Shuford, Elissabeth—Smyer, John
Shuford, Elizabeth—Shireman, Michael
Shuford, Elizabeth—Hoyle, Noah
Shuford, Elizabeth—Blackburn, Saml
Shuford, Elizabeth—Avery, Absalom
Shuford, Elizabeth M—Butts, David
Shuford, Eve—Summy, Jacob
Shuford, Eve—Ramsour, Jonas
Shuford, Fanny—Cansler, Henry
Shuford, Francis—Doggett, John R
Shuford, M Caroline—Johnston, Robert E
Shuford, Polly—Hines, Philip
Shuford, Sally—Rhyne, John
Shuford, Sarah—Link, Jacob
Shuford, Sarah—Miller, Caleb
Shuford, Sarah E—Ramsaur, Henry F
Shuford, Susan—Reinhardt, Lawson A
Shuford, Susen E—Colding, J D
Shulahr, Rosie—Mitchael, Jacob
Shull, Barbara—Brown, Absalom
Shull, Elizabeth—Buthof, Gasper
Shull, Frances—Black, Joseph
Shull, Martha A—Houser, Joseph
Shull, Mary—Beam, Aron
Shull, Mary—Raynalls, Calib
Shull, Mary Ann—Anthony, Gideon
Shutley, Levina—Stroup, John
Shutley, Sophia—Rodes, Christian
Shutly, Polly—Bradshaw, John
Sides, Ann—Sitze, John
Sides, Ann—Hawn, Daniel
Sides, Anny—Lawing, David
Sides, Barbary—Hinkle, Anthony
Sides, Hannah—Dillinger, John
Sides, Hannah—Cowan, Richard D
Sides, Louisa—Blaylock, David, Jr
Sides, Rachel—Warlick, David E
Sides, Rebecca—Clay, David
Sides, Sarah—Summerour, Henry
Sides, Sarah—Hawn, David
Sides, Susanna—Hinkle, Jacob
Sides, Susanna—Walker, Henry
Siffert, Belinda—Mcintosh, Alexander
Sifford, Mariah—Little, Wm P
Sifford, Maxamelia—Morris, Stephen
Sifford, V N—Derr, John H
Sigman, Agaline—Smith, Frederick
Sigman, Betty An—Spencer, Israel
Sigman, Catharina—Moser, Tobias
Sigman, Catherine—Thronebargh, William
Sigman, Catherine—Whitener, Daniel
Sigman, Delilah—Huffman, Joseph
Sigman, Dorethea—Gordan, John
Sigman, Elissabeth—Setser, Mathias
Sigman, Elizabeth—Sigman, George
Sigman, Fanny—Christofar, Peter
Sigman, Harriet- Barger, Thomas

Sigman, Harriett C—Gabriel, John W
Sigman, Katrine—Taar, Adam
Sigman, Margred—Dellinger, Joseph
Sigman, Maria—Mingus, Conrad
Sigman, Mary—Sigman, William
Sigman, Mary A—Megee, Jacob
Sigman, Mary A—Sigman, George H
Sigman, Peggy—Null, George
Sigman, Polly—Baker, Philip
Sigman, Polly—Hunsicker, John
Sigman, Polly—Cline, Mathias
Sigman, Polly—Johnson, Leander R
Sigman, Regena—Fulbright, William
Sigman, Sally—Bolick, Joseph
Sigman, Sarah—Reed, Jacob
Sigman, Susy—Setser, William
Sigmon, Catharine—Crup, Martin
Simmon, Addy Celena—Eckerd, Jonathan
Simmons, Elisabeth—Wisom, John
Simmons, Jemima—Setzer, Paul
Simmons, Patsy—Sadler, John
Simmons, Susana—Hamilton, William
Simms, Sarah—Edmond, Francis M
Simon, Catharina—Smith, John
Simon, Lidia—Harmon, Peter, Jr
Simon, Rachael—Bolick, David
Simon, Rachel—Carpenter, James
Simon, Susanah—Bolick, Daniel
Simons, Melinda—Huffman, Alferd
Simpson, Sarah A—Bobo, Charles D
Sims, Elizabeth—Robeson, Isaac
Simson, Ann—Bluford, Daniel
Sinclair, Jane—Dickey, Alexander
Singleton, Seussanah—McCormick, John S
Sites, Anny—Moll, Daniel
Skidmore, Ann—Huson, George
Skidmore, Cynthia—Chrisman, Henry
Skrimshire, Elisabeth—Moore, Elisha
Slade, Elizabeth A—Frisbie, Samuel
Slade, Virginia B—Moss, Z A
Slagle, Elizabeth—Wyont, Noah
Slagle, Mary—Moore, John
Slagle, Peggy—Lingerfelt, Jacob
Slagle, Susannah—Peterson, Henry
Slate, Elizabeth—Grissom, Moses
Slate, Nancey—Grissom, Milton W
Sleagle, Sarar—Campbell, John
Slinkard, Susanah—Simpson, William
Sloan, Sarah—Smith, David
Slown, Margaret—McKee, Isaac
Smith, Ann—Sigman, Ely
Smith, Anne—Phillips, David
Smith, Anny—Kistler, Paul
Smith, Barbara—Willims, Isaac
Smith, Barbara—Niel, Andrew
Smith, Barbra—Hullet, Moses
Smith, Betcy—Conrad, John
Smith, Betcy—Miller, Samuel
Smith, Betsy—Elmore, Edward
Smith, C Catharine—Gilbert, Alfred
Smith, Catherine—Warlick, Daniel
Smith, Catherine—Houser, Isaac
Smith, Cathrine—Hoke, Frederick
Smith, Clarissa—Settlemyer, Paul
Smith, Cleresa—Hefner, George
Smith, Elisabeth—Goins, Philip P
Smith, Eliza—Bradley, Alexander

Smith, Eliza—Rousche, F A
Smith, Elizabeth—Jinkens, Wiatt
Smith, Elizabeth—Smyer, Elias
Smith, Elizabeth—Pendleton, Hiream
Smith, Elizabeth—Roderick, Elisha W
Smith, Elizabeth—Davis, Michall
Smith, Ellen—Morrison, John
Smith, Esbel—Rhoads, Bennet
Smith, Eugenia B—Payne, J W A
Smith, Evilene—Canseler, Philip, Jr
Smith, Hariet E—Hope, Henry
Smith, Harriet—Paysaur, Jonas W
Smith, Jane—Beatey, John
Smith, Jane E—Barnet, James
Smith, Lena—Smith, John W
Smith, Magdalin—Fry, Daniel
Smith, Malinda—Hauss, J C
Smith, Margaret—Holdtree, Joseph
Smith, Margaret—Hull, John
Smith, Margarett—Hull, Major
Smith, Martha—Weathers, George
Smith, Martha—Erwin, Alexander
Smith, Martha—Capps, Thomas B
Smith, Mary—Mousar, George
Smith, Mary—Lufsey, Levi
Smith, Mary—Hoke, Henry
Smith, Mary—Torrence, John C
Smith, Mary—Weathers, William
Smith, Mary J—Hoffman, Frederick
Smith, Mary R—McCombs, J J
Smith, Nancey—Rhyne, Jacob
Smith, Nancy—Moore, Aron
Smith, Nancy—Allison, Greenberry
Smith, Nancy L—Cathey, Cyrus
Smith, Peggy—Jenkins, Edward
Smith, Polly—Deshaser, Hardy
Smith, Polly—Petree, John
Smith, Rachel—Brooks, Walter
Smith, Rachel—Oliver, John
Smith, Rosannah—Ray, George W
Smith, Sabina—Sigman, William
Smith, Sally—Rodes, John
Smith, Sally—Hoke, Daniel
Smith, Sally—Sain, Jacob
Smith, Sarah—Park, Patrick
Smith, Sarah—Smith, Jacob
Smith, Sarah—Oates, William
Smith, Sarah—Stowe, William
Smith, Sarah—Cansler, Daniel
Smith, Sarah—Relph, John W
Smith, Sarah—Huffstetler, Caleb A
Smith, Sarah Ann—Black, Ephraim
Smith, Sarah M—Reinhardt, Franklin M
Smith, Sophia—Carpenter, Andrew
Smoyer, Percidia—Green, Oliver C
Smyer, Cathrine—Deal, William
Smyer, Margaret M—Frazer, Alexander
Smyer, Salley—Boovey, David
Smyre, Adaline—Bost, Eli
Smyre, Mahala—Setzer, George
Sommet, Sally—Ligal, Henry
Sommit, Anna—Dietz, Israel
South, Rachel—Scott, Moses
Southard, Nancy—Stacy, Jeremiah
Spain, Betcy—Blaloc, John
Spain, Nancy—Foy, James
Spain, Patcy—Proctor, Richard

Spake, Caroline—Davis, John
Spake, Catharine—Bangle, John
Spake, Mary—Reep, Samuel
Spake, Vica—Detter, John
Spangler, Barbara—Hauser, Joseph
Spangler, Mary—Miller, John
Spangler, Sarah—Willis, Henry
Spangler, Susanah—Houser, Joseph
Speagle, Elizabeth—Shitle, Philip
Speak, Sally—Avery, Daniel
Speck, Barbara—Hudson, Ephraim
Speck, Barbara A—Crowder, Paschal P
Speck, Mary Ann—Padgett, Mansfield
Speck, Polly—Temples, Needham
Spencer, Ann—Wood, William
Spencer, Anne B—McCarver, Wm H
Spencer, Caty—Featherston, William
Spencer, Eliza—McAllister, Joseph
Spencer, Eliza Clark—Jones, Isaac
Spencer, Elizabeth—Turner, George
Spencer, Isabella—Bonham, John
Spencer, Isabella—Dunn, William M
Spencer, Jane—McAlister, Joseph
Spencer, Jemimay—Spencer, Ganaway
Spencer, Mary—Vaughn, Hempsel
Spencer, Nancy—Hazlet, John
Spencer, Nanny—Withers, Logan
Spencer, Sally—Ash, William
Spencer, Sally—White, Joseph P G
Spenser, Sarah—Baird, Adam
Sprat, Katey—Sullivan, Elijah
Spratt, Jane—Grigg, Berry P
Spratt, Jane—Alexander, David M
Spratt, Margaret—Felmet, C F
Spratt, Nancy—Shull, Pearson
Springs, Margaret—Bulingar, George F
Springs, Mary L—Little, William
Spurlin, Elizabeth—Ponder, Silas
Spurlin, Polley—Gladen, Aaron
Spurling, Rebeca—Pigg, John
Sraunce, Elizabeth—Keener, Henry
Sronce, Barbara R—Crouse, David E
Sronce, Elizabeth Catharine—Helderman, George Franklin
Sronce, Nancy—Edgin, Samuel
Sronce, Peggy—Parker, Wilson
Sronce, Salley—Beal, Christopher
Sronce, Sarah—Ingle, Michael
Srum, Barbara—Duderow, Michael
Srum, Barbara—Engle, Andrew
Srum, Catharine—Keener, Michael
Srum, Poly—Srum, Solomon
Stacia, Selina—Hull, Benjamin
Stacy, Nelly—Wilson, John
Stamay, Salley—McElroy, David
Stamey, Adaline—Boils, John W
Stamey, Barbara—Ritchy, J Thomas
Stamey, Barbary—Robinson, Jonathan
Stamey, Eliza—Leonard, George
Stamey, Eliza—Howser, John
Stamey, Lucinda—Helton, William
Stamey, Luiza—Rhodes, Henry
Stamey, Mary M—Mooney, A J
Stamey, Peggy—Moores, James
Stamey, Sally—Aby, Henry
Stamey, Sally—Shuford, Philip
Stamey, Sarah A—Pixley, Noah H

Stamey, Sufroney Matilda—Reep, Jonas
Stark, Elissabeth—Fry, Philip
Starns, Nancy—Harbison, Alberto
Starr, Ester—Miller, John
Starr, Polly—Thronburgh, George
Starr, Susannah—Cline, William
Starret, Dinny Adeline—Stanford, Lyman
Starret, Rebecca—Vanata, Peter
Starret, Ruth—Swan, James
Starrett, Elisabeth—Gillespie, John
Starriat, Mary—Hanks, James
Starrit, Elezebeth—Magginnas, John
Statia, Lucrecie—Cruthers, Edmond
Statia, Nancy—Beel, John
Statia, Sally—Heaker, John
Staymey, Maria—Martin, Philip
Steasy, Elizabeth—Edwards, Mathew
Steel, Ann—Mehafey, Joseph
Steel, Rosanah—Willson, Andrew
Steel, Ruth—Campble, Matthew
Steeley, Luveey—Cobb, Stephen
Steely, Lurany—Hager, Aron
Stevenson, Jancey—Sherrill, Jacob
Stevenson, Myra—Neill, John
Steward, Caroline—Davis, Anderson
Steward, Mary A—Fisher, James E
Stewinter, Margaret—James, James
Stierwalt, Elizebeth—Hoke, Frederick
Stiles, Elender—Clubb, Jacob
Stiles, Elizabeth—Colwell, William
Stiles, Nancy—Wilkinson, James
Stiles, Rebeckah—Ingle, Michael
Stilwell, Nancey—Coulter, Daniel
Stilwell, Sarah—Whitener, David
Stillwell, Margaret—Abee, James
Stillwell, Theresa—Lucky, David
Stine, Catharine—Baker, Joseph
Stine, Mary—White, Wesley
Stine, Molly—Simon, John
Stine, Sally—Isenhower, Henry
Stinson, Martina—Bradley, James A
Stockinger, Christina—Conrad, Rudolph
Stockininger, Elisabeth—Felker, Peter
Stowe, Catherine—Davis, Thomas
Stowe, Margaret—Cox, William
Stowe, Marthew—Hasley, Richard R
Stowe, Mary—Pegram, Winchester
Stowe, Mary—Nichols, John
Stroud, Fanny—Finn, Jesse
Stroup, Ann—Nance, Lawson
Stroup, Barbara—Dillinger, George
Stroup, Carline—Anders, Elias M
Stroup, Caty—Rhyne, Jacob
Stroup, Delaney—Hovis, Philip
Stroup, Dinny—Keever, Henry
Stroup, Elisabeth—Head, A S
Stroup, Elizabeth—Master, John
Stroup, Elizabeth—Hager, Daniel
Stroup, Esther—Hallman, Daniel
Stroup, Eve—Vaughan, W B
Stroup, Hannah—Posten, Daniel
Stroup, Joannah—Philips, S H
Stroup, Katherine—Dillinger, Phillip
Stroup, Mary—Reel, George
Stroup, Mary—Dellinger, Moses N
Stroup, Miriam—see Armstrong, Miriam
Stroup, Nancy—Stroup, Jacob

Stroup, Nancy Jane—Huggins, M H
Stroup, Rebeckah—Black, Thomas
Stroup, Sarah Ann—Hovis, David
Stroup, Sarah Ann—Blackwood, John
Strutt, Mahala—Holebrooks, Joshua
Strutt, Nancy—Smith, David G
Styles, Polley—Painter, Samuel
Styles, Rebecca—Bomgarner, Philip G
Suford, Jane I—Johnston, Wilis
Sulivan, Mariah—Keener, Daniel
Sullivan, Betsey—Moore, Samuel
Sullivan, Catherine—Moore, Moses
Sullivan, Harriet C—Hudson, Enoch
Sullivan, Margaret—Cline, John
Sullivan, Margaret—Spratt, J L
Sullivan, Martha A—Cornwell, John
Sullivan, Mary Ann—Mauney, Peter
Sullivan, Mary E—Mauney, Michael
Sullivan, Nancy—Taylor, James
Sullivan, Nancy—Abernathy, Elijah
Sullivan, Nancy J—Hoke, John E
Sullivan, Nancy M—Hauss, John R
Sullivan, Polley—Clyne, Henry
Sullivan, Sally—Hoppes, John
Sulvent, Sary—Hermon, Daniel
Sumee, Persilla—Sigman, William
Sumerour, Mary—Finger, David
Sumerour, Susanah—Finger, Jonas
Summerow, Adaline E—McLurd,
   Robinson L
Summerow, Ann—Keener, Lewis
Summerow, Catharine—Dellinger, Henry
Summerow, Margaret—Dellinger, Noah
Summerów, Margaret C—Self, Rufus
Summerow, Salome A—Wingate, Norris A
Summerow, Sarah—Gilbert, John F
Summerrow, Louisa F—Eddlemon, David F
Summet, Catherine—Huit, Henry
Summet, Sarah—Kistler, Elias
Summett, Catharine—Robinson, Andrew
Summett, Polly—Sullivan, Samuel
Summey, Ann—Hovis, Solomon
Summey, Anne—Hoyl, Solomon
Summey, Barbara L—Alexander, Elias J
Summey, Caroline Amanda—Dusenberry,
   E La Fayette
Summey, Catharine—Berry, Thomas
Summey, Catharine—Ramsey, Thomas
Summey, Catharine Elmina—McKee,
   Peter C
Summey, Catherine—Hartsog, John
Summey, Elizabeth—Carpenter, Joshua
Summey, Lavina—Queen, Maraday
Summey, Lovena—Wilfong, John, Jr
Summey, Susanah—Ramsaur, John
Summey, Susanah—Sronce, Jacob
Summit, Barbara—Kistler, Noah
Summit, Betsey—Thornbury, David
Summit, Eliza—Moose, Andrew
Summit, Levina—Litten, Gilbert
Summit, Magdlin—Thronbarg, Jacob
Summit, Nancy—Huit, David
Summit, Polly—Abernathy, David
Summit, Rebeckah—Scronce, James
Summner, Ann—Summner, Daniel
Summy, Barbara—Ramsour, Jacob
Summy, Betsey—Ramsour, David

Summy, Catharine—Hoyle, Jacob
Summy, Katharine—Perkins, Isaac
Summy, Polly—Hufstetler, Jacob
Summy, Salley—Ramsaur, Philip
Sumner, Georgiana T—Hoke, William J
Sumner, M E—McBee, Vardry A
Sumpter, Anne—Morrison, Thos
Sumrour, Margarett E—Hallman, Jacob
Sumrow, Barbara—Hollman, Wile
Sumrow, Catherine—Finger, Daniel
Sumrow, Elmira—Hudspeth, Wesley
Sumy, M J—Ramsey, W W
Surratt, Susannah—Wilfong, George
Suttlemyer, Sally—Mull, Abraham
Sutton, Betsy—Bealk, Payton
Swanson, Dyza—Clipard, David
Swareingame, Eleanor—Conner, John
Swarengame, Hannah—Mauney, Christian
Swaringame, Delila—Conner, James
Swaringame, Nancy—Bookout, Levi
Swaringgame, Mary—Harris, Tarlton
Swearingame, Malinda—Wiatt, Caleb
Swearingham, Jane—Wiatt, James
Swearingin, Masny—Conner, Jacob
Swenson, Lydicia—Dougherty, Bernard

Tabb, Elizabeth—Smith, John
Tallent, Malinda—Long, Henry
Tarr, Rebeckah—Abernathy, Berryman
Taylor, Ann—Adams, Andrew
Taylor, Catherine—Wilson, Andrew
Taylor, Elizabeth—Snider, John
Taylor, Jane—Spencer, William
Taylor, Louisa—Smoyer, Pinkny
Taylor, Martha—Towery, Adam
Taylor, Mary—Cline, Andrew
Taylor, Mary—Hoil, Jonas C
Taylor, Nancy—Eaton, Adam
Taylor, Polly—Waterson, John
Taylor, Rachel—Maples, Thomas
Taylor, Sally—McGinnas, Lawson
Taylor, Sarah—Lacky, David
Taylor, Susanah—Laurence, William
Taylor, Susanah—Grigg, Jesse
Teavebaugh, Catharine—Etris, Henry
Temple, Elisabeth—Letherman, Jonas
Temples, Sufiar—Page, James Matison
Terry, Martha—Cunniham, James
Tetherow, Mary—King, William
Tetherro, Hannah—Keener, Martin
Tethrow, Salley—Plunk, Jacob
Tevebough, Betsey—Arney, John
Thomas, Anna—Maxwell, S D
Thomas, Mary—Sparrow, Patrick J
Thompson, Ann—Litton, Wesley
Thompson, Ann—Stoner, Isaac
Tompson, Betsy—Lockman, Elihu
Thompson, Elizabeth—Lucas, Isaac
Thompson, Elizabeth E—Wise, William F
Thompson, Martha—Fleming, Archa
Thompson, Martha—Cloninger, William
Thompson, Martha Ann—Wells, Henry W
Thompson, Mary—Hager, George
Thompson, Mary M—Shelton, Young
Thompson, Polley—Williams, Joseph
Thompson, Rachel—Johnston, John

Thompson, Sarah A—Patterson, James A
Thomson, Sally—Cherry, Robert
Thonbery, Margerett—Singeltun, Starling
Thorman, Mary—Wallis, Joseph N
Thornbery, Mary—Paysour. Manasseh
Thornbury, Cathern—Forbes, John H
Thronbary, Barbre—Shook, Fred, Jr
Thronburg, Cloah M—Wilson, Joseph C
Throneberg, Matilda—Helms, John
Titerbeam, _____—Reynolds, Thomas
Titman, Eliza—Reeves, Jennings R
Titman, Violet—Porter, James M
Titmon, Cathrine—Armstrong, Mathew
Titmon, Mary M—Porter, James M
Tompson, Polly—Philips, Joseph
Torance, Anna—Robinson, William
Torrance, Margaret J I—Robinson, Zimri
Torrance, Martha S—Lovey, Thomas
Torrance, Mary B—Robinson, Samuel C
Torrence, Mary B—Mendenhull, Nathan
Totherow, Christina—Kerns, Washington
Tounsen, Cathrine—Throrneburgh, Eli
Towery, Mime—Willis, Joseph
Townsend, Elizabeth—Holler, Peter
Townsend, Sally A—Ornt, Henry
Trefelstatt, Sally—Hawn, Jacob
Trefeastat, Cathrine—Sigman, John
Treffelstad, Susanna—Haun, David
Treffelstet, Mary—Setzer, Jacob
Trevelstedt, Betsy—Bollinger, Daniel
Triplet, Lavina—Bumgarner, Andrew
Trit, Sally—Herman, Daniel
Tritt, Elizabeth—Justice, Moses
Tritt, Molley—James, James
Tronbierg, Rachel—Gilbert, Andrew
Troughbach, Betcy—Ingle, Michael
Troughbock, Barbara—Ashabraner, John
Trout, Margret—Shoup, Gabriel
Trout, Nelly—Hause, David
Troutman, Elisabeth—Ingle, Martin
Troutman, Mary Ann—Bumgarner, Melcher
Troutman, Nancy—Keener, Jacob
Troutman, Polly—Finger, John
Troutman, Susanah—Finger, Jacob
Troutmon, Adaline—Lehmans, William M
Truigs, Elizabeth—Self, Williams
Tucker, Belsora A—Oats, Saml R
Tucker, Eliza—Baty, Gabriel
Tucker, Louisa—Collier, Henry
Tucker, Margret—Dameron, William
Tucker, Mary—Tipps, Thomas
Tucker, Matilda Ann—Hager, Henry
Tucker, Nancy—Seine, Jacob
Tucker, Nancy—Wamac, Starling
Tucker, Patsy A—Pryor, Wiley
Tucker, Polly—Pryor, Thos J
Tucker, Rebecah—Nixson, William
Tucker, Rebecca—Hovis, Levi
Tucker, Sophia—Harry, John H
Turbefield, Elvira—Fisher, Benjamin
Turbifield, Polly—Abernathy, Wiliferd
Turbyfield, Elizabeth—Petry, William
Turbyfield, Nancy—Long, John
Turbyfield, Sally—Tuttle, William
Turbyfill, Ann—Shook, John H
Turbyfill, Anna—Fisher, Rufus
Turbyfill, Elisabeth—Lee, James

Turbyfill, Holly—Roberts, John
Turner, Betsey—Ward, Lawson
Turner, Elizabeth—Connor, John
Turner, Sarah—Ward, William
Turner, Zelpha—Sumeroua, Jacob
Turpin, Delphy Taylor—Hunter, Michael
Twitty, Abella—Magness, Joseph
Twitty, Charlott—Miles, Daniell

Umphry, Jane—Shittle, Jacob
Underwood, Betcy—McKee, James
Upchurch, Clement—Thorpe, Robert W
Uton, Rachael—Shadden, David

Vanderver, Nancy—Chapman, George
Vanhorn, Sary—Jackson, John
Vaughan, Harriet—Spencer, John
Vaughen, Patsey—Kincaid, David
Vaughen, Suckey—Abernathy, Aaron
Vence, Christiana—Richards, Jno
Vendike, Aney—Cox, Robert
Vendike, Salley—Arney, Christian
Vestal, Rachel—Baker, Silas
Vials, Betcy—Birk, James
Vickars, Mary—Gardiner, John
Vickers, Alice—Gardiner, Andrew
Vickers, Louisa—Deck, Peter
Vickers, Peggy—Prece, Isaac
Vickers, Polley—Smith, James M
Vines, Agness—Fewours, William
Vines, Susannah—Felps, Samuel
Vinsant, Elisabeth—Kuykendall, Abram

Wacaser, Mahala—Farmer, Caleb
Wacaser, Mary Ann—Helms, William
Wagener, Polley—Caldwell, Andrew
Waggoner, Rachel—Howard, William H
Waggoner, Rebecah—Caldwell, William
Waggoner, Susanna—Crow, John
Waist, Mary—M'Ashlin, William
Walker, Cena—Sides, Daniel
Walker, Jenet—Wilson, John
Walker, Mary—Baily, Cox
Walker, Mary—Sides, Simon
Walker, Rachel—Whiteside, Edward
Walker, Susan—Norman, Robert
Walker, Susanah—Seitz, Levi
Walker, Winna—Clifton, Samuel
Wallace, Ann—Humphreys, Richard R
Wallace, Elisabeth D—Hendricks, Tiberius
Wallace, Jenny—Riggs, George
Wallace, Kitty G—Brem, George
Wallace, Sally—West, Barney
Wallice, Juliet C—Glenn, Enos B
Wallice, Katharine—Summey, Peter
Wallis, _____—Spencer, William
Wallis, Polly—Merit, Thomas
Wallis, Ruthey—Helton, John
Walls, Betsey—Gantt, Henry
Walters, Luisa—Costner, Peter
Wamick, Elizabeth—Childris, Alfred
Ward, Betcy—Hanes, Jesse
Ward, Betcy A—Setser, George
Ward, Catharine—Deal, Jacob

Ward, Elizabeth—Samson, James
Ward, Elizabeth—Fry, Henry
Ward, Francess—Earp, Philip
Ward, Katrine—Bumgarner, John
Ward, Margaret L—Ford, Jno N
Ward, Mira—Burch, Thos F
Ward, Nancy—Harriss, Wm
Ward, Nancy—Nolin, David
Ward, Nancy—Null, John
Ward, Rebecky B—Hildrman, John
Ward, Rue—Abernathy, Jeremiah
Ward, Ruth—Earley, Charles
Ward, Sally—Ward, Charles
Ward, Sally—Holler, John
Ward, Sarah—Sugg, George
Warlick, Abigail—Carpenter, Alford
Warlick, Barbara—Kerr, Robert
Warlick, Barbara—Warlick, Solomon
Warlick, Barbara—Link, John
Warlick, Barbara—Goode, John T
Warlick, Catharine—Ellis, Stanford
Warlick, Catharine—Finger, Peter
Warlick, Eliza—Roberts, Thomas
Warlick, Eliza—Ramsour, George S
Warlick, Elizabeth—Ramsour, Solomon
Warlick, Julia—Reinhardt, Abram
Warlick, Levica—Guyton, Abram J
Warlick, Levina—Wilkins, Anderson S
Warlick, Maggie—Bechtler, J A
Warlick, Margaret—Shuford, John M
Warlick, Mary—Belew, John
Warlick, Mary Ann—Eaker, Peter
Warlick, Mary R—Robinson, Henry C
Warlick, Nina—Shuford, Henry
Warlick, Rachel—Hallman, Henry
Warlick, Rachel—Finger, Michael
Warlick, Rachel E—Blackburn, George
Warlick, Sally—Wray, William
Warlick, Sarah—Ramsaur, Eli
Warlick, Sarah—Beam, M R
Warlick, Susannah—Beam, Micheal
Warran, Martha—Smith, William
Warren, Margaret—Miller, George
Waterson, Jenny—Waterson, John
Wates, Elender—Bumgarner, Peter
Watson, Mary L—Slagle, John J
Wattson, Peggy B—Knox, Robert
Weahon, Catharine—Goolman, Jacob
Wear, Charlotte D—Clark, William A C
Weathers, Barbara—Rhyne, Michael
Weathers, Catharine—Ryne, David
Weathers, Eliza—Lay, William B
Weathers, Elizabeth—Hanks, John
Weathers, Frances M—Hager, John
Weathers, Franky—Smith, John
Weathers, Jemima—Smith, John
Weathers, Leanna—Bess, Peter
Weathers, Leusia—Dameron, Dixon
Weathers, Margaret A—Weathers,
   Simpson F
Weathers, Margaret R—Hannah,
   Thomas M
Weathers, Mary—Clemmer, George
Weathers, Mary—Loftin, Lafayett
Weathers, Mary S—Robinson, Alexander S
Weathers, Minerva—Ward, David
Weathers, Nancy—Tethro, Jacob

Weathers, Polly—Hawkins, Samuel
Weathers, Polly—Rhyne, Emanuel
Weathers, Sarah—Rhoads, Jacob
Weathers, Sarah—Hufman, Joseph
Weathers, Sarah Ann—Keener, Simon
Weathers, Sousee—Strain, Alexander
Weatherspoon, Eliza—Hovis, Elias
Weatherspoon, Pelina—Cloninger, Noah
Weaver, Elizabeth—Carpenter, Jacob
Weaver, Eve—Harris, Valentine
Weaver, Malinda—Black, Lorenzo D
Weaver, Sallema—Fisher, Joseph
Weaver, Sarah—Whitener, John
Weaver, Susan—Cornwill, James
Weaver, Susanna—Miller, John
Web, Peggey—Wats, Enoch
Webb, Rebeckah—Coxe, Vinson
Weer, Peggy—Huffsticklar, Daniel
Weever, Eve—Smith, Cuddious
Wehon, Catherine—Eaby, Andrew
Wehunt, M A—Childers, W C
Weir, Elizabeth—Costner, Levi
Weir, Elizabeth M—McCarter, Michael
Weir, Matsey Graham—Crow,
   Robert Armstrong
Weir, Sally—Huffstetsler, Logan
Welch, Polley—Hamilton, John
Wells, Catharine—Fronabarger, Ambrose
Wells, Caty—Wiatt, Abrihan
Wells, Dolly—Hoyl, John
Wells, Elizabeth—Dunn, Moses M
Wells, Elizabeth—Killian, Jacob B
Wells, Mrs Fanny—Fite, Solomon
Wells, Frances A—Alexander, James L
Wells, Julia A—Speck, John F
Wells, Martha—Hoyl, Nathen M
Wells, Mary—Hannah, John
Wells, Mary—Henry, Isaac
Wells, Mary—Gaston, James A
Wells, Nancy—Fite, Jacob
Wells, Nancy—Jinkins, Jinkey
Wells, Nancy—Ewing, Robert A
Wells, Peggy—Weathers, Thomas
Wells, Peggy—Dunn, Simon
Wells, Polly—Jinkins, Elijah
Wells, Polly—Blackburn, John
Wells, Rachel—Dunn, James
Wells, Sarah—Patterson, Alexander
Wells, Sarah—Angle, David
Wells, Sarah—Faires, Elias M
Wells, Susanah—Christenbury, Daniel F
Wells, Susannah—Horton, Nimrod
Wells, Wille—Connolly, James D
Welmon, Rebeccah—Connor, James
Weon, Matleaner—Saine, Samuel
Werble, Senna—Havner, Nicholas
Wesson, Rose—Boncard, Oscar T de
Wesson, Rose—Welsh, David
West, Amanda—McCoy, William T
West, Amey—Hawkins, Samuel
West, Barbara—Troutman, Jacob
West, Dulcina—Pixley, N H
West, Fereby—Rees, James
West, Hanah—Lyons, William
West, Izabellar—Abernathy, Michal
West, Juliet—Dickson, John M
West, Martha—Ballard, James

West, Mary—Bealt, William
West, Mary—Cox, William
West, Nancy—Chrisman, Henry
West, Phereby—Belt, Isaac
West, Salley—Belt, Stephen
West, Sarah—Baker, John
West, Sophia—Ramsey, John M
West, Visey—Armstrong, John
Westmoreland, Rhoda—Harwell, Buckner
Weston, Nancy—Weaver, Conrad
Wethers, Ebby—Palmer, Jacob
Wethers, Jane—Rhyne, Adam A
Wethers, Leeanna—Johnston, Alexander
Wethers, Mary—Shutley, John
Wethers, Nancy Lavina—Carroll, Henry W
Whealer, Reachel—McMin, William
Wheard, Catherine—Carpenter, Nicholas
Wheard, Eliza—Clark, Jacob F
Wheeler, Ann—Gevin, George
Wheon, Susannah—Hallman, David
Wheton, Polley—Williams, William
Whetston, Susana—Stricker, Daniel
Whetstone, Salina—Kistler, Jacob
Whienand, Caty—Parker, Nicholas
Whise, Rhody C—Lutz, Daniel
Whisenhant, Catherine—Abernathy, David
Whisenhunt, Anne—Carpenter, John
Whisenhunt, Barbara—Daugherty, John
Whisenhunt, Unica—Peters, Francis
Whisnant, Martha—Porter, Samuel G
White, Achsah—Link, Moses
White, Ann—Hettrick, Conrad
White, Anna—Jones, William
White, Bega—Kerk, William
White, Betcy—Robinson, David
White, Betsy—Nance, James
White, Cynthia Winslow—Stroup, Benjamin
White, Elizabeth—Bradshaw, Jonas
White, Elvarna—Lowe, Green
White, Erixene—Torrance, Samuel A
White, Fanny—Keever, George
White, Gane—Rooker, Daniel
White, Jane—Gilleland, Allen
White, Lillis—Oats, Robert
White, Lucy—Oates, James
White, Martha H—Robinson, John
White, Mary C—White, James
White, Nancey—Cauble, Harrison
White, Nancey W—Elmore, David
White, Rebecca—Propst, Wilson
White, Sally—Bradshaw, Pride
White, Sarah—Irvin, David
White, Sarah—Hager, Jonathan
White, Sarah H—Ramsour, Jacob H
White, Susannah—Stroup, Jessee
Whiteley, Elisabeth—Miller, Jacob
Whitenbarger, Cristina—Best, Petter
Whitener, Anna—Willkie, George J
Whitener, Barbara—Sigman, David
Whitener, Barbara—Ward, John
Whitener, Catherine—Stacy, Zachary
Whitener, Catherine—Bullinger, Michael
Whitener, Elisabeth—Yount, John
Whitener, Elizabeth—Naugle, Henry
Whitener, Emeline—Sigmon, Abel
Whitener, Fanney—Abernathy, Turner
Whitener, Hannah—Haun, Sampson

Whitener, Lovina P—Daliner, John A
Whitener, Mary—Miller, Absalom
Whitener, Polly—Sigman, Cristopher
Whitener, Polly—Miller, Jacob
Whitener, Rachel—Miller, Caleb
Whitener, Rhoda—Bollinger, Jacob A
Whitener, Sally—Link, Michael
Whitener, Sarah—Yoder, John, Jr
Whitener, Sarah—Settlemyer, Henry
Whitener, Sarah M—Hoyle, Reuben
Whitener, Susanna—Fisher, Joseph
Whitener, Susannah—Hawn, John
Whiteside, Jean—Wilson, Thomas
Whiteside, Kathrine—Jenkins, John
Whitesides, Isebella—Carson, Andrew
Whitley, Mary—Derr, Andrew
Whitner, Anna M—Jarrett, Daniel
Whitner, Betsey—Sumerow, Henry
Whitner, Linna—Tipps, William
Whitner, Mary M—Seitz, Abel
Whitner, Mary M—Whitener, Moses B
Whitney, Elizabeth—Eaton, John
Whitney, Mina—Ballard, William L
Whitney, Nancy—Robinson, John
Whitnor, Molliana—Robinson, Jesse
Whitson, Margaret—Litten, Thomas
Wial, Nancy—Rhodes, David
Wiatt, Rachel—Conar, Hugh E
Wiatt, Susanna—Thornburgh, Jacob M
Wiells, Katrine—Winebarier, Conrad
Wier, Margaret—Hager, Solomon
Wier, Martha—Gladen, Andrew
Wier, Mary A—Kizer, Ezekias
Wier, Milly—Cordell, Calven
Wike, Febe—Dugless, James
Wike, Polly—Setzer, Daniel
Wike, Susanna—Cline, Daniel
Wilbourn, Rebecah—Crowder, Anderson
Wiley, Elinor—Thompson, William F
Wiley, Ellen—Cathey, Archibald
Wilfong, Anna—Ramsaur, David A
Wilfong, Barbara—Simpson, S P
Wilfong, Catherine—Harrell, Hugh H
Wilfong, Elisabeth—Cline, Jacob
Wilfong, Elizabeth—Bandy, William
Wilfong, Eve—Abernathy, Andrew
Wilfong, Mary M—Hamilton, Ninian
Wilfong, Polley—Robinson, Henry W
Wilfong, Salley—Clodfelter, Peter
Wilfong, Sarah—Ramsaur, David
Wilians, Mary T—Pirkins, Richard
Wilkerson, Elizabeth—Sherrill, Lawson
Wilkerson, Ibby—Killian, Levi E
Wilkerson, Milly—Hooper, Edley
Wilkerson, Patsey—Linbarger, Daniel
Wilkinson, Dove—Sherrill, Gabriel
Wilkinson, E E—Robinson, John S
Wilkinson, Effy—Linebarger, Martin
Wilkinson, Emala—Thompson, John
Wilkinson, Margaret L—Anthony, John J
Wilkinson, Martha S—Black, Thomas P
Wilkinson, Salina—Connor, Columbia
Wilkiser, Marey—Beam, David
Wilkison, Nancy—Linebarger, Frederick
Willbanks, Elizabeth—Bird, Benjamin
Willhight, Barbara—Miller, Henry
Williams, ____ney—Chapman, Jones

Williams, Amia—Mitcham, Joshua
Williams, Amy—Hull, Benjamin
Williams, Ann—Thompson, Henry
Williams, Ann—Biles, Charles
Williams, Anna—Hambright, Christian
Williams, Anna—Boggs, Thomas D
Williams, Barbara—Taylor, Franklin
Williams, Betsey—Beal, Benjamin
Williams, Catharine—Falls, George L
Williams, Catherine—Rhyne, Peter
Williams, Dicy—Brendel, David
Williams, Elisabeth—Clore, Elisha
Williams, Elisabeth—Williams, Charles
Williams, Elizabeth—Tucker, Butler
Williams, Elizabeth—Ekeart, David
Williams, Elizabeth—Bynum, John S
Williams, Elizabeth M—Steward, Thos W
Williams, Ellender—Rogers, Nicles
Williams, Judith—Rector, John
Williams, Laura—Pendleton, William
Williams, Lizur—Parker, Peter
Williams, Margaret—Linster, A J
Williams, Margaret—Medlin, Columbus
Williams, Martha—Carpenter, Christopher
Williams, Martha—Caldwell, J F
Williams, Mary—Bynum, Arthur
Williams, Mary—Deck, John
Williams, Mary—Muckelvein, Calep
Williams, Mary—Williams, William T
Williams, Mary Ann—Bracket, George
Williams, Mary Ann—Wise, George W
Williams, Nancy—Wallace, David H
Williams, Nancy—Leatherman, Solomon
Williams, Nelley—Stamey, John R
Williams. Polly—Stacy, Elisha
Williams, Polly—Club, John
Williams, Polly—Brindle, John
Williams, Polly—Williams, Isaiah
Williams, Rebecca—Wilson, Thomas
Williams, Rebecca—Duncan, Turner
Williams, Sally—Rodgers, Aaron
Williams, Saly—Edwards, Benjamin
Williams, Sarah—Beenick, Henry
Williams, Sarah—Williams, Millinton
Williams, Susan—Brooks, Abram
Williams, Susanna—Powel, Wm
Williams, Susannah—Singleton, James
Williams, Susannah—Chapman, Thomas
Williams, Tempe—Helton, Jessy
Williams, Vicey M—Lutz, M Luther
Williams, Winifred—Bradley, Richard
Williamson, Elizabeth—Thompson, William
Williamson, Sarah—Happoldt, John M
Willis, Dolly—Gladen, John
Willis, Mary—Martin, George
Willis, Nancy—Norman, Wilson
Willis, Rosena—Campbell, Daniel
Willis, Susannah—Bailes, John
Wills, Barbay—Hinkle, Jacob
Wills, Catharine—Stroder, Alexander
Wills, Christiana—Dillinger, Michael
Wills, Dinna Adaline—West, Ebenezer
Willson, Eliza—Powell, Smith L A
Willson, Mary—Love, Andrew
Willson, Minervy—Hoover, Ephraim
Wilson, Agness—Patton, David
Wilson, Ann—Lackey, John

Wilson, Anne—Robinson, William
Wilson, Belina—Bost, Jesse
Wilson, Betey—Elders, Thomas
Wilson, Catherine—Whitesides, James
Wilson, E M—Huss, P M
Wilson, Eidey—Bigger, James
Wilson, Elaner, Jr—Lindsey, Samuel
Wilson, Eliza—Yoakley, John
Wilson, Elizabeth—Stroup, Matthew
Wilson, Elizabeth—Bess, Hiram
Wilson, Isabella—Bigham, William
Wilson, Jane—Robinson, Elijah
Wilson, Jane—McGalliard, William
Wilson, Lavina—Lynck, L L
Wilson, Lettitia—Wilson, Samuel
Wilson, Malinda—Coulter, Elkanah P
Wilson, Margaret—Caslin, Matthew
Wilson, Margaret—Ingol, Peter
Wilson, Mariah C—Wilkinson, Franklin
Wilson, Martha—Houston, John
Wilson, Martha—Detter, John
Wilson, Mary—Welmon, Wilkins
Wilson, Mary—Torrence, Ephraim
Wilson, Mary—Anthony, John P
Wilson, Mary—Byres, Franklin
Wilson, Milissa—Travelstedt, William
Wilson, Nancy—Torrance, Mathew
Wilson, Peggy—Robinson, John
Wilson, Polley—Alexander, Moses
Wilson, Polly—Robinson, Isaac
Wilson, Polly—Taylor, James
Wilson, Priscilla—Wilson, Joshua
Wilson, Priscilla R—Holland, Franklin H
Wilson, Rebeca—Wilson, Joshua
Wilson, Rebecca K—Kiser, George
Wilson, Rebekah—Kibler, Jacob
Wilson, Rosanah L—Robinson, David
Wilson, Ruth—Angel, John
Wilson, Ruth—Yoder, David
Wilson, Sarah—Bigger, Samuel
Wilson, Sarah A—Torrence, William W
Wilson, Sarah A—McCoy, Abner
Wilson, Sarah Emet—Canipe, Joseph J
Winbargner, Lidda—Harmen, George
Winebarger, Katherine—Treffanstet, Daniel
Wingate, Jane—Linebarger, A P
Wingate, Martha M—Killian, John
Wingate, Mary—Wingate, Risdon
Wingate, Sophia—Davis, John
Winkler, Mary—Spencer, Benjamin
Winn, Mary—Constable, Thomas
Winter, Mary—Nile, William
Winters, Margaret—Adams, Joseph W
Winters, Mime—Black, William, Sr
Wion, Barbara—Lingerfelt, David
Wion, Christeener—Hover, Ephraim
Wion, Sally—Hartsec, David
Wise, Anna—Cook, Christian
Wise, Barbara—Sain, Jacob
Wise, Catharine A—Gilbert, J M
Wise, Catherine E—Armstrong, A S
Wise, Clara—Flanigan, Jacob
Wise, Elisebeth—Morison, Moses
Wise, Elizabeth—Paysour, George
Wise, Elizabeth—Hubberd, David
Wise, Fanney—Costner, Frederick
Wise, Mary—Trobaugh, John

Wise, Mary L—Williams, Jacob
Wise, Mary M—Armstrong, W J
Wise, Salley—Temples, Daniel
Wise, Sussana—Mitchem, Banks
Wisenhunt, Sarah—Whitener, Eli
Wishon, Mary—Wright, Solomon
Wisnant, Elisabeth—Riggs, Israel
Witherow, Mary—Rankin, Robert
Witherspoon, Anna—Lowrance, Isaac
Witherspoon, Anne—Lewis, James
Witherspoon, Emeline—Lourance, Lawson
Witherspoon, Ruth—Gordon, John
Witt, Jane—Pinner, Demsy
Womac, Milly—Nixon, Robert
Wood, Maryann—Wise, George
Wood, Sally—Gross, David
Wood, Sarah—Hildebrand, Marcus V
Wood, Susan A—Boyles, Marcus W
Woodring, Polly—Shook, Daniel
Woods, Mary—Price, James
Woods, Nancy—Long, Jonathan
Woods, Nancy—Farmer, David
Woods, Sally—Rohm, Isaac
Word, Elisabeth—Crysler, George
Workman, Nancy A—Eaker, Jesse
Wowicks, Susanah—Hulbard, Isaac
Wrenweeks, Sally—Black, Joseph
Wright—see also Right
Wright, Agness—McEntire, Alexander
Wright, Betcy—Thompson, John
Wright, Elenor—Elmore, Jesse
Wright, Else—McEntire, John
Wright, Isabela—Lindsey, James
Wright, Jane S—Wagner, Randolph
Wright, Lucinda—Partlow, James M
Wright, Mary—Nickles, John
Wright, Salley—Ferguson, Thomas, Jr
Wright, Sarah—Clark, Johnston
Wyant, Elizabeth—Reinhardt, Isaac
Wyatt, Elisabeth—Armour, Robert
Wyatt, Susanah—Levan, William
Wyatte, Sarah—Grant, Charles
Wycoff, Polly—Ward, Thomas
Wycough, Margaret—Ward, Alexander
Wycough, Sarah—Woodford, Lyman
Wyett, Nancey—Gosnell, Peter
Wyont, Mary—Boggs, Joseph
Wyrim, Mary—Wyatt, James

Yarber. Elisebeth—Parker, Jonathan
Yarber, Martha—Redmon, James A
Yarberough, Sally—Whisenhant, Lauson H
Yarboro, Elizbeth—Mathus, Peter
Yarborough, Elizabeth—Bridges, Moses
Yarbrough, Polly—Shook, Daniel
Yates, Nancy—McClain, Edward
Yoder, Barbera—Reep, David
Yoder, Cathn—Baker, John
Yoder, Cristeena—Weaver, Jacob
Yoder, Eliza C—Heavner, Daniel M
Yoder, Lavina—Kilain, Jesse
Yong, Mary C—Johnson, Henry
Yont, Polly—Hunsicker, Joseph
York, Eliza—Baulding, Alfred
Young, Catharine—Shikle, Henry
Young, Elizabeth—Willis, Robert
Young, Elizabeth E—Yount, Samuel

Young, Faney—Boils, David
Young, Katrine—Graves, Anthoney
Young, Levina—Hanks, Richard
Young, Martha—Thomas, James
Young, Mary—Self, Isaac R
Young, Sary—Ritchey, John S
Young, Susan—Bandy, Alexander M
Yount, Catherine—Hetrick, Philip
Yount, Elizabeth—Hurbenson, George T
Yount, Elizer—Elmore, Wm
Yount, Leah—Williams, Hartwell Spain
Yount, Sally—Deal, Solomon
Yount, Sarah—Miller, Jacob
Yount, Sarey—Odom, William
Yount, Susannah—Deal, William

Zimmerman, Ann E—Peck, Willis
Zimmerman, Clary L—Jarrett, Samuel
Zimmerman, Elisebeth—Froy, David
Zimmerman, Elizabeth—Jarrett, George
Zimmerman, Mary A—Hoke, Franklin A

------, ------—Alexander, Robert
------, ------—Baldon, Squire
------, ------—Braneman, Christian
------, ------—Bridgers, Nicholas
------, ------—Bridges, Elisha L
------, ------—Byers, Wm
----er, Martha—Cherry, John
------, ------—Cline, John
------, ------—Cobb, William
------, ------—Dyer, Elisha
------, ------—Edwards, Alexander
------, ------—Gaines, Robert
------, ------—Hall, Fergus A
------, Nancy—Harris, Wilie
------, ------—Harwell, Thomas
------, Savina—Herman, Andrew
------, ------—Hill, Thomas
------, ------—Howard, Francis R
----, Elizabeth—Howser, John
------, ------—Hubburd, Kearby
------, ------—Ivins, David
------, ------—Jones, Miles
------, ------—Lambert, Peter
------, ------—Leeper, James
--niger, ----—Linebarger, Michael
------, ------—Lourance, Alexr
------, ------—Lowrie, Samuel
------, ------—Miarse, Henry
------, ------—Moreland, John
------, ------—Mullin, Alexander
------, ------—Niell, Alexander
------, ------—Pettillo, James
------, ------—Petre, Henry
------, ------—Prevett, Matthew
------, ------—Propst, Daniel
------, ------—Ransom, Demse
----, Elisabeth—Robertson, Alexander
------, ------—Rutledge, James
------, ------—Sherill, Nelson
----, Charity—Sifford, Lewis
------, ------—Turner, Fielden
------, ------—Vandike, Joseph
------, ------—Williams, Samuel
------, ------—Wycough, S B

www.ingramcontent.com/pod-product-compliance
Lightning Source LLC
Chambersburg PA
CBHW061738270326
41928CB00011B/2293